IT'S ONLY ROCK 'N' ROLL

IT'S ONLY ROCK 'N' ROLL

THE ULTIMATE GUIDE TO THE ROLLING STONES

JAMES KARNBACH AND CAROL BERNSON

Facts On File, Inc.

"Without music, life would be a mistake."
—*Friedrich Wilhelm Nietzsche (1844–1900)*

This book is dedicated to all the fans of the Rolling Stones—past, present and future—
and to the Force that started the Rolling Stones and has kept them going for more than thirty-five years.
Long live rock 'n' roll.

IT'S ONLY ROCK 'N' ROLL: The Ultimate Guide to the Rolling Stones

Copyright © 1997 by James Karnbach and Carol Bernson

Facts On File, Inc.
11 Penn Plaza
New York NY 10001

Library of Congress Cataloging-in-Publication Data

Karnbach, James.
It's only rock 'n' roll: The ultimate guide to the Rolling Stones / James Karnbach and Carol Bernson.
p. cm.
Includes index.
ISBN 0-8160-3035-9.—ISBN 0-8160-3547-4 (pbk.)
1. Rolling Stones. 2. Rolling Stones—History—Chronology.
3. Rolling Stones—Discography. I. Bernson, Carol. II. Title.
ML421.R64K37 1997
782.42166'092'2—dc21
[B]   97–1056

Facts On File books are available at special discounts when purchased in bulk quantities for businesses, associations, institutions or sales promotions. Please call our Special Sales Department in New York at (212) 967-8800 or (800) 322-8755.

You can find Facts On File on the World Wide Web at http://www.factsonfile.com

Text and cover design by Cathy Rincon
Layout by Robert Yaffe

Printed in the United States of America

VB FOF 10 9 8 7 6 5 4 3 2 1

This book is printed on acid-free paper.

Contents

FOREWORD   VII

ACKNOWLEDGMENTS   IX

INTRODUCTION   XI

CHRONOLOGY   1

TOURS AND CONCERTS   53

SESSIONOGRAPHY   217

DISCOGRAPHY (US & UK)   261

FILMS   313

TELEVISION APPEARANCES   331

PROMOTIONAL FILMS AND VIDEOS   381

BOOTLEGS   393

INDEX   398

Foreword

This book is an historical and factual account of the musical endeavors of the Rolling Stones from their early days until the present. It is the product of many hours' (years') research by James Karnbach and Carol Bernson. They are both good friends of mine.

Carol is a talented photographer and writer and James's passion is anything and everything to do with the Rolling Stones' recorded history—audios, videos, jam sessions, intakes, outtakes—you name it, he knows about it. Since they've been collaborating on this book, it has become a labor of love, and an obsession for both of them.

I have spent many hours, sometimes long into the night, at their apartments in Manhattan, trying to identify various jam sessions (leftovers and unrealized ideas not included on any official albums). I know from personal experience that trying to analyze and identify any method in such radical musical madness is mostly futile. The best music, the best art is always mostly spontaneous, without calculation and too much thinking.

But, anyway, here it is, the most definitive and accurate account of everything that went onto tape.

It is a perceptive insight into the way real people make real music—a truly absorbing and interesting story of the life and soul of one of the world's greatest and most enduring rock 'n' roll bands and will be on my bookshelves with all my other musical books from Mozart to Frank Zappa—as soon as I find a place to live. Enjoy.

—*Mick Taylor (A Rolling Stone Forever)*

Mick Taylor (with Valerie Taylor—back to camera) greets the press at the Rock and Roll Hall of Fame induction ceremonies at New York's Waldorf-Astoria.
(CAROL BERNSON)

Acknowledgments

This book would not have been possible without the help, input and resources of many, many people and organizations. First on the list are our families, whose unconditional love and support got us through all those dark hours when most people were sleeping. Thank you Bernsons and Karnbachs, you'll never know how much you helped us make sense of it all.

Gathering data on the Stones and making sense of it all has been our primary goal, but that process and this project began many years before we decided to collaborate on writing a book. All the early legwork, data collection and research was done only by one of us. Therefore, all thanks must reflect events that took place well before we started to work together.

Confessing the Blues

I would like to acknowledge various people whom I have either interviewed or spoken with casually over the years about details of the musical history of the Rolling Stones. Those conversations were substantive and have helped me analyze new data. All of that input has somehow found its way into the book. So, thanks Bill Wyman, Keith Richards, Mick Jagger, Ronnie Wood, Ian Stewart, Jimmy Miller, Chuck Berry, Al Kooper, Bobby Keys, Jerry Brandt, Chris Barber, Harold Pendleton, Ted Newman Jones, James Brown, B. B. King, Andy Warhol, Pete Townshend, Keith Moon, Billy Preston, John Belushi, Dezo Hoffman, Peter Rudge, Marybeth Medley, Derek vonLindt, Alexis Korner, Ian McLagan, George Thorogood, Andrew Wilkins, Art Collins, David Maysles, Peter Clifton, Les Paul, Arno Hecht, Bob Funk, Michael Lindsay-Hogg, Anita, Marianne, Mary Clayton, Giorgio Gomelski, Chip Monck . . .

—*James Karnbach*

Yesterday's Papers

Initially, our collaboration was a novel and untried amalgam of two individuals with seemingly disparate talents and backgrounds but equally intense, music-loving personalities. One physicist-turned-music-archivist and one anthropologist-turned-photojournalist. Had I not received an assignment to photograph Mick Taylor in November 1986, James would have written this book with someone else. So, my thanks to Bob Chamberlin and Larry Armstrong of the *Los Angeles Times* for setting off an apparently inexorable chain of events. And, of course, to Mick, for knowing how to have a good time while being photographed.

—*Carol Bernson*

The authors wish to acknowledge the kind assistance of the staffs of the British Newspaper Library, the British Sound Archive, the New York City Public Library–Lincoln Center Branch and the Performing Rights Society of Great Britain. Additionally, our thanks go to the many colleagues at newspapers, magazines, wire services and radio and television stations worldwide that passed on clippings, captions and contacts throughout our quest. Specific gratitude to our friends at London Weekend Television, BBC–UK and BBC–Bristol, and MTV–US and UK for all those specifics. Our appreciation to ABKCO Records, for their graciousness and their generosity in granting permission to reproduce photographs and phonorecord sleeves. Mention must be made of the incalculable value of the online databases of ASCAP and BMI, and those of the U.S. Library of Congress and Copyright Office, all of which were consulted in the preparation of this manuscript.

Special thanks go to the following individuals for, among other things, their substantive contributions, steadfast support, nurturing nagging, patience and understanding, and all else so freely given—as each knows much better than we could possibly state here:

Gary Levinson, database designer, for that early, invaluable key role; Hilary Poole, our editor, who will doubtless be elevated to sainthood forthwith; Tom Beach, the collector's collector; Sandy Beach, for loaning us his sunscreen; Ron Furmanek (in a league of his own); Daniel Gardin, a true friend and Stones afficionado; Bob Gruen, one heck of great guy (PS: throws great parties); Virginia Lohle, friend first, #1 in the photo biz; Phyllis and Stuart Lattner (great photographer and great desserts); Dick Taylor (never too busy to help); Colin Golding (new insight into the wintry past personified); Phil Windeatt (Fabulous Phil—beyond the call of duty); the Brothers

Johns, Andy and Glyn, for help in settling debates; Mick Avory, for the fax facts; George Chkiantz (alias "Irish O' Duffy" Chkiantz); Ed Dorso (Philly's finest); John Platt, for imparting his English touch; Bill German, for getting us into this mess in the first place; Sally Stevens, Esq. (advice, counsel, and unbelievable patience); Jon Marko (knows what he's talking about); Terry Hood, for keeping the dream alive and for understanding; Freddy and Larry Sessler, for always coming through in the clutch; Valerie Taylor (the best, through it all); Alan Copeland, Sensei, for focus and focus and an open helping hand as always; the late Howard Chapnick, for underscoring the second half of the word *photojournalist*; Jane Rose, for taking the time; Jim Callaghan (generous J.C.—for all those places none of us never expected to go); Giorgio Gomelsky, for his memory and providing, yet again, a Crawdaddy-like stage debut; Stash (so many untold stories, still waiting); Sam and Cheryl Rivera of Rivera Technics, magical Macintosh medics, for rescuing the Quacker—and us—from those deadline crashes; Jason Delfos and Glen Davis of Spectra Photo/Digital, for eleventh-hour artistry, emergency mindreading and elegant professionalism; Mick Taylor, for friendship—and wondrous music; and to Dax "Are You Done Yet?" Wexper, Dawn Wolf and Billie Greenfield, for keeping the faith.

And finally, our appreciation goes to the following for their part in making this book a reality: Pat Andrews, Al Arthur and Ruth Kahn, Brian Auger, Long John Baldry, Dick Bangham, Chris Barber, Rob Barnett, Magnus Bartlett, Bob Bender, Brad Blanc, Victor Bockris, Bruce Botnick, Geoff Bradford, Helen, Stasia and JoAnne Brown, Peter Brown, Bugsy, Woody Camp, Cathy Carapella/Diamond Time, Clem Cattini, Tony Chapman, Ben Chapnick, Michael Chertok, Sam Cutler, David Dalton, Jim Dickinson, Frank Esslinger, Rosanne Fontana, Rob Fabroni, Bruce Greenfield, Art Greenslade, Alex Gregson, Perry Handelman, Richard Hattrell, Mark Haverkos, D.V.M., Dick Heckstall-Smith, Ed Hemwall, Bob Herman, Andy Hoogenboom, Alan Hope, Wayne Hyde, Yuji Ikeda and Stone People Japan, Brian Jones, Theresa Kereakes, Bobby Keys, Tony King, Malcolm Klein, Brian Knight, Eddie Kramer, J.P. Laffont, Dean Lance, Shelley Lazar, Chuck Leavell, Peter Lee, Malcolm Leo, Carlo Little, D. Lope, Gered Mankowitz, Ray Manzarek, Roy Martin, Joe Marvullo, Bob Mascaro, Phil May, Sam Merrell, Anthony Monteforte, Tom Moulton, Andrew Neeley, Robert O'Dell, Jerry O'Neill, Carl Palomes, Karen Palomes, George Paulus, Dave Peck, Gene Pitney, Billy & Mary Lou Regan, Mark Roberty, Mick Rock, Tony Russell, Freddy Sall, Keith Scott, Francine Silberstein, Keith Sluchansky, Andy Solt, Starfile Photos, Big Jim Sullivan, Paul Surratt, David (Screaming Lord) Sutch, Jonathan Venn, Mickey Waller, Rob Weingartner, Mark & Debbie Zakrin, Nico Zentgraf and Mark Zubotkin. Those of you whose names we missed—it was unintentional.

Thank you, Rolling Stones, we love you.

—*James Karnbach and Carol Bernson*
New York

Introduction

Ladies and gentlemen, welcome to the musical career of those "five [sic] singing boys from England who've sold a lot of albums—the Rolling Stones!"[*]

This book has taken three years to prepare, a process that initially resulted in twice the number of words required by contractual agreement. After our finetoothed chainsaw achieved an approximately 50 percent reduction, the book finally found a resting place.

To say our project has been a labor of love is an understatement—it could not have happened otherwise once we started. The long, long road to a true Stones history turned out to be strewn with obstacles and prone to mirages. The "truth" as it existed then was not a pretty picture—it was a jumble of contradictions plus factoids and rumor upgraded to mythological truisms by the passage of time. The brain bell jangling we began to experience was surely enough to make any normal person totally batty; any sane human would have walked away from such a situation before trying to make sense out of such nonsense.

These authors, on the other hand, chose to battle the amnesia of various people affiliated with the Stones, and to challenge the embellishment and incorrect information of earlier books that had become fact by default. That included dubious details from James Karnbach's own private mountain of Stones data. If we were to chronicle three and a half decades of the Rolling Stones, we resolved, we weren't going to perpetuate those errors if at all possible, nor did we want to give credence to the masses of new ones coming in large part from the liner notes of an explosion of bootleg CDs (an issue that is discussed in the text).

We weren't interested in the dirt—no exposés of sub rosa Stones shenanigans offstage, no listings of illegal albums or videos—our concern was to provide correct factual information about the career and official output of "the world's greatest rock 'n' roll band"—in other words, the work.

We were always looking for the definitive, official "Yeah, that's right!" or "No, not really"—a herculean task if ever there was one. Our most time-consuming, toughest decisions came when two or more primary sources—people who were there—gave us three or more entirely different versions of the same incident. Resolving those questions, we knew, would always be a no-win situation—the other person or persons would no doubt disagree with our choice. Still, we forged ahead.

In plotting this crusade, we had to limit the degree of detail in the various categories. Sorry, but that constraint was applied to data like matrix numbers, details of various label configurations, length in minutes and seconds of multiple song versions, guitar tablatures and chord progressions of numbers performed live, etc. You won't find that in here. Had we gone that route, each chapter would have easily been a book in itself.

What you will find is the story of how one English rock 'n' roll band came into existence and survived to continue to create, perform and record music together for 35 years and counting. The Rolling Stones' story is very clearly told by their work. How they did it and who they are can be found by looking at this book's listings—their records and the studio and live recording sessions that produced them, their concert performances and tours, their television appearances and promo films and music videos, their feature film contributions—and in the band chronology that gathers up salient bits from each chapter and a few facts with no other home and (it is hoped) provides a framework for it all.

One thing that will be immediately obvious is that the biggest chapter is Tours and Concerts. This is neither an accident nor a case of editorial laxness. The Stones began as a live band and still are—most likely it's one of the secrets of their success as well as having been a source of much of their own frustration since the beginning. Getting the sound, feeling and energy of the Stones' music that you heard and they felt they played in concert onto something that can be purchased in a record store has always been the band's often elusive goal—not a simple proposition either in a recording studio or from the stage.

A Rolling Stones show, like the band itself, has always been more than music and musicians, and certainly more than a rock 'n' roll band plus the pyrotechnics and multimillion-dollar sets of the stadium rock era or cutting-edge technology in or out of the recording studio. The Stones' long career took off from the tiny stages of British clubs. Less than a year after the band's first gig, those clubs were bursting with frenzied fans, electrified by black

---

[*] As the band was introduced for the first time on US network television (June 13, 1964) by Dean Martin

American rhythm and blues performed by six white working-class English kids who defied almost every other social convention of the time along with their chosen repertoire. Their dynamic attraction to fiercely devoted fans and the almost palpable lust in the air at Stones concerts did not end when the band began writing its own songs or even when the personnel changed. No other band still fills stadiums around the world, sells records and elicits such strong public and personal reactions after 35 years.

It was a combination of many factors—the personalities, the times, the music—that became an immeasurable force that pulled it all together, giving the Stones something "extra-musical," as Mick Taylor describes it.

However, another clue to the process of the band's early and continued success can be found in their highly effective use of the visual media—particularly television and the music promo film—the latter now well known and ever-present as the music video. There was no MTV or VH1 in 1963, yet in July of that year, the Rolling Stones provided a public peek at what the club crowds were screaming about, making the first of what would be a steady, career-long stream of television appearances. When their first single was released pop music programs were proliferating, fast becoming staples in British viewers' television diets; the Stones' first spot on television came a month later. Appearances on the more established shows of the small screen both in the UK and abroad afforded them a chance to broaden their reach and put their music in the face of an initially unsuspecting general public. Whether audience response was thrill or disgust, and it was both, the Stones were unforgettable. Considering the fact that four Stones (past and present)[*] had training and avid interests in the visual arts, the band's acute perception of the power of television and film shouldn't be at all surprising. The details are set forth in the appropriate chapters (Television Appearances; Promotional Films and Videos; and Films).

None of this should be taken as a put-down of the prodigious creative output of the Rolling Stones as it appears on record (cassette, CD, what-have-you). The band has put untold hours of recording studio time into getting it "just right" and into our homes, a procedure that, from all we've been fortunate to learn from Mick Taylor, could definitely make a grown man cry.

Our primary task in the sessionography and discography chapters was to undertake a major housecleaning effort on that messy historical record, so that the recording sessionography listings would illustrate how, where, when and with whom the material that was recorded ended up

on the various official releases, along with similarly correlated information on as many unreleased titles (outtakes) as possible. A few things became quite clear to us as we mopped our brows (and our tears) and wrote it all down. The creative process is exactly that—a process—and not always linear; we were able to nail down many definitive recording dates from previously vague references, but there will always be Stones tracks that were really done in sessions somewhere in the ether. The Rolling Stones didn't get to where they are just by being in the right place at the right time or because of their looks, or because they had good karma—they worked very hard.

So, whether your heart's been with the Stones since the '60s, you're a '70s "can't you hear them rocking" Stones afficionado or an '80s Stones fan caught between a rock and a hard place, or even if you happen to be a new '90s type who's just gone wild over the Stones—there will be amusing tidbits and startling revelations for everyone in the pages that follow.

We'd like to offer one last thought. The Rolling Stones were in the vanguard of the rock 'n' roll revolution at the beginning of their career—seen as the Beatles' antithesis, they were the bad-boy pioneers best known for habitually confronting and resisting the conventional. As rebels, they were just as often the scapegoats of the established, but rapidly changing, social order of the 1960s and '70s. Still, they always took the creative and individual chances that, as a result, made the way easier for artists who followed; at the same time, the Stones' music became an inseparable portion of the cultural soundtrack for that very intense era.

At this writing, with the Steel Wheels and Voodoo Lounge tours behind them and scheduled to embark on yet another year-long world tour in September 1997, the Rolling Stones will have made what is perhaps one of their greatest breakthroughs and lasting contributions—debunking the common wisdom that rock 'n' roll is for and only to be played by the young. Over or close to 50 years old, those "singing boys from England" have packed stadiums worldwide, played great new tunes, sold a lot of albums and demonstrated that if you're creative, good at what you do best, willing to stay on the edge and work hard—you are never too old to rock 'n' roll! In the years to come, rock 'n' roll bands will no longer be burdened with the fallacious notion of mandatory retirement at age 35–40, but will know they can go on as long as they want to. Because it is possible—the Stones have proved it.

—JPK & CB
New York, New York

---

[*]Keith (Sidcup Art College), Charlie (Harrow School of Art, left his ad agency job at Hobson and Gray to join the Stones), Ronnie (art school, paints and exhibits internationally to this day), and Mick Taylor (among other things, had a job as a graphic artist before joining John Mayall's band).

Chronology

OCTOBER 24, 1936 The eldest of six children, William George Perks (Bill Wyman) born, Lewisham, London, England, to William and Kathleen "Molly" May Jeffrey Perks. After he got into the Stones, Bill took the modified name of an army buddy, Lee Whyman, as his stage name. In February 1963, less than a month after adopting his friend's full name, he substituted his own first name and kept the rest. He had a legal name change in July 1964.

JULY 18, 1938 Ian Stewart born in the fishing village of Pittenweem, Fife, Scotland. The pianist who answered an advertisement placed by Brian Jones in 1962, became the second founding member of the original Rollin' Stones and would remain an integral, irreplaceable part of the group until his untimely death on December 12, 1985.

JUNE 2, 1941 Charles Robert Watts born, Islington, London, England, to Charles Richard Watts, a parcel truck driver, and Lillian "Lilly" Charlotte Watts.

FEBRUARY 28, 1942 Lewis Brian Hopkin-Jones (Brian Jones) born, Cheltenham, Gloucestershire, England. Brian's father, Lewis Blount Jones, was an aeronautical engineer; his mother, Louisa Beatrice Simmonds Jones, taught piano. A sister, Barbara, was born three years later.

JULY 26, 1943 Michael Philip Jagger born, Dartfort, Kent, England, to Basil "Joe" Fanshawe Jagger, a physical education teacher, and Eva Ensley Scutts Jagger, a hairdresser. A brother, Chris, was born in 1947.

DECEMBER 18, 1943 Keith Richards born, Dartford, Kent, England, the only child of Herbert "Bert" William Richards and Doris Maude Lydia Dupree Richards. Bert worked for General Electric all his life after returning, wounded, from World War II. Doris drove a bakery van during the war, sold washing machines and played the ukulele. Keith's parents separated when he was in his teens; father and son remained estranged until 1982. Andrew Oldham persuaded Keith to drop the "s"—à la Cliff Richard—for a slicker stage name, but Keith never legally changed it. He used Richard for quite a while, and it's printed both ways on record covers and other Stones-related material from many time periods. But Keith returned to his real "Richards" in the late '70s, insisting on it after the trouble that began in Canada on February 27, 1977 (see below).

JUNE 1, 1947 Ron Wood born. His father, Arthur, was a tugboat captain and a harmonica player. His mother, Mercy Leah Elizabeth, was a photographic hand-colorist. Art and Ted, Ronnie's two older brothers, preceded him onto the British music scene.

JANUARY 17, 1949 Michael Kevin Taylor born, Hatfield, Hertfordshire, England, to Lionel and Joyce Basil Taylor. Almost all Stones reference books list Taylor's birth year as 1948; he was, in fact, born in 1949. The error, says Taylor, probably happened when his first passport was issued (although once he jokingly blamed it all on his mum). He has a sister, Marilyn.

1961

OCTOBER 1961 Sometime in late October, Mick Jagger is at the Dartford, Kent train station on his way to classes at the London School of Economics, carrying some imported R&B records he has acquired via mail order from Chess Records in Chicago. He runs into Keith Richards, bound for Sidcup Art College. Though they had gone to elementary school together, the two had traveled in different circles since then. But Mick's armful of Muddy Waters and Chuck Berry piques Keith's interest and, well, the rest is. . . .

NOVEMBER 1961 Keith Richards joins Little Boy Blue & the Blue Boys. They are a real house band. The group will never play a live club gig, but serves to keep Mick and Keith in touch both physically and musically until things begin to roll. The group also includes Dick Taylor, Bob Beckwith and Allen Etherington. Rehearsing together in each other's homes, they play a lot of Jimmy Reed and Chuck Berry. Chuck Berry's music is as special to Keith Richards as Elmore James's is to Brian Jones—an unknown factor in '61 that will become an important one in '62.

1962

MARCH 17, 1962 St. Patrick's Day of 1962 will prove to be a very lucky date for the Rolling Stones. This Saturday night is the first gig of a standing weekly engagement for Alexis Korner's Blues Incorporated at the Ealing Jazz Club in West London. Korner's band played rhythm and blues and very few clubs in the UK booked R&B acts in the early '60s. Not only was the music not generally heard live or available on record at the time, but there was also much resistance to it from the traditional jazz community. Korner not only loved playing the music himself but was also a great supporter of other musicians, young and old, black and white, English and foreign. Traveling players always knew they would have a place to sleep in London—on Korner's kitchen floor. Blues Inc. itself nurtured the early careers of many now-famous musicians, including the Rolling Stones. Korner became a mentor first to Brian, then to both Mick and Keith.

Charlie Watts was Blues Inc.'s drummer at the Ealing Club on this date. Korner played electric guitar, and the balance of the group consisted of Cyril Davies on harmonica, Dick Heckstall-Smith on tenor sax, Dave Stevens on piano and Andy Hoogenboom on bass. Interestingly, Jack Bruce (later of Cream fame) took Hoogenboom's place two weeks after this gig. Brian gives Alexis a tape entitled *Elmo & Paul*—three songs he'd recorded with mate Paul Pond (a.k.a. Paul Jones).

MARCH 24, 1962 Onstage at the Ealing Club, Alexis Korner introduces a guest guitarist named "Elmo Lewis" who'd come "all the way from Cheltenham" to play "Dust My Broom." Brian Jones who'd been in the audience at Blues Inc.'s debut the week before comes onstage to play. Charlie Watts is on drums; he has been playing regularly with Korner's group and will continue doing so until June, when he leaves and is replaced by Ginger Baker.

MARCH 31, 1962 Brian Jones's response to columnist Jack Good's definition of R&B is published by *DISC* magazine. Good, now more well known as the producer of "Shindig" and many other television shows in the UK ("Oh Boy," "6.5 Special," *et al.*), has raised Jones's hackles. Jones's letter pleads for someone to please "play Jack Good a Muddy Waters or a Howlin' Wolf disc so that he can hear what R and B really is?" (See photo page 3.)

APRIL 7, 1962 Little Boy Blue & the Blue Boys, minus Bob Beckwith, visit the Ealing Club to hear Blues Inc. Brian Jones and Paul Pond (a.k.a. Paul Jones, a.k.a. J. P. Jones), performing as "Elmo & Paul," have a guest spot at the interval. Cyril Davies introduces Elmo Lewis on slide guitar and, in a bit of typical Cyril Davies humor, "perpetually pissed Pond" on vocals. The guys from Kent are blown away by Brian's slide playing and are almost convinced they're hearing the real Elmore James. Jones is a total blues fanatic—the "Elmo Lewis" (his quirky homage to James) just adds to the mystique. The Blue Boys meet Brian at the bar after the set, and an animated discussion ensues. Until that night, each group thought it was the only bunch of young blokes in England wanting to play the blues, Keith has said of that meeting.

APRIL 16, 1962 Alexis Korner receives a tape, sent by Mick, of "Little Boy Blue" playing Berry's "Around & Around" and "Reelin' & Rockin'," plus "Bright Lights, Big City" by Jimmy Reed and Richie Valens's "La Bamba." (Historical note: 33 years later, these very songs will be found on the "early Stones tape" that is auctioned

DISC, April 7, 1962   **5**

Rules of thumb are fine for thumbs
—but lousy for records

I don't know where rock ends or R & B begins

by **JACK GOOD**

TREVOR PEACOCK . . . striking similarities between himself and Johnny Worth.

WHERE does rock 'n' roll end and rhythm and blues begin? I wish I knew for certain. It must be great to be able to have everything tied up in nice little packages, all neatly labelled. People who can do that don't get accused, as I was last week by a reader in " Post Bag," of not knowing true R and B.

I was told to go away and listen to Muddy Waters and Howlin' Wolf. Fine, and as I say, it must be nice to be a purist. You don't have to think or feel, you just apply a rule of thumb. Thus Billy Fury is a rock 'n' roll singer, so his records must be rock 'n' roll records.

Trouble is that rules of thumb are all right for thumbs but lousy for records. For instance, Acker Bilk is a trad band leader and therefore " Stranger On The Shore " is traditional jazz. It's not as easy as that, is it?

Let us take Howlin' Wolf's recording of " Little Baby." The tune and even the guitar figure in the accompaniment are almost identical to Ricky Nelson's recording of " My Babe."

Complications

Now the aforementioned reader tells me that Howlin' Wolf sings—R and B. Therefore, " Little Baby " is R and B. But " Little Baby " is the same as " My Babe." Therefore, " My Babe " is R and B. But " My Babe " is sung by Ricky Nelson, who is a rock and roll singer. Therefore " My Babe " can't be rhythm and blues.

See the mess you get into by applying rules of thumb?

Actually, although " Little Baby " and " My Babe " are so similar one is R and B and the other is R and R. The difference lies purely in the " feel " of the thing.

And you can't analyse and define a feel with the precision that you can analyse a bottle of medicine. One thing is certain, however—the idiom of a record is not revealed by the name of the artist on the label. If you don't believe me listen to the new Lonnie Donegan.

---

done before, by the Americans.

It may put some life back into British music. — HUGH BOYLE, 52, Dundonald Road, Gallowhill, Paisley.

that " Teach will be a hit,

THIS IS IT

" RHYTHM and blues " seems to be a term which needs defining, judging by Jack Good's column (DISC, 17-3-62).

It is a genuine blues style, evolved directly from the earlier, less sophisticated country blues. R and B in turn gave birth to a commercial offspring, universally known as rock 'n' roll. Billy Fury is a rock 'n' roll singer— not an R and B vocalist.

I listened to all the records quoted by Jack Good in his article, and all except one were rock 'n' roll records. The one exception was the Barbara George disc " I Know."

Please will somebody play Jack Good a Muddy Waters or a Howlin' Wolf disc so that he can hear what R and B really is?— BRIAN JONES, 23, Christchurch Road, Cheltenham, Gloucestershire.

As ardent twister that she takes this by Gary Edwards merits.—J. THORO P. THOMAS, K. SHORT, S. EDWA SHARPE, Fry Hal College, Eltham, L

THE LOT

I AGREE with S letter (DISC 1 have some music " get-up-and-go " i with these dreary, concoctions.

Variety is what '

~~~~~~~~~ **Bonus winner for March** ~~~

THOMAS ROOKES, 29 Addison Drive, St. Gil

~~~~~~~~~~~~~~~~~~

who better to give 1 than Jerry Lee L country and western blues. He can c **EDDIE GAMMA** Winton Road, An

JOAN REC couldn't have nicer person.

The first-ever appearance in print of a Rolling Stone: Brian Jones's letter to DISC *magazine, questioning columnist Jack Good's knowledge of R&B music. Jack Good's reply to Brian Jones's letter requires an entire article in* DISC. *Ironically, Jack Good will play an important, positive role in the Stones' future.* (JPK/CB)

off at Christie's on May 25, 1995. The Christie's tape has a total of 18 separate tracks but only 13 song titles, the four sent to Korner in 1962 plus nine others. The extra five tracks were alternate takes of certain songs—among them the ones Korner received.)

APRIL 21, 1962 Mick, Keith, and Dick Taylor have their own guest spot onstage at the Ealing Club, performing Chuck Berry's "Around & Around" with Cyril Davies and Charlie Watts and the rest of Blues Inc.

MAY 1962 Brian Jones places an ad in *Jazz News*, looking for players with whom to form his own R&B band. The first response comes from pianist Ian Stewart, known as Stu. Andy Wren, who also played piano (with Screaming Lord Sutch) but wanted to sing, shows up at Brian's first rehearsal at the White Bear pub in Leicester Square. Wren's style doesn't mesh with the Jimmy Reed/Howlin' Wolf/Muddy Waters sound that Jones favors, but Stu's boogie-woogie playing does and he sticks around. There are two or three rehearsals a week in the beginning at the White Bear—until Brian gets caught filching cigarettes from the bar and they move to another pub, the Bricklayer's Arms in Soho. The eviction is no major setback. Word of Brian's search had spread— with a bit of help from Alexis Korner—and other musicians like guitarist Geoff Bradford and harp player Brian Knight have begun showing up to play with Brian and Stu. Jones tries to persuade singer Paul Pond (later known as Paul Jones of Manfred Mann) to join the rehearsals, but Pond,

Singer joins Korner

A 19 - YEAR - OLD Dartford rhythm and blues singer, Mick Jagger, has joined the Alex Korner group, Blues Incorporated, and will sing with them regularly on their Saturday dates at Ealing and their Thursday sessions at the Marquee Jazz Club, London.

Jagger, at present completing a course at the London School of Economics, also plays harmonica.

First mention of Mick Jagger in print—Mick begins singing with Alexis Korner and this item appears in the May 19, 1962 issue of DISC, *the British music weekly.*
(JPK/CB)

who has been appearing with Blues Inc. like Jagger and others, declines.

MAY 19, 1962 *DISC* magazine reports that Mick Jagger has joined Alexis Korner's band and will be singing with them at their regular resident gigs at the Marquee and Ealing jazz clubs. Jagger's one-song guest spot has been worked into a segment of four classic blues numbers in the Blues Inc. show. The end of the month finds him gigging with the band three nights a week, performing songs like Muddy Waters's "Got My Mojo Working" or Big Bill Broonzy's "Ride 'Em on Down," attending the London School of Economics by day, and still living with his parents in Dartford.

MAY 25, 1962 Mick goes down to the Bricklayer's Arms to check out Brian and Stu's rehearsals, bringing Keith and Dick Taylor. Brian wants Jagger to join them, but isn't so sure about Keith and his passion for Chuck Berry: Brian doesn't include Berry in his own pantheon of blues idols. But Mick won't sing without Keith, so Brian hasn't much choice. Keith coaxes Brian into playing some Berry tunes along with his beloved Jimmy Reed and Elmore James classics.

JUNE 1962 Jagger leaves Korner's band to concentrate on working with the group that will become the Stones. It is not yet a "band," but that is what the group all want it to become. Brian is the acknowledged leader. The pub players now include Brian Jones on slide guitar, Mick Jagger on vocals, Keith Richards on guitar, Dick Taylor on bass, Geoff Bradford on guitar, and Ian Stewart on piano. Bradford doesn't stick around long and the rhythm section needs sorting out. There are many drummers at these rehearsals, among them Mick Avory (who later joined the Kinks), Tony Chapman and Charlie Watts. Watts's participation is purely recreational, at most. With a good steady job at an ad agency, he has no thoughts of joining at this point. Tony Chapman plays with another group, the Cliftons, but is often found in the drummer's chair at the mostly regular Wednesday and Friday rehearsals. The sessions move again—to the Wetherby Arms, Chelsea. Chuck Berry was apparently not such a hard sell. Getting Charlie Watts to join them proves to be more difficult.

JUNE 30, 1962 *DISC*, the UK music weekly, scoops the rest of the British music press by at least a week with an item announcing Alexis Korner's Blues Incorporated's upcoming radio debut. Blues Inc. is to appear on the venerated BBC program "Jazz Club" on July 12, 1962.

JULY 7, 1962 "Korner Cancels" reads the headline of an item in *DISC* on this date. The article explains that

Korner's R and B group debuts on radio

ALEXIS KORNER and his R & B group Blues Incorporated will make their radio debut in the Light Programme's "Jazz Club" on July 12.

They are rush‑recording a single for Decca next Monday, under Jack Good's supervision for which they will be joined by the American Servicemen vocal team The Stripes of Glory, who made their debut with the band at the Marquee last Thursday with great success. Top side title will be "Geneva."

Korner and the group will present an R & B and gospel concert with the Stripes at the Richmond Jazz Festival on July 28 and 29.

The event that gave the Rolling Stones the chance to play their first gig—replacing Long John Baldry and His Kansas City Blue Boys as Alexis Korner's interval band. Baldry moved up to headline that evening's show at the Marquee. June 30, 1962 DISC (JPK/CB)

since Alexis Korner is to be appearing with Blues Inc. on the BBC "Jazz Club" broadcast on July 12, he and his band will not be featured on that date at the Marquee, their usual Thursday evening spot. "Instead," the magazine reports, "their place will be taken by a new rhythm and blues group, Mick Jagger and the Rolling Stones, together with another group headed by Long John Baldry."

KORNER CANCELS

OWING to a "Jazz Club" broadcast on July 12, Alexis Korner and his Blues Incorporated will not be featured in their weekly session at the Marquee that night.

Instead, their place will be taken by a new rhythm and blues group, Mick Jagger and the Rolling Stones, together with another group headed by Long John Baldry.

As far as we know, this item in the July 7, 1962 issue of DISC is the first-ever mention of the Rolling Stones in print. The announcement in Jazz News came on July 11. (JPK/CB)

So, your humble authors theorize, the Stones must have had a name somewhat earlier than most (including us) have thought. *DISC* is a weekly publication; its cover date refers to the first day of the week that issue is on sale, which means the July 7 edition was printed before July 6, and any information contained in it had to have been known prior to that. And, if Alexis Korner and Mick Jagger had already had their discussion and Korner had negotiated the Stones' debut with Harold Pendleton (see TOURS AND CONCERTS) prior to *DISC*'s June 30 issue, then the birthdate of the Rolling Stones would have been even earlier. Ergo, the Stones had a name sometime in the last week of *June*, first few days of July at the very latest.

JULY 11, 1962 The following item appears in the British music weekly, *Jazz News:* "Mick Jagger, R&B vocalist, is taking an R&B group into the Marquee tomorrow night while Blues Incorporated do their 'Jazz Club' radio broadcast gig. Called the Rolling Stones, the line-up is: Mick Jagger (vocals), Keith Richards and Elmo Lewis (guitars), Dick Taylor (bass), Ian Stewart (piano) and Mick Avory (drums).

Their first gig, their first advertised appearance, and the ad copy is not quite correct. The first of two groups scheduled to appear Thursday, July 12, according to the club's calendar-style ad, is: "Mick Jagger and the Rolling Stones." But Brian had named them the "Rollin' Stones,"

The pre–Charlie Watts Stones were making themselves known on the British R&B scene—reflected by this page in Jazz News *from September 1962. (Charlie was around....)* (JPK/CB)

after the line in Muddy Waters's Song "Mannish Boy," and spelled it like the track entitled "Rollin' Stone Blues."

Furthermore, Mick Avory did not play: it was Tony Chapman who filled in on drums. Chapman's "disappearing act" is what brought Avory to the band's rehearsals for the Marquee gig, only to be replaced two rehearsals later. When Chapman is finally reached, he confirms that he'll be at the show.

JULY 12, 1962 The Rollin' Stones' first gig, at the Marquee Jazz Club in Oxford Street. They're paid £20, but they earn the chance to do more. Owner Harold Pendleton later described the band's wardrobe, saying that Jagger wore a "colorful pullover" while Richards had on a "necktie and banker's suit." Brian Jones had picked the name—from a line in Muddy Waters's song "Mannish Boy,"—some say it was just the week before, but see July 7, 1962 above—when the unnamed band found it had scored a real gig. The others went along with Brian's choice (Ian Stewart later said he hated the name). (See TOURS AND CONCERTS)

The Marquee Jazz Club's advertisement in *Melody Maker* doesn't reflect any change in the club's calendar for this week; the ad copy indicates only that Alexis Korner's Blues Incorporated is appearing July 12, as usual, and does not mention the Rollin' Stones.

Alexis Korner does the "Jazz Club" radio show. Charlie Watts is the drummer on this broadcast. It was thought that Ginger Baker had replaced him at this gig, but a recently discovered tape of this program has proved conclusively that the drummer was indeed Charlie Watts.

AUGUST 1, 1962 Mick rents the flat that will become infamous—102 Edith Grove in Chelsea—and, with

Brian, moves in. Pat Andrews, Brian's girlfriend and the mother of one of his sons, joins them. Keith subsequently leaves Dartford for good and installs himself at Edith Grove.

SEPTEMBER 29, 1962 The Rollin' Stones first recording session, at Curly Clayton Sound Studios in London. Three tracks are recorded. Dick Taylor leaves the Stones to prepare his portfolio for consideration by the Royal College of Art and returns to his studies at Sidcup (though he later cofounds the Pretty Things). The band at this session consists of Mick, Keith, Brian, Dick Taylor and Ian Stewart, with Tony Chapman on drums. (See SESSIONOGRAPHY and TOURS AND CONCERTS)

DECEMBER 1962 Bill Wyman goes with Tony Chapman to hear the Stones at the Red Lion Pub in Surrey. Chapman introduces Bill to Ian Stewart and they get talking. Stu mentions that the Stones are looking for a bass player and invites him down to the Wetherby Arms two days later. (Bill Wyman, in *Stone Alone* and elsewhere, has said that Chapman took him to see the Presidents and that this Red Lion event took place on December 5, 1962, which was a Wednesday. However Glyn Johns, who sang with the Presidents, has confirmed that the Presidents played at the Surrey pub on Fridays—the only day there was *any* music there. Not only that, Glyn elaborated that it was the Stones who played the Red Lion on Friday,

Again, the Stones roll into a fortuitous vacancy left by Alexis Korner. An item in DISC announces that Alexis Korner's band is leaving their Ealing Club Saturday night residency, to be replaced by the Rolling Stones. (JPK/CB)

JAZZ NEWS & REVIEW — Thursday, 27th December, 1962 **Page 15**

R & B
by
BILL CAREY

top three or four in the country.........by the way, **GUITARIST** wanted quickly.........

THE RICKY TICK up in **WINDSOR** at the 'Star & Garter' looks as if it is going to one of the regular homes of regular R & B...then there's the growing custom at the PICCA...

of personnel...Cyril is planning a record.....**DAVE HUNT** (new tel bookings WES 9373) reaching five gigs per week...**ROLLIN' STONES** (wanted one **BASSIST**-must be Rhythm & Blues slanted) are heav-

ily booked over the season ...gigging at the Green Man, Black Heath on few dates...On 4th January they are at the Red Lion, Sutton...with a chance of fortnightly residency......

A portion of a newspaper item (in a December 27, 1962 issue) in which the Stones advertised for a bass player—oddly enough, Wyman had already auditioned for the spot.

December 7—and the Presidents performed on alternate weeks. The Stones and the Presidents never played together at the Red Lion. One example of why and how our dates here and elsewhere may differ from other published reports.) (See TOURS AND CONCERTS)

DECEMBER 4, 1962 Hearing the other Stones bemoaning their lack of a bassist during a break at their Ealing Club gig, Tony Chapman mentions that he knows a guy, a bandmate in the Cliftons. His bass player friend, he tells them, also has his own amp. Chapman is urged to bring him to the next rehearsal.

DECEMBER 9, 1962 Wyman arrives at the "audition" with his monster amp. He has plenty of experience —quite a bit more than the others, in truth. In addition to a day job, Wyman (whose real surname is Perks) has been playing regular gigs with the Cliftons, a South London band. But by all accounts, including his own, it's his equipment that most likely clinches the deal. He calls the amplifier his "spare"—it is later dubbed "the wardrobe"—and observes the impoverished Stones' eyes fixed upon it. They ask him back. (This event took place two days after Bill Wyman spoke to Ian Stewart at the Red Lion, by Wyman's own account. December 9 was a Sunday in 1962, although it is not clear whether the group rehearsed on Sundays—the bassist's first meeting with the Stones may actually have been on December 10.)

DECEMBER 15, 1962 Bill Wyman's first gig with the Stones. Personality-wise, there hadn't been a lot of chemistry at the Wetherby Arms audition. Wyman is older than the others—married, with an infant son and a day job as a clerk—and a lot straighter. But musically they got along and continued to get along at their second rehearsal together, the day before this gig.

DECEMBER 18, 1962 Wyman's second gig with the band. The Stones have played other gigs without him in the intervening days, having agreed that Wyman, with family and work responsibilities, could pass on the low-paying jobs. A nice sentiment, but at this point, they're all low-paying jobs, if that. But the process of Bill's absorption into the band has begun. The boys seem to have warmed up to him.

DECEMBER 25, 1962 Although Wyman may have felt accepted by the group, he may not have been aware that the Stones were still advertising for a bass player.

1963

JANUARY 17, 1963 Charlie Watts's first gig as an official band member—at the Marquee Jazz Club in London's Soho district—thus, the first gig played by the "Rolling Stones." Watts sat in with the band before this date, but only as a favor, to fill the frequently vacant drummer's slot. After leaving Blues Inc., Watts still played with Blues By Six, but he hadn't given up his day job as a graphic artist at an advertising agency. Brian had been pursuing him all along. (See TOURS AND CONCERTS)

FEBRUARY 24, 1963 First gig at Giorgio Gomelsky's Crawdaddy Club, located at the Station Hotel, Richmond, Surrey. The Stones' big break happens by fluke when bad weather causes the scheduled act, the Dave Hunt Band, to cancel on February 17 and Giorgio calls them to play on the 24th. This will become a regular Sunday residency and, in essence, where the Stones are discovered by those outside the jazz club circuit. Gomelsky becomes an ardent supporter, intent on managing and promoting the band.

MARCH 11, 1963 The band records five tracks at IBC Studios, where Glyn Johns works as an engineer when he's not singing with the Presidents. This studio time costs the Stones no money, but the material they cut here is owned and represented by IBC management. This is the studio's customary arrangement. If an artist or group preferred not to be represented by IBC—who were not very well versed in the rock 'n' roll end of the music business—all they had to do was pay for the session.

APRIL 13, 1963 The first major article about the Rolling Stones appear in a newspaper, the *Richmond and Twickenham Times*, a local weekly. Barry May's five-column story is full of colorful details about the band's appearance and about their audience, which, in a mere six weeks, had grown by word-of-mouth from less than a handful to more than 300 avid, dancing fans. It results in a deluge of interest in the Stones and a torrent of new business on Sunday nights—and eventual headaches for the club in subsequent weeks as the rowdy audience spills out into the surrounding streets.

APRIL 14, 1963 Taping an appearance on "Thank Your Lucky Stars," the Beatles meet old friend Giorgio Gomelsky. Giorgio's presence at the taping was, he has told us, for the purpose of giving the Beatles a movie script he had written. The plot called for the Fab Four (in starring roles) to act like "goons"—English for jumping around and acting silly—à la *Hard Day's Night*. After giving them the script, Giorgio invites the Beatles to stop off at his club in Richmond to see the new group that has begun attracting a huge following—besides, he tells them, the road back to London passes right past the Station Hotel.

   The Beatles do stop by, and catch the last 20 minutes of the last set. Afterwards, Giorgio, the Beatles and the Stones all go back to Edith Grove.

APRIL 21, 1963 Giorgio Gomelsky films the Stones at the Station Hotel for a planned documentary about the band. The filming takes place during the day, prior to the regular Sunday Crawdaddy Club gig. Five days earlier, on April 16, Gomelsky had taken the band into R. G. Jones Studio to record the two tracks used in the film. (See SESSIONOGRAPHY and FILMS)

APRIL 28, 1963 Tipped off by a phone call from journalist Peter Jones, Andrew Loog Oldham attends the Stones' Crawdaddy Club gig at the Station Hotel, Richmond. The band's performance and the crowd's reaction set Oldham in motion. He approaches Brian and Mick in the bar for a little chat: though this conversation does not include an offer of a management contract with Easton/Oldham, it will lead to one very shortly. Giorgio

Gomelsky, the group's de facto manager, is in Switzerland attending his father's funeral during this critical period. Oldham is very creative, very sharp and poised for his own big break, just like the Stones. Previously, he had done a bit of publicity work with Brian Epstein for the Beatles and knew that the music industry was ripe for a radical change. Oldham sees the Stones' potential (and his own) as major players in this process and wants to cement a relationship with them.

MAY 5, 1963 Andrew Oldham brings partner Eric Easton to the Crawdaddy Club to see the Stones for himself. Easton is an old hand in the music business, a respected artist's manager and former movie theater organist who has just teamed up with the highly motivated, and much younger Oldham. It will prove to be a dynamic combination for the Stones.

MAY 6, 1963 The Rolling Stones' management agreement with Andrew Loog Oldham and Eric Easton's newly formed company, Impact Sound, becomes effective. Signed by Brian Jones on behalf of the Stones, the contract is for a term of three years.

MAY 8, 1963 Ian Stewart is informed by either Andrew Oldham or Brian Jones that he will not be a front line member of the Rolling Stones. The reason: his image doesn't mesh with the one the band is trying to project—so Stu is told. And, on top of that, he's told that it's easier for fans to remember a group of five people than one containing six. The meaning: he has a big chin and looks too rough—and too straight. He will be treated as a band member behind the scenes, he is promised, and is urged to stay on. Incredibly, he does—despite what appears to be an outrageous affront—Stu has been around from the beginning and, essentially, helped Brian start the band. Years later, when asked about his being fired, Stu replied, "I had nothing else better to do at the time so I figured I would stay with them anyway, and travel." He becomes a kind of (semi-) silent partner/road manager, using his transit van to ferry the band to and from gigs in these early days, and continues to play piano in the studio and onstage. The band relies on him totally from this point until his death in December 1985.

MAY 9, 1963 Brian Jones, again for the band, signs a three-year recording contract with Impact Sound (Andrew Oldham and Eric Easton) that gives the five Stones (but not Stu!) a 6% share (to be divided among them) of royalties received by Impact. During his discussions the band's new managers, Jones had mentioned that the band had already recorded some demos with Glyn Johns at IBC Studios on March 11. Easton and Oldham shrewdly decide to get those tapes back and deputize Brian to retrieve them. Jones does so, paying studio director George Clewson the band's £106 session bill while leading him to believe that the band is breaking up and merely wants the tapes as a souvenir of their brief time together.

MAY 10, 1963 Beatle George Harrison judges the Lancashire and Cheshire Beat Group Contest at Philharmonic Hall, Liverpool. With him on the panel is "the man who turned down the Beatles," Decca A&R chief Dick Rowe. Harrison gives him a tip: go see the Rolling Stones at the Station Hotel and sign them.

MAY 10, 1963 The Rolling Stones record Chuck Berry's "Come On" at Olympic Sound Studios in London. Andrew Oldham produces. (A week later, they record it again at Decca, at the suggestion of the record company, but the use the first one, in the end.)

MAY 11, 1963 The Stones play the *News of the World* Charity Gala at Battersea Park. This is the first booking secured for them by their new managers, Andrew Loog Oldham and Eric Easton. Many books have said this event took place on May 4, 1963 but it didn't.

MAY 12, 1963 Decca's Dick Rowe (hoping, one would think, for a chance to again hold his head up in the music industry) heeds George Harrison's advice and ventures down to Richmond to see the Stones perform.

MAY 14, 1963 Dick Rowe signs the Stones. A two-year contract, in the form of a "tape-lease agreement" is executed by Decca Records and Impact Sound (Oldham and Easton). Despite what might appear to be a miniscule royalty provision in their Impact Sound contract, the Stones (well, Oldham and Easton) still own their masters: the record company merely leases the right to use them. This is not only shrewd dealing, but was unheard of in the industry at the time. Not only that, the Stones' percentage with Impact is higher than the Beatles are receiving at the time.

JUNE 7, 1963 The Stones' first single, "Come On" b/w "I Want to Be Loved" is released in the UK.

JUNE 13, 1963 The *Daily Mirror*'s Patrick Doncaster breaks the Stones' story to the British nation. This is the first time the band is the subject of an article in a national, daily newspaper. Like earlier stories in the *Richmond and Twickenham Times* and other local papers, Doncaster's piece attempts to describe Britain's newest cultural phenomenon—currently on view Sundays at the Station Hotel in suburban Richmond.

JULY 13, 1963 The band makes its television debut, performing "Come On" on the ITV pop music program, "Thank Your Lucky Stars." Reluctantly, they wear identical outfits—velvet-collared houndstooth jackets, complete with coordinated ties and trousers.

AUGUST 23, 1963 First appearance on the Friday "Ready, Steady, Go!" television show. The program's motto: "The weekend starts here."

SEPTEMBER 9, 1963 The compilation album *Thank Your Luck Stars, Vol. 2* is released by Decca in the UK, marking the Stones' first appearance on an LP. Their contribution is a single track on the B-side, "Come On."

SEPTEMBER 10, 1963 Andrew Oldham brings John Lennon and Paul McCartney to Studio 51, where the Stones are rehearsing. Learning that the Stones are searching for a followup single to "Come On," the two Beatles offer a partially finished song to them. The Stones accept and John and Paul quickly complete "I Wanna Be Your Man." The next day, Lennon and McCartney rush into the studio to record it themselves, releasing it some time later.

SEPTEMBER 29, 1963 The Stones begin their first UK tour, as the support act for the Everly Brothers and Bo Diddley, at the New Victoria Theatre in London. Little Richard will join the bill on October 5 and remain for the rest of the 32-date package which ends on November 3 at London's Hammersmith Odeon Theatre.

NOVEMBER 1, 1963 UK release date of the band's second single, "I Wanna Be Your Man," written by John Lennon and Paul McCartney. The B-side, "Stoned," is the first release of a track with the songwriting credit of "Nanker Phelge," thus the Stones' first recording of one of their own compositions.

DECEMBER 20, 1963 Gene Pitney's single "That Girl Belongs to Yesterday," is released. This is the first time a Jagger/Richards song is released, though George Bean was, in fact, the first artist to *record* one of the team's compositions—"It Should Be You." However, Bean's disc wasn't shipped to record stores until January 1964.

1964

JANUARY 2, 1964 The band appears on the premiere broadcast of BBC-TV's "Top of the Pops," performing the Lennon/McCartney song "I Wanna Be Your

Man," their second UK single, which had reached number 12 on the UK charts.

JANUARY 6, 1964 The Stones' second UK tour, but their first time as headliners. This two-week outing is marked by concerts filled with crazed fans and garners much press attention. (See TOURS AND CONCERTS for the support acts and more info.)

JANUARY 7, 1964 Cyril Davies, one of the founding fathers of the British R & B movement, dies at the age of 32, of leukemia. Like Alexis Korner, Chris Braber and Giorgio Gomelsky, Davies had been responsible for some of Britain's earliest exposure to the authentic blues and had booked Muddy Waters's first UK tour in the late '50s. A blues purist, Davies introduced English clubgoers to the blues harmonica, which he played in various groups, notably as a member of Alexis Korner's Blues Incorporated, then as the leader of his own group, the Cyril Davies All-Stars.

JANUARY 10, 1964 *The Rolling Stones*, the band's first EP, is released in the UK by Decca. (See DISCOGRAPHY)

JANUARY 18, 1964 Little known fact: On this day both a Lennon/McCartney composition and a Jagger/Richards composition enter the US charts for the first time. The Beatles' tune was "I Wanna Hold Your Hand" and the Jagger/Richards song was "That Girl Belongs to Yesterday" recorded by Gene Pitney.

MARCH 6, 1964 The Stones' first US single, "Not Fade Away" b/w "I Wanna Be Your Man," is released by London Records. A US promo with a different B-side—"Stoned"—had been pressed some weeks earlier. However, London Records, afraid of that title's innuendo, stopped the commercial release of the original single and issued one with the Lennon/McCartney song on the flipside.

MARCH 19, 1964 The Rolling Stones tape their appearance on BBC Radio's "Blues & Rhythm" program hosted by Long John Baldry—whose stentorian opening line is a rousing "Ladies and gentlemen this is Rhythm *and* Blues!" Also appearing on the show were George Fame & the Blue Flames. This event was particularly noteworthy as it was to be the BBC's (Light Programme) first-ever stereo broadcast. That in itself was a rather bizarre idea since there were few stereo radios in British households in March 1964. To the age old philosophical query, slightly mangled and updated, "would anybody hear it?" the experimental station BBC3 proffered the two-radio theory. Transmitting the program over two additional frequencies, they instructed listeners with two ordinary radios to tune one receiver to one frequency for the left channel and the other to the second frequency for the right side. And, voilà—stereo. Presumably, the show was also transmitted intact at the assigned frequency for those with only one radio. So, one could also say it was Britain's first stereo "simulcast." The Stones performed for nearly an hour before a select audience at the BBC's Camden Theatre, although only 15 minutes of their show was actually aired on the program broadcast on May 9, 1964.

MARCH 27, 1964 Mick and Marianne Faithfull meet for the first time at a birthday party for teen singer Adrienne Posta (then known by her real surname, Poster). The Jagger-Faithfull encounter is actually a nonevent; Marianne comes away from it decidedly unimpressed, preferring her more refined boyfriend (and later, husband) John Dunbar, to the likes of Mick and the rest of the band. But the party produces another introduction that will nonetheless draw her into the Stones' web. Andrew Oldham, in his quest to become Brian Epstein and Phil Spector rolled into one, had just produced the birthday girl's single of Mick and Keith's fluffy "Shang A Doo Lang" (Poster/Posta's first had been "Only Fifteen" in '63. She was 14 at the time). Drink in hand and on the lookout for fresh talent, Oldham zeros in on blonde 17-year-old Marianne. He and Dunbar have met before, and their conversation easily leads to one with Faithfull. Her name alone (not to mention her looks) is Oldham-the-publicist's dream; he proposes a recording session straightaway, her singing ability, if any, irrelevant to him. Marianne is, understandably, skeptical of the "I can make you a star" line, but within two months finds herself recording "As Tears Go By" for Decca and being managed by Andrew.

MAY 2, 1964 Their very first album is released in the UK. Titled *The Rolling Stones*, the LP's cover art is only an unadorned photograph of the five Stones—without the band's name, or any information, for that matter. The omission is intentional and a record industry first. (Until the "no-title" idea materialized, the short list for the album's name included "12 x 5.") The LP replaces *With the Beatles* at number one on the UK album charts, and breaks the Beatles' year-long lock on the top spot.

MAY 29, 1964 London Records releases the band's first US LP *The Rolling Stones—England's Newest Hitmakers*, which, like their first UK album, includes "Tell Me," the first Jagger/Richards composition recorded by the Stones. But, the UK and US albums have different track listings. (See DISCOGRAPHY)

JUNE 2, 1964 The Rolling Stones' first US television appearance, on the "Les Crane Show," a New York local late-night program. On June 1, the band had arrived at New York's Kennedy airport—on BOAC Flight 505—to begin their first concert tour of the United States.

JUNE 3, 1964 They tape their appearance on the "Hollywood Palace" show for later broadcast. Little did they know. . . . (See TELEVISION APPEARANCES)

JUNE 5, 1964 The Stones' first US tour begins at the Swing Auditorium in San Bernardino, CA. The band plays only nine dates on the tour, and audience reaction across the country is decidedly mixed. The last show is at Carnegie Hall. (See TOURS AND CONCERTS)

JUNE 6, 1964 At their second US gig, the Stones get to know Bobby Keys, the saxophonist with Bobby Vee's band. Vee appeared in San Bernardino the day before and is also on this day's bill at the San Antonio State Fair. Born in Lubbock, TX on the same day as Keith Richards, Bobby Keys will play a major role with the Rolling Stones in later years, in countless recording ses-

sions and on many tours. (See SESSIONOGRAPHY and TOURS AND CONCERTS)

JUNE 10, 1964 The band's own monthly magazine, *The Rolling Stones Book*, premieres on London newsstands.

JUNE 10–11, 1964 The Stones' first recording session in the United States—at Chicago's famed Chess Studios. This is the proverbial dream-come-true for the band—to record at the same studio in which their idols made the music that started the Stones' own journey. And, to work with engineers who know and understand the type of sound they want to end up on tape, one that British engineers are unable to achieve. This booking and those later at RCA in Hollywood are a result of the group's acquaintance with American record producer, Phil Spector, whom they met in the UK in January '64.

JUNE 12, 1964 The first US release of a Jagger/Richards composition. The single "Tell Me," b/w Willie Dixon's "I Just Want to Make Love to You" is released by London Records.

Bill Wyman, circa 1964 (TOM BEACH COLLECTION)

JUNE 13, 1964   Their first US network television appearance, on "Hollywood Palace," is broadcast on ABC. This could be characterized as an enlightening experience for the band (or a reality check). (See TELEVISION APPEARANCES)

JUNE 20, 1964   At the end of their first US tour, the Stones play two shows at Carnegie Hall.

JUNE 26, 1964   Release in the UK of "It's All Over Now" b/w "Good Times, Bad Times," the first Stones' single to reach number one in the UK.

JULY 4, 1964   The infamous Stones' "Juke Box Jury" appearance is aired. (See TELEVISION APPEARANCES)

CA. JULY 10, 1964   Bill Perks's name is officially changed to Bill Wyman.

JULY 18, 1964   "It's All Over Now" reaches the top of the UK charts—the Stones' first number one single.

AUGUST 8, 1964   The Stones' first gig in Europe outside of the UK and Ireland is a short one in The Netherlands. The concert, at the Kurhaus, Scheveningen, The Hague, is scheduled to last only about half an hour but the audience goes insane as soon as the Stones come on, and the show is essentially over after the second song. Crazed fans rushed the stage and were immediately met by a merciless platoon of police who very efficiently removed them from the front and, not sparing the truncheons, tossed them out of the hall. Despite the escalating riot, which left the historic venue in a total shambles, the Stones tried to continue performing—first without vocals when the mikes lost their cables, then with only percussion when police cut the power. It became clear that it was neither the time nor place to try an acoustic set and they finally gave up. This engagement had been booked by the same promoter who brought the Beatles to Holland. Apparently, he didn't realize the Rolling Stones weren't a "family show."

AUGUST 10, 1964   First known Stones brush with the law. Mick Jagger gets a speeding ticket in Liverpool. He is also cited for driving without insurance and is fined £32.

AUGUST 22, 1964   *England's Newest Hitmakers —The Rolling Stones*, the band's first US LP, is released.

SEPTEMBER 16, 1964   Andrew Loog Oldham marries painter Sheila Klein (no relation to Allen) in Glasgow, Scotland.

OCTOBER 9, 1964   The band retracts an earlier announcement of a projected South African tour, stating that they wish to comply with the Musicians Union policy of opposition to apartheid.

OCTOBER 14, 1964   Charlie Watts marries sculptress Shirley Ann Shepherd in Bradford, Yorkshire, England.

OCTOBER 25, 1964   The Rolling Stones' first appearance on "The Ed Sullivan Show." The band is in the US again for their second American tour.

OCTOBER 27, 1964   The Stones' first recording session at RCA Studios, Hollywood, CA.

OCTOBER 28–29, 1964   The Stones take part in the filmed concerts at the Santa Monica (CA) Civic Auditorium for the movie, *The T.A.M.I. Show*. This is the band's first appearance in a full-length film. (See FILMS)

NOVEMBER 2, 1964   Mayor Ralph Locher of Cleveland, OH, the same city that will erect the Rock and Roll Hall of Fame & Museum 30 years later, threatens to forbid the use of public facilities for rock shows. Locher's opinion—that rock 'n' roll doesn't contribute to his city's culture, and tends to cause riots—is widely quoted in news reports. The Rolling Stones are to perform at the Public Auditorium in Cleveland on November 3, the next day. (See TOURS AND CONCERTS)

DECEMBER 5, 1964   "Little Red Rooster" hits number one on the UK singles chart.

DECEMBER 18, 1964   The US single, "Heart of Stone" b/w "What a Shame" is released by London Records. This is the group's first single to contain only Jagger/Richards original songs.

1965

JANUARY 20, 1965   The Stones' first appearance on the US television show, "Shindig" (ABC) is broadcast. They had taped this spot in November 1964 in the UK. "Shindig" is produced by Jack Good, also producer of the hugely successful UK "Ready, Steady, Go!," among others. (See TELEVISION APPEARANCES)

JANUARY 22, 1965   The band begins its first tour in the Far East, which is actually made up of three weeks of concerts in Australia and New Zealand and a final two-show date in Singapore.

JANUARY 22, 1965 Charlie Watts's book, *Ode to a Highflying Bird*, is published by Beat Publications in London. The homage to saxophone legend Charlie Parker had been written and illustrated by Watts in 1961.

FEBRUARY 6, 1965 *The Rolling Stones No. 2* is number one on the UK charts.

MARCH 18, 1965 The infamous "pissing" incident. This occurs on the way back to London after a show at the ABC Theatre in Romford, Essex, the last gig of a two-week UK tour. The band's first priority after their last number has become getting out of any concert venue quickly and, hopefully, unscathed; such departures usually preclude final pit stops. By the time the Stones' Daimler reaches West Ham, Bill Wyman's self-described weak bladder needs attention, and they make the obvious decision. However, the Romford Road gas station's mechanic, Charles Keeley, for whatever reason, chooses not to open the "private" facilities and tells them to leave. The band, no doubt still energized from performing (and getting out alive), is irate, and takes up Jagger's vinegarish reply to Keeley as a chant. A dancing Stones chorus of "we will piss anywhere, man" accompanies Wyman, Jones and Jagger as they urinate on the garage wall. They then speed off, hands protruding from the Daimler's windows, bidding Keeley one-fingered adieux. But, this isn't to be, precisely, farewell (see July 22, 1965).

MARCH 26, 1965 During their pre-show sound check at the Fyns Forum in Odense, Denmark, the two microphones Jagger is holding make contact and produce a 220-volt arc, the force of which throws him into Brian, who then smashes into Bill Wyman, who gets knocked unconscious. Wyman comes to in several minutes and the band is able to play its first concert of seven in Scandinavia.

MAY 25, 1965 A baby boy, Sean, is born to Sheila and Andrew Loog Oldham.

JUNE 4, 1965 The Rolling Stones' first US number-one single, "(I Can't Get No) Satisfaction" b/w "The Under-Assistant West Coast Promotion Man" is released by London Records.

JUNE 11, 1965 The band's first live record, the UK EP *Got Live If You Want It!* is released on Decca.

JULY 10, 1965 "(I Can't Get No) Satisfaction" becomes the Stones' first number-one single in the US. It remains at the top of the charts for four weeks.

JULY 22, 1965 Brian Jones, Mick Jagger and Bill Wyman are found guilty of having committed "insulting behavior" at the Romford Road filling station on March 18, 1965. The West Ham magistrate gives them the obligatory lecture and orders each to pay a fine of £5 plus court costs. The hearing provides great grist for the national media mill; reports of the bad boys' behavior are splattered all over the next day's tabloids.

JULY 30, 1965 London Records releases *Out of Our Heads*, the Stones' first LP to top the US charts. It is also the first Stones' album recorded entirely in the United States.

AUGUST 1, 1965 The band's first booking at the famed London Palladium. They play two shows. (Not to be confused with the ITV's television program "Sunday Night at the London Palladium"! (See January 22, 1967, and TELEVISION APPEARANCES)

AUGUST 21, 1965 *Out of Our Heads* becomes the Stones' first number-one album in the US.

AUGUST 28, 1965 The Stones sign a deal with Allen Klein; the contract names Andrew Loog Oldham and Klein as the group's comanagers (Klein handles all the business affairs from his US base, Oldham continues to stick with the band on the road). The two men had met in 1964, when Oldham's work for the Stones took him to a business meeting in London that, serendipitously, was also attended by Klein. They clicked: it was there that Allen Klein issued the oft-quoted grabber, "How would you like to be a millionaire?" It would appear that Oldham thought it an okay idea, and gave Klein a positive response. While the combination of Andrew Oldham and Eric Easton had been perfect for the "adolescence" of the Rolling Stones—Easton's own history in the music business lent both the band and Oldham much-needed credibility—by 1965 they needed a new, more dynamic hand.

SEPTEMBER 14, 1965 The Stones play the Circus Kronebau, in Munich. Brian Jones and Anita Pallenberg meet for the first time.

SEPTEMBER 24, 1965 UK *Out of Our Heads* is released by Decca. This is the first Stones LP to be issued in both mono and "stereo" versions in the UK. It is not true stereo, however.

OCTOBER 29, 1965 The fourth North American tour kicks off with a bang at Montreal's Forum. Forty female fans are taken to hospital as nearly 450 of both sexes rush the stage. The band's final quick exit is foiled when Keith and Bill are trapped onstage for 20 minutes by the fracas, which also leaves Brian's forehead slashed and Charlie's jacket in tatters.

Have VOX ...will travel

There's no doubt that for quality, reliability and purity of tone, VOX Sound Equipment has no equal.   VOX Sound Equipment is part of the Stones way of life . . . It'll stand up to any amount of hammering on countrywide tours.   That is why the Stones choose VOX . . . for top performance.   ANY TIME, ANY PLACE

JMI   **JENNINGS MUSICAL INDUSTRIES LTD**   DARTFORD · KENT · Telephone: 22471

Printed by Hastings Printing Company   Telephone Hastings 2450

The ROLLING STONES play HOHNER HARMONICAS

HOHNER

Obtainable from Music Shops Everywhere

Advertising wasn't just an '80s thing for the Stones. Here's one 1966 band endorsement, and one by Mick Jagger, a 1966 ad for Hohner harmonicas.
(TOM BEACH COLLECTION)

Mick, Keith and Charlie at RCA Studios in Hollywood during recording sessions for the Between the Buttons *LP.*
(TOM BEACH COLLECTION)

NOVEMBER 29, 1965 A state-wide "Rolling Stones Day" is declared by Colorado Governor John A. Love. The band's evening performance at the Denver Coliseum is a sellout.

DECEMBER 3, 1965 An electrical shock knocks out Keith Richards as he plays "The Last Time" at the Sacramento (CA) Memorial Auditorium. Ten months earlier, the February 8 issue of *Melody Maker* quoted Keith predicting, "I'll probably die of an electric shock." It would be neither the first (see March 26, 1965) nor the last near-electrocution onstage for any band member.

1966

As the year opens, the Rolling Stones are virtually a household name, having achieved worldwide recogni-

tion following the huge international success of "Satisfaction." They are elevated to "superstardom" and from this year on, unlike some artists who reach this heady status only to disappear after a few years, the Stones manage to stay there for the next 30.

FEBRUARY 18, 1966 The second Australia/New Zealand tour begins. It will end on March 2.

MARCH 21, 1966 The Stones win the Carl Alan Award for the most outstanding group of 1965.

MARCH 26, 1966 The Stones begin an 11-day European tour, to end on April 5.

MARCH 30, 1966 Fans riot at the Stones' show at the Musicorama in Marseilles, literally tearing up the place. Mick Jagger narrowly misses losing an eye when a flying theater seat connects with his forehead. Eight stitches are needed to close the nasty gash a few millimeters above his left eyebrow. The police are pounded with their own truncheons (and at least one gets bitten) and make more than 80 arrests. All but the biter are released the next day.

APRIL 1, 1966 The Stones' first "greatest hits" album, *Big Hits (High Tide & Green Grass)*, is released in the US. The UK version doesn't appear until November 4, 1966.

APRIL 15, 1966 Decca releases *Aftermath*, the first Rolling Stones LP to contain only Jagger/Richards songs. The British label had refused to issue the album the band had submitted for an early March release because of its title, "Could You Walk on the Water." Much conflict, many rounds of negotiations and much brouhaha ensued. By the time a settlement was reached, the content of the LP was different; the Stones had been in the studio in the interim and substituted a couple of new tracks. Finally —and appropriately—the title was changed. The US version of *Aftermath* also comprises only Jagger/Richards compositions (though the track listings of the albums are not the same), but London Records does not release it until July 1.

JUNE 23, 1966 The Stones board Allen Klein's yacht, *SS Sea Panther*, anchored at Manhattan's westside 79th Street boat basin, where they spend the night prior to the kickoff of their fifth North American tour. The same day, a story in the UK *Daily Mirror* reports that the Stones are filing a £1,750,000 lawsuit against 14 New York hotels that refused their reservations, alleging injury to their reputations and seeking damages. The article mentions that the band's complaint makes use of American civil rights laws, in that the hotels' actions amount to "discrimination on the basis of national origin." The next day, the band hosts a party aboard ship for selected New York and music press. In fact, the "no room at the inn" routine and the reported lawsuit turn out to be bogus. The whole event was a publicity ploy; the *Sea Panther* stay had been planned for some time and the Stones used the vessel as tour headquarters.

JUNE 24, 1966 The fifth North American tour opens at the Manning Bowl in Lynn, MA. The tour is another sellout, but sustains a major loss right away when thieves rip off the band's newly upgraded equipment. The haul includes Brian Jones's unique, custom-built electronic dulcimer. The tour ends July 28, in Honolulu, HI (Brian's last US gig), where an airline strike grounds them unexpectedly for several days. The band finally flies back to Los Angeles for a planned week of recording at RCA

Studios, rescheduled to begin on August 3. (See TOURS AND CONCERTS and SESSIONOGRAPHY)

AUGUST 25, 1966 Mick and Chrissie Shrimpton are unhurt, but Mick's Aston Martin DB6 is smashed to the tune of £700, in a collision in Marylebone, London. Even for the Stones, traffic accidents happen close to home, which in this case is Mick's.

SEPTEMBER 10, 1966 The Stones dress in drag for their controversial promo film for "Have You Seen Your Mother, Baby, Standing in the Shadows?" shot in New York City. Peter Whitehead's film was quite a radical departure from the other rock promos being made in 1966. (See PROMOTIONAL FILMS AND VIDEOS)

NOVEMBER 10, 1966 The band records new material, back at Olympic Studios in London after some two and a half years of sessions elsewhere. They also announce that the 30th issue of *The Rolling Stones Book* will be the last one.

1967

This was probably the most stressful period in Rolling Stones history. If there was to be an early finale for the band, this was the time for it to happen and these were the events that would make the curtain fall—it didn't, but 1967 left its mark on all of the Stones. For Brian Jones, 1967 was the year his overindulgence became the catalyst for his eventual demise. Although Brian's lifestyle most closely resembled the sex-drugs-rock'n'roll stereotype, his personality always had a sensitive and needy side, fraught with insecurity that now bordered on paranoia. His chronic asthma and other health problems multiplied along with the psychological, legal, and interpersonal stresses of being the founder, but not the front man, of one of the two best-known rock bands in the world.

FEBRUARY 1967 Late February 1967. Brian Jones writes the score for the Volker Schlöndorff film, *A Degree of Murder* (*Mord und Totschlag*), which stars Anita Pallenberg. With the assistance of Glyn Johns and producer/arranger Mike Leander, he records the soundtrack at IBC Studios in London. Jones himself plays sitar, organ, autoharp, harmonica and dulcimer and the music also includes strings and other orchestral accompaniment in addition to the services of session musicians like Nicky Hopkins and Jimmy Page.

FEBRUARY 5, 1967 Mick Jagger's name appears in the second of five newspaper articles on the drug consumption habits of pop stars. The London tabloid *News of the World* reports that Jagger once dropped acid with the Moody Blues. Enraged, Mick responds that night in a scheduled appearance on ITV's "Eamonn Andrews Show," announcing his intention to sue the paper for libel and defamation. This is the opening salvo in the drug war against the Rolling Stones.

FEBRUARY 10, 1967 Mick, Keith and Marianne attend the Beatles' orchestral recording session for their song, "A Day in the Life" in Studio One at EMI's Abbey Road recording complex. The session is filmed for a possible Beatles promo, but is never released.

FEBRUARY 12, 1967 8:00 P.M. Acting on information gleaned from an "anonymous" phone call received in the afternoon and armed with a search warrant, 18 police officers raid a party at Redlands, Keith Richards's new Sussex home, looking for drugs. Four Italian pep pills are found in Mick's jacket pocket and a total of 32 pills (two dozen of which turn out to be heroin) are discovered in art dealer Robert Fraser's clothing. The police proceed to confiscate "various substances of a suspicious nature" from the premises, and Keith is informed that he will face charges for any drugs the police can't connect to anyone else. It is later revealed that the tipoff came from someone at *News of the World* and that one member of the party, a Californian "friend-of-a-friend" named David Schneidermann, a.k.a. "Acid King David," was in all probability a "plant" (no pun intended) and had informed the newspaper. Other than Jagger and Fraser, he is the only person found with any drugs—hash and grass—in his possession. He also has a briefcase that everyone at Redlands knows is full of LSD and lots more cannabis, at the very least. When asked by police to open it, he tells them it is full of exposed film that will be ruined by light. That answer is—strangely—satisfactory. The case is not searched. Schneidermann disappears that night, presumably with his luggage and a return airline ticket that the police also saw and declined to confiscate. He is neither arrested nor charged (though police later say that a warrant was issued for him on "February 13 or 14"). "Acid King David" is never seen again.

FEBRUARY 25, 1967 Keith meets driver Tom Keylock at the Hotel George V in Paris, and they prepare to motor down to Morocco in Keith's Bentley for a holiday. Brian, Anita and Deborah Dixon (friend of director Donald Cammell) are the other passengers. Mick, Marianne, Robert Fraser, photographer Michael Cooper and Christopher Gibbs are to meet them in Tangier.

FEBRUARY 28, 1967 Brian's twenty-fifth birthday. He is in hospital near Toulouse, France, having become seriously ill on the way to Morocco. Keith and the others have continued on, per Brian's instructions, and are in Barcelona. Jones sends a telegram to Anita, demanding she return to Toulouse and pick him up. She ignores it. Deborah Dixon flies back to Paris. Keylock drives Keith and Anita to Marbella, where they spend four nights.

MARCH 5, 1967 Richards, Pallenberg and Keylock arrive in Tangier, where they meet up with Mick and Marianne and find a pile of frantic cables from Brian. Marianne accompanies Anita on her journey back to collect Brian in Toulouse. The (soon-to-be former) couple, plus Marianne, are back in London two days later.

MARCH 11, 1967 Marianne, Brian and Anita fly to Tangier following Brian's release from West London Hospital, and go on to meet the others in Marrakesh.

MARCH 15, 1967 Cecil Beaton photographs Mick in Marrakesh, where the group is now staying. The next day, artist Brion Gyson takes Brian Jones to the Atlas Mountains to hear the music of the Master Musicians of JouJouka. When they return to the hotel, Jones finds that everyone is gone. Essentially, Keith has finally rescued Anita from Brian's abuse. Jones had blown up at her while in Marrakesh, ending up injuring himself instead—not the first instance of physical violence in their relationship (or in Brian's other liaisons with women). Anita will return to London on her own one week later and Brian will meet her plane. But everything has irrevocably changed, for Brian and for the Rolling Stones.

APRIL 13, 1967 The band plays Warsaw. The Stones' first gig behind the then Iron Curtain takes place in the Polish capital's Palace of Culture. (See TOURS AND CONCERTS)

MAY 10, 1967 Mick, Keith and Robert Fraser appear before Chichester Crown Court, West Sussex to hear charges stemming from the Redlands bust. Jagger is charged with unlawful possession of amphetamines (four tablets called Stenamina, purchased over the counter in Italy, found to be composed of amphetamine sulphate and methylamphetamine hydrochloride). Richards, as the householder, is cited with allowing the smoking of cannabis to take place on his property. Gallery owner Robert Fraser is accused of the unlawful possession of heroin and of methylamphetamine hydrochloride. All three plead "not guilty" and elect to be tried by jury. They are released on bail, set at £100 each, pending trial in West Sussex Quarter Sessions to begin on June 27, 1967.

MAY 10, 1967 Having just returned to London from the Cannes Film Festival (where *A Degree of Murder* was screened), Brian Jones and friend "Stash" (Prince Stanislas Klossowski de Rola) are arrested when police raid Jones's flat in Courtfield Road. Armed with a search warrant, detectives "find" a purple wallet containing marijuana, some speed and a vial containing minute traces of cocaine. They also confiscate cigarette butts, ashtrays, pipes and other potential evidence of drug possession. Stash and Brian are also seized and taken—past a television crew positioned outside the flat—to the Kensington police station, where more news media is waiting. They are charged with possession of cannabis (the other substances are to be analyzed) and released pending their appearance in court the next day.

MAY 11, 1967 Brian and Stash appear before the West London magistrate. Detective-Sergeant Norman Pilcher of Scotland Yard requests the court grant enough time for thorough laboratory analysis of the seized evidence, and the magistrate adjourns the proceedings until June 2. The two defendants, neither having said a word at the hearing, each post £250 bail and are released.

Paul McCartney offers his house in St. Johns Wood to Stash to help lower his and Brian's public profile and, hopefully, keep them out of the media's easy reach. McCartney is quite upset at police harassment of the Stones versus their kid-glove handling of the Beatles; particularly in view of the fact that the Fab Four's lifestyle was equally well known at the time.

MAY 11, 1967 Instead of recording "Baby, You're a Rich Man" at Abbey Road as usual, the Beatles go where the Stones go—to Olympic Sound Studios. Mick attends the session. That he did so shouldn't be surprising, and not just because it was convenient. Rock'n'roll fans may have split themselves into two camps—Beatles versus Stones—but no such rivalry existed between the groups themselves. In a sense, the Beatles had more than a little to do with the Stones' early success. The Stones' first hit single had been a Lennon/McCartney song, "I Wanna Be Your Man," for one thing. The musicians were still socializing and attending each other's sessions in 1967.

JUNE 8, 1967 The Beatles ask Brian Jones to sit in with them on the recording of "You Know My Name (Look Up the Number)" at EMI's studios in Abbey Road. He plays alto sax on the John Lennon tune.

JUNE 25, 1967 Mick, Keith, Brian and Marianne join the audience of friends of the Beatles at Abbey Road for the televised recording of "All You Need Is Love," part of the Beatles' segment of the landmark BBC-TV show, "Our World." This program was the first live global television broadcast ever, and was seen by an estimated 400 million people. Only Mick, Keith and Marianne are readily visible on the program, but Brian attended as well, as did Eric Clapton, Keith Moon and many others.

JUNE 27, 1967 Mick's, Keith's, and Robert Fraser's Redlands drug trials begin, West Sussex Quarter Sessions, Chichester Crown Court, before Judge Leslie Block. Fraser, whose case is heard first, has changed his plea to "guilty" but his counsel's valiant efforts to offer as mitigating circumstances his client's distinguished military service record and successful treatment for heroin addiction aren't enough. He is found guilty. Mick is found guilty following the jury's five-minute deliberation, the judge having decreed that Jagger's own doctor's testimony—that he had okayed his patient's use of the tablets—could not be considered a defense. Justice Block defers the sentencing of both Jagger and Fraser until after Keith's trial, which will begin the next day. Thus, after police walk them, handcuffed, past a throng of spectators into a waiting police van, the two spend the night of June 27 in Lewes prison.

JUNE 28, 1967 Keith Richard's trial (on the charge of allowing the smoking of cannabis to take place on his property) begins. The jury is told to disregard the identities, though not the actions, of other persons present at the Redlands party on the night in question; they are to be concerned only with Keith, the sole defendant. This does keep Marianne Faithfull, Christopher Gibb, photographer Michael Cooper, Nicky Cramer and Robert Fraser's Moroccan servant Ali out of the legal soup, but somehow it also allows the court to use evidence (a substantial amount of marijuana and hashish) taken off David Schneidermann against Keith without attaching any responsibility for it to Schneidermann, who is long gone (see February 12, 1967). Several of the arresting officers describe the scene, and the actions and demeanor of certain unnamable Redlands guests during the raid. Much attention is focused on a "technically anonymous" lone female who was allegedly in an "euphoric state" and "in the nude" when the Sussex constabulary presented their warrant. The prosecution draws conclusions for the jury that the reason for the woman's "merry mood" and "vague unconcern" his witnesses observed was that she had been smoking hemp.

Only two women had been at Keith's home on February 12. Patti Harrison had left Redlands (with husband George Harrison) before the police (including two policewomen) arrived, and that left Marianne Faithfull. Anonymity was a sham—it was never difficult to identify the players in court or in the press. Since the raid, the *News of the World* (and the rest of Fleet Street) had been having an ongoing field day with suggestive stories about the interrupted party. Tabloid insinuations were particularly obvious with regard to Marianne, who was clothed only in a fur rug the size of a bedspread, after a bath, when the law showed up. Along with the first news reports, a now-legendary kinky rumor began to spread—the cops had walked in on a major orgiastic happening at Redlands, the participants having included Marianne and a Mars candy bar which was *in* her person and about to be consumed in an imaginative way. One can only speculate as to the rumor's origin. In fact, there had been some Mars bars in the room, on a piece of furniture, but candy wasn't among the items proffered as evidence at trial. In addition to the drugs, the prosecution contends that bits of incense and joss sticks are particularly damning. The fur piece is a major defense exhibit that Keith's counsel, Michael Havers, drapes across the judge's bench as a graphic demonstration of its size. While the day's proceedings are in session, Mick and Robert Fraser languish in holding cells in the courthouse basement. They are taken back to spend another night at Lewes Prison when court is adjourned, to resume the following day.

JUNE 29, 1967 The third day of trial proceedings in the Redlands drug bust cases. Following their second overnight stay in Lewes Prison, Jagger and Fraser are transported back to the courthouse holding cell to await a verdict in Keith's case and sentencing for all three of them. Keith takes the stand in his own defense. His lawyer, Michael Havers, has managed to get the police to confirm that they'd been tipped off by the *News of the World* and uses all the innuendo about the party and character defamation of the Stones and Marianne Faithfull to further illustrate his case—that the Stones were set up by the tabloid and the bust occurred as a result of Mick's libel suit against the *News of the World* for their February 5, 1967 story. Under questioning by prosecutor Malcolm Morris, Keith details how Schneidermann (to whom Keith had been introduced in New York the previous year) conveniently happened on the Stones scene in London just after the "drug habits of pop stars" story, got himself invited to the Redlands house party and showed up there with a bag full of illegal substances. Richards denies that either he or his friends partook in any of these. And he did not smell anything unusual, he says, he often burns incense. The prosecutor pushes on, to the question of the "naked" lady who must have been under the influence to be so attired in a roomful of men, or so he wants the jury to believe. Richards doesn't find this attitude on the woman's part a bit unusual? Keith replies with the famous line, "We are not old men. We are not worried about petty morals."

The jury takes just over an hour to find Keith guilty. The judge deliberates for 10 minutes, then sentences him to a year in prison and orders him to pay £500 in costs. Mick,

who with Robert Fraser has been brought from the holding cell into the courtroom to face the music with his bandmate, gets three months for the four "uppers," plus £100 fine. Fraser's heroin possession nets him a six-month jail term and a £200 court-cost bill. In handcuffs and tears, Jagger is taken to Brixton prison. Richards and Fraser are chained together and go to Wormwood Scrubs. The defense attorneys rush to get their appeal forms written.

JUNE 30, 1967 The High Court of Criminal Appeal finds grounds for the appeals of Mick's and Keith's convictions and grants their attorneys' requests for bail. Each must pay £5,000 in bail and post two £1,000 surety bonds, surrender his passport and remain in England until the appeals are heard. The Stones' publicist Les Perrin, accountant Stan Blackbourn and solicitor Peter Howard take Keith's Bentley and, at 4:25 P.M., retrieve Mick from Brixton prison. Forty minutes later, the car picks up Keith at Wormwood Scrubs.

JULY 1, 1967 The *Times* of London runs an editorial entitled "Who Breaks a Butterfly on a Wheel" (after a line from Alexander Pope's *Epistle to Dr. Arbuthnot, Prologue to the Satires*), written by chief editor William Rees-Mogg. The piece, in a break from the usually ultraconservative *Times*, strongly criticizes the decision in Mick's Redlands trial and denounces the sentence handed down by Judge Block. Calling the charge for four pills "a technical offence" and "about as mild a drug case" as could ever be brought before the courts, Rees-Mogg maintains that Jagger was treated much more severely than anyone else because of his celebrity. Rees-Mogg argues that many may resent or dislike the Stones and their music, even think Jagger "got what he deserved," but "if we are going to make any case a symbol of the conflict between the sound traditional values of Britain and the new hedonism, then we must be sure that the sound traditional values include those of tolerance and equity." The editorial's effect is stunning. Public opinion ran the gamut amidst raging debate, but unexpected support for the Stones was voiced in the legal community and the less liberal sectors of the population. The *Times* piece gives public outcry the establishment stamp of approval that will turn the case around.

JULY 12, 1967 Lennon and McCartney record backing vocals for the Stones' "We Love You" at Olympic. (See SESSIONOGRAPHY)

JULY 22, 1967 Robert Fraser loses his appeal and goes to jail for six months.

JULY 31, 1967 Keith Richards's conviction in the Redlands case is overturned by the Court of Appeal. The evidence was improper and the jury had been erroneously instructed by Judge Block. Mick's conviction, however, is not overturned but he is given a year's "conditional discharge," or probation. If he stays "out of trouble for the next 12 months," says the court, the conviction will not go on his record. Upon leaving the courthouse, Keith sends flowers to his mother and hops on a plane to meet Anita in Italy. Mick and Marianne are followed and filmed by Granada TV for most of the rest of the day, and are transported by car and helicopter from London press conference to pre-arranged "great debate" at a manse in Essex. (See TELEVISION APPEARANCES)

OCTOBER 31, 1967 Brian and Stash appear for trial on drug charges following their arrests on May 10. The case against Stash is dropped after Brian heeds his counsel's advice and pleads guilty to possession of cannabis and to permitting the use of cannabis on his premises, but not guilty to possessing cocaine and methedrine. The court opts to drop the hard drugs charges, and sentences

Keith Richards on guitar with Charlie Watts (back to camera) on bongos during sessions at Olympic Studios in June 1968 (COURTESY OF ABKCO)

Jones to nine months in jail for allowing cannabis use on his premises plus a concurrent three months for possession. He is ordered to pay some £265 in court costs and is led off to a van that transports him to Wormwood Scrubs prison. The court gives Stash a "paltry cost award" that hardly makes a dent, he says, in his actual expenses. He goes home after the session. The same evening a demonstration is held in Kings Road to protest Brian's sentence. Eight people are arrested. One of them is Chris Jagger, Mick's brother, who is charged with obstructing a police officer and abusive behavior.

NOVEMBER 1, 1967 At a hearing in the chambers of High Court Judge Donaldson, Brian's lawyers' plea for bail pending consideration of appeal is granted. Two of Jones's doctors have presented additional evidence of his fragile physical and psychological condition. The court agrees to release him upon payment of a total of £750 in bail and sureties with the condition that he see a court-appointed psychiatrist on the outside. His lawyer, Paul Howard, picks him up at Wormwood Scrubs.

DECEMBER 12, 1967 Brian Jones's jail sentence is set aside and replaced by a £1,000 fine and three years' probation.

1968

Student demonstrations worldwide, the war in Vietnam and the assassinations of Martin Luther King and Robert F. Kennedy were all notes in an inescapable political and social cacophony heard by people around the world in 1968. For the Rolling Stones, the addition of producer Jimmy Miller along with the now-mature songwriting team of Jagger and Richards allowed the band to make Beggars Banquet, an album that reflected the times perfectly and spoke directly to its audience. Mick and Keith went back to their blues roots to write more socially conscious lyrics for grittier numbers closer to the struggles of the common people.

JANUARY 20, 1968 Brian adds saxophone to a song for Paul McCartney's brother Mike McGear's solo album.

JANUARY 21, 1968 Brian Jones attends Jimi Hendrix's recording session at Olympic Studios. Hendrix is recording "All Along the Watchtower." Brian plays piano on takes 20 and 21. Neither is on the released version.

FEBRUARY 28, 1968 The band announces the hiring of an American record producer, Jimmy Miller, who will work with them on a new album.

MARCH 18, 1968 Charlie and Shirley Watts's daughter, Serafina, is born.

MAY 12, 1968 The Stones play the *New Musical Express* Poll-Winners Concert at Empire Pool, Wembley. This is the last public show Brian Jones plays with the Stones. The band's appearance was not advertised; they would only play as "surprise guests" at the concert.

MAY 21, 1968 Brian Jones is arrested for possession of cannabis in his Kings Road flat. Marlborough Street Magistrates' Court sets bail at £200 and orders him to appear in three weeks to answer charges.

MAY 24, 1968 Decca releases the UK single of "Jumpin' Jack Flash" (b/w "Child of the Moon"), the Stones' first effort with new producer Jimmy Miller. It will reach number one in Britain.

JUNE 5, 1968 French avant-garde director Jean-Luc Godard begins filming the Stones in sessions at Olympic Studios for *One Plus One*. Over the following week, Godard's crew chronicles the development of a single song, "Sympathy for the Devil," in the studio, providing a rare inside look at the process of making a Rolling Stones record. As it happens, the crew is also present on June 10, still covering an all-nighter at 4:00 A.M. when fire breaks out and the whole studio is evacuated. The fire footage is not part of *One Plus One* (also released as *Sympathy for the Devil*), but is used later in *Voices*, another Godard film.

JUNE 11, 1968 Complying with authorities in connection with his latest drug case, Brian appears in court. His not-guilty plea to the charge of marijuana possession is entered and trial is set for September 26.

AUGUST 2, 1968 Accompanied by his new girlfriend, Suki Poitier, Brian Jones returns to Morocco to record the music of the Master Musicians of JouJouka. He first heard the ancient tribal sounds in 1967 while attending the annual JouJouka festival with artist Brion Gyson. Rolling Stones Records will release an album in 1971, *Brian Jones Presents the Pipes of Pan*, two years after Jones's death.

AUGUST 14, 1968 Brian plays on the Beatles' unreleased track, "What's the New Mary Jane?"

SEPTEMBER 3, 1968 Radio stations in Chicago, IL, still smarting from the violence of the Democratic National Convention, ban the Stones' "Street Fighting Man" single from the airwaves. Closing the barn door in the windy city doesn't fire up much free publicity, unfortunately. This record only makes it to number 48 on the charts.

SEPTEMBER 12, 1968 Mick Jagger begins work on the Nicholas Roeg/Donald Cammell film, *Performance*, in London. He plays a burnt-out rock star opposite James Fox. The movie also features more experienced thespain, Anita Pallenberg, whose acting advice to Mick was, she recalls, terse and to the point: "Just be Brian." (Pallenberg and Keith Richards have been together since the fateful Morocco trip of March '67, the end of her liaison with Jones. See above.)

SEPTEMBER 26, 1968 Brian Jones is found guilty of cannabis possession and fined £50 plus costs of £105, but is not jailed. Mick, Keith and Suki Poitier attend the trial.

OCTOBER 3, 1968 Decca wins their summer-into-fall battle with the Stones over the cover art for *Beggars Banquet*. In August, the record company rejected the Stones' photograph, a graffiti-covered bathroom wall over the tank and raised seat of a grungy toilet, on grounds of poor taste and sensationalism. Mick Jagger says in the British press that he finds a picture of an exploding atom bomb on Tom Jones's *Atomic Jones* LP released by the same company more upsetting and offensive.

NOVEMBER 21, 1968 Brian Jones buys Cotchford Farm in Sussex. The property was once owned by A. A. Milne, author of *Winnie the Pooh*.

NOVEMBER 29, 1968 One Plus One premieres in London.

DECEMBER 5, 1968 The Stones host a luncheon press reception for the long-delayed release of *Beggars Banquet* at the upscale Gore Hotel in London. The absurdity of the interminable cover photo battle is finally matched by the silliness of the custard pie-throwing stunt that ends this event. All the guests (Decca execs, press, titled and chic Londoners) as well as the Stones and their minions end up covered in pie. Except Keith, who for mysterious reasons arrives too late for the pie throwing but not for some photos. The *Daily Mail* runs the story the next day under the headline, "Top of the Plops."

DECEMBER 7, 1968 The *New Musical Express* Pop Poll rates the Rolling Stones as '68's "Best British R&B Band."

DECEMBER 10–12, 1968 The *Rolling Stones' Rock 'n' Roll Circus* is filmed at InterTel Studios in Wembley. The feature-length production, intended for broadcast as a television special, is an original Stones idea developed over the past year. A variety show in another guise, the *Circus* mixes a traditional "big top" production with rock'n'roll, and includes the tent. Mick Jagger is the ringmaster to clowns, trapeze artists, John Lennon, Yoko Ono, Marianne Faithfull, Taj Mahal, The Who, Mitch Mitchell, Jethro Tull, Eric Clapton, the Stones and more. The special never aired after two days of shooting (the second day went into the wee hours of the 12th) and later editing. The Stones weren't satisfied with it and, in time, the project was shelved. Rumors of its imminent release were rampant and greatly exaggerated for many years afterward—until October 1996, when the *Circus* had its premiere, finally, at the New York Film Festival. This is Brian Jones's last performance (outside of the recording studio) with the Stones.

1969

The Rolling Stones had toured every year since its formation and had spent at least 75% of its time on the road from 1963 through 1966. So, their nearly three-year absence from the concert trail (with the exception of a short March/April European tour in '67) was very apparent by January 1969. The Stones knew they needed that unique energy that only comes from playing live. But Brian Jones was now in such a depressed physical and mental condition that he'd likely not have the endurance to withstand the stresses of the road. Furthermore, Jones's arrest record would make a US tour impossible. So it is in this year that Brian Jones gets extracted from "his" band by Mick, Keith and Charlie. It is not a totally unexpected event. The year 1969 brings true tragedy to the Stones on July 2, when Brian dies. Then, the year closes with the concert event that will be linked with the Stones forever— Altamont, the "anti-Woodstock" show.

MAY 28, 1969 London-based narcs raid Mick and Marianne's Chelsea residence and arrest them for possession of hashish (cannabis resin).

MAY 30, 1969 Mick Taylor's first session with the Stones, at Olympic Studios. He has no idea they want him to join the band, merely thinking they want him to play on some tracks being recorded for *Let It Bleed*. Most recently a member of John Mayall's Bluesbreakers, Taylor has just become unemployed, as have others in that band after Mayall's decision to form a new, acoustic group after their last US tour. But Mayall recommends him highly when Mick Jagger calls for advice about a new guitarist, then rings Mick Taylor to tell him to expect a call from the Stones. Mayall is vague about the extent of their interest. It is, by the way, Ian Stewart who phones to invite Mick Taylor down to Olympic Studios.

JUNE 5, 1969 Mick, Keith and Charlie visit Brian at Cotchford Farm and fire him from the band. Their 20-minute meeting is friendly; Jones is offered a settlement of £100,000, to be paid in installments.

It is implied, when they meet, that Brian might be able to rejoin the band when they tour Europe, if he wants to (though both sides know it isn't going to happen). But, when official word goes out, it is that he is leaving for good and that 20-year-old Mick Taylor has been brought into the group to replace him.

JUNE 7, 1969 Mick Jagger and Marianne Faithfull and at least 80,000 other people attend Blind Faith's free concert in London's Hyde Park. The successful, pleasant outdoor event is the first of its kind in England. The free-admission policy has drawn such a huge appreciative crowd that it strikes Jagger as an ideal format for a much-needed Rolling Stones "comeback" concert in the very near future. Jagger begins laying the groundwork for their own free show before Blind Faith's has ended.

JUNE 8, 1969 The Rolling Stones and Brian Jones officially part company. Both Jones and the band issue statements indicating that insurmountable "artistic differences" are the reason for the breakup. Mick Taylor is announced as Brian Jones's replacement.

JUNE 13, 1969 The Stones introduce Mick Taylor to the visual media at a press conference/photo call in Hyde Park.

JULY 2–3, 1969 Brian Jones is found, dead, at the bottom of his Cotchford Farm swimming pool. Authorities arrive shortly after midnight (July 3) and witness the official pronouncement of death by a local doctor who, along with an ambulance crew, is already at the scene. However, the post mortem pathologist later states that 27-year-old Jones died after 10:30 P.M. and *before midnight*, July 2, although even his tombstone reads "July 3."

This is but one of innumerable conflicting points and theories surrounding this mysterious and tragic event. The original Stone was a good swimmer, but drowned in his own pool. He had a history of asthma and his inhaler is found beside the pool, but the autopsy finds absolutely no evidence of either an asthma attack or of overuse or abuse of the medication. Nor does the medical examiner find that Jones had ingested enough alcohol to kill him. Statements taken that night from all three primary witnesses at Cotchford Farm conflict on crucial points and raise even more questionable issues. Most of Jones's friends discount the possibility of suicide or even of accidental drug overdose. Despite the traumatic nature of Jones's recent separation from the Stones, he had not appeared overly depressed to friends or family when they had last seen him; he had also successfully stayed away from drugs of late. The coroner's inquest finally rules "death by misadventure," but the mystery remains. It is quite odd that after Jones's body was removed that night his house was robbed —all of his instruments, clothing, rugs, antiques and jewelry were totally cleaned out by morning. Whole books, not to mention film scripts and reams of newspaper and magazine articles, have since been written about Brian Jones's untimely death.

JULY 5, 1969 The free concert in London's Hyde Park, which the band had planned as their re-entry into the limelight and Mick Taylor's stage baptism, unexpectedly becomes a wake for Brian Jones. The show goes on, with an estimated 300,000 people in attendance, in spite of public controversy and the band's own qualms about the propriety of doing it at all. The band has put a great deal of effort into the organization of such a large-scale event. They have hired Sam Cutler, who worked with Blackhill Enterprises, the producers of Blind Faith's Hyde Park show. The London chapter of the Hell's Angels has been asked to do security (and did so very nicely). But, when Brian died, the Stones' first thought was to cancel the gig. After a band meeting, they decided to go ahead with the concert as a tribute to the founding father of the Rolling Stones, instead of as their own comeback.

Jagger, dressed in a filmy white thigh-length tunic and flared trousers and wearing heavy makeup, a leather choker and a crucifix, starts it off by reading two stanzas from Shelley's "Adonais." White butterflies are released as an additional tribute to Brian, then the music starts. Granada TV's documentary, fortunately, captures the historic nature of the concert, which was clearly a difficult one for the Stones to play, and not their best, musically. (See TOURS AND CONCERTS and TELEVISION APPEARANCES)

JULY 6, 1969 Mick Jagger and Marianne Faithfull arrive in Sydney, Australia, prior to beginning work on the Tony Richardson film, *Ned Kelly*. Jagger's contract with the film company makes it impossible for him to attend Brian's funeral.

JULY 8, 1969 Marianne Faithfull is found in her and Jagger's Sydney hotel room, comatose from a drug overdose. She regains consciousness five days later, but is replaced by another actress, Diane Craig, in *Ned Kelly*.

JULY 9, 1969 Bill and Diane Wyman divorce.

JULY 10, 1969 Brian Jones's funeral takes place in Cheltenham. Keith, Bill and Charlie attend, as do many fellow musicians and friends. The town is packed with mourning fans as Cheltenham's "prodigal son" is laid to rest. His parents have chosen as his epitaph their son's plea for understanding he wired to them after his May 11, 1967 drug bust: "Please don't judge me too harshly."

JULY 13, 1969 In Melbourne, the filming of *Ned Kelly* begins with Mick Jagger in the title role. Jagger's participation has brought armies of press people down under, but the production garners even more international coverage when irate locals mount protests over the casting of a long-haired (read: sissy) British rock star as the legendary Australian outlaw and (more macho) folk hero. Meanwhile, in Sydney, the press continues its regular bulletins as Marianne comes out of her drug-induced coma, her mother at her bedside. Faithfull is on the road to a full medical recovery, while her relationship with Jagger is rapidly deteriorating.

JULY 26, 1969 An interview with Keith appears in the July 26 issue of *DISC* magazine. In it, he talks about sound—in general—and in particular, the sound of the Stones' upcoming album. Keith says he has enjoyed making this new LP much more than *Beggars Banquet*; working with new Stone, Mick Taylor, has been one factor. Taylor's joining the band has resulted in more energetic music, according to Richards, although he only appears on three tracks on the forthcoming LP to be titled "*Sticky Fingers*" (this is not a misprint—the original title for the LP actually released as *Let It Bleed* was *Sticky Fingers*!)

AUGUST 12, 1969 Marlon Richards, a son, is born to Anita Pallenberg and Keith Richards at King's College Hospital, London.

AUGUST 18, 1969 Mick Jagger receives a self-inflicted gunshot wound to his hand during the filming of *Ned Kelly* in Australia. The injury is not serious and he returns to the set within a few days.

OCTOBER 20, 1969 Shortly after they arrive in Los Angeles to prep for the '69 tour, the Stones hold their first US press conference in the Sans Souci Room of the Beverly Wilshire Hotel in Beverly Hills. The issue of the day is, of course, money. Journalists are anxious for a Stones response to underground and establishment press stories of massive fan discontent over high ticket prices at Rolling Stones concerts.

The top price for a ticket to a '69 Stones show in L.A. is US$7.50 (about £3, then), but that's not entirely the point. This media grilling has more to do with the once obviously anti-establishment Rolling Stones having been seen and photographed living like rich rock stars. Woodstock took place in August and the Stones themselves played London's Hyde Park for free in July. Will they do a free show for the hardworking American fans? An interesting question, one that will have most unexpected results. It won't be answered until later in the tour, in New York City.

NOVEMBER 7, 1969 The Stones' sixth North American tour begins with a concert in Fort Collins, CO.

NOVEMBER 20, 1969 Realizing that the West Palm Beach Pop Festival is scheduled for November 30, an overzealous county commissioner with a mission seeks to have the International Speedway (the site of the festival) re-zoned so as to bar the festival from happening. Promoter David Rupp issues a counter-statement: he'll do evrything and anything—even go to jail—to fight this action against the concert. Rock wins; the concert goes on as planned.

NOVEMBER 26, 1969 The Stones' second US press conference of the '69 tour takes place at the Rainbow Room atop Manhattan's Rockefeller Center. A reporter asks a question and the eminently quotable Jagger gives her what she wants; journalists will recast the question over the next 25 years, trying for a sound bite as memorable as this: "Mr. Jagger, some time ago you recorded a song, '(I Can't Get No) Satisfaction.' Are the Stones more satisfied today?" Jagger responds, "Sexually, d'you mean, or philosophically?" "Both," she replies. And Mick says, "Sexually—more satisfied. Financially—dissatisfied. Philosophically—still trying." On the subject of dissatisfaction and money, the Stones announce that as a way of thanking their fans for a successful tour, they'll hold that free concert the Los Angeles press mentioned. It will be on December 6, probably in San Francisco's Golden Gate Park, says Mick. As it turns out later, he's half right; the date is correct.

NOVEMBER 30, 1969 The final *official* concert of the North American tour, at the West Palm Beach Pop Festival in Florida.

DECEMBER 6, 1969 The real end of the tour and, many think, of the spirit of the '60s: Altamont. One of the most famous Stones shows ever, it's clearly their most

The Stones and the Hells Angels and everyone else—the onstage scene at Altamont. (COPYRIGHT ALAN COPELAND, COURTESY OF THE PHOTOGRAPHER)

infamous. However, all the incidents commonly thought of as peculiar to Altamont—death, stabbings, fans with guns, the use of the Hell's Angels as a security force—had happened before at various Rolling Stones concerts through the years, just not all at once.

Altamont was trouble from the beginning, when San Francisco city officials vetoed the choice of Golden Gate Park for the venue. Then it escalated to a major hassle, as constant negotiations were required to produce the second-string site, Sears Point Raceway, which was not in the city proper but an hour south of it. Finally, it became a true miracle that they pulled it off at all. The Stones' crew had built and rigged the stage at Sears Point, but were then forced to move the whole thing to Altamont Speedway, nearly 30 miles away in Livermore, CA less than 24 hours before the show opened. (See FILMS for why this happened. And, see TOURS AND CONCERTS)

Like the band itself, Altamont is cloaked in myth. Due to erroneous press reports in 1969, many Stones fans are still under the mistaken impression that gun-wielding Altamont audience member Meredith Hunter was killed while the band performed "Sympathy for the Devil." Untrue. The Stones were performing "Under My Thumb" when the incident occurred, as anyone who has

carefully viewed the Maysles Brothers' film *Gimme Shelter* can confirm. Contrary to more mythic fiction passed on by '60s tale-spinners, not only were the Stones *not* playing "Sympathy" when Hunter was killed, but they also had no apparent compunctions about playing it afterwards. The band played the song at their next two gigs following Altamont, in London in December 1969, and it remained part of their set during the 1970 European tour. "Sympathy for the Devil" was next performed in the US in 1975.

There are more obvious Altamont questions. For example, what happened to the Angel who did the actual stabbing? Alan Passaro was brought to trial and acquitted on all charges in January 1971. What, if anything, did the Stones say or do about the murder and the victim? The band was obviously distressed and saddened and felt a horrific crime had occurred. Privately, the Stones' organization made financial restitution to the Hunter family. Also, at first, Mick Jagger was vehemently opposed to the Maysles Brothers' suggestion that the filmed murder scene be included in *Gimme Shelter*. He changed his mind only after being convinced by fellow musicians—members of the Grateful Dead and Jefferson Airplane (whose guitarist, Marty Balin, had been seriously beaten by Angels at Altamont)—who made a special trip to London to explain the historical importance of the footage and the necessity of its inclusion in the Maysles' film.

DECEMBER 19, 1969 Mick Jagger's and Marianne Faithfull's cannabis possession cases before the Marlborough Street Magistrates' Court end with a guilty verdict for him and an acquittal for her. He pays court costs plus a fine of £200 and they both go home.

1970

A new decade, and a new band. Mick Taylor is an official member of the Rolling Stones, with the appropriate privileges and percentages. The band's contract with Decca/London/ABKCO runs out, and Rolling Stones Records is born. But, there are still many unreleased songs written during the ABKCO days that need inclusion on the Stones' upcoming LPs, and many ABKCO-era hits are now ripe for re-release and compilation. What to do—who does it and who gets what? The unknotting of a mass of legal entanglements begins in 1970, to stretch out over many years.

JANUARY 20, 1970 The Rolling Stones news of the day: the building of the "mighty mobile." Industry scuttlebutt says the boys have commissioned the retro-fitting of a full recording studio into a semi (tractor-trailer truck). The Stones begin using it during the summer and will rent it out to other bands when they aren't.

FEBRUARY 3, 1970 Distribution of *LiveR Than You'll Ever Be*, the first mass-produced bootleg recording of a live Rolling Stones concert, has reached such epic proportions that Decca is forced to pursue a lawsuit on behalf of London Records against several Los Angeles record stores for selling the album. Within a week, UK imports of the bootleg skyrocket and British copyright authorities take steps to ban its sale there. In February, *Rolling Stone Magazine*'s unprecedented review of the illegal disc, a recording of the band's November 9, 1969 Oakland (CA) Coliseum show, give major exposure to a live bootleg for the first time, and cause the Stones great concern. So much so that the band rushes to finish and release their own live album, *Get Yer Ya-Ya's Out!*, in order to compete with the bootleg. (See DISCOGRAPHY)

MARCH 11, 1970 Godard's *Sympathy for the Devil* (a.k.a. *One Plus One*) premieres in the US.

JUNE 24, 1970 *Ned Kelly* premieres in London.

JULY 28, 1970 *Ned Kelly* premieres near Melbourne in Glenrowan, Australia, the site of the film's famous battle.

JULY 30, 1970 The band begins to sever its relationship with Allen Klein. The Stones announce in a statement that Klein and ABKCO (and anyone else) no longer have the right to negotiate contracts on the band's behalf.

JULY 31, 1970 The recording contract between Decca and the Stones expires. The band owes the company one more single, so they submit the unreleasable "Cocksucker Blues." In fact, the song does get released once, in Germany in 1983, but only for a very short time as a bonus single to a limited edition boxed set (*The Rest of the Best: The Rolling Stones Story—Part 2*) that is quickly withdrawn and reissued without it. (See DISCOGRAPHY)

AUGUST 1, 1970 The expiration of Decca's contract with the five original band members means that the group is free to make Mick Taylor an official Rolling Stone, and they do.

SEPTEMBER 2, 1970 The Rolling Stones begin their first European tour in three years, with a concert at the Olympic Stadium in Helsinki. Stones roadshows enter a new era on this outing, with the introduction of their own travelling stage set, designed by Chip Monck. The set includes lighting, curtains, and steel support rigging, and needs two semis and a forklift to erect and transport.

SEPTEMBER 4, 1970 *Get Yer Ya-Ya's Out* is released, some nine months after the appearance of its bootleg competition.

SEPTEMBER 22, 1970 Mick meets Bianca Perez Morena de Macias for the first time at the Hotel Georges V party following the Stones' Paris concert at L'Olympia.

OCTOBER 30, 1970 John Dunbar and Marianne Faithfull are divorced. Mick Jagger is named as co-respondent in the proceedings.

DECEMBER 6, 1970 *Gimme Shelter*, David and Albert Maysles's '69 tour documentary, premieres in New York.

1971

The Stones' move to France brings them back to the '60s as well, to the closeness of group living very much like their early experience, but this time with a lot more money. Although each Stone has his own home, Keith's house at Villefranche-sur-Mer is where they all congregate to work (and play). Nellcôte is a vile, druggy villa of upscale squalor and creative (and destructive) energy. But, this "Edith Grove on £500 a day" atmosphere is what gives Exile on Main Street *the "certain something" that separates it from later LPs written when the group is dispersed.*

JANUARY 4, 1971 *Performance* is finally premiered in the UK; Keith and Anita attend the charity event. Warner Brothers did not want to release the film because of its drug-related plot; although the company's public statements cite Mick Jagger's "unintelligible Cockney accent" as their reason for holding it back. However, a deal was struck whereby the studio agreed to screen *Performance* to benefit Release, an organization devoted to helping persons arrested on drug-related offenses, and the film opens at the Warner West End Cinema in London. It is pulled back two weeks later.

JANUARY 6, 1971 Mick and Rose Miller Taylor's daughter, Chloe, is born at Wimbledon Hospital, London, England.

MARCH 4, 1971 The Stones' "Good Bye Britain" tour begins with a concert at City Hall, Newcastle-upon-Tyne. Rampant rumors that the whole band was going into tax exile in France were finally confirmed when the tour itinerary was announced less than a month earlier. The press has a field day and the tour is sold out.

MARCH 20, 1971 All five Stones sign an open letter voicing their strong disapproval of Decca's just-released *Stone Age* compilation album; they declare they had no part in it and that the LP is "below the standard we try to keep up, both in choice of content and cover design." The letter runs as an advertisement in British music publications. (See DISCOGRAPHY)

APRIL 1, 1971 Marshall Chess is announced as head of Rolling Stones Records, the Rolling Stones' new label, in the United States, with Trevor Churchill to be his UK counterpart. Marshall once worked at the Chicago record company owned by his father, Leonard, filling mail orders such as those for Chess Records' classic blues albums requested by a young Mike Jagger.

APRIL 6, 1971 The Rolling Stones sign a distribution deal with the Kinney Group that covers the worldwide release of all product on the Rolling Stones Records label. Kinney is the parent corporation to Atlantic Records, which will be the US distributor. The band prom-

ises to give them something to sell, agreeing to produce six albums over the next four years. The contract signing takes place in Cannes. The Stones have each moved into new homes and are settling in to life in the South of France. Their visits to Britain are now legally limited to no more than 90 days a year.

APRIL 16, 1971 The first single on Rolling Stones Records, "Brown Sugar," b/w "Bitch," is released in both the US and UK. The British version is a maxi-single with the live "Let It Rock" as the bonus track.

APRIL 23, 1971 *Sticky Fingers* is released, the band's first LP on Rolling Stones Records. The Stones now owe five albums to Atlantic Records/Kinney, according to their one-week-old contract. (See DISCOGRAPHY and SESSIONOGRAPHY)

MAY 12, 1971 Mick Jagger and Bianca Perez Morena de Macias are married in St. Tropez, first in a civil ceremony, then in a religious rite by the Reverend Lucien Baud. Bianca made it a condition of their marriage that Mick first take Roman Catholic religious instruction, which he did. Supposedly a secret, the wedding and reception is attended by Stones, Beatles, family, friends and hordes of press. Paparazzi and pencil-press had dogged the band, Mick and Bianca in particular, since the very public beginning of their "exile." Articles and photographs appeared regularly as the tabloids followed the development of Jagger's new romance with the "exotic" 21-year-old Nicaraguan. The couple repeatedly denied planning to marry, even as reporters caught Mick buying rings in Paris and discovered the marriage application they had made to French authorities. On the day, Jagger delays the ceremony, complaining that he doesn't want to be married in a fishbowl, but the St. Tropez mayor refuses to evict the journalists from the town hall, a public place; the media's response to Mick's ire is a collective "Then why did you tell us about it?"

The vows are exchanged and the groom joins his guests in an all-star jam (minus Keith, who is passed out cold on the floor) at the reception, which ends at 4:00 A.M. The new Mrs. Jagger makes only a brief appearance at the party before splitting for the bridal suite alone. Photographs of the occasion reveal a very unhappy bride whose most uncatholic taste in wedding attire leaves no question as to her physical condition, either (see October 21, 1971). The couple spend their two-week honeymoon in a secluded chateau accessible only by yacht. Among the Jaggers' many wedding presents is a white bicycle-built-for-two from Mick and Rose Taylor.

MAY 26, 1971 Keith is charged with assault when police are summoned to the scene of an altercation between Richards and an Italian tourist. The argument comes after Keith's Jaguar has plowed into the Italian's vehicle on the road near Beaulieu-sur-Mer. Keith is ordered to appear in court in one month's time, then continues on to his original destination, the screening of *Gimme Shelter* at the Cannes film festival.

JUNE 3, 1971 Arrested at Nice airport for assaulting and swearing at French customs inspectors and airport officials, Shirley Watts is sentenced *in absentia* to a six-month jail term and receives a fine of £30.

JULY 31, 1971 Keith and Anita attend the UK premiere of *Gimme Shelter* in London.

AUGUST 5, 1971 An Aix-en-Provence judge reduces Shirley Watts's jail term for abusing French customs officials from six months' incarceration to a 15-day suspended sentence.

AUGUST 31, 1971 Mick, Keith, Bill, Charlie and Brian Jones's father file suit in the British High Court against Andrew Oldham and Eric Easton, claiming the Stones' former managers fraudulently deprived the band of their proper percentage of royalties by means of secret agreements with Decca and coercion. Decca's contract gave 14% to Impact Sound but Easton and Oldham made Brian Jones accept 6% as the band's total share. In addition, Oldham took a management cut of 25%.

In another court action, the four original Stones plus Lewis Jones sue Allen Klein for $29,000,000, alleging that Klein failed to represent the musicians' best interests by convincing them to sign over all their North American music publishing and synchronization rights to Nanker Phelge Music, Inc., which the Stones had thought was their own company. In reality, they later discovered, it was controlled solely by Klein.

OCTOBER 8, 1971 Rolling Stones Records releases *Brian Jones Presents the Pipes of Pan*. (See DISCOGRAPHY)

OCTOBER 21, 1971 Mick and Bianca Jagger's daughter, Jade, is born at the Belvedere Nursing Home, Paris.

DECEMBER 3, 1971 Keith pleads self-defense in explaining his May 26th roadside fight with an Italian motorist near Beaulieu-sur-Mer. The French magistrate goes along with him and drops the charges.

1972

The Stones have become living legends—just about everybody knows about their music, their anti-establishment attitudes, their nonconformity. The word is out: if you haven't seen them live, don't miss this tour, it could be the last one. The current wisdom, circa 1972, was nobody goes on this long, especially a group. So the Stones, in typical fashion, tour North America and the world. 1972 is the point at which the band's "performance" becomes the event. Things change: it's now first-class hotels and food, and their own private plane on tour. But, as usual, the Stones are still the Stones; they still have their trials and tribulations—like being arrested in Rhode Island.

FEBRUARY 26, 1972 ABKCO secures a preliminary injunction in New York State against Atlantic Records (that is, the Stones); preventing them from releasing a compilation album entitled *Hot Rocks 1964–1971*, the same title as an almost identical anthology released by ABKCO/London in mid-December 1971. On January 21, the Stones had instituted legal action against ABKCO for releasing that first *Hot Rocks* without the band's okay.

APRIL 17, 1972 Anita Pallenberg and Keith Richards's daughter, Dandelion (later changed to Angela), is born in Geneva, Switzerland.

APRIL 29, 1972 *New Musical Express*, it is reported, sells an unprecedented 300,000 copies of its current issue, which contains a free Rolling Stones flexi-disc, an *Exile on Main Street* promo maxi-single.

MAY 10, 1972 The Stones and Allen Klein/ABKCO announce they have settled their differences, and the band will now assist Klein in pursuing their pending lawsuit against Eric Easton.

MAY 17, 1972 The band begins rehearsals in Montreux, Switzerland for their '72 North American tour.

JUNE 3, 1972 The '72 tour begins with a bang in Vancouver, BC. The Stones' first North American concert is sold out, but that doesn't stop an estimated 2,000 ticketless fans from trying to get into the Pacific Coliseum to see the show. Thirty police are injured trying to quell the riot in which eight people are arrested. There will be a few more gatecrashing incidents and fan riots along the way, but not with the same frequency as in the past. Security and tightly managed tour organization become of prime importance to the Stones in '72. Which isn't to say that it all runs like clockwork, however. . . .

JULY 17, 1972 An explosion, caused by a bomb allegedly planted by Quebecois separatists, decimates a truck containing the Stones' equipment in Montreal. Replacement gear is rounded up by a local band manager (see March 4, 1977), and the band's Montreal Forum concert is delayed by only 45 minutes. Still, 3,000 very irate people without seats—the innocent victims of a counterfeit ticket scam—are engaged in a riot outside the gates. The mood inside is also intense: Mick Jagger gets hit by a flying bottle during the performance.

JULY 18, 1972 The band departs Montreal for their evening concert at the Boston Garden, but their flight plan gets nixed on approach; Logan Airport is fogged in, and the plane is forced to land in Warwick, Rhode Island. Theoretically, the Stones can make the 60-mile trip to Boston by car in about an hour. But an enterprising local newspaper photographer had gotten wind of the Stones' unscheduled visit and met them on the runway. He made his exclusive pictures but wanted more. Jagger, becoming irritated, asked him to stop. Unfathomably, the photographer refused, choosing to ignore tour manager Peter Rudge's last ditch plea to limit the picture-taking. The photographer's reward for his misplaced persistence came swiftly—a roundhouse punch from Keith Richards.

As police arrive at the Warwick airport, Stones fans are beginning to trickle into South Boston. Recently the scene of mass racial violence, the neighborhood surrounding the Boston Garden is still a powder keg. Boston mayor Kevin White, on hearing of the airport fiasco, realizes that his fragile peace will disappear in a multiracial bloodbath sparked by 15,000 mostly white Stones ticketholders if they don't get what they've paid for. White puts it to the Warwick police quite clearly—either they let the Stones go or the blood will be on Rhode Island's hands. While Boston police escort the Stones' high-speed motorcade to the gig, Stevie Wonder plays a two-hour opening set and Chip Monck recites *Jonathan Livingston Seagull*. The Stones come on five hours late, but hero Kevin White gets a standing ovation from the fans at the Garden for saving the day, which ends peacefully. Mick, Keith, *et al.*, have a court date in Warwick in September.

AUGUST 28, 1972 Keith Richards moves his household to a chalet in the mountain village of Villars, near Montreux, Switzerland.

SEPTEMBER 7, 1972 French police in Nice who have been working overtime gathering information in order to bust the Stones for drugs, arrest Charlie Watts and Bill Wyman and indicate that they also plan to arrest the other band members who are not currently in France. Wyman and Watts are charged with possession of drugs,

per informants' reports of the Stones use of narcotics at Nellcôte. Police surveillance had been going on for over a year without clearly implicating anyone other than Keith and Anita, but the Stones had failed to appear for questioning prior to the US tour; these arrests were a kind of hostage-taking of the entire band by authorities.

SEPTEMBER 11, 1972 The Stones' Rhode Island court appearance is continued until December 13.

OCTOBER 10, 1972 The Stones' legal battles continue in the British High Court as lawsuits and countersuits are filed. Eric Easton sues Andrew Oldham, Allen Klein, Decca Records, London Records, and Nanker Phelge Music; Mick Jagger joins the defendants' party in a countersuit against Easton.

NOVEMBER 6, 1972 Bill Wyman gets a £20 fine for speeding and his driving license is suspended for six months by the Chelmsford Magistrate.

DECEMBER 2, 1972 Official warrants are issued in Nice for the arrests of Keith Richards and Anita Pallenberg.

DECEMBER 3, 1972 Keith buys his home, Point of View, in Ocho Rios, Jamaica.

DECEMBER 4, 1972 Mick Jagger and Mick Taylor, together with Bill Wyman and Charlie Watts meet with French police and clear up the matter of their alleged drug charges. The authorities declare them "clean" and uninvolved in any drug violations. The police publicly state that their misinformation had come by way of the arrests of a disgruntled former cook at Nellcôte and at least two other young French "Stones fans." Despite being cleared of any wrongdoing, the Rolling Stones will continue to be haunted by the specter of the French drug difficulties.

DECEMBER 23, 1972 Bianca Jagger's hometown of Managua, Nicaragua is hit by a devastating earthquake.

DECEMBER 28, 1972 Unable to locate her family by telephone or other means, Bianca and Mick charter a private jet in Kingston, Jamaica and fly to Nicaragua. Three days after they arrive and deliver the 2,000 units of typhoid vaccine and other medical supplies they have brought with them, the Jaggers finally locate Bianca's mother in a nearby suburb. She and other missing family members have safely escaped the disaster.

1973

Mick Taylor makes his last live concert tour with the Rolling Stones on the band's European outing during the last part of the year. 1973 was also quite trying for Keith Richards, with another drug bust, the death of very close friend, Gram Parsons, and a major fire at his Sussex home, Redlands. This year marks the release of the last Stones LP produced by Jimmy Miller, Goat's Head Soup.

JANUARY 8, 1973 The Japanese government announces that it will not allow the Stones to enter their country because of Mick Jagger's 1966 drug conviction.

JANUARY 10, 1973 The Rolling Stones are voted Best Band of 1972 by *Billboard* magazine.

JANUARY 11, 1973 The Stones announce the cancellation of the Japan portion of their upcoming Far East/Australia tour. The band, refused entry into Japan on account of Jagger's 1966 drug conviction, is forced to cancel six sold-out Japanese concerts. This results in a major gap in the tour, due to begin January 21 in Hawaii, and is a major financial loss for the Rolling Stones. (See TOURS AND CONCERTS)

JANUARY 18, 1973 The Stones headline a star-studded concert in Los Angeles, arranged by Mick Jagger as a benefit for victims of the Nicaraguan earthquake. (See TOURS AND CONCERTS)

JANUARY 21, 1973 The first gig of the 1973 Far East (not!)/Australia tour takes place in Hawaii. (See TOURS AND CONCERTS)

FEBRUARY 5, 1973 Contrary to their original tour itinerary, the Stones do *not* play two shows in Hong Kong on this date. (See TOURS AND CONCERTS)

FEBRUARY 27, 1973 The band finishes up their winter tour in Sydney, Australia. (See TOURS AND CONCERTS)

JUNE 13, 1973 The Stones are voted Band of the Year and Best Live Act by the American magazine, *Creem*, which also names *Exile on Main Street* as Best Album and Bill Wyman as number-one bass player.

JUNE 18, 1973 Actress Marsha Hunt files suit against Mick Jagger in Marylebone Magistrates Court for child support payments for their daughter, Karis. Despite the fact that the child's paternity is well known, Mick

denies the allegations and the matter drags on in the courts for two years. He makes a private settlement with Hunt in 1975.

JUNE 26, 1973 The drug squad raids Keith and Anita's house in Cheyne Walk, London. Richards and Pallenberg, together with friend, Stash, are charged with possession of cannabis. Keith is additionally charged with possession of unregistered firearms (including the .38 revolver Keith had packed throughout last year's US tour) and ammunition. The next day, he pays £1,000 bail, but the court returns his passport, allowing him to tour with the Stones prior to trial.

JULY 31, 1973 Redlands, Keith's West Sussex home, is ravaged by fire. Keith, Anita, Marlon and Dandelion are asleep at the time. No one is injured and a few precious items are saved, but the place is badly damaged.

AUGUST 22, 1973 The Spanish government bans all Rolling Stones records from its territory, citing anti-Franco remarks made by Mick Jagger. Jagger responds with an unqualified denial, saying he never made any such statements.

AUGUST 25, 1973 The Stones' planned Pembroke Castle concert, on the coast of Wales, is cancelled due to local officials' fear of "another Altamont." This is the second time this month that the Welsh have balked at allowing the Stones to play. When the Cardiff local council nixed the band's planned outdoor show there, Pembroke Castle became the substitute venue.

SEPTEMBER 1, 1973 The 1973 European tour opens at the Stadthalle, Vienna, Austria.

SEPTEMBER 18, 1973 "Rolling Stones form a new publishing company," says *Billboard* magazine. The article outlines the band's restructuring of their business affairs now that contracts with Decca/London and ABKCO are no longer in force. Promopub, B.V. is the name of the publishing company, with two other divisions: Promotone, B.V. will handle recordings and Promoright Music, B.V., licensing.

SEPTEMBER 19, 1973 Keith Richards's pal, Gram Parsons, dies of an overdose in a motel room in California. Parsons is cremated at Joshua Tree National Monument, per Parsons's wishes, though hardly the law's. A friend had grabbed the body from a baggage area at the Los Angeles airport and transported it to the national park. The Stones are in concert in Birmingham, England.

OCTOBER 15, 1973 The French court in Nice hands down suspended prison sentences in the pending drug cases of Keith Richards, Anita Pallenberg and Bobby Keys. Fines of £500 are also imposed on Keith and Anita. The Stones play the Palais de Sport, in Antwerp, Belgium.

OCTOBER 20, 1973 An item in *Billboard* announces that Lawrence Belling will head the European branch of Jimmy Miller Productions and will handle the Cuban band, Kracker.

OCTOBER 24, 1973 The Marlborough Street Magistrates Court imposes a £205 fine on Keith Richards and gives Anita Pallenberg a one-year conditional discharge on charges stemming from the June 26 Cheyne Walk raid. Keith has pled guilty to possession of cannabis, Chinese heroin, Mandrax (British Quaaludes), a revolver, a shotgun and ammunition. Anita's offense was possession of 25 Mandrax tablets.

1974

1974 will be the first year the Rolling Stones as a group do not perform even once in public, only getting together in a film studio to make three promos for their It's Only Rock 'n' Roll *album. In late 1974 Mick Taylor decides to leave the band. The Stones set out to find a new guitarist; one of them is later quoted as saying, "When we saw Woody we knew he was what we were looking for."*

FEBRUARY 13, 1974 The French government officially bans Keith, Anita and Bobby Keys from entering the country.

FEBRUARY 16, 1974 US president Gerald Ford reveals in a televised interview that he has no clue about Mick Jagger. He's never heard of him, but asks "Mick Jagger? Isn't he the motorcycle rider?"

APRIL 14, 1974 *Ladies and Gentlemen, the Rolling Stones* has its US premiere at the Ziegfeld Theater, New York City.

JULY 13–14, 1974 Keith joins Ron Wood onstage at the Kilburn State Cinema in London, where Wood is playing. In the spring, Keith, Mick Jagger, Mick Taylor, George Harrison and Eric Clapton had all participated in sessions for Woody's first solo LP, *I've Got My Own Album to Do.* Keith shows up at Kilburn again the next day.

JULY 27, 1974 *New Musical Express* calls Keith Richards "The World's Most Elegantly Wasted Human Being."

OCTOBER 1974 An at-home photo story about Mick and Bianca Jagger is published in the London *Sunday Times.* The photographs were taken by Leni Reifenstahl, whose wartime employer had been Adolf Hitler. As a young woman in Germany, Reifenstahl had been the Third Reich's visual propagandist, having made such epics as *Triumph of the Will* and *Olympiad* to advance the Nazi cause.

NOVEMBER 29, 1974 Mick Taylor informs the Stones—via a phone call to the office—he's leaving the band. Jagger preempts his visit to Managua and flies back to the UK to talk with Taylor.

DECEMBER 4, 1974 Mick Taylor tells Mick Jagger again that he is leaving the Stones. They have attended Eric Clapton's concert at London's Hammersmith Odeon and discuss the matter at a post-gig party at Robert Stigwood's home. The Stones are scheduled to begin recording sessions in three days in Munich, Germany.

DECEMBER 13, 1974 The official announcement of Mick Taylor's resignation is made. He states that he will be joining the Jack Bruce Band. Jagger's legendary response to reporters' questions about replacing Taylor: "No doubt we can find a brilliant 6'3" blond guitarist who can do his own makeup." Jagger wishes him success and happiness. The Rolling Stones continue recording at Musicland Studios in Munich.

1975

In contrast with 1974, 1975 is a year of tour, tour, tour. They always seem to be doing something unique this year, from holding tour rehearsals on Andy Warhol's estate in Montauk, Long Island (there's a rundown inn nearby called Memory Hotel) to announcing the tour via a flatbed truck press conference in Manhattan to staging their tour performances on unfolding lotus petals.

JANUARY 1, 1975 With Mick Taylor's unexpected departure in December 1974, the Rolling Stones are once again placed in the predicament of finding a new guitartist with whom to record their upcoming LP and most likely join them on an imminent US tour. Unlike that of '69, the guitarist hunt of '74–'75 isn't the band members' idea, nor are they able to keep it quiet—every-

The infamous inflatable rises, 1975 US tour.

body knows that all of a sudden one of the best gigs in the music business is up for grabs. Guitarists from both sides of the Atlantic converge on recording studios in Munich and then in Rotterdam, where the Stones are working. The band carries on with recording, adopting an outwardly relaxed attitude toward the recruiting thing. The Stones have been together for more than 12 years and much has happened, and changed, particularly in the past five. There will be no hasty decisions. In choosing a potential new Stone, there are several factors to consider: 1) musical compatibility with both Keith and Charlie; 2) attitude; and 3) physical and mental stamina to withstand the grueling lifestyle of the road . . . like a Rolling Stone.

The roster of fine players who come by for the impromptu, casual auditions includes such noteworthy names as Jeff Beck, Roy Gallagher, Harvey Mandel, and Wayne Perkins. After a time it appears that Perkins, an American, has the position as "new Stone" all but locked up. Then, in walks The Faces' Ron Wood—and all bets are off. We mention Wayne Perkins's nationality because of much fan and press speculation and debate (at the time and since) over the issue of a quintessentially British rock

'n' roll band like the Stones hiring an American guitarist: many deemed it a very slim possibility. In truth, however, Woody's real trump card was his roadworthiness—he knew how to handle the grind of a major concert tour. This was something that experienced session man Wayne Perkins had not yet mastered.

MARCH 15, 1975 Press reports indicate the parties have reached an out-of-court settlement in Marsha Hunt's 1973 paternity suit against Mick Jagger. Hunt sought child support payments for daughter, Karis, whom Jagger, initially, denied fathering. The monetary amount of the settlement was not disclosed.

APRIL 14, 1975 The Stones announce that Ron Wood will fill the guitarist's slot left vacant by Mick Taylor's resignation, but only for the upcoming US tour. Wood is not leaving the Faces.

MAY 1, 1975 The Rolling Stones announce their upcoming "Tour of the Americas" and tie up Manhattan traffic by driving down Fifth Avenue while playing

"Brown Sugar" from the back of a flatbed truck. The movable stage slows down upon reaching "Feathers" at 10th Street in Greenwich Village, where unsuspecting newspeople await the Stones' arrival for, they have assumed by that point, the late start of a conventional press conference. Surprise! The band flings tour press briefings to jangled journalists who hastily exit the bar for the street, then the truck moves off through a growing crowd of fans. Tickets go on sale at Madison Square Garden this day.

MAY 21, 1975 The official unveiling of the band's hydraulic lotus stage takes place at an aircraft hangar in Newburgh, NY's Stewart Airport. Designed by Mick Jagger and Charlie Watts and built by Robin Wagner, the stage unfolds and extends its five petals into the audience. In fact, there are two lotus stages; while one is being used for a performance, the other is being set up in the next city along the tour route.

JUNE 1, 1975 The 1975 tour of the Americas opens at Louisiana State University, Baton Rouge. The concert inaugurates the Stones new lotus stage, but a surprise addition to the production comes out during "Star Star"—a.k.a. "Starfucker"—a 20-foot long inflatable penis, ridden by Mick Jagger.

JUNE 3, 1975 The City of San Antonio is not amused by reports of the Stones' plans to erect a giant "obscenity" onstage at the San Antonio Convention Center and calls in the police vice squad. The Stones decide they'd rather not be arrested and keep the inflatable phallus zipped up while in San Antonio. Somehow, the organ is never the same; alterations are made so that it never again quite resembles its anatomical inspiration in later tour performances.

JUNE 6, 1975 ABKCO releases *Metamorphosis.* This is the last album of new Stones material released to date by ABKCO.

JUNE 22, 1975 Eric Clapton joins the Stones onstage at their Madison Square Garden show, sitting in on "Sympathy for the Devil" (see TOURS AND CONCERTS). After that show, the Stones showed up at Electric Lady Studios in Greenwich Village where Clapton was recording. Several takes of a track called "Carnival to Rio" were laid down that night. The lineup: Mick Jagger, vocals; Billy Preston, clavinet; Dick Sims, organ; Marcy Levy and Yvonne Elliman, vocals; Jamie Oldaker and Charlie Watts, drums; Bill Wyman and Carl Radle, bass; Ollie Brown, congas; Keith Richards, Ronnie Wood and George Terry, guitars; plus Eric Clapton on lead vocals and guitar. Each guitarist soloed on the tune, which was about eight minutes long. Reportedly, a good time was had by all, but the

track was never released "due to contractual difficulties." Clapton rerecorded "Carnival to Rio" the following year as "Carnival."

JUNE 27, 1975 Carlos Santana joins the Stones onstage for "Sympathy for the Devil" at the band's Madison Square Garden show.

JULY 5, 1975 Instead of flying from Memphis with the others, Keith and Woody decide, at the airport, to take the southern scenic route to their July 6 Cotton Bowl gig and drive to Dallas. Tour manager Peter Rudge is concerned and sends Stones security man Jim Callaghan along as driver/minder in the nondescript American Sedan Keith has procured. All is well until the group, which includes Keith's pal (and 50-year-old Holocaust survivor) Fred Sessler, decides to have a burger in Fordyce, Arkansas (pop. 4,000). As they sample the local cuisine, the two Stones draw a crowd of local teenagers and the town police are alerted. When Keith unintentionally burns rubber upon exiting the drive-in, the car is stopped, searched under the pretense of what the officer describes as billowing marijuana smoke emanating from the vehicle's windows, and the four are brought to the Fordyce jail. Keith is charged with possession of a concealed weapon (actually a utility knife with can opener and horse's hoof pick) and reckless driving. Callaghan and Wood are not charged. Sessler, described as a "hitchhiker" in press reports, is charged with possession of cocaine that police have found after opening the car trunk with a crowbar. Stones attorney and former Kennedy administration Secret Service man, Bill Carter, comes to the rescue within two and a half hours: arguing illegal search and seizure; he persuades local officials to release Richards on $162.75 bail and Sessler on $5,000. After posing for pictures with the judge, Keith and Woody, Callaghan and Sessler join Carter in a police motorcade to the local airport, board Carter's waiting chartered plane, and take off for Dallas. Keith's confiscated knife is now enshrined on a plaque hanging on the Fordyce courtroom wall.

AUGUST 6, 1975 The 1975 tour of the Americas ends with a fan riot at Rich Stadium in Buffalo, NY, all Latin American dates having been cancelled. The final statistics in Buffalo: 600 people injured, 170 arrests; total tour gross, $13,000,000 or so; 45 performances in 27 cities.

DECEMBER 26, 1975 Year-end kudos for the Rolling Stones include: *Performance Magazine*'s poll of US concert promoters rates the Stones the band with most audience drawing power; *Creem* honors the Rolling Stones with awards of Best Group, Best R&B Band, and Best Live Band and votes *Made in the Shade* Best Reissue Album. *Creem* also names Ron Wood as Most Valuable Player.

1976

*The year starts off with the official pronounce-
ment—Ron Wood is a full-fledged member of
the Rolling Stones. In May, the 1976 tour begins,
which means, essentially, that the '75 tour continues
into Europe with material from the just-released
Black & Blue LP showing up on the Stones' live
setlists. While Europeans see television promos for
Black & Blue, stateside album hype got off to a mis-
erable start because of public outcry over the band's
choice of promotional imagery that the
Stones don't promote the LP on US television.
The offending design is a photograph of a bound
and bruised woman manacled and suspended
spreadeagled over the opened album cover (a highly
graphic Hiro photograph bearing just the faces of
the Rolling Stones) with the legend, "'Black &
Blue.' The Rolling Stones." The billboard comes
down, the store displays are pulled, and the
album goes to number one in the US.
Midway through the tour, while the Stones are recording their Paris shows for another end-of-record
contract live LP, Keith and Anita's 10-week-old
son, Tara, dies. But the show, and tour, and plan
for a different kind of live album all go on.*

JANUARY 3, 1976 *New Musical Express* places
Mick Jagger at the top of its "Best Dressed Musician" list.
Keith is number seven.

FEBRUARY 28, 1976 The band makes its long-
awaited formal announcement of Mick Taylor's replacement—Ron Wood is an official Rolling Stone. This would
have been Brian Jones's thirty-fourth birthday.

MARCH 26, 1976 Tara Jo Jo Gunne Richards, a son,
is born to Keith Richards and Anita Pallenberg in Geneva,
Switzerland.

APRIL 28, 1976 The European tour opens at the
Festhalle in Frankfurt, West Germany.

MAY 10–11, 1976 The Stones play the Apollo.
The Apollo Theatre in Glasgow, Scotland, that is.

MAY 15, 1976 Eric Clapton joins the Stones onstage at Grandby Hall, Leicester. The Stones last played
this venue on July 26, 1965.

MAY 19, 1976 Keith totals his Bentley when he
rams into the central divider on the M1 motorway just
north of London. Fortunately, none of the car's occupants

—Keith, Anita and Marlon—are injured. Unfortunately,
police at the scene find a suspicious "substance" in the car,
arrest Keith and take him to the police station at Newport
Pagnell. He is released, pending identification of the
"substance."

MAY 22, 1976 Mick meets Jerry Hall for the first
time when she and then-boyfriend Bryan Ferry come
backstage to visit during the Stones' gig at Earl's Court
Arena.

JUNE 6, 1976 In Geneva, Switzerland, Keith and
Anita's 10-week-old son, Tara, dies in his crib. Keith hears
of the tragedy just prior to the Stones' third concert at Les
Abattoirs in Paris but a grief-stricken Richards demands
that the sad news be embargoed so as not to disrupt the
tour. This evening's performance is one of the Stones',
particularly Keith's, most intense ever. Recorded for *Love
You Live*, like the other Les Abattoirs dates, only this
evening's tracks are on the album. (See DISCOGRAPHY)

AUGUST 2, 1976 Keith appears in court in Newport Pagnell and is charged with possession of cocaine and
LSD as well as three driving offenses. He pays £100 bail
and is released pending another court appearance in one
month's time.

AUGUST 21, 1976 The Stones play their longest
show, with the most songs in any setlist in the band's
history, before their largest ever paying audience (over
200,000 people). The concert, at the Knebworth Festival,
was done to replace a cancelled gig. (See TOURS AND
CONCERTS)

SEPTEMBER 1976 Keith Harwood, longtime
Stones sound engineer, is killed in an automobile crash.
Mick McKenna, also a Stones engineer, is seriously injured
but eventually recovers. Bill Wyman sets up a trust fund
for Harwood's family.

SEPTEMBER 6, 1976 Keith Richards appears in
Newport Pagnell court again. His case is continued to
October 6.

OCTOBER 6, 1976 Keith's excuse for arriving two
and a half hours late for his court appearance—that he was
waiting for his pants to come back from the cleaners—
prompts Newport Pagnell Chairman of Magistrates, Mrs.
Mary Durbridge, to utter one of Stones fans' favorite
quotes: "It strikes me as extraordinary that any gentleman
of his stature can only afford one pair of trousers." It also
moves her to rule that Richards's original £100 bail be
forfeited. He elects to go to trial and pays renewed bail of
£5,000.

OCTOBER 30, 1976 Ron and Krissie Wood's son, Jesse James Wood, is born in Hollywood, CA.

1977

A mostly inactive year, musically, but one of major turmoil and a severe turning point for the band, with the arrest of Keith Richards in Toronto. By now, the Stones have become old pros at stressful drug-related legal situations, but the Canadian charges are life-sentence serious in a judicial climate that is anything but lenient. Keith's future and that of the Stones looks very grim—and rests in the hands of the judicial system. The music business maintains a wait-and-see attitude about negotiating any new deals with the almost-free agents until after the live LP is released.

JANUARY 10–11, 1977 Keith's trial on drug charges arising out of his May 19, 1976 car crash near Newport Pagnell takes place at Aylesbury Crown Court. Mick Jagger is present in court to support his mate.

JANUARY 12, 1977 Keith is found guilty of possession of cocaine (the drug was inside a silver tube and coke spoon necklace discovered by police in the wreckage of Keith's Bentley), and LSD (found inside folded paper in his jacket pocket). The court orders him to pay a fine of £750 plus £250 in costs.

JANUARY 22, 1977 The Stones obtain a court order enjoining the UK tabloid, the *News of the World*, from publishing the illegally obtained screenplay and still photographs from *Cocksucker Blues*, Robert Frank's film about the Stones' 1972 US tour. The following day, the newspaper reports that the band's attorneys asked Frank to return his personal copy of the film and quotes the filmmaker's public refusal to part with his property.

FEBRUARY 16, 1977 With the Stones' deal with WEA about to expire, the band announces that EMI will distribute the Rolling Stones Records label worldwide, except in the United States and Canada. The new contract guarantees EMI six albums plus a portion of Jagger/Richards song publishing rights. No exact monetary figure is released, which results in, naturally, much speculation. A North American distributor is not named, yet.

FEBRUARY 18, 1977 Keith pays a fine of £25 for driving without payment of tax, a vehicle infraction with which he had been additionally charged in connection with his May '76 crash on the M1.

FEBRUARY 24, 1977 The Rolling Stones, wanting more material for their scheduled live album release, decide to play and record some small club gigs. They settle on the 350-seat El Mocambo in Toronto, Canada and arrange to meet there, without announcing it to the press or public. Keith Richards and Anita Pallenberg arrive with seven-year-old Marlon, four days later than expected, at Toronto International Airport. Keith and Marlon clear customs easily, but Anita's 28 pieces of luggage set the inspectors on alert and they get out the fine-toothed comb. Officials discover 10 grams of hash and some paraphernalia, a burnt spoon and hypodermic syringe with traces of what turns out to be heroin. Pallenberg is arrested by Constable Hachinski of the Royal Canadian Mounted Police. Keith and Marlon are gathered up by Stones personnel and driven to the band's headquarters hotel, the Hilton Harbour Castle. Anita is booked and released upon her promise to appear in court.

FEBRUARY 27, 1977 Exhausted after travel, the airport fiasco, and all-night rehearsals for El Mocambo, a totally knackered Keith Richards is rudely grabbed—well, it took about an hour to wake him, in truth—from his Harbour Castle bed by Constable Hachinski and four other mounties. Unbeknownst to the band, the RCMP have been watching the Stones since their arrival in Canada; surveillance was merely stepped up after Anita's arrest. Looking for Anita, the warrant-bearing mounties find Keith (after combing the hotel for some two hours!) search his room, and haul him in. They find enough evidence to charge him with possession of heroin for the purpose of trafficking and (though the second charge comes to light a bit later) possession of cocaine. Should Keith be convicted by the extremely strict Canadian courts on the heroin trafficking charge—22 grams was confiscated—he'd be looking at a possible sentence of life in prison. Seven years is Canada's statutory minimum on that offense alone. Keith is booked, released on $1,000 bail, and has returned to the Harbour Castle by evening.

MARCH 4, 1977 The Rolling Stones play their first night at El Mocambo. Originally, the shows were to be on March 11 and 12, but were moved up because of Keith's impending situation. Opening for them is April Wine, a local band. Why them, you might ask? Remember the bomb, allegedly planted by French separatists, that blew up the Stones' equipment truck in Montreal back in 1972? Well, it seems that April Wine's manager knew Skippy Snaire, the one guy in the whole Dominion of Canada who knew where and how to get enough replacement gear to save the Stones' act that night in '72.

The show is a roaring success. Seated in the audience is Margaret Trudeau, wife of Canadian prime minister Pierre Trudeau, who has come, solo, to see the Stones play

Toronto on her wedding anniversary. Registered as Margaret Sinclair, her maiden name, she's booked into—you guessed it—the Harbour Castle Hilton.

MARCH 5, 1977 The second El Mocambo show. Mme. Trudeau is again present. The Canadian press, already in a major Stones feeding frenzy over Keith's troubles, goes ballistic over their young first lady's antics, imagined or not. While some financial writers portend a major devaluation of the Canadian dollar on the world market, the political stock of the Trudeau government begins a real decline.

MARCH 7, 1977 After being cheered, then grabbed by the hair and verbally assaulted at the entrance, Keith appears in Toronto's Old City Hall Court. His hearing on the monster heroin charge is continued for a week, but the RCMP's analysts produce the evidence needed to formally add possession of cocaine to the government's case.

MARCH 8, 1977 The RCMP rearrests Keith on the cocaine charge as he enters the courthouse for a secret hearing arranged the previous day. This is all legal under Canadian law, which allows notice of certain "sensitive" proceedings to be kept from the Canadian press and public —in addition to the judge's imposition of the usual order preventing the Canadian press from reporting on trials in progress. Keith's attorneys' maneuverings prevent his being summarily jailed and he is released on $25,000 cash bail. The Canadians still hold his passport.

MARCH 14, 1977 Anita Pallenberg pleads guilty to possessing heroin and hash. She pays fines of $200 per offense. Keith appears in court and is remanded on bail until June 27. He gets his passport back. Over the past week, the rest of the band has left, all but Charlie having flown to New York, as has Maggie Trudeau. The Canadian papers are still debating that one when she returns to Ottawa on March 12. Ian Stewart remains in Toronto (as do Anita and Marlon) working at Interchange Studios with Keith, while legal eagles figure out Richards's next move.

APRIL 1, 1977 Keith, Anita and Marlon leave Toronto for Philadelphia. The Stones organization has secured medical visas from US immigration for Richards and Pallenberg on the condition that they have rapid treatment for heroin addiction. They've also wrangled special dispensation so they can avail themselves of the "black box" cure pioneered by Dr. Margaret Paterson. (The technique had gotten both Eric Clapton and Pete Townshend off dope, painlessly, they'd told Keith, who adamantly refused the official alternative, methadone

withdrawal.) Keith can't move out of a 25-mile radius of where he's being cured, is never without a guard, and the press can't know anything. Keith agrees, indicating his sincerity to kick the habit.

Meanwhile, it is announced that the Rolling Stones have re-signed with Atlantic for their North American distribution, a deal reportedly worth $21 million for six albums. At the same time, Marshall Chess is replaced by Earl McGrath as head of Rolling Stones Records.

JUNE 27, 1977 Keith misses his Toronto court appearance. His attorney requests a continuance on the grounds that Richards is in drug treatment. The judge grants a postponement until July 19.

JULY 19, 1977 Keith misses another date with Canadian justice; he is now being treated at Stevens Clinic in New York City. His next appearance is scheduled for December 2.

JULY 20, 1977 Premiere of the Japanese animated film, *Metamorphosis*. The soundtrack contains the *Goats Head Soup* outtake, "Criss Cross." The Stones grant permission for the unreleased song's inclusion in the film —the first time the band has allowed this kind of usage in a non-Stones project.

DECEMBER 2, 1977 Keith finally makes it to Toronto. He is ordered to appear before the Canadian High Court in February 1978.

1978

The Stones continue their every-three-years custom of US touring with judgment on Keith's future still in question. In fact, a "Saturday Night Live" skit in which Keith appeared was, of necessity, dropped after dress rehearsal—too many drug references, such as his one-liner: "Every February, I go to Switzerland to get my blood changed."

FEBRUARY 6, 1978 In Toronto, Keith's lawyers get his court date put off until March 6.

FEBRUARY 16, 1978 In London, Krissie Wood is involved in an automobile accident and is admitted to hospital with minor injuries.

MARCH 6, 1978 The Canadian High Court orders that Keith Richards's trial commence on October 23.

MARCH 9, 1978 Krissie Wood files for divorce against Ronnie, naming Jo Howard as co-respondent.

MAY 3, 1978 The Rolling Stones sign the second artist to their record label—reggae great Peter Tosh. Tosh will open for the Stones throughout their upcoming 1978 North American tour.

MAY 14, 1978 Bianca Jagger files for divorce from Mick in London. It takes nine months for her lawyers to serve the papers on him, in New York.

JUNE 10, 1978 The Rolling Stones' 1978 North American tour begins in Lakeland, Florida. It will finish up in Oakland, CA on July 26. (See TOURS AND CONCERTS)

JULY 8, 1978 Mick, Keith and Woody drop in at The Quiet Knight in Chicago to catch a Muddy Waters gig. After a while, Keith leaves their table, grabs a guitar and joins Muddy onstage. Then, a bit later, Mick follows suit, leaving Ronnie to save their seats—but he comes onstage shortly afterward and joins the impromtu jam taking place there. The next time such a "spontaneous" event happens (in 1981), the Stones' camera crew films it.

JULY 10, 1978 Bill Wyman is literally knocked out after the band's St. Paul (Minnesota) Coliseum performance. As he exits the stage, Wyman walks through a curtain and off the stage, unaware of the sheer drop of several feet beyond the curtain. He is revived; the tour continues with a performance the next evening in St. Louis, MO.

JULY 18, 1978 In Ft. Worth, TX, Fiddler Doug Kershaw joins the Stones onstage at the Will Rogers Auditorium, sitting in on "Faraway Eyes."

JULY 21, 1978 Linda Ronstadt shows up in Tucson to sing along with Mick on "Tumbling Dice."

AUGUST 21, 1978 Les Perrin, the Rolling Stones' longtime publicist, dies at the age of 57 in London.

SEPTEMBER 13, 1978 Charlie and Bill attend Keith Moon's funeral. The Who's drummer had died in London on September 7.

OCTOBER 22, 1978 Ron Wood and Jo Howard's daughter, Leah, is born in Los Angeles.

OCTOBER 23, 1978 Keith's trial begins in the Canadian High Court before Judge Lloyd Graburn. As a result of massive plea bargaining between defense and prosecution, the original charge of heroin possession for the purpose of trafficking has been dropped to simple possession of heroin. Keith pleads guilty.

OCTOBER 24, 1978 Keith returns to Judge Graburn's courtroom for sentencing. It is a hearing of much impassioned oratory all around. Keith's attorney, Austin Cooper, argues strongly for probation. He reiterates Keith's testimony of the day before, of his client's firm resolve to stay off heroin after a long struggle with addiction, and adds that Richards has pledged to make a $1,000,000 donation to a rehab clinic. Judge Graburn's sentence turns some classic fatherly advice inside out. To pay for his crime, in addition to a one-year suspended jail term, Keith must play a special concert at the Canadian Institute for the Blind within six months. Plus, continue treatment and report to a Toronto probation officer three times at six-month intervals beginning today. The courtroom explodes with cheers, Keith sees the probation officer, and splits for the airport and back to New York. Canadian reaction to Graburn's decision runs the gamut. Government officials voice outrage and push for an appeal. Sentiment in the press is mixed, with Canada's largest paper calling it "a model of enlightened sentencing." Some—particularly Keith—attribute it to divine intervention, of one sort or the other.

DECEMBER 28, 1978 *Rolling Stone* announces its Critics Awards. The Rolling Stones are Artists of the Year, and *Some Girls* is Album of the Year.

1979

Keith does his time by playing for the blind. The rest of the Stones, at their own expense, fly in to join him onstage even though the Rolling Stones are not on the bill. Ron Wood's newly formed group, the New Barbarians, with Keith, open the show. Then the Stones make their "surprise appearance," that everyone knew about all along.

How Judge Graburn arrived at such a novel solution is, naturally, anybody's guess. But, as Keith Richards tells it, Richards once noticed a young blind woman who, like many sighted fans, followed the Stones from town to town. He flipped over her chutzpah, but worried about her, being blind, female and on the road. So, he befriended her, and made sure someone saw that she got to shows safely and got in. Keith Richards's "blind angel," he says, must've gone to the good judge's house as he pondered Keith's fate, and told him her story. Works for us. . . .

JANUARY 15, 1979   While rehearsing in a Soho studio for their upcoming "showcase" gig at Trax in New York City, prospective Rolling Stones Records recording artist Neon Leon and his band are suprised by two guests. Mick Jagger and Rolling Stones Records president Earl McGrath have come by for a listen. Jagger decides to join the band's session and sings three numbers with Leon: "Heart of Stone," "The Last Time" and John Lee Hooker's "Dimples." "Heart of Stone" was later released as a maxi-single on Big Deal Records, an independent label. The other two tracks remain unreleased.

JANUARY 20, 1979   *New Musical Express* award for "Best Dressed Album of 1978" goes to *Some Girls*.

APRIL 22, 1979   Keith Richards with Ron Wood and the New Barbarians—and the Stones—play two concerts at Oshawa Civic Auditorium to benefit the Canadian Institute for the Blind. (See TOURS AND CONCERTS)

JULY 20, 1979   Seventeen-year-old Scott Cantrell of Norwalk, CT shoots himself in the head at the home of Anita Pallenberg and Keith Richards in South Salem, NY (though Keith is rarely there). The young man had been depressed of late and that day had been talking of Russian roulette, according to Anita, who was in the room at the time of the incident. While Pallenberg tidied up her bedroom, Cantrell, who was sitting on the bed watching television and playing with the .38 revolver, shot himself. He is pronounced dead at Westchester Hospital after midnight on July 21.

JULY 21, 1979   The .38 with which Scott Cantrell shot himself is found to have been stolen in Ft. Lauderdale. Anita Pallenberg is charged with possession of stolen property and released on $500 bail.

SEPTEMBER 2, 1979   In Las Vegas, Bill Wyman plays with Ringo Starr, Dave Mason, Todd Rundgren and Kiki Dee at the "Jerry Lewis Telethon for Muscular Dystrophy."

Keith and Ronny at Oshawa, April 22, 1979, doing what they do best   (1979, PHYLLIS LATTNER)

SEPTEMBER 17, 1979 The Ontario (Canada) Court of Appeal rejects the Toronto prosecutor's petition for appeal in Keith Richards's heroin case.

NOVEMBER 2, 1979 Bianca and Mick Jagger are divorced. Custody of their daughter, Jade, is granted to Bianca.

NOVEMBER 19, 1979 The Westchester (NY) Grand Jury clears Anita Pallenberg of any involvement in Scott Cantrell's death but indicts her on two misdemeanor counts of illegal possession of a weapon.

DECEMBER 18, 1979 Keith Richards meets model Patti Hansen during his birthday party at Roxy Roller Disco in New York City.

DECEMBER 31, 1979 Anita pleads guilty to one count of illegal possession of a weapon. The second charge is dropped. Sentencing will be on March 3, 1980.

1980

The Rolling Stones release Emotional Rescue *and the band members seem to have free time and energy to put into other projects and travel a lot, especially Mick who is the major social butterfly in 1980. No tour is planned and no real studio session time is scheduled until the end of the year. And then, the death of John Lennon deals the world a crushing blow. The Stones are personally devastated: each has lost a friend and kindred spirit. Someone who touched us all.*

JANUARY 13, 1980 Milwaukee fans riot at a New Barbarians concert. Neither Keith nor Ian McLagan play the gig, which was arranged as settlement for a lawsuit between the Milwaukee promoter and the band.

FEBRUARY 22, 1980 Ron Wood and Jo Howard (later Jo Howard Wood) are arrested and charged with possession of 200 grams of cocaine in St. Maarten, Netherlands Antilles.

FEBRUARY 26, 1980 Ron and Jo are released by the St. Maarten police and the cocaine possession charges are dropped when an investigation reveals that the drugs had been planted on them.

MARCH 3, 1980 Anita Pallenberg is ordered to pay a $1,000 fine and given a one-year conditional discharge on the New York weapon possession charge.

Jim Carroll and Keith jam together on Carroll's "People Who Died" at Trax, New York City, June 26, 1980. Carroll was the eighth artist featured on Rolling Stones Records. (1980, PHYLLIS LATTNER)

JUNE 26, 1980 After a promotional party for the Stones' *Emotional Rescue* LP at Manhattan's Danceteria, the action moves to another New York City club, Trax, where poet/musician Jim Carroll is performing. Keith sits in on Carroll's cult hit, "All the People Who Died, Died."

AUGUST 1, 1980 Earl McGrath resigns as president of Rolling Stones Records. VP Art Collins will fill in.

SEPTEMBER 16–21, 1980 Robert Frank's 1972 tour film, *Cocksucker Blues*, is finally shown to the public at New York City's Whitney Museum of American Art. The filmmaker and the Stones have finally reached an agreement that allows the film to be shown in public—but only for educational purposes and Frank must be physically present at each screening.

DECEMBER 8, 1980 John Lennon is shot dead in front of his apartment building in New York City. The Dakota, where John lived with Yoko and Sean, is just a few blocks from Mick's home.

DECEMBER 27, 1980 Mick Jagger and Jerry Hall journey to Peru for the filming of Werner Herzog's *Fitzcarraldo*, in which Mick is to star. In February, they leave along with much of the crew and actress Claudia Cardinale, as shooting comes to a halt when numerous disasters (including Amazonian Indian attacks) occur at the film's jungle location. Although the beleaguered production is scheduled to restart in May, Jagger decides to forget it altogether.

1981

1981 begins with the band engaged in solo work, semi-solo projects, and vacationing. Mid-year, the Stones mount their three-year US tourcycle again, prior to which they warm up for the road at their first-ever US small-club show at Sir Morgan's Cove in Worcester, MA. The trip ends in December with the Stones' first television pay-per-view concert broadcast. The tour is also filmed for the feature-length film, Let's Spend the Night Together.

JUNE 1981 Keith and Patti go to see Chuck Berry play the Ritz in New York City. After the performance, Keith goes backstage to visit Chuck, who punches him in the eye. Berry hasn't recognized him.

AUGUST 14, 1981 The Rolling Stones convene at Long View Farm in Brookfield, MA to begin rehearsing for their 1981 tour, which they haven't yet announced.

AUGUST 26, 1981 Mick Jagger, on his own at JFK Stadium in Philadelphia, makes the official announcement—the Stones will begin a major North American tour on September 25, right there in Philly.

SEPTEMBER 1, 1981 The Stones and Jovan, Inc. announce that the band's 1981 tour will be underwritten by the Chicago-based perfume manufacturer, making this the first time the Stones go on the road with corporate sponsorship.

SEPTEMBER 14, 1981 The Cockroaches and Blue Sunday play Sir Morgan's Cove, capacity 350, in Worcester, Massachusetts. That's how the bill reads for the Stones' supposedly secret 1981 tour warm-up gig. Some 275 tickets are distributed from the windows of unmarked cars driving around the town by Ian Stewart, Stones tour personnel and Worcester radio station WAAF staffers to anyone displaying the station's logo (T-shirts, hats, bumper stickers, etc.). The station has announced on the air that the Stones will play, but not where. However, the secrecy is blown by a much larger, jealous station in the Boston metro area which broadcasts the name of the club upon hearing of little WAAF's coup. This brings out about 4,000 people, as well as the riot squad with helicopter assistance. For once, the police offer an intelligent solution, and the massed fans hear the gig through the club's wide-open doors. Amazingly, this is the first club

gig the Stones ever played in the United States. (Remember, El Mocambo is in Canada!)

SEPTEMBER 18–19, 1981 Two more scheduled warmup shows, at the Orpheum in Boston, are cancelled by the once-intrepid but now fearful Mayor Kevin White after the trouble in Worcester. The band tries, unsuccessfully, to book another pre-tour show in Providence, but Rhode Island officials aren't any more inspired than the last time they heard the band's name.

SEPTEMBER 21, 1981 Mick Jagger grants his only face-to-face interview of the 1981 tour warm-up period to two junior high school girls, aged 12 and 13, on assignment for the North Brookfield (MA) Jr. High School newspaper. Jagger had said no to requests from virtually every major newspaper, magazine, wire service and television network.

SEPTEMBER 25, 1981 The Rolling Stones play the first official concert of their 1981 tour at JFK Stadium in Philadelphia, PA.

OCTOBER 1, 1981 The band plays, by popular demand, in Rockfold, Illinois. The Stones added the concert at the 9,000-seat Metro to their itinerary as a result of a petition plea spearheaded by two radio DJs (Dennis Logan and Dallas Cole of WZOK) and sent to promoter Bill Graham. The 9,000 lucky attendees were chosen from the petition's 36,000 signers.

OCTOBER 20, 1981 In San Francisco, Mick Jagger has a full day with the ladies. First, he lends his support to a "Save the Cable Cars" drive by taping a public service

Mick appears solo to announce the Stones' '81 tour at a press conference at JFK Stadium in Philadelphia—and the city presents him with his very own Liberty Bell.
(1981, PHYLLIS LATTNER)

Charlie and Keith onstage at Largo, Maryland, December 7, 1981 (1981, PHYLLIS LATTNER)

television spot with the city's mayor Dianne Feinstein. In the evening, he has dinner with Jacqueline Onassis.

NOVEMBER 22, 1981 The night before the tour's first Chicago performance, Mick, Keith and Woody visit the Windy City's Checkerboard Lounge to see Muddy Waters. Muddy invites Keith and Woody onstage with him for a jam with Buddy Guy and Junior Wells. Then, Mick comes up and joins the fun. A good time is had by all, and is captured on film by the Stones' crew who have come along on the evening's outing.

DECEMBER 14, 1981 For the first time since their 1973 European tour, Mick Taylor plays in concert with the Rolling Stones, at the band's Kemper Arena show. Taylor, in Kansas City for his own gig, had come by the band's hotel "just to say hello" to his former bandmates. All were still enjoying the reunion when it came time to go to the show, so Keith and Woody asked him to go along. Taylor figured they'd just continue hanging out before the show, but Mick and Keith ask him to sit in. He

borrows one of Keith's guitars, comes on early in the set, and plays until the end. Taylor doesn't remember his first number with the Stones that night in Kansas City, nor, it seems, does anyone else. On tapes of this show he is introduced right before "Let Me Go"—a non–Taylor/Stones song. It seems strange Taylor would come out for this number.

DECEMBER 18, 1981 The next-to-last show of the tour, at Hampton Roads Coliseum in Hampton, VA, and the Rolling Stones' first live pay-per-view television concert broadcast. It is also both Keith's and Bobby Keys's birthday.

1982

Touring-wise, the band does in Europe pretty much what it did in the US in '81. But, the Rolling Stones play the UK for the first time in six years on the 1982 European tour, having missed the 1979 tour cycle there.

FEBRUARY 3, 1982 Mick, Keith and Hal Ashby meet in Los Angeles to work on Ashby's film of the '81 US tour, which is, eventually, titled *Let's Spend the Night Together.*

MARCH 4, 1982 *Rolling Stone*'s Readers' Awards seem to be a Rolling Stones sweep. The stats: Best Band of the Year—The Rolling Stones; Best Male Vocalist—Mick Jagger; Album of the Year—*Tattoo You*; Best Single—"Start Me Up"; Best Songwriters—Mick Jagger and Keith Richards; Best Instrumentalist—Keith Richards. The magazine's Critics Awards give honors of Artist of the Year to the Rolling Stones; Best Album to *Tattoo You*; and Best Single to "Start Me Up."

APRIL 28, 1982 Mick officially announces the Rolling Stones' 1982 European tour at a press conference at the London disco, Le Beat Route. The tickets for the first concert he names, on June 2 in Rotterdam, are already sold out.

MAY 26, 1982 The 1982 European tour's actual, but not official, first concert takes place at the Capitol Theatre in Aberdeen, Scotland. The Stones play the Apollo in Glasgow the next night, for the second time in their career—and the last before the fabled venue is razed.

MAY 31, 1982 The band plays a surprise show at the 400-seat 100 Club in London. Neither this nor the two Scotland shows are part of the official tour itinerary.

JUNE 1, 1982 The 1982 European tour officially opens with a concert at Feyenoord Stadium in Rotterdam, Holland.

JULY 25, 1982 The last concert of the '82 European tour takes place in Yorkshire at Roundhay Park, Leeds. Promoter Bill Graham finds that his very rare map of the '81 US tour has gone missing.

AUGUST 8, 1982 Bill Graham offers a £1,000 reward for his tour map. Graham's copy is special; each venue is marked with his own notes and handwritten messages from band members are all over it.

SEPTEMBER 1, 1982 Another major fire breaks out at Redlands, Keith's thatch-roofed, moated manse in West Wittering. Fortunately, there are no injuries and the only serious damage is to the roof.

1983–1988

Six whole years and only two new Rolling Stones LPs are released—Undercover in '83 and Dirty Work in '86—and there isn't a three-year tourcycle in sight. The band is fairly well dispersed doing their own things, making solo albums, getting married, having babies, rattling around. The death of Ian Stewart, in December of 1985 hits hard. The only live show the Stones did during this entire six-year period was a memorial for Stu at the 100 Club in London on February 23, 1986.

1983

JANUARY 18, 1983 *Let's Spend the Night Together* is screened privately at Loew's Astor Theater on 44th Street in New York City. All the Stones except Bill Wyman are there. A party follows at Tavern on the Green.

FEBRUARY 10, 1983 Another private screening of *Let's Spend the Night Together* in Manhattan, this time at Loew's East 66th Theater. Again, all Stones but Wyman are present. The party is held at Corso's Restaurant on East 86th Street.

FEBRUARY 11, 1983 The New York premiere of Hal Ashby's film of the Stones' 1981 tour, *Let's Spend the Night Together*, is held at Loew's East 66th Street Theater.

AUGUST 20, 1983 Ron Wood and Jo Howard's son, Tyrone, is born at Mt. Sinai Hospital, New York City.

DECEMBER 18, 1983 Keith marks his fortieth birthday by marrying Patti Hansen. The ceremony, kept secret from the press, is held at the Finisterra Hotel in Cabo San Lucas, Mexico. Mick is Keith's best man and is the only other member of the band present.

1984

JANUARY 1, 1984 Alexis Korner dies at the age of 55, in London.

MARCH 2, 1984 Mick Jagger and Jerry Hall's daughter, Elizabeth Scarlett, is born at Lenox Hill Hospital in New York. Jagger is in the delivery room.

APRIL 16, 1984 Jagger testifies in a New York City courtroom as part of the Stones' lawsuit over their contract with former manager, Allen Klein.

APRIL 23, 1984 Klein and the Stones reach a settlement and the Stones drop the lawsuit.

NOVEMBER 14, 1984 The first music promo "greatest hits" compilation, *Video Rewind*, is released (with the assistance of archivist/author James Karnbach) by Vestron Video. The tape contains classic promo films and videos, some never previously released. (See PROMOTIONAL FILMS AND VIDEOS)

1985

JANUARY 2, 1985 Ron Wood and Jo Howard are married at St. Mary's Church, Denham, Buckinghamshire, England.

FEBRUARY 4, 1985 Mick Jagger's first solo record, the single "Just Another Night" b/w "Turn the Girl Loose," is released in both the UK and US by CBS.

MARCH 4, 1985 *She's the Boss*, Mick Jagger's first solo album, is released by CBS.

MARCH 18, 1985 Patti and Keith Richards's daughter, Theodora Dupree, is born, with Keith in the delivery room, at New York Hospital.

JULY 13, 1985 Live Aid—Bob Geldof's gigantic transatlantic benefit, with stages in Wembley Stadium and JFK Stadium in Philadelphia, hooked up via satellite and beamed worldwide. Mick Jagger performs solo backed by Hall and Oates, and then with Tina Turner, from Philadelphia. Also from JFK Stadium, Keith and Woody play with Bob Dylan to close the show.

AUGUST 19, 1985 Charlie Watts falls in the cellar of his home in Devon, breaking his leg in three places. Doctors tell him he's out of action until November.

AUGUST 28, 1985 Mick Jagger and Jerry Hall's son, James Leroy Augustine, is born at Lenox Hill Hospital.

NOVEMBER 18, 1985 Charlie Watts's Big Band opens a week-long engagement at Ronnie Scott's Jazz Club in London.

DECEMBER 5, 1985 The Stones last recording session until *Steel Wheels*, at Right Track Studios in New York. Also Ian Stewart's last session.

DECEMBER 12, 1985 Ian Stewart, 47, dies of a massive heart attack as he leaves his doctor's office following a complete physical examination. He had been having respiratory problems of late. He is survived by former wife, Cynthia and their son, Giles, 15.

Stu, as he was called by the band, though always out of the limelight, kept the Stones in focus. He was the one who brought them back to their musical roots and sensibilities when superstardom, adulation and flash threatened to throw the Stones off course and apart. He was the no-nonsense one, there from the beginning to keep them in touch and *remind* them—his "little shower of shit" he'd called them as he hustled them from countless dressing rooms onto stages—when necessary. The loss is unspeakable.

DECEMBER 20, 1985 Ian Stewart's funeral takes place at Randall's Park Crematorium, Leatherhead, Surrey. All the Stones and many other friends and family are present.

1986

JANUARY 2, 1986 Reggae artist Patrick Alley announces he is suing Mick Jagger for plagiarism. The Jamaican singer contends that Jagger copied "Just Another Night" from Alley's 1982 album, *A Touch of Patrick Alley*.

JANUARY 23, 1986 Keith Richards inducts Chuck Berry as the first member of the Rock 'n' Roll Hall of Fame at the inaugural awards presentation in New York.

FEBRUARY 23, 1986 The Stones play a private show at London's 100 Club as a memorial to Ian Stewart. The wake is attended by a select group of family and friends, some of whom are musicians but only a few of them sit in. The setlist is unique—all 11 numbers are Stu's favorite kind, classic blues songs. It was not the Rolling Stones doing a "Stones show," but, rather, a tribute in Stu's style, a set full of songs that he'd do. (See TOURS AND CONCERTS)

JUNE 28, 1986 Patti and Keith Richards's daughter, Alexandra Nicole, is born at Lenox Hill Hospital, in New York City.

DECEMBER 1, 1986 Columbia Records releases the Charlie Watts Orchestra's first LP, *Live at Fulham Town Hall*.

1987

JANUARY 21, 1987 Jerry Hall is arrested by customs officials at the Barbados Airport and charged with importing 20 pounds of marijuana. The bust is an obvious set-up. The facts: Jerry goes to the airport to pick up her own clothing and makeup that has been shipped to her from Mustique. An airline employee tells her there is another package for her. Hall is not expecting anything else and the Mustique Airways clerk says it's "unlabelled," so she suggests Hall open it to see if it is hers. It's full of grass. She gets arrested and spends the night in jail. Officials don't inform Mick of the arrest for six hours. Mick forks over $5,000 to bail her out; she is ordered to surrender her passport and must report to the Holetown police twice a week until her trial on February 13.

FEBRUARY 13, 1987 Jerry Hall's trial. She denies knowing anything about the mysterious marijuana from Mustique. Her attorneys (Elliott Mottley of Barbados and Peter Partcher of New York) call witnesses who back up her testimony. The trial adjourns until February 16.

FEBRUARY 16, 1987 The trial of Jerry Hall resumes. The defense rips apart the prosecution's case; under her advocates' questioning, the customs supervisor admits he lied to the court, changes his story several times, and reveals that police primed him to look for a particular package. Court testimony seems to point to an "ambush" of Jerry Hall, perpetrated by Barbadian police and customs officials. Magistrate Frank King keeps Hall hanging for a while longer by adjourning until February 20 before announcing his decision.

FEBRUARY 20, 1987 Jerry Hall is found not guilty.

APRIL 13, 1987 Bill Wyman holds a press conference at the Champagne Exchange in London to announce his AIMS Project, his not-for-profit endeavor to record unknown bands in order to give them that "first big break." The acronym stands for Ambition, Ideas, Motivation, Success. Bill plans to use the Stones' Mighty Mobile and produce the groups without taking either a producer's fee or a percentage from record sales for himself.

JULY 15, 1987 Keith Richards signs with Virgin Records, his first solo record deal.

SEPTEMBER 11, 1987 Peter Tosh, 42, is shot and killed at his home near Kingston, Jamaica. Two of Tosh's friends, with him at the time, are also killed. Initial statements by Kingston police list robbery as the motive for the crime, for which they have no suspects. Official statements later agree with those of Tosh insiders, who believed that the unknown perpetrator or perpetrators knew the reggae star and that the crime was an act of revenge.

OCTOBER 3, 1987 *Hail! Hail! Rock 'n' Roll* premieres at the New York Film Festival. The film is a tribute to Chuck Berry, directed by Taylor Hackford from an idea of Keith's, who was also the project's musical director. Both Keith and Chuck Berry are in the Lincoln Center audience.

OCTOBER 29, 1987 Ron Wood's one-man show —of paintings—opens at the Katherine Hamnett Gallery.

NOVEMBER 4, 1987 The Gunslingers' Tour— Ron Wood and Bo Diddley—begins with a gig at the Newport Music Hall in Columbus, OH. The last date of the tour is at the Ritz in New York City.

DECEMBER 19, 1987 Ron Wood's new club/restaurant/gallery, Woody's on the Beach, officially opens in Miami. Woody and Bo Diddley inaugurate the stage.

1988

JANUARY 7–8, 1988 Mick Taylor plays Woody's on the Beach. Woody and Bobby Keys join Taylor and his band onstage.

JANUARY 20, 1988 Mick Jagger inducts "the four-headed monster"—the Beatles—into the Rock 'n' Roll Hall of Fame at the annual ceremony at New York's Waldorf-Astoria Hotel. Jagger joins George Harrison, Bruce Springsteen, Ringo, Bob Dylan and Jeff Beck onstage for the closing all-star jam.

MARCH 15, 1988 In Osaka's Castle Hall, Mick Jagger plays the first concert of his 10-day, seven-show tour of Japan. It is his first solo tour and the first time any of the original Rolling Stones has played Japan. Tina Turner will join him in onstage duets of "Brown Sugar" and "It's Only Rock 'n' Roll" at the Tokyo Korakuen Dome on March 23.

APRIL 18–26, 1988 Reggae artist Patrick Alley's $7 million copyright infringement suit against Mick Jagger goes to trial in US Federal Court in White Plains, NY. At issue is the song "Just Another Night," which appears on Jagger's 1985 solo LP, *She's the Boss*. Alley maintains he wrote music and lyrics in 1979 for the song which was released on his own 1982 album and that Jagger copied it. Witnesses include drummer Sly Dunbar who played on Jagger's LP and, allegedly, on Alley's and Mick Jagger, both of whom perform before the court as part of official testimony. The verdict goes against Alley and absolves Jagger of the charges.

JULY 22, 1988 Bill Wyman reportedly receives a sizable advance from Viking/Penguin in the UK and Viking/NAL in the US for what is eventually titled *Stone Alone*, the bassist's autobiography. Though an exact figure is not released, the publishers are said to be paying around £3 million for world English language rights.

SEPTEMBER 17, 1988 In Sydney, about to begin his Australian tour, Mick Jagger gives a surprise performance for 400 people at the Kardomah Cafe.

SEPTEMBER 23, 1988 Virgin Records releases "Take It So Hard" b/w "I Could Have Stood You Up," Keith Richards's first solo single off his upcoming solo album.

SEPTEMBER 29, 1988 A party/opening is held at London's Hamilton Gallery to fete the UK publication of Ron Wood's book, *The Works*, along with the exhibition of some of Wood's new paintings.

OCTOBER 4, 1988 Keith's first solo album, *Talk is Cheap*, is released by Virgin.

NOVEMBER 24, 1988 Keith begins his first tour fronting his own band, The X-Pensive Winos, with a concert at the 4,000-seat Fox Theater in Atlanta. Along with Keith on guitar and lead vocals, the Winos include Steve Jordan, drums; Charley Drayton, bass (Jordan and Drayton switch places on a couple of numbers); Waddy Wachtel, guitar; Ivan Neville, keyboards; Bobby Keys, sax; and Sarah Dash, backup vocals. The tour consists of 15 US shows at various sized venues in a dozen cities, ending up on December 17 at New Jersey's Brendan Byrne Arena.

1989

After almost eight years off that three-year cycle and not together much in the public eye for the past seven—the Rolling Stones go bigtime. New promoter Michael Cohl of CPI will handle their tour and guarantees the Stones an unprecedented $70 million. This will not be an "oldies tour," but a new production with new material from a new LP, Steel Wheels. The Stones again set attendance records across the country. Their show is over two hours and

Mick and Keith on the podium at the band's induction into the Rock and Roll Hall of Fame, Waldorf-Astoria, New York City (1989, CAROL BERNSON, ALL RIGHTS RESERVED)

packed with raw energy: the 1989 Rolling Stones are not a bunch of decrepit old men playing rock'n'roll, they're as young and strong as their music and—still—the epitome of what a rock'n'roll band is meant to be.

JANUARY 18, 1989 Pete Townshend inducts the Rolling Stones into the Rock and Roll Hall of Fame at the Waldorf-Astoria in Manhattan. Present at the ceremonies are Mick, Keith, Woody and Mick Taylor. Wyman declined to appear (reportedly calling the honor "too little, too late"), and Charlie just couldn't make it to New York in time. All current and former Stones are remembered and inducted. Particular tribute is paid to the late Brian Jones and Ian Stewart. The traditional closing all-star jam features the two Micks, Keith and Woody along with Little Richard, Tina Turner and the rest of the inductees, inductors and members of Paul Shaffer's World's Most Dangerous Band in various combinations and permutations, solos, duets and mishmashes.

JANUARY 21, 1989 Woody, along with Percy Sledge, Bo Diddley, Willie Dixon and Koko Taylor, play one of US President George Bush's inaugural balls, at the Washington, DC Convention Center. Ronnie, Billy Preston, Albert Collins and Steve Cropper jam later in the evening, joined by George Bush on (bogus) guitar—he fakes it.

FEBRUARY 18, 1989 Bill Wyman plays in the benefit concert for the Kampuchea Appeal, held in Ringwood Recreation Center, Southampton.

MARCH 15, 1989 The Rolling Stones and Toronto-based Concert Productions International sign the largest financial deal in rock'n'roll history. Headed by Michael Cohl, CPI and its merchandising division, Brockum, agree to sponsor and promote the Stones' upcoming, but as yet unannounced, North American tour, their first in seven years. The Stones are guaranteed something in the neighborhood of $70 million for about 60 concerts. The contract is signed in Barbados, where the band has been working on tracks for the album which will become *Steel Wheels.*

MAY 9, 1989 Bill Wyman's restaurant in London's Kensington district, Sticky Fingers, has its opening party, which is attended by various stars, Stones, relatives and friends. The public will be able to eat there and check out the rock memorabilia on the walls beginning May 17.

MAY 31, 1989 Eric Clapton presents Keith Richards with the Living Legend Award (a 12-inch-high

Elvis) at the first annual International Rock Awards, held at the Armory in New York City.

JUNE 2, 1989 Bill Wyman, 52, and (his girlfriend of six years) Mandy Smith, 19, are secretly married in the registry office at Bury St. Edmonds, Suffolk, England. The ceremony is witnessed by Stephen Wyman, Bill's son, and Mandy's sister, Nicole, who are the only guests. Naturally, this relationship has been fodder for the tabloids for a while, for reasons hopefully apparent to even the worst students of arithmetic.

JUNE 5, 1989 Bill and Mandy have the "white wedding" she wanted, as their marriage is blessed by Reverend Thaddeus Birchard of Louisiana at the Anglican Church of St. John the Evangelist in London. The ceremony is attended by 170 guests and the number swells to 400 at the Grosvenor House Hotel reception which follows. All the Stones and spouses and various other musicians, friends and usual suspects attend. Mick Jagger's gift to the happy couple is reported to be an original Picasso etching.

JUNE 16–17, 1989 Mick, Keith, Ronnie (covered by a crew from BBC-TV) record the sounds discovered by the late Brian Jones, the Master Musicians of JouJouka in Tangier, Morocco. The ancient pipe music will become part of "Continental Drift" on *Steel Wheels.* (See DISCOGRAPHY)

JULY 11, 1989 Steel Wheels, the tour (and accompanying album), is announced after the Stones arrive, an hour late, on a train that rolls into Grand Central Station for an extremely sweaty press conference attended by too many (some say 500) journalists and more ecstatic fans. The advancing ages of the Stones become the most overused rock'n'roll topic for jokes, story hooks and boring conversation pieces from this day on. (See TOURS AND CONCERTS)

AUGUST 12, 1989 The Stones give a surprise performance for 700 mostly unsuspecting people at Toad's Place in New Haven, CT, as a warmup for Steel Wheels. The lucky music lovers who'd come to the club for that night's billed event—"Rock Dance Party with the Cruiser"—paid a paltry $3.00 cover charge and got to see just under an hour of the Rolling Stones—11 songs from their new show.

AUGUST 31, 1989 The opening show of the Stones' Steel Wheels North American tour, 1989 takes place at Veterans Stadium in Philadelphia, PA.

SEPTEMBER 6, 1989 The Stones appear at the MTV Video Awards. It was taped three days earlier, but

MTV doesn't make that too clear. (See TELEVISION APPEARANCES)

NOVEMBER 26, 1989 The Stones perform a Steel Wheels show they hadn't scheduled—at Death Valley Stadium in Clemson, SC—and donate part of the proceeds to relief efforts for the victims of that state's Hurricane Hugo.

DECEMBER 19, 1989 After 32 cities, 59 shows and four Canadian border crossings, the Stones' Steel Wheels North American tour ends in Atlantic City with a concert that's broadcast live over pay-per-view cable television. (See TOURS AND CONCERTS and TELEVISION APPEARANCES)

1990

1990 is a milestone year for Japan and the Rolling Stones. For the first time, Japanese fans get to see the Rolling Stones perform live in their own country. Though individual Stones have played Japan in recent years, the Japanese portion of Steel Wheels is the first time the Rolling Stones, as a group, have ever performed there. The Stones are very well received; likewise, the band truly enjoys the reception given them by the fans and the country.
The band winds up 1990 touring Europe, changing pace and show, now calling the tour Urban Jungle, using new set designs and varying the setlist from their Steel Wheels shows. Once again, the Stones prove they haven't lost a thing in their eight-year absence from the concert trail—the road they began traveling some 28 years earlier.

FEBRUARY 14–27, 1990 A half million Japanese fans finally get to see the Rolling Stones perform live in their country during the band's 10 sold-out shows at Tokyo's Korakuen Dome. Short, but very sweet, Steel Wheels—Japan is the first time the Rolling Stones have ever done (or been allowed to do) a Japanese tour.

MARCH 22, 1990 Mick Jagger announces the details of the upcoming European version of the Stones' ongoing world tour in a press conference at the Tabernacle Club in London. The band's 1990 tour of Europe will begin in Rotterdam on May 18, but it won't be the same old Steel Wheels of North America and Japan—it will have a new stage, new songs and a new name—Urban Jungle 1990.

MAY 18, 1990 Urban Jungle opens with its first concert at Feyenoord Stadium, Rotterdam, Holland.

JUNE 6, 1990 ABC-TV's International Rock Awards bestows its "Tour of the Year" honor on the Rolling Stones for Steel Wheels and names Charlie Watts "MVP Drummer." The broadcast includes the Stones' taped acceptance speeches and concert performance of "It's Only Rock 'n' Roll."

JULY 9, 1990 Keith's right index finger, which he cut on July 7, becomes infected. Although he makes it through this evening's performance in Glasgow, the band cancels three upcoming Urban Jungle concerts: on July 11 in Cardiff and July 13 and 14 at Wembley Stadium. This is the first time in 28 years of performing that the Stones have canceled a show due to a band injury. The tour resumes in Cardiff on July 16 and two replacement Wembley dates are tacked on to the itinerary. (See TOURS AND CONCERTS)

AUGUST 25, 1990 Urban Jungle ends after 46 shows in 26 cities with a final concert at Wembley Stadium.

1991

JANUARY 7, 1991 Rolling into London's Hit Factory Studio, the band begins recording two tracks—"Highwire" and "Sex Drive"—to be added to their upcoming live world tour album—*Flashpoint*. "Highwire" is political, topical, and—natch—controversial because of its reference to the critical situation in the Persian Gulf at the time. "Sex Drive" is a classic Stones foil.

JANUARY 29–30, 1991 Keith produces two tracks for legendary pianist Johnnie Johnson's upcoming album in New York.

FEBRUARY 14, 1991 Mick begins work in Atlanta, GA on the film *Freejack*, costarring with Emilio Estevez.

MARCH 1, 1991 The Stones' "Highwire" video, directed by Julien Temple, is shot at Pier 3, Brooklyn, NY, without Bill Wyman.

APRIL 3, 1991 The Charlie Watts Quintet debuts at Ronnie Scott's in London to promote the release of their new album, *From One Charlie*, which includes a new edition of *Ode to a High Flying Bird*, Charlie Watts's 1964 book about Charlie Parker.

MAY 2, 1991 The Stones are honored for their "Outstanding Contribution to British Music" at the Ivor Novello Awards at the Grosvenor House Hotel in London. Bill Wyman and Ron Wood are present to accept the award on behalf of the Stones.

OCTOBER 25, 1991 The cutting-edge *At the MAX* Stones concert film premieres in eight theaters worldwide. Shot in the IMAX format, it can be shown only in the 100 specially-equipped theaters in existence—on a superwide (100-foot) screen. It has since been marketed, somehow, on home video. (See PROMOTIONAL FILMS AND VIDEOS)

NOVEMBER 12, 1991 Ronnie and Jo are involved in a major traffic accident on the M-4 motorway at Swindon, Wiltshire, returning from the funeral of Jo's father in Devon. With Jo behind the wheel, their BMW hit an oil slick and spun out of control, landing in the fast lane, whereupon another car plowed into it. Jo's back and Woody's left shoulder were injured at this point. Woody then stepped out of the car, at which moment a third vehicle hit car #2 which again hit the BMW, sandwiching Ron in between and breaking both of his legs. He was, in fact, fortunate: the BMW served as a buffer, keeping him from being tossed back into the traffic. Woody wears two knee-length casts for a month.

NOVEMBER 19, 1991 The Rolling Stones sign with Virgin Records. The mother of all mega-deals.

NOVEMBER 21, 1991 Mick Jagger and Jerry Hall are married on the island of Bali.

DECEMBER 10, 1991 The plaster casts are removed from Ron Wood's legs, broken on the M-4 motorway on November 12, 1991.

1992

JANUARY 15, 1992 Keith inducts Leo Fender into the Rock 'n' Roll Hall of Fame at the annual awards dinner at New York's Waldorf-Astoria Hotel. He joins Jimmy Page and Johnny Cash in the finale jam.

JANUARY 16, 1992 *Freejack* is premiered at Mann's Chinese Theater in Hollywood, and Mick attends.

MARCH 18, 1992 Keith begins recording his second solo album at the Site in San Rafael, CA.

JULY 2, 1992 Mick Jagger becomes a grandfather. Daughter Jade, age 20, gives birth to a baby girl, to be named Assissi. Jagger is the first Rolling Stone to become a grandfather. The day also marks Jerry Hall's 36th birthday.

AUGUST 3, 1992 Keith attends Woody's CD release party for *Slide On This* at Tatou in Manhattan.

OCTOBER 20, 1992 *Main Offender*, Keith's second solo LP, is released by Virgin Records.

OCTOBER 28, 1992 Woody begins his 20-gig Slide On This tour in New Britain, CT. The tour ends on December 5 in Philadelphia.

NOVEMBER 27, 1992 Keith and the X-Pensive Winos kick off an 11-show, seven-nation European tour supporting *Main Offender*. The run ends in London on December 18, Keith's birthday.

DECEMBER 31, 1992 Keith does his Guy Lombardo impression, playing a New Year's eve concert at the Academy in New York City. Actually, CBS broadcasts part of the show live (see TELEVISION APPEARANCES), and Keith does say "Who knows? Maybe I could end up as the next Guy Lombardo."

1993

JANUARY 6, 1993 In an appearance on the British television program "London Tonight," Bill Wyman makes the official announcement—he has quit the Rolling Stones after 30 years with the band. "I really don't want to do it anymore," says Wyman.

JANUARY 10–14, 1993 Ron Wood plays four solo gigs in Japan.

JANUARY 17, 1993 Keith and the Winos begin a 22-show US Main Offender tour in Seattle, WA. They end up at the Beacon Theater in New York City on February 24.

FEBRUARY 5, 1993 Ron Wood and Rod Stewart tape MTV's "Unplugged" in Los Angeles. (See TELEVISION APPEARANCES)

FEBRUARY 6, 1993 Jagger appears on "Saturday Night Live." (See TELEVISION APPEARANCES)

FEBRUARY 9, 1993 Atlantic Records releases *Wandering Spirit*, Mick Jagger's third solo album. In the evening, he plays a private show at New York's Webster Hall.

APRIL 20, 1993 Jagger and Richards are off to Barbados to begin the songwriting part of the process of making a new Rolling Stones album.

APRIL 30, 1993 Charlie Watts goes down to join Mick and Keith in Barbados.

JULY 9, 1993 Sessions begin for what is to become *Voodoo Lounge* at Ron Wood's house in Ireland. (See SESSIONOGRAPHY)

NOVEMBER 2, 1993 Final recording begins for *Voodoo Lounge*, with Darryl Jones on bass, at Windmill Studios in Dublin, Ireland.

1994

JANUARY 9, 1994 The mixing of *Voodoo Lounge*, which will take four months, begins with Mick's arrival in Los Angeles.

JANUARY 14, 1994 Keith joins Mick and producer Don Was in Los Angeles. Charlie and Ronnie arrive in February.

MAY 3, 1994 The Stones sail down the Hudson aboard the yacht *Honey Fitz* and disembark at Pier 60 where the press awaits. With the new *Voodoo Lounge* graphic emblazoned on a banner behind them, the band holds court with the assembled journalists from a portable stage inside the Chelsea Pier building to announce "the Rolling Stones' world tour of 1994–1995," play a bit of the album, and talk about Darryl Jones, the bassist. (See TOURS AND CONCERTS)

JUNE 20, 1994 Voodoo Lounge tour rehearsals begin in Toronto.

JULY 19, 1994 The Stones play their now-traditional small-club unannounced warmup gig at Toronto's RPM Club. This is bassist Darryl Jones's first public appearance with the Rolling Stones. (See TOURS AND CONCERTS)

AUGUST 1, 1994 The Rolling Stones perform at RFK Stadium in Washington, DC; this is the first official concert of Voodoo Lounge. (See TOURS AND CONCERTS)

SEPTEMBER 6, 1994 Longtime contributor to the Stones albums, tours and all-around musical life, keyboard player Nicky Hopkins dies of complications from previous intestinal surgeries, in Nashville. He was 50. Never physically robust, Nicky suffered from chronic stomach problems throughout his life, yet was featured on at least 74 Stones songs and almost every Stones album from *Between the Buttons* in 1966 to *Tattoo You* in 1981 —besides working with the Beatles, the Who, the Kinks, Jefferson Airplane, Jeff Beck and many, many others. He is sorely missed.

OCTOBER 22, 1994 Producer Jimmy Miller, 52, dies of liver failure at University Hospital in Denver, Colorado while awaiting organ transplant surgery. An American, Miller had moved to London in 1965 to produce albums by Spencer Davis and Traffic; he was hired by the Stones in 1968 when they decided that an American producer might help them reach a new level in their music. He went on to produce *Beggars Banquet*, *Let It Bleed*, *Exile on Main Street*, *Sticky Fingers* and *Goat's Head Soup* —among the most popular of all Stones LPs. Miller's style

Keith during Steel Wheels

of producing meant he wasn't stuck at a console in a studio control room—he often played drums or other percussion and can be heard on many a famous track. His tenure with the band was arguably the Stones' most prolific period; his joining them when he did probably saved them from themselves and group self-destruction. He produced many, many other records, many hits for other musicians after leaving the Stones, the latest of which was Primal Scream's single "Movin' On Up" in 1991.

NOVEMBER 18, 1994 The band gives new meaning to the phrase "world tour" as the first five songs of the evening's concert at Dallas' (TX) Cotton Bowl are broadcast over the Internet's fledgling MBONE system. The Stones' first live performance in cyberspace is the first for a major group and, naturally, gets much media attention before and after. But the virtual Voodoo Lounge, while demonstrating the band's willingness to break new ground, is disappointing. Only 200 computers worldwide are reported to have seen and heard the show live (there are subsequent rebroadcasts) as the powerful hardware needed to receive it is well beyond the means of most computer users. Those who do see it, see something like a slide show sometimes accompanied by music. However, this is only one of the Stones' official cyber promotions—the band had begun rolling down the info superhighway on the '94 tour with an "Official Rolling Stones Internet Provider" (Delphi), a "home page" on the World Wide Web, with more to follow.

NOVEMBER 28, 1994 The Stones hold a press conference at the Four Seasons Hotel in Palm Beach, FL to discuss plans for the next portion of Voodoo Lounge.

1995

JANUARY 7, 1995 The Stones are in Mexico City for rehearsals prior to beginning the Latin American portion of Voodoo Lounge.

JANUARY 14–20, 1995 The Stones play four nights at Mexico City's Rodriguez Stadium (Autodromo Hermanos Rodriguez).

FEBRUARY 2–19, 1995 The South American leg of Voodoo Lounge begins in Rio and ends in Santiago, Chile.

FEBRUARY 24–25, 1995 Voodoo Lounge in Johannesburg, South Africa. Winnie Mandela raises a ruckus, but the Stones still play two dates at Ellis Park Stadium. Everything's the same about the shows, except

for the cobra—the huge structure that is usually part of the set is left behind to cut costs: it needs its own plane.

MARCH 3, 1995 The Stones hold a press conference at Toshiba EMI Studios in Tokyo, Japan. They announce their plans for the Japanese leg of Voodoo Lounge.

MARCH 6–23, 1995 Voodoo Lounge in Japan. The Stones play March 6–17 in Tokyo and March 22–23 in Fukuoka.

MARCH 28, 1995 The Australia/New Zealand leg of Voodoo Lounge begins. The band plays Sydney, Adelaide, Perth, Brisbane and Auckland.

APRIL 17, 1995 Voodoo Lounge winds up Down Under. These have been the first Australian shows the Stones have played in 22 years.

MAY 25, 1995 The earliest known audio recording of Mick and Keith playing together—a 30-minute reel-to-reel tape made in 1961—goes on the auction block at Christie's in London. The tape, containing 13 songs performed by "Little Boy Blue & the Blue Boys," was recorded in a group member's living room (neither Mick's nor Keith's). Christie's identifies the seller only as a former member of "Little Boy Blue," now a "British senior civil servant" whose teenage daughter is a Stones fan. The tape reportedly fetches £50,250 (about $81,400), slightly less than the £55,000 ($89,000) the auctioneers predicted. Christie's does not, officially, name the purchaser. Within 48 hours of the sale, the British press, citing sources inside Christie's, reveals that the "anonymous buyer" is none other than Mick Jagger.

MAY 26–27, 1995 Just prior to the official beginning of the European leg of Voodoo Lounge, the Stones perform two concerts at the Paradiso in Amsterdam. Both performances are videotaped for future video projects and television broadcasts, and recorded for what will become *Stripped*, the Stones' next album. (See TOURS AND CONCERTS)

MAY 28, 1995 The Rolling Stones hold a press conference at Cirkus Kungl in Stockholm, Sweden, to announce their plans for the final leg of the Voodoo Lounge world tour. The European dates will begin in Stockholm on June 3. The tour ends on August 30 in Rotterdam, though the Rotterdam gig is not revealed at this press conference.

OCTOBER 28, 1995 *New Musical Express* reports that Eric Easton has died at the age of 67. A former music hall and movie theater organist, Easton had become a booking agent and artist's manager in the 1950s. In 1963, he formed Impact Sound in partnership with Andrew Loog Oldham, and with him became the first to manage the Rolling Stones.

JULY 16, 1995 Former Stones bass player Bill Wyman stops by to say hello to his ex-bandmates at their Wembley Stadium show. He attends the concert. All is very congenial.

1996

JANUARY 26, 1996 Bill German, writer, editor and publisher of *Beggars Banquet*, the Rolling Stones' official fanzine, announces that this issue (Vol. 3, No. 29) of the publication is the last one. No more *Banquet*s, he's had enough after 17 years. The last 'zine contains handwritten thank-you notes from the Stones as well as official confirmation that the band's proposed but unconfirmed 1996 tour of the Far East and South America isn't happening, citing "foreseen scheduling and staging problems" as the Stones' final deciding factor. German predicts that the band will occupy themselves with solo projects throughout 1996.

MAY 29, 1996 Grandpa is a Rolling Stone (we couldn't resist): Keith Richards and Anita Pallenberg's son, Marlon, and his wife, supermodel Lucie de la Falaise, become the proud parents of Ella Rose Richards. The 7lb., 13oz. baby girl is born today in Connecticut and joyously greeted by the "houseful of women" gathered at the Richards home in anticipation of the event, which occurred somewhat later than expected. Father and grandfather (the latter, reportedly, sought refuge in the studio whenever possible before labor's onset) are equally ecstatic.

OCTOBER 12, 1996 Most thought they'd never see it and no one ever dreamed it would be under such circumstances. *The Rock 'n' Roll Circus* (newly edited) has its premiere at the Lincoln Center—at the New York Film Festival—a joint entry of ABKCO and the Stones. Seven screenings of the band's mythic 1968 project take place within two days, October 12 and 13.

OCTOBER 15, 1996 The official, long-awaited release of *The Rock 'n' Roll Circus* on VHS and laserdisc and of the film's soundtrack on CD.

Tours and Concerts

The blues were born in America well before 1962, but the entity we now know as the Rolling Stones was only in the throes of creation that year. The early nucleus —Brian, Mick, Keith and Stu—was in place, four nearly penniless young Englishmen drawn together by a passion to play American black music. But the *band* was still incomplete, and undeveloped, and the thread of the music was most uncommon for that time and place.

So, what else could four poor boys do? They played, and they paid some dues. Unnamed at first, then as the "Rollin' Stones," and finally as we know them, the Rolling Stones labored to become a rhythm and blues band throughout 1962. Largely because of Brian Jones's persistence, using an unplanned rotation of drummers and bassists (1963 was nearly a month old before both Bill and Charlie were permanently in the picture), they landed gigs whenever possible. Still, it was by no means an easy delivery.

England's popular music scene wasn't a particularly nurturing atmosphere for any rhythm and blues band when the Stones first got together. R&B wasn't considered "pop" or "jazz"—clubs and audiences were fairly well split into those two camps. The jazz clubs were more approachable for new artists, but as the 1960s began the UK jazz scene was conventional, if not stodgy. The question of R&B's musical legitimacy was hotly debated among jazz fans, club owners and in the music press. Consequently, most jazz clubs offered "trad jazz," not daring to book blues or R&B artists for fear of alienating loyal customers.

R&B received most of its early exposure in the UK along with rock'n'roll in the spate of American pop music films that hit the British Isles from the mid-1950s. Teenagers flocked to their local cinemas to see Frank Tashlin's *The Girl Can't Help It*, Bert Stern's *Jazz On a Summer's Day*, Fred Sears's *Rock around the Clock*, Richard Brooks's *Blackboard Jungle* and others. In those audiences were the new generation of British music lovers—kids like Keith Richards, Ray Davies, Rod Stewart, Mick Jagger, John Lennon, Pete Townshend, Bill Wyman and so on. The music in these and similar films left a lasting impression that became a craving to hear more, on record, at home. Bill Haley's "Rock around the Clock," Jerry Lee Lewis's "Great Balls of Fire" and Elvis Presley's "Heartbreak Hotel" were all transatlantic hits that were available in UK record stores along with Britain's own "Rock Island Line" by Lonnie Donegan. But recordings by artists like Chuck Berry could only be obtained as imports, a somewhat arduous and expensive process nevertheless undertaken by both Mick Jagger and Bill Wyman, independently, so strongly had they been affected by their initial glimpses of Berry and his music. Berry's R&B was unlike anything Mick, Keith and those other musically inclined moviegoers had heard at a time when music was already becoming a liberating force in the lives of much of Britain's postwar generation. The aforementioned "Rock Island Line," sung by Lonnie (né Tony) Donegan with the Chris Barber Band, became a number one hit in the UK in 1956, and its driving rhythm and energy was so infectious that it sparked what is known as the "skiffle craze." Like many of their contemporaries, all of the Stones (except Charlie Watts, who was captivated by modern jazz), found a way to express themselves musically in a local skiffle group. Skiffle was a social leveler—anyone could form a band and play a homemade instrument, even a washboard or a stewpot. The skiffle movement was also the beginning of British rock'n'roll.

Not content with skiffle music, like-minded fans of R&B began forming their own rough groups to try playing this new, raw music themselves. At the same time, they sought out places to hear the real thing performed live by R&B artists.

Unlike their British counterparts, most clubgoing fans in the United States had never even heard of Muddy Waters or Howlin' Wolf. Racism and segregation kept their so-called "race records" from getting regular airplay, except by those radio stations geared to all-black audiences. But Muddy, Howlin' Wolf, and other American blues and R&B artists did tour the UK. There was a small but fervent group of blues afficionados in England at the beginning of the 1960s. Many were musicians themselves—like Chris Barber, Alexis Korner and Cyril Davies—and it was these people who were largely responsible for bringing the music and the musicians across the Atlantic. Chris Barber acted as UK booking agent, while Harold Pendleton's Marquee jazz clubs became the first London venues for Barber and Davies's initial self-sponsored "rhythm and blues nights." These evenings attracted tiny audiences at first, but those who did attend might have caught Sonny Boy Williamson or Big Bill Broonzy. The real thing.

The anti-trad jazz scene in London, in contrast with what was happening in the rest of Britain, moved quite quickly out of skiffle into an almost cult-like environment for the development of British R&B. New music in Liverpool, for example, evolved more slowly out of the skiffle movement toward the pop end of the spectrum in its progress toward rock and away from trad jazz. The disparity would disappear as rhythm and blues gained legitimacy throughout Britain. The first breakthrough came by way of an annual event—The American Folk Festival—staged by Willie Dixon and Horst Leibman. Beginning in 1959 and occurring each year for 10 years, the festival brought blues musicians from the US to Britain and attracted fans from throughout the country. The same musicians—Muddy Waters, Sonny Boy Williamson, Big Boy Broonzy, Sister Rosetta Thorpe—then played clubs all over Britain. Once the music was out there, the stage was set for what Giorgio Gomelsky calls "BRRB"—BRitish Rhythm & Blues.

The British homegrown style of Alexis Korner's band, Blues Incorporated, was the incubator for most of what became British rock. Its members included at one time or another such familiar names as Ginger Baker, Jack Bruce, Long John Baldry, Charlie Watts and Mick Jagger. Alexis was mentor to all aspiring blues musicians, and to each of the Stones individually (to varying degrees) before they knew each other. It was Alexis, by design and by chance, who provided some of the Stones' earliest support and the opportunity to transform a shared passion into performance. He was not the only one. Nevertheless, it was the Stones themselves, who had to take it from there.

HOW TO READ THE CONCERT LISTINGS

We've tried to make these entries easy to read, without taking up too much space with redundancies or extraneous detail. Our method of balancing these considerations has been to give detailed information at the beginning of each year, each transitional period in the Stones' history, and in the first listing for each tour, but not to keep repeating facts that are relatively constant—like the band members' names—unless something changes. When one of the Stones doesn't perform, the setlist changes, a special guest comes on stage, or something else is different, that information will appear in the entry for the date on which it occurred. The information in TOURS AND CONCERTS is broken down into the following categories:

DATE: The first entry for a tour has both the beginning date and ending date for that tour. The concert engagements within that tour have only the *date* for each venue, as do individual gigs that were not part of any tour. There is one entry per date per venue, even if two shows were performed at the same place that day.

TOUR: The name of the tour. If a gig is not part of a tour, this category does not appear.

VENUE: The name of the club, stadium, arena etc., where the performance was given. The title of this heading changes to Where in the initial listing for each tour, and indicates the countries visited on that tour.

PERSONNEL: The members of the Rolling Stones and, in later years, regular tour personnel who performed. Again, we've listed all members of the Rolling Stones under the heading Personnel at the beginning of each year. Additional personnel (if any) are listed in the first entry for each major tour. If the regular lineup changed for any reason, it will be indicated on the date it occurs.

SPECIAL GUESTS: Any musician who made a guest appearance with the Rolling Stones during a Stones show. The category only appears at the beginning of a tour during which a guest or guests appeared (all guests' names for that tour are provided), and on the actual date of each guest's appearance.

OPENING/OTHER ACTS: Other artists on the bill for any individual concert or throughout a tour. All acts that appeared at concerts within a single tour are indicated in the initial summary for that tour; the names of those who actually perform on a given date can be found with the appropriate concert entry. If the category does not appear, either the information is unknown (primarily in the early years) or there were no other acts. The Stones did not start their career as headliners, naturally, and there were later occasions when they didn't top the bill. The artists' positions in the lineup for a gig are clarified where necessary.

SONGS: Confirmed setlist information is given wherever possible with individual concert listings. In the early years, as described in the following pages, only a "typical set" for a given time period may be available. As the Stones became famous, their shows and the songs they played onstage became matters of intense interest to the music-oriented press as well as to their fans, some of whom began coming to gigs with pen and paper and jotting down the songs they heard. Of course, detail-oriented individuals weren't always present, and even they made mistakes as late as the Voodoo Lounge tour. But, by 1994, international Stones fans were communicating over the Internet, and correcting each other's errors and those published in the various fanzines throughout the world. Most of the time. In any event, the authors have attempted to provide an accurate picture of the content of all Rolling Stones' shows throughout the years, including accurate song titles in the proper sequence for each show. Arrows between song titles indicate a medley.

As a general rule, if no setlist is provided, refer to the most recent complete set chronologically preceding the gig in question for a guide to what the Stones were then playing—most likely, the set hadn't changed much, if at all. From the late '70s until Voodoo Lounge, the absence of a setlist indicates no gross change; for dates prior to that, a show may have been different from the last confirmed entry, but we cannot be certain either way. In the 1960s, for example, if only a few titles are listed for a gig—and they weren't included in an earlier setlist—we've ascertained that they were performed as of that date but cannot confirm how the rest of the set changed; that is, which, if any, older titles were taken out to make room for the new ones or if the songs were merely added. Once a new number is listed, it could be included in any performance after that, in theory. In reality, it may not have worked and the band chucked it out of the show. Check the next set or few sets in the chapter for comparison and look for any additional information in the Notes for the gig in question.

NOTES: As in the other sections of the book, any available information not included in the earlier categories of an entry, and any clarification of the briefer categorical data, can be found in Notes, where appropriate.

1962

Though reliable reports about the infancy of the Stones' career are somewhat sparse and frequently contradictory, enough factual information exists to visualize those early performances. While the minute details of all the band's 1962 gigs are unconfirmable, in creating this chapter the dates and places of all shows on record have been re-checked and confirmed, and other dates have been added as new, trustworthy facts have arisen. We have a good idea of the likely content of these early engagements and who was present, and when and where they were performed—information that has been somewhat more sketchily presented in the past. We make no claims of infallibility, but merely have tried our best to set this section of the record as straight as possible.

The **1962 Repertoire** is a compilation of all song titles known to have been in the Stones' repertoire for the year 1962. As far as can be determined, the band rehearsed and/or performed each of the numbers mentioned at some point during their first year—really six months—together (officially, there were no "Rollin' Stones" until they played the Marquee Club on July 12). Except for that very first paying gig, which was documented by the late Ian Stewart in his diary and has been widely quoted by others, records of individual (complete) setlists for 1962 are almost nonexistent. We have confirmed that some songs were played on particular occasions and, using confirmed facts from many sources along with deduction, provided likely setlists at various gigs listed in 1962 as well as later in 1963. Be advised that in all such cases, unless otherwise noted, the order of play is not known.

That no one was writing everything down shouldn't be surprising, for many reasons. In the early 1960s, it was common practice in British clubs for groups to play three or more sets in an evening or weekend afternoon. During their first year (1962 to mid–1963), the Stones were frequently booked as the "interval band," and played as many as five short (30–40 minutes) sets in between the headliners' shows. Consider also that being a band and performing together in public was a new experience for the Stones, but at the same time the music they were playing was equally new to their audiences. It would be more surprising to find that the band prepared five setlists for a gig and stuck to them; it is much more likely that as the evening progressed and the crowd responded, they picked the next song to play, on-the-fly, from those they'd rehearsed. Press reports for this time period are spotty at best and are most reliable when they concentrate on the phenomenon of the Stones' rise, but are not always so accurate on details like the setlist. It's clear enough from all descriptions that early fans were into dancing, not documenting. Finally, even after Bill Wyman joined them—the early Stones appear to have been more concerned with the idea of making records than with keeping them. That's as it should be.

Despite all the above, when asked nicely, people do remember things that impressed them even three decades ago. We have discovered quite a lot about the songs the Stones knew and performed, based on information gathered from reliable primary (and a few secondary) sources, a bit of deduction, and more questions. While individual listings for the Stones' early performances only contain song titles if positive confirmation has been obtained, it's a good bet that the setlist for any 1962 show would have been made up of songs from the following list (*plus* any others we've not yet found):

1962 REPERTOIRE: Ain't That Loving You Baby (Reed) / Back in the U.S.A. (Berry) / Bad Boy (Taylor) / Beautiful Delilah (Berry) / Big Boss Man (Dixon) / Blueberry Hill (Stock, Lewis, Rose) / Blues before Sunrise (James) / Bo Diddley (McDaniel) / Bright Lights, Big City (Reed) / Close Together (Reed) / Confessin' the Blues (McShann, Brown) / Crawling King Snake (Hooker) / Dimples (Hooker) / Don't Stay Out All Night (Arnold) / Down the Road Apiece (Raye) / Fortune Teller (Neville) / Happy Home (Reed) / Hey Crawdaddy (McDaniel) / Honey What's Wrong (Reed) / Hush Hush (Reed) / I Ain't Got You (Carter) / I Ain't Got No Money (Arnold) / I Believe I'll Dust My Broom (Robt. Johnson) / I Got My Brand on You (Morganfield) / I Got My Mojo Working (Morganfield) / I'm a Hog for You, Baby (Leiber, Stoller) / I'm Moving On (Snow) / I'm Your Hoochie Coochie Man (Dixon) / If You Need Me (Pickett, Bateman, Sanders) / I Want You to Love Me (Morganfield) / Johnny B. Goode (Berry) / Kansas City (Leiber, Stoller) / Kind of Lonesome (Reed) / La Bamba (Valens) / Let Me Love You, Baby (Dixon) / Little Baby (Dixon) / The Moon Is Rising (Reed) / My Baby (Dixon) / No Money Down (Berry) / Nursery Rhyme (McDaniel) / Pretty Thing (McDaniel) / Ride 'Em on Down (Broonzy) / Road Runner (McDaniel) / Roll over Beethoven (Berry) / Smokestack Lightning (Burnett) / Soon Forgotten (Oden) / Still a Fool (Morganfield) / The Sun Is Shining (Reed) / Sweet Little Sixteen (Berry) / Talkin' 'Bout You (Berry) / Tell Me That You Love Me (Reed) / Tiger in Your Tank (Dixon) / You Better Move On (Alexander) / You Can't Judge a Book (By Looking at the Cover) (Dixon)

1962 ROTATION: Bill Wyman had not yet joined the band at the time of their first performance on July 12; in fact, he did not play with them at all until late 1962. Charlie Watts didn't join until early 1963, though he may have sat in on drums at one or two gigs in 1962 as a favor and is said to have been at several rehearsals during that year. What could be called the "1962 rotation" consisted of various musicians, primarily drummers and bassists, who performed with the band on a rotational basis during

MARQUEE

THE LONDON JAZZ CENTRE
165, Oxford Street, W.1.

Wednesday, July 11th
★ DOUG RICHFORD'S JAZZMEN
(Members: 4/-
Guests: 5/-)

Thursday, July 12th
★ MICK JAGGER and the ROLLING STONES
★ LONG JOHN BALDRY'S KANSAS CITY BLUE BOYS
(Members: 4/-
Guests: 5/-)

Friday, July 13th
★ FAIRWEATHER — BROWN ALL STARS
(Members: 4/-
Guests: 5/-)

Saturday, July 14th
★ JOE HARRIOTT QUINTET
★ RONNIE ROSS QUARTET
(Members: 6/-
Guests: 7/6d)

Sunday, July 15th
★ DANKWORTH NIGHT
(Members: 4/-
Guests: 5/-)

Monday, July 16th
★ CYRIL PRESTON JAZZ BAND
★ COLIN KINGWELL'S JAZZ BANDITS
(Members: 4/-
Guests: 5/-)

The first advertisement for the Rolling Stones' first gig, July 1962 (JPK/CB)

that year. Those players are: Dick Taylor (bass); Ricky Fenson—also known as Ricky Brown—(bass); Colin Golding (bass); Tony Chapman (drums); Carlo Little (drums); and Steve Harris (drums). Guitarist Geoff Bradford and drummer Mick Avory were among the Bricklayer's Arms rehearsal players during 1962, but neither actually performed with the Rollin' Stones. Almost every written history of the band to date has named Avory as the Stones' drummer at their first gig; however, the authors have learned otherwise. See the July 12, 1962, entry.

In the 1962 concert listings that follow, personnel names printed in italics denote the *likely* players on a given date. In other words, an italicized name is an educated guess based on various known facts that the musician in question appeared on the specified date. A few examples: In September 1962, Dick Taylor decided to quit in order to prepare his portfolio for consideration by the Royal Colllege of Art while continuing his course at Sidcup Art College (he later cofounded the Pretty Things). This left Ricky Fenson as the only bassist in the rotation for a couple of months or so. Then, in November and December of 1962, Colin Golding (of the Presidents) began filling in on bass somewhat regularly until Bill Wyman joined. Also, Tony Chapman played with another band, the Cliftons, until the end of September and was not always available as the Rollin' Stones' drummer. The Stones' "engine," as Keith Richards has called their rhythm section, was hardly a finely tuned machine in 1962. One or two parts would often be missing at showtime. Nevertheless, they muddled through. Thus, the *probable* rhythm player for a particular gig is noted in italics—if a player's name is *not* italicized in a listing, then his participation has been confirmed for that date.

1962

JULY 12, 1962

VENUE: Marquee Jazz Club, London, England

PERSONNEL: Mick Jagger, Keith Richards, Elmo Lewis (a.k.a. Brian Jones), Dick Taylor, Ian Stewart, Tony Chapman

OPENING/OTHER ACT(S): Long John Baldry's Kansas City Blue Boys (headlined—Stones played the intermission)

SONGS: Kansas City (Leiber, Stoller) / Honey What's Wrong (Reed) / Confessin' the Blues (McShann, Brown) / Bright Lights, Big City (Reed)/ I Believe I'll Dust My Broom (Robt. Johnson) / Down the Road Apiece (Raye) / I Want You To Love Me (Morganfield) / Bad Boy (Taylor) / I Ain't Got You (Carter) / Hush Hush (Reed) / Ride 'Em on Down (Broonzy) / Back in the U.S.A. (Berry) / Kind of Lonesome (Reed) / Blues before

Sunrise (James) / Big Boss Man (Dixon) / Don't Stay out All Night (Arnold) / Tell Me that You Love Me (Reed) / Happy Home (Reed)

NOTES: The first public performance—the baptismal gig for the newly named "Rollin' Stones" (without a "g") who were, ironically, advertised by the club as "Mick Jagger and the Rolling Stones" (with the "g"). Prior to this first booking, the "band" was unnamed, as yet a variable collection of players brought together by Brian Jones for semi-regular rehearsals in a pub. Their big chance was, in fact, an opportunity seized for them by Mick Jagger when the Marquee's regular Thursday group, Alexis Korner's Blues Incorporated, got a better offer for July 12. Alexis's band was invited to make its nationwide radio debut on the BBC's prestigious "Jazz Club" program. As it happened, the parsimonious "Beeb" would only pay for a six-player band: Mick's brief stint as Blues Inc.'s vocalist made him the seventh. This invitation was the first of its kind for *any* R&B band, not only Blues Inc.'s first shot at a national audience. Still, Korner's loyalty to his players made him inclined to turn down the BBC, even though Jagger had only been with them for a short time. But Mick, aware of the "Jazz Club" spot's significance and also his own Stones agenda, persuaded Korner to accept it without him. The club replaced Blues Inc. by shifting Long John Baldry's Kansas City Blue Boys from support band to headliners, and agreed to let Jagger and his pals take their spot as the "interval" act.

Upon learning that they actually had a gig, Brian quickly chose to name his group after a line in "Mannish Boy" (perhaps because he identified with the song's lyrics)—"I'm a lover's man—I'm a rolling stone"—but dropped the "g," as Muddy Waters had done in the title of "Rollin' Stone Blues," much to the others' dismay. Ian Stewart particularly hated the name, but, like his bandmates, went along with Brian. The Marquee Club's ad in *Melody Maker* listed Blues Inc. as appearing as usual. Ironically, however, the club's ad in another, smaller circulation, music paper offered "Mick Jagger and the Rolling Stones" and Long John Baldry's Kansas City Blue Boys as July 12's attractions. Understandably, Brian Jones was not at all pleased with this billing—not only had he started the group, but he felt they were a band, not a backup group for Mick Jagger.

In all fairness, the authors believe that the "Mick Jagger and the Rolling Stones" bit was *not* a Jagger scam. Most likely, it was the club's idea. Advertising "Mick Jagger and the Rolling Stones" could at least take advantage of Mick's short tenure with Alexis—he was the only one of the Stones with any name recognition at all. Prior to this time, there had been a few trade press mentions of Blues Inc.'s new vocalist (Jagger). But alone, the Rollin' Stones—or the Rolling Stones—was just an unknown group, with or without the "g." They became the Rolling Stones (officially with "g") in 1963, though the name was printed both ways until their first record came out.

It has been written that the Stones' first gig was played to just a few lonely old souls. Not true. In fact, the Marquee Club was nearly full that night. Apparently their advertising strategy, if that's what it was, worked.

The accepted history of the band's birth has also stated that Stones' lineup for this engagement included the following: Mick Jagger, vocals; Keith Richards and Brian Jones (who called himself "Elmo Lewis" during this period—see CHRONOLOGY), guitars; Dick Taylor, bass; Ian Stewart, piano; and Mick Avory, drums. Avory (who later joined the Kinks) was part of the rotating cast of drummers, guitarists, and bassists who played with the 1962 Rollin' Stones, and supposedly "just happened" to get the drummer's slot at the Marquee that night. However it happened, he played the gig, according to nearly everything in and out of print. An advance item did run in the music press, which might explain some of the confusion. The small story announced the Stones' upcoming Marquee gig and identified Avory along with the other band members by name and instrument. There were no reviews after the show, nothing to contradict the details in the advance piece, as far as we have determined.

Two things seem odd about this: Avory's name never appeared as a member of the Stones lineup in later articles and nobody ever explained why he left—which led to our contacting him. In response to our queries, Mick Avory told us emphatically that he did *not* play that night—Tony Chapman was the drummer at the Stones' first performance—though Avory had indeed rehearsed with the band prior to July 12. It seems he'd been told to contact Mick Jagger by a friend's father, a drummer named Syd Payne. Payne regularly advertised his own services in the "Engagements Wanted" column of *Melody Maker's* classified section. He'd learned of an opportunity with a newly formed R&B band that seemed better suited to a younger drummer, and passed the information on to Avory. Mick attended a rehearsal, and learned that the Stones were looking for a permanent drummer, a position that he couldn't commit to because of his day job. They asked if

he could stay on to play their upcoming Marquee gig and rehearse once more prior to the date, and he agreed. After Avory's second practice at the Bricklayers Arms, he got a phone call. Apparently, a more permanent percussionist had turned up. The drummer the Stones had been using —Tony Chapman—he was told, would be able to play the Marquee. And thank you very much.

Somehow, the drummer's identity at the Stones' first performance has been misremembered, misquoted, or confused and then serially misprinted over the years, along with several other early details, for example, Dick Taylor's presence on bass at the band's first recording session (see SESSIONOGRAPHY). Actually, Dick Taylor played twice as hard as anyone else on July 12, 1962—Long John Baldry's bassist didn't make it to the Marquee Club gig, so Taylor filled in for him *and* played with the Stones.

Songs, above, lists the 18 tunes the Stones played that night. Each set was, at most, 30 to 40 minutes in length, as was the custom for intermission bands in those days. The authors found it a bit difficult to imagine the Rollin' Stones doing 18 numbers in a single set at their first gig —even nine was a stretch. Yet, we've confirmed that the group did indeed make two trips to the bandstand that evening.

JULY 28, 1962

VENUE: Ealing Jazz Club, London, England
PERSONNEL: Mick Jagger, Keith Richards, Elmo Lewis (a.k.a. Brian Jones), Ian Stewart, Dick Taylor, Tony Chapman
OPENING/OTHER ACT(S): Alexis Korner's Blues Incorporated (headlined)

AUGUST 4, 1962

VENUE: Wm. Morris Hall, South Oxhey (Nr. Watford), Hertfordshire, England
PERSONNEL: Mick Jagger, Keith Richards, Elmo Lewis (a.k.a. Brian Jones), Ian Stewart, Dick Taylor, Tony Chapman
SONGS: Dimples (Hooker) / Peepin' 'n' Hidin' (Reed) / I Got My Brand on You (Morganfield) / The Moon Is Rising (Reed) / I'm Moving On (Snow)
NOTES: Dick Taylor remembers playing these songs at this venue.

SEPTEMBER 8, 1962

VENUE: Ealing Jazz Club, London, England
PERSONNEL: Mick Jagger, Keith Richards, Elmo Lewis (a.k.a. Brian Jones), Ian Stewart, Dick Taylor, *Tony Chapman* or *Steve Harris*
OPENING/OTHER ACT(S): Alexis Korner's Blues Incorporated

An ad from fall 1962 (JPK/CB)

NOTES: The Stones were the support band—not the headliners—playing the interval between Blues Inc.'s sets

SEPTEMBER 15, 1962

VENUE: Ealing Jazz Club, London, England

PERSONNEL: Mick Jagger, Keith Richards, Elmo Lewis (a.k.a. Brian Jones), Ian Stewart, Dick Taylor, *Tony Chapman* or *Steve Harris*

NOTES: The September 15 issue of *DISC* announced that Alexis Korner's band had left their Saturday Ealing Jazz Club residency for a spot at Maton Hall, Putney, as of this evening—and that the Rollin' Stones would be taking their place.

SEPTEMBER 22, 1962

VENUE: Ealing Jazz Club, London, England

PERSONNEL: Mick Jagger, Keith Richards, Elmo Lewis (a.k.a. Brian Jones), Ian Stewart, Dick Taylor, Tony Chapman

SONGS: Crawling King Snake (Hooker) / Dimples (Hooker) / Bo Diddley (McDaniel) / I Believe I'll Dust My Broom (Robt. Johnson)

SEPTEMBER 27, 1962

VENUE: Marquee Jazz Club, London, England

PERSONNEL: Mick Jagger, Keith Richards, Elmo Lewis (a.k.a. Brian Jones), Ian Stewart, Dick Taylor, Tony Chapman

OPENING/OTHER ACT(S): Alexis Korner's Blues Incorporated (headlined)

NOTES: This date is not 100% confirmed. 1962 repertoire and rhythm section rotation.

SEPTEMBER 29, 1962

VENUE: Ealing Jazz Club, London, England

PERSONNEL: Mick Jagger, Keith Richards, Elmo Lewis (a.k.a. Brian Jones), Ian Stewart, Dick Taylor, Tony Chapman

OCTOBER 5, 1962

VENUE: Woodstock Hotel, North Cheam, Surrey, England

PERSONNEL: Mick Jagger, Keith Richards, Elmo Lewis (a.k.a. Brian Jones), Ian Stewart, *Dick Taylor* or *Ricky Fenson*, Tony Chapman

SONGS: Roll Over Beethoven (Berry) / Road Runner (McDaniel) / Tell Me That You Love Me (Reed) / Tiger in Your Tank (Dixon) / Bright Lights, Big City (Reed) / Pretty Thing (McDaniel) / Nursery Rhyme (McDaniel) / Confessin' the Blues (McShann, Brown) / You Can't Judge a Book (by Looking at the Cover) (Dixon) / The

A SHOT OF RHYTHM AND BLUES
★ THE REAL THING ★
THE ROLLIN' STONES
EVERY WED. — Wm. MORRIS HALL, Sth. OXHEY
— 7.30 P.M. (TUBE TO CARPENDERS PARK)
AVAILABLE FOR BOOKINGS: GER 6601 or
MANAGEMENT — 102 EDITH GROVE S.W.10

Another bit of self-promotion from late 1962 (JPK/CB)

Sun Is Shining (Reed) / Let Me Love You, Baby (Dixon) / I'm a Hog for You, Baby (Leiber, Stoller) / Honey What's Wrong (Reed) / Close Together (Reed) / Johnny B. Goode (Berry) / Beautiful Delilah (Berry)

NOTES: Several sources have mentioned the above songs as having been in Stones' shows at this point in time, although the order in which they were played remains unknown.

OCTOBER 6, 1962

VENUE: Ealing Jazz Club, London, England

PERSONNEL: Mick Jagger, Keith Richards, Elmo Lewis (a.k.a. Brian Jones), Ian Stewart, *Dick Taylor* or *Ricky Fenson*, Tony Chapman

OCTOBER 13, 1962

VENUE: Ealing Jazz Club, London, England

PERSONNEL: Mick Jagger, Keith Richards, Elmo Lewis (a.k.a. Brian Jones), Ian Stewart, Dick Taylor or *Ricky Fenson*, Tony Chapman

OCTOBER 20, 1962

VENUE: Ealing Jazz Club, London, England

PERSONNEL: Mick Jagger, Keith Richards, Elmo Lewis (a.k.a. Brian Jones), Ian Stewart, *Dick Taylor* or *Ricky Fenson*, Tony Chapman

OCTOBER 27, 1962

VENUE: Ealing Jazz Club, London, England

PERSONNEL: Mick Jagger, Keith Richards, Elmo Lewis (a.k.a. Brian Jones), Ian Stewart, *Dick Taylor* or *Ricky Fenson*, Tony Chapman

NOVEMBER 6, 1962

VENUE: Ealing Jazz Club, London, England

PERSONNEL: Mick Jagger, Keith Richards, Elmo Lewis (a.k.a. Brian Jones), Ian Stewart, *Ricky Fenson*, Tony Chapman

NOTES: The band's Ealing gigs changed to Tuesdays at this point in November (November 6).

NOVEMBER 7, 1962

VENUE: Wm. Morris Hall, South Oxhey (Nr. Watford), Hertfordshire, England

PERSONNEL: Mick Jagger, Keith Richards, Elmo Lewis (a.k.a. Brian Jones), Ian Stewart, *Ricky Fenson*, Tony Chapman

NOTES: At this point in time, Ricky Fenson had left Screamin' Lord Sutch but had not yet committed to playing regularly with Cyril Davies. Hence, it is quite possible that he filled in on bass with the Stones at this and other gigs around this time.

NOVEMBER 13, 1962

VENUE: Ealing Jazz Club, London, England

PERSONNEL: Mick Jagger, Keith Richards, Elmo Lewis (a.k.a. Brian Jones), Ian Stewart, *Ricky Fenson*, Tony Chapman

NOVEMBER 14, 1962

VENUE: Wm. Morris Hall, South Oxhey (Nr. Watford), Hertfordshire, England

PERSONNEL: Mick Jagger, Keith Richards, Elmo Lewis (a.k.a. Brian Jones), Ian Stewart, *Ricky Fenson,* Tony Chapman

NOVEMBER 18, 1962

VENUE: Studio 51, London England

PERSONNEL: Mick Jagger, Keith Richards, Elmo Lewis (a.k.a. Brian Jones), Ian Stewart, Tony Chapman

OPENING/OTHER ACT(S): Blues By Six

NOTES: Brian Knight's Blues By Six were supported by five Rollin' Stones, instead of the usual six. We have been unable to confirm a bass player for this gig. Moreover, we have confirmed that the 1962 Rollin' Stones—after Dick Taylor left—often performed without a bass player. This was not by choice, of course. Nor was it a particularly comfortable situation for the other musicians, particularly the drummer, who in this case was Tony Chapman. Chapman has confirmed our working hypothesis of the existence of a five-piece Rollin' Stones at several 1962 gigs. This theory arose when we were consistently unable to name any possible bass player for various gigs before the Stones met Colin Golding (read on, to find out who Colin Golding might be, and more on the mystery of the missing bass player).

NOVEMBER 20, 1962

VENUE: Ealing Jazz Club, London, England

PERSONNEL: Mick Jagger, Keith Richards, Elmo Lewis (a.k.a. Brian Jones), Ian Stewart, Tony Chapman

NOTES: Have you ever tried playing drums without a bass player? Tony Chapman did on this and several other occasions in 1962. The Stones, according to Chapman and others we have spoken to, were often without half a rhythm section.

NOVEMBER 21, 1962

VENUE: Wm. Morris Hall, South Oxhey (Nr. Watford), Hertfordshire, England

PERSONNEL: Mick Jagger, Keith Richards, Elmo Lewis (a.k.a. Brian Jones), Ian Stewart, Tony Chapman

NOVEMBER 23, 1962

VENUE: Red Lion Pub, Sutton, Surrey, England

PERSONNEL: Mick Jagger, Keith Richards, Elmo Lewis (a.k.a. Brian Jones), Ian Stewart, Colin Golding, Tony Chapman

NOTES: This was the Rollin' Stones' first time at this venue, a small local pub in Surrey. The usual 1962 choices—songs and player rotation—with a bit of a twist. Recording engineer Glyn Johns, a good friend (and at one point, flatmate) of Ian Stewart's, managed the Presidents, a local band that had been the Red Lion's regular Friday evening group for some time. At this point, though, conflicting schedules and more lucrative gigs at parties and society functions was making it difficult for the Presidents to appear every week at the pub. They played the Red Lion dates, according to Glyn and bassist Colin Golding, primarily for their friends who wouldn't hear them otherwise. Word-of-mouth publicity alone usually brought a large crowd on Fridays, which pleased the landlord. It was a nice scene all around. If he happened to be there, Ian Stewart might sit in on piano with the Presidents. Even Glyn, who sang well but was more interested in recording and producing, occasionally did a few numbers with his friends. But if the Presidents continued to miss gigs, it surely meant that the often disappointed bunch of Friday Red Lion regulars would look for another pub. Stu suggested that Glyn hire the Stones to play every other Friday, and Glyn agreed to give it a try. He'd be able to advertise the Stones' biweekly Red Lion gigs as a "Rhythm and Blues Night," like other small clubs and pubs were doing. He could tap into the growing popularity of R&B to bring the non-locals down to Sutton and, hopefully, keep the regulars.

On this first night, Stu and the Presidents' bass player, Colin Golding (also a close friend), had to pick up Mick, Keith and Brian at a prearranged location because the Stones had no idea how to find the Red Lion once they got off the train. When Stu and Colin drove up to the small coffee shop they'd agreed upon, they found three nearly frostbitten Rollin' Stones sitting outside on the stoop. It seems that the restaurant manager had considered them too scruffy-looking for his establishment and tossed the lads out! The Stones had no bassist of their own with them that night—a fairly regular occurrence at the time—so Colin Golding filled in. Golding would go on to play five to seven gigs with the Stones, at the Red Lion and elsewhere, until Bill Wyman joined the group for good. Glyn Johns as well as his brother, Andy, would later become the Stones' recording engineers. After leaving the Stones' employ, both would go on to a successful careers as record producers.

Another important link in the chain of Stones history began to take shape at the first Red Lion gig. In attendance that night was Giorgio Gomelsky. Seeing them play for the first time impressed him and led to a booking at the Piccadilly Jazz Club on November 30. (See also SESSIONOGRAPHY, DISCOGRAPHY and CHRONOLOGY)

NOVEMBER 25, 1962

VENUE: Studio 51, London, England
PERSONNEL: Mick Jagger, Keith Richards, Elmo Lewis (a.k.a. Brian Jones), Ian Stewart, Tony Chapman
OPENING/OTHER ACT(S): Blues By Six
NOTES: This gig and the one on November 18, 1962 at Studio 51 (the same physical location as the Ken Colyer Jazz Club) were not formal bookings for the Stones. The Stones wanted to play, so they asked if they could do the interval set—for free, to sharpen their "chops"—they needed practice in front of an audience. Note that again, we have not listed a bass player. There wasn't one, as far as we can determine. Neither asking to play for free nor the lack of a bassist at this time seem to have done the Stones any harm. They were hungry—and it paid off. The band landed a weekly residency here in early '63, which became a two-day weekly standing engagement not long afterwards.

NOVEMBER 27, 1962

VENUE: Ealing Jazz Club, London, England
PERSONNEL: Mick Jagger, Keith Richards, Elmo Lewis (a.k.a. Brian Jones), Ian Stewart, Colin Golding, Tony Chapman

NOVEMBER 28, 1962

VENUE: Wm. Morris Hall, South Oxhey (Nr. Watford), Hertfordshire, England
PERSONNEL: Mick Jagger, Keith Richards, Elmo Lewis (a.k.a. Brian Jones), Ian Stewart, *Tony Chapman* or *Steve Harris*
NOTES: No Bassist

NOVEMBER 30, 1962

VENUE: Piccadilly Jazz Club, London, England
PERSONNEL: Mick Jagger, Keith Richards, Elmo Lewis (a.k.a. Brian Jones), Ian Stewart, *Ricky Fenson*, Tony Chapman
OPENING/OTHER ACT(S): Alexis Korner's Blues Incorporated with Ron Jones, Dave Hunt's R&B Band with Hamilton King
NOTES: The Rollin' Stones opened the first show of this "Rhythm 'n' Blues Special" evening. Korner's band, with US serviceman Ron Jones as a special guest, topped the bill. This gig was booked by Giorgio Gomelsky, the Russian-Italian filmmaker and promoter who, in the next few months, would become a strong early influence and mentor and help the Rollin' Stones launch their career.

DECEMBER 2, 1962

VENUE: Studio 51, London, England
PERSONNEL: Mick Jagger, Keith Richards, Elmo Lewis (a.k.a. Brian Jones), Ian Stewart, Tony Chapman
OPENING/OTHER ACT(S): Blues By Six
NOTES: No Bassist

DECEMBER 4, 1962

VENUE: Ealing Jazz Club, London, England
PERSONNEL: Mick Jagger, Keith Richards, Elmo Lewis (a.k.a. Brian Jones), Ian Stewart, Colin Golding, Tony Chapman
SONGS: Sweet Little Sixteen (Berry) / Blues Before Sunrise (James) / Soon Forgotten (Oden) / La Bamba (Valens) / Smokestack Lightning (Burnett) / My Baby (Dixon)
NOTES: "La Bamba" was played here—according to several reports of varying trustworthiness.

DECEMBER 5, 1962

VENUE: Wm. Morris Hall, South Oxhey (Nr. Watford), Hertfordshire, England
PERSONNEL: Mick Jagger, Keith Richards, Elmo Lewis (a.k.a. Brian Jones), Ian Stewart, *Ricky Fenson*, Tony Chapman

DECEMBER 7, 1962

VENUE: Red Lion Pub, Sutton, Surrey, England
PERSONNEL: Mick Jagger, Keith Richards, Elmo Lewis (a.k.a. Brian Jones), Ian Stewart, Colin Golding, Tony Chapman
SONGS: Talkin' 'Bout You (Berry) / Bright Lights, Big City (Reed) / I'm a Hog for You, Baby (Leiber, Stoller) / Tiger in Your Tank (Dixon) / If You Need Me (Pickett, Bateman, Sanders) / I Ain't Got No Money (Arnold) / Still a Fool (Morganfield) / The Sun Is Shining (Reed) /

I Got My Mojo Working (Morganfield) / I'm Your Hoochie Coochie Man (Dixon) / Blueberry Hill (Stock, Lewis, Rose) / Fortune Teller (Neville) / Sweet Little Sixteen (Berry) / Road Runner (McDaniel) / Hey Crawdaddy (McDaniel)

NOTES: The Stones' second gig at the Red Lion. This was a typical selection of songs in the band's setlists at this point in '62.

DECEMBER 9, 1962

VENUE: Studio 51, London England
PERSONNEL: Mick Jagger, Keith Richards, Elmo Lewis (a.k.a. Brian Jones), Ian Stewart, Tony Chapman
OPENING/OTHER ACT(S): Blues By Six
NOTES: No bassist. Another interval gig, because they wanted to play.

DECEMBER 11, 1962

VENUE: Ealing Jazz Club, London, England
PERSONNEL: Mick Jagger, Keith Richards, Elmo Lewis (a.k.a. Brian Jones), Ian Stewart, Colin Golding, Tony Chapman
NOTES: No bassist. Again, Tony Chapman remembered playing the Ealing Club without a bass player.

DECEMBER 12, 1962

VENUE: Sidcup Art College, Sidcup, Kent, England
PERSONNEL: Mick Jagger, Keith Richards, Elmo Lewis (a.k.a. Brian Jones), Ian Stewart, *Ricky Fenson*, Tony Chapman
NOTES: The art school attended by both Keith Richards and Dick Taylor. Taylor did *not* play this gig, an annual dance at Sidcup, but he hired his ex-bandmates for it. The arrangements—including the band and the venue—were essentially left up to the students, Taylor among them. Taylor remembers booking both the Stones and a public hall in the town for the event (it was not held on the school grounds that year). He also recalls being a member of the audience and not the band that night. He says the evening remotivated him and Phil May to start their own band the following year. That band became known as the Pretty Things.

DECEMBER 15, 1962

VENUE: Youth Club, St. Mary's Church Hall, Putney, London, England
PERSONNEL: Mick Jagger, Keith Richards, Elmo Lewis (a.k.a. Brian Jones), Ian Stewart, Bill Perks (Bill Wyman), Tony Chapman
NOTES: Bill Wyman's first gig with the Stones, though he was going by his real name, Bill Perks. He would use "Lee Wyman," the name of an army buddy (slightly altered from the original Whyman), as a stage name for a short time at the beginning of 1963, and then become "Bill Wyman" at about the same time Brian Jones stopped being "Elmo Lewis"—the beginning of February 1963. Early in the show, Brian's amplifier blew a fuse. He played the rest of the gig acoustic, without an amp.

DECEMBER 18, 1962

VENUE: Ealing Jazz Club, London, England
PERSONNEL: Mick Jagger, Keith Richards, Elmo Lewis (a.k.a. Brian Jones), Ian Stewart, Bill Perks (Bill Wyman), Tony Chapman

DECEMBER 21, 1962

VENUE: Red Lion Pub, Sutton, Surrey, England
PERSONNEL: Mick Jagger, Keith Richards, Elmo Lewis (a.k.a. Brian Jones), Ian Stewart, Colin Golding, Tony Chapman
NOTES: Perks/Wyman did not play at this gig. Colin Golding, bassist for the Presidents, filled in. See November 23 and December 7, 1962, above.

DECEMBER 22, 1962

VENUE: Sandover Hall, Richmond, England
PERSONNEL: Mick Jagger, Keith Richards, Elmo Lewis (a.k.a. Brian Jones), Ian Stewart, *Ricky Fenson*, Tony Chapman/*Steve Harris*
SONGS: Tiger in Your Tank (Dixon)
NOTES: Two shows—7:30 P.M. and 10:30 P.M. A Saturday evening. In addition to the one confirmed number, the songs in the Stones' sets came from the 1962 list, as usual.

DECEMBER 26, 1962

VENUE: Piccadilly Jazz Club, London, England
PERSONNEL: Mick Jagger, Keith Richards, Elmo Lewis (a.k.a. Brian Jones), Ian Stewart, *Ricky Fenson, Carlo Little*
NOTES: There was very poor attendance at this Boxing Day evening gig.

DECEMBER 29, 1962

VENUE: Sandover Hall, Richmond, England *and/or* Ealing Jazz Club, London, England
PERSONNEL: Mick Jagger, Keith Richards, Elmo Lewis (a.k.a. Brian Jones), Ian Stewart, Tony Chapman
NOTES: Some evidence points to the Stones having played *both* of these venues on this date; neither gig is as yet confirmed without doubt, nor is Bill Wyman's presence at either location.

LATE DECEMBER 1962

VENUE: The Green Man, Blackheath, England

PERSONNEL: Mick Jagger, Keith Richards, Elmo Lewis (a.k.a. Brian Jones), *Ricky Fenson* or *Bill Perks (Bill Wyman)*, Ian Stewart, Tony Chapman

EPILOGUE

As autumn of 1962 faded, the band had fallen into a groove of its own. Since July, the Rollin' Stones had been playing the raw, down-home blues onstage—sitting on stools, taking breaks between songs for a beer or a fag, chatting between themselves about the next song. There was no real setlist—they played what they wanted and what got the best response. If Jimmy Reed went over well, it would be more Reed songs that night. If Wolf, or Waters, were getting the audience going, their songs would be highlighted. December's cold brought with it more heat in the clubs—from new fans. As the group became more popular, so did their repertoire. The original, naked R&B sound of July 12 was increasingly relegated to a solo spot in a more pop-y setlist as '62 ended, much to the dismay of blues purist Brian Jones. But in hindsight, this metamorphosis set the Rolling Stones on the road to becoming the greatest rock'n' roll band in the world.

1963

As 1963 began, the Rollin' Stones lost the apostrophe and gained a drummer. Although they were officially called the Rolli*ng* Stones when Charlie Watts joined up on the evening of January 11 (playing his first gig as a member on the 17th), the band's composition—in superficial detail—had not quite gelled at that point. But things begin to fall into place during the balance of January and February.

On January 10, Bill Perks dropped his surname and modified that of his best buddy in the army, Lee Whyman, to become "Lee Wyman" onstage. This lasted until the beginning of February when he opted to keep the new last name, but use his own given name. So, it was Bill Wyman from then on, and he had a legal name change in 1964. Concurrently with Bill's final transformation, Lewis Brian Hopkin-Jones (his full name) dropped the Elmo Lewis persona, to be known forevermore as Brian Jones. There was one more change in personnel in 1963. On May 8th, Ian Stewart was told he was no longer a member of the band. As detailed in the TELEVISION APPEARANCES and CHRONOLOGY sections, Stu stayed on as road manager, officially. In fact, he continued to play piano onstage and in the studio along with his other duties—and kept the band together—until his untimely death in 1985. The

Stones always considered him a member and so do we. Therefore, Ian Stewart is listed along with all other official band personnel in the appropriate Concert entries, even after Andrew Oldham's axe fell in July 1963.

1963 was the true inaugural year for the Rolling Stones—on stage, in the studio, and everywhere else. Some details of their performing life are found in this chapter along with the individual entries for each concert, more are in the CHRONOLOGY. It is, however, the big picture that is the most telling. The Rolling Stones had some 265 individual bookings in 1963, playing two shows at many, if not most, of them. In addition, for many months in '63 the band played two different venues on the same day once or twice a week. In other words, as their career took off, the number of performances grew exponentially. Moreover, the band began appearing on television and making records this year—all this activity started almost concurrently in the summer of 1963.

Unfortunately for us all, there didn't yet exist in '63 the coterie of fact-finding Stones fanatics that became visible in the '70s and '80s. Nevertheless, even if there isn't a setlist database covering each and every 1963 gig, there is documentation of many performances that year.

1963 REPERTOIRE: Ain't That Loving You Baby (Reed) / Around & Around (Berry) / Beautiful Delilah (Berry) / Bright Lights, Big City (Reed) / Bye Bye Johnny (Berry) / Can I Get a Witness (Holland, Holland, Dozier) / Close to You (Dixon) / Close Together (Reed) / Come On (Berry) / Crackin' Up (McDaniel) / Diddley Daddy (McDaniel) / Fortune Teller (Neville) / Hey Crawdaddy (McDaniel) / Honest I Do (Reed) / Honey What's Wrong (Reed) / I Can Tell (Berry) / I Just Want to Make Love to You (Dixon) / I Wanna Be Your Man (Lennon, McCartney) / I Want to Be Loved (Dixon) / I Want You to Know (Domino) / I'm a Hog for You, Baby (Leiber, Stoller) / I'm a King Bee (Moore) / I'm Alright (McDaniel) / I'm Bad Like Jesse James (Hooker) [*] / It's All Right Babe (McDaniel) / Johnny B. Goode (Berry) / Little Egypt (Leiber, Stoller) / Love Potion #9 (Leiber, Stoller) / Memphis Tennessee (Berry) / Mona (I Need You Baby) (McDaniel) / Money (Gordy Jr., Bradford) / Nadine (Berry) / Poison Ivy (Leiber, Stoller) / Pretty Thing (McDaniel) / Road Runner (McDaniel) / Roll Over Beethoven (Berry) / Route 66 (Troup) / Shame, Shame, Shame (Reed) / Soon Forgotten (Oden) / Susie Q (Broadwater, Lewis, Hawkins) / Sweet Little Sixteen (Berry) / Talkin' 'Bout You (Berry) / Twist & Shout (Berns) / Walking the Dog (Thomas) / You Better Move On (Alexander) / You Can Make It If You Try (Jarrett) / You Can't Judge a Book (by Looking at the Cover) (Dixon)

---

[*] Unconfirmed at the time of writing.

A TYPICAL SET FOR EARLY 1963: Talkin' 'Bout You (Berry) / Poison Ivy (Leiber, Stoller) / Fortune Teller (Neville) / Come On (Berry) / Money (Gordy Jr., Bradford) / Roll Over Beethoven (Berry) / You Better Move On (Alexander) / Beautiful Delilah (Berry) / Honest I Do (Reed) / Road Runner (McDaniel) / Pretty Thing (McDaniel) / Hey Crawdaddy (McDaniel)

1963

JANUARY 3, 1963

VENUE: Marquee Jazz Club, London, England
PERSONNEL: Mick Jagger, Keith Richards, Elmo Lewis (a.k.a. Brian Jones), Ian Stewart, Tony Chapman
OPENING/OTHER ACT(S): Cyril Davies' R&B All-Stars (headlined)
NOTES: A Thursday "Rhythm & Blues Night" at the Marquee. No bassist. Charlie Watts wasn't in the lineup until January 17, 1963. The group was now officially known as "The Rolling Stones"—with a "g"—though Brian was still "Elmo Lewis." Clubs and journalists persistently spelled the band's name either way or both ways simultaneously. But, June and the band's first single seemingly validated the existence of the "Rolling Stones" as an entity and somehow that helped standardize their billing.

JANUARY 4, 1963

VENUE: Red Lion Pub, Sutton, Surrey, England
PERSONNEL: Mick Jagger, Keith Richards, Elmo Lewis (a.k.a. Brian Jones), Ian Stewart, Colin Golding, Tony Chapman
NOTES: Tony Chapman was on drums; Colin Golding was on bass.

JANUARY 5, 1963

VENUE: Sandover Hall, Richmond, London, England
PERSONNEL: Mick Jagger, Keith Richards, Elmo Lewis (a.k.a. Brian Jones), Ian Stewart, *Ricky Fenson*, Tony Chapman
NOTES: Tony Chapman was on drums.

JANUARY 7, 1963

VENUE: Flamingo Jazz Club, London, England
PERSONNEL: Mick Jagger, Keith Richards, Elmo Lewis (a.k.a. Brian Jones), Ian Stewart, Tony Chapman
OPENING/OTHER ACT(S): "Special Guest"
NOTES: Still no Charlie. The bill for this gig, according to *Melody Maker*, included the Rolling Stones "and guests." No bass player. Chapman was on drums.

JANUARY 10, 1963

VENUE: Marquee Jazz Club, London, England
PERSONNEL: Mick Jagger, Keith Richards, Elmo Lewis (a.k.a. Brian Jones), Lee (Bill) Wyman, Ian Stewart, Tony Chapman
OPENING/OTHER ACT(S): Cyril Davies's R&B All-Stars (headlined)
NOTES: The Stones opened for Cyril Davies's R&B All-Stars; pianist Nicky Hopkins, drummer Carlo Little and bass player Ricky Fenson were often among those playing with the All-Stars. It was at this gig that Bill Perks began to use "Lee Wyman" as his *nom de musique*, deciding that his former army buddy's appellation sounded better than his own. Not too radical for anyone, apparently, they were still introducing Brian as "Elmo Lewis." But Bill's new performing identity wasn't cast in concrete—he would mix it up a bit at the beginning of February.

JANUARY 11, 1963

VENUE: Ricky Tick Club, Star and Garter Pub, Windsor, Berkshire, England
PERSONNEL: Mick Jagger, Keith Richards, Elmo Lewis (a.k.a. Brian Jones), Ian Stewart, Tony Chapman
NOTES: See note for January 12, 1963.

JANUARY 12, 1963

VENUE: Sandover Hall, Richmond, England
PERSONNEL: Mick Jagger, Keith Richards, Elmo Lewis (a.k.a. Brian Jones), Ian Stewart, *Ricky Fenson*, Tony Chapman
NOTES: Either this or the Ricky Tick Club gig of January 11, 1963 was the last for Tony Chapman. Contrary to the many stories making the rounds over 35 years, Chapman was not fired after the Stones' gig at the Ricky Tick Club on January 11 or Sandover Hall on January 12. On January 12 or 13, Chapman received a telephone call at home from Ian Stewart. Stu told him that the Flamingo Club was unhappy with the Stones, especially the drummer, and if they were to get any more gigs there they would have to get a new drummer. Chapman was told he would have to sit out the Flamingo and Marquee dates, but could still be in the band for the rest. "Well," Chapman told us he replied, "I'm either in the band or I'm not. So piss off!"

Steve Harris could have played either gig, Watts did not play them. It was probably Carlo Little, from what we have been able to determine in conversations with him and others. We can only assume that Charlie had other commitments at the time, prior to his actual first gig with the Stones on (what we believe was) January 17.

JANUARY 14, 1963

VENUE: Flamingo Jazz Club, London, England

PERSONNEL: Mick Jagger, Keith Richards, Elmo Lewis (a.k.a. Brian Jones), Ian Stewart, Ricky Fenson, Carlo Little

OPENING/OTHER ACT(S): "Special Guest"

SONGS: Mona (I Need You Baby) (McDaniel) / Tiger in Your Tank (Dixon) / Cops & Robbers (McDaniel) / No Money Down (Berry) / Dimples (Hooker) / Pretty Thing (McDaniel) / Bright Lights, Big City (Reed) / Honest I Do (Reed) / Around & Around (Berry) / Beautiful Delilah (Berry) / Jaguar & the Thunderbird (Berry)

NOTES: Underlined song titles are new to the performance repertoire as of this listing.

JANUARY 17, 1963

VENUE: Marquee Jazz Club, London, England

PERSONNEL: Mick Jagger, Keith Richards, Elmo Lewis (a.k.a. Brian Jones), Lee (Bill) Wyman, Ian Stewart, Charlie Watts

OPENING/OTHER ACT(S): Cyril Davies's R&B All-Stars (headlined), plus The Velvettes

NOTES: Charlie sits in on this date, but does not become the permanent member as agreed until probably January 31, possibly as late as February 7. He was still playing with Blues By Six at the time of his decision to join the Stones; it is likely that he honored his previous commitment to Brian Knight's group and did not leave them drummerless while they searched for a replacement. Knight swears that Watts was in the Blues By Six drum chair on February 7 at the Harringay Jazz Club at the Manor House Pub and did not play with the Stones during their set that night. Who are we to argue with that? Of course, Bill Wyman has said it was Charlie on drums with the Stones that night . . . This is the evidence, draw your own conclusions.

JANUARY 18, 1963

VENUE: Red Lion Pub, Sutton, Surrey, England

PERSONNEL: Mick Jagger, Keith Richards, Elmo Lewis (a.k.a. Brian Jones), Charlie Watts, Ian Stewart, Colin Golding

JANUARY 19, 1963

VENUE: Sandover Hall, Richmond, England

PERSONNEL: Mick Jagger, Keith Richards, Elmo Lewis (a.k.a. Brian Jones), Ian Stewart, Ricky Fenson, Carlo Little

JANUARY 21, 1963

VENUE: Flamingo Jazz Club, London, England

PERSONNEL: Mick Jagger, Keith Richards, Elmo Lewis (a.k.a. Brian Jones), Ian Stewart, Ricky Fenson, Carlo Little

OPENING/OTHER ACT(S): "and Guests"

NOTES: The Flamingo's mysterious advertisement announced the evening's bill as reported above—"Rolling Stones and Guests."

JANUARY 24, 1963

VENUE: Marquee Jazz Club, London, England

PERSONNEL: Mick Jagger, Keith Richards, Elmo Lewis (a.k.a. Brian Jones), Charlie Watts, Lee (Bill) Wyman, Ian Stewart

OPENING/OTHER ACT(S): Cyril Davies's R&B All-Stars (headlined), The Velvettes

JANUARY 25, 1963

VENUE: Red Lion Pub, Sutton, Surrey, England

PERSONNEL: Mick Jagger, Keith Richards, Elmo Lewis (a.k.a. Brian Jones), Charlie Watts, Lee (Bill) Wyman, Ian Stewart

JANUARY 26, 1963

VENUE: Ealing Jazz Club, London, England

PERSONNEL: Mick Jagger, Keith Richards, Elmo Lewis (a.k.a. Brian Jones), Charlie Watts, Lee (Bill) Wyman, Ian Stewart

NOTES: The Stones took over for Alexis Korner's band at the Ealing this evening. Up to this point, the Stones had played Sandover Hall on Saturdays. They no longer appeared there after January 19.

JANUARY 28, 1963

VENUE: Flamingo Jazz Club, London, England

PERSONNEL: Mick Jagger, Keith Richards, Elmo Lewis (a.k.a. Brian Jones), Charlie Watts, Lee (Bill) Wyman, Ian Stewart

OPENING/OTHER ACT(S): The Graham Bond Trio ("featuring the Hammond Organ")

NOTES: The last gig at the Flamingo. Another quote from one of their ads.

JANUARY 31, 1963

VENUE: Marquee Jazz Club, London, England

PERSONNEL: Mick Jagger, Keith Richards, Elmo Lewis (a.k.a. Brian Jones), Charlie Watts, Lee (Bill) Wyman, Ian Stewart

OPENING/OTHER ACT(S): Cyril Davies's R&B All-Stars (headlined). The Velvettes, Long John Baldry, Colin Bannigan Trio

Notes: Another Thursday "Rhythm and Blues Night" and the Stones' last gig at the Marquee Club—until March 26, 1971. Losing the argument with the club's owners over a pay hike (the Stones wanted one) causes the band to take a hike.

FEBRUARY 1, 1963

Venue: Red Lion Pub, Sutton, Surrey, England
Personnel: Mick Jagger, Keith Richards, Brian Jones, Charlie Watts, Bill Wyman, Ian Stewart
Notes: Alternate Friday residency (usually). Brian finally drops the "Elmo Lewis" bit—and Wyman opts to use his own first name from now on.

FEBRUARY 5, 1963

Venue: Ealing Jazz Club, London, England

FEBRUARY 7, 1963

Venue: Harringay Jazz Club, Manor House Pub, London, England
Opening/Other Act(s): Blues By Six featuring Brian Knight (headlined), other acts
Notes: The Rolling Stones' first gig at this club's opening night, supporting Brian Knight and Blues by Six, the headliners. There were (unknown) other acts.

FEBRUARY 8, 1963

Venue: Red Lion Pub, Sutton, Surrey, England
Notes: According to the music press, the Stones played two venues on February 8. See January 11, 1963, above.

FEBRUARY 8, 1963

Venue: Ricky Tick Club, Star and Garter Pub, Windsor, Berkshire, England

FEBRUARY 9, 1963

Venue: Ealing Jazz Club, London, England

FEBRUARY 14, 1963

Venue: Harringay Jazz Club, Manor House Pub, London, England
Opening/Other Act(s): Blues By Six (headlined)

FEBRUARY 16, 1963

Venue: Ealing Jazz Club, London, England

FEBRUARY 22, 1963

Venue: Red Lion Pub, Sutton, Surrey, England

FEBRUARY 23, 1963

Venue: Ealing Jazz Club, London, England

FEBRUARY 24, 1963

Venue: Station Hotel, Richmond, Surrey, England
Notes: The Stones' first gig at the club that would become their launching pad. The promoter Giorgio Gomelsky knew all too well that the Stones needed and wanted a good gig—Brian Jones had been bending his ear since November. Until the week prior to this, however, the Dave Hunt Band regularly filled the bill for Gomelsky's Sunday event in Richmond. Unfortunately for that group, they had lately become almost chronically incapable of making it to the Station Hotel on time or at all. Gomelsky had grown increasingly irritated at the situation and had finally fired them the previous Sunday. Persistence paid off for the Stones, yet again. Gomelsky telephoned them (by calling Stu at work—the only phone available to them at the time) on Monday, February 18, and asked them to play on this date. Gomelsky's Sunday Stones offerings would become known as the "Crawdaddy Club," after the Bo Diddley song that was a trademark of the Stones' show at the time.

FEBRUARY 28, 1963

Venue: Harringay Jazz Club, Manor House Pub, London, England
Opening/Other Act(s): Blues By Six (headlined)

MARCH 2, 1963

Venue: Ealing Jazz Club, London, England
Notes: The last gig for the Stones at the Ealing Jazz Club.

MARCH 3, 1963

Venue: Ken Colyer Jazz Club At Studio 51, London, England
Notes: First gig at this club, from 4:00 P.M. till 6:30 P.M. on a Sunday afternoon. This would become a regular Sunday residency for the group along with another—in the evening at the Station Hotel.

MARCH 3, 1963

Venue: Station Hotel, Richmond, Surrey, England
Songs: Route 66 (Troup) / Little Egypt (Leiber, Stoller) / Poison Ivy (Leiber, Stoller) / I'm Alright (McDaniel) / I'm a King Bee (Moore) / You Better Move On (Alexander) / Nadine (Berry) / You Can't Judge a Book (By Looking at the Cover) (Dixon) / Honest I Do (Reed) / I Want to Be Loved (Dixon) / Beautiful Delilah (Berry) / Memphis Tennessee (Berry) / Walking the Dog

(Thomas) / Pretty Thing (McDaniel) / Hey Crawdaddy (McDaniel)

NOTES: The second gig of the day. These songs are typical of those the Stones would play in two sets at the Station Hotel and in other clubs at this time. The tunes are listed in no particular order, except for the band's closing numbers in Richmond, usually either "Pretty Thing" or "Hey Crawdaddy."

MARCH 7, 1963

VENUE: Harringay Jazz Club, Manor House Pub, London, England

OPENING/OTHER ACT(S): Blues By Six

MARCH 8, 1963

VENUE: Red Lion Pub, Sutton, Surrey, England

MARCH 8, 1963

VENUE: Ricky Tick Club, Star and Garter Pub, Windsor, Berkshire, England

MARCH 9, 1963

VENUE: Wooden Bridge Hotel, Guildford, Surrey, England

NOTES: Their first time at this venue.

MARCH 10, 1963

VENUE: Ken Colyer Jazz Club At Studio 51, London, England

NOTES: Another two-gig Sunday. The Stones played from 4:00 P.M. until 6:30 P.M. then went on to Richmond.

MARCH 10, 1963

VENUE: Station Hotel, Richmond, Surrey, England

NOTES: The second gig of the day.

MARCH 14, 1963

VENUE: Harringay Jazz Club, Manor House Pub, London, England

OPENING/OTHER ACT(S): Blues By Six

MARCH 17, 1963

VENUE: Ken Colyer Jazz Club At Studio 51, London, England

NOTES: The weekly Sunday double feature, part one.

MARCH 17, 1963

VENUE: Station Hotel, Richmond, Surrey, England

NOTES: The second Sunday show.

MARCH 22, 1963

VENUE: Red Lion Pub, Sutton, Surrey, England

NOTES: Alternate Friday residency

MARCH 22, 1963

VENUE: Ricky Tick Club, Star and Garter Pub, Windsor, Berkshire, England

MARCH 24, 1963

VENUE: Ken Colyer Jazz Club At Studio 51, London, England

NOTES: First of the Stones' two regular Sunday engagements.

MARCH 24, 1963

VENUE: Station Hotel, Richmond, Surrey, England

NOTES: The band's second gig on March 24, 1963.

MARCH 29, 1963

VENUE: Wooden Bridge Hotel, Guildford, Surrey, England

MARCH 31, 1963

VENUE: Ken Colyer Jazz Club At Studio 51, London, England

NOTES: First gig of two on the last day of March 1963.

MARCH 31, 1963

VENUE: Station Hotel, Richmond, Surrey, England

NOTES: Second show of the day.

APRIL 5, 1963

VENUE: Red Lion Pub, Sutton, Surrey, England

APRIL 7, 1963

VENUE: Ken Colyer Jazz Club At Studio 51, London, England

APRIL 7, 1963

VENUE: Station Hotel, Richmond, Surrey, England

APRIL 14, 1963

VENUE: Ken Colyer Jazz Club At Studio 51, London, England

APRIL 14, 1963

VENUE: Crawdaddy Club, Station Hotel, Richmond, Surrey, England

NOTES: The second of two gigs on April 14, 1963. Gomelsky's Sunday offering in Richmond had by now become a huge success and known as the "Crawdaddy Club." The Stones had popularized Bo Diddley's "Hey Crawdaddy" and their fans made a dance craze out of "doin' the Crawdaddy" at the now crowded Station Hotel.

APRIL 19, 1963

VENUE: Wooden Bridge Hotel, Guildford, Surrey, England

APRIL 21, 1963

VENUE: Crawdaddy Club, Station Hotel, Richmond, Surrey, England
NOTES: There was no Ken Colyer Club gig on this particular Sunday afternoon: the Stones were busy being filmed by Giorgio Gomelsky at the Station Hotel before their evening Crawdaddy Club show. (See CHRONOLOGY)

APRIL 24, 1963

VENUE: Eel Pie Island, Twickenham, Middlesex, England
NOTES: The first time the Stones played Eel Pie Island. This became their Wednesday night residency through the end of the summer, 1963.

APRIL 26, 1963

VENUE: Ricky Tick Club, Star and Garter Pub, Windsor, Berkshire, England
NOTES: "Giraffes Not Admitted" warned the Ricky Tick's advertisement for this show.

APRIL 28, 1963

VENUE: Ken Colyer Jazz Club At Studio 51, London, England
NOTES: First of two. The Stones returned to their Sunday afternoon residency after a week off.

APRIL 28, 1963

VENUE: Crawdaddy Club, Station Hotel, Richmond, Surrey, England
SONGS: Ain't That Loving You Baby (Reed) / Bright Lights, Big City (Reed) / Close Together (Reed) / Soon Forgotten (Oden) / Shame, Shame, Shame (Reed) / Talkin' 'Bout You (Berry) / Memphis Tennessee (Berry) / Close to You (Dixon) / I Just Want to Make Love to You (Dixon) / I Want You to Know (Domino) / I'm Bad Like Jesse James (Hooker) [*] / Little Egypt (Leiber, Stoller) / I'm Alright (McDaniel) / Pretty Thing (McDaniel) / Hey Crawdaddy (McDaniel)
NOTES: The second show of two on April 28. The Stones' Crawdaddy Club shows had changed since the beginning of their residency, as can be seen from this list. They still ended sets with either "Pretty Thing" or "Hey Crawdaddy," but had added many new tunes to their onstage repertoire. Again, other than the closers, the songs are not necessarily listed in performance order. (See CHRONOLOGY)

MAY 1, 1963

VENUE: Eel Pie Island, Twickenham, Middlesex, England
NOTES: Wednesday residency

MAY 5, 1963

VENUE: Ken Colyer Jazz Club At Studio 51, London, England
NOTES: A two-fer day. This is the first gig on the 5th of May.

MAY 5, 1963

VENUE: Crawdaddy Club, Station Hotel, Richmond, Surrey, England
NOTES: The second of two engagements.

MAY 8, 1963

VENUE: Eel Pie Island, Twickenham, Middlesex, England
NOTES: Wednesday residency

MAY 11, 1963

VENUE: "News of the World" Charity Gala, Battersea Park, London, England
OPENING/OTHER ACT(S): The Dowlands (with the Soundtracks), Brian Howard & The Silhouettes, The Saracens, The Washington DCs
NOTES: The Stones' performance was part of the gala opening of the Battersea Pleasure Gardens and was the first booking secured for them by Eric Easton and Andrew Oldham. The Stones and the other artists played on a bandstand by the boating pool. The event was sponsored by *News of the World* (a newspaper that would later contribute most negatively to the Stones' career [see 1967

---

[*]It has been reported that the Stones played the John Lee Hooker tune "I'm Bad Like Jesse James," but independent confirmation of this "factoid" had not yet been secured at press time. This gig was the first one attended by Andrew Loog Oldham, who would become the Stones' comanager (with Eric Easton, who was not at the Station Hotel on this date).

in CHRONOLOGY]), and was held annually to benefit the Variety Club children's charities.

MAY 12, 1963

VENUE: Ken Colyer Jazz Club At Studio 51, London, England

MAY 12, 1963

VENUE: Station Hotel, Richmond, Surrey, England

MAY 17, 1963

VENUE: Wooden Bridge Hotel, Guildford, Surrey, England

MAY 19, 1963

VENUE: Ken Colyer Jazz Club At Studio 51, London, England

MAY 19, 1963

VENUE: Station Hotel, Richmond, Surrey, England
NOTES: Unusually, no advertisements appeared for this or the following Sunday's performance at the Station Hotel. It is possible that the Stones did not play on May 19 and/or May 26. It is also possible that they did play but Giorgio Gomelsky was too angry with them at the time to place his customary ads in the music papers. (See CHRONOLOGY)

MAY 22, 1963

VENUE: Eel Pie Island, Twickenham, Middlesex, England
NOTES: Another Wednesday at Eel Pie Island.

MAY 24, 1963

VENUE: Ricky Tick Club, Star and Garter Pub, Windsor, Berkshire, England

MAY 26, 1963

VENUE: Ken Colyer Jazz Club At Studio 51, London, England

MAY 26, 1963

VENUE: Crawdaddy Club, Station Hotel, Richmond, Surrey, England
NOTES: The second show of the day, in theory. No newspaper advertisement announced this performance, which was abnormal. The Stones may or may not have played the Crawdaddy on either May 26 or May 19. See May 19, 1963.

MAY 29, 1963

VENUE: Eel Pie Island, Twickenham, Middlesex, England
NOTES: Wednesday residency

JUNE 2, 1963

VENUE: Ken Colyer Jazz Club At Studio 51, London, England
NOTES: First of two Sunday gigs.

JUNE 2, 1963

VENUE: Crawdaddy Club, Station Hotel, Richmond, Surrey, England
NOTES: Second gig on this date. Apparently, the band still had their Sunday evening Crawdaddy Club residency —Gomelsky's ads began running again. For this show, at least.

JUNE 3, 1963 (VERY DOUBTFUL)

VENUE: Ken Colyer Jazz Club At Studio 51, London, England
NOTES: It has been written that as of this date the Stones had secured a Monday booking in addition to their Sunday afternoon residency at this club. However, no independent information has been found to confirm this for the month of June 1963. Ken Colyer's regular display ads in *Melody Maker* and other publications are hard to miss. None of his June ads billed the Stones on any Monday, whereas other groups are listed. The band's Sunday performances in June were announced quite clearly. However, the club's *July* ads, beginning with schedules for July 7 and July 8, confirm two Stones performances weekly— on Sunday and Monday. Therefore, we believe they did *not* appear at the Ken Colyer Jazz Club on this or any other Monday in June, and so are not including any Monday shows at this club until July 8.

JUNE 5, 1963

VENUE: Eel Pie Island, Twickenham, Middlesex, England
NOTES: Wednesday residency

JUNE 7, 1963

VENUE: Wooden Bridge Hotel, Guildford, Surrey, England
NOTES: Another Friday in Guildford.

JUNE 9, 1963

VENUE: Ken Colyer Jazz Club At Studio 51, London, England
NOTES: First of two gigs on this Sunday in 1963.

JUNE 9, 1963

VENUE: Crawdaddy Club, Station Hotel, Richmond, Surrey, England

NOTES: Second of two gigs on this date.

JUNE 12, 1963

VENUE: Eel Pie Island, Twickenham, Middlesex, England

NOTES: Wednesday residency

JUNE 14, 1963

VENUE: Ricky Tick Club, Star and Garter Pub, Windsor, Berkshire, England

NOTES: Friday residency

JUNE 16, 1963

VENUE: Ken Colyer Jazz Club At Studio 51, London, England

NOTES: The first of two gigs on this date.

JUNE 16, 1963

VENUE: Crawdaddy Club, Station Hotel, Richmond, Surrey, England

NOTES: The second engagement of the day, but the band's last gig at the Crawdaddy Club in this location. The Sunday evening crowds had grown so huge that the Station Hotel could not accommodate them all. Neighboring residents were disturbed by the overflow of dancing, drinking, frenzied Stones fans clogging the streets around the club, forcing Gomelsky to find another venue or shut down altogether. Two weeks later, on June 30, he was back in business nearby.

JUNE 19, 1963

VENUE: Eel Pie Island, Twickenham, Middlesex, England

NOTES: Wednesday residency

JUNE 20, 1963

VENUE: Scene Club, London, England

NOTES: First time at this club.

JUNE 21, 1963

VENUE: Wooden Bridge Hotel, Guildford, Surrey, England

JUNE 23, 1963

VENUE: Ken Colyer Jazz Club At Studio 51, London, England

NOTES: Sunday afternoon residency. No Crawdaddy Club gig this week, as explained above. See June 16, 1963.

JUNE 26, 1963

VENUE: Eel Pie Island, Twickenham, Middlesex, England

NOTES: Wednesday residency

JUNE 27, 1963

VENUE: Scene Club, London, England

JUNE 28, 1963

VENUE: Ricky Tick Club, Star and Garter Pub, Windsor, Berkshire, England

JUNE 30, 1963

VENUE: Studio 51, London, England

NOTES: First of two gigs on this Sunday.

JUNE 30, 1963

VENUE: Crawdaddy Club, Athletic Ground, Richmond, Surrey, England

NOTES: First gig at the Crawdaddy Club's new venue; the second engagement of the day.

JULY 3, 1963

VENUE: Eel Pie Island, Twickenham, Middlesex, England

NOTES: Wednesday residency

JULY 4, 1963

VENUE: Scene Club, London, England

JULY 5, 1963

VENUE: Ricky Tick Club, Star and Garter Pub, Windsor, Berkshire, England

NOTES: Friday residency

JULY 7, 1963

VENUE: Studio 51, London, England

NOTES: Sunday residency. The Stones' gigs were now listed in the ads for Studio 51, the same location as Ken Colyer's jazz club—essentially the same place. Rather than being the name of a physical venue, the word "club" often indicated who promoted an evening's entertainment at the site. The "Crawdaddy Club," for example, was not the name of the Station Hotel; it was Giorgio Gomelsky's Sunday night event at the Station Hotel, or the Richmond Athletic Ground, or wherever. The same was true of John Mansfield's Ricky Tick Clubs, which existed in many different places. Studio 51 was the site of many "clubs"—Ken Colyer's, the All-Nighter, and others. A private club was allowed to serve liquor and stay open well past the rigidly enforced hours of Britain's public houses (pubs, restaurants or any non-membership facility). The business and legal reasons are obvious. Catering to specific musical tastes might be another factor in naming and promoting a club.

JULY 8, 1963

VENUE: Studio 51, London, England
NOTES: The new Monday residency begins (see June 3, above).

JULY 10, 1963

VENUE: Eel Pie Island, Twickenham, Middlesex, England
NOTES: Wednesday residency

JULY 11, 1963

VENUE: Scene Club, London, England

JULY 12, 1963

VENUE: Twickenham Design College, Eel Pie Island, Twickenham, Middlesex, England
NOTES: A Friday gig.

JULY 13, 1963

VENUE: Alcove Club, Middlesbrough, Yorkshire, England
OPENING/OTHER ACT(S): The Hollies (headlined)
NOTES: The Stones opened for the Hollies. This club was in the north of England, a good half-day's travel from London—one way—they returned to London for two gigs the next day. July 1963's packed performance schedule is but one indication of the band's mushrooming popularity. (See DISCOGRAPHY, TELEVISION APPEARANCES and CHRONOLOGY)

JULY 14, 1963

VENUE: Studio 51, London, England
NOTES: First of two gigs on Sunday, July 14. After Saturday night in North Yorkshire.

JULY 14, 1963

VENUE: Crawdaddy Club, Athletic Ground, Richmond, Surrey, England
OPENING/OTHER ACT(S): The Muleskinners
NOTES: Second gig on this Sunday.

JULY 15, 1963

VENUE: Studio 51, London, England
NOTES: Monday residency

JULY 16, 1963

VENUE: British Legion Hall, Stoke Road, Slough, Buckinghamshire, England

JULY 17, 1963

VENUE: Eel Pie Island, Twickenham, Middlesex, England
NOTES: Wednesday residency

JULY 19, 1963

VENUE: Debutante Ball, Hastings, Sussex, England (cancelled but attended)
PERSONNEL: Mick Jagger, Keith Richards, Charlie Watts, Bill Wyman, Ian Stewart
OPENING/OTHER ACT(S): Chris Andrews
NOTES: Brian Jones had become ill and was unable to play by the time the Stones arrived at this engagement, so he remained in the car: the rest of the band just joined the party.

JULY 20, 1963

VENUE: Corn Exchange, Wisbech, Cambridgeshire, England
PERSONNEL: Mick Jagger, Keith Richards, Brian Jones, Charlie Watts, Bill Wyman, Ian Stewart
NOTES: The Stones' first ballroom gig.

JULY 21, 1963

VENUE: Studio 51, London, England
NOTES: The first of two engagements on this date, a Sunday. As detailed above, the band had Sunday residencies here and at the Crawdaddy Club in Surrey during much of 1963. However, this Sunday's Crawdaddy gig was not advertised.

JULY 21, 1963

VENUE: Crawdaddy Club, Athletic Ground, Richmond, Surrey, England
NOTES: The second gig of the day, customarily. This one was not advertised, however, and should be considered unconfirmed.

JULY 22, 1963

VENUE: Studio 51, London, England
NOTES: Monday residency

JULY 23, 1963

VENUE: British Legion Hall, Stoke Road, Slough, Buckinghamshire, England

JULY 24, 1963

VENUE: Eel Pie Island, Twickenham, Middlesex, England

NOTES: Wednesday residency

JULY 26, 1963

VENUE: Ricky Tick Club, Star and Garter Pub, Windsor, Berkshire, England

NOTES: The last gig at this club in this location. It moved to the Thames Hotel, also in Windsor, where the Stones played beginning in August.

JULY 27, 1963

VENUE: California Ballroom, Dunstable, Bedfordshire, England

JULY 28, 1963

VENUE: Studio 51, London, England

NOTES: Sunday afternoon residency. No Crawdaddy Club gig was advertised on this date and no other confirmation has been obtained for a July 28 Crawdaddy gig; hence, no listing.

JULY 29, 1963

VENUE: Studio 51, London, England

NOTES: Monday residency

JULY 30, 1963

VENUE: British Legion Hall, Stoke Road, Slough, Buckinghamshire, England

NOTES: The band played here on Tuesdays in July. "Triffids welcome," promised the advertisements in the music press; the British sci-fi film *Day of the Triffids*, had just come out.

JULY 31, 1963

VENUE: Eel Pie Island, Twickenham, Middlesex, England

NOTES: Wednesday residency

AUGUST 2, 1963

VENUE: Wooden Bridge Hotel, Guildford, Surrey, England

AUGUST 3, 1963

VENUE: St. Leonard's Hall, Horsham, Sussex, England

OPENING/OTHER ACT(S): Freddie Starr and the Midnighters

AUGUST 4, 1963

VENUE: Studio 51, London, England

NOTES: The first of two confirmed gigs on this Sunday.

AUGUST 4, 1963

VENUE: Crawdaddy Club, Athletic Ground, Richmond, Surrey, England

OPENING/OTHER ACT(S): The Muleskinners

NOTES: The second of two confirmed gigs.

AUGUST 5, 1963

VENUE: Botwell House, Hayes, Middlesex, England

AUGUST 6, 1963

VENUE: Thames Hotel, Windsor, Berkshire, England

NOTES: Tuesday at the new Ricky Tick.

AUGUST 7, 1963

VENUE: Eel Pie Island, Twickenham, Middlesex, England

NOTES: Wednesday residency

AUGUST 9, 1963

VENUE: California Ballroom, Dunstable, Bedfordshire, England

AUGUST 10, 1963

VENUE: Plaza Theatre, Handsworth, Birmingham, Warwickshire, England

NOTES: This was the first of two Plaza Theatres in the Birmingham area that the Stones played on August 10. The second was in Oldhill.

AUGUST 10, 1963

VENUE: Plaza Theatre, Oldhill, Birmingham, Warwickshire, England

NOTES: The second Birmingham-area Plaza Theatre the band played on this date!

AUGUST 11, 1963

VENUE: Studio 51, Ken Colyer Club, London, England

NOTES: The first of two gigs on this Sunday—the Stones' second performance was at the Richmond Jazz Festival in Surrey.

AUGUST 11, 1963

VENUE: Third Richmond Jazz Festival, Athletic Ground, Richmond, Surrey, England

OPENING/OTHER ACT(S): Acker Bilk's Paramount Jazz Band, Terry Lightfoot's Jazzmen, Freddy Randall Band, Blue Note Jazz Band, Cyril Davies's All-Stars, Long John Baldry, The Velvettes

NOTES: The Stones' second gig on this Sunday was a spot near the end of the bill on the second and final day of the Third National Jazz Festival in Richmond. To be included in the weekend's lineup wasn't just a coup for the Stones, it also signified for the many other R&B bands on the bill that the British jazz establishment had loosened up a lot in the past year.

AUGUST 12, 1963

VENUE: Studio 51, Ken Colyer Club, London, England
NOTES: Monday evening residency

AUGUST 13, 1963

VENUE: Town Hall, High Wycombe, Buckinghamshire, England

AUGUST 14, 1963

VENUE: Eel Pie Island, Twickenham, Middlesex, England
NOTES: Wednesday residency

AUGUST 15, 1963

VENUE: Dreamland Ballroom, Margate, Kent, England

AUGUST 16, 1963

VENUE: Winter Gardens, Banbury, Oxfordshire, England

AUGUST 17, 1963

VENUE: Memorial Hall, Northwich, Cheshire, England
OPENING/OTHER ACT(S): Lee Curtis

AUGUST 18, 1963

VENUE: Studio 51, Ken Colyer Club, London, England
NOTES: The afternoon gig of the Stones' regular '63 Sunday double feature.

AUGUST 18, 1963

VENUE: Crawdaddy Club, Athletic Ground, Richmond, Surrey, England
OPENING ACT(S): The Muleskinners
NOTES: The band's second performance on August 18. The Stones were back at the Crawdaddy after the previous Sunday's jazz festival appearance.

AUGUST 19, 1963

VENUE: Atlanta Ballroom, Woking, Surrey, England

AUGUST 20, 1963

VENUE: Ricky Tick Club, Thames Hotel, Windsor, Berkshire, England
NOTES: The band's appearances at the Ricky Tick Club's new site were on Tuesdays, instead of their Friday bookings at the Star and Garter Pub.

AUGUST 21, 1963

VENUE: Eel Pie Island, Twickenham, Middlesex, England
NOTES: Wednesday residency

AUGUST 24, 1963

VENUE: Il Rondo Ballroom, Leicester, Leicestershire, England

AUGUST 25, 1963

VENUE: Studio 51, London, England
NOTES: Regular Sunday afternoon gig, the first of two on this date.

AUGUST 25, 1963

VENUE: Crawdaddy Club, Athletic Ground, Richmond, Surrey, England
NOTES: Second Sunday residency

AUGUST 26, 1963

VENUE: Studio 51, London, England
NOTES: The band's Monday evening residency, a standing 8:00 P.M. gig in London.

AUGUST 27, 1963

VENUE: Ricky Tick Club, Thames Hotel, Windsor, Berkshire, England
PERSONNEL: Mick Jagger, Keith Richards, Charlie Watts, Bill Wyman, Ian Stewart
NOTES: No Brian Jones—he was ill on this Tuesday.

AUGUST 28, 1963

VENUE: Eel Pie Island, Twickenham, Middlesex, England
PERSONNEL: Mick Jagger, Keith Richards, Charlie Watts, Bill Wyman, Ian Stewart
NOTES: Wednesday residency. Again without Brian.

AUGUST 30, 1963

VENUE: Oasis Club, Manchester, Lancashire, England

PERSONNEL: Mick Jagger, Keith Richards, Brian Jones, Charlie Watts, Bill Wyman, Ian Stewart

NOTES: Brian returns. The Stones were originally booked to appear along with Brian Poole and the Tremeloes at the New Brighton Tower on this date, but that engagement was cancelled due to a fire at the venue. They played the Oasis Club instead.

AUGUST 31, 1963

VENUE: Royal Lido Ballroom, Prestatyn, Wales

SEPTEMBER 1, 1963

VENUE: Studio 51, London, England

NOTES: The first of the two regular Sunday gigs.

SEPTEMBER 1, 1963

VENUE: Crawdaddy Club, Athletic Ground, Richmond, Surrey, England

NOTES: The second performance on Sunday, September 1.

SEPTEMBER 2, 1963

VENUE: Studio 51, London, England

NOTES: Monday standing engagement for the Stones during this period.

SEPTEMBER 3, 1963

VENUE: Ricky Tick Club, Thames Hotel, Windsor, Berkshire, England

NOTES: Tuesday gig

SEPTEMBER 4, 1963

VENUE: Eel Pie Island, Twickenham, Middlesex, England

PERSONNEL: Mick Jagger, Keith Richards, Brian Jones, Charlie Watts, Bill Wyman, Ian Stewart

NOTES: The Stones played the second set of this gig without Brian Jones, who became ill, his face having broken out in large red blotches, according to Bill Wyman. The other band members sent Jones home after the first set. He had collapsed from "nervous exhaustion" during rehearsals in late August, missed two gigs, but then made it through the subsequent week of performances. However, he was too sick to play for the band's next three engagements after this one.

SEPTEMBER 5, 1963

VENUE: Strand Palace Theatre, Walmer, Kent, England

PERSONNEL: Mick Jagger, Keith Richards, Charlie Watts, Bill Wyman, Ian Stewart

OPENING/OTHER ACT(S): The Paramounts

NOTES: The band performed without Brian Jones, who was still too ill to play.

SEPTEMBER 6, 1963

VENUE: Grand Hotel Ballroom, Lowestoft, Suffolk, England

PERSONNEL: Mick Jagger, Keith Richards, Charlie Watts, Bill Wyman, Ian Stewart

NOTES: The Stones without Brian again.

SEPTEMBER 7, 1963

VENUE: Kings Hall, Aberystwyth, Wales

PERSONNEL: Mick Jagger, Keith Richards, Charlie Watts, Bill Wyman, Ian Stewart

NOTES: The band's third gig in as many days without Brian. According to Bill Wyman, Jones had been suffering from "nervous exhaustion" since rehearsals in late August (see September 4, 1963).

SEPTEMBER 9, 1963

VENUE: Studio 51, London, England

PERSONNEL: Mick Jagger, Keith Richards, Brian Jones, Charlie Watts, Bill Wyman, Ian Stewart

NOTES: Monday residency. Brian Jones returned to perform with the band after missing three and a half gigs due to illness.

SEPTEMBER 10, 1963

VENUE: Ricky Tick Club, Thames Hotel, Windsor, Berkshire, England

NOTES: Tuesday residency

SEPTEMBER 11, 1963

VENUE: Eel Pie Island, Twickenham, Middlesex, England

NOTES: Wednesday residency

SEPTEMBER 12, 1963

VENUE: Cellar Club, Kingston-upon-Thames, Surrey, England

SEPTEMBER 13, 1963

VENUE: California Ballroom, Dunstable, Bedfordshire, England

SEPTEMBER 14, 1963

VENUE: Ritz Ballroom, Kings Heath, Birmingham, Warwickshire, England

NOTES: The first of two engagements in the Birmingham area on this Saturday.

SEPTEMBER 14, 1963

VENUE: Plaza Theatre, Oldhill, Birmingham, Warwickshire, England
NOTES: The band's second gig on this Saturday in 1963. They also played two gigs the next day!

SEPTEMBER 15, 1963

VENUE: Great Pop Prom, Royal Albert Hall, London, England
OPENING/OTHER ACT(S): The Beatles (headlined), Susan Maughan
NOTES: The first of two gigs this Sunday. While the Stones regularly performed twice on Sundays in 1963, this particular show was hardly one of those standing engagements. And while it was the second time that year they appeared at the Albert Hall, it was the first time they played, not just schlepped, guitars. (See April 18, 1963 in the CHRONOLOGY, or check out February 1, 1964 and September 23, 1966, in this chapter.)

SEPTEMBER 15, 1963

VENUE: Crawdaddy Club, Athletic Ground, Richmond, Surrey, England
NOTES: The second gig of the day, at one of the clubs where the band had a regular Sunday residency. For the first gig, they played the Royal Albert Hall instead of the usual Ken Colyer's.

SEPTEMBER 16, 1963

VENUE: Studio 51, London, England
NOTES: Regular Monday residency

SEPTEMBER 17, 1963

VENUE: British Legion Hall, Harrow-on-the-Hill, London, England

SEPTEMBER 18, 1963

VENUE: Eel Pie Island, Twickenham, Middlesex, England
NOTES: Wednesday residency

SEPTEMBER 19, 1963

VENUE: St. John's Hall, Watford, Hertfordshire, England

SEPTEMBER 20, 1963

VENUE: Savoy Ballroom, Southsea, Hampshire, England

SEPTEMBER 21, 1963

VENUE: Corn Exchange, Peterborough, Northamptonshire, England

SEPTEMBER 22, 1963

VENUE: Studio 51, London, England
NOTES: First of two gigs on this Sunday.

SEPTEMBER 22, 1963

VENUE: Crawdaddy Club, Athletic Ground, Richmond, Surrey, England
NOTES: The second gig of the day. The Stones' last resident performance at the Crawdaddy Club.

SEPTEMBER 23, 1963

VENUE: Studio 51, London, England
NOTES: Last resident performance at Studio 51.

SEPTEMBER 24, 1963

VENUE: Ricky Tick Club, Thames Hotel, Windsor, Berkshire, England
NOTES: Last resident performance at the Ricky Tick Club.

SEPTEMBER 25, 1963

VENUE: Eel Pie Island, Twickenham, Middlesex, England
NOTES: Last resident performance at this club. The Stones were entering a new era in their career as a band. Bigger venues, real touring—they were taking off.

SEPTEMBER 27, 1963

VENUE: Teen Beat Night, Floral Hall, Morecambe, Lancashire, England
OPENING/OTHER ACT(S): Dave Berry & the Cruisers, The Merseybeats, Doodles Black

SEPTEMBER 28, 1963

VENUE: Assembly Hall, Walthamstow, London, England

SEPTEMBER 29, 1963 – NOVEMBER 3, 1963

TOUR: First British tour

LOCATION: England, Scotland and Wales
PERSONNEL: Mick Jagger, Keith Richards, Brian Jones, Charlie Watts, Bill Wyman, Ian Stewart
SPECIAL GUESTS: None
OPENING/OTHER ACT(S): The Everly Brothers, Bo Diddley, Little Richard (headliners), Julie Grant, Mickie Most, The Flintstones, The Rattles, Ray Cameron/ Johnny Kidd & the Pirates
SONGS: Poison Ivy (Leiber, Stoller) / Fortune Teller (Neville) / Come On (Berry) / Money (Gordy, Jr., Bradford) / Route 66 (Troup) / Memphis Tennessee (Berry) / Talkin' 'Bout You (Berry) / Roll Over Beethoven (Berry) / You Better Move On (Alexander) / Down in the Bottom (Dixon) / High Heel Sneakers (Higginbotham) / Down the Road Apiece (Raye) / E: Beautiful Delilah (Berry) / E: Bye Bye Johnny (Berry)
NOTES: The Stones' first major tour of the UK. The Everly Brothers, Bo Diddley and Little Richard were the headliners: the Stones and the other acts listed opened for them. However, Little Richard did not join the tour package until October 5, the Everly Brothers did not appear on some dates, and Johnny Kidd & the Pirates only performed at one confirmed engagement. Such instances are indicated where appropriate in the following listings. The songs listed above are the ones the band is known to have performed on this tour but it is not a setlist *per se*. The titles are not listed in any particular order, except that the Stones often closed these performances with either "Beautiful Delilah" or "Bye Bye Johnny." The band's actual sets comprised nine to 11 numbers. Note the omission of all Bo Diddley (Ellas McDaniel) compositions from the repertoire. This is not an error. Bo Diddley was one of the headliners, and one of the Stones' idols, but either out of respect or for fear of comparison they avoided playing any of his songs as they normally would have—not "Pretty Thing," "Mona" or even "Hey Crawdaddy"—on this first tour. A few of the band's engagements detailed below have been documented well enough to provide actual song titles for those shows, though none have either a confirmed playing order or complete setlist.

SEPTEMBER 29, 1963

TOUR: First British tour
VENUE: New Victoria Theatre, London, England
OPENING/OTHER ACT(S): The Everly Brothers, Bo Diddley, Julie Grant, Mickie Most, The Flintstones, The Rattles, Ray Cameron
SONGS: Poison Ivy (Leiber, Stoller) / Fortune Teller (Neville) / Come On (Berry) / Money (Gordy, Jr., Bradford) / Route 66 (Troup) / Roll Over Beethoven (Berry) / Talkin' 'Bout You (Berry) / Bye Bye Johnny (Berry)

NOTES: The first gig of the Stones' first tour. Confirmed song titles; not the complete set or sequence.

OCTOBER 1, 1963

TOUR: First British tour
VENUE: Odeon Theatre, Streatham, London, England
OPENING/OTHER ACT(S): The Everly Brothers, Bo Diddley, Julie Grant, Mickie Most, The Flintstones, The Rattles, Ray Cameron
NOTES: Two shows

OCTOBER 2, 1963

TOUR: First British tour
VENUE: Regal Theatre, Edmonton, London, England
OPENING/OTHER ACT(S): The Everly Brothers, Bo Diddley, Julie Grant, Mickie Most, The Flintstones, The Rattles, Ray Cameron
NOTES: Two shows

OCTOBER 3, 1963

TOUR: First British tour
VENUE: Odeon Theatre, Southend, Essex, England
OPENING/OTHER ACT(S): The Everly Brothers, Bo Diddley, Julie Grant, Mickie Most, The Flintstones, The Rattles, Ray Cameron
NOTES: Two shows

OCTOBER 4, 1963

TOUR: First British tour
VENUE: Odeon Theatre, Guildford, Surrey, England
OPENING/OTHER ACT(S): The Everly Brothers, Bo Diddley, Julie Grant, Mickie Most, The Flintstones, The Rattles, Ray Cameron
NOTES: Two shows

OCTOBER 5, 1963

TOUR: First British tour
VENUE: Gaumont Theatre, Watford, Hertfordshire, England
OPENING/OTHER ACT(S): The Everly Brothers, Bo Diddley, Little Richard, Julie Grant, Mickie Most, The Flintstones, The Rattles, Ray Cameron
NOTES: Two shows. Little Richard joined the tour on this date.

OCTOBER 6, 1963

TOUR: First British tour
VENUE: Capitol Theatre, Cardiff, Wales
OPENING/OTHER ACT(S): Bo Diddley, Little Richard, Julie Grant, Mickie Most, The Flintstones, The Rattles, Ray Cameron

SONGS: Poison Ivy (Leiber, Stoller) / Talkin' 'Bout You (Berry) / Roll Over Beethoven (Berry) / Money (Gordy, Jr., Bradford) / Fortune Teller (Neville) / Bye Bye Johnny (Berry)
NOTES: Two shows. The Everly Brothers did not play this date.

OCTOBER 8, 1963

TOUR: First British tour
VENUE: Odeon Theatre, Cheltenham, Gloucestershire, England
OPENING/OTHER ACT(S): The Everly Brothers, Bo Diddley, Little Richard, Julie Grant, Mickie Most, The Flintstones, The Rattles, Ray Cameron
NOTES: They played two shows at this gig in Brian Jones's hometown.

OCTOBER 9, 1963

TOUR: First British tour
VENUE: Gaumont Theatre, Worcester, Worcestershire, England
OPENING/OTHER ACT(S): The Everly Brothers, Bo Diddley, Little Richard, Julie Grant, Mickie Most, The Flintstones, The Rattles, Ray Cameron
NOTES: Two shows

OCTOBER 10, 1963

TOUR: First British tour
VENUE: Gaumont Theatre, Wolverhampton, Staffordshire, England
OPENING/OTHER ACT(S): The Everly Brothers, Bo Diddley, Little Richard, Julie Grant, Mickie Most, The Flintstones, The Rattles, Ray Cameron
NOTES: Two shows

OCTOBER 11, 1963

TOUR: First British tour
VENUE: Gaumont Theatre, Derby, Derbyshire, England
OPENING/OTHER ACT(S): The Everly Brothers, Bo Diddley, Little Richard, Julie Grant, Mickie Most, The Flintstones, The Rattles, Ray Cameron
NOTES: Two shows

OCTOBER 12, 1963

TOUR: First British tour
VENUE: Gaumont Theatre, Doncaster, Yorkshire, England
OPENING/OTHER ACT(S): The Everly Brothers, Bo Diddley, Little Richard, Julie Grant, Mickie Most, The Flintstones, The Rattles, Ray Cameron

NOTES: Two shows

OCTOBER 13, 1963

TOUR: First British tour
VENUE: Odeon Theatre, Liverpool, Lancashire, England
OPENING/OTHER ACT(S): The Everly Brothers, Bo Diddley, Little Richard, Julie Grant, Mickie Most, The Flintstones, The Rattles, Ray Cameron
NOTES: Two shows

OCTOBER 15, 1963

TOUR: First British tour
VENUE: Majestic Ballroom, Kingston-upon-Hull, Yorkshire, England
OPENING/OTHER ACT(S): Bo Diddley, Little Richard, Julie Grant, Mickie Most, The Flintstones, The Rattles, Ray Cameron, Johnny Kidd & the Pirates
NOTES: No Everly Brothers, But Johnny Kidd & the Pirates joined the lineup for this show.

OCTOBER 16, 1963

TOUR: First British tour
VENUE: Odeon Theatre, Manchester, Lancashire, England
OPENING/OTHER ACT(S): The Everly Brothers, Bo Diddley, Little Richard, Julie Grant, Mickie Most, The Flintstones, The Rattles, Ray Cameron
NOTES: Two shows. The Everlys are back.

OCTOBER 17, 1963

TOUR: First British tour
VENUE: Odeon Theatre, Glasgow, Scotland
OPENING/OTHER ACT(S): The Everly Brothers, Bo Diddley, Little Richard, Julie Grant, Mickie Most, The Flintstones, The Rattles, Ray Cameron
NOTES: Two shows

OCTOBER 18, 1963

TOUR: First British tour
VENUE: Odeon Theatre, Newcastle-upon-Tyne, Northumberland, England
OPENING/OTHER ACT(S): The Everly Brothers, Bo Diddley, Little Richard, Julie Grant, Mickie Most, The Flintstones, The Rattles, Ray Cameron
NOTES: Two shows

OCTOBER 19, 1963

TOUR: First British tour
VENUE: Gaumont Theatre, Bradford, Yorkshire, England

OPENING/OTHER ACT(S): The Everly Brothers, Bo Diddley, Little Richard, Julie Grant, Mickie Most, The Flintstones, The Rattles, Ray Cameron
NOTES: Two shows

OCTOBER 20, 1963

TOUR: First British tour
VENUE: Gaumont Theatre, Hanley, Staffordshire, England
OPENING/OTHER ACT(S): The Everly Brothers, Bo Diddley, Little Richard, Julie Grant, Mickie Most, The Flintstones, The Rattles, Ray Cameron
NOTES: Two shows

OCTOBER 22, 1963

TOUR: First British tour
VENUE: Gaumont Theatre, Sheffield, Yorkshire, England
OPENING/OTHER ACT(S): The Everly Brothers, Bo Diddley, Little Richard, Julie Grant, Mickie Most, The Flintstones, The Rattles, Ray Cameron
NOTES: Two shows

OCTOBER 23, 1963

TOUR: First British tour
VENUE: Odeon Theatre, Nottingham, Nottinghamshire, England
OPENING/OTHER ACT(S): Bo Diddley, Little Richard, Julie Grant, Mickie Most, The Flintstones, The Rattles, Ray Cameron
NOTES: Two shows. No Everly Brothers.

OCTOBER 24, 1963

TOUR: First British tour
VENUE: Odeon Theatre, Birmingham, Warwickshire, England
OPENING/OTHER ACT(S): The Everly Brothers, Bo Diddley, Little Richard, Julie Grant, Mickie Most, The Flintstones, The Rattles, Ray Cameron
NOTES: Two shows. The Everlys return.

OCTOBER 25, 1963

TOUR: First British tour
VENUE: Gaumont Theatre, Taunton, Somerset, England
OPENING/OTHER ACT(S): Bo Diddley, Little Richard, Julie Grant, Mickie Most, The Flintstones, The Rattles, Ray Cameron
NOTES: Two shows. No Everly Brothers.

OCTOBER 26, 1963

TOUR: First British tour

VENUE: Gaumont Theatre, Bournemouth, Hampshire, England
OPENING/OTHER ACT(S): The Everly Brothers, Bo Diddley, Little Richard, Julie Grant, Mickie Most, The Flintstones, The Rattles, Ray Cameron
NOTES: Two shows. They're (The Everly Brothers, that is) back!

OCTOBER 27, 1963

TOUR: First British tour
VENUE: Gaumont Theatre, Salisbury, Wiltshire, England
OPENING/OTHER ACT(S): The Everly Brothers, Bo Diddley, Little Richard, Julie Grant, Mickie Most, The Flintstones, The Rattles, Ray Cameron
NOTES: Two shows

OCTOBER 29, 1963

TOUR: First British tour
VENUE: Gaumont Theatre, Southampton, Hampshire, England
OPENING/OTHER ACT(S): The Everly Brothers, Bo Diddley, Little Richard, Julie Grant, Mickie Most, The Flintstones, The Rattles, Ray Cameron
NOTES: Two shows

OCTOBER 30, 1963

TOUR: First British tour
VENUE: Odeon Theatre, St. Albans, Hertfordshire, England
OPENING/OTHER ACT(S): The Everly Brothers, Bo Diddley, Little Richard, Julie Grant, Mickie Most, The Flintstones, The Rattles, Ray Cameron
NOTES: Two shows

OCTOBER 31, 1963

TOUR: First British tour
VENUE: Odeon Theatre, Lewisham, London, England
OPENING/OTHER ACT(S): The Everly Brothers, Bo Diddley, Little Richard, Julie Grant, Mickie Most, The Flintstones, The Rattles, Ray Cameron
NOTES: Two shows. And, among the many who came to the Lewisham Odeon to see the Stones' and The Everlys', was Beatle George Harrison.

NOVEMBER 1, 1963

TOUR: First British tour
VENUE: Odeon Theatre, Rochester, Kent, England
OPENING/OTHER ACT(S): The Everly Brothers, Bo Diddley, Little Richard, Julie Grant, Mickie Most, The Flintstones, The Rattles, Ray Cameron

NOTES: Two shows

NOVEMBER 2, 1963

TOUR: First British tour
VENUE: Odeon Theatre, Ipswich, Suffolk, England
OPENING/OTHER ACT(S): The Everly Brothers, Bo Diddley, Little Richard, Julie Grant, Mickie Most, The Flintstones, The Rattles, Ray Cameron
NOTES: Two shows

NOVEMBER 3, 1963

TOUR: First British tour
VENUE: Odeon Theatre, Hammersmith, London, England
OPENING/OTHER ACT(S): The Everly Brothers, Bo Diddley, Little Richard, Julie Grant, Mickie Most, The Flintstones, The Rattles, Ray Cameron
NOTES: Two shows. The last night of the Stones' first British tour.

Here is a typical Rolling Stones set from the last month of 1963—post-first tour, pre-first of the year: Talkin' 'Bout You (Berry) / I'm a King Bee (Moore) / You Can Make It If You Try (Jarrett) / Honest I Do (Reed) / Can I Get a Witness (Holland, Holland, Dozier) / Bye Bye Johnny (Berry) / You Better Move On (Alexander) / Memphis Tennessee (Berry) / E: Beautiful Delilah (Berry)

NOVEMBER 4, 1963

VENUE: Top Rank Ballroom, Preston, Lancashire, England
NOTES: The Stones played on a revolving stage at this venue.

NOVEMBER 5, 1963

VENUE: Cavern Club, Liverpool, Lancashire, England
NOTES: The Beatles' home turf!

NOVEMBER 6, 1963

VENUE: Queens Hall, Leeds, Yorkshire, England

NOVEMBER 8, 1963

VENUE: Whiskey à Go-Go, Newcastle-upon-Tyne, Northumberland, England

NOVEMBER 9, 1963

VENUE: Club à Go-Go, Whitley Bay, Northumberland, England

NOVEMBER 10, 1963

VENUE: Town Hall, Crewe, Cheshire, England

NOVEMBER 11, 1963

VENUE: Pavilion Ballroom, Bath, Somerset, England
OPENING/OTHER ACT(S): Colin Anthony Combo

NOVEMBER 12, 1963

VENUE: Town Hall, High Wycombe, Buckinghamshire, England
OPENING/OTHER ACT(S): Sonny Boy Williamson (headlined)

NOVEMBER 13, 1963

VENUE: City Hall, Sheffield, Yorkshire, England
OPENING/OTHER ACT(S): The Big Three, Wayne Fontana and the Mindbenders, The Sheffields, Johnny Tempest & the Cadillacs, The Vantennas, The Four + One, Karen Young
NOTES: It was on this night that the "black vest look" ended forever. No longer would the Stones' stage wardrobes be uniform in any way—though they would continue to be pressured to conform to the conventional for some time.

NOVEMBER 15, 1963

VENUE: Co-op Ballroom, Nuneaton, Warwickshire, England
OPENING/OTHER ACT(S): The Liverbirds
NOTES: Two shows, matinee and evening. The Liverbirds were an all-female Beatle cover band.

NOVEMBER 16, 1963

VENUE: Matrix Ballroom, Coventry, Warwickshire, England

NOVEMBER 19, 1963

VENUE: State Ballroom, Kilburn, London, England

NOVEMBER 20, 1963

VENUE: Chiswick Polytechnic Dance, Athletic Club, Richmond, Surrey, England

NOVEMBER 21, 1963

VENUE: McIlroys Ballroom, Swindon, Wiltshire, England

NOVEMBER 22, 1963

VENUE: Town Hall, Greenwich, London, England

NOVEMBER 23, 1963

VENUE: The Baths, Leyton, London, England
NOTES: The first of two gigs on this date.

NOVEMBER 23, 1963

VENUE: Chez Don Club, Dalston, London, England
NOTES: The second of two gigs on this Saturday in 1963.

NOVEMBER 24, 1963

VENUE: Studio 51, London, England
NOTES: The first of two gigs on this date, a Sunday.

NOVEMBER 24, 1963

VENUE: Majestic Ballroom, Luton, Bedfordshire, England
NOTES: The second gig on this Sunday.

NOVEMBER 25, 1963

VENUE: Parr Hall, Warrington Tower, Warrington, Lancashire, England

NOVEMBER 26, 1963

VENUE: Stamford Hall, Altrincham, Cheshire, England

NOVEMBER 27, 1963

VENUE: ABC Theatre, Wigan, Lancashire, England
NOTES: The first of two gigs.

NOVEMBER 27, 1963

VENUE: Memorial Hall, Northwich, Cheshire, England
NOTES: The second of two gigs on this date, a Wednesday.

NOVEMBER 29, 1963

VENUE: The Baths, Urmston, Lancashire, England

NOVEMBER 30, 1963

VENUE: Kings Hall, Stoke-on-Trent, Staffordshire, England

DECEMBER 1, 1963

VENUE: Oasis Club, Manchester, Lancashire, England
OPENING/OTHER ACT(S): The Shirelles

DECEMBER 2, 1963

VENUE: Assembly Rooms, Tamworth, Staffordshire, England

DECEMBER 3, 1963

VENUE: Floral Hall, Southport, Lancashire, England

DECEMBER 4, 1963

VENUE: The Baths, Doncaster, Yorkshire, England

DECEMBER 5, 1963

VENUE: Gaumont Theatre, Worcester, Worcestershire, England
OPENING/OTHER ACT(S): Gerry & the Pacemakers, The Overlanders, The Original Checkmates
NOTES: Two shows

DECEMBER 6, 1963

VENUE: Odeon Theatre, Romford, Essex, England
OPENING/OTHER ACT(S): Gerry & the Pacemakers, The Overlanders, The Original Checkmates

Poster advertising the Stones' first show in New York, at Carnegie Hall. (JAMES KARNBACH COLLECTION)

NOTES: Two shows

DECEMBER 7, 1963

VENUE: Fairfield Halls, Croydon, Surrey, England
OPENING/OTHER ACT(S): Gerry & the Pacemakers, The Overlanders, The Original Checkmates
NOTES: Two shows

DECEMBER 8, 1963

VENUE: Olympia Ballroom, Reading, Berkshire, England
OPENING/OTHER ACT(S): The Searchers
NOTES: First engagement on this day.

DECEMBER 8, 1963

VENUE: Gaumont Theatre, Watford, Hertfordshire, England
OPENING/OTHER ACT(S): Gerry & the Pacemakers, The Overlanders, The Original Checkmates
NOTES: The Stones played two shows at this gig, their second booking this Sunday.

DECEMBER 11, 1963

VENUE: Bradford Arts Ball, King and Queens Hall, Bradford, Yorkshire, England

DECEMBER 12, 1963

VENUE: Locarno Ballroom, Liverpool, Lancashire, England
OPENING/OTHER ACT(S): Paul Ryan & the Streaks

DECEMBER 13, 1963

VENUE: Hillside Ballroom, Hereford, Herefordshire, England

DECEMBER 14, 1963

VENUE: The Epsom Baths, Epsom, Surrey, England
OPENING/OTHER ACT(S): The Presidents
NOTES: The only time the Presidents ever shared a bill with the Stones. One year earlier, the Stones began alternating Friday night gigs with the Presidents at the Red Lion Pub in Sutton (also in Surrey). Those gigs had been booked by Glyn Johns, who also managed the Presidents.

DECEMBER 15, 1963

VENUE: Civil Hall, Guildford, Surrey, England
OPENING/OTHER ACT(S): The Graham Bond Organization, Georgie Fame and the Blue Flames, Carter Lewis & the Southerners, The Yardbirds

DECEMBER 17, 1963

VENUE: Town Hall, High Wycombe, Buckinghamshire, England

DECEMBER 18, 1963

VENUE: Corn Exchange, Bristol, Gloucestershire, England
OPENING/OTHER ACTS: Chet and the Triumphs

DECEMBER 20, 1963

VENUE: Lido Ballroom, Winchester, Hampshire, England

DECEMBER 21, 1963

VENUE: Kayser Bondor Ballroom, Baldock, Hertfordshire, England

DECEMBER 22, 1963

VENUE: St. Mary's Hall, Putney, London, England
OPENING/OTHER ACT(S): The Detours (a.k.a. the Who)

DECEMBER 24, 1963

VENUE: Town Hall, Leek, Staffordshire, England
NOTES: Christmas eve in Leek. The Stones arrived two hours late, so they did a single one-hour show instead of the scheduled two 30-minute shows.

DECEMBER 26, 1963

VENUE: Selby's Restaurant, London, England
NOTES: Back in London for Boxing Day.

DECEMBER 27, 1963

VENUE: Town Hall, Reading, Berkshire, England

DECEMBER 28, 1963

VENUE: "All Night Rave," Club Noreik, Tottenham, London, England
OPENING/OTHER ACT(S): Dave Davani & the D-Men, Keith Conway & the Aristokats
NOTES: They weren't kidding about the billing for this show—the Stones played from midnight until 6:00 A.M.

DECEMBER 30, 1963

VENUE: Studio 51, London, England
OPENING/OTHER ACT(S): Jimmy Powell & the Five Dimensions

DECEMBER 31, 1963

VENUE: Drill Hall, Lincoln, Lincolnshire, England
NOTES: New Year's Eve in Lincolnshire.

1964

1964 REPERTOIRE: Ain't That Loving You Baby (Reed) / Around & Around (Berry) / Boys [sung as "Girls"] (Dixon, Farrell) / Bye Bye Johnny (Berry) / Can I Get a Witness (Holland, Holland, Dozier) / Carol (Berry) / Come On (Berry) / Confessin' the Blues (McShann, Brown) / Congratulations / Cops & Robbers (McDaniel) / Don't Lie to Me (Berry) / Down in the Bottom (Dixon) / Down the Road Apiece (Raye) / Empty Heart (Nanker Phelge) / Heart of Stone / High Heel Sneakers (Higginbotham) / I Can Tell (Berry) / I Can't be Satisfied (Morganfield) / I Just Want to Make Love to You (Dixon) / I Wanna Be Your Man (Lennon, McCartney) / I'm a King Bee (Moore) / I'm Alright (McDaniel) / I'm Moving On (Snow) / If You Need Me (Pickett, Bateman, Sanders) / It's All Over Now (Womack, Womack) / Jaguar & the Thunderbird (Berry) / Little By Little (Phelge, Spector) / Little Red Rooster (Dixon) / Memphis Tennessee (Berry) / Mona (I Need You Baby) (McDaniel) / Money (Gordy Jr., Bradford) / Not Fade Away (Petty, Hardin) / Off the Hook (Nanker Phelge) / Oh Baby (We Got a Good Thing Goin') (Ozen) / Pretty Thing (McDaniel) / Road Runner (McDaniel) / Roll Over Beethoven (Berry) / Route 66 (Troup) / Susie Q (Broadwater, Lewis, Hawkins) / Talkin' 'Bout You (Berry) / Tell Me / Time Is on My Side (Meade) / Walking the Dog (Thomas) / You Better Move On (Alexander) / You Can Make It If You Try (Jarrett)

JANUARY 3, 1964

VENUE: Glenlyn Ballroom, Forest Hill, London, England
PERSONNEL: Mick Jagger, Keith Richards, Brian Jones, Charlie Watts, Bill Wyman, Ian Stewart
OPENING/OTHER ACT(S): The Detours (a.k.a. the Who)
SONGS: Boys [sung as "Girls"] (Dixon, Farrell) / Come On (Berry) / Mona (I Need You Baby) (McDaniel) / You Better Move On (Alexander) / Roll Over Beethoven (Berry) / I Wanna Be Your Man (Lennon, McCartney) / Money (Gordy Jr., Bradford) / Memphis Tennessee (Berry) / Pretty Thing (McDaniel) / I Can Tell (Berry) / Road Runner (McDaniel) / Bye Bye Johnny (Berry)
NOTES: This would have been a *typical* Stones set in the early months of 1964, but is not the *exact* set for this gig.

JANUARY 4, 1964

VENUE: Town Hall, Oxford, Oxfordshire, England
NOTES: See above for a typical set for early '64.

JANUARY 5, 1964

VENUE: Olympia Ballroom, Reading, Berkshire, England

JANUARY 6, 1964 – JANUARY 27, 1964

TOUR: Second British tour
VENUE: England and Scotland
PERSONNEL: Mick Jagger, Keith Richards, Brian Jones, Charlie Watts, Bill Wyman, Ian Stewart
OPENING/OTHER ACT(S): The Ronettes, Marty Wilde & the Wildcats, The Swinging Blue Jeans, Dave Berry & the Cruisers, Al Paige, The Cheynes, Freddie & the Dreamers, Joe Brown, Bern Elliot & the Fenmen
SONGS: Boys [sung as "Girls"] (Dixon, Farell) / Come On (Berry) / Mona (I Need You Baby) (McDaniel) / You Better Move On (Alexander) / Roll Over Beethoven (Berry) / I Wanna Be Your Man (Lennon, McCartney) / Money (Gordy Jr., Bradford) / Memphis Tennessee (Berry) / Pretty Thing (McDaniel) / I Can Tell (Berry) / Road Runner (McDaniel) / Bye Bye Johnny (Berry)
NOTES: Though this was the Rolling Stones' second major tour of the UK, it was their first as headliners. "Opening/Other act(s)" above lists all other artists who performed at shows on this tour. Occasionally, the lineup would differ, in that one or more of the other acts might not perform at a particular gig, or an artist might appear on the bill for a single concert only. "Songs," above, reflects a typical set the Stones played in early 1964. It must be remembered that titles were added to the repertoire as the year progressed, as the "typical set" for a particular period indicates.

JANUARY 6, 1964

TOUR: Second British tour
VENUE: Granada Theatre, Harrow-on-the-Hill, London, England
OPENING/OTHER ACT(S): The Ronettes, Marty Wilde & the Wildcats, The Swinging Blue Jeans, Dave Berry & the Cruisers, Al Paige, The Cheynes
SONGS: Boys [sung as "Girls"] (Dixon, Farrell) / Come On (Berry) / Mona (I Need You Baby) (McDaniel) / You Better Move On (Alexander) / Roll Over Beethoven (Berry) / I Wanna Be Your Man (Lennon, McCartney) / Money (Gordy Jr., Bradford) / Memphis Tennessee (Berry) / Pretty Thing (McDaniel) / I Can Tell (Berry) / Road Runner (McDaniel) / Bye Bye Johnny (Berry)

NOTES: First engagement of the Stones' second UK tour, their first time with top billing. They played two shows here, as they would at most of the venues that followed. This is a *typical* set for the period, not the confirmed show for this venue.

JANUARY 7, 1964

TOUR: Second British tour
VENUE: Adelphi Theatre, Slough, Buckinghamshire, England
OPENING/OTHER ACT(S): The Ronettes, Marty Wilde & the Wildcats, The Swinging Blue Jeans, Dave Berry & the Cruisers, Al Paige, The Cheynes
NOTES: Two shows

JANUARY 8, 1964

TOUR: Second British tour
VENUE: Granada Theatre, Maidstone, Kent, England
OPENING/OTHER ACT(S): The Ronettes, Marty Wilde & the Wildcats, The Swinging Blue Jeans, Dave Berry & the Cruisers, Al Paige, The Cheynes
NOTES: Two shows

JANUARY 9, 1964

TOUR: Second British tour
VENUE: Granada Theatre, Kettering, Northamptonshire, England
OPENING/OTHER ACT(S): The Ronettes, Marty Wilde & the Wildcats, The Swinging Blue Jeans, Dave Berry & the Cruisers, Al Paige, The Cheynes
NOTES: Two shows

JANUARY 10, 1964

TOUR: Second British tour
VENUE: Granada Theatre, Walthamstow, London, England
OPENING/OTHER ACT(S): The Ronettes, Marty Wilde & the Wildcats, The Swinging Blue Jeans, Dave Berry & the Cruisers, Al Paige, The Cheynes, Bern Elliott & the Fenmen
NOTES: Two shows. Bern Elliott & the Fenmen made a special appearance at this gig.

JANUARY 11, 1964

TOUR: Second British tour
VENUE: The Epsom Baths, Epsom, Surrey, England
OPENING/OTHER ACT(S): Marty Wilde & the Wildcats, The Swinging Blue Jeans, Dave Berry & the Cruisers, Al Paige, The Cheynes, The Quiet 5 with Patrick Dane

NOTES: The Ronettes had another engagement and did not appear with the Stones on this date. The Quiet 5 and Patrick Dane were added to the evening's bill.

JANUARY 12, 1964

TOUR: Second British tour
VENUE: Granada Theatre, Tooting, London, England
OPENING/OTHER ACT(S): The Ronettes, Marty Wilde & the Wildcats, The Swinging Blue Jeans, Dave Berry & the Cruisers, Al Paige, The Cheynes
NOTES: Two shows

JANUARY 13, 1964

TOUR: Second British tour
VENUE: Barrowlands Ballroom, Glasgow, Scotland
OPENING/OTHER ACT(S): Marty Wilde & the Wildcats, The Swinging Blue Jeans, Dave Berry & the Cruisers, Al Paige, The Cheynes
NOTES: No Ronettes

JANUARY 14, 1964

TOUR: Second British tour
VENUE: Granada Theatre, Mansfield, Nottinghamshire, England
OPENING/OTHER ACT(S): The Ronettes, Marty Wilde & the Wildcats, The Swinging Blue Jeans, Dave Berry & the Cruisers, Al Paige, The Cheynes, Joe Brown
NOTES: Two shows. Joe Brown joined the lineup for this engagement.

JANUARY 15, 1964

TOUR: Second British tour
VENUE: Granada Theatre, Bedford, Bedfordshire, England
OPENING/OTHER ACT(S): The Ronettes, Marty Wilde & the Wildcats, The Swinging Blue Jeans, Dave Berry & the Cruisers, Al Paige, The Cheynes
NOTES: Two shows

JANUARY 16, 1964

TOUR: Second British tour
VENUE: McIlroys Ballroom, Swindon, Wiltshire, England
OPENING/OTHER ACT(S): Marty Wilde & the Wildcats, The Swinging Blue Jeans, Dave Berry & the Cruisers, Al Paige, The Cheynes
NOTES: The Ronettes had another engagement, so were not on the bill here.

JANUARY 17, 1964

TOUR: Second British tour

VENUE: Salisbury City Hall, Salisbury, Wiltshire, England

OPENING/OTHER ACT(S): Marty Wilde & the Wildcats, The Swinging Blue Jeans, Dave Berry & the Cruisers, Al Paige, The Cheynes

NOTES: The Ronettes did not perform.

JANUARY 18, 1964

TOUR: Second British tour

VENUE: Hastings Pier Ballroom, Hastings, Sussex, England

OPENING/OTHER ACT(S): Marty Wilde & the Wildcats, The Swinging Blue Jeans, Dave Berry & the Cruisers, Al Paige, the Cheynes

NOTES: No Ronettes that night, they had other plans.

JANUARY 19, 1964

TOUR: Second British tour

VENUE: Coventry Theatre, Coventry, Warwickshire, England

OPENING/OTHER ACT(S): The Ronettes, Marty Wilde & the Wildcats, The Swinging Blue Jeans, Dave Berry & the Cruisers, Al Paige, The Cheynes, Freddie & the Dreamers

NOTES: The Ronettes returned and Freddie & the Dreamers joined the bill; the Stones played two shows.

JANUARY 20, 1964

TOUR: Second British tour

VENUE: Granada Theatre, Woolwich, London, England

OPENING/OTHER ACT(S): The Ronettes, Marty Wilde & the Wildcats. The Swinging Blue Jeans, Dave Berry & the Cruisers, Al Paige, The Cheynes

NOTES: Two shows

JANUARY 21, 1964

TOUR: Second British tour

VENUE: Granada Theatre, Aylesbury, Buckinghamshire, England

PERSONNEL: Mick Jagger, Keith Richards, Charlie Watts, Bill Wyman, Ian Stewart

OPENING/OTHER ACT(S): The Ronettes, Marty Wilde & the Wildcats, The Swinging Blue Jeans, Dave Berry & the Cruisers, Al Paige, The Cheynes

NOTES: The band played two shows as usual, but without Brian Jones, who was ill.

JANUARY 22, 1964

TOUR: Second British tour

VENUE: Granada Theatre, Shrewsbury, Shropshire, England

PERSONNEL: Mick Jagger, Keith Richards, Brian Jones, Charlie Watts, Bill Wyman, Ian Stewart

OPENING/OTHER ACT(S): The Ronettes, Marty Wilde & the Wildcats, The Swinging Blue Jeans, Dave Berry & the Cruisers, Al Paige, The Cheynes

NOTES: Two shows

JANUARY 23, 1964

TOUR: Second British tour

VENUE: Pavilion, Lowestoft, Suffolk, England

OPENING/OTHER ACT(S): Marty Wilde & the Wildcats, The Swinging Blue Jeans, Dave Berry & the Cruisers, Al Paige, The Cheynes

NOTES: No Ronettes

JANUARY 24, 1964

TOUR: Second British tour

VENUE: The Palais, Wimbledon, London, England

OPENING/OTHER ACT(S): Marty Wilde & the Wildcats, The Swinging Blue Jeans, Dave Berry & the Cruisers, Al Paige, The Cheynes

NOTES: No Ronettes

JANUARY 25, 1964

TOUR: Second British tour

VENUE: California Ballroom, Dunstable, Bedfordshire, England

OPENING/OTHER ACT(S): Marty Wilde & the Wildcats, The Swinging Blue Jeans, Dave Berry & the Cruisers, Al Paige, The Cheynes

NOTES: No Ronettes

JANUARY 26, 1964

TOUR: Second British tour

VENUE: De Montfort Hall, Leicester, Leicestershire, England

OPENING/OTHER ACT(S): The Ronettes, Marty Wilde & the Wildcats, The Swinging Blue Jeans, Dave Berry & the Cruisers, Al Paige, The Cheynes

NOTES: The Ronettes return. The Stones play two shows.

JANUARY 27, 1964

TOUR: Second British tour

VENUE: Colston Hall, Bristol, Gloucestershire, England

OPENING/OTHER ACT(S): The Ronettes, Marty Wilde & the Wildcats, The Swinging Blue Jeans, Dave Berry & the Cruisers, Al Paige, The Cheynes

NOTES: The last gig of the Stones' second UK tour. Two shows.

JANUARY 31, 1964

VENUE: Public Hall, Preston, Lancashire, England

SONGS: Boys [sung as "Girls"] (Dixon, Farrell) / Come On (Berry) / Mona (I Need You Baby) (McDaniel) / You Better Move On (Alexander) / Roll Over Beethoven (Berry) / I Wanna Be Your Man (Lennon, McCartney) / Money (Gordy Jr., Bradford) / Memphis Tennessee (Berry) / Pretty Thing (McDaniel) / I Can Tell (Berry) / Road Runner (McDaniel) / Bye Bye Johnny (Berry)

NOTES: Typical early 1964 set.

FEBRUARY 1, 1964

VENUE: Valentine Charity Pop Show, Royal Albert Hall, London, England

OPENING/OTHER ACT(s): The Heartbeats, Terry Judge & the Barristers, The Original Checkmates, Brian Poole & the Tremeloes, Alan Randall, The Seekers, Dusty Springfield, The Swinging Blue Jeans

FEBRUARY 2, 1964

VENUE: Country Club, Hampstead, London, England

FEBRUARY 5, 1964

VENUE: Ballroom, Willenhall, Staffordshire, England

FEBRUARY 8, 1964 – MARCH 7, 1964

TOUR: Third British tour—"All Star '64"

VENUE: England and Wales

PERSONNEL: Mick Jagger, Keith Richards, Brian Jones, Charlie Watts, Bill Wyman, Ian Stewart

OPENING/OTHER ACT(s): John Leyton, Mike Berry, The Innocents, Jet Harris, Don Spencer, Billie Davies, The LeRoys, Billy Boyle, The Swinging Blue Jeans, Bern Elliott & the Fenmen, The Paramounts, The Dowlands

SONGS: Talkin' 'Bout You (Berry) / Walking the Dog (Thomas) / Pretty Thing (McDaniel) / Cops & Robbers (McDaniel) / Jaguar & the Thunderbird (Berry) / Don't Lie to Me (Berry) / I Wanna Be Your Man (Lennon, McCartney) / Roll Over Beethoven (Berry) / I'm Moving On (Snow) / Road Runner (McDaniel) / Route 66 (Troup) / Bye Bye Johnny (Berry)

NOTES: This group of songs reflects a typical Stones set for this time period and this tour. As in the rest of this chapter, documented, confirmed setlist information is given whenever possible with individual concert listings. If no setlist is provided, refer to the most recent complete set chronologically preceding the gig in question for a guide to what the Stones were then playing—most likely, the set hadn't changed much. If only a few titles are listed

—and they weren't included in an earlier setlist—we've ascertained that they were performed as of that date but cannot confirm how the rest of the set changed (i.e., which, if any, older titles were taken out to make room for new ones or whether were they just added). Once a new song is listed, it could have been included in any performance after that, in theory. In reality, it may not have worked. Check the next typical set and any additional information in the Notes. Compare the songs in a "typical set" for this third British tour with the last one, using the year's repertoire as a reference.

All personnel changes are indicated where appropriate. Assume that all members of the current Rolling Stones played on any date after the beginning of the year or the beginning of a major tour. If names are listed in the Personnel category, something happened. Check the Notes for information. On this tour, The Swinging Blue Jeans and Bern Elliott & the Fenmen were part of the supporting lineup for only two weeks out of the month-long concert series; details of this nature are described in the Notes and specific artist names are provided in the Opening/Other Act(s) category for each gig.

FEBRUARY 8, 1964

TOUR: Third British tour—"All Star '64"

VENUE: Regal Theatre, Edmonton, London, England

OPENING/OTHER ACT(s): John Leyton, Mike Berry, The Innocents, Jet Harris, Don Spencer, Billie Davies, The LeRoys, Billy Boyle, The Swinging Blue Jeans, The Dowlands

NOTES: The Stones played two shows here at the Regal Theatre, followed by a second engagement at Club Noreik (without John Leyton) on this first date of their third UK tour.

FEBRUARY 8, 1964

TOUR: Third British tour—"All Star '64"

VENUE: "All Star '64" All-Night Rave, Club Noreik, Tottenham, London, England

OPENING/OTHER ACT(s): Mike Berry, The Innocents, Jet Harris, Don Spencer, Billie Davies, The LeRoys, Billy Boyle, The Swinging Blue Jeans, The Dowlands

NOTES: Second gig of the day. John Leyton was not on the bill.

FEBRUARY 9, 1964

TOUR: Third British tour—"All Star '64"

VENUE: De Montfort Hall, Leicester, Leicestershire, England

OPENING/OTHER ACT(s): John Leyton, Mike Berry, The Innocents, Jet Harris, Don Spencer, Billie Davies, The LeRoys, Billy Boyle, The Swinging Blue Jeans

Tour program from the "All Star '64" British tour
(TOM BEACH COLLECTION)

NOTES: Two shows. John Leyton returned to the bill.

FEBRUARY 10, 1964

TOUR: Third British tour—"All Star '64"
VENUE: Odeon Theatre, Cheltenham, Gloucestershire, England
OPENING/OTHER ACT(S): John Leyton, Mike Berry, The Innocents, Jet Harris, Don Spencer, Billie Davies, The LeRoys, Billy Boyle, The Swinging Blue Jeans
NOTES: Two shows

FEBRUARY 11, 1964

TOUR: Third British tour—"All Star '64"
VENUE: Granada Theatre, Rugby, Warwickshire, England
OPENING/OTHER ACT(S): John Leyton, Mike Berry, The Innocents, Jet Harris, Don Spencer, Billie Davies, The LeRoys, Billy Boyle, The Swinging Blue Jeans
NOTES: Two shows

FEBRUARY 12, 1964

TOUR: Third British tour—"All Star '64"
VENUE: Odeon Theatre, Guildford, Surrey, England
OPENING/OTHER ACT(S): John Leyton, Mike Berry, The Innocents, Jet Harris, Don Spencer, Billie Davies, The LeRoys, Billy Boyle, The Swinging Blue Jeans
NOTES: Two shows

FEBRUARY 13, 1964

TOUR: Third British tour—"All Star '64"
VENUE: Granada Theatre, Kingston-upon-Thames, Surrey, England
OPENING/OTHER ACT(S): John Leyton, Mike Berry, The Innocents, Jet Harris, Don Spencer, Billie Davies, The LeRoys, Billy Boyle, The Swinging Blue Jeans
NOTES: Two shows

FEBRUARY 14, 1964

TOUR: Third British tour—"All Star '64"
VENUE: Gaumont Theatre, Watford, Hertfordshire, England
OPENING/OTHER ACT(S): John Leyton, Mike Berry, The Innocents, Jet Harris, Don Spencer, Billie Davies, The LeRoys, Billy Boyle, The Swinging Blue Jeans
NOTES: Two shows

FEBRUARY 15, 1964

TOUR: Third British tour—"All Star '64"
VENUE: Odeon Theatre, Rochester, Kent, England
OPENING/OTHER ACT(S): John Leyton, Mike Berry, The Innocents, Jet Harris, Don Spencer, Billie Davies, The LeRoys, Billy Boyle, The Dowlands (replaced The Swinging Blue Jeans at this gig only)
NOTES: Two shows

FEBRUARY 16, 1964

TOUR: Third British tour—"All Star '64"
VENUE: The Guildhall, Portsmouth, Hampshire, England
OPENING/OTHER ACT(S): John Leyton, Mike Berry, The Innocents, Jet Harris, Don Spencer, Billie Davies, The LeRoys, Billy Boyle, The Swinging Blue Jeans
NOTES: Two shows

FEBRUARY 17, 1964

TOUR: Third British tour—"All Star '64"
VENUE: Granada Theatre, Greenford, Middlesex, England
OPENING/OTHER ACT(S): John Leyton, Mike Berry, The Innocents, Jet Harris, Don Spencer, Billie Davies, The LeRoys, Billy Boyle, The Swinging Blue Jeans
NOTES: Two shows

FEBRUARY 18, 1964

TOUR:　Third British tour—"All Star '64"
VENUE:　Rank Theatre, Colchester, Essex, England
OPENING/OTHER ACT(S):　John Leyton, Mike Berry, The Innocents, Jet Harris, Don Spencer, Billie Davies, The LeRoys, Billy Boyle, The Swinging Blue Jeans
NOTES:　Two shows

FEBRUARY 19, 1964

TOUR:　Third British tour—"All Star '64"
VENUE:　Rank Theatre, Stockton-on-Tees, Durham, England
OPENING/OTHER ACT(S):　John Leyton, Mike Berry, The Innocents, Jet Harris, Don Spencer, Billie Davies, The LeRoys, Billy Boyle, The Swinging Blue Jeans
NOTES:　Two shows

FEBRUARY 20, 1964

TOUR:　Third British tour—"All Star '64"
VENUE:　Rank Theatre, Sunderland, Durham, England
OPENING/OTHER ACT(S):　John Leyton, Mike Berry, The Innocents, Jet Harris, Don Spencer, Billie Davies, The LeRoys, Billy Boyle, The Swinging Blue Jeans
NOTES:　Two shows

FEBRUARY 21, 1964

TOUR:　Third British tour—"All Star '64"
VENUE:　Gaumont Theatre, Hanley, Staffordshire, England
OPENING/OTHER ACT(S):　John Leyton, Mike Berry, The Innocents, Jet Harris, Don Spencer, Billie Davies, The LeRoys, Billy Boyle, The Swinging Blue Jeans, The Dowlands
NOTES:　Two shows

FEBRUARY 22, 1964

TOUR:　Third British tour—"All Star '64"
VENUE:　Winter Gardens, Bournemouth, Hampshire, England
OPENING/OTHER ACT(S):　John Leyton, Mike Berry, The Innocents, Jet Harris, Don Spencer, Billie Davies, The LeRoys, Billy Boyle, The Swinging Blue Jeans
NOTES:　Two shows. The Swinging Blue Jeans leave the tour after this gig.

FEBRUARY 23, 1964

TOUR:　Third British tour—"All Star '64"
VENUE:　Hippodrome Theatre, Birmingham, Warwickshire, England
OPENING/OTHER ACT(S):　John Leyton, Mike Berry, The Innocents, Jet Harris, Don Spencer, Billie Davies, The LeRoys, Billy Boyle, Bern Elliott & the Fenmen
NOTES:　Two shows. Bern Elliott & the Fenmen join the tour here.

FEBRUARY 24, 1964

TOUR:　Third British tour—"All Star '64"
VENUE:　Odeon Theatre, Southend, Essex, England
OPENING/OTHER ACT(S):　John Leyton, Mike Berry, The Innocents, Jet Harris, Don Spencer, Billie Davies, The LeRoys, Billy Boyle, Bern Elliott & the Fenmen
NOTES:　Two shows

FEBRUARY 25, 1964

TOUR:　Third British tour—"All Star '64"
VENUE:　Odeon Theatre, Romford, Essex, England
OPENING/OTHER ACT(S):　John Leyton, Mike Berry, The Innocents, Jet Harris, Don Spencer, Billie Davies, The LeRoys, Billy Boyle, Bern Elliott & the Fenmen
NOTES:　Two shows

FEBRUARY 26, 1964

TOUR:　Third British tour—"All Star '64"
VENUE:　Rialto Theatre, York, Yorkshire, England
OPENING/OTHER ACT(S):　John Leyton, Mike Berry, The Innocents, Jet Harris, Don Spencer, Billie Davies, The LeRoys, Billy Boyle, Bern Elliott & the Fenmen
NOTES:　Two shows

FEBRUARY 27, 1964

TOUR:　Third British tour—"All Star '64"
VENUE:　City Hall, Sheffield, Yorkshire, England
OPENING/OTHER ACT(S):　John Leyton, Mike Berry, The Innocents, Jet Harris, Don Spencer, Billie Davies, The LeRoys, Billy Boyle, Bern Elliott & the Fenmen
NOTES:　Two shows

FEBRUARY 28, 1964

TOUR:　Third British tour—"All Star '64"
VENUE:　Sophia Gardens, Cardiff, Wales
OPENING/OTHER ACT(S)　John Leyton, Mike Berry, The Innocents, Jet Harris, Don Spencer, Billie Davies, The LeRoys, Billy Boyle, Bern Elliott & the Fenmen
NOTES:　Two shows

FEBRUARY 29, 1964

TOUR:　Third British tour—"All Star '64"
VENUE:　Hippodrome, Brighton, Sussex, England

OPENING/OTHER ACT(S): John Leyton, Mike Berry, The Innocents, Jet Harris, Don Spencer, Billie Davies, The LeRoys, Billy Boyle, Bern Elliott & the Fenmen
NOTES: Two shows

MARCH 1, 1964

TOUR: Third British tour—"All Star '64"
VENUE: Empire Theatre, Liverpool, Lancashire, England
OPENING/OTHER ACT(S): John Leyton, Mike Berry, The Innocents, Jet Harris, Don Spencer, Billie Davies, The LeRoys, Billy Boyle, Bern Elliott & the Fenmen
NOTES: Two shows

MARCH 2, 1964

TOUR: Third British tour—"All Star '64"
VENUE: Albert Hall, Nottingham, Nottinghamshire, England
OPENING/OTHER ACT(S): John Leyton, Mike Berry, The Innocents, Jet Harris, Don Spencer, Billie Davies, The LeRoys, Billy Boyle, Bern Elliott & the Fenmen, The Paramounts
NOTES: Two shows

MARCH 3, 1964

TOUR: Third British tour—"All Star '64"
VENUE: Opera House, Blackpool, Lancashire, England
OPENING/OTHER ACT(S): John Leyton, Mike Berry, The Innocents, Jet Harris, Don Spencer, Billie Davies, The LeRoys, Billy Boyle, Bern Elliott & the Fenmen, The Paramounts
NOTES: Two shows

MARCH 4, 1964

TOUR: Third British tour—"All Star '64"
VENUE: Gaumont Theatre, Bradford, Yorkshire, England
OPENING/OTHER ACT(S): John Leyton, Mike Berry, The Innocents, Jet Harris, Don Spencer, Billie Davies, The LeRoys, Billy Boyle, Bern Elliott & the Fenmen
NOTES: Two shows

MARCH 5, 1964

TOUR: Third British tour—"All Star '64"
VENUE: Odeon Theatre, Blackburn, Lancashire, England
OPENING/OTHER ACT(S): John Leyton, Mike Berry, The Innocents, Jet Harris, Don Spencer, Billie Davies, The LeRoys, Billy Boyle, Bern Elliott & the Fenmen, The Paramounts
NOTES: Two shows

MARCH 6, 1964

TOUR: Third British tour—"All Star '64"
VENUE: Gaumont Theatre, Wolverhampton, Staffordshire, England
OPENING/OTHER ACT(S): John Leyton, Mike Berry, The Innocents, Jet Harris, Don Spencer, Billie Davies, The LeRoys, Billy Boyle, Bern Elliott & the Fenmen
NOTES: Two shows

MARCH 7, 1964

TOUR: Third British tour—"All Star '64"
VENUE: Winter Gardens, Morecambe, Lancashire, England
OPENING/OTHER ACT(S): John Leyton, Mike Berry, The Innocents, Jet Harris, Don Spencer, Billie Davies, The LeRoys, Billy Boyle, Bern Elliott & the Fenmen
NOTES: Two shows. The last gig of this tour.

MARCH 15, 1964

VENUE: Invicta Ballroom, Chatham, Kent, England
PERSONNEL: Mick Jagger, Keith Richards, Brian Jones, Mickey Waller, Bill Wyman, Ian Stewart
SONGS: Not Fade Away (Petty, Hardin) / Down the Road Apiece (Raye) / Route 66 (Troup) / Cops & Robbers (McDaniel) / You Better Move On (Alexander) / Money (Gordy, Jr., Bradford) / I Wanna Be Your Man (Lennon, McCartney) / Mona (I Need You Baby) (McDaniel) / Walking the Dog (Thomas) / Bye Bye Johnny (Berry)
NOTES: This set was typical for March 1964. The Stones played this gig without Charlie Watts, who had not returned from a post-tour vacation with his wife Shirley. Inclement weather and airport closings had delayed the couple's flight for an indeterminate amount of time. So, with showtime approaching, the band set out to find a last-minute substitute, a somewhat daunting task. More than a year had elapsed since the Stones had last been drummerless, but they could hardly have forgotten what it was like without Charlie. By March 15, 1964, the Rolling Stones had played some 315 gigs together. They had become a unit. This was a ballroom show—not a small club—and there wasn't time for rehearsal either. They took the logical step and called at the home of the last of the rotating drummers. Unfortunately, as he reminisced more than three decades later, Carlo Little wasn't at home when the Stones dropped by; his mother told them she thought he'd most likely not return in time for the gig. Mickey Waller, the drummer for Marty Wilde's Wildcat's, was available. Waller had been friends with the Stones since those lean times of 1962 and early 1963; they'd been on many bills together, even if Waller hadn't been on the Stones' drum chair—until now. He was quick to oblige,

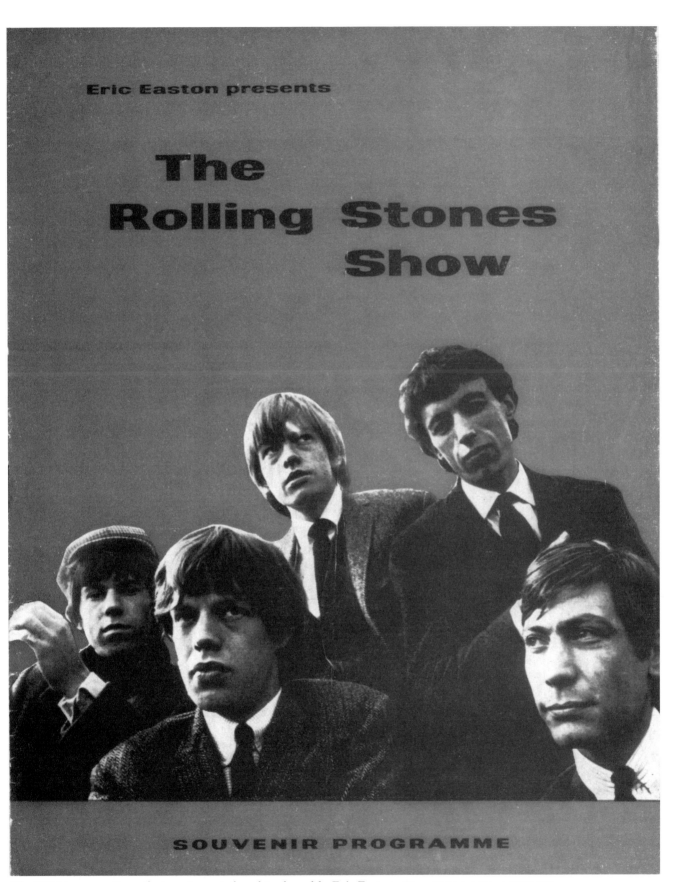

The 1964 program from the tour promoted and packaged by Eric Easton (TOM BEACH COLLECTION)

and the gig was a successful one. Reportedly, after the show Waller was equally quick to complain about a measly sum of £12 (or £16, depending on which story one hears) that he was paid for his services. Partially untrue, says Waller now. It wasn't a lot of money, for sure. "But," he assured us, "I didn't complain about it."

MARCH 17, 1964

VENUE: Assembly Hall, Tunbridge Wells, Kent, England
PERSONNEL: Mick Jagger, Keith Richards, Brian Jones, Charlie Watts, Bill Wyman, Ian Stewart

MARCH 18, 1964

VENUE: City Hall, Salisbury, Wiltshire, England
SONGS: Talkin' 'Bout You (Berry) / Walking the Dog (Thomas) / Pretty Thing (McDaniel) / Cops & Robbers (McDaniel) / Jaguar & the Thunderbird (Berry) / Don't Lie to Me (Berry) / I Wanna Be Your Man (Lennon, McCartney) / Roll Over Beethoven (Berry) / I'm Moving On (Snow) / Road Runner (McDaniel) / Route 66 (Troup) / Bye Bye Johnny (Berry)
NOTES: Setlist according to Bill Wyman.

MARCH 21, 1964

VENUE: Whitehall, East Grinstead, Sussex, England

MARCH 22, 1964

VENUE: Pavilion, Ryde, Isle of Wight, Hampshire, England

MARCH 23, 1964

VENUE: Guildhall, Southampton, Hampshire, England

MARCH 25, 1964

VENUE: Town Hall, Birmingham, Warwickshire, England
NOTES: Two shows

MARCH 26, 1964

VENUE: Town Hall, Kidderminster, Worcestershire, England
NOTES: Two shows

MARCH 27, 1964

VENUE: Ex-Serviceman's Club, Windsor, Berkshire, England
NOTES: This is a fateful date for Jagger. After this gig, Mick and Andrew Oldham went to singer Adrienne

Posta's birthday party where Mick met Marianne Faithfull for the first time. (See CHRONOLOGY)

MARCH 28, 1964

VENUE: Wilton Hall, Bletchley, Buckinghamshire, England
NOTES: First of two gigs on this date.

MARCH 28, 1964

VENUE: Club Noreik, Tottenham, London, England
NOTES: Second of two gigs on this date, a Saturday.

MARCH 30, 1964

VENUE: Ricky Tick Club, Plaza Ballroom, Guildford, Surrey, England
OPENING/OTHER ACT(S): Chris Farlowe
NOTES: Yet another location for the Ricky Tick Club. The show was from 3:00–5:30 P.M., the first of two gigs on this Easter Monday.

MARCH 30, 1964

VENUE: Olympia Ballroom, Reading, Berkshire, England
OPENING/OTHER ACT(S): Chris Farlowe
NOTES: Second gig of the day. March 30, 1964 was the first time singer Chris Farlowe and the Stones met. It was the beginning of a long friendship and professional relationship. Beginning in January of 1966, Farlowe would release a string of covers of Stones songs, his sessions produced primarily by Mick Jagger. Farlowe became quite popular in the UK as a result.

MARCH 31, 1964

VENUE: West Cliff Hall, Ramsgate, Kent, England

APRIL 1, 1964 – MAY 31, 1964

TOUR: Fourth British tour
VENUE: England and Scotland
PERSONNEL: Mick Jagger, Keith Richards, Brian Jones, Charlie Watts, Bill Wyman, Ian Stewart
OPENING/OTHER ACT(S): David John & the Mood, Tony Marsh, Julie Grant, Peter & Gordon, The Caravelles, Duke D'Mond & the Barron Knights, The Overlanders, Freddie & the Dreamers, Dave Berry & the Cruisers, Mark Peters & the Silhouettes, Millie & the Five Embers, Cilla Black, The Fourmost, Kathy Kirby, Billy J. Kramer & the Dakotas, Kenny Lynch, Manfred Mann, The Merseybeats, The Searchers, Sounds Inc., Gene Vincent and the Shouts.

NOTES: Opening acts listed above include those that appeared at non-tour engagements within this time period. The actual tour package program listed the following acts in running order: David John & the Mood, Tony Marsh (comedian and tour compère), Julie Grant, Peter & Gordon (all gigs except Coventry), The Caravelles (replaced Peter & Gordon in Coventry only)—intermission—Duke D'Mond & the Barron Knights, The Overlanders. Tony Marsh returned to the stage following The Overlanders' set and introduced the headliners, the Rolling Stones.

APRIL 1, 1964

TOUR: Fourth British tour
VENUE: Locarno Ballroom, Stevenage, Hertfordshire, England
OPENING/OTHER ACT(S): David John & the Mood, Tony Marsh, Julie Grant, Peter & Gordon, Duke D'Mond & the Barron Knights, the Overlanders
SONGS: Not Fade Away (Petty, Hardin) / Talkin' 'Bout You (Berry) / You Better Move On (Alexander) / I Wanna Be Your Man (Lennon, McCartney) / High Heel Sneakers (Higginbotham) / Roll Over Beethoven (Berry) / Don't Lie to Me (Berry) / I Just Want to Make Love to You (Dixon) / Carol (Berry) / You Can Make It If You Try (Jarrett) / Mona (I Need You Baby) (McDaniel) / Walking the Dog (Thomas) / I'm Alright (McDaniel)
NOTES: This is a fairly typical set for April–May 1964. Shows now opened with "Not Fade Away" and Charlie introduced "I Wanna Be Your Man."

APRIL 3, 1964

TOUR: Fourth British tour
VENUE: The Palais, Wimbledon, London, England
OPENING/OTHER ACT(S): David John & the Mood, Tony Marsh, Julie Grant, Peter & Gordon, Duke D'Mond & the Barron Knights, The Overlanders

APRIL 4, 1964

TOUR: Fourth British tour
VENUE: Leas Cliff Hall, Folkestone, Kent, England
OPENING/OTHER ACT(S): David John & the Mood, Tony Marsh, Julie Grant, Peter & Gordon, Duke D'Mond & the Barron Knights, The Overlanders

APRIL 5, 1964

TOUR: Fourth British tour
VENUE: Gaumont Theatre, Ipswich, Suffolk, England
OPENING/OTHER ACT(S): David John & the Mood, Tony Marsh, Julie Grant, Peter & Gordon, Duke D'Mond & the Barron Knights, The Overlanders
NOTES: Two shows

APRIL 6, 1964

TOUR: Fourth British tour
VENUE: Royal Hotel Ballroom, Lowestoft, Suffolk, England
OPENING/OTHER ACT(S): David John & the Mood, Tony Marsh, Julie Grant, Peter & Gordon, Duke D'Mond & the Barron Knights, The Overlanders

APRIL 8, 1964

VENUE: "*Ready, Steady, Go!* Rave Mad Mod Ball," Empire Pool, Wembley, Middlesex, England
OPENING/OTHER ACT(S): Cilla Black, The Fourmost, Freddie & the Dreamers, Kathy Kirby, Billy J. Kramer & the Dakotas, Kenny Lynch, Manfred Mann, The Merseybeats, The Searchers, Sounds, Inc.
SONGS: Walking the Dog (Thomas) / Not Fade Away (Petty, Hardin) / High Heel Sneakers (Higginbotham) / I'm Alright (McDaniel)
NOTES: The Stones were *not* the headliners.

APRIL 9, 1964

TOUR: Fourth British tour
VENUE: McIlroys Ballroom, Swindon, Wiltshire, England
OPENING/OTHER ACT(S): David John & the Mood, Tony Marsh, Julie Grant, Peter & Gordon, Duke D'Mond & the Barron Knights, The Overlanders

APRIL 10, 1964

TOUR: Fourth British tour
VENUE: The Baths, Leyton, London, England
OPENING/OTHER ACT(S): David John & the Mood, Tony Marsh, Julie Grant, Peter & Gordon, Duke D'Mond & the Barron Knights, The Overlanders

APRIL 11, 1964

TOUR: Fourth British tour
VENUE: Pier Ballroom, Hastings, Sussex, England
OPENING/OTHER ACT(S): David John & the Mood, Tony Marsh, Julie Grant, Peter & Gordon, Duke D'Mond & the Barron Knights, The Overlanders

APRIL 12, 1964

TOUR: Fourth British tour
VENUE: Fairfield Halls, Croydon, Surrey, England
OPENING/OTHER ACT(S): David John & the Mood, Tony Marsh, Julie Grant, Peter & Gordon, Duke D'Mond & the Barron Knights, The Overlanders
NOTES: Two shows

APRIL 16, 1964

TOUR: Fourth British tour
VENUE: Cubi-Club, Rochdale, Lancashire, England (abandoned)
OPENING/OTHER ACT(S): David John & the Mood, Tony Marsh, Julie Grant, Peter & Gordon, Duke D'Mond & the Barron Knights, The Overlanders
NOTES: The gig had to be abandoned, according to Bill Wyman. Nothing else was known at time of writing.

APRIL 17, 1964

TOUR: Fourth British tour
VENUE: Locarno Ballroom, Coventry, Warwickshire, England
OPENING/OTHER ACT(S): David John & the Mood, Tony Marsh, Julie Grant, The Caravelles, Duke D'Mond & the Barron Knights, The Overlanders
NOTES: Peter & Gordon were replaced by The Caravelles in the opening lineup at this gig.

APRIL 18, 1964

TOUR: Fourth British tour
VENUE: Royalty Theatre, Chester, Cheshire, England
OPENING/OTHER ACT(S): David John & the Mood, Tony Marsh, Julie Grant, Peter & Gordon, Duke D'Mond & the Barron Knights, The Overlanders, Miss Olivia Dunn (pianist), "a bunch of sailors"

APRIL 22, 1964

TOUR: Fourth British tour
VENUE: Carlton Ballroom, Slough, Buckinghamshire, England
OPENING/OTHER ACT(S): David John & the Mood, Tony Marsh, Julie Grant, Peter & Gordon, Duke D'Mond & the Barron Knights, The Overlanders

APRIL 24, 1964

TOUR: Fourth British tour
VENUE: Gaumont Theatre, Norwich, Norfolk, England
OPENING/OTHER ACT(S): David John & the Mood, Tony Marsh, Julie Grant, Peter & Gordon, Duke D'Mond & the Barron Knights, The Overlanders
NOTES: Two shows

APRIL 25, 1964

TOUR: Fourth British tour
VENUE: Odeon Theatre, Luton, Bedfordshire, England
OPENING/OTHER ACT(S): David John & the Mood, Tony Marsh, Julie Grant, Peter & Gordon, Duke D'Mond & the Barron Knights, The Overlanders
NOTES: Two shows

APRIL 26, 1964

VENUE: New Musical Express Poll Winners Concert, Empire Pool, Wembley, Middlesex, England
OPENING/OTHER ACT(S): The Beatles, The Dave Clark Five
SONGS: Not Fade Away (Petty, Hardin) / I Just Want to Make Love to You (Dixon) / I'm Alright (McDaniel)
NOTES: The New Musical Express Poll Winners Concert was the band's first gig of two on this date. An afternoon show. Charlie introduced "I'm Alright," as he had been doing at the Stones' regular shows around this time. This concert was filmed by BBC-TV for a two-part "Big Beat" program—one segment headlined by the Stones, the other by the Beatles. (See TELEVISION APPEARANCES, May 3, 1964)

APRIL 26, 1964

TOUR: Fourth British tour
VENUE: Empire Pool, Wembley, Middlesex, England
OPENING/OTHER ACT(S): David John & the Mood, Tony Marsh, Julie Grant, Peter & Gordon, Duke D'Mond & the Barron Knights, The Overlanders
NOTES: Evening show; the Stones' second performance of the day in the same location. This was a different show, with a different artist lineup from that of the afternoon's Poll Winners Concert held in the same location.

APRIL 27, 1964

VENUE: Pop Prom, Royal Albert Hall, London, England
NOTES: Two shows

APRIL 28, 1964

TOUR: Fourth British tour
VENUE: Public Hall, Wallington, Surrey, England
OPENING/OTHER ACT(S): David John & the Mood, Tony Marsh, Julie Grant, Peter & Gordon, Duke D'Mond & the Barron Knights, The Overlanders

APRIL 30, 1964

TOUR: Fourth British tour
VENUE: Majestic Ballroom, Birkenhead, Cheshire, England
OPENING/OTHER ACT(S): David John & the Mood, Tony Marsh, Julie Grant, Peter & Gordon, Duke D'Mond & the Barron Knights, The Overlanders
NOTES: The Stones only played two songs before a wild reception became an audience riot and the show was ended.

MAY 1, 1964

TOUR: Fourth British tour

VENUE: Imperial Ballroom, Nelson, Lancashire, England

OPENING/OTHER ACT(S):   David John & the Mood, Tony Marsh, Julie Grant, Peter & Gordon, Duke D'Mond & the Barron Knights, The Overlanders

MAY 2, 1964

TOUR: Fourth British tour

VENUE: Spa Royal Hotel, Bridlington, Yorkshire, England

OPENING/OTHER ACT(S):   David John & the Mood, Tony Marsh, Julie Grant, Peter & Gordon, Duke D'Mond & the Barron Knights, The Overlanders

MAY 3, 1964

TOUR: Fourth British tour

VENUE: Palace Theatre, Manchester, Lancashire, England

OPENING/OTHER ACT(S):   David John & the Mood, Tony Marsh, Julie Grant, Peter & Gordon, Duke D'Mond & the Barron Knights, The Overlanders

MAY 7, 1964

TOUR: Fourth British tour

VENUE: Savoy Ballroom, Southsea, Hampshire, England

OPENING/OTHER ACT(S):   David John & the Mood, Tony Marsh, Julie Grant, Peter & Gordon, Duke D'Mond & the Barron Knights, The Overlanders

MAY 8, 1964

TOUR: Fourth British tour

VENUE: Town Hall, Hove, Sussex, England

OPENING/OTHER ACT(S):   David John & the Mood, Tony Marsh, Julie Grant, Peter & Gordon, Duke D'Mond & the Barron Knights, The Overlanders

MAY 9, 1964

TOUR: Fourth British tour

VENUE: Savoy Ballroom, Catford, London, England

OPENING/OTHER ACT(S):   David John & the Mood, Tony Marsh, Julie Grant, Peter & Gordon, Duke D'Mond & the Barron Knights, The Overlanders

NOTES: The Stones arrived late, having been to see Chuck Berry perform for the very first time at Finsbury Park. Seeing Berry live took precedence over punctuality for their own show.

MAY 10, 1964

TOUR: Fourth British tour

VENUE: Colston Hall, Bristol, Gloucestershire, England

OPENING/OTHER ACT(S):   Gene Vincent, The Shouts, Millie

NOTES: The band played two shows, but the first was without Brian. He had been delayed by a major traffic tieup caused by a vehicle accident. The story of this gig is truly strange. Brian chose to leave a bit later and drive up on his own to join the others for two shows in Bristol. The emcee for the evening was a sometime promoter named, coincidentally, Brian Jones. He was quite concerned that the concert should proceed without a hitch, well aware of the riotous conditions that had become the norm at Stones shows. Of prime importance was the band's welfare, and to that end, Jones (the promoter) issued strict instructions to his staff that no one was to be allowed backstage without a pass. As it happened, by the time Rolling Stone Jones arrived at the venue, the place was packed and all outer doors were under guard. Reaching the stage entrance, Jones introduced himself to a security man who scanned the Rolling Stones's face and shook his head smartly. "Oh no you ain't," he said adamantly. "I've already met him and he told me to watch out for people like you." According to Brian-the-promoter, Brian-the-Stone spent the next 45 minutes trying to get in, having no luck with verbal persuasion nor any form of identification. Luckily, when he appealed to local authorities, Brian had remembered the press clipping he carried in his wallet. The police looked doubtful at first, but were finally convinced when he pointed to the photo in the paper; indeed, this was the same Brian Jones of the Rolling Stones as in the creased bit of newsprint. His identity confirmed, Brian made it into the hall past a crowd of not-so-lucky fans and through the same door, held open by the same guard, who merely shrugged. The Stones were already onstage, a good 10 minutes into their show, Emcee Jones had introduced the band members at the start, making a vain attempt to acknowledge Brian Jones's absence (the screaming crowd merely got louder, as if he had actually walked on); the emcee now watched from the wings, for the moment unaware of the reason for his namesake's absence. Jones was totally suprised when he was then confronted by an irate Brian Jones, who grabbed him by the throat and growled, "don't you ever effin' do that again!" As promoter Jones tells it now, the other Brian was understandably angry at what he'd been put through. The promoter, who had booked the Stones (as well as the Beatles among others) for several other engagements, was dumbfounded. Security followed his orders, probably too well; "It didn't cross my mind that a real . . . musician couldn't get in to his own show," he now says. The two

Brians quickly cooled off and watched the first show together from the wings. Our Brian then went on as usual for the second and Bristol Brian took up his position in the wings.

MAY 11, 1964

TOUR: Fourth British tour
VENUE: Winter Gardens, Bournemouth, Hampshire, England
OPENING/OTHER ACT(S): David John & the Mood, Tony Marsh, Julie Grant, Peter & Gordon, Duke D'Mond & the Barron Knights, The Overlanders
NOTES: Two shows

MAY 13, 1964

TOUR: Fourth British tour
VENUE: City Hall, Newcastle-upon-Tyne, Northumberland, England
OPENING/OTHER ACT(S): David John & the Mood, Tony Marsh, Julie Grant, Peter & Gordon, Duke D'Mond & the Barron Knights, The Overlanders
NOTES: Two shows

MAY 14, 1964

TOUR: Fourth British tour
VENUE: St. Georges Hall, Bradford, Yorkshire, England
OPENING/OTHER ACT(S): David John & the Mood, Tony Marsh, Julie Grant, Peter & Gordon, Duke D'Mond & the Barron Knights, The Overlanders
NOTES: Two shows

MAY 15, 1964

TOUR: Fourth British tour
VENUE: Trentham Gardens, Stoke-on-Trent, Staffordshire, England
OPENING/OTHER ACT(S): David John & the Mood, Tony Marsh, Julie Grant, Peter & Gordon, Duke D'Mond & the Barron Knights, The Overlanders
NOTES: Two shows

MAY 16, 1964

TOUR: Fourth British tour
VENUE: Regal Theatre, Edmonton, London, England
OPENING/OTHER ACT(S): David John & the Mood, Tony Marsh, Julie Grant, Peter & Gordon, Duke D'Mond & the Barron Knights, The Overlanders
NOTES: Two shows

MAY 17, 1964

TOUR: Fourth British tour
VENUE: Odeon Theatre, Folkestone, Kent, England
OPENING/OTHER ACT(S): David John & the Mood, Tony Marsh, Julie Grant, Peter & Gordon, Duke D'Mond & the Barron Knights, The Overlanders
NOTES: Two shows

MAY 18, 1964

TOUR: Fourth British tour
VENUE: Chantinghall Hotel, Hamilton, Lanarkshire, Scotland
OPENING/OTHER ACT(S): David John & the Mood, Tony Marsh, Julie Grant, Peter & Gordon, Duke D'Mond & the Barron Knights, The Overlanders

MAY 19, 1964

TOUR: Fourth British tour
VENUE: Capitol Theatre, Aberdeen, Scotland
OPENING/OTHER ACT(S): David John & the Mood, Tony Marsh, Julie Grant, Peter & Gordon, Duke D'Mond & the Barron Knights, The Overlanders
NOTES: Two shows

MAY 20, 1964

TOUR: Fourth British tour
VENUE: Caird Hall, Dundee, Scotland
OPENING/OTHER ACT(S): David John & the Mood, Tony Marsh, Julie Grant, Peter & Gordon, Duke D'Mond & the Barron Knights, The Overlanders
NOTES: Two shows

MAY 21, 1964

TOUR: Fourth British tour
VENUE: Regal Theatre, Edinburgh, Scotland
OPENING/OTHER ACT(S): David John & the Mood, Tony Marsh, Julie Grant, Peter & Gordon, Duke D'Mond & the Barron Knights, The Overlanders
NOTES: Two shows

MAY 23, 1964

TOUR: Fourth British tour
VENUE: Leicester University, Leicester, Leicestershire, England
OPENING/OTHER ACT(S): David John & the Mood, Tony Marsh, Julie Grant, Peter & Gordon, Duke D'Mond & the Barron Knights, The Overlanders

MAY 24, 1964

TOUR: Fourth British tour
VENUE: Coventry Theatre, Coventry, Warwickshire, England

OPENING/OTHER ACT(S): David John & the Mood, Tony Marsh, Julie Grant, The Caravelles, Duke D'Mond & the Barron Knights, The Overlanders
NOTES: Two shows

MAY 25, 1964

TOUR: Fourth British tour
VENUE: Granada Theatre, East Ham, London, England
OPENING/OTHER ACT(S): David John & the Mood, Tony Marsh, Julie Grant, Peter & Gordon, Duke D'Mond & the Barron Knights, The Overlanders
NOTES: Two shows

MAY 26, 1964

TOUR: Fourth British tour
VENUE: Town Hall, Birmingham, Warwickshire, England
OPENING/OTHER ACT(S): David John & the Mood, Tony Marsh, Julie Grant, Peter & Gordon, Duke D'Mond & the Barron Knights, The Overlanders
NOTES: Two shows

MAY 27, 1964

TOUR: Fourth British tour
VENUE: Danilo Theatre, Cannock, Staffordshire, England
OPENING/OTHER ACT(S): David John & the Mood, Tony Marsh, Julie Grant, Peter & Gordon, Duke D'Mond & the Barron Knights, The Overlanders
NOTES: Two shows

MAY 28, 1964

TOUR: Fourth British tour
VENUE: Essoldo Theatre, Stockport, Cheshire, England
OPENING/OTHER ACT(S): David John & the Mood, Tony Marsh, Julie Grant, Peter & Gordon, Duke D'Mond & the Barron Knights, The Overlanders
NOTES: Two shows

MAY 29, 1964

TOUR: Fourth British tour
VENUE: City Hall, Sheffield, Yorkshire, England
OPENING/OTHER ACT(S): David John & the Mood, Tony Marsh, Julie Grant, Peter & Gordon, Duke D'Mond & the Barron Knights, The Overlanders
NOTES: Two shows

MAY 30, 1964

TOUR: Fourth British tour
VENUE: Adelphi Theatre, Slough, Buckinghamshire, England

OPENING/OTHER ACT(S): David John & the Mood, Tony Marsh, Julie Grant, Peter & Gordon, Duke D'Mond & the Barron Knights, The Overlanders
NOTES: Two shows

MAY 31, 1964

TOUR: Fourth British tour
VENUE: Pop Hit Parade, Empire Pool, Wembley, Middlesex, England
OPENING/OTHER ACT(S): Peter & Gordon, Freddie & the Dreamers, Dave Berry & the Cruisers, Mark Peters & the Silhouettes, Millie & the Five Embers
NOTES: Afternoon show. First of two shows that day.

MAY 31, 1964

TOUR: Fourth British tour
VENUE: Empire Pool, Wembley, Middlesex, England
OPENING/OTHER ACT(S): Peter & Gordon, Freddie & the Dreamers, Dave Berry & the Cruisers, Mark Peters & the Silhouettes, Millie & the Five Embers
NOTES: Evening show, second gig of the day.

JUNE 5, 1964 – JUNE 20, 1964

TOUR: First North American tour
VENUE: US
PERSONNEL: Mick Jagger, Keith Richards, Brian Jones, Charlie Watts, Bill Wyman, Ian Stewart
OPENING/OTHER ACT(S): George Jones, The Chiffons, Bobby Vee, Bobby Comstock, Bobby Goldsboro, The Rivieras, Jay & the Americans, circus and animal acts, rodeo show and western trick riders
SONGS: Not Fade Away (Petty, Hardin) / Talkin' 'Bout You (Berry) / I Wanna Be Your Man (Lennon, McCartney) / High Heel Sneakers (Higginbotham) / Route 66 (Troup) / Walking the Dog (Thomas) / Tell Me / Beautiful Delilah (Berry) / Can I Get a Witness (Holland, Holland, Dozier) / I Just Want to Make Love to You (Dixon) / I'm Alright (McDaniel)
NOTES: A typical setlist for the Stones' first US tour and the one they played at the first gig are listed above in the first group of Songs. The songs Carol (Berry), I'm a King Bee (Moore) and Down the Road Apiece (Raye) were also played on the tour, but the specific instances are unknown at this time. The Stones' reception by audiences on their initial trip to the States was, figuratively, all over the map, from riotous approval to being booed off the stage. The other acts on the bill varied from city to city, and the Stones weren't always the headliners.

JUNE 5, 1964

TOUR: First North American tour

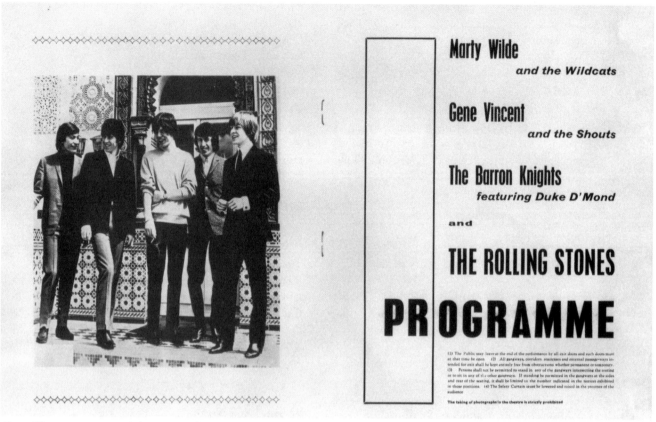

Marty Wilde
and the Wildcats

Gene Vincent
and the Shouts

The Barron Knights
featuring Duke D'Mond

and

THE ROLLING STONES

PROGRAMME

Gene Vincent was one of the acts on the bill for the 1964 UK tour. (TOM BEACH COLLECTION)

VENUE: Swing Auditorium, San Bernardino, CA, USA
OPENING/OTHER ACT(S): The Chiffons,* Bobby Vee, Bobby Comstock, Bobby Goldsboro
SONGS: Not Fade Away (Petty, Hardin) / Talkin' 'Bout You (Berry) / I Wanna Be Your Man (Lennon, McCartney) / High Heel Sneakers (Higginbotham) / Route 66 (Troup) / Walking the Dog (Thomas) / Tell Me / Beautiful Delilah (Berry) / Can I Get a Witness (Holland, Holland, Dozier) / I Just Want to Make Love to You (Dixon) / I'm Alright (McDaniel)
NOTES: First gig of the Stones' first US tour.

JUNE 6, 1964

TOUR: First North American tour
VENUE: Teen Fair, Texas State Fair, San Antonio, TX, USA
OPENING/OTHER ACT(S): George Jones, Bobby Vee, chimpanzees and elephant acts, trampolinist, western acts
NOTES: Two shows—afternoon and evening.

JUNE 7, 1964

TOUR: First North American tour

---

*Unconfirmed, all other opening acts confirmed.

VENUE: Teen Fair, Texas State Fair, San Antonio, TX, USA
OPENING/OTHER ACT(S): George Jones, Bobby Vee, rodeo show and western trick (horseback) riders
NOTES: Two shows—afternoon and evening. Playing saxophone with Bobby Vee was Texas-native Bobby Keys, born the same day as Keith Richards. The San Antonio Teen Fair marked the beginning of a long relationship between Keys and the Stones. He would tour and record with them many times in the future.

JUNE 12, 1964

TOUR: First North American tour
VENUE: Big Reggie's Danceland Ballroom, Excelsior Fair, Minneapolis, MN, USA
OPENING/OTHER ACT(S): The Rivieras (headlined)
NOTES: The Rivieras headlined this show, *not* the Stones.

JUNE 13, 1964

TOUR: First North American tour
VENUE: Music Hall, Omaha, NB, USA

OPENING/OTHER ACT(S): The Chiffons, Bobby Vee, Bobby Comstock, Bobby Goldsboro

JUNE 14, 1964

TOUR: First North American tour
VENUE: Olympia Stadium, Detroit, MI, USA
OPENING/OTHER ACT(S): The Chiffons, Bobby Vee, Bobby Comstock, Bobby Goldsboro

JUNE 17, 1964

TOUR: First North American tour
VENUE: Westview Park, Pittsburgh, PA, USA
OPENING/OTHER ACT(S): The Chiffons, Bobby Vee, Bobby Comstock, Bobby Goldsboro

JUNE 19, 1964

TOUR: First North American tour
VENUE: Farm Show Arena, Harrisburg, PA, USA
OPENING/OTHER ACT(S): The Chiffons, Bobby Vee, Bobby Comstock, Bobby Goldsboro

JUNE 20, 1964

TOUR: First North American tour
VENUE: Carnegie Hall, New York, NY, USA
OPENING/OTHER ACT(S): Bobby Goldsboro, Jay & the Americans
SONGS: Not Fade Away (Petty, Hardin) / Talkin' 'Bout You (Berry) / I Wanna Be Your Man (Lennon, McCartney) / High Heel Sneakers (Higginbotham) / Route 66 (Troup) / Walking the Dog (Thomas) / Tell Me / Beautiful Delilah (Berry) / Can I Get a Witness (Holland, Holland, Dozier)/ I Just Want to Make Love to You (Dixon) / I'm Alright (McDaniel)
NOTES: Two shows—afternoon and evening. The Stones had a mixed reception across the country, but wound up playing Carnegie Hall anyway on the last date of their first US tour. A memorable occasion in another respect, in that it was the first time they met Bob Dylan and schmoozed with hip New York. Jay & the Americans closed the show, to cool down the kids.

JUNE 22, 1964

VENUE: Magdalen College Commemorative Ball, Oxford University, Oxford, England
NOTES: This date had been booked for quite a while. Contrary to popular belief via a bit of flackery (as in public relations), the Rolling Stones did not have to shell out for round-trip first-class airline tickets in order to play this last-minute gala at Oxford and return to the US in time for the final gig of their first American tour. So respectable and respectful underneath it all, aren't they? (See CHRONOLOGY)

JUNE 26, 1964

VENUE: Alexandra Palace, London, England

JULY 11, 1964

VENUE: Spa Royal Hotel, Bridlington, Yorkshire, England

JULY 12, 1964

VENUE: Queens Hall, Leeds, Yorkshire, England
OPENING/OTHER ACT(S): Garth Cawood (compère), Ray Kennon & the Guvnors, Ryles Bros. with Dallas, Lulu & the Luvvers, Ray Anton & the Peppermintmen
SONGS: Walking the Dog (Thomas) / High Heel Sneakers (Higginbotham) / You Can Make It If You Try (Jarrett) / Not Fade Away (Petty, Hardin) / Can I Get a Witness (Holland, Holland, Dozier) / I Just Want to Make Love to You (Dixon) / It's All Over Now (Womack, Womack)
NOTES: Two shows. Garth Cawood introduced the bands. There was an intermission after Lulu & the Luvvers' set. Ray Anton & the Peppermintmen led the second half of the show, followed by the Stones. They played on a revolving stage in the center of the hall.

JULY 18, 1964

VENUE: Beat City Club, London, England
OPENING/OTHER ACT(S): Tom Jones
NOTES: "Up and coming English singing sensation"— Tom Jones (and his band)—opened.

JULY 19, 1964

VENUE: Hippodrome, Brighton, Sussex, England
NOTES: Two shows

JULY 24, 1964

VENUE: Empress Ballroom, Blackpool, Lancashire, England
NOTES: The site of a major riot during the Stones' performance. Charlie had borrowed a drum kit from the LeRoy's drummer, who was reportedly seen crying as it got destroyed in the melee.

JULY 25, 1964

VENUE: Imperial Ballroom, Nelson, Lancashire, England

JULY 26, 1964

VENUE: De Montfort Hall, Leicester, Leicestershire, England

OPENING/OTHER ACT(S): Marty Wilde & the Wildcats, Gene Vincent and the Shouts, Duke D'Mond & the Barron Knights
NOTES: Two shows

JULY 31, 1964

VENUE: Ulster Hall, Belfast, Northern Ireland
OPENING/OTHER ACT(S): The Banshees, The Original Checkmates, The Gonks, Twinkle
SONGS: I Wanna Be Your Man (Lennon, McCartney) / It's All over Now (Womack, Womack) / I Just Want to Make Love to You (Dixon) / High Heel Sneakers (Higginbotham) / Not Fade Away (Petty, Hardin) / I'm Alright (McDaniel) / Walking the Dog (Thomas)
NOTES: First of two gigs on this date. The second half of the program, following the intermission, was opened by The Gonks. The Stones played last.

JULY 31, 1964

VENUE: Flamingo Ballroom, Ballymena, Northern Ireland
OPENING/OTHER ACT(S): The Banshees, The Original Checkmates, The Gonks, Twinkle
NOTES: Second of two engagements in Northern Ireland on July 31, 1964.

AUGUST 1, 1964

VENUE: Pier Ballroom, Hastings, Sussex, England

AUGUST 2, 1964

VENUE: Longleat House, Warminster, Wiltshire, England
SONGS: Walking the Dog (Thomas) / I Wanna Be Your Man (Lennon, McCartney) / It's All Over Now (Womack, Womack) / I Just Want to Make Love to You (Dixon)

AUGUST 7, 1964

VENUE: Fourth National Jazz & Blues Festival, Richmond Athletic Ground, Richmond, Sussex, England
OPENING/OTHER ACT(S): The T-Bones, The Authentics, The Grebbels

AUGUST 8, 1964

VENUE: Kurhaus, Scheveningen, The Hague, The Netherlands
OPENING/OTHER ACT(S): Andre Van Duin, The Telstars, The Joe Brinks
SONGS: Walking the Dog (Thomas) / High Heel Sneakers (Higginbotham) / Susie Q (Broadwater, Lewis, Hawkins) / Not Fade Away (Petty, Hardin)

NOTES: The Stones first concert on the European continent. The audience went nuts as soon as the band came on, rushing the stage and tearing up the place. Police cut the power to the stage after the crazed fans pulled the microphone cables loose, and though the band tried to carry on, the show was stopped. The above songs are not necessarily in order of play, but no one heard them anyway.

AUGUST 9, 1964

VENUE: New Elizabethan Ballroom, Belle Vue, Manchester, Lancashire, England
OPENING/OTHER ACT(S): The Mysteries

AUGUST 10, 1964

VENUE: Tower Ballroom, New Brighton, Cheshire, England
OPENING/OTHER ACT(S): Twelve finalists from a local beat group contest

AUGUST 11, 1964

VENUE: Winter Gardens, Blackpool, Lancashire, England (cancelled)
NOTES: The reason for cancellation? The Blackpool riot two weeks earlier on July 24.

AUGUST 13, 1964

VENUE: Palace Ballroom, Douglas, Isle of Man, UK
SONGS: Not Fade Away (Petty, Hardin) / I Just Want to Make Love to You (Dixon) / Walking the Dog (Thomas) / If You Need Me (Pickett, Bateman, Sanders) / Around & Around (Berry) / High Heel Sneakers (Higginbotham) / I Wanna Be Your Man (Lennon, McCartney) / I'm a King Bee (Moore) / You Can Make It If You Try (Jarrett) / Down in the Bottom (Dixon) / Carol (Berry) / Tell Me / It's All Over Now (Womack, Womack)

AUGUST 14, 1964

VENUE: The Palais, Wimbledon, London, England

AUGUST 18, 1964

VENUE: St. Georges Hall, New Theatre Ballroom, Guernsey, Channel Islands, UK

AUGUST 19, 1964

VENUE: St. Georges Hall, New Theatre Ballroom, Guernsey, Channel Islands, UK

AUGUST 20, 1964

VENUE: St. Georges Hall, New Theatre Ballroom, Guernsey, Channel Islands, UK

AUGUST 21, 1964

VENUE: Springfield Hall, St. Helier, Jersey, Channel Islands, UK

AUGUST 22, 1964

VENUE: Springfield Hall, St. Helier, Jersey, Channel Islands, UK

AUGUST 23, 1964

VENUE: Gaumont Theatre, Bournemouth, Hampshire, England

OPENING/OTHER ACT(S): Duke D'Mond & the Barron Knights, Worryin' Kind, The Overlanders, The Paramounts, Julie Grant

NOTES: Two shows. This was the beginning of a mini-tour that lasted until the end of August. Opening acts are listed in sequence. There was an intermission after the Overlanders' set. The Paramounts later evolved into the group known as Procol Harum.

AUGUST 24, 1964

VENUE: Gaumont Theatre, Weymouth, Dorset, England

OPENING/OTHER ACT(S): Duke D'Mond & the Barron Knights, Worryin' Kind, The Overlanders, Millie & the Five Embers

NOTES: Two shows. The second half of the program, beginning with Millie & the Five Embers' set, differed from the Bournemouth gig.

AUGUST 25, 1964

VENUE: Odeon Theatre, Weston-super-Mare, Somerset, England

OPENING/OTHER ACT(S): Duke D'Mond & the Barron Knights, Worryin' Kind, The Overlanders, Millie & the Five Embers

NOTES: Two shows

AUGUST 26, 1964

VENUE: Odeon Theatre, Exeter, Devon, England

OPENING/OTHER ACT(S): Duke D'Mond & the Barron Knights, Worryin' Kind, The Overlanders, Millie & the Five Embers

NOTES: Two shows

AUGUST 27, 1964

VENUE: ABC Theatre, Plymouth, Devon, England

OPENING/OTHER ACT(S): Duke D'Mond & the Barron Knights, Worryin' Kind, The Overlanders, Millie & the Five Embers

NOTES: Two shows

AUGUST 28, 1964

VENUE: Gaumont Theatre, Taunton, Somerset, England

OPENING/OTHER ACT(S): Duke D'Mond & the Barron Knights, Worryin' Kind, The Overlanders, Millie & the Five Embers

NOTES: Two shows

AUGUST 29, 1964

VENUE: Town Hall, Torquay, Devon, England

OPENING/OTHER ACT(S): Duke D'Mond & the Barron Knights, Worryin' Kind, The Overlanders, Patrick Dane & the Quiet 5, Julie Grant

NOTES: Two shows. Again, the first half of the program was the same but new acts performed after the intermission.

AUGUST 30, 1964

VENUE: Gaumont Theatre, Bournemouth, Hampshire, England

OPENING/OTHER ACT(S): Duke D'Mond & the Barron Knights, Worryin' Kind, The Overlanders, Long John Baldry & the Hoochie-Coochie Men, Julie Grant

NOTES: Two shows. Long John Baldry opened the second half of the show.

SEPTEMBER 5, 1964 – OCTOBER 11, 1964

TOUR: Fifth British tour

VENUE: England, Scotland and Wales

PERSONNEL: Mick Jagger, Keith Richards, Brian Jones, Charlie Watts, Bill Wyman, Ian Stewart

OPENING/OTHER ACT(S): The Innocents, Don Spencer (compère), Mike Berry, The Mojos, The LeRoys, Simon Scott, Inez & Charlie Foxx

SONGS: I Just Want to Make Love to You (Dixon) / Walking the Dog (Thomas) / Not Fade Away (Petty, Hardin) / If You Need Me (Pickett, Bateman, Sanders) / Carol (Berry) / Time Is on My Side (Meade) / Around & Around (Berry) / Tell Me / It's All Over Now (Womack, Womack) / High Heel Sneakers (Higginbotham) / You Can Make It If You Try (Jarrett) / I'm a King Bee (Moore) / I'm Alright (McDaniel)

ALSO PERFORMED: Off the Hook (Nanker Phelge) / Susie Q (Broadwater, Lewis, Hawkins)

NOTES: These were songs typically included in sets of this period. A partial setlist is included for the first show of the tour, below. Opening acts are listed in the running order of the shows on this tour, but each show was divided in half by an intermission. The Mojos closed the first half, the LeRoys opened the second and the Stones came on last, following Inez & Charlie Foxx.

SEPTEMBER 5, 1964

TOUR: Fifth British tour

VENUE: Astoria Theatre, Finsbury Park, London, England

OPENING/OTHER ACT(S): The Innocents, Don Spencer (compère), Mike Berry, The Mojos, The LeRoys, Simon Scott, Inez & Charlie Foxx.

SONGS: I Just Want to Make Love to You (Dixon) / Walking the Dog (Thomas) / If You Need Me (Pickett, Bateman, Sanders) / I'm Alright (McDaniel) / Around & Around (Berry) / It's All Over Now (Womack, Womack)

NOTES: Two shows

SEPTEMBER 6, 1964

TOUR: Fifth British tour

VENUE: Odeon Theatre, Leicester, Leicestershire, England

OPENING/OTHER ACT(S): The Innocents, Don Spencer (compère), Mike Berry, The Mojos, The LeRoys, Simon Scott, Inez & Charlie Foxx

NOTES: Two shows

SEPTEMBER 8, 1964

TOUR: Fifth British tour

VENUE: Odeon Theatre, Colchester, Essex, England

OPENING/OTHER ACT(S): The Innocents, Don Spencer (compère), Mike Berry, The Mojos, The LeRoys, Simon Scott, Inez & Charlie Foxx

NOTES: Two shows

SEPTEMBER 9, 1964

TOUR: Fifth British tour

VENUE: Odeon Theatre, Luton, Bedfordshire, England

OPENING/OTHER ACT(S): The Innocents, Don Spencer (compère), Mike Berry, The Mojos, The LeRoys, Simon Scott, Inez & Charlie Foxx

NOTES: Two shows

SEPTEMBER 10, 1964

TOUR: Fifth British tour

VENUE: Odeon Theatre, Cheltenham, Gloucestershire, England

OPENING/OTHER ACT(S): The Innocents, Don Spencer (compère), Mike Berry, The Mojos, The LeRoys, Simon Scott, Inez & Charlie Foxx

NOTES: Two shows. Brian's home town.

SEPTEMBER 11, 1964

TOUR: Fifth British tour

VENUE: Capitol Theatre, Cardiff, Wales

OPENING/OTHER ACT(S): The Innocents, Don Spencer (compère), Mike Berry, The Mojos, The LeRoys, Simon Scott, Inez & Charlie Foxx

NOTES: Two shows

SEPTEMBER 14, 1964

TOUR: Fifth British tour

VENUE: ABC Theatre, Chester, Cheshire, England

OPENING/OTHER ACT(S): The Innocents, Don Spencer (compère), Mike Berry, The Mojos, The LeRoys, Simon Scott, Inez & Charlie Foxx

NOTES: Two shows

SEPTEMBER 15, 1964

TOUR: Fifth British tour

VENUE: Odeon Theatre, Manchester, Lancashire, England

OPENING/OTHER ACT(S): The Innocents, Don Spencer (compère), Mike Berry, The Mojos, The LeRoys, Simon Scott, Inez & Charlie Foxx

NOTES: Two shows

SEPTEMBER 16, 1964

TOUR: Fifth British tour

VENUE: ABC Theatre, Wigan, Lancashire, England

OPENING/OTHER ACT(S): The Innocents, Don Spencer (compère), Mike Berry, The Mojos, The LeRoys, Simon Scott, Inez & Charlie Foxx

NOTES: Two shows

SEPTEMBER 17, 1964

TOUR: Fifth British tour

VENUE: ABC Theatre, Carlisle, Cumberland, England

OPENING/OTHER ACT(S): The Innocents, Don Spencer (compère), Mike Berry, The Mojos, The LeRoys, Simon Scott, Inez & Charlie Foxx

NOTES: Two shows

SEPTEMBER 18, 1964

TOUR: Fifth British tour

VENUE: Odeon Theatre, Newcastle-upon-Tyne, Northumberland, England

OPENING/OTHER ACT(S): The Innocents, Don Spencer (compère), Mike Berry, The Mojos, The LeRoys, Simon Scott, Inez & Charlie Foxx

NOTES: Two shows

SEPTEMBER 19, 1964

TOUR: Fifth British tour

VENUE: Usher Hall, Edinburgh, Scotland

OPENING/OTHER ACT(S): The Innocents, Don Spencer (compère), Mike Berry, The Mojos, The LeRoys, Simon Scott, Inez & Charlie Foxx

NOTES: Two shows

SEPTEMBER 20, 1964

TOUR: Fifth British tour

VENUE: Globe Theatre, Stockton-on-Tees, Durham, England

OPENING/OTHER ACT(S): The Innocents, Don Spencer (compère), Mike Berry, The Mojos, The LeRoys, Simon Scott, Inez & Charlie Foxx

NOTES: Two shows

SEPTEMBER 21, 1964

TOUR: Fifth British tour

VENUE: ABC Theatre, Kingston-upon-Hull, Yorkshire, England

OPENING/OTHER ACT(S): The Innocents, Don Spencer (compère), Mike Berry, The Mojos, The LeRoys, Simon Scott, Inez & Charlie Foxx

NOTES: Two shows

SEPTEMBER 22, 1964

TOUR: Fifth British tour

VENUE: ABC Theatre, Lincoln, Lincolnshire, England

OPENING/OTHER ACT(S): The Innocents, Don Spencer (compère), Mike Berry, The Mojos, The LeRoys, Simon Scott, Inez & Charlie Foxx

NOTES: Two shows

SEPTEMBER 24, 1964

TOUR: Fifth British tour

VENUE: Gaumont Theatre, Doncaster, Yorkshire, England

OPENING/OTHER ACT(S): The Innocents, Don Spencer (compère), Mike Berry, The Mojos, The LeRoys, Simon Scott, Inez & Charlie Foxx

NOTES: Two shows

SEPTEMBER 25, 1964

TOUR: Fifth British tour

VENUE: Gaumont Theatre, Hanley, Staffordshire, England

OPENING/OTHER ACT(S): The Innocents, Don Spencer (compère), Mike Berry, The Mojos, The LeRoys, Simon Scott, Inez & Charlie Foxx

NOTES: Two shows

SEPTEMBER 26, 1964

TOUR: Fifth British tour

VENUE: Odeon Theatre, Bradford, Yorkshire, England

OPENING/OTHER ACT(S): The Innocents, Don Spencer (compère), Mike Berry, The Mojos, The LeRoys, Simon Scott, Inez & Charlie Foxx

NOTES: Two shows

SEPTEMBER 27, 1964

TOUR: Fifth British tour

VENUE: Hippodrome Theatre, Birmingham, Warwickshire, England

OPENING/OTHER ACT(S): The Innocents, Don Spencer (compère), Mike Berry, The Mojos, The LeRoys, Simon Scott, Inez & Charlie Foxx

NOTES: Two shows

SEPTEMBER 29, 1964

TOUR: Fifth British tour

VENUE: Odeon Theatre, Guildford, Surrey, England

OPENING/OTHER ACT(S): The Innocents, Don Spencer (compère), Mike Berry, The Mojos, The LeRoys, Simon Scott, Inez & Charlie Foxx

NOTES: Two shows

OCTOBER 1, 1964

TOUR: Fifth British tour

VENUE: Colston Hall, Bristol, Gloucestershire, England

OPENING/OTHER ACT(S): The Innocents, Don Spencer (compère), Mike Berry, The Mojos, The LeRoys, Simon Scott, Inez & Charlie Foxx

NOTES: Two shows

OCTOBER 2, 1964

TOUR: Fifth British tour

VENUE: Odeon Theatre, Exeter, Devon, England

OPENING/OTHER ACT(S): The Innocents, Don Spencer (compère), Mike Berry, The Mojos, The LeRoys, Simon Scott, Inez & Charlie Foxx

NOTES: Two shows

OCTOBER 3, 1964

TOUR: Fifth British tour

VENUE: Regal Theatre, Edmonton, London, England

OPENING/OTHER ACT(S): The Innocents, Don Spencer (compère), Mike Berry, The Mojos, The LeRoys, Simon Scott, Inez & Charlie Foxx

NOTES: Two shows

OCTOBER 4, 1964

TOUR: Fifth British tour

VENUE: Gaumont Theatre, Southampton, Hampshire, England

OPENING/OTHER ACT(S): The Innocents, Don Spencer (compère), Mike Berry, The Mojos, The LeRoys, Simon Scott, Inez & Charlie Foxx

NOTES: Two shows

OCTOBER 5, 1964

TOUR: Fifth British tour

VENUE: Gaumont Theatre, Wolverhampton, Staffordshire, England

OPENING/OTHER ACT(S): The Innocents, Don Spencer (compère), Mike Berry, The Mojos, The LeRoys, Simon Scott, Inez & Charlie Foxx

NOTES: Two shows

OCTOBER 6, 1964

TOUR: Fifth British tour

VENUE: Gaumont Theatre, Watford, Hertfordshire, England

OPENING/OTHER ACT(S): The Innocents, Don Spencer (compère), Mike Berry, The Mojos, The LeRoys, Simon Scott, Inez & Charlie Foxx

NOTES: Two shows

OCTOBER 8, 1964

TOUR: Fifth British tour

VENUE: Odeon Theatre, Lewisham, London, England

OPENING/OTHER ACT(S): The Innocents, Don Spencer (compère), Mike Berry, The Mojos, The LeRoys, Simon Scott, Inez & Charlie Foxx

NOTES: Two shows

OCTOBER 9, 1964

TOUR: Fifth British tour

VENUE: Gaumont Theatre, Ipswich, Suffolk, England

OPENING/OTHER ACT(S): The Innocents, Don Spencer (compère), Mike Berry, The Mojos, The LeRoys, Simon Scott, Inez & Charlie Foxx

NOTES: Two shows

OCTOBER 10, 1964

TOUR: Fifth British tour

VENUE: Odeon Theatre, Southend, Essex, England

OPENING/OTHER ACT(S): The Innocents, Don Spencer (compère), Mike Berry, The Mojos, The LeRoys, Simon Scott, Inez & Charlie Foxx

NOTES: Two shows

OCTOBER 11, 1964

TOUR: Fifth British tour

VENUE: Hippodrome Theatre, Brighton, Sussex, England

OPENING/OTHER ACT(S): The Innocents, Don Spencer (compère), Mike Berry, The Mojos, The LeRoys, Simon Scott, Inez & Charlie Foxx

NOTES: Two shows. The last night of the Stones' fifth UK tour.

OCTOBER 20, 1964

VENUE: Olympia Theatre, Paris, France

OPENING/OTHER ACT(S): Vince Taylor Band, Ron & Mel

SONGS: Not Fade Away (Petty, Hardin) / Walking the Dog (Thomas) / If You Need Me (Pickett, Bateman, Sanders) / Carol (Berry) / Time Is on My Side (Meade) / Tell Me / Around & Around (Berry) / It's All Over Now (Womack, Womack) / I'm Alright (McDaniel)

NOTES: The one opening act, the Vince Taylor Band, was a jazz group. The other artists, Ron & Mel, were a quadrilingual singing duet; that is, they sang in four languages.

OCTOBER 24, 1964 – NOVEMBER 15, 1964

TOUR: Second North American tour

VENUE: USA

PERSONNEL: Mick Jagger, Keith Richards, Brian Jones, Charlie Watts, Bill Wyman, Ian Stewart

OPENING/OTHER ACT(S): The Shangri-Las, Joey Paige

SONGS: Not Fade Away (Petty, Hardin) / Walking the Dog (Thomas) / If You Need Me (Pickett, Bateman, Sanders) / Carol (Berry) / Time Is on My Side (Meade) / Around & Around (Berry) / Tell Me / It's All Over Now (Womack, Womack) / High Heel Sneakers (Higginbotham) / You Can Make It If You Try (Jarrett) / I'm a King Bee (Moore) / I'm Alright (McDaniel)

ALSO PERFORMED: Off the Hook (Nanker Phelge) / Susie Q (Broadwater, Lewis, Hawkins)

NOTES: This is a typical set from the Stones' second North American tour. The Shangri-Las opened several shows, Joey Paige appeared in San Diego.

OCTOBER 24, 1964

TOUR: Second North American tour

VENUE: Academy of Music, New York, NY, USA

OPENING/OTHER ACT(S): The Shangri-Las

NOTES: Beginning of the band's second US tour. Two shows—afternoon and evening.

OCTOBER 26, 1964

TOUR: Second North American tour
VENUE: Sacramento Memorial Auditorium, Sacramento, CA, USA
OPENING/OTHER ACT(S): The Shangri-Las

OCTOBER 28, 1964

TOUR: Second North American tour
VENUE: The T.A.M.I. Show, Santa Monica Civic Auditorium, Santa Monica, CA, USA
OPENING/OTHER ACT(S): Marvin Gaye with the Blossoms, James Brown & the Flames, Smokey Robinson & the Miracles, The Supremes, The Beach Boys, Gerry & the Pacemakers, Chuck Berry, Lesley Gore, Jan & Dean, Billy J. Kramer & the Dakotas, The Barbarians
SONGS: Not Fade Away (Petty, Hardin) / Around & Around (Berry) / Off the Hook (Nanker Phelge) / Tell Me / It's All Over Now (Womack, Womack) / Time Is On My Side (Meade) / I Just Want to Make Love to You (Dixon) / I'm Alright (McDaniel) plus Get Together (cast finale, with Jagger doing live vocal)
NOTES: The Stones' appearance on the T.A.M.I.—"Teenage Awards Music International"—Show came about through their association with Phil Spector and Sonny Bono and was a prime career opportunity. It not only granted them exposure to US television audiences as part of an all-star cast, but it also gave them the chance to meet American celebrities, other talented musicians and influential music industry types. Many stories of behind-the-scenes competitive nastiness at the T.A.M.I. Show have circulated over the years, including rumors about James Brown and the Stones. The "buzz" was that Brown was determined to "blow away" the young upstarts once he got onstage, and elaborate tales were told of conspicuous offstage friction between the boys and Brown. In reality, the backstage scene was quite the opposite. Over the course of T.A.M.I.'s two days of rehearsals and filmed performances, James Brown and Brian Jones struck up a friendship, and Brown went on to establish friendly relationships with both Mick and Keith in later years. Certainly, there must have been some tension before the show —amongst the Stones. They had a terrific spot in the lineup: just two years in the business and they were to go on after the Godfather of Soul. The Stones performed eight songs (plus the encore/finale) at the Santa Monica Civic Auditorium, though only five of these were seen in the final cut of the film. (For more about it, see PROMOTIONAL FILMS AND VIDEOS.)

OCTOBER 29, 1964

TOUR: Second North American tour

VENUE: The T.A.M.I. Show, Santa Monica Civic Auditorium, Santa Monica, CA, USA
OPENING/OTHER ACT(S): Marvin Gaye, James Brown & the Flames, Smokey Robinson & the Miracles, The Supremes, The Beach Boys, Gerry & the Pacemakers, Chuck Berry, Lesley Gore, Jan & Dean, Billy J. Kramer & The Dakotas, The Barbarians
NOTES: More on these concerts can be found with the October 28, 1964 show, above, and in PROMOTIONAL FILMS AND VIDEOS.

OCTOBER 31, 1964

TOUR: Second North American tour
VENUE: Swing Auditorium, San Bernardino, CA, USA
OPENING/OTHER ACT(S): The Shangri-Las
SONGS: Not Fade Away (Petty, Hardin) / Time Is on My Side (Meade) / I'm Alright (McDaniel) / It's All Over Now (Womack, Womack) / If You Need Me (Pickett, Bateman, Sanders) / Carol (Berry) / I'm a King Bee (Moore) *and several others*

NOVEMBER 1, 1964

TOUR: Second North American tour
VENUE: Long Beach Civic Auditorium, Long Beach Arena, Long Beach, CA, USA
OPENING/OTHER ACT(S): The Shangri-Las
NOTES: Afternoon show—the first of two shows in Southern California that day.

NOVEMBER 1, 1964

TOUR: Second North American tour
VENUE: Balboa Park Bowl, San Diego, CA, USA
OPENING/OTHER ACT(S): The Shangri-Las, Joey Paige
NOTES: Evening show, the second gig of the day.

NOVEMBER 3, 1964

TOUR: Second North American tour
VENUE: The Public Auditorium, Cleveland, OH, USA
OPENING/OTHER ACT(S): The Shangri-Las

NOVEMBER 4, 1964

TOUR: Second North American tour
VENUE: Loews Theatre, Providence, RI, USA
OPENING/OTHER ACT(S): The Shangri-Las

NOVEMBER 11, 1964

TOUR: Second North American tour
VENUE: Milwaukee Auditorium, Milwaukee, WI, USA
PERSONNEL: Mick Jagger, Keith Richards, Charlie Watts, Bill Wyman, Ian Stewart
OPENING/OTHER ACT(S): The Shangri-Las

NOTES: Brian did not perform because of illness.

NOVEMBER 12, 1964

TOUR: Second North American tour
VENUE: Coliseum, Fort Wayne, IN, USA
PERSONNEL: Mick Jagger, Keith Richards, Charlie Watts, Bill Wyman, Ian Stewart
OPENING/OTHER ACT(S):   The Shangri-Las
NOTES: Again without Brian.

NOVEMBER 13, 1964

TOUR: Second North American tour
VENUE: Hara Arena, Dayton, OH, USA
PERSONNEL: Mick Jagger, Keith Richards, Charlie Watts, Bill Wyman, Ian Stewart
OPENING/OTHER ACT(S):   The Shangri-Las
NOTES: Still no Brian.

NOVEMBER 14, 1964

TOUR: Second North American tour
VENUE: Memorial Auditorium, Louisville, KY, USA
PERSONNEL: Mick Jagger, Keith Richards, Charlie Watts, Bill Wyman, Ian Stewart
OPENING/OTHER ACT(S):   The Shangri-Las
NOTES: The Stones went on again without an ailing Brian Jones.

NOVEMBER 15, 1964

TOUR: Second North American tour
VENUE: Arie Crown Theatre, Chicago, IL, USA
PERSONNEL: Mick Jagger, Keith Richards, Brian Jones, Charlie Watts, Bill Wyman, Ian Stewart
OPENING/OTHER ACT(S):   The Shangri-Las
NOTES: The last gig of the tour, Brian returned to play.

NOVEMBER 20, 1964

VENUE: Glad Rag Ball, Empire Pool, Wembley, Middlesex, England
OPENING/OTHER ACT(S):   Long John Baldry, The Pretty Things, Gene Vincent, The Animals, Cliff Bennett

DECEMBER 4, 1964

VENUE: Fairfield Halls, Croydon, Surrey, England
NOTES: Two shows

1965

1965 REPERTOIRE   Around & Around (Berry) / Carol (Berry) / Cry to Me (Russell) / Down the Road Apiece (Raye) / Everybody Needs Somebody to Love (Russell, Burke, Wexler) / Everybody Needs Somebody to Love (Russell, Burke, Wexler) → Pain in My Heart (Neville), LMV / Everybody Needs Somebody to Love (Russell, Burke, Wexler) → Around & Around (Berry), LMV / Fanny Mae (Brown, Robinson) / Get off of My Cloud / Good Times (Cooke) / Heart of Stone / Hey Crawdaddy (McDaniel) / Hitch Hike (Gaye, Stevenson, Paul) / I Can't Be Satisfied (Morganfield) / (I Can't Get No) Satisfaction / I'm Alright (McDaniel) / I'm Moving On (Snow) / It's All Over Now (Womack, Womack) / Little Red Rooster (Dixon) / Mercy Mercy (Covay, Miller) / Off the Hook (Nanker Phelge) / Oh Baby (We Got a Good Thing Goin') (Ozen) / One More Try / Pain in My Heart (Neville) / Play with Fire (Nanker Phelge) / Route 66 (Troup) / She Said Yeah (Christy, Jackson) / That's How Strong My Love Is (Jamison) / The Last Time / The Spider and the Fly (Nanker Phelge) / The Under-Assistant West Coast Promotion Man (Nanker Phelge) / Time Is on My Side (Meade) / Under the Boardwalk (Resnick, Young) / Walking the Dog (Thomas)

The Rolling Stones played these songs—not all at one gig, hopefully—in their shows from the beginning until the end of this year. Quite a few titles had been in the band's live shows since they began doing shows, for sure, but some of these tunes wouldn't be played again until the year was well under way, as typical sets later in 1965 indicate. Note that in the early '65 setlists "Everybody Needs Somebody to Love (Russell, Burke, Wexler) → Pain in My Heart (Neville), LMV" is a medley (LMV = Live Medley Version)—usually performed as a short take on "Everybody Needs Somebody to Love" sliding into "Pain in My Heart" at or near the beginning of a show. Generally, the band would reprise "Everybody Needs Somebody" later on in the performance, most of the time playing the song in its entirety as the finale or encore number. Also, they might make a medley out of "Everybody Needs Somebody to Love" and "Around & Around" as they did in April '65 at the Olympia in Paris. The first one (with "Pain in My Heart") was the more common of the medleys in 1965.

TYPICAL SET FOR EARLY 1965:   Everybody Needs Somebody to Love (Russell, Burke, Wexler) Pain in My Heart (Neville), LMV / Off the Hook (Nanker Phelge) / Route 66 (Troup) / Down the Road Apiece (Raye) / I'm Moving On (Snow) / Little Red Rooster (Dixon) / I'm Alright (McDaniel) / The Last Time / E: Everybody Needs Somebody to Love (Russell, Burke, Wexler)

JANUARY 6, 1965

VENUE: ABC Theatre, Belfast, Northern Ireland
NOTES: The first gig of 1965—they played two shows. This was the first of three Irish bookings in as many days.

See the band's 1965 setlist repertoire and a typical set for this year, above, for an idea of what they played; comparing 1965's with the last 1964 set wouldn't hurt, either. The Stones also appeared on Belfast television (see TELEVISION APPEARANCES) on this date, then left British-held Northern Ireland for Dublin and two days of shows.

JANUARY 7, 1965

VENUE: Adelphi Theatre, Dublin, Eire
NOTES: The Stones performed another two shows on the second day of their Irish jaunt.

JANUARY 8, 1965

VENUE: Savoy Theatre, Cork, Eire
NOTES: Two shows. The Stones would be returning to Ireland in September, for more gigs—and to be in their own movie. (See PROMOTIONAL FILMS AND VIDEOS)

JANUARY 10, 1965

VENUE: ABC Commodore Theatre, Hammersmith, London, England
OPENING/OTHER ACT(S): Zoot Money's Big Roll Band, Julie Grant, Marianne Faithfull, The Original Checkmates, Tony Jackson & the Vibrations, Tony Marsh, The Quiet Five
NOTES: Two shows, 5:45 P.M. and 8:15 P.M.; this Sunday gig was billed as the Stones' "only London appearance prior to their Australian tour."

JANUARY 22, 1965 – FEBRUARY 17, 1965

TOUR: 1965 Australia/Far East tour
VENUE: Australia, New Zealand and Singapore
PERSONNEL: Mick Jagger, Keith Richards, Brian Jones, Charlie Watts, Bill Wyman, Ian Stewart
OPENING/OTHER ACT(S): Roy Orbison, Rolf Harris, The Newbeats, Ray Columbus & the Invaders
SONGS: Not Fade Away (Petty, Hardin) / Walking the Dog (Thomas) / Under the Boardwalk (Resnick, Young) / Little Red Rooster (Dixon) / Around & Around (Berry) / Heart of Stone / Time Is on My Side (Meade) / **E:** It's All Over Now (Womack, Womack)
NOTES: The Stones' 1965 Australia/Far East tour setlists rarely differed from this basic lineup. "It's All Over Now" was played as the encore tune throughout the tour. These shows are a bit different from those done in the UK, Europe and the US. Tastes differed here, according to Brian Jones's reports published in *Melody Maker* during this tour. See January 25, 1965, below.

JANUARY 22, 1965

TOUR: 1965 Australia/Far East tour
VENUE: Manufacturers Auditorium, Agricultural Hall, Sydney, Australia
OPENING/OTHER ACT(S): Rolf Harris, The Newbeats
NOTES: Two shows. Roy Orbison had transportation problems (and/or laryngitis, depending on which reports one believes) and arrived in Australia too late to perform at this first gig, but opened for the Stones as scheduled from January 23 on.

JANUARY 23, 1965

TOUR: 1965 Australia/Far East tour
VENUE: Manufacturers Auditorium, Agricultural Hall, Sydney, Australia
OPENING/OTHER ACT(S): Roy Orbison, Rolf Harris, The Newbeats
NOTES: Afternoon show on this date. There were also two evening performances; see below.

JANUARY 23, 1965

TOUR: 1965 Australia/Far East tour
VENUE: Manufacturers Auditorium, Agricultural Hall, Sydney, Australia
OPENING/OTHER ACT(S): Roy Orbison, Rolf Harris, The Newbeats
NOTES: Two evening shows. These were in addition to an afternoon performance on the same day in the same place.

JANUARY 25, 1965

TOUR: 1965 Australia/Far East tour
VENUE: City Hall, Brisbane, Australia
OPENING/OTHER ACT(S): Roy Orbison, Rolf Harris, The Newbeats
SONGS Not Fade Away (Petty, Hardin) / Walking the Dog (Thomas) / Under the Boardwalk (Resnick, Young) / Little Red Rooster (Dixon) / Around & Around (Berry) / Heart of Stone / Time Is on My Side (Meade) / **E:** It's All Over Now (Womack, Womack)
NOTES: Two shows. With the headline "Stones Gas Aussies!", *Melody Maker* devoted the front page of its January 30, 1965 issue to the Stones in Australia. Much of the "coverage" consisted of quotes from a telephone conversation with Brian Jones. In the article entitled "Brian Jones Phones From Down Under," Brian reported from Brisbane that all five Sydney shows had been sellouts, that the Stones had played to 25,000 people in two days there, and that "the most popular number is 'Little Red Rooster,'" which Jones thought "funny considering we didn't want it released in any country except England!" "We've had a lot of singles out here," Brian was quoted

as saying, "even including 'Walking the Dog.'" Following Brisbane, the Stones returned to Sydney for two more shows, and it was then Jagger's turn to phone. *Melody Maker*'s next issue quoted Mick's audience totals—35,000 for seven shows in Sydney.

JANUARY 26, 1965

TOUR: 1965 Australia/Far East tour
VENUE: City Hall, Brisbane, Australia
OPENING/OTHER ACT(S): Roy Orbison, Rolf Harris, The Newbeats
NOTES: Two shows

JANUARY 27, 1965

TOUR: 1965 Australia/Far East tour
VENUE: Manufacturers Auditorium, Agricultural Hall, Sydney, Australia
OPENING/OTHER ACT(S): Roy Orbison, Rolf Harris, The Newbeats
NOTES: Two evening shows

JANUARY 28, 1965

TOUR: 1965 Australia/Far East tour
VENUE: Palais Theatre, St. Kilda, Melbourne, Australia
OPENING/OTHER ACT(S): Roy Orbison, Rolf Harris, The Newbeats
NOTES: Two shows

JANUARY 29, 1965

TOUR: 1965 Australia/Far East tour
VENUE: Palais Theatre, St. Kilda, Melbourne, Australia
OPENING/OTHER ACT(S): Roy Orbison, Rolf Harris, The Newbeats
NOTES: Afternoon show. And they did two more shows (see below) on this date, in the evening.

JANUARY 29, 1965

TOUR: 1965 Australia/Far East tour
VENUE: Palais Theatre, St. Kilda, Melbourne, Australia
OPENING/OTHER ACT(S): Roy Orbison, Rolf Harris, The Newbeats
NOTES: Two evening shows

FEBRUARY 1, 1965

TOUR: 1965 Australia/Far East tour
VENUE: Theatre Royal, Christchurch, New Zealand
OPENING/OTHER ACT(S): Roy Orbison, Rolf Harris, The Newbeats
NOTES: Two shows

FEBRUARY 2, 1965

TOUR: 1965 Australia/Far East tour
VENUE: Civic Theatre, Invercargill, New Zealand
OPENING/OTHER ACT(S): Roy Orbison, Rolf Harris, The Newbeats, The Echophones
NOTES: Two shows

FEBRUARY 3, 1965

TOUR: 1965 Australia/Far East tour
VENUE: Town Hall, Dunedin, New Zealand
OPENING/OTHER ACT(S): Roy Orbison, Rolf Harris, The Newbeats
NOTES: Two shows

FEBRUARY 6, 1965

TOUR: 1965 Australia/Far East tour
VENUE: Town Hall, Auckland, New Zealand
OPENING/OTHER ACT(S): Roy Orbison, Rolf Harris, The Newbeats
NOTES: Afternoon show. Plus two evening shows; see below.

FEBRUARY 6, 1965 (EVENING)

TOUR: 1965 Australia/Far East tour
VENUE: Town Hall, Auckland, New Zealand
OPENING/OTHER ACT(S): Roy Orbison, Rolf Harris, The Newbeats
NOTES: Two evening shows

FEBRUARY 8, 1965

TOUR: 1965 Australia/Far East tour
VENUE: Town Hall, Wellington, New Zealand
OPENING/OTHER ACT(S): Roy Orbison, Rolf Harris, The Newbeats
NOTES: Two shows

FEBRUARY 10, 1965

TOUR: 1965 Australia/Far East tour
VENUE: Palais Theatre, St. Kilda, Melbourne, Australia
OPENING/OTHER ACT(S): Roy Orbison, Rolf Harris, The Newbeats
NOTES: Two shows

FEBRUARY 12, 1965

TOUR: 1965 Australia/Far East tour
VENUE: Centennial Hall, Adelaide, Australia
OPENING/OTHER ACT(S): Roy Orbison, Rolf Harris, The Newbeats

NOTES: Two shows. These were the last shows on the tour for The Newbeats, who did not continue on to Perth with the tour.

FEBRUARY 13, 1965

TOUR: 1965 Australia/Far East tour
VENUE: Capitol Theatre, Perth, Australia
OPENING/OTHER ACT(S): Roy Orbison, Rolf Harris
NOTES: Afternoon show. In addition, the Stones did two evening shows here that day. The Newbeats were not on the bill after the Adelaide gig on February 12; Roy Orbison and Rolf Harris finished touring in Perth and didn't play Singapore.

FEBRUARY 13, 1965

TOUR: 1965 Australia/Far East tour
VENUE: Capitol Theatre, Perth, Australia
OPENING/OTHER ACT(S): Roy Orbison, Rolf Harris
NOTES: Two evening shows. On top of one that afternoon; see above.

FEBRUARY 16, 1965

TOUR: 1965 Australia/Far East tour
VENUE: Badminton Stadium, Singapore
OPENING/OTHER ACT(S): Sylvia Desayles, The Castaways
NOTES: Two shows. The last day of this tour, with two new opening acts.

MARCH 5, 1965 – MARCH 18, 1965

TOUR: Sixth British tour
VENUE: England
PERSONNEL: Mick Jagger, Keith Richards, Brian Jones, Charlie Watts, Bill Wyman, Ian Stewart
OPENING/OTHER ACT(S): The Konrads, Dave Berry & the Cruisers, The Hollies, The Original Checkmates, Goldie & the Gingerbreads, Johnny Ball (compère)
SONGS: Everybody Needs Somebody to Love (Russell, Burke, Wexler) → Pain in My Heart (Neville), LMV / Off the Hook (Nanker Phelge) / Route 66 (Troup), LV1 / Down the Road Apiece (Raye) / Time Is on My Side (Meade) / I'm Moving On (Snow) / Little Red Rooster (Dixon) / I'm Alright (McDaniel), LV1 / The Last Time / **E:** Everybody Needs Somebody to Love (Russell, Burke, Wexler)
NOTES: The Stones' EP, *Got Live If You Want It*, was recorded on this tour. These songs reflect all numbers played during this outing, though not necessarily in order. The Righteous Brothers had been booked to open for the Stones, but, citing a packed and conflicting schedule in the US, they cancelled out while the Stones were in the

Far East. The Hollies replaced the Righteous Brothers at the head of the pack of support acts. In fact, the way the program was arranged, The Konrads, then Dave Berry & the Cruisers opened for "special guests" the Hollies for the first section of the show. Then there was an intermission. The Original Checkmates opened the second half, then Goldie & the Gingerbreads played and, finally, the Stones came on and closed the show. There were two complete shows at each of the 14 consecutive stops on this tour.

MARCH 5, 1965

TOUR: Sixth British tour
VENUE: Regal Theatre, Edmonton, London, England
OPENING/OTHER ACT(S): The Konrads, Dave Berry & the Cruisers, The Hollies, The Original Checkmates, Goldie & the Gingerbreads, Johnny Ball (compère)
SONGS: Everybody Needs Somebody to Love (Russell, Burke, Wexler) → Pain in My Heart (Neville), LMV / Down the Road Apiece (Raye) / Time Is on My Side (Meade) / I'm Alright (McDaniel), LV1 / Little Red Rooster (Dixon) / Route 66 (Troup), LV1 / I'm Moving On (Snow) / The Last Time / **E:** Everybody Needs Somebody to Love (Russell, Burke, Wexler)
NOTES: First night of the sixth UK tour. Two shows. This was a typical setlist for the tour. The Stones played the entire "Everybody Needs Somebody to Love" as their encore (**E:**), performed much like the long version of the song on the band's second UK LP. (See DISCOGRAPHY and SESSIONOGRAPHY)

MARCH 6, 1965

TOUR: Sixth British tour
VENUE: Empire Theatre, Liverpool, Lancashire, England
OPENING/OTHER ACT(S): The Konrads, Dave Berry & the Cruisers, The Hollies, The Original Checkmates, Goldie & the Gingerbreads, Johnny Ball (compère)
SONGS: Everybody Needs Somebody to Love (Russell, Burke, Wexler) → Pain in My Heart (Neville), LMV / Down the Road Apiece (Raye) / Time Is on My Side (Meade) / I'm Alright (McDaniel) / Little Red Rooster (Dixon) / Route 66 (Troup) / I'm Moving On (Snow) / The Last Time / **E:** Everybody Needs Somebody to Love (Russell, Burke, Wexler)
NOTES: Two shows

MARCH 7, 1965

TOUR: Sixth British tour
VENUE: Palace Theatre, Manchester, Lancashire, England

OPENING/OTHER ACT(S): The Konrads, Dave Berry & the Cruisers, The Hollies, The Original Checkmates, Goldie & the Gingerbreads, Johnny Ball (compère)

SONGS: Everybody Needs Somebody to Love (Russell, Burke, Wexler) → Pain in My Heart (Neville), LMV / Down the Road Apiece (Raye) / Time Is on My Side (Meade) / I'm Alright (McDaniel) / Little Red Rooster (Dixon) / Route 66 (Troup) / I'm Moving On (Snow) / The Last Time / **E:** Everybody Needs Somebody to Love (Russell, Burke, Wexler)

NOTES: Two shows

MARCH 8, 1965

TOUR: Sixth British tour

VENUE: Futurist Theatre, Scarborough, Yorkshire, England

OPENING/OTHER ACT(S): The Konrads, Dave Berry & the Cruisers, The Hollies, The Original Checkmates, Goldie & the Gingerbreads, Johnny Ball (compère)

NOTES: Two shows

MARCH 9, 1965

TOUR: Sixth British tour

VENUE: Odeon Theatre, Sunderland, Durham, England

OPENING/OTHER ACT(S): The Konrads, Dave Berry & the Cruisers, The Hollies, The Original Checkmates, Goldie & the Gingerbreads, Johnny Ball (compère)

NOTES: Two shows

MARCH 10, 1965

TOUR: Sixth British tour

VENUE: ABC Theatre, Huddersfield, Yorkshire, England

OPENING/OTHER ACT(S): The Konrads, Dave Berry & the Cruisers, The Hollies, The Original Checkmates, Goldie & the Gingerbreads, Johnny Ball (compère)

NOTES: Two shows

MARCH 11, 1965

TOUR: Sixth British tour

VENUE: City Hall, Sheffield, Yorkshire, England

OPENING/OTHER ACT(S): The Konrads, Dave Berry & the Cruisers, The Hollies, The Original Checkmates, Goldie & the Gingerbreads, Johnny Ball (compère)

NOTES: Two shows

MARCH 12, 1965

TOUR: Sixth British tour

VENUE: Trocadero Theatre, Leicester, Leicestershire, England

OPENING/OTHER ACT(S): The Konrads, Dave Berry & the Cruisers, The Hollies, The Original Checkmates, Goldie & the Gingerbreads, Johnny Ball (compère)

NOTES: Two shows

MARCH 13, 1965

TOUR: Sixth British tour

VENUE: Granada Theatre, Rugby, Warwickshire, England

OPENING/OTHER ACT(S): The Konrads, Dave Berry & the Cruisers, The Hollies, The Original Checkmates, Goldie & the Gingerbreads, Johnny Ball (compère)

NOTES: Two shows

MARCH 14, 1965

TOUR: Sixth British tour

VENUE: Odeon Theatre, Rochester, Kent, England

OPENING/OTHER ACT(S): The Konrads, Dave Berry & the Cruisers, The Hollies, The Original Checkmates, Goldie & the Gingerbreads, Johnny Ball (compère)

NOTES: Two shows

MARCH 15, 1965

TOUR: Sixth British tour

VENUE: Odeon Theatre, Guildford, Surrey, England

OPENING/OTHER ACT(S): The Konrads, Dave Berry & the Cruisers, The Hollies, The Original Checkmates, Goldie & the Gingerbreads, Johnny Ball (compère)

NOTES: Two shows

MARCH 16, 1965

TOUR: Sixth British tour

VENUE: Granada Theatre, Greenford, Middlesex, England

OPENING/OTHER ACT(S): The Konrads, Dave Berry & the Cruisers, The Hollies, The Original Checkmates, Goldie & the Gingerbreads, Johnny Ball (compère)

NOTES: Two shows

MARCH 17, 1965

TOUR: Sixth British tour

VENUE: Odeon Theatre, Southend, Essex, England

OPENING/OTHER ACT(S): The Konrads, Dave Berry & the Cruisers, The Hollies, The Original Checkmates, Goldie & the Gingerbreads, Johnny Ball (compère)

NOTES: Two shows

MARCH 18, 1965

TOUR: Sixth British tour

VENUE: ABC Theatre, Romford, Essex, England

OPENING/OTHER ACT(S): The Konrads, Dave Berry & the Cruisers, The Hollies, The Original Checkmates, Goldie & the Gingerbreads, Johnny Ball (compère)
NOTES: Two shows. Last night of this tour. (See CHRONOLOGY for what happened on the way home.)

MARCH 26, 1965 – APRIL 18, 1965

TOUR: 1965 Scandinavia/France tour
VENUE: Denmark, Sweden and France
PERSONNEL: Mick Jagger, Keith Richards, Brian Jones, Charlie Watts, Bill Wyman, Ian Stewart
SONGS: Everybody Needs Somebody to Love (Russell, Burke, Wexler) → Around & Around (Berry), LMV / Time Is on My Side (Meade) / Tell Me / It's All Over Now (Womack, Womack) / Little Red Rooster (Dixon) / Route 66 (Troup) / The Last Time / E: I'm Alright (McDaniel)
NOTES: Individual concert setlists were drawn from the 1965 set repertoire and resembled those played on the sixth British tour, with a few interesting changes (see March 5, 1965 for comparison). Note that the New Musical Express (NME) Poll Winners Concert at Wembley falls within the dates of this tour.

MARCH 26, 1965

TOUR: 1965 Scandinavia/France tour
VENUE: Fyns Forum, Odense, Denmark
NOTES: Two shows

MARCH 28, 1965

TOUR: 1965 Scandinavia/France tour
VENUE: Koncert Sal, Tivoli Gardens, Copenhagen, Denmark
NOTES: Two shows

MARCH 30, 1965

TOUR: 1965 Scandinavia/France tour
VENUE: Koncert Sal, Tivoli Gardens, Copenhagen, Denmark
NOTES: Two shows

MARCH 31, 1965

TOUR: 1965 Scandinavia/France tour
VENUE: Masshallen, Gothenberg, Sweden
SONGS: Everybody Needs Somebody to Love (Russell, Burke, Wexler) / Tell Me / Around & Around (Berry) / Time Is on My Side (Meade) / It's All Over Now (Womack, Womack) / Little Red Rooster (Dixon) / Route 66 (Troup) / The Last Time
NOTES: Two shows

APRIL 1, 1965

TOUR: 1965 Scandinavia/France tour
VENUE: Kungliga Tennishallen, Stockholm, Sweden
NOTES: Two shows

APRIL 2, 1965

TOUR: 1965 Scandinavia/France tour
VENUE: Kungliga Tennishallen, Stockholm, Sweden

APRIL 11, 1965

VENUE: NME Poll Winners Concert, Empire Pool, Wembley, Middlesex, England
SONGS: Everybody Needs Somebody to Love (Russell, Burke, Wexler) → Pain in My Heart (Neville), LMV / Around & Around (Berry) / The Last Time / Everybody Needs Somebody to Love (Russell, Burke, Wexler)
NOTES: Afternoon show. "Everybody Needs Somebody to Love → Pain in My Heart" was a medley that the Stones often played to open shows at this time. They would usually close these performances with the complete version of "Everybody Needs Somebody to Love," as they did on this evening. Note that this gig fell within the dates of the 1965 Scandinavia/France tour, but was not actually part of it.

APRIL 16, 1965

TOUR: 1965 Scandinavia/France tour
VENUE: Olympia Theatre, Paris, France
NOTES: The first of three nights at L'Olympia. The entry below, for the second concert on April 17, 1965 includes a definitive setlist.

APRIL 17, 1965

TOUR: 1965 Scandinavia/France tour
VENUE: Olympia Theatre, Paris, France
SONGS: Everybody Needs Somebody to Love (Russell, Burke, Wexler) → Around & Around (Berry), LMV / Off the Hook (Nanker Phelge) / Time Is on My Side (Meade) / Carol (Berry) / It's All Over Now (Womack, Womack) / Little Red Rooster (Dixon) / Route 66 (Troup) / Everybody Needs Somebody to Love (Russell, Burke, Wexler) / The Last Time / I'm Alright (McDaniel) / Hey Crawdaddy (McDaniel)
NOTES: The actual setlist from this performance.

APRIL 18, 1965

TOUR: 1965 Scandinavia/France tour
VENUE: Olympia Theatre, Paris, France
NOTES: Last gig of the tour.

APRIL 23, 1965 – MAY 30, 1965

TOUR: Third North American tour
VENUE: US and Canada
PERSONNEL: Mick Jagger, Keith Richards, Brian Jones, Charlie Watts, Bill Wyman, Ian Stewart
OPENING/OTHER ACT(S): The Byrds, The Beach Boys, The Righteous Brothers, Marty Robbins & Skeeter Davis, Herman's Hermits, Little Anthony & the Imperials, Bobby Vee, Freddy Cannon, Reparata & the Delrons, Brenda Holloway, The Hondells, The Ikettes, Paul Revere & the Raiders
SONGS: Everybody Needs Somebody to Love (Russell, Burke, Wexler) → Around & Around (Berry), LMV / Off the Hook (Nanker Phelge) / Time Is on My Side (Meade) / Carol (Berry) / It's All Over Now (Womack, Womack) / Little Red Rooster (Dixon) / Route 66 (Troup) / Everybody Needs Somebody to Love (Russell, Burke, Wexler) / The Last Time
NOTES: Typical set for this tour. The long version of "Everybody Needs Somebody to Love" wasn't always the last song this time. Opening acts varied from city to city; though Herman's Hermits, Little Anthony & the Imperials, Bobby Vee, Freddy Cannon, Reparata & the Delrons, Brenda Holloway, The Hondells, and The Ikettes were part of the "Dick Clark's Caravan of Stars" package and opened only once for the Stones, in Philadelphia on May 1.

APRIL 23, 1965

TOUR: Third North American tour
VENUE: Maurice Richard Arena, Montreal, Canada
SONGS: Everybody Needs Somebody to Love (Russell, Burke, Wexler) → Around & Around (Berry), LMV / Off the Hook (Nanker Phelge) / Time Is on My Side (Meade) / Carol (Berry) / It's All Over Now (Womack, Womack) / Little Red Rooster (Dixon) / Route 66 (Troup) / Everybody Needs Somebody to Love (Russell, Burke, Wexler) / The Last Time
NOTES: The Stones' first gig in Canada, and their first set on the first night of the tour.

APRIL 24, 1965

TOUR: Third North American tour
VENUE: YMCA Auditorium, Ottawa, Ontario, Canada

APRIL 25, 1965

TOUR: Third North American tour
VENUE: Maple Leaf Gardens, Toronto, Ontario, Canada

APRIL 26, 1965

TOUR: Third North American tour

VENUE: Treasure Island Gardens, London, Ontario, Canada

APRIL 29, 1965

TOUR: Third North American tour
VENUE: Palace Theatre, Albany, NY, USA
NOTES: Two shows

APRIL 30, 1965

TOUR: Third North American tour
VENUE: Worcester Memorial Auditorium, Worcester, MA, USA

MAY 1, 1965

TOUR: Third North American tour
VENUE: Academy of Music, New York, NY, USA
NOTES: Afternoon show. Their evening show on this day was in Philadelphia.

MAY 1, 1965

TOUR: Third North American tour
VENUE: Convention Hall, Philadelphia, PA, USA
OPENING/OTHER ACT(S): (Dick Clark's Caravan of Stars) Herman's Hermits, Little Anthony & the Imperials, Bobby Vee, Freddy Cannon, Reparata & the Delrons, Brenda Holloway, The Hondells, The Ikettes, *et al.*
NOTES: Evening show. The Stones were a late addition to this bill, having been asked to add this appearance to their tour itinerary—reportedly to boost sagging ticket sales for this "Dick Clark's Caravan of Stars" show.

MAY 4, 1965

TOUR: Third North American tour
VENUE: Georgia Southern College Auditorium, Statesboro, GA, USA

MAY 6, 1965

TOUR: Third North American tour
VENUE: Jack Russell Stadium, Clearwater, FL, USA

MAY 7, 1965

TOUR: Third North American tour
VENUE: Legion Field Stadium, Birmingham, AL, USA
OPENING/OTHER ACT(S): The Beach Boys, The Righteous Brothers, Marty Robbins & Skeeter Davis

MAY 8, 1965

TOUR: Third North American tour
VENUE: Jacksonville Coliseum, Jacksonville, FL, USA

MAY 9, 1965

TOUR: Third North American tour
VENUE: Arie Crown Theatre, McCormick Place, Chicago, IL, USA

MAY 14, 1965

TOUR: Third North American tour
VENUE: New Civic Auditorium, San Francisco, CA, USA
OPENING/OTHER ACT(S): Paul Revere & the Raiders, The Byrds

MAY 15, 1965

TOUR: Third North American tour
VENUE: Swing Auditorium, San Bernardino, CA, USA

MAY 16, 1965

TOUR: Third North American tour
VENUE: Civic Auditorium, Long Beach Arena, Long Beach, CA, USA
OPENING/OTHER ACT(S): The Byrds
SONGS: Everybody Needs Somebody to Love (Russell, Burke, Wexler) → Around & Around (Berry), LMV / Off the Hook (Nanker Phelge) / Little Red Rooster (Dixon) / Time Is on My Side (Meade) / I'm Alright (McDaniel) / Pain in My Heart (Neville) / The Last Time
NOTES: Afternoon show. "Everybody Needs Somebody to Love → Around & Around, LMV" is the two-song medley the band used as an opener during this period.

MAY 17, 1965

TOUR: Third North American tour
VENUE: Convention Hall, Community Concourse, San Diego, CA, USA

MAY 21, 1965

TOUR: Third North American tour
VENUE: Civic Auditorium, San Jose, CA, USA

MAY 22, 1965

TOUR: Third North American tour
VENUE: Convention Hall, Ratcliffe Stadium, Fresno, CA, USA
NOTES: Afternoon show

MAY 22, 1965

TOUR: Third North American tour
VENUE: Sacramento Municipal Auditorium, Sacramento, CA, USA
NOTES: Evening show

MAY 29, 1965

TOUR: Third North American tour
VENUE: Academy of Music, New York, NY, USA
NOTES: Afternoon show

MAY 30, 1965

TOUR: Third North American tour
VENUE: Academy of Music, New York, NY, USA
NOTES: Two evening shows. The last night of the tour.

JUNE 15, 1965 – JUNE 29, 1965

TOUR: 1965 Scotland/Scandinavia tour
VENUE: Scotland, Norway, Finland, Denmark and Sweden
PERSONNEL: Mick Jagger, Keith Richards, Brian Jones, Charlie Watts, Bill Wyman, Ian Stewart
OPENING/OTHER ACT(S): (Scotland only) Moody Blues, The Hollies, The Cannon Brothers, The Checkmates
SONGS (SCOTLAND SET [NOT IN SEQUENCE]): Route 66 (Troup) / Pain in My Heart (Neville) / Little Red Rooster (Dixon) / Not Fade Away (Petty, Hardin) / It's All Over Now (Womack, Womack) / The Last Time / Play with Fire (Nanker Phelge) / Come On (Berry) / Off the Hook (Nanker Phelge)
NOTES: The Stones reportedly played the "Scotland Set" during the short Scottish portion of this tour. This information came from the band's own monthly magazine. What is most surprising is the inclusion of "Come On" in that list, a tune that band members have repeatedly denied ever playing again after 1963.

JUNE 15, 1965

TOUR: 1965 Scotland/Scandinavia tour
VENUE: Odeon Theatre, Glasgow, Scotland
OPENING/OTHER ACT(S): Moody Blues, The Hollies, The Cannon Brothers, The Checkmates
NOTES: Two shows

JUNE 16, 1965

TOUR: 1965 Scotland/Scandinavia tour
VENUE: Usher Hall, Edinburgh, Scotland
OPENING/OTHER ACT(S): Moody Blues, The Hollies, The Cannon Brothers, The Checkmates
NOTES: Two shows

JUNE 17, 1965

TOUR: 1965 Scotland/Scandinavia tour
VENUE: Caird Hall, Dundee, Scotland

OPENING/OTHER ACT(S): Moody Blues, The Hollies, The Cannon Brothers, The Checkmates
NOTES: Two shows

JUNE 18, 1965

TOUR: 1965 Scotland/Scandinavia tour
VENUE: Capitol Theatre, Aberdeen, Scotland
OPENING/OTHER ACT(S): Moody Blues, The Hollies, The Cannon Brothers, The Checkmates
NOTES: Two shows

JUNE 24, 1965

TOUR: 1965 Scotland/Scandinavia tour
VENUE: Messhallen, Oslo, Norway
OPENING/OTHER ACT(S): The Pussycats

JUNE 25, 1965

TOUR: 1965 Scotland/Scandinavia tour
VENUE: Yyteri Beach, Pori, Finland

JUNE 26, 1965

TOUR: 1965 Scotland/Scandinavia tour
VENUE: K. B. Hallen, Copenhagen, Denmark
NOTES: Two shows

JUNE 29, 1965

TOUR: 1965 Scotland/Scandinavia tour
VENUE: Baltiska Hallen, Malmö, Sweden
NOTES: Two shows. Last night of this tour.

JULY 16, 1965

VENUE: Odeon Theatre, Exeter, Devon, England
OPENING/OTHER ACT(S): The Walker Brothers, Steampacket, Elkie Brooks, Tommy Quickly, Thee
NOTES: Two shows

JULY 17, 1965

VENUE: The Guildhall, Portsmouth, Hampshire, England
OPENING/OTHER ACT(S): The Walker Brothers, Steampacket, Elkie Brooks
NOTES: Two shows

JULY 18, 1965

VENUE: Gaumont Theatre, Bournemouth, Hampshire, England
OPENING/OTHER ACT(S): The Paramounts, Steampacket, Twinkle
NOTES: Two shows

JULY 25, 1965

VENUE: ABC Theatre, Great Yarmouth, Norfolk, England
OPENING/OTHER ACT(S): The Walker Brothers, Steampacket, Elkie Brooks
NOTES: Two shows

AUGUST 1, 1965

VENUE: London Palladium, London, England
OPENING/OTHER ACT(S): The Quiet 5, Ray Cameron, Sugar Pie Desanto, The Fourmost, Steampacket, The Moody Blues, Julie Grant
NOTES: Two shows. Opening acts included American Blues and gospel singer, Sugar Pie Desanto.

AUGUST 22, 1965

VENUE: Futurist Theatre, Scarborough, Yorkshire, England
OPENING/OTHER ACT(S): The Walker Brothers, Steampacket, Elkie Brooks
NOTES: Two shows

SEPTEMBER 3, 1965 – SEPTEMBER 17, 1965

TOUR: 1965 Ireland/UK/West Germany/Austria tour
VENUE: Eire, Northern Ireland, Isle of Man, West Germany and Austria
PERSONNEL: Mick Jagger, Keith Richards, Brian Jones, Charlie Watts, Bill Wyman, Ian Stewart
NOTES: The short Irish portion of this tour, both on and offstage, was filmed by Peter Whitehead for the yet-to-be-released (as of writing) *Charlie Is My Darling*. (See below and also PROMOTIONAL FILMS AND VIDEOS)

SEPTEMBER 3, 1965

TOUR: 1965 Ireland/UK/West Germany/Austria tour
VENUE: Adelphi Theatre, Dublin, Eire
NOTES: Two shows. These performances and those of September 4 were filmed by Peter Whitehead for *Charlie Is My Darling*. The black-and-white documentary-style movie (á la *Hard Day's Night*) was never released by the band, though a 1997 official video/laserdisc of the film was rumored when we went to press. (See PROMOTIONAL FILMS AND VIDEOS)

SEPTEMBER 4, 1965

TOUR: 1965 Ireland/UK/West Germany/Austria tour
VENUE: ABC Theatre, Belfast, Northern Ireland
NOTES: Two shows. Filmed for *Charlie Is My Darling* by Peter Whitehead (see September 3, above).

SEPTEMBER 8, 1965

TOUR: 1965 Ireland/UK/West Germany/Austria tour
VENUE: Palace Ballroom, Douglas, Isle of Man, UK

SEPTEMBER 11, 1965

TOUR: 1965 Ireland/UK/West Germany/Austria tour
VENUE: Münsterland Halle, Münster, West Germany
NOTES: Two shows

SEPTEMBER 12, 1965

TOUR: 1965 Ireland/UK/West Germany/Austria tour
VENUE: Gruga Halle, Essen, West Germany
NOTES: Two shows

SEPTEMBER 13, 1965

TOUR: 1965 Ireland/UK/West Germany/Austria tour
VENUE: Ernst Merck Halle, Hamburg, West Germany
NOTES: Two shows

SEPTEMBER 14, 1965

TOUR: 1965 Ireland/UK/West Germany/Austria tour
VENUE: Circus-Krone-Bau, Munich, West Germany
NOTES: Two shows

SEPTEMBER 15, 1965

TOUR: 1965 Ireland/UK/West Germany/Austria tour
VENUE: Waldbühne Halle, West Berlin, West Germany
SONGS: Everybody Needs Somebody to Love (Russell, Burke, Wexler) → Pain in My Heart (Neville), LMV / Around & Around (Berry) / Time Is on My Side (Meade) / I'm Moving On (Snow) / The Last Time / (I Can't Get No) Satisfaction / I'm Alright (McDaniel)

SEPTEMBER 17, 1965

TOUR: 1965 Ireland/UK/West Germany/Austria tour
VENUE: Wiener Stadthalle, Vienna, Austria
NOTES: Last gig of tour.

SEPTEMBER 24, 1965 – OCTOBER 17, 1965

TOUR: Seventh British tour
VENUE: England, Scotland and Wales
PERSONNEL: Mick Jagger, Keith Richards, Brian Jones, Charlie Watts, Bill Wyman, Ian Stewart
OPENING/OTHER ACT(S): The End, The Original Checkmates, Unit 4 + 2, The Moody Blues, The Habits, Charles Dickens, Spencer Davis Group, Ray Cameron (compère)

SONGS: She Said Yeah (Christy, Jackson) / Mercy Mercy (Covay, Miller) / Cry to Me (Russell) / The Last Time / That's How Strong My Love Is (Jamison) / I'm Moving On (Snow) / Talkin' 'Bout You (Berry) / Hitch Hike (Gaye, Stevenson, Paul) / Oh Baby (We Got a Good Thing Goin') (Ozen) / (I Can't Get No) Satisfaction
NOTES: Rehearsals for this tour were held at Westbourne Grove. The above represents a master setlist for these gigs, based on those rehearsals. As the three weeks of engagements progressed, the band's show varied somewhat in the order and number of songs performed, but not a lot. The program at each performance was divided into two parts. Unit 4 + 2 closed the first half at all but the Hanley, Chester and Wigan dates, where they were replaced by the Moody Blues. After an intermission, the Habits opened the second half and the Stones closed the show.

SEPTEMBER 24, 1965

TOUR: Seventh British tour
VENUE: Astoria Theatre, Finsbury Park, London, England
OPENING/OTHER ACT(S): The End, The Original Checkmates, Unit 4 + 2, The Habits, Charles Dickens, Spencer Davis Group

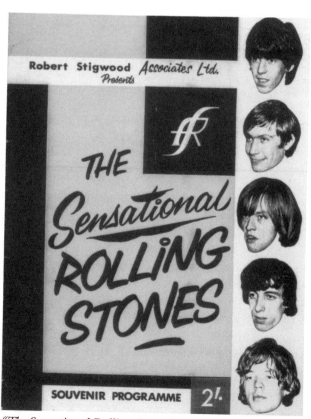

"The Sensational Rolling Stones" tour program from the 1965 UK tour, packaged by Robert Stigwood (TOM BEACH COLLECTION)

programme

The Management reserve to themselves the right to refuse admission to the theatre and to make any change, vary or omit any part of the programme without previous notice.

In accordance with the requirements of the local authority:
1.—The public may leave at the end of the performance or exhibitions by all exit doors and such doors must at that time be open. 2.—All gangways, corridors, staircases and external passageways intended for exit shall be kept entirely free from obstruction whether permanent or temporary. 3.—Persons shall not be permitted to stand or sit in any of the gangways intersecting the seating or to sit in any of the other gangways. If standing be permitted in the gangways at the sides and the rear of the seating, it shall be limited to the numbers indicated in notices exhibited in those positions. 4.—The safety curtain must be lowered and raised in the presence of each audience.

At HANLEY, CHESTER and WIGAN
UNIT FOUR + TWO
will be replaced by
THE MOODY BLUES

THE END

THE CHECKMATES

UNIT FOUR + 2

INTERVAL

THE HABITS

CHARLES DICKENS

SPENCER DAVIS GROUP

THE SENSATIONAL
ROLLING STONES

Compere - Ray Cameron

The inside of the official program for "The Sensational Rolling Stones" tour, packaged by Robert Stigwood (TOM BEACH COLLECTION)

SONGS: She Said Yeah (Christy, Jackson) / Mercy Mercy (Covay, Miller) / Cry to Me (Russell) / The Last Time / That's How Strong My Love Is (Jamison) / I'm Moving On (Snow) / Talkin' 'Bout You (Berry) / Oh Baby (We Got a Good Thing Goin') (Ozen) / (I Can't Get No) Satisfaction
NOTES: Two shows

SEPTEMBER 25, 1965

TOUR: Seventh British tour
VENUE: Gaumont Theatre, Southampton, Hampshire, England
OPENING/OTHER ACT(S): The End, The Original Checkmates, Unit 4 + 2, The Habits, Charles Dickens, Spencer Davis Group

NOTES: Two shows

SEPTEMBER 26, 1965

TOUR: Seventh British tour
VENUE: Colston Hall, Bristol, Gloucestershire, England
OPENING/OTHER ACT(S): The End, The Original Checkmates, Unit 4 + 2, The Habits, Charles Dickens, Spencer Davis Group
NOTES: Two shows

SEPTEMBER 27, 1965

TOUR: Seventh British tour
VENUE: Odeon Theatre, Cheltenham, Gloucestershire, England

OPENING/OTHER ACT(S):   The End, The Original Checkmates, Unit 4 + 2, The Habits, Charles Dickens, Spencer Davis Group
NOTES: Two shows

SEPTEMBER 28, 1965

TOUR: Seventh British tour
VENUE: Capitol Theatre, Cardiff, Wales
OPENING/OTHER ACT(S):   The End, The Original Checkmates, Unit 4 + 2, The Habits, Charles Dickens, Spencer Davis Group
SONGS: Hitch Hike (Gaye, Stevenson, Paul) / She Said Yeah (Christy, Jackson) / Oh Baby (We Got a Good Thing Goin') (Ozen) / Mercy Mercy (Covay, Miller) / Cry to Me (Russell) / That's How Strong My Love Is (Jamison) / The Last Time / I'm Moving On (Snow) / (I Can't Get No) Satisfaction
NOTES: Two shows

SEPTEMBER 29, 1965

TOUR: Seventh British tour
VENUE: Granada Theatre, Shrewsbury, Shropshire, England
OPENING/OTHER ACT(S):   The End, The Original Checkmates, Unit 4 + 2, The Habits, Charles Dickens, Spencer Davis Group
NOTES: Two shows

SEPTEMBER 30, 1965

TOUR: Seventh British tour
VENUE: Gaumont Theatre, Hanley, Staffordshire, England
OPENING/OTHER ACT(S):   The End, The Original Checkmates, The Moody Blues, The Habits, Charles Dickens, Spencer Davis Group
NOTES: Two shows. The Moody Blues replaced Unit 4 + 2 in the opening lineup at this gig and in Chester and Wigan.

OCTOBER 1, 1965

TOUR: Seventh British tour
VENUE: ABC Theatre, Chester, Cheshire, England
OPENING/OTHER ACT(S):   The End, The Original Checkmates, The Moody Blues, The Habits, Charles Dickens, Spencer Davis Group
NOTES: Two shows

OCTOBER 2, 1965

TOUR: Seventh British tour
VENUE: ABC Theatre, Wigan, Lancashire, England

OPENING/OTHER ACT(S):   The End, The Original Checkmates, The Moody Blues, The Habits, Charles Dickens, Spencer Davis Group
NOTES: Two shows

OCTOBER 3, 1965

TOUR: Seventh British tour
VENUE: Odeon Theatre, Manchester, Lancashire, England
OPENING/OTHER ACT(S):   The End, The Original Checkmates, Unit 4 + 2, The Habits, Charles Dickens, Spencer Davis Group
NOTES: Two shows. Keith was knocked unconscious by an unidentifeid flying object thrown from the audience and was carried offstage. He came back to finish the show.

OCTOBER 7, 1965

TOUR: Seventh British tour
VENUE: City Hall, Newcastle-upon-Tyne, Northumberland, England
OPENING/OTHER ACT(S):   The End, The Original Checkmates, Unit 4 + 2, The Habits, Charles Dickens, Spencer Davis Group
NOTES: Two shows

OCTOBER 8, 1965

TOUR: Seventh British tour
VENUE: ABC Theatre, Stockton-on-Tees, Durham, England
OPENING/OTHER ACT(S):   The End, The Original Checkmates, Unit 4 + 2, The Habits, Charles Dickens, Spencer Davis Group
NOTES: Two shows

OCTOBER 9, 1965

TOUR: Seventh British tour
VENUE: Odeon Theatre, Leeds, Yorksire, England
OPENING/OTHER ACT(S):   The End, The Original Checkmates, Unit 4 + 2, The Habits, Charles Dickens, Spencer Davis Group
NOTES: Two shows

OCTOBER 10, 1965

TOUR: Seventh British tour
VENUE: Empire Theatre, Liverpool, Lancashire, England
OPENING/OTHER ACT(S):   The End, The Original Checkmates, Unit 4 + 2, The Habits, Charles Dickens, Spencer Davis Group
NOTES: Two shows

OCTOBER 11, 1965

TOUR: Seventh British tour
VENUE: Gaumont Theatre, Sheffield, Yorkshire, England
OPENING/OTHER ACT(S): The End, The Original Checkmates, Unit 4 + 2, The Habits, Charles Dickens, Spencer Davis Group
NOTES: Two shows

OCTOBER 12, 1965

TOUR: Seventh British tour
VENUE: Gaumont Theatre, Doncaster, Yorkshire, England
OPENING/OTHER ACT(S): The End, The Original Checkmates, Unit 4 + 2, The Habits, Charles Dickens, Spencer Davis Group
NOTES: Two shows

OCTOBER 13, 1965

TOUR: Seventh British tour
VENUE: De Montfort Hall, Leicester, Leicestershire, England
OPENING/OTHER ACT(S): The End, The Original Checkmates, Unit 4 + 2, The Habits, Charles Dickens, Spencer Davis Group
NOTES: Two shows

OCTOBER 14, 1965

TOUR: Seventh British tour
VENUE: Odeon Theatre, Birmingham, Warwickshire, England
OPENING/OTHER ACT(S): The End, The Original Checkmates, Unit 4 + 2, The Habits, Charles Dickens, Spencer Davis Group
NOTES: Two shows

OCTOBER 15, 1965

TOUR: Seventh British tour
VENUE: Regal Theatre, Cambridge, Cambridgeshire, England
OPENING/OTHER ACT(S): The End, The Original Checkmates, Unit 4 + 2, The Habits, Charles Dickens, Spencer Davis Group
NOTES: Two shows

OCTOBER 16, 1965

TOUR: Seventh British tour
VENUE: ABC Theatre, Northampton, Northamptonshire, England
OPENING/OTHER ACT(S): The End, The Original Checkmates, Unit 4 + 2, The Habits, Charles Dickens, Spencer Davis Group
NOTES: Two shows

OCTOBER 17, 1965

TOUR: Seventh British tour
VENUE: Granada Theatre, Tooting, London, England
OPENING/OTHER ACT(S): The End, The Original Checkmates, Unit 4 + 2, The Habits, Charles Dickens, Spencer Davis Group
NOTES: Two shows. The last of this tour.

OCTOBER 29, 1965 – DECEMBER 6, 1965

TOUR: Fourth North American tour
VENUE: US and Canada
PERSONNEL: Mick Jagger, Keith Richards, Brian Jones, Charlie Watts, Bill Wyman, Ian Stewart
OPENING/OTHER ACT(S): Rockin' Ramrods, Patti LaBelle & the Blue Belles, The Vibrations, the Shangri-Las, The Catalinas, Zacherley (guest MC), Bo Diddley, The Righteous Brothers, The Byrds, We Five, Paul Revere & the Raiders
SONGS: She Said Yeah (Christy, Jackson) / Hitch Hike (Gaye, Stevenson, Paul) / Heart of Stone /Mercy Mercy (Covay, Miller) / That's How Strong My Love Is (Jamison) / Play With Fire (Nanker Phelge) / The Last Time / Good Times (Cooke) / Oh Baby (We Got a Good Thing Goin') (Ozen) / Get Off of My Cloud I'm Moving On (Snow) / (I Can't Get No) Satisfaction
PERFORMED: It's All over Now (Womack, Womack) / Talkin' Bout You (Berry) / I'm Alright (McDaniel)
NOTES: The basic tour setlist of 12 songs is listed above, followed by songs that were rotated into North American shows during fall '65. Multi-instrumentalist Brian Jones was featured on electric organ on "That's How Strong My Love Is," on harmonica on "Play with Fire," and on tambourine on "I'm Moving On."

OCTOBER 29, 1965

TOUR: Fourth North American tour
VENUE: Forum, Montreal, Quebec, Canada
OPENING/OTHER ACT(S): The Vibrations, Rockin' Ramrods, Patti LaBelle & the Blue Belles

OCTOBER 30, 1965

TOUR Fourth North American Tour
VENUE Barton Hall, Cornell University, Ithaca, NY, USA

OPENING/OTHER ACT(S)   Rockin' Ramrods, Patti La-
Belle & the Blue Belles
NOTES: Afternoon gig, the first of two performances in
the State of New York on October 30, 1965.

OCTOBER 30, 1965

TOUR: Fourth North American tour
VENUE: War Memorial Auditorium, Syracuse, NY, USA
OPENING/OTHER ACT(S):   Rockin' Ramrods, Patti La-
Belle & the Blue Belles
NOTES: Evening show, the second New York booking
on day two of the tour.

OCTOBER 31, 1965

TOUR: Fourth North American tour
VENUE: Maple Leaf Gardens, Toronto, Ontario, Canada
OPENING/OTHER ACT(S):   Rockin' Ramrods, Patti La-
Belle & the Blue Belles

NOVEMBER 1, 1965

TOUR: Fourth North American tour
VENUE: Memorial Auditorium, Rochester, NY, USA
OPENING/OTHER ACT(S):   Rockin' Ramrods, Patti La-
Belle & the Blue Belles
NOTES: Police stopped the show as nearly 3,000 fans
rushed the stage.

NOVEMBER 3, 1965

TOUR: Fourth North American tour
VENUE: The Public Auditorium, Providence, RI, USA
OPENING/OTHER ACT(S):   Rockin' Ramrods, Patti La-
Belle & the Blue Belles

NOVEMBER 4, 1965

TOUR: Fourth North American tour
VENUE: Loew's State Theater, New Haven, CT, USA
OPENING/OTHER ACT(S):   Rockin' Ramrods, Patti La-
Belle & the Blue Belles
NOTES: Two shows

NOVEMBER 5, 1965

TOUR: Fourth North American tour
VENUE: The Boston Garden, Boston, MA, USA
OPENING/OTHER ACT(S):   Rockin' Ramrods, Patti La-
Belle & the Blue Belles

NOVEMBER 6, 1965

TOUR: Fourth North American tour
VENUE: Academy of Music, New York, NY, USA

OPENING/OTHER ACT(S):   Rockin' Ramrods, Patti La-
Belle & the Blue Belles
NOTES: Afternoon gig the first of two performances in
two states that day.

NOVEMBER 6, 1965

TOUR: Fourth North American tour
VENUE: Convention Hall, Philadelphia, PA, USA
OPENING/OTHER ACT(S):   Bo Diddley, The Righteous
Brothers, The Byrds, We Five, Paul Revere & the Raiders,
The Vibrations, Patti LaBelle & the Blue Belles
NOTES: Evening engagement, their second show of the
day. A Dick Clark Caravan of Stars package date.

NOVEMBER 7, 1965

TOUR: Fourth North American tour
VENUE: Symphony Hall, Newark, NJ, USA
OPENING/OTHER ACT(S):   Patti LaBelle & the Blue
Belles, The Catalinas, Rockin' Ramrods, special guest
MC: Zacherley
NOTES: Two shows. Orchestra seats were $4.50 apiece
at the afternoon performance. The special guest M.C. was
a popular New Jersey radio DJ with an established cult
following. Zacherley (a.k.a. John K. Zacherle) had made
tristate-area fame on local television in the late
1950s/early 1960s as the satirical horror-movie host of
"Shock Theatre" and other programs. Some confusion
exists about this concert, because the venue, Symphony
Hall, is remembered by many as "The Mosque Theater."
That *was* its name. Apparently, the new name hadn't sunk
in at the time of the Stones' show. Even the October 1965
issue of *The Rolling Stones Book*, the band's monthly, listed
"The Mosque Theater" on their tour schedule. However,
the site was officially "Symphony Hall" on November 7,
1965, as concert tickets and press reports have confirmed.

NOVEMBER 10, 1965

TOUR: Fourth North American tour
VENUE: Reynolds Coliseum, Raleigh, NC, USA
OPENING/OTHER ACT(S):   Rockin' Ramrods, Patti La-
Belle & the Blue Belles

NOVEMBER 12, 1965

TOUR: Fourth North American tour
VENUE: Memorial Auditorium (War Memorial Hall),
Greensboro, NC, USA
OPENING/OTHER ACT(S):   Rockin' Ramrods, Patti La-
Belle & the Blue Belles

NOVEMBER 13, 1965

TOUR: Fourth North American tour

VENUE: Washington Coliseum, Washington, DC, USA
OPENING/OTHER ACT(S): Rockin' Ramrods, Patti La-Belle & the Blue Belles, The Vibrations
SONGS: Everybody Needs Somebody to Love (Russell, Burke, Wexler) / Play With Fire (Nanker Phelge) / Mercy Mercy (Covay, Miller) / Around & Around (Berry) / The Last Time / That' How Strong My Love Is (Jamison) / Get Off of My Cloud / **E:** (I Can't Get No) Satisfaction
NOTES: Afternoon gig. The evening show was in Baltimore.

NOVEMBER 13, 1965

TOUR: Fourth North American tour
VENUE: Baltimore Civic Centre, Baltimore, MD, USA
OPENING/OTHER ACT(S): Rockin' Ramrods, Patti La-Belle & the Blue Belles, The Vibrations
NOTES: Evening show

NOVEMBER 14, 1965

TOUR: Fourth North American tour
VENUE: Civic Coliseum Auditorium, Knoxville, TN, USA
OPENING/OTHER ACT(S): Rockin' Ramrods, Patti La-Belle & the Blue Belles

NOVEMBER 15, 1965

TOUR: Fourth North American tour
VENUE: The Coliseum, Charlotte, NC, USA
OPENING/OTHER ACT(S): Patti LaBelle & the Blue Belles

NOVEMBER 16, 1965

TOUR: Fourth North American tour
VENUE: Nashville Municipal Auditorium, Nashville, TN, USA
OPENING/OTHER ACT(S): Rockin' Ramrods, Patti La-Belle & the Blue Belles

NOVEMBER 17, 1965

TOUR: Fourth North American tour
VENUE: Mid-South Coliseum, Memphis, TN, USA
OPENING/OTHER ACT(S): Rockin' Ramrods, Patti La-Belle & the Blue Belles

NOVEMBER 20, 1965

TOUR: Fourth North American tour
VENUE: State Fair Youth Centre, Shreveport, LA, USA
OPENING/OTHER ACT(S): Rockin' Ramrods, Patti La-Belle & the Blue Belles

NOVEMBER 21, 1965

TOUR: Fourth North American tour
VENUE: Will Rogers Auditorium, Fort Worth, TX, USA
OPENING/OTHER ACT(S): Rockin' Ramrods, Patti La-Belle & the Blue Belles
NOTES: Afternoon gig

NOVEMBER 21, 1965

TOUR: Fourth North American tour
VENUE: Memorial Auditorium, Dallas, TX, USA
OPENING/OTHER ACT(S): Rockin' Ramrods, Patti La-Belle & the Blue Belles
NOTES Evening engagement

NOVEMBER 23, 1965

TOUR: Fourth North American tour
VENUE: Assembly Center, Tulsa, OK, USA
OPENING/OTHER ACT(S): Rockin' Ramrods, Patti La-Belle & the Blue Belles

NOVEMBER 24, 1965

TOUR: Fourth North American tour
VENUE: Civic Center Arena, Pittsburgh, PA, USA
OPENING/OTHER ACT(S): Rockin' Ramrods, Patti La-Belle & the Blue Belles

NOVEMBER 25, 1965

TOUR: Fourth North American tour
VENUE: Milwaukee Arena, Milwaukee, WI, USA
OPENING/OTHER ACT(S): Rockin' Ramrods, Patti La-Belle & the Blue Belles

NOVEMBER 26, 1965

TOUR: Fourth North American tour
VENUE: Cobo Hall, Detroit, MI, USA
OPENING/OTHER ACT(S): Rockin' Ramrods, Patti La-Belle & the Blue Belles, The Shangri-Las

NOVEMBER 27, 1965

TOUR: Fourth North American tour
VENUE: Hara Arena, Dayton, OH, USA
OPENING/OTHER ACT(S): Rockin' Ramrods, Patti La-Belle & the Blue Belles
NOTES: Afternoon gig

NOVEMBER 27, 1965

TOUR: Fourth North American tour
VENUE: The Cincinnati Garden, Cincinnati, OH, USA
OPENING/OTHER ACT(S): Rockin' Ramrods, Patti La-Belle & the Blue Belles

NOTES: Evening engagement

NOVEMBER 28, 1965

TOUR: Fourth North American tour
VENUE: Arie Crown Theatre, McCormick Place, Chicago, IL, USA
OPENING/OTHER ACT(S): Rockin' Ramrods, Patti La-Belle & the Blue Belles
NOTES: Two shows

NOVEMBER 29, 1965

TOUR: Fourth North American tour
VENUE: Denver Coliseum, Denver, CO, USA
OPENING/OTHER ACT(S): Rockin' Ramrods, Patti La-Belle & the Blue Belles

NOVEMBER 30, 1965

TOUR: Fourth North American tour
VENUE: Veterans Memorial Coliseum, Phoenix, AZ, USA
OPENING/OTHER ACT(S): Rockin' Ramrods, Patti La-Belle & the Blue Belles

DECEMER 1, 1965

TOUR: Fourth North American tour
VENUE: PNE Agrodome, Vancouver, British Columbia, Canada
OPENING/OTHER ACT(S): Rockin' Ramrods, Patti La-Belle & the Blue Belles

DECEMBER 2, 1965

TOUR: Fourth North American tour
VENUE: The Coliseum, Seattle, WA, USA
OPENING/OTHER ACT(S): Rockin' Ramrods, Patti La-Belle & the Blue Belles

DECEMBER 3, 1965

TOUR: Fourth North American tour
VENUE: Sacramento Memorial Auditorium, Sacramento, CA, USA
OPENING/OTHER ACT(S): Rockin' Ramrods, Patti La-Belle & the Blue Belles

DECEMBER 4, 1965

TOUR: Fourth North American tour
VENUE: San Jose Municipal Auditorium, San Jose, CA, USA
OPENING/OTHER ACT(S): Rockin' Ramrods, Patti La-Belle & the Blue Belles
NOTES: Two shows

DECEMBER 5, 1965

TOUR: Fourth North American tour
VENUE: Main Auditorium, Community Concourse, San Diego, CA, USA
OPENING/OTHER ACT(S): Rockin' Ramrods, Patti La-Belle & the Blue Belles
NOTES: Afternoon show

DECEMBER 5, 1965

TOUR: Fourth North American tour
VENUE: L. A. Sports Arena, Los Angeles, CA, USA
OPENING/OTHER ACT(S): Rockin' Ramrods, Patti La-Belle & the Blue Belles
NOTES: Evening performance. The last performance of this tour.

1966

1966 REPERTOIRE: Around & Around (Berry) / Doncha' Bother Me / Get Off of My Cloud / Have You Seen Your Mother, Baby, Standing in the Shadow? / (I Can't Get No) Satisfaction / I'm Alright (McDaniel) / I'm Moving On (Snow) / Lady Jane / Mercy Mercy (Covay, Miller) / Mother's Little Helper / 19th Nervous Breakdown / Not Fade Away (Petty, Hardin) / Paint It, Black / Play with Fire (Naker Phelge) / She Said Yeah (Christy, Jackson) / Stupid Girl / That's How Strong My Love Is (Jamison) / The Last Time / The Spider and the Fly (Nanker Phelge) / Time Is on My Side (Meade) / Under My Thumb

Individual concert set list—in the UK, Australia, New Zealand, Europe and North America—were taken from this group of songs.

FEBRUARY 18, 1966 – MARCH 2, 1966

TOUR: 1966 Australia/New Zealand tour
VENUE: Australia and New Zealand
PERSONNEL: Mick Jagger, Keith Richards, Brian Jones, Charlie Watts, Bill Wyman, Ian Stewart
OPENING/OTHER ACT(S): The Searchers, Max Merritt & the Meteors
SONGS: The Last Time / Mercy Mercy (Covay, Miller) / She Said Yeah (Christy, Jackson) / Play with Fire (Nanker Phelge) / Not Fade Away (Petty, Hardin) / The Spider and the Fly (Nanker Phlege) / That's How Strong My Love Is (Jamison) / Get Off of My Cloud / 19th Nervous Breakdown / I'm Moving On (Snow) / (I Can't Get No) Satisfaction
NOTES: This was a typical setlist for this tour.

FEBRUARY 18, 1966

TOUR: 1966 Australia/New Zealand tour

VENUE: Commemorative Auditorium, Showgrounds, Sydney, Australia

OPENING/OTHER ACT(S): The Searchers, Max Merritt & the Meteors

SONGS: Mercy Mercy (Covay, Miller) / She Said Yeah (Christy, Jackson) / Play with Fire (Nanker Phelge) / Not Fade Away (Petty, Hardin) / The Spider and the Fly (Nanker Phelge) / That's How Strong My Love Is (Jamison)

NOTES: Two shows. The list of songs consitutes a confirmed portion of the show.

FEBRUARY 19, 1966

TOUR: 1966 Australia/New Zealand tour

VENUE: Commemorative Auditorium, Showgrounds, Sydney, Australia

OPENING/OTHER ACT(S): The Searchers, Max Merritt & the Meteors

NOTES: Afternoon show

FEBRUARY 19, 1966

TOUR: 1966 Australia/New Zealand tour

VENUE: Commemorative Auditorium, Showgrounds, Sydney, Australia

OPENING/OTHER ACT(S): The Searchers, Max Merritt & the Meteors

NOTES: Two evening shows

FEBRUARY 21, 1966

TOUR: 1966 Australia/New Zealand tour

VENUE: City Hall, Brisbane, Australia

OPENING/OTHER ACT(S): The Searchers, Max Merritt & the Meteors

NOTES: Two shows

FEBRUARY 22, 1966

TOUR: 1966 Australia/New Zealand tour

VENUE: Centennial Hall, Adelaide, Australia

OPENING/OTHER ACT(S): The Searchers, Max Merritt & the Meteors

FEBRUARY 24, 1966

TOUR: 1966 Australia/New Zealand tour

VENUE: Palais Theatre, St. Kilda, Melbourne, Australia

OPENING/OTHER ACT(S): The Searchers, Max Merritt & the Meteors

NOTES: Two shows

FEBRUARY 25, 1966

TOUR: 1966 Australia/New Zealand tour

VENUE: Palais Theatre, St. Kilda, Melbourne, Australia

OPENING/OTHER ACT(S): The Searchers, Max Merritt & the Meteors

NOTES: Two shows

FEBRUARY 26, 1966

TOUR: 1966 Australia/New Zealand tour

VENUE: Palais Theatre, St. Kilda, Melbourne, Australia

OPENING/OTHER ACT(S): The Searchers, Max Merritt & the Meteors

NOTES: Two shows

FEBRUARY 28, 1966

TOUR: 1966 Australia/New Zealand tour

VENUE: Town Hall, Wellington, New Zealand

OPENING/OTHER ACT(S): The Searchers, Max Merritt & the Meteors

NOTES: Two shows

MARCH 1, 1966

TOUR: 1966 Australia/New Zealand tour

VENUE: Civic Theatre, Auckland, New Zealand

OPENING/OTHER ACT(S): The Searchers, Max Merritt & the Meteors

MARCH 2, 1966

TOUR: 1966 Australia/New Zealand tour

VENUE: Capitol Theatre, Perth, Australia

OPENING/OTHER ACT(S): The Searchers, Max Merritt & the Meteors

NOTES: Last night of this tour.

MARCH 26, 1966 – APRIL 5, 1966

TOUR: 1966 European tour

VENUE: Holland, Belgium, France, Sweden and Denmark

PERSONNEL: Mick Jagger, Keith Richards, Brian Jones, Charlie Watts, Bill Wyman, Ian Stewart

OPENING/OTHER ACT(S): Wayne Fontana & the Mindbenders, Ian Whitcomb, Chuck Berry

SONGS: The Last Time / Mercy Mercy (Covay, Miller) / She Said Yeah (Christy, Jackson) / Play with Fire (Nanker Phelge) / Not Fade Away (Petty, Hardin) / That's How Strong My Love Is (Jamison) / I'm Moving On (Snow) / The Spider and the Fly (Nanker Phelge) / Time Is on My Side (Meade) / 19th Nervous Breakdown / Around & Around (Berry) / Get Off of My Cloud / I'm Alright (McDaniel) / (I Can't Get No) Satisfaction

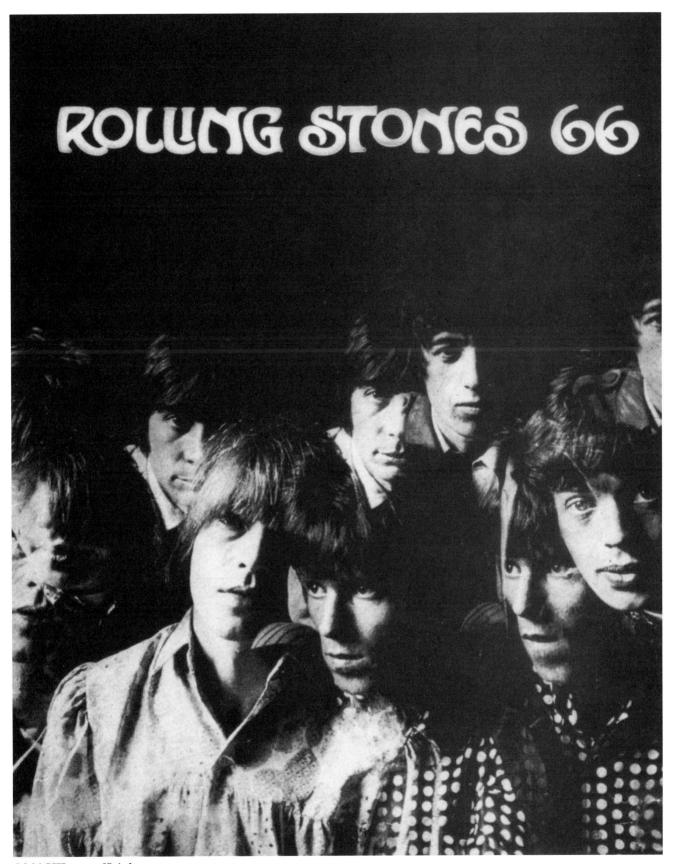

1966 UK tour official program (TOM BEACH COLLECTION)

NOTES: This was a typical setlist for this tour. See March 29, 1966, below.

MARCH 26, 1966

TOUR: 1966 European tour
VENUE: Brabant Hall, Den Bosche, The Hague, Holland

MARCH 27, 1966

TOUR: 1966 European tour
VENUE: Palais des Sports, Brussels, Belgium

MARCH 29, 1966

TOUR: 1966 European tour
VENUE: Olympia Theatre, Paris, France
OPENING/OTHER ACT(S): Wayne Fontana & the Mindbenders, Ian Whitcomb
SONGS: The Last Time / Mercy Mercy (Covay, Miller) / She Said Yeah (Christy, Jackson) / Play with Fire (Nanker Phelge) / Not Fade Away (Petty, Hardin) / That's How Strong My Love Is (Jamison) / I'm Moving On (Snow) / The Spider and the Fly (Nanker Phelge) / Time Is on My Side (Meade) / 19th Nervous Breakdown / Around & Around (Berry) / Get Off of My Cloud / I'm Alright (McDaniel) / (I Can't Get No) Satisfaction
NOTES: The Stones played two shows on this date at L'Olympia. This was their Paris setlist.

MARCH 30, 1966

TOUR: 1966 European tour
VENUE: Salle Vallier, Marseilles, France
OPENING/OTHER ACT(S): Chuck Berry
NOTES: Chuck Berry opened here only.

MARCH 31, 1966

TOUR: 1966 European tour
VENUE: Palais d'Hiver, Lyon, France
NOTES: Two shows

APRIL 3, 1966

TOUR: 1966 European tour
VENUE: Kungliga Tennishallen, Stockholm, Sweden
NOTES: Two shows

APRIL 5, 1966

TOUR: 1966 European tour
VENUE: K. B. Hallen, Copenhagen, Denmark
NOTES: Two shows. The last night of this tour.

MAY 1, 1966

VENUE: NME Poll Winners Concert, Empire Pool, Wembley, Middlesex, England
OTHER ACT(S): The Beatles; Spencer Davis Group; Dave Dee; Dozy, Beary, Mick & Tich; The Fortunes; Roy Orbison; The Overlanders; The Alan Price Set; Cliff Richard; The Seekers; The Shadows; Sounds, Inc.; Dusty Springfield; Crispian St. Peters; The Walker Brothers; The Who; The Yardbirds; Herman's Hermits
SONGS: Play with Fire (Nanker Phelge) / (I Can't Get No) Satisfaction / Paint It, Black
NOTES: Afternoon show. The "Other Acts" listed above were the honorees who performed at this conert. Due to contractual disagreements, the Stones and the Beatles asked that the BBC's cameras be turned off during their performances and the entire musical program was not filmed as it normally would have been.

JUNE 24, 1966 – JULY 28, 1966

TOUR: Fifth North American tour
VENUE: US and Canada
PERSONNEL: Mick Jagger, Keith Richards, Brian Jones, Charlie Watts, Bill Wyman, Ian Stewart
OPENING/OTHER ACT(S): The Standells, The McCoys, The Tradewinds, Buffalo Springfield, The Byrds, Richie & the Renegades
SONGS: Not Fade Away (Petty, Hardin) / The Last Time / Paint It, Black / Stupid Girl / Lady Jane / The Spider and the Fly (Nanker Phelge) / Mother's Little Helper / Get Off of My Cloud / 19th Nervous Breakdown / E: (I Can't Get No) Satisfaction
ALSO PERFORMED: Under My Thumb / Play with Fire (Nanker Phelge) / Doncha' Bother Me
NOTES: The group of songs above reflects the Stones' typical 1966 US tour setlist; the three additional songs were rotated into their performance at some shows along the route. Buffalo Springfield and the Byrds performed only in California, while Richie & the Renegades were only part of the lineup at the first gig.

JUNE 24, 1966

TOUR: Fifth North American tour
VENUE: Manning Bowl, Lynn, MA, USA
OPENING/OTHER ACT(S): The Standells, Riche & the Renegades, The Tradewinds
SONGS: Not Fade Away (Petty, Hardin) / The Last Time / Paint It, Black / Stupid Girl / Lady Jane / The Spider and the Fly (Nanker Phelge) / Mother's Little Helper / Get Off of My Cloud / 19th Nervous Breakdown / E: (I Can't Get No) Satisfaction

NOTES: This is the actual setlist from this concert. Richie & the Renegades, a local band, joined the opening lineup at the Manning Bowl.

JUNE 25, 1966

TOUR: Fifth North American tour
VENUE: Civic Center Arena, Pittsburgh, PA, USA
OPENING/OTHER ACT(S): The Standells, The McCoys, The Tradewinds
NOTES: Evening show

JUNE 26, 1966

TOUR: Fifth North American tour
VENUE: Urhlien Arena (a.k.a. the Washington Coliseum), Washington, DC, USA

OPENING/OTHER ACT(S): The Standells, The McCoys, The Tradewinds
NOTES: Afternoon show. There was an evening gig, too —in Baltimore.

JUNE 26, 1966

TOUR: Fifth North American tour
VENUE: Baltimore Civic Centre, Baltimore, MD, USA
OPENING/OTHER ACT(S): The Standells, The McCoys, The Tradewinds
NOTES: Evening show

JUNE 27, 1966

TOUR: Fifth North American tour
VENUE: Dillon Stadium, Hartford, CT, USA

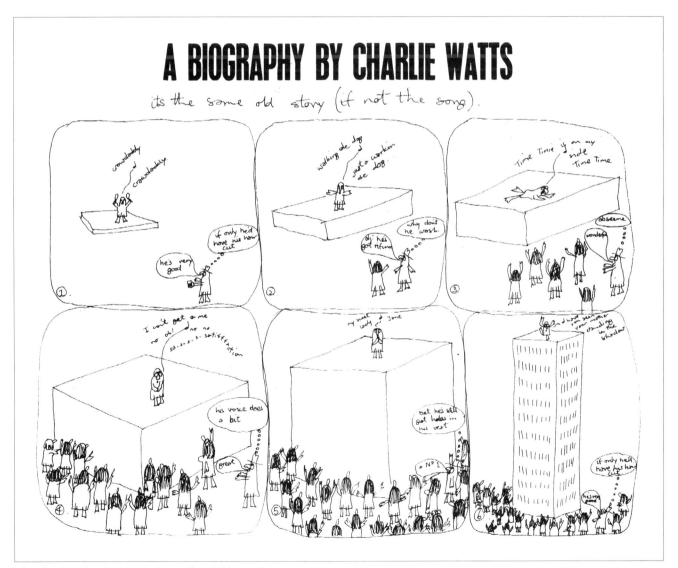

Sketches by Charlie Watts, from the 1966 tour program (TOM BEACH COLLECTION)

OPENING/OTHER ACT(S): The Standells, The McCoys, The Tradewinds

JUNE 28, 1966

TOUR: Fifth North American tour

VENUE: War Memorial Auditorium Buffalo, NY, USA

OPENING/OTHER ACT(S): The Standells, The McCoys, The Tradewinds

JUNE 29, 1966

TOUR: Fifth North American tour

VENUE: Maple Leaf Gardens, Toronto, Ontario, Canada

OPENING/OTHER ACT(S): The Standells, The McCoys, The Tradewinds

JUNE 30, 1966

TOUR: Fifth North American tour

VENUE: Forum, Montreal, Quebec, Canada

OPENING/OTHER ACT(S): The Standells, The McCoys, The Tradewinds

JULY 1, 1966

TOUR: Fifth North American tour

VENUE: Marine Ballroom, Steel Pier, Atlantic City, NJ, USA

OPENING/OTHER ACT(S): The Standells, The McCoys, The Tradewinds

JULY 2, 1966

TOUR: Fifth North American tour

VENUE: Forest Hills Tennis Stadium, Queens, NY, USA

OPENING/OTHER ACT(S): The Standells, The McCoys, The Tradewinds

SONGS: Not Fade Away (Petty, Hardin) / The Last Time / Paint It, Black / Under My Thumb / Lady Jane / The Spider and the Fly (Nanker Phelge) / Mother's Little Helper / Get Off of My Cloud / 19th Nervous Breakdown / E: (I Can't Get No) Satisfaction

NOTES: This is the setlist from the Stones' 1966 concert at Forest Hills Tennis Stadium, perhaps better known as the site of the US Open.

JULY 3, 1966

TOUR: Fifth North American tour

VENUE: Convention Hall, Asbury Park, NJ, USA

OPENING/OTHER ACT(S): The Standells, The McCoys, The Tradewinds

JULY 4, 1966

TOUR: Fifth North American tour

VENUE: The Virginia Beach Dome, Virginia Beach, VA, USA

OPENING/OTHER ACT(S): The Standells, The McCoys, The Tradewinds

SONGS: Not Fade Away (Petty, Hardin) / The Last Time / Paint It, Black / Lady Jane / Doncha' Bother Me / Mother's Little Helper / Get Off of My Cloud / 19th Nervous Breakdown / E: (I Can't Get No) Satisfaction

NOTES: This is the setlist from Virginia Beach, 1966.

JULY 6 1966

TOUR: Fifth North American tour

VENUE: War Memorial Hall, Syracuse, NY, USA

OPENING/OTHER ACT(S): The Standells, The McCoys, The Tradewinds

JULY 8, 1966

TOUR: Fifth North American tour

VENUE: Cobo Hall, Detroit, MI, USA

OPENING/OTHER ACT(S): The Standells, The McCoys, The Tradewinds

JULY 9, 1966

TOUR: Fifth North American tour

VENUE: Indiana State Fairgrounds Coliseum, Indianapolis, IN, USA

OPENING/OTHER ACT(S): The Standells, The McCoys, The Tradewinds

JULY 10, 1966

TOUR: Fifth North American tour

VENUE: Arie Crown Theatre, McCormick Place, Chicago, IL, USA

PERSONNEL: Mick Jagger, Keith Richards, Charlie Watts, Bill Wyman, Ian Stewart

OPENING/OTHER ACT(S): The Standells, The McCoys, The Tradewinds

NOTES: Brian Jones was ill and did not appear at the Stones' Chicago concert in 1966.

JULY 11, 1966

TOUR: Fifth North American tour

VENUE: Sam Houston Coliseum, Houston, TX, USA

PERSONNEL: Mick Jagger, Keith Richards, Brian Jones, Charlie Watts, Bill Wyman, Ian Stewart

OPENING/OTHER ACT(S): The Standells, The McCoys, The Tradewinds

JULY 12, 1966

TOUR: Fifth North American tour
VENUE: Kiel Convention Hall, St. Louis, MO, USA
OPENING/OTHER ACT(S): The Standells, The McCoys, The Tradewinds

JULY 14, 1966

TOUR: Fifth North American tour
VENUE: Winnipeg Stadium, Winnipeg, Manitoba, Canada
OPENING/OTHER ACT(S): The Standells, The McCoys, The Tradewinds

JULY 15, 1966

TOUR: Fifth North American tour
VENUE: Omaha Civic Auditorium, Omaha, NE, USA
OPENING/OTHER ACT(S): The Standells, The McCoys, The Tradewinds

JULY 19, 1966

TOUR: Fifth North American tour
VENUE: Pacific National Exhibition Forum Park, Vancouver, British Columbia, Canada
OPENING/OTHER ACT(S): The Standells, The McCoys, The Tradewinds

JULY 20, 1966

TOUR: Fifth North American tour
VENUE: Seattle Coliseum, Seattle, WA, USA
OPENING/OTHER ACT(S): The Standells, The McCoys, The Tradewinds

JULY 21, 1966

TOUR: Fifth North American tour
VENUE: Memorial Coliseum, Portland, OR, USA
OPENING/OTHER ACT(S): The Standells, The McCoys, The Tradewinds

JULY 22, 1966

TOUR: Fifth North American tour
VENUE: Sacramento Memorial Auditorium Sacramento, CA, USA
OPENING/OTHER ACT(S): The Standells, The McCoys, The Tradewinds

JULY 23, 1966

TOUR: Fifth North American tour
VENUE: The Davis County Lagoon, Salt Lake City, UT, USA
OPENING/OTHER ACT(S): The Standells, The McCoys, The Tradewinds
NOTES: Afternoon show

JULY 24, 1966

TOUR: Fifth North American tour
VENUE: Bakersfield Civic Auditorium, Bakersfield, CA, USA
OPENING/OTHER ACT(S): The Standells, The McCoys, The Tradewinds
NOTES: Two shows

JULY 25, 1966

TOUR: Fifth North American tour
VENUE: Hollywood Bowl, Los Angeles, CA, USA
OPENING/OTHER ACT(S): Buffalo Springfield, The Byrds, The Standells, The McCoys, The Tradewinds

JULY 26, 1966

TOUR: Fifth North American tour
VENUE: Cow Palace, San Francisco, CA, USA
OPENING/OTHER ACT(S): The Byrds, The Standells, The McCoys, The Tradewinds

JULY 28, 1966

TOUR: Fifth North American tour
VENUE: International Sports Centre, Honolulu, HI, USA
SONGS: Not Fade Away (Petty, Hardin) / The Last Time / Paint It, Black / Under My Thumb / Lady Jane / Play with Fire (Nanker Phelge) / Mother's Little Helper / Get Off of My Cloud / 19th Nervous Breakdown / E: (I Can't Get No) Satisfaction
NOTES: Last gig of tour, and Brian Jones's last US performance. An airline strike kept them all island-bound for several days after the gig; the band was forced (!) to hang out in Hawaii a bit longer before returing to Los Angeles.

SEPTEMBER 23, 1966 – OCTOBER 9, 1966

TOUR: Eighth British tour
VENUE England, Scotland and Wales
PERSONNEL: Mick Jagger, Keith Richards, Brian Jones, Charlie Watts, Bill Wyman, Ian Stewart
OPENING/OTHER ACT(S): Ike & Tina Turner & the Ikettes, The Yardbirds, Peter Jay & the New Jaywalkers, The Kings of Rhythm Orchestra, Jimmy Thomas, Bobby John, Long John Baldry

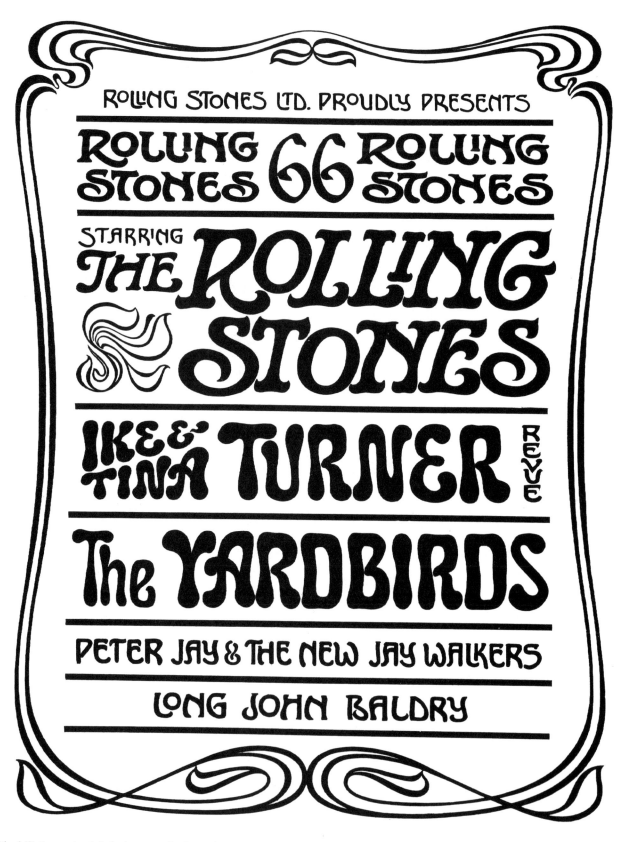

ROLLING STONES LTD. PROUDLY PRESENTS

ROLLING STONES 66 ROLLING STONES

STARRING THE ROLLING STONES

IKE & TINA TURNER REVUE

The YARDBIRDS

PETER JAY & THE NEW JAY WALKERS

LONG JOHN BALDRY

The bill for each night's show on the Stones' 1966 tour, from the official program (TOM BEACH COLLECTION)

SONGS: The Last Time / Meercy Mercy (Covay, Miller) / She Said Yeah (Christy, Jackson) / Play with Fire (Nanker Phelge) / Not Fade Away (Petty, Hardin) / That's How Strong My Love Is (Jamison) / I'm Moving On (Snow) / The Spider and the Fly (Nanker Phelge) / Time Is on My Side (Meade) / 19th Nervous Breakdown / Around & Around (Berry) / Get Off of My Cloud / I'm Alright (McDaniel) / (I Can't Get No) Satisfaction / Paint It, Black / Mother's Little Helper / Lady Jane / Under My Thumb / Have You Seen Your Mother, Baby, Standing in the Shadow?

NOTES: Sets came from this list. On this tour, Charlie Watts introduced "Lady Jane."

SEPTEMBER 23, 1966

TOUR: Eighth British tour

VENUE: Royal Albert Hall, London, England

OPENING/OTHER ACT(S): Ike & Tina Turner & the Ikettes, The Yardbirds, Peter Jay & the New Jaywalkers, The Kings of Rhythm Orchestra, Jimmy Thomas, Bobby John, Long John Baldry

NOTES: First night of tour. The Royal Albert Hall has quite a history of its own, and for the Stones it has been the site of a couple of important occasions in their career. The first time the band entered the hall on April 18, 1963, they were guests of the Beatles but posed as their roadies and carried their guitars in a ploy to come backstage (and not have to pay for tickets). The Stones weren't nearly as famous as the Beatles then and had their first experience with a fan frenzy that night when Brian Jones was attacked at the stage door by a fan who mistook him for one of Fab Four.

September 23, 1966 was not the first time the Stones had headlined a show at the Albert Hall, but the concert that night was filmed and recorded for the first time. The audio became part of their first live LP, *Got Live If You Want It!*, and the film ended up as part of the promo for the UK "Have You Seen Your Mother, Baby?" single. Both of these live performance products helped show the Stones in a new perspective, which couldn't be captured in a studio LP.

SEPTEMBER 24, 1966

TOUR: Eighth British tour

VENUE: Odeon Theatre, Leeds, Yorkshire, England

OPENING/OTHER ACT(S): Ike & Tina Turner & the Ikettes, The Yardbirds, Peter Jay & the New Jaywalkers, The Kings of Rhythm Orchestra, Jimmy Thomas, Bobby John, Long John Baldry

NOTES: Two shows

SEPTEMBER 25, 1966

TOUR: Eighth British tour

VENUE: Empire Theatre, Liverpool, Lancashire, England

OPENING/OTHER ACT(S): Ike & Tina Turner & the Ikettes, The Yardbirds, Peter Jay & the New Jaywalkers, The Kings of Rhythm Orchestra, Jimmy Thomas, Bobby John, Long John Baldry

NOTES: Two shows

SEPTEMBER 28, 1966

TOUR: Eighth British tour

VENUE: ABC Theatre, Ardwick, Manchester, Lancashire, England

OPENING/OTHER ACT(S): Ike & Tina Turner & the Ikettes, The Yardbirds, Peter Jay & the New Jaywalkers, The Kings of Rhythm Orchestra, Jimmy Thomas, Bobby John, Long John Baldry

NOTES: Two shows

SEPTEMBER 29, 1966

TOUR: Eighth British tour

VENUE: ABC Theatre, Stockton-on-Tees, Durham, England

OPENING/OTHER ACT(S): Ike & Tina Turner & the Ikettes, The Yardbirds, Peter Jay & the New Jaywalkers, The Kings of Rhythm Orchestra, Jimmy Thomas, Bobby John, Long John Baldry

NOTES: Two shows

SEPTEMBER 30, 1966

TOUR: Eighth British tour

VENUE: Odeon Theatre, Glasgow, Scotland

OPENING/OTHER ACT(S): Ike & Tina Turner & the Ikettes, The Yardbirds, Peter Jay & the New Jaywalkers, The Kings of Rhythm Orchestra, Jimmy Thomas, Bobby John, Long John Baldry

NOTES: Two shows

OCTOBER 1, 1966

TOUR: Eighth British tour

VENUE: City Hall, Newcastle-upon-Tyne, Northumberland, England

OPENING/OTHER ACT(S): Ike & Tina Turner & the Ikettes, The Yardbirds, Peter Jay & the New Jaywalkers, The Kings of Rhythm Orchestra, Jimmy Thomas, Bobby John, Long John Baldry

NOTES: Two shows

OCTOBER 2, 1966

TOUR: Eighth British tour
VENUE: Gaumont Theatre, Ipswich, Suffolk, England
OPENING/OTHER ACT(S): Ike & Tina Turner & the Ikettes, The Yardbirds, Peter Jay & the New Jaywalkers, The Kings of Rhythm Orchestra, Jimmy Thomas, Bobby John, Long John Baldry
NOTES: Two shows

OCTOBER 6, 1966

TOUR: Eighth British tour
VENUE: Odeon Theatre, Birmingham, Warwickshire, England
OPENING/OTHER ACT(S): Ike & Tina Turner & the Ikettes, The Yardbirds, Peter Jay & the New Jaywalkers, The Kings of Rhythm Orchestra, Jimmy Thomas, Bobby John, Long John Baldry
NOTES: Two shows

OCTOBER 7, 1966

TOUR: Eighth British tour
VENUE: Colston Hall, Bristol, Gloucestershire, England
OPENING/OTHER ACT(S): Ike & Tina Turner & the Ikettes, The Yardbirds, Peter Jay & the New Jaywalkers, The Kings of Rhythm Orchestra, Jimmy Thomas, Bobby John, Long John Baldry
NOTES: Two shows

OCTOBER 8, 1966

TOUR: Eighth British tour
VENUE: Capitol Theatre, Cardiff, Wales
OPENING/OTHER ACT(S): Ike & Tina Turner & the Ikettes, The Yardbirds, Peter Jay & the New Jaywalkers, The Kings of Rhythm Orchestra, Jimmy Thomas, Bobby John, Long John Baldry
NOTES: Two shows

OCTOBER 9, 1966

TOUR: Eighth British tour
VENUE: Gaumont Theatre, Southampton, Hampshire, England
OPENING/OTHER ACT(S): Ike & Tina Turner & the Ikettes, The Yardbirds, Peter Jay & the New Jaywalkers, The Kings of Rhythm Orchestra, Jimmy Thomas, Bobby John, Long John Baldry
NOTES: Two shows. Last night of tour.

1967

MARCH 25, 1967 – APRIL 17, 1967

TOUR: 1967 European tour
VENUE: Sweden, West Germany, Austria, Italy, France, Poland, Switzerland, Holland and Greece
PERSONNEL: Mick Jagger, Keith Richards, Brian Jones, Charlie Watts, Bill Wyman, Ian Stewart
OPENING/OTHER ACT(S): The Easybeats, The Creations, The Batman, Achim Reichel, The Move, The Sevens, Les Sauterelles, The Times, Heiner Hepp & the Waltl Anselmo Set, The Dogs
SONGS: The Last Time / Paint It, Black / 19th Nervous Breakdown / Lady Jane / Get Off of My Cloud → Yesterday's Papers → Get Off of My Cloud, LMV / She Smiled Sweetly / Under My Thumb / Connection / Ruby Tuesday / It's All Over Now (Womack, Womack) / Let's Spend the Night Together / Goin' Home / (I Can't Get No) Satisfactory, LMV
NOTES: This tour is noteworthy in two respects. First, it was the last tour Brian Jones would do with the Stones, though not his last public performance. But second, the Rolling Stones marked a major milestone on this trip, their first concerts behind the then "Iron Curtain." The 1967 sets included two medleys. The first came mid-show —"Get Off of My Cloud → Yesterday's Papers → Get Off of My Cloud." The second was a combination of "Goin' Home" and "Satisfaction" used for the encore. Opening-act information for this tour is somewhat sparse; all other artists are listed collectively above and individually with the appropriate concert, if known.

MARCH 25, 1967

TOUR: 1967 European tour
VENUE: Idrottens Hus Paskafton, Halsingborg, Sweden
NOTES: First night of tour. Two shows.

MARCH 27, 1967

TOUR: 1967 European tour
VENUE: Vinterstadium, Ørebro, Sweden
NOTES: Two shows

MARCH 29, 1967

TOUR: 1967 European tour
VENUE: Stadthalle, Bremen, West Germany
OPENING/OTHER ACT(S): The Easybeats, The Creations, The Batman, Achim Reichel
NOTES: Two shows

MARCH 30, 1967

TOUR: 1967 European tour
VENUE: Sporthalle, Cologne, West Germany
OPENING/OTHER ACT(S): The Easybeats, The Creations
NOTES: Two shows

MARCH 31, 1967

TOUR: 1967 European tour
VENUE: Westfallenhalle, Dortmund, West Germany
OPENING/OTHER ACT(S): The Easybeats, The Creations

APRIL 1, 1967

TOUR: 1967 European tour
VENUE: Ernst Merck Halle, Hamburg, West Germany
OPENING/OTHER ACT(S): The Easybeats, The Creations
NOTES: Two shows

APRIL 2, 1967

TOUR: 1967 European tour
VENUE: Stadthalle, Vienna, Austria
NOTES: Two shows

APRIL 5, 1967

TOUR: 1967 European tour
VENUE: Palazzo dello Sport, Bologna, Italy
OPENING/OTHER ACT(S): The Move
NOTES: Two shows

APRIL 6, 1967

TOUR: 1967 European tour
VENUE: Palazzo dello Sport, Rome, Italy
OPENING/OTHER ACT(S): The Move
NOTES: Two shows

APRIL 8, 1967

TOUR: 1967 European tour
VENUE: Palazzo dello Sport, Milan, Italy
OPENING/OTHER ACT(S): The Move
NOTES: Two shows

APRIL 9 , 1967

TOUR: 1967 European tour
VENUE: Palazzo dello Sport, Genoa, Italy
OPENING/OTHER ACT(S): The Move
NOTES: Two shows

APRIL 11, 1967

TOUR: 1967 European tour
VENUE: Olympia Theatre, Paris, France
OPENING/OTHER ACT(S): The Move
NOTES: Two shows. At the first show, an equipment glitch developed with the organ Brian played on "She Smiled Sweetly." The band stopped and restarted the song three times before the problem with the recalcitrant instrument was solved.

APRIL 13, 1967

TOUR: 1967 European tour
VENUE: Sala Kongresowej, Palace of Culture, Warsaw, Poland
NOTES: Two shows. In contrast to more stringent practices in the former Soviet Union and other Eastern Bloc states, Polish cultural censorship somehow allowed the black market in Western records (like those of the Stones) to flourish, while banning their legal import or broadcast by state-controlled radio and television. However, "underground" Radio Luxembourg, as well as the BBC's Central European Service and the US-backed anticommunist Radio Free Europe and Voice of America, did play the music. The diligent no doubt picked up the US Armed Forces network as well. The result: in 1967, the Stones had a huge, vocal fan base in Poland that the Polish government chose not to ignore.

Polish officials may have sanctioned the concerts hoping to avert civil insurrection or, perhaps, merely to appear less repressive. Unfortunately for them in retrospect, it was the proverbial no-win situation: a riot immediately broke out among the thousands of fans outside who couldn't get into the first show. Inside, the luckier audiences were equally frenzied—in their appreciation, like Stones fans all over—despite the fact that, and unbeknownst to the band, the first five rows were reserved for Polish Communist Party members and their families.

Caught between rock 'n 'roll and hard line politics, the government called in the troops for the second show, expecting that water cannons would deter another riot outside the venue. They didn't. The military solution just sparked a second melee and more bad press. International news organizations covered the Stones journey, "behind the Iron Curtain"—the whole kielbasa was captured on film.

APRIL 15, 1967

TOUR: 1967 European tour
VENUE: Hautreust Hall, The Hague, Holland

APRIL 17, 1967

TOUR: 1967 European tour
VENUE: Panathinaikos Football Stadium, Athens, Greece

NOTES: Last gig of tour.

1968

MAY 12, 1968

VENUE: NME Poll Winners Concert, Empire Pool, Wembley, Middlesex, England

PERSONNEL: Mick Jagger, Keith Richards, Brian Jones, Charlie Watts, Bill Wyman, Ian Stewart

OPENING/OTHER ACT(S):   Status Quo; The Move; Dusty Springfield; The Herd; The Association; The Bee Gees; Lulu; Don Partridge; Amen Corner; Cliff Richard & the Shadows; Dave Dee; Dozy, Beaky, Mick & Tich; The Tremeloes

SONGS: Jumpin' Jack Flash / (I Can't Get No) Satisfaction

NOTES: Brian Jones's last live public performance with the Stones. The Stones appeared on the condition their name would not be used to promote the show. Actor Roger Moore (007, The Saint) introduced the Stones and presented them with their NME awards.

1969

JULY 5, 1969

VENUE: Free Concert, Hyde Park, London, England

PERSONNEL: Mick Jagger, Keith Richards, Mick Taylor, Charlie Watts, Bill Wyman, Ian Stewart

SPECIAL GUESTS: Rocky Dijon, Ginger Johnson & His African Drummers

OPENING/OTHER ACT(S):   Third Ear Band, King Crimson, Screw, Alexis Korner's New Church, Battered Ornaments, Family

SONGS: I'm Yours and I'm Hers (J. Winter) / Jumpin' Jack Flash / Mercy Mercy (Covay, Miller) / Down Home Girl (Leiber, Butler) / Stray Cat Blues / No Expectations / I'm Free / Loving Cup / Love in Vain (Robt. Johnson) / (I Can't Get No) Satisfaction / Honky Tonk Women / Midnight Rambler / Street Fighting Man / Sympathy for the Devil

NOTES: On June 7, 1969, Jagger and Marianne Faithfull had attended the short-lived super group Blind Faith's (Eric Clapton, Ginger Baker, Steve Winwood and Rick Grech) free concert in Hyde Park. Mick was impressed—and overwhelmed by the 80,000 plus attendance. The Stones had been beset by troubles for some time, and after the June 8 announcements of Brian Jones's leaving the band and Taylor's hiring, Jagger felt obligated to show the fans that the Rolling Stones were stronger than ever. A free "comeback" concert in Hyde

Park seemed the perfect solution, and the date was set for July 5. This was Mick Taylor's first public appearance with the band.

But, Brian Jones died suddenly on July 3, and the mood in Hyde Park two days later was hardly what had been expected. Jagger read portions of Shelley's "Adonais" and thousands of white butterflies were released as memorials to Brian—along with the music. Still, the concert was a success. Six bands warmed up the crowd, beginning with the Third Ear Band and, in the above order, ending with Family.

The Stones' show began uniquely with the Johnny Winter song, "I'm Yours and I'm Hers," and the song "Loving Cup" was introduced as "Give Me a Little Drink." There were no other particular curiosities in the setlist—save their playing the just-released "Honky Tonk Women" and two songs from the yet-to-be-released *Let It Bleed* LP fro the first time live at this concert. What is most unusual, at least to the authors, is the inclusion of the Winter song to open the set. Not much, if any, notice has been paid to the reason: it was one of Brian Jones's favorites.

Their last song was "Sympathy for the Devil," accompanied by Rocky Dijon (who had played congas in the studio session) along with Ginger Johnson & his African Drummers. Oddly, these were the first guest musicians ever to join the Stones onstage. (The 1964 T.A.M.I. Show did have a musical finale—the entire star-studded cast gathered for the song "Get Together" to close the concert. But T.A.M.I. was not a "Stones show" and the whole band wasn't even playing on the closing number—Mick Jagger's ad libbed vocal was the only Rolling Stones contribution.)

NOVEMBER 7, 1969 – DECEMBER 6, 1969

TOUR: Sixth North American tour

VENUE: USA

PERSONNEL: Mick Jagger, Keith Richards, Charles Watts, Bill Wyman, Ian Stewart

OPENING/OTHER ACT(S):   B. B. King, Ike & Tina Turner, Terry Reid & the Pack, Chuck Berry

SONGS: Jumpin' Jack Flash / Carol (Berry) / Sympathy for the Devil / Stray Cat Blues / Prodigal Son (Rev. Wilkins) / You Gotta Move (McDowell, Davis) / Love in Vain (Robt. Johnson) / I'm Free / Under My Thumb / Midnight Rambler / Live with Me / Gimme Shelter / Little Queenie (Berry) / (I Can't Get No) Satisfaction / Honky Tonk Women / Street Fighting Man / Brown Sugar / The Sun Is Shinning (Reed)

1969 TOUR REHEARSALS: Jumpin' Jack Flash / Carol (Berry) / Sympathy for the Devil / Stray Cat Blues

/ Prodigal Son (Rev. Wilkins) / You Gotta Move (McDowell, Davis) / Love in Vain (Robt. Johnson) / I'm Free / Under My Thumb / Midnight Rambler / Live with Me / Gimme Shelter / Little Queenie (Berry) / (I Can't Get No) Satisfaction / Honky Tonk Women / Street Fighting Man / Bad Boy (Taylor) [never played on '69 tour] / Monkey Man (never played on '69 tour) / Let It Bleed (never played on '69 tour)

Notes: Mick Taylor's first tour as a Stone. He receives a salary, not a percentage, until the band's current record contracts run out. When the Stones sign with Atlantic Records, Taylor becomes a full-fledged member, with a cut. B. B. King, Ike & Tina Turner (backed by the Ikettes), and Terry Reid & the Pack were the opening acts throughout the tour. But because of prior commitments, B. B. King and Ike & Tina were unable to appear at dates in four cities in the middle of the tour, so the Stones called in a replacement—Chuck Berry.

The basic setlist varied slightly from show to show during the tour. "I'm Free" and "Under My Thumb" were performed as a medley much of the time, the length of each portion differed. "Street Fighting Man" was the usual encore. However, at the ill-fated Altamont free concert at the end of the tour, two songs showed up that hadn't been played elsewhere in '69—"Brown Sugar" and the Jimmy Reed tune, "The Sun Is Shining." Thus, the numbers listed above in "Songs" were all performed on the tour; subtract the last two for a "typical set," check out the ones in "1969 Tour Rehearsals" for comparison and see how the set developed from the first show of the tour in Fort Collins, CO to the last one in West Palm Beach, FL. Altamont is listed as the last show, which it was in too many respects, but the official tour really ended on November 30.

November 7, 1969

Tour: Sixth North American tour
Venue: Colorado State University, Fort Colliins, CO, USA
Opening/Other Act(s): B. B. King, Terry Reid & the Pack
Songs: Jumpin' Jack Flash / Carol (Berry) / Sympathy for the Devil / Stray Cat Blues / Midnight Rambler / Under My Thumb / Prodigal Son (Rev. Wilkins) / Love in Vain (Robt. Johnson) / I'm Free / Little Queenie (Berry) / Gimme Shelter / (I Can't Get No) Satisfaction / Honky Tonk Women / E: Street Fighting Man

November 8, 1969

Tour: Sixth North American tour
Venue: L.A. Forum, Inglewood, CA, USA
Personnel: Mick Jagger, Keith Richards, Mick Taylor, Charlie Watts, Bill Wyman, Ian Stewart

Opening/Other Act(s): B. B. King, Ike & Tina Turner, Terry Reid & the Pack
Notes: Two shows

November 9, 1969

Tour: Sixth North American tour
Venue: Oakland Coliseum, Oakland, CA, USA
Opening/Other Act(s): B. B. King, Ike & Tina Turner, Terry Reid & the Pack
Songs: Jumpin' Jack Flash / Prodigal Son (Rev. Wilkins) / You Gotta Move / Carol (Berry) / Sympathy for the Devil / Stray Cat Blues / Love in Vain (Robt. Johnson) / I'm Free / Under My Thumb / Midnight Rambler / Live With Me / Little Queenie (Berry) / Gimme Shelter / (I Can't Get No) Satisfaction / Honky Tonk Women / E: Street Fighting Man
Notes: There were 2 shows. The setlist order varied from the norm during the first show because of electrical power failures. B. B. King did not play the early show, but did open the "late late" show.

November 10, 1969

Tour: Sixth North American tour
Venue: Sports Arena, San Diego, CA, USA
Opening/Other Act(s): B. B. King, Ike & Tina Turner, Terry Reid & the Pack

November 11, 1969

Tour: Sixth North American tour
Venue: Coliseum, Phoenix, AZ, USA
Opening/Other Act(s): B. B. King, Ike & Tina Turner, Terry Reid & the Pack

November 13, 1969

Tour: Sixth North American tour
Venue: Moody Coliseum, Dallas, TX, USA
Opening/Other Act(s): Chuck Berry, Terry Reid & the Pack
Notes: Chuck Berry opened for the Stones, replacing B. B. King and Ike & Tina.

November 14, 1969

Tour: Sixth North American tour
Venue: University Coliseum, Auburn, AL, USA
Opening/Other Act(s): Chuck Berry, Terry Reid & the Pack
Notes: Two shows. Chuck Berry opened for the Stones, again replacing B. B. King and Ike & Tina. However, at the second show, Berry was the only pre-Stones act. The first show had started almost an hour later than scheduled and ran longer than anticipated. When the

second show got off to an even later start, management decided to cut Terry Reid's opening set altogether.

NOVEMBER 15, 1969

TOUR: Sixth North American tour
VENUE: Assembly Hall, University of Illinois, Champaign, IL, USA
OPENING/OTHER ACT(S): Chuck Berry, Terry Reid & the Pack
NOTES: Two shows. Again Chuck Berry replaced B. B. King and Ike & Tina on the opening bill.

NOVEMBER 16, 1969

TOUR: Sixth North American tour
VENUE: International Amphitheatre, Chicago, IL, USA
OPENING/OTHER ACT(S): Chuck Berry, Terry Reid & the Pack
NOTES: Chuck Berry travelled with the band to the Chicago gig, and replaced Ike & Tina and B. B. King for the last time on the '69 tour.

NOVEMBER 20, 1969

TOUR: Sixth North American tour
VENUE: L.A. Forum, Inglewood, CA, USA
OPENING/OTHER ACT(S): B. B. King, Tina Turner, Terry Reid & the Pack

NOVEMBER 24, 1969

TOUR: Sixth North American tour
VENUE: Olympia Stadium, Detroit, MI, USA
OPENING/OTHER ACT(S): B. B. King, Ike & Tina Turner, Terry Reid & the Pack
NOTES: Two shows

NOVEMBER 25, 1969

TOUR: Sixth North American tour
VENUE: Spectrum, Philadelphia, PA, USA
OPENING/OTHER ACT(S): B. B. King, Ike & Tina Turner, Terry Reid & the Pack
SONGS: Jumpin' Jack Flash / Carol (Berry) / Sympathy for the Devil / Stray Cat Blues / Love in Vain (Robt. Johnson) / Prodigal Son (Rev. Wilkins) / Under My Thumb / Midnight Rambler / Live with Me / Little Queenie (Berry) / (I Can't Get No) Satisfaction / Honky Tonk Women / **E:** Street Fighting Man

NOVEMBER 26, 1969

TOUR: Sixth North American tour
VENUE: Civic Centre, Baltimore, MD, USA
OPENING/OTHER ACT(S): B. B. King, Ike & Tina Turner, Terry Reid & the Pack

SONGS: Jumpin' Jack Flash / Carol (Berry) / Sympathy for the Devil / Stray Cat Blues / Love in Vain (Robt. Johnson) / You Gotta Move (McDowell, Davis) / Under My Thumb / I'm Free / Midnight Rambler / Live with Me / Little Queenie (Berry) / (I Can't Get No) Satisfaction / Honky Tonk Women / **E:** Street Fighting Man
NOTES: This gig was recorded for the live LP that became *Get Yer Ya-Ya's Out*. (See SESSIONOGRAPHY and DISCOGRAPHY)

NOVEMBER 27, 1969

TOUR: Sixth North American tour
VENUE: Madison Square Garden, New York, NY, USA
OPENING/OTHER ACT(S): B. B. King, Ike & Tina Turner, Terry Reid & the Pack
SONGS: Jumpin' Jack Flash / Carol (Berry) / Sympathy for the Devil / Stray Cat Blues / Love in Vain (Robt. Johnson) / Prodigal Son (Rev. Wilkins) / Under My Thumb / Midnight Rambler / Live with Me / Little Queenie (Berry) / (I Can't Get No) Satisfaction / Honky Tonk Women / **E:** Street Fighting Man
NOTES: Also recorded for *Get Yer Ya-Ya's Out*.

NOVEMBER 28, 1969

TOUR: Sixth North American tour
VENUE: Madison Square Garden, New York, NY, USA
OPENING/OTHER ACT(S): B. B. King, Ike & Tina Turner, Terry Reid & the Pack
SONGS: Jumpin' Jack Flash, LV / Carol (Berry), LV / Sympathy for the Devil, LV / Stray Cat Blues, LV / Love in Vain (Robt. Johnson) / You Gotta Move (McDowell, Davis) / Prodigal Son (Rev. Wilkins) / Under My Thumb / Midnight Rambler, LV / Live with Me, LV / Little Queenie (Berry), LV / (I Can't Get No) Satisfaction / Honky Tonk Women, LV / **E:** Street Fighting Man, LV
NOTES: The band did two shows here on this date, both recorded for *Ya-Ya's*.

NOVEMBER 29, 1969

TOUR: Sixth North American tour
VENUE: The Boston Garden, Boston, MA, USA
OPENING/OTHER ACT(S): B. B. King, Ike & Tina Turner, Terry Reid & the Pack
NOTES: Two shows. This gig was also recorded for *Ya-Ya's*.

NOVEMBER 30, 1969

TOUR: Sixth North American tour
VENUE: West Palm Beach Pop Festival, International Raceway, West Palm Beach, FL, USA

OPENING/OTHER ACT(S): Janis Joplin, Johnny Winter, Jefferson Airplane, Iron Butterfly, Vanilla Fudge, Spirit, Grand Funk Railroad, Country Joe and the Fish

SONGS: Jumpin' Jack Flash / Carol (Berry) / Sympathy for the Devil / Stray Cat Blues / Love in Vain (Robt. Johnson) / Under My Thumb / Midnight Rambler / Gimme Shelter, LV / Live with Me, LV / Little Queenie (Berry) / (I Can't Get No) Satisfaction / Honky Tonk Woman / E: Street Fighting Man

NOTES: This was a pop festival—Janis Joplin and Johnny Winter were among the other artists on the bill along with the Stones. The Stones arrived at the last minute and went onstage at 5:00 AM. The Maysles' cameras were there.

DECEMBER 6, 1969

TOUR: Sixth North American tour

VENUE: Altamont Speedway, Livermore, CA, USA (free concert)

OPENING/OTHER ACT(S): Santana, Flying Burrito Brothers, Crosby, Stills, Nash & Young, Jefferson Airplane.

SONGS: Jumpin' Jack Flash / Carol (Berry) / Sympathy for the Devil / The Sun Is Shining (Reed) / Stray Cat Blues / Love in Vain (Robt. Johnson) / Under My Thumb / Brown Sugar / Midnight Rambler / Live with Me / Gimme Shelter, LV / Little Queenie (Berry) / (I Can't Get No) Satisfaction / Honky Tonk Women / Street Fighting Man

NOTES: The sun was certainly not shining at Altamont, but the Stones played the Jimmy Reed song and "Brown Sugar" here and nowhere else on the '69 tour. "Brown Sugar" wasn't even recorded until the official tour was over (see SESSIONOGRAPHY). "Sun Is Shining" hadn't been part of a Stones setlist since their 1962–63 club gigs. Thus, the band's Altamont set consisted of those two songs plus the usual 1969 tour set with "Prodigal Son," "You Gotta Move" and "I'm Free" taken off the list. Santana, the Flying Burrito Brothers, Crosby, Stills, Nash & Young and Jefferson Airplane were the opening acts. The Grateful Dead were supposed to follow the Stones and play until dawn to close the festival, but changed their minds about performing at all after the audience/Angels mayhem during the Stones' set. It was the Dead's management team of Sam Cutler and Rock Scully who helped plan the event and who had recommended the local Hell's Angels to the Stones to function as concert security. (Cutler, English but experienced with US rock 'n' roll touring, was hired prior to Hyde Park to comanage the Stones' '69 tour. He did not continue on to the 1970 European tour; neither Sam Cutler nor Rock Scully worked with the Stones again after Altamont.) Since the Stones had used the London Angels for security without incident at Hyde Park in July, they had agreed. But bad drugs, abundant alcohol and a whole different kind of Angel made for a totally different vibe here.

That something wasn't quite right became obvious when Stones blood was spilled immediately upon their arrival at Altamont Speedway. As Mick Jagger made his way to a backstage trailer, an irate (and most likely inebriated and/or stoned) "fan" punched the singer in the mouth. Bill Wyman decided to travel by car, separately from the other band members, who were flown in. The same helicopter would get the Stones all back to San Francisco in a harrowing getaway after their performance. Even though all concerned hoped the setting of the sun might cool things out, the Stones' coming on late didn't help the overly tense, mostly out-of-control situation. Actually, the only "control" was in the hands of the Hell's Angels who, provided with free beer as partial compensation for "crowd control" services, took the job way too seriously.

Brandishing pool cues, knives, tire irons, beer bottles and whatever else was handy, the bikers used force summarily on anyone in the crowd or onstage whose actions displeased them. There were many varieties of drugs, hard and soft, circulating at the hastily arranged event, which took place on a site with inadequate facilities and amenities. Many spectators were drunk or stoned (some on alleged bad LSD) like the Hell's Angels, and fights broke out between audience members in addition to the many Angel/audience confrontations. The Rolling Stones were themselves fortunate to have escaped injury; earlier, several Angels had brutally beaten Marty Balin of Jefferson Airplane as he attempted to stop them from pounding a spectator. Because of all this, the atmosphere when the Stones mounted the stage was very, very scary.

The band started, stopped, then restarted their performances of "Sympathy for the Devil" and "Under My Thumb" because of mounting disturbances and confusion emanating from the audience. As is well documented in news footage and the Maysles Brothers film *Gimme Shelter*, audience member Meredith Hunter was stabbed repeatedly and literally stomped to death by an overzealous Angel. It happened as the band began "Under My Thumb"—one of those false starts—but the Stones weren't aware of exactly *what* had happened until much later. Not only could they not see the fans beyond the ones being clubbed at the very front, but the stage itself was overcrowded with non-musicians. In addition to having overabundant, leather-clad, beer-swilling, uncompromising "security" almost on top of them, the band was literally hemmed in behind by roadies, press, and others seeking refuge from the escalating chaos beneath. There were four deaths *and* four births, plus numerous injuries, at the incredibly bad trip that was Altamont. (See CHRONOLOGY)

DECEMBER 14, 1969

VENUE: Saville Theatre, London, England
OPENING/OTHER ACT(S): Conjurer David Berglass, Mighty Baby, Shakin' Stevens & the Sunset
SONGS: Jumpin' Jack Flash / Carol (Berry) / Sympathy for the Devil / Stray Cat Blues / Prodigal Son (Rev. Wilkins) / You Gotta Move (McDowell, Davis) / Love in Vain (Robt. Johnson) / I'm Free / Under My Thumb / Midnight Rambler / Live with Me / Gimme Shelter / Little Queenie (Berry) / (I Can't Get No) Satisfaction / Honky Tonk Women / Street Fighting Man
NOTES: Two shows

DECEMBER 21, 1969

VENUE: Lyceum Theatre, London, England
OPENING/OTHER ACT(S): Yes
SONGS: Jumpin' Jack Flash / Carol (Berry) / Sympathy for the Devil / Stray Cat Blues / Prodigal Son (Rev. Wilkins) / You Gotta Move (McDowell, Davis) / Love in Vain (Robt. Johnson) / I'm Free / Under My Thumb / Midnight Rambler / Live with Me / Gimme Shelter / Little Queenie (Berry) / (I Can't Get No) Satisfaction / Honky Tonk Women / Street Fighting Man
NOTES: Two shows. Yes, there was an opening act—the band named Yes.

1970

AUGUST 30, 1970 – OCTOBER 9, 1970

TOUR: 1970 European tour
VENUE: Sweden, Finland, Denmark, West Germany, France, Austria, Italy and Holland
PERSONNEL: Mick Jagger, Keith Richards, Mick Taylor, Charlie Watts, Bill Wyman, Ian Stewart, Bobby Keys, Jim Price
SPECIAL GUESTS: Stephen Stills
OPENING/OTHER ACT(S): Buddy Guy & Junior Wells (and special guest Eric Clapton—one show)
SONGS: Jumpin' Jack Flash / Roll Over Beethoven (Berry) / Sympathy for the Devil / Stray Cat Blues / Love in Vain (Robt. Johnson) / Prodigal Son (Rev. Wilkins) / You Gotta Move (McDowell, Davis) / Dead Flowers / Midnight Rambler / Live with Me / Little Queenie (Berry) / Let It Rock (Anderson) / Brown Sugar / Gimme Shelter / Honky Tonk Women / Street Fighting Man
NOTES: In addition to Ian Stewart on his usual piano, the Stones were backed on this tour by Bobby Keys on saxophone and Jim Price on trombone. Buddy Guy and

Junior Wells opened for the Stones throughout the tour, with a surprise guest at one Paris show. "Gimme Shelter" was not performed at Malmö, but sets contained 14 to 15 songs elsewhere on this tour with or without it.

AUGUST 30, 1970

TOUR: 1970 European tour
VENUE: Baltiska Hallen, Malmö, Sweden
OPENING/OTHER ACT(S): Buddy Guy & Junior Wells
SONGS: Jumpin' Jack Flash / Roll Over Beethoven (Berry) / Sympathy for the Devil / Stray Cat Blues / Love in Vain (Robt. Johnson) / Prodigal Son (Rev. Wilkins) / You Gotta Move (McDowell, Davis) / Dead Flowers / Midnight Rambler / Live with Me / Little Queenie (Berry) / Let It Rock (Anderson) / Brown Sugar / Honky Tonk Women / Street Fighting Man

SEPTEMBER 2, 1970

TOUR: 1970 European tour
VENUE: Olympiastadium, Helsinki, Finland
OPENING/OTHER ACT(S): Buddy Guy & Junior Wells

SEPTEMBER 4, 1970

TOUR: 1970 European tour
VENUE: Rasunda Stadium, Stockholm, Sweden
OPENING/OTHER ACT(S): Buddy Guy & Junior Wells

SEPTEMBER 6, 1970

TOUR: 1970 European tour
VENUE: Liseberg, Gothenburg, Sweden
OPENING/OTHER ACT(S): Buddy Guy & Junior Wells

SEPTEMBER 9, 1970

TOUR: 1970 European tour
VENUE: Tennis Stadium, Aarhus, Denmark
OPENING/OTHER ACT(S): Buddy Guy & Junior Wells

SEPTEMBER 12, 1970

TOUR: 1970 European tour
VENUE: Forum, Copenhagen, Denmark
OPENING/OTHER ACT(S): Buddy Guy & Junior Wells

SEPTEMBER 14, 1970

TOUR: 1970 European tour
VENUE: Ernst Merck Halle, Hamburg, West Germany
OPENING/OTHER ACT(S): Buddy Guy & Junior Wells

SEPTEMBER 16, 1970

TOUR: 1970 European tour
VENUE: Deutschlandhalle, West Berlin, West Germany

OPENING/OTHER ACT(S):   Buddy Guy & Junior Wells

SEPTEMBER 18, 1970

TOUR: 1970 European tour
VENUE: Sporthalle, Cologne, West Germany
OPENING/OTHER ACT(S):   Buddy Guy & Junior Wells
NOTES: Sporthalle, a.k.a. "Building Number 11."

SEPTEMBER 20, 1970

TOUR: 1970 European tour
VENUE: Killesberg, Stuttgart, West Germany
OPENING/OTHER ACT(S):   Buddy Guy & Junior Wells

SEPTEMBER 22, 1970

TOUR: 1970 European tour
VENUE: Palais des Sports, Paris, France
OPENING/OTHER ACT(S):   Buddy Guy & Junior Wells
(with special guest Eric Clapton)
NOTES: Eric Clapton left his seat in the audience and came onstage to play with Buddy Guy and Junior Wells —on "Money"—during their opening set. He did not sit in with the Stones.

SEPTEMBER 23, 1970

TOUR: 1970 European tour
VENUE: Palais des Sports, Paris, France
OPENING/OTHER ACT(S):   Buddy Guy & Junior Wells

SEPTEMBER 24, 1970

TOUR: 1970 European tour
VENUE: Palais des Sports, Paris, France
OPENING/OTHER ACT(S):   Buddy Guy & Junior Wells

SEPTEMBER 27, 1970

TOUR: 1970 European tour
VENUE: Stadthalle, Vienna, Austria
OPENING/OTHER ACT(S):   Buddy Guy & Junior Wells

SEPTEMBER 29, 1970

TOUR: 1970 European tour
VENUE: Palazzo dello Sport, Rome, Italy
OPENING/OTHER ACT(S):   Buddy Guy & Junior Wells

OCTOBER 3, 1970

TOUR: 1970 European tour
VENUE: Palais des Sports, Lyons, France
OPENING/OTHER ACT(S):   Buddy Guy & Junior Wells

OCTOBER 5, 1970

TOUR: 1970 European tour
VENUE: Festhalle, Frankfurt, West Germany
OPENING/OTHER ACT(S):   Buddy Guy & Junior Wells

OCTOBER 6, 1970

TOUR: 1970 European tour
VENUE: Festhalle, Frankfurt, West Germany
OPENING/OTHER ACT(S):   Buddy Guy & Junior Wells

OCTOBER 7, 1970

TOUR: 1970 European tour
VENUE: Grugahalle, Essen, West Germany
OPENING/OTHER ACT(S):   Buddy Guy & Junior Wells

OCTOBER 9, 1970

TOUR: 1970 European tour
VENUE: Rai-Halle, Amsterdam, Holland
SPECIAL GUESTS: Stephen Stills
OPENING/OTHER ACT(S):   Buddy Guy & Junior Wells
NOTES: Stephen Stills made a guest appearance on piano with the Stones on "Dead Flowers." Last gig of the 1970 tour.

1971

MARCH 4, 1971 – MARCH 26, 1971

TOUR: Ninth British tour ("Good Bye Britain")
VENUE: England and Scotland
PERSONNEL: Mick Jagger, Keith Richards, Mick Taylor, Charlie Watts, Bill Wyman, Ian Stewart, Nicky Hopkins, Bobby Keys, Jim Price
OPENING/OTHER ACT(S):   The Groundhogs
SONGS: Jumpin' Jack Flash / Live with Me / Dead Flowers / Stray Cat Blues / Love in Vain (Robt. Johnson) / I Got the Blues / Midnight Rambler / Bitch / Honky Tonk Women / (I Can't Get No) Satisfaction / Little Queenie (Berry) / Brown Sugar / Street Fighting Man / Let It Rock (Anderson)
NOTES: Nicky Hopkins was on piano, Keys on sax, and Price on trumpet. A typical set for this "tour before exile." But see the second show on March 4, below, for how much the set could vary.

MARCH 4, 1971

TOUR: Ninth British tour ("Good Bye Britain")
VENUE: City Hall, Newcastle-upon-Tyne, Northumberland, England
OPENING/OTHER ACT(S):   The Groundhogs

SONGS: Jumpin' Jack Flash / Live with Me / Dead Flowers / Stray Cat Blues / Love in Vain (Robt. Johnson) / Prodigal Son (Rev. Wilkins) / Midnight Rambler / Bitch / Honky Tonk Women / Little Queenie (Berry) / Brown Sugar / Street Fighting Man / **E1:** Sympathy for the Devil / **E2:** Let It Rock (Anderson)
NOTES: Two shows. This is the setlist for the second show. The band played two songs as an encore, their first encore of any kind in three years.

MARCH 5, 1971

TOUR: Ninth British tour ("Good Bye Britain")
VENUE: Free Trade Hall, Manchester, Lancashire, England
OPENING/OTHER ACT(S): The Groundhogs

MARCH 6, 1971

TOUR: Ninth British tour ("Good Bye Britain")
VENUE: Coventry Theatre, Coventry, Warwickshire, England
OPENING/OTHER ACT(S): The Groundhogs
NOTES: Two shows

MARCH 8, 1971

TOUR: Ninth British tour ("Good Bye Britain")
VENUE: Green's Playhouse, Glasgow, Scotland
OPENING/OTHER ACT(S): The Groundhogs

MARCH 9, 1971

TOUR: Ninth British tour ("Good Bye Britain")
VENUE: Colston Hall, Bristol, Gloucestershire, England
OPENING/OTHER ACT(S): The Groundhogs

MARCH 10, 1971

TOUR: Ninth British tour ("Good Bye Britain")
VENUE: Big Apple, Brighton, Sussex, England
OPENING/OTHER ACT(S): The Groundhogs

MARCH 12, 1971

TOUR: Ninth British tour ("Good Bye Britain")
VENUE: Empire Theatre, Liverpool, Lancashire, England
OPENING/OTHER ACT(S): The Groundhogs

MARCH 13, 1971

TOUR: Ninth British tour ("Good Bye Britain")
VENUE: Leeds University, Leeds, Yorkshire, England
OPENING/OTHER ACT(S): The Groundhogs
SONGS: Let It Rock (Anderson), LV

NOTES: This is where the only officially released version of "Let It Rock" was recorded and the version name is noted here for that reason. The Stones played the tune throughout this tour.

MARCH 14, 1971

TOUR: Ninth British tour ("Good Bye Britain")
VENUE: Roundhouse, Chalk Farm, London, England
OPENING/OTHER ACT(S): The Groundhogs
NOTES: Two shows, both sellouts. These were the last "Good Bye Britain" concerts open to the public; the Marquee Club show on March 26 was done before an audience of invited guests, and was filmed for broadcast as a television special in Britain and Europe.

MARCH 26, 1971

TOUR: Ninth British tour ("Good Bye Britain")
VENUE: Marquee Jazz Club, London, England
NOTES: This performance, a milestone of sorts, was filmed for a television special. The Stones had last played the Marquee on January 31, 1963. They did two shows: one for fans, the other for friends and family. There was no opening act at the Marquee.

1972

JUNE 3, 1972 – JULY 26, 1972

TOUR: Seventh (1972) North American tour
VENUE: US and Canada
PERSONNEL: Mick Jagger, Keith Richards, Mick Taylor, Charlie Watts, Bill Wyman, Ian Stewart, Nicky Hopkins, Bobby Keys, Jim Price
SPECIAL GUESTS: Stevie Wonder
OPENING/OTHER ACT(S): Stevie Wonder, Dorothy Ellis
SONGS: Brown Sugar / Bitch / Rocks Off / Ventilator Blues (Jagger, Richards, Taylor) / Torn and Frayed / Loving Cup / Gimme Shelter / Happy / Tumbling Dice / Love in Vain (Robt. Johnson) / Sweet Virginia / You Can't Always Get What You Want / All Down the Line / Midnight Rambler / Bye Bye Johnny (Berry) / Rip This Joint / Jumpin' Jack Flash / Street Fighting Man / Honky Tonk Women / Don't Lie to Me (Berry) / Uptight → Satisfaction, LMV
NOTES: This was the archetypical Stones tour, the one that's been immortalized in print and on film from many angles, sublime to ridiculous and really raunchy. It all makes for engaging reading and interesting viewing. (See other sections for books and films.) Much of the legend is true in some portion, a lot isn't. The dirt can be found elsewhere; here are some facts. Except for one booking on

The Rolling Stones—1972 tour (l. Mick Taylor, with Mick Jagger and airborne rose petals during encore)

June 25 in Houston, Stevie Wonder was the opening act throughout the Stones' seventh North American tour, also known as the "STP" tour after the inscription on the Stones Touring Party's official passes (and a few other explanations). "Ventilator Blues," "Torn and Frayed" and "Loving Cup" were all played in Vancouver; then, in Seattle, the first two were dropped but "Loving Cup" was done at both shows. These three songs never were played again on the '72 tour. Chuck Berry's "Don't Lie to Me" was only performed in Dallas/Fort Worth, where it was captured on film for *Ladies and Gentlemen, the Rolling Stones.* A snippet of "Let it Rock," not listed above, ended a San Francisco performance at Winterland. And, in a first for the band, they were joined onstage on the last leg of the tour (Boston, New York, Philadelphia) by Stevie Wonder for an encore medley of "Uptight" and "Can't Get No Satisfaction," which they first tried out in St. Louis

on July 9. Prior to those performances and with the exception of the one time in Los Angeles and the first show in Boston (July 18, 1972), "Street Fighting Man" had been the encore. The setlist, as it changed, is noted in the following listings. Backing the Stones, as on their two previous tours, were Nicky Hopkins on piano, Bobby Keys on sax, and Jim Price on trumpet. "Sweet Black Angel" appeared only once—at the first show in Fort Worth on June 24. "Dead Flowers" was also played at that performance, and turned up again at the early show in Houston on June 25. Chuck Berry's "Don't Lie to Me" made a single setlist appearance at the second Fort Worth show. The making of the movie, in fact, was behind the unexpected appearance of such songs in the Texas shows, and was also a perfect opportunity to add new titles to the Stones' filmed repertoire.

JUNE 3, 1972

TOUR: Seventh (1972) North American tour
VENUE: Canadian Pacific Coliseum, Vancouver, British Columbia, Canada
OPENING/OTHER ACT(S):   Stevie Wonder
SONGS: Brown Sugar / Rocks Off / Gimme Shelter / Bitch / Tumbling Dice / Happy / Honky Tonk Women / Loving Cup / Torn and Frayed / Sweet Virginia / You Can't Always Get What You Want / Ventilator Blues (Jagger, Richards, Taylor) / Midnight Rambler / All Down the Line / Bye Bye Johnny (Berry) / Rip This Joint / Jumpin' Jack Flash / **E:** Street Fighting Man
NOTES: The first performance of the Stones' seventh North American tour. This was the setlist at the beginning of the tour.

JUNE 4, 1972

TOUR: Seventh (1972) North American tour
VENUE: Coliseum, Seattle, WA, USA
OPENING/OTHER ACT(S):   Stevie Wonder
SONGS: Brown Sugar / Bitch / Rocks Off / Loving Cup / Gimme Shelter / Happy / Tumbling Dice / Love in Vain (Robt. Johnson) / Sweet Virginia / You Can't Always Get What You Want / All Down the Line / Midnight Rambler / Bye Bye Johnny (Berry) / Rip This Joint / Jumpin' Jack Flash / Street Fighting Man
NOTES: Two shows. "Ventilator Blues" and "Torn and Frayed" were out of the set. These were the songs played in both shows (in no particular order).

JUNE 6, 1972

TOUR: Seventh (1972) North American tour
VENUE: Winterland, San Francisco, CA, USA
OPENING/OTHER ACT(S):   Stevie Wonder
SONGS: Brown Sugar / Bitch / Rocks Off / Gimme Shelter / Happy / Tumbling Dice / Love in Vain (Robt. Johnson) / Sweet Virginia / You Can't Always Get What You Want / All Down the Line / Midnight Rambler / Bye Bye Johnny (Berry) / Rip This Joint / Jumpin' Jack Flash / Street Fighting Man
NOTES: Two shows. Note that the setlist changed. "Loving Cup" was not performed here, the band dropped three songs in all after Seattle.

JUNE 8, 1972

TOUR: Seventh (1972) North American tour
VENUE: Winterland, San Francisco, CA, USA
OPENING/OTHER ACT(S):   Stevie Wonder
SONGS: "Let It Rock" (Anderson), ELV

NOTES: Two shows. Same songs as on June 6, except for the one-time addition of a 1:40 blip—or edited live version—of "Let It Rock" at the end of "Street Fighting Man."

JUNE 9, 1972

TOUR: Seventh (1972) North American tour
VENUE: Hollywood Palladium, Hollywood, CA, USA
OPENING/OTHER ACT(S):   Stevie Wonder

JUNE 10, 1972

TOUR: Seventh (1972) North American tour
VENUE: Pacific Terrace Center, Long Beach, CA, USA
OPENING/OTHER ACT(S):   Stevie Wonder

JUNE 11, 1972

TOUR: Seventh (1972) North American tour
VENUE: L.A. Forum, Inglewood, CA, USA
OPENING/OTHER ACT(S):   Stevie Wonder
SONGS: Brown Sugar / Bitch / Rocks Off / Gimme Shelter / Happy / Tumbling Dice / Love in Vain (Robt. Johnson) / Sweet Virginia / You Can't Always Get What You Want / All Down the Line / Midnight Rambler / Bye Bye Johnny (Berry) / Rip This Joint / Jumpin' Jack Flash / **E1:** Street Fighting Man / **E2*:** Honky Tonk Women
NOTES: Two shows.*

JUNE 13, 1972

TOUR: Seventh (1972) North American tour
VENUE: International Sports Arena, San Diego, CA, USA
OPENING/OTHER ACT(S):   Stevie Wonder

JUNE 14, 1972

TOUR: Seventh (1972) North American tour
VENUE: Civic Arena, Tucson, AZ, USA
OPENING/OTHER ACT(S):   Stevie Wonder

JUNE 15, 1972

TOUR: Seventh (1972) North American tour
VENUE: University of New Mexico, Albuquerque, NM, USA
OPENING/OTHER ACT(S):   Stevie Wonder

JUNE 16, 1972

TOUR: Seventh (1972) North American tour
VENUE: Coliseum, Denver, CO, USA

---

*At the second show the Stones played "Honky Tonk Women" as the encore. There were no more changes until Fort Worth, Texas on June 24.

OPENING/OTHER ACT(S): Stevie Wonder

JUNE 18, 1972

TOUR: Seventh (1972) North American tour
VENUE: Metropolitan Sports Center, Minneapolis, MN, USA
OPENING/OTHER ACT(S): Stevie Wonder

JUNE 19, 1972

TOUR: Seventh (1972) North American tour
VENUE: International Amphitheatre, Chicago, IL, USA
OPENING/OTHER ACT(S): Stevie Wonder

JUNE 20, 1972

TOUR: Seventh (1972) North American tour
VENUE: International Amphitheatre, Chicago, IL, USA
OPENING/OTHER ACT(S): Stevie Wonder
NOTES: Two shows

JUNE 22, 1972

TOUR: Seventh (1972) North American tour
VENUE: Municipal Auditorium, Kansas City, KS, USA
OPENING/OTHER ACT(S): Stevie Wonder

JUNE 24, 1972

TOUR: Seventh (1972) North American tour
VENUE: Will Rogers Auditorium, Fort Worth, TX, USA
OPENING/OTHER ACT(S): Stevie Wonder
SONGS: (First Show) Brown Sugar / Bitch / Rocks Off / Gimme Shelter / Dead Flowers / Sweet Black Angel / Happy / Tumbling Dice / Love in Vain / Sweet Virginia / You Can't Always Get What You Want / All Down the Line / Midnight Rambler / Rip this Joint / Jumpin' Jack Flash / **E:** Street Fighting Man (Second Show) Brown Sugar / Bitch / Rocks Off / Gimme Shelter / Don't Lie to Me (Berry) / Love in Vain / Sweet Virginia / You Can't Always Get What You Want / Tumbling Dice / Happy / All Down the Line / Midnight Rambler / Bye Bye Johnny (Berry) / Rip This Joint / Jumpin' Jack Flash / **E:** Street Fighting Man
NOTES: Two shows. Note the addition of the Chuck Berry song "Don't Lie to Me," which was performed here at the evening show only, filmed for *Ladies and Gentlemen, the Rolling Stones,* but didn't make it into the film's final cut. Stevie Wonder did not miss opening these concerts in the 4,800-seat Will Rogers Auditorium (as has often been published; he missed Houston, not Ft. Worth); his band was minus the drummer who'd begun having a nervous breakdown in Chicago.

JUNE 25, 1972

TOUR: Seventh (1972) North American tour
VENUE: Hofheinz Pavilion, Houston, TX, USA
SONGS: Brown Sugar / Bitch / Rocks Off / Gimme Shelter / Happy / Tumbling Dice / Love in Vain (Robt. Johnson) / Sweet Virginia / You Can't Always Get What You Want / All Down the Line / Midnight Rambler / Bye Bye Johnny (Berry) / Rip This Joint / Jumpin' Jack Flash / Street Fighting Man
NOTES: Two shows. The setlist was back to "normal" after the addition of "Don't Lie to Me" in Fort Worth (second show) and "Sweet Black Angel" (Ft. Worth, first show).

JUNE 27, 1972

TOUR: Seventh (1972) North American tour
VENUE: Municipal Auditorium, Mobile, AL, USA
OPENING/OTHER ACT(S): Stevie Wonder (returns to the tour)

JUNE 28, 1972

TOUR: Seventh (1972) North American tour
VENUE: University of Alabama, Tuscaloosa, AL, USA
OPENING/OTHER ACT(S): Stevie Wonder

JUNE 29, 1972

TOUR: Seventh (1972) North American tour
VENUE: Municipal Auditorium, Nashville, TN, USA
OPENING/OTHER ACT(S): Stevie Wonder

JULY 4, 1972

TOUR: Seventh (1972) North American tour
VENUE: Robert F. Kennedy Memorial Stadium, Washington, DC, USA
OPENING/OTHER ACT(S): Stevie Wonder, Dorothy Ellis
NOTES: Gospel singer Dorothy Ellis joined the opening bill for this July 4 performance in the nation's capital.

JULY 5, 1972

TOUR: Seventh (1972) North American tour
VENUE: The Scope, Norfolk, VA, USA
OPENING/OTHER ACT(S): Stevie Wonder

JULY 6, 1972

TOUR: Seventh (1972) North American tour
VENUE: Coliseum, Charlotte, NC, USA
OPENING/OTHER ACT(S): Stevie Wonder

JULY 7, 1972

TOUR: Seventh (1972) North American tour

VENUE: Civic Arena, Knoxville, TN, USA
OPENING/OTHER ACT(S): Stevie Wonder

JULY 9, 1972

TOUR: Seventh (1972) North American tour
VENUE: Kiel Auditorium, St. Louis, MO, USA
OPENING/OTHER ACT(S): Stevie Wonder
SONGS: Uptight / Satisfaction LMV
NOTES: This was the first night Stevie Wonder joined the Stones onstage for the encore jam medley of "Uptight" and "Satisfaction" that became a regular feature at the end of the tour.

JULY 11, 1972

TOUR: Seventh (1972) North American tour
VENUE: Rubber Bowl, Akron, OH, USA
OPENING/OTHER ACT(S): Stevie Wonder

JULY 12, 1972

TOUR: Seventh (1972) North American tour
VENUE: Convention Center, Indianapolis, IN, USA
OPENING/OTHER ACT(S): Stevie Wonder

JULY 13, 1972

TOUR: Seventh (1972) North American tour
VENUE: Cobo Hall, Detroit, MI, USA
OPENING/OTHER ACT(S): Stevie Wonder

JULY 14, 1972

TOUR: Seventh (1972) North American tour
VENUE: Cobo Hall, Detroit, MI, USA
OPENING/OTHER ACT(S): Stevie Wonder

JULY 15, 1972

TOUR: Seventh (1972) North American tour

Stevie Wonder and Mick Jagger, 1972 US tour

VENUE: Maple Leaf Gardens, Toronto, Ontario, Canada

OPENING/OTHER ACT(S): Stevie Wonder

NOTES: Two shows

JULY 17, 1972

TOUR: Seventh (1972) North American tour

VENUE: Forum, Montreal, Quebec, Canada

OPENING/OTHER ACT(S): Stevie Wonder

JULY 18, 1972

TOUR: Seventh (1972) North American tour

VENUE: The Boston Garden, Boston, MA, USA

OPENING/OTHER ACT(S): Stevie Wonder

SONGS: Brown Sugar / Bitch / Rocks Off / Gimme Shelter / Happy / Tumbling Dice / Love in Vain (Robt. Johnson) / Sweet Virginia / All Down the Line / Midnight Rambler / Bye Bye Johnny (Berry) / Rip This Joint / Jumpin' Jack Flash / Street Fighting Man / E: Honky Tonk Woman

NOTES: The band arrived late to this gig, Mick and Keith having been arrested in Warwick, RI but ordered sprung and motorcaded to the venue with a police escort by Boston's mayor, Kevin White, who was contending with near-riot conditions both inside and outside the Boston Garden. (See CHRONOLOGY)

JULY 19, 1972

TOUR: Seventh (1972) North American tour

VENUE: The Boston Garden, Boston, MA, USA

SPECIAL GUESTS: Stevie Wonder

OPENING/OTHER ACT(S): Stevie Wonder

SONGS: Brown Sugar / Bitch / Rocks Off / Gimme Shelter / Happy / Tumbling Dice / Love in Vain (Robt. Johnson) / Sweet Virginia / You Can't Always Get What You Want / All Down the Line / Midnight Rambler / Bye Bye Johnny (Berry) / Rip This Joint / Jumpin' Jack Flash / Street Fighting Man / E: Uptight → Satisfaction, LMV

NOTES: From this date until the end of the tour, Stevie Wonder joined the Stones onstage at all but a couple of performances for the encore number, a medley version of "Uptight" and "Satisfaction." This was a "first" in the band's history.

JULY 20, 1972

TOUR: Seventh (1972) North American tour

VENUE: Spectrum, Philadelphia, PA, USA

SPECIAL GUESTS: Stevie Wonder

OPENING/OTHER ACT(S): Stevie Wonder

SONGS: Brown Sugar / Bitch / Rocks Off / Gimme Shelter / Happy / Tumbling Dice / Love in Vain (Robt. Johnson) / Sweet Virginia / You Can't Always Get What You Want / All Down the Line / Midnight Rambler / Bye Bye Johnny (Berry) / Rip This Joint / Jumpin' Jack Flash / Street Fighting Man / Uptight → Satisfaction, LMV

JULY 21, 1972

TOUR: Seventh (1972) North American tour

VENUE: Spectrum, Philadelphia, PA, USA

SPECIAL GUESTS: Stevie Wonder

OPENING/OTHER ACT(S): Stevie Wonder

SONGS: Brown Sugar / Bitch / Rocks Off / Gimme Shelter / Happy / Tumbling Dice / Love in Vain (Robt. Johnson) / Sweet Virginia / You Can't Always Get What You Want / All Down the Line / Midnight Rambler / Bye Bye Johnny (Berry) / Rip This Joint / Jumpin' Jack Flash / **E***: Street Fighting Man / **E***: Uptight → Satisfaction, LMV

NOTES: Two shows.

JULY 22, 1972

TOUR: Seventh (1972) North American tour

VENUE: Civic Center Arena, Pittsburgh, PA, USA

OPENING/OTHER ACT(S): Stevie Wonder

SONGS: Brown Sugar / Bitch / Rocks Off / Gimme Shelter / Happy / Tumbling Dice / Love in Vain (Robt. Johnson) / Sweet Virginia / You Can't Always Get What You Want / All Down the Line / Midnight Rambler / Bye Bye Johnny (Berry) / Rip This Joint / Jumpin' Jack Flash / Street Fighting Man

NOTES: No medley

JULY 24, 1972

TOUR: Seventh (1972) North American tour

VENUE: Madison Square Garden, New York, NY, USA

SPECIAL GUESTS: Stevie Wonder

OPENING/OTHER ACT(S): Stevie Wonder

SONGS: Brown Sugar / Bitch / Rocks Off / Gimme Shelter / Happy / Tumbling Dice / Love in Vain (Robt. Johnson) / Sweet Virginia / You Can't Always Get What You Want / All Down the Line / Midnight Rambler / Bye Bye Johnny (Berry) / Rip This Joint / Jumpin' Jack Flash / Street Fighting Man / E: Uptight → Satisfaction, LMV

JULY 25, 1972

TOUR: Seventh (1972) North American tour

VENUE: Madison Square Garden, New York, NY, USA

---

*The live jam medley wasn't performed at the afternoon show.

Mick and Keith during "Brown Sugar," 1972 US tour (USED BY PERMISSION OF BOB GRUEN, ALL RIGHTS RESERVED)

SPECIAL GUESTS: Stevie Wonder

OPENING/OTHER ACT(S): Stevie Wonder

SONGS: Brown Sugar / Bitch / Rocks Off / Gimme Shelter / Happy / Tumbling Dice / Love in Vain (Robt. Johnson) / Sweet Virginia / You Can't Always Get What You Want / All Down the Line / Midnight Rambler / Bye Bye Johnny (Berry) / Rip This Joint / Jumpin' Jack Flash / **E:** Street Fighting Man / **E:** Uptight → Satisfaction, LMV

NOTES: Two shows. The early (afternoon) show was filmed for the ABC-TV "Dick Cavett Show," and the final medley was only performed in the evening.

JULY 26, 1972

TOUR: Seventh (1972) North American tour

VENUE: Madison Square Garden, New York, NY, USA

SPECIAL GUESTS: Stevie Wonder

OPENING/OTHER ACT(S): Stevie Wonder

SONGS: Brown Sugar / Bitch / Rocks Off / Gimme Shelter / Happy / Tumbling Dice / Love in Vain (Robt. Johnson) / Sweet Virginia / You Can't Always Get What You Want / All Down the Line / Midnight Rambler / Bye Bye Johnny (Berry) / Rip This Joint / Jumpin' Jack Flash / Street Fighting Man / **E:** Uptight → Satisfaction, LMV

NOTES: The last performance of the 1972 tour.

1973

JANUARY 18, 1973

TOUR: Nicaraguan Earthquake benefit concert
VENUE: L.A. Forum, Inglewood, CA, USA
PERSONNEL: Mick Jagger, Keith Richards, Mick Taylor, Charlie Watts, Bill Wyman
OPENING/OTHER ACT(S): Santana, Cheech & Chong, Tower of Power
SONGS: Brown Sugar / Bitch / Rocks Off / Gimme Shelter / Route 66 (Troup) / It's All Over Now (Womack, Womack) / Happy / Tumbling Dice / No Expectations / Sweet Virginia / You Can't Always Get What You Want / Dead Flowers / Stray Cat Blues / Live with Me / All Down the Line / Rip This Joint / Jumpin' Jack Flash / Street Fighting Man / Midnight Rambler
NOTES: In response to the huge December 23 earthquake which struck Bianca Jagger's home town of Managua, the Stones topped the bill at this one-nighter, which raised over half a million dollars for Nicaraguan quake relief. Santana, Cheech & Chong and Tower of Power were the opening acts at this show. Mick Taylor played the entire opening act set with Billy Preston.

JANUARY 21, 1973 – FEBRUARY 27, 1973

TOUR: 1973 Far East winter tour
VENUE: Hawaii, New Zealand and Australia
PERSONNEL: Mick Jagger, Keith Richards, Mick Taylor, Charlie Watts, Bill Wyman, Bobby Keys, Jim Price
SONGS: Brown Sugar / Bitch / Rocks Off / Gimme Shelter / Happy / Tumbling Dice / Love in Vain (Robt. Johnson) / Sweet Virginia / You Can't Always Get What You Want / Honky Tonk Women / All Down the Line / Dead Flowers / Midnight Rambler / Little Queenie (Berry) / Rip This Joint / Jumpin' Jack Flash / Street Fighting Man / It's All Over Now (Womack, Womack) / Route 66 (Troup) / No Expectations / Live with Me
NOTES: "It's All Over Now," "Route 66," "No Expectations" and "Live with Me" were added occasionally to individual performances: where the set varies from the norm, it is noted in the following listings. The usual encore was "Street Fighting Man." In one of the weirder coincidences in Stones history, Mick Taylor was to make his last US live concert appearance as a member of the band on this tour in the same place (Hawaii) as had his predecessor, Brian Jones. The Stones had booked January 28 through February 2 at Tokyo's Nippon Budokan Hall, but were forced to cancel all six sold-out concerts when the Japanese government denied Mick Jagger's entry visa because of his 1967 drug conviction. Japanese television negotiated a deal to film the Hawaii shows to appease

Stones fans in Japan, but the Stones had a change of heart at the last moment and refused to allow the crew access to the concerts. The Rolling Stones didn't play Japan until the 1990 Steel Wheels tour but, in another twist, Mick Jagger was the first original band member to perform there—on his first, solo tour in March 1988. Contrary to the somewhat widespread belief, the band did *not* play Hong Kong on this tour.

JANUARY 21, 1973

TOUR: 1973 Far East winter tour
VENUE: International Sports Centre, Honolulu, HI, USA
NOTES: Japanese television was slated to film the Hawaii shows when the band had to cancel all six Tokyo concerts. It never happened. See prior listing.

JANUARY 22, 1973

TOUR: 1973 Far East winter tour
VENUE: International Sports Centre, Honolulu, HI, USA
SONGS: Brown Sugar / Bitch / Rocks Off / Gimme Shelter / It's All Over Now (Womack, Womack) / Happy / Tumbling Dice / Sweet Virginia / Dead Flowers / You Can't Always Get What You Want / All Down the Line / Midnight Rambler / Rip This Joint / Jumpin' Jack Flash / Street Fighting Man
NOTES: Two shows. This is the set performed at the 6:00 P.M. show. The second show was Mick Taylor's last US performance as a Rolling Stone. Curiously, Brian Jones's last US performance with the band had been here as well, on July 28, 1966.

JANUARY 28 – FEBRUARY 2, 1973

TOUR: 1973 Far East winter tour
VENUE: Nippon Budokan Hall, Tokyo, Japan (cancelled)
NOTES: Six sold-out performances had to be cancelled when the Japanese denied Mick Jagger an entry visa, ostensibly because of his 1967 conviction on drug charges. The whole band, of course, had ongoing loud legal hassles, most recently with the French police in December 1972. Warrants had been issued against Keith Richards and Anita Pallenberg on heroin charges, and Jagger tried to counter reports of the other members' involvement via categorical denials to the press. The Japanese, however, were unmoved. The Stones were not pleased either. Japanese television stepped in and negotiated to broadcast the Stones performing in Hawaii, a deal that might have appeased the fans and helped the band's finances. Nevertheless, the filming was nixed by the band in Honolulu.

FEBRUARY 5, 1973

TOUR: 1973 Far East winter tour
VENUE: Football Club Stadium, Hong Kong (canceled)

FEBRUARY 11, 1973

TOUR: 1973 Far East winter tour
VENUE: Western Springs Stadium, Auckland, New Zealand

FEBRUARY 13, 1973

TOUR: 1973 Far East winter tour
VENUE: Milton Park Tennis Courts, Brisbane, Australia

FEBRUARY 14, 1973

TOUR: 1973 Far East winter tour
VENUE: Milton Park Tennis Courts, Brisbane, Australia

FEBRUARY 17, 1973

TOUR: 1973 Far East winter tour
VENUE: Kooyong Tennis Courts, Melbourne, Australia
OPENING/OTHER ACT(S): Madderlake
SONGS: Brown Sugar / Bitch / Rocks Off / Gimme Shelter / Happy / Tumbling Dice / Love in Vain (Robt. Johnson) / Sweet Virginia / You Can't Always Get What You Want / Honky Tonk Women / All Down the Line / Midnight Rambler / Bye Bye Johnny (Berry) / Jumpin' Jack Flash / Street Fighting Man

FEBRUARY 18, 1973

TOUR: 1973 Far East winter tour
VENUE: Kooyong Tennis Courts, Melbourne, Australia
OPENING/OTHER ACT(S): Madderlake
SONGS: Brown Sugar / Bitch / Rocks Off / Gimme Shelter / Happy / Tumbling Dice / Love in Vain (Robt. Johnson) / Sweet Virginia / You Can't Always Get What You Want / Honky Tonk Women / All Down the Line / Midnight Rambler / Bye Bye Johnny (Berry) / Jumpin' Jack Flash / Street Fighting Man
NOTES: Two shows

FEBRUARY 20, 1973

TOUR: 1973 Far East winter tour
VENUE: Memorial Drive Park, Adelaide, Australia

FEBRUARY 21, 1973

TOUR: 1973 Far East winter tour
VENUE: Memorial Drive Park, Adelaide, Australia
SONGS: Brown Sugar / Bitch / Rocks Off / Gimme Shelter / Happy / Tumbling Dice / Love in Vain (Robt. Johnson) / Sweet Virginia / You Can't Always Get What You Want / Honky Tonk Women / All Down the Line / Midnight Rambler / Bye Bye Johnny (Berry) / Jumpin' Jack Flash / Street Fighting Man

FEBRUARY 24, 1973

TOUR: 1973 Far East winter tour
VENUE: Western Australia Cricket Ground, Perth, Australia

FEBRUARY 26, 1973

TOUR: 1973 Far East winter tour
VENUE: Royal Randwick Racecourse, Sydney, Australia
OPENING/OTHER ACT(S): Madderlake, Rockery
SONGS: Brown Sugar / Bitch / Rocks Off / Gimme Shelter / Happy / Tumbling Dice / Love in Vain (Robt. Johnson) / Sweet Virginia / You Can't Always Get What You Want / Honky Tonk Women / All Down the Line / Midnight Rambler / Little Queenie (Berry) / Rip This Joint / Jumpin' Jack Flash / Street Fighting Man

FEBRUARY 27, 1973

TOUR: 1973 Far East winter tour
VENUE: Royal Randwick Racecourse, Sydney, Australia
OPENING/OTHER ACT(S): Madderlake, Rockery
SONGS: Brown Sugar / Bitch / Rocks Off / Gimme Shelter / Happy / Tumbling Dice / Love in Vain (Robt. Johnson) / Sweet Virginia / You Can't Always Get What You Want / Honky Tonk Women / All Down the Line / Midnight Rambler / Little Queenie (Berry) / Rip This Joint / Jumpin' Jack Flash / Street Fighting Man
NOTES: Last gig of the 1973 winter tour.

SEPTEMBER 1, 1973 – OCTOBER 19, 1973

TOUR: 1973 European tour
VENUE: Austria, West Germany, UK, Switzerland, Denmark, Sweden, Holland and Belgium
PERSONNEL: Mick Jagger, Keith Richards, Mick Taylor, Charlie Watts, Bill Wyman, Ian Stewart, Nicky Hopkins (kb), Billy Preston (kb), Bobby Keys (sax), Jim Price (tpt), Trevor Lawrence (sax), Steve Madaio (tpt)
OPENING/OTHER ACT(S): Billy Preson, Kracker
SONGS: Brown Sugar / Bitch / Gimme Shelter / Happy / Tumbling Dice / 100 Years Ago / Star Star / Angie / Sweet Virginia / You Can't Always Get What You Want / Dancing with Mr. D / Doo Doo Doo Doo Doo (Heartbreaker) / Midnight Rambler / Silver Train / Honky Tonk Women / All Down the Line / Rip this Joint / Jumpin' Jack Flash / Street Fighting Man

NOTES: Opening acts on this tour were: Billy Preston, who also backed the Stones on piano during their set; and Kracker, a Cuban band out of Brooklyn discovered by Jimmy Miller that became the first act signed to Rolling Stones Records (before Peter Tosh). On this tour, Mick Taylor joined Preston during his opening set but in disguise. Taylor donned a huge Afro wig, as if changing his appearance could mask the guitarist's identity. . . . In addition to the keyboards of Preston, Nicky Hopkins and Stu, the Stones' backup players included a horn section: Bobby Keys on sax, Jim Price and Steve Madaio on trumpet and, at some shows, Trevor Lawrence on sax.

Above is a list of all songs included in sets throughout the tour. "100 Years Ago," "Sweet Virginia" and "Bitch" were only performed in Vienna and Cologne, and in London on September 7 only. "Doo Doo Doo Doo (Heratbreaker)" and "Dancing with Mr. D," on the other hand, were somewhat regularly rotated; neither was played at every concert.

SEPTEMBER 1, 1973

TOUR: 1973 European tour
VENUE: Stadthalle, Vienna, Austria
OPENING/OTHER ACT(S): Billy Preston, Kracker
SONGS: Brown Sugar / Bitch / Gimme Shelter / Happy / Tumbling Dice / 100 Years Ago / Star Star / Angie / Sweet Virginia / You Can't Always Get What You Want / Dancing with Mr. D / Midnight Rambler / Silver Train / Honky Tonk Women / All Down the Line / Rip This Joint / Jumpin' Jack Flash / Street Fighting Man
NOTES: The band played every song—except for "Doo Doo Doo Doo Doo (Heartbreaker)"—that they'd perform on the entire '73 tour.

SEPTEMBER 3, 1973

TOUR: 1973 European tour
VENUE: Eisstadion, Mannheim, West Germany
OPENING/OTHER ACT(S): Billy Preston, Kracker
SONGS: Brown Sugar / Bitch / Gimme Shelter / Happy / Tumbling Dice / 100 Years Ago / Star Star / Angie / Sweet Virginia / You Can't Always Get What You Want / Dancing with Mr. D / Doo Doo Doo Doo Doo (Heartbreaker) / Midnight Rambler / Honky Tonk Women / All Down the Line / Rip This Joint / Jumpin' Jack Flash / Street Fighting Man
NOTES: "Silver Train" comes out, "Heartbreaker" goes in. "100 Years Ago," "Sweet Virginia" and "Bitch" are performed in Mannheim, but for the last time on the '73 tour.

SEPTEMBER 4, 1973

TOUR: 1973 European tour

VENUE: Sporthalle, Cologne, West Germany
OPENING/OTHER ACT(S): Billy Preston, Kracker
NOTES: Two shows

SEPTEMBER 7, 1973

TOUR: 1973 European Tour
VENUE: Empire Pool, Wembley, Middlesex, England
OPENING/OTHER ACT(S): Billy Preston, Kracker
SONGS: Brown Sugar / Gimme Shelter / Happy / Tumbling Dice / Star Star / Angie / You Can't Always Get What You Want / Dancing with Mr. D / Doo Doo Doo Doo Doo (Heartbreaker) / Midnight Rambler / Silver Train / Honky Tonk Women / All Down the Line / Rip This Joint / Jumpin' Jack Flash / Street Fighting Man

SEPTEMBER 8, 1973

TOUR: 1973 European tour
VENUE: Empire Pool, Wembley, Middlesex, England
OPENING/OTHER ACT(S): Billy Preston, Kracker
SONGS: Brown Sugar / Gimme Shelter / Happy / Tumbling Dice / Star Star / Angie / You Can't Always Get What You Want / Dancing with Mr. D / Doo Doo Doo Doo Doo (Heartbreaker) / Midnight Rambler / Honky Tonk Women / All Down the Line / Rip This Joint / Jumpin' Jack Flash / Street Fighting Man
NOTES: Two shows.

SEPTEMBER 9, 1973

TOUR: 1973 European tour
VENUE: Empire Pool, Wembley, Middlesex, England
OPENING/OTHER ACT(S): Billy Preston, Kracker
SONGS: Brown Sugar / Gimme Shelter / Happy / Tumbling Dice / Star Star / Angie / You Can't Always Get What You Want / Dancing with Mr. D / Doo Doo Doo Doo Doo (Heartbreaker) / Midnight Rambler / Honky Tonk Women / All Down the Line / Rip This Joint / Jumpin' Jack Flash / Street Fighting Man

SEPTEMBER 11, 1973

TOUR: 1973 European tour
VENUE: King's Hall, Belle Vue, Manchester, Lancashire, England
OPENING/OTHER ACT(S): Billy Preston, Kracker

SEPTEMBER 12, 1973

TOUR: 1973 European tour
VENUE: King's Hall, Belle Vue, Manchester, Lancashire, England
OPENING/OTHER ACT(S): Billy Preston, Kracker

SEPTEMBER 13, 1973

TOUR: 1973 European tour
VENUE: City Hall, Newcastle-upon-Tyne, Northumberland, England
OPENING/OTHER ACT(S): Billy Preston, Kracker
NOTES: Two shows

SEPTEMBER 16, 1973

TOUR: 1973 European tour
VENUE: Apollo Theatre, Glasgow, Scotland
OPENING/OTHER ACT(S): Billy Preston, Kracker

SEPTEMBER 17, 1973

TOUR: 1973 European tour
VENUE: Apollo Theatre, Glasgow, Scotland
OPENING/OTHER ACT(S): Billy Preston, Kracker

SEPTEMBER 19, 1973

TOUR: 1973 European tour
VENUE: Odeon Theatre, Birmingham, Warwickshire, England
OPENING/OTHER ACT(S): Billy Preston, Kracker
NOTES: Two shows

SEPTEMBER 20, 1973

TOUR: 1973 European tour
VENUE: Cardiff and Pembroke Castles, Wales (both canceled)
NOTES: Though these gigs were cancelled, posters adorned with a dragon were printed to advertise them. Some of these still exist and are, naturally, collectors' items.

SEPTEMBER 23, 1973

TOUR: 1973 European tour
VENUE: Eishalle, Innsbruck, Austria
OPENING/OTHER ACT(S): Billy Preston, Kracker

SEPTEMBER 25, 1973

TOUR: 1973 European tour
VENUE: Festhalle, Berne, Switzerland
OPENING/OTHER ACT(S): Billy Preston, Kracker

SEPTEMBER 26, 1973

TOUR: 1973 European tour
VENUE: Festhalle, Berne, Switzerland
OPENING/OTHER ACT(S): Billy Preston, Kracker
NOTES: Two shows

SEPTEMBER 28, 1973

TOUR: 1973 European tour
VENUE: Olympiahalle, Munich, West Germany
OPENING/OTHER ACT(S): Billy Preston, Kracker
SONGS: Brown Sugar / Gimme Shelter / Happy / Tumbling Dice / Star Star / Dancing with Mr. D / Angie / You Can't Always Get What You Want / Midnight Rambler / Honky Tonk Women / All Down the Line / Rip This Joint / Jumpin' Jack Flash / Street Fighting Man
NOTES: Two shows

SEPTEMBER 30, 1973

TOUR: 1973 European tour
VENUE: Festhalle, Frankfurt, West Germany
OPENING/OTHER ACT(S): Billy Preston, Kracker
NOTES: Two shows

OCTOBER 2, 1973

TOUR: 1973 European tour
VENUE: Ernst Merck Halle, Hamburg, West Germany
OPENING/OTHER ACT(S): Billy Preston, Kracker
NOTES: Two shows

OCTOBER 4, 1973

TOUR: 1973 European tour
VENUE: Bejlby Riiskonhallen, Aarhus, Denmark
OPENING/OTHER ACT(S): Billy Preston, Kracker

OCTOBER 6, 1973

TOUR: 1973 European tour
VENUE: Skandinavium, Gothenberg, Sweden
OPENING/OTHER ACT(S): Billy Preston, Kracker

OCTOBER 7, 1973

TOUR: 1973 European tour
VENUE: Brandby Hallen, Copenhagen, Denmark
OPENING/OTHER ACT(S): Billy Preston, Kracker
SONGS: Brown Sugar / Gimme Shelter / Happy / Tumbling Dice / Star Star / Doo Doo Doo Doo Doo (Heartbreaker) / Angie / You Can't Always Get What You Want / Midnight Rambler / Honky Tonk Women / All Down the Line / Rip This Joint / Jumpin' Jack Flash / Street Fighting Man
NOTES: Two shows. "Dancing with Mr. D" replaces "Heartbreaker" at the second show.

OCTOBER 9, 1973

TOUR: 1973 European tour
VENUE: Gruga Halle, Essen, West Germany
OPENING/OTHER ACT(S): Billy Preston, Kracker

OCTOBER 10, 1973

TOUR: 1973 European tour
VENUE: Gruga Halle, Essen, West Germany
OPENING/OTHER ACT(S): Billy Preston, Kracker

OCTOBER 11, 1973

TOUR: 1973 European tour
VENUE: Gruga Halle, Essen, West Germany
OPENING/OTHER ACT(S): Billy Preston, Kracker

OCTOBER 13, 1973

TOUR: 1973 European tour
VENUE: Ahoy Hall, Rotterdam, Holland
OPENING/OTHER ACT(S): Billy Preston, Kracker

OCTOBER 14, 1973

TOUR: 1973 European tour
VENUE: Ahoy Hall, Rotterdam, Holland
OPENING/OTHER ACT(S): Billy Preston, Kracker
NOTES: Two shows

OCTOBER 15, 1973

TOUR: 1973 European tour
VENUE: Palais des Sports, Antwerp, Belgium
OPENING/OTHER ACT(S): Billy Preston, Kracker

OCTOBER 17, 1973

TOUR: 1973 European tour
VENUE: Forêt Nationale, Brussels, Belgium
OPENING/OTHER ACT(S): Billy Preston, Kracker
SONGS: Brown Sugar / Gimme Shelter / Happy / Tumbling Dice / Star Star / Dancing with Mr. D / Angie / You Can't Always Get What You Want / Midnight Rambler / Honky Tonk Women / All Down the Line / Rip This Joint / Jumpin' Jack Flash / Street Fighting Man
NOTES: Two shows

OCTOBER 19, 1973

TOUR: 1973 European tour
VENUE: Deutschlandhalle, West Berlin, West Germany
OPENING/OTHER ACT(S): Billy Preston, Kracker
SONGS: Brown Sugar / Gimme Shelter / Happy / Tumbling Dice / Star Star / Dancing with Mr. D / Angie / You Can't Always Get What You Want / Midnight Rambler / Honky Tonk Women / All Down the Line / Rip This Joint / Jumpin' Jack Flash / **E:** Street Fighting Man
NOTES: Last gig of the Stones' 1973 European tour, and the last gig for Mick Taylor as a member of the band.

A thankful Mick Jagger, 1975 US tour (USED BY PER-MISSION OF BOB GRUEN, ALL RIGHTS RESERVED)

1975

JUNE 1, 1975 – AUGUST 8, 1975

TOUR: 1975 Tour of the Americas
VENUE: US and Canada
PERSONNEL: Mick Jagger, Keith Richards, Ron Wood, Charlie Watts, Bill Wyman, Ian Stewart, Billy Preston, Ollie Brown
SPECIAL GUESTS: Elton John, Eric Clapton, Carlos Santana, Jesse Ed Davis (tpt), Steve Madaio (tpt), Trevor Lawrence (sax), Bobby Keys (sax)
OPENING/OTHER ACT(S): The Meters, The Eagles, Rufus, The Crusaders, The J. Geils Band, Tower of Power, Steel Drummers, The Commodores, Mighty Clouds of Joy, The Charlie Daniels Band, Furry Lewis, Montrose, Trapeze, The Wailers
SONGS: Honky Tonk Women / All Down the Line / If You Can't Rock Me → Get Off of My Cloud, LMV / Rocks Off / Ain't Too Proud to Beg (Whitfield, Holland) / Star Star / Gimme Shelter / You Gotta Move (McDowell, Davis) / Cherry Oh Baby (Donaldson) / You Can't Always Get What You Want / Happy / Tumbling Dice / Luxury / Fingerprint File, LV1 / Brown Sugar / Dance

Little Sister / It' Only Rock 'n' Roll, LV1 / Sure the One You Need / Doo Doo Doo Doo Doo (Heartbreaker) / That's Life (Preston) / Outta Space (Preston, Green) / Angie / Wild Horses / Midnight Rambler / Rip This Joint / Street Fighting Man / Jumpin' Jack Flash / **E:** Sympathy for the Devil

NOTES: The Stones' 1975 "Tour of the Americas" was so named because it had been slated to conclude in Latin America. But all gigs there were canceled—six dates in Mexico City, four in Rio, four in São Paulo, and four in Caracas, Venezuela. The tour had been announced to the press and public on May 1, when the band played down New York's Fifth Avenue on the back of a flatbed truck. It was Ron Wood's first outing with the Stones, though he wasn't "official" until the following February. The tour-long backing musicians were Billy Preston on keyboards and Ollie Brown on percussion. There were, however, cameo players and a variety of opening acts throughout the tour. Elton John made a surprise guest appearance in Boulder, and Eric Clapton and Carlos Santana joined the Stones onstage at Madison Square Garden. Four horn players materialized at the Forum in LA. Their names and those of the opening artists are listed above and with individual concert entries.

This song list contains all titles performed at any time on the '75 tour. A short recorded excerpt of Aaron Copland's "Fanfare for the Common Man" served as an intro/overture to the actual show. Three numbers were dropped from the regular lineup after the first gig in Baton Rouge—"Rocks Off," "Luxury" and "Dance Little Sister"—but the latter two appeared at the occasional performance later on. "Sympathy for the Devil," accompanied by a group of Brooklyn-based West Indian steel drummers (all members of the Steel Band Association of America), was added as the encore in New York and Los Angeles only. "Cherry Oh Baby" was performed in New York. "Sure the One You Need" was played only in Kansas City and Milwaukee. Two *Love You Live* tracks came from one Toronto show. The Stones backed Billy Preston on his two solo numbers in the middle of the set. Dancing, Jagger would join him onstage. Then—in the indoor venues—Mick used what he'd learned from his dad back in 1957 (see TELEVISION APPEARANCES) for a crowd-pleasing surprise. Clinging to a rope dropped like some jungle vine from the rafters, the singer would hoist himself up and leap off the stage to swoop into the air, swing back and forth over the audience and land, finally, back onstage.

JUNE 1, 1975

TOUR: 1975 Tour of the Americas
VENUE: Louisiana State University, Baton Rouge, LA, USA
OPENING/OTHER ACT(S): The Meters

SONGS: Honky Tonk Women / All Down the Line / If You Can't Rock Me → Get Off of My Cloud, LMV / Rocks Off / Ain't Too Proud to Beg (Whitfield, Holland) / Star Star / Gimme Shelter / You Gotta Move (McDowell, Davis) / You Can't Always Get What You Want / Happy / Tumbling Dice / Luxury / Fingerprint File / That's Life (Preston) / Outta Space (Preston, Green) / Brown Sugar / Dance Little Sister / It's Only Rock 'n' Roll / Jumpin' Jack Flash / Rip This Joint / Street Fighting Man / **E:** Midnight Rambler

NOTES: Two shows, 3:30 P.M. and 9:00 P.M. The Meters opened both performances. Check out this setlist! In an uncommon move, the Stones played "Midnight Rambler" as their encore at LSU. They'd done it once before—at the Nicaraguan earthquake benefit at the L.A. Forum in January 1973. Amazingly, the band played two shows on this date, each over two and a half hours long. Five hours plus of rock 'n' roll on the first day of the tour!

JUNE 3, 1975

TOUR: 1975 Tour of the Americas
VENUE: San Antonio Convention Center, San Antonio, TX, USA
OPENING/OTHER ACT(S): The Meters
SONGS: Honky Tonk Women / All Down the Line / If You Can't Rock Me → Get Off of My Cloud, LMV / Ain't Too Proud to Beg (Whitfield, Holland) / Star Star / Gimme Shelter / You Gotta Move (McDowell, Davis) You Can't Always Get What You Want / Happy / Tumbling Dice / Fingerprint File / Brown Sugar / It's Only Rock 'n' Roll / Doo Doo Doo Doo Doo (Heartbreaker) / That's Life (Preston) / Outta Space (Preston, Green) / Angie / Wild Horses / Midnight Rambler / Rip This Joint / Street Fighting Man / **E:** Jumpin' Jack Flash

NOTES: The Meters opened for the Stones. This is the usual setlist, with the initial removal of "Rocks Off," "Luxury," and "Dance Little Sister."

JUNE 4, 1975

TOUR: 1975 Tour of the Americas
VENUE: San Antonio Convention Center, San Antonio, TX, USA
OPENING/OTHER ACT(S): The Meters
NOTES: The Meters opened the show.

JUNE 6, 1975

TOUR: 1975 Tour of the Americas
VENUE: Arrowhead Stadium, Kansas City, MO, USA
OPENING/OTHER ACT(S): The Eagles, Rufus
SONGS: Honky Tonk Women / All Down the Line / If You Can't Rock Me → Get Off of My Cloud, LMV / Ain't Too Proud to Beg (Whitfield, Holland) / Star Star

/ Gimme Shelter / You Gotta Move (McDowell, Davis) / You Can't Always Get What You Want / Happy / Tumbling Dice / Fingerprint File / Brown Sugar / It's Only Rock 'n' Roll / Sure the One You Need / Doo Doo Doo Doo Doo (Heartbreaker) / That's Life (Preston) / Outta Space (Preston, Green) / Angie / Wild Horses / Midnight Rambler / Rip This Joint / Street Fighting Man / E: Jumpin' Jack Flash

NOTES: One show. Opening acts were the Eagles and Rufus. "Sure the One You Need," with Keith Richards on vocals, was performed here.

JUNE 8, 1975

TOUR: 1975 Tour of the Americas
VENUE: Milwaukee County Stadium, Milwaukee, WI, USA
OPENING/OTHER ACT(S): The Eagles, Rufus
SONGS: Honky Tonk Women / All Down the Line / If You Can't Rock Me → Get Off of My Cloud, LMV / Ain't Too Proud to Beg (Whitfield, Holland) / Star Star / Gimme Shelter / You Gotta Move (McDowell, Davis) / You Can't Always Get What You Want / Happy / Tumbling Dice / Fingerprint File / Brown Sugar / It's Only Rock 'n' Roll / Sure the One You Need / Doo Doo Doo Doo Doo (Heartbreaker) / That's Life (Preston) / Outta Space (Preston, Green) / Angie / Wild Horses / Midnight Rambler / Rip This Joint / Street Fighting Man / E: Jumpin' Jack Flash
NOTES: A single 2:00 P.M. show was opened by Rufus and The Eagles. Keith sang "Sure the One You Need" again. But the song did not appear in a Tour of the Americas set.

JUNE 9, 1975

TOUR: 1975 Tour of the Americas
VENUE: St. Paul Civic Center, St. Paul, MN, USA
OPENING/OTHER ACT(S): Rufus
SONGS: Honky Tonk Women / All Down the Line / If You Can't Rock Me → Get Off of My Cloud, LMV / Ain't Too Proud to Beg (Whitfield, Holland) / Star Star / Gimme Shelter / You Gotta Move (McDowell, Davis) / You Can't Always Get What You Want / Happy / Tumbling Dice / Fingerprint File / Brown Sugar / It's Only Rock 'n' Roll / Doo Doo Doo Doo Doo (Heartbreaker) / That's Life (Preston) / Outta Space (Preston, Green) / Angie / Wild Horses / Midnight Rambler / Rip This Joint / Street Fighting Man / E: Jumpin' Jack Flash
NOTES: Rufus was the opening act at the Stones' single St. Paul show. The set returned to normal.

JUNE 11, 1975

TOUR: 1975 Tour of the Americas

VENUE: The Boston Garden, Boston, MA, USA
OPENING/OTHER ACT(S): The Crusaders
NOTES: The Crusaders opened for the Stones. They played a single show each night of a two day stint at the Boston Garden.

JUNE 12, 1975

TOUR: 1975 Tour of the Americas
VENUE: The Boston Garden, Boston, MA, USA
OPENING/OTHER ACT(S): The Crusaders
NOTES: One show

JUNE 14, 1975

TOUR: 1975 Tour of the Americas
VENUE: Cleveland Municipal Stadium, Cleveland, OH, USA
OPENING/OTHER ACT(S): The J. Geils Band, Tower of Power
NOTES: One show. J. Geils and Tower of Power opened for the Stones.

JUNE 15, 1975

TOUR: 1975 Tour of the Americas
VENUE: Buffalo Memorial Auditorium, Buffalo, NY, USA
OPENING/OTHER ACT(S): The Crusaders
NOTES: The Crusaders opened for the Stones' single show in Buffalo.

JUNE 17, 1975

TOUR: 1975 Tour of the Americas
VENUE: Maple Leaf Gardens, Toronto, Ontario, Canada
OPENING/OTHER ACT(S): The Crusaders
NOTES: The Crusaders opened for the Stones on this and the next night's Maple Leaf Gardens shows. Two tracks on *Love You Live*—"Fingerprint File," LV1 and "It's Only Rock 'n' Roll," LV1—came from recordings done at this show.

JUNE 18, 1975

TOUR: 1975 Tour of the Americas
VENUE: Maple Leaf Gardens, Toronto, Ontario, Canada
OPENING/OTHER ACT(S): The Crusaders, Rufus

JUNE 22, 1975

TOUR: 1975 Tour of the Americas
VENUE: Madison Square Garden, New York, NY, USA
SPECIAL GUESTS: Eric Clapton, Steel Band Association of America

OPENING/OTHER ACT(S): Steel Band Association of America

SONGS: Honky Tonk Women / All Down the Line / If You Can't Rock Me → Get Off of My Cloud, LMV / Ain't Too Proud to Beg (Whitfield, Holland) / Star Star / Gimme Shelter / You Gotta Move (McDowell, Davis) / You Can't Always Get What You Want / Happy / Tumbling Dice / Fingerprint File / Brown Sugar / It's Only Rock 'n' Roll / Doo Doo Doo Doo Doo (Heartbreaker) That's Life (Preston) / Outta Space (Preston, Green) / Angie / Wild Horses / Midnight Rambler / Rip This Joint / Street Fighting Man / Jumpin' Jack Flash / **E:** Sympathy for the Devil

NOTES: Eric Clapton made a surprise guest appearance with the Stones at this concert, sitting in on "Sympathy for the Devil." This was the first of six consecutive Madison Square Garden shows on the tour. The steel drummers (most of whom came from Brooklyn, NY) and were members of the Steel Band Association of America were the opening act for each of the NYC dates, and also appeared with the band on "Sympathy for the Devil."

JUNE 23, 1975

TOUR: 1975 Tour of the Americas
VENUE: Madison Square Garden, New York, NY, USA
SPECIAL GUESTS: Steel Band Association of America
OPENING/OTHER ACT(S): Steel Band Association of America
SONGS: Honky Tonk Women / All Down the Line / If You Can't Rock Me → Get Off of My Cloud, LMV / Ain't Too Proud to Beg (Whitfield, Holland) / Star Star / Gimme Shelter / You Gotta Move (McDowell, Davis) / You Can't Always Get What You Want / Happy / Tumbling Dice / Fingerprint File / Brown Sugar / It's Only Rock 'n' Roll / Doo Doo Doo Doo Doo (Heartbreaker) / That's Life (Preston) / Outta Space (Preston, Green) / Angie / Wild Horses / Midnight Rambler / Rip This Joint / Street Fighting Man / Jumpin' Jack Flash / **E:** Sympathy for the Devil

JUNE 24, 1975

TOUR: 1975 Tour of the Americas
VENUE: Madison Square Garden, New York, NY, USA
SPECIAL GUESTS: Steel Band Association of America

Keith, 1975 US tour

OPENING/OTHER ACT(S): Steel Band Association of America

SONGS: Honky Tonk Women / All Down the Line / If You Can't Rock Me → Get Off of My Cloud, LMV / Ain't Too Proud to Beg (Whitfield, Holland) / Star Star / Gimme Shelter / You Gotta Move (McDowell, Davis) / You Can't Always Get What You Want / Happy / Tumbling Dice / Fingerprint File / Brown Sugar / It's Only Rock 'n' Roll / Doo Doo Doo Doo Doo (Heartbreaker) / That's Life (Preston) / Outta Space (Preston, Green) / Angie / Wild Horses / Midnight Rambler / Rip This Joint / Street Fighting Man / Jumpin' Jack Flash / E: Sympathy for the Devil

JUNE 25, 1975

TOUR: 1975 Tour of the Americas
VENUE: Madison Square Garden, New York, NY, USA
SPECIAL GUESTS: Steel Band Association of America
OPENING/OTHER ACT(S): Steel Band Association of America
SONGS: Honky Tonk Women / All Down the Line / If You Can't Rock Me → Get Off of My Cloud, LMV / Ain't Too Proud to Beg (Whitfield, Holland) / Star Star / Gimme Shelter / You Gotta Move (McDowell, Davis) / You Can't Always Get What You Want / Happy / Tumbling Dice / Fingerprint File / Brown Sugar / It's Only Rock 'n' Roll / Doo Doo Doo Doo Doo (Heartbreaker) / That's Life (Preston) / Outta Space (Preston, Green) / Angie / Wild Horses / Midnight Rambler / Rip This Joint / Street Fighting Man / Jumpin' Jack Flash / E: Sympathy for the Devil

JUNE 26, 1975

TOUR: 1975 Tour of the Americas
VENUE: Madison Square Garden, New York, NY, USA
SPECIAL GUESTS: Steel Band Association of America
OPENING/OTHER ACT(S): Steel Band Association of America
SONGS: Fanfare for the Common Man (Copland) / Honky Tonk Women / All Down the Line / If You Can't Rock Me → Get Off of My Cloud, LMV / Ain't Too Proud to Beg (Whitfield, Holland) / Star Star / Gimme Shelter / You Gotta Move (McDowell, Davis) / Cherry Oh Baby (Donaldson) / You Can't Always Get What You Want / Happy / Tumbling Dice / Fingerprint File / Brown Sugar / It's Only Rock 'n' Roll / Doo Doo Doo Doo Doo (Heartbreaker) / That's Life (Preston) / Outta Space (Preston, Green) / Angie / Wild Horses / Midnight Rambler / Rip This Joint / Street Fighting Man / Jumpin' Jack Flash / E: Sympathy for the Devil
NOTES: The band performed "Cherry Oh Baby" at this performance and on the following night, then dropped it from the set for the duration of the '75 tour.

JUNE 27, 1975

TOUR: 1975 Tour of the Americas
VENUE: Madison Square Garden, New York, NY, USA
SPECIAL GUESTS: Carlos Santana, Steel Band Association of America
OPENING/OTHER ACT(S): Steel Band Association of America
SONGS: Honky Tonk Women / All Down the Line / If You Can't Rock Me → Get Off of My Cloud, LMV / Ain't Too Proud to Beg (Whitfield, Holland) / Star Star / Gimme Shelter / You Gotta Move (McDowell, Davis) / Cherry Oh Baby (Donaldson) / You Can't Always Get What You Want / Happy / Tumbling Dice / Fingerprint File / Brown Sugar / It's Only Rock 'n' Roll / Doo Doo Doo Doo Doo (Heartbreaker) / That's Life (Preston) / Outta Space (Preston, Green) / Angie / Wild Horses / Midnight Rambler / Rip This Joint / Street Fighting Man / Jumpin' Jack Flash / E: Sympathy for the Devil
NOTES: Carlos Santana was the "Sympathy For The Devil" guest artist at this show, the last of Six New York City dates on this tour. As with the other Madison Square Garden shows, the Brooklyn-based steel drummers, members of the Steel Band Association of America, were the opening act and joined the Stones onstage for the "Sympathy for the Devil" encore.

JUNE 29, 1975

TOUR: 1975 Tour of the Americas
VENUE: Spectrum, Philadelphia, PA, USA
OPENING/OTHER ACT(S): The Commodores
SONGS: Fanfare for the Common Man (Copland) / Honky Tonk Women / All Down the Line / If You Can't Rock Me → Get Off of My Cloud, LMV / Ain't Too Proud to Beg (Whitfield, Holland) / Star Star / Gimme Shelter / You Gotta Move (McDowell, Davis) / You Can't Always Get What You Want / Happy / Tumbling Dice / Fingerprint File / Brown Sugar / It's Only Rock 'n' Roll / Doo Doo Doo Doo Doo (Heartbreaker) / That's Life (Preston) / Outta Space (Preston, Green) / Angie / Wild Horses / Midnight Rambler / Rip This Joint / Street Fighting Man / Jumpin' Jack Flash
NOTES: There was one show each night of the Stones' two-night engagement at the Spectrum. The Commodores opened each performance. Both "Cherry Oh Baby" and "Sympathy for the Devil" were off the setlist after Madison Square Garden.

JUNE 30, 1975

TOUR: 1975 Tour of the Americas
VENUE: Spectrum, Philadelphia, PA, USA
OPENING/OTHER ACT(S): The Commodores
NOTES: The Commodores opened.

JULY 1, 1975

TOUR: 1975 Tour of the Americas
VENUE: Capitol Center, Largo, MD, USA
OPENING/OTHER ACT(S): Mighty Clouds of Joy
NOTES: Mighty Clouds of Joy opened for the Stones at both Capitol Center dates.

JULY 2, 1975

TOUR: 1975 Tour of the Americas
VENUE: Capitol Center, Largo, MD, USA
OPENING/OTHER ACT(S): Mighty Clouds of Joy
NOTES: Mighty Clouds of Joy opened.

JULY 4, 1975

TOUR: 1975 Tour of the Americas
VENUE: Memphis Memorial Stadium, Memphis, TN, USA
OPENING/OTHER ACT(S): The J. Geils Band, The Charlie Daniels Band, The Meters, Furry Lewis
NOTES: Four acts, including fabled blues man Furry Lewis, opened the Memphis show.

JULY 6, 1975

TOUR: 1975 Tour of the Americas
VENUE: Cotton Bowl, Dallas, TX, USA
OPENING/OTHER ACT(S): The Eagles, Montrose, Trapeze
NOTES: The opening acts were The Eagles, Montrose and Trapeze.

JULY 9, 1975

TOUR: 1975 Tour of the Americas
VENUE: L.A. Forum, Inglewood, CA, USA
SPECIAL GUESTS: Steel Band Association of America, Jesse Ed Davis (tpt), Steve Madaio (tpt), Trevor Lawrence (sax), Bobby Keys (sax)
OPENING/OTHER ACT(S): Steel Band Association of America
SONGS: Honky Tonk Women / All Down the Line / If You Can't Rock Me → Get Off of My Cloud, LMV / Ain't Too Proud to Beg (Whitfield, Holland) / Star Star / Gimma Shelter / You Gotta Move (McDowell, Davis) / You Can't Always Get What You Want / Happy / Tumbling Dice / Fingerprint File / Brown Sugar / It's Only Rock 'n' Roll / Doo Doo Doo Doo Doo (Heartbreaker) / That's Life (Preston) / Outta Space (Preston, Green) / Angie / Wild Horses / Midnight Rambler / Rip This Joint / Street Fighting Man / Jumpin' Jack Flash / E: Sympathy for the Devil
NOTES: The first of five Los Angeles performances in as many days. The Los Angeles Forum and the Los Angeles

airport are both located in Inglewood, a city in Los Angeles county, and very much within the vast L.A. metropolitan area. As on the Rolling Stones' New York City programs, members of the Steel Band Association of America were the opening act at all five LA dates. The steel drummers reappeared for the Stones' "Sympathy for the Devil" encore, along with the entire guest brass section. Only Trevor Lawrence played saxophone during "You Can't Always Get What You Want." But, when he came on again at the close of the Forum shows, he brought Jesse Ed Davis, Bobby Keys and Steve Madaio with him.

JULY 10, 1975

TOUR: 1975 Tour of the Americas
VENUE: L.A. Forum, Inglewood, CA, USA
SPECIAL GUESTS: Steel Band Association of America, Jesse Ed Davis (tpt), Steve Madaio (tpt), Trevor Lawrence (sax), Bobby Keys (sax)
OPENING/OTHER ACT(S): Steel Band Association of America
SONGS: Honky Tonk Women / All Down the Line / If You Can't Rock Me → Get Off of My Cloud, LMV / Ain't Too Proud to Beg (Whitfield, Holland) / Star Star / Gimme Shelter / You Gotta Move (McDowell, Davis) / You Can't Always Get What You Want / Happy / Tumbling Dice / Fingerprint File / Brown Sugar / It's Only Rock 'n' Roll / Doo Doo Doo Doo Doo (Heartbreaker) / That's Life (Preston) / Outta Space (Preston, Green) / Angie / Wild Horses / Midnight Rambler / Rip This Joint / Street Fighting Man / Jumpin' Jack Flash / E: Sympathy for the Devil
NOTES: The second of five Los Angeles shows.

JULY 11, 1975

TOUR: 1975 Tour of the Americas
VENUE: L.A. Forum, Inglewood, CA, USA
SPECIAL GUESTS: Steel Band Association of America, Jesse Ed Davis (tpt), Steve Madaio (tpt), Trevor Lawrence (sax), Bobby Keys (sax)
OPENING/OTHER ACT(S): Steel Band Association of America
SONGS: Honky Tonk Women / All Down the Line / If You Can't Rock Me → Get Off of My Cloud, LMV / Ain't Too Proud to Beg (Whitfield, Holland) / Star Star / Gimme Shelter / You Gotta Move (McDowell, Davis) / You Can't Always Get What You Want / Happy / Tumbling Dice / Fingerprint File / Brown Sugar / It's Only Rock 'n' Roll / Doo Doo Doo Doo Doo (Heartbreaker) / That's Life (Preston) / Outta Space (Preston, Green) / Angie / Wild Horses / Midnight Rambler / Rip This Joint / Street Fighting Man / Jumpin' Jack Flash / E: Sympathy for the Devil
NOTES: The third of five Los Angeles shows.

JULY 12, 1975

TOUR: 1975 Tour of the Americas

VENUE: L.A. Forum, Inglewood, CA, USA

SPECIAL GUESTS: Steel Band Association of America, Jesse Ed Davis (tpt), Steve Madaio (tpt), Trevor Lawrence (sax), Bobby Keys (sax)

OPENING/OTHER ACT(S): Steel Band Association of America

SONGS: Honky Tonk Women / All Down the Line / If You Can't Rock Me → Get Off of My Cloud, LMV / Ain't Too Proud to Beg (Whitfield, Holland) / Star Star / Gimme Shelter / You Gotta Move (McDowell, Davis) / You Can't Always Get What You Want / Happy / Tumbling Dice / Fingerprint File / Brown Sugar / It's Only Rock 'n' Roll / Doo Doo Doo Doo Doo (Heartbreaker) / That's Life (Preston) / Outta Space (Preston, Green) / Angie / Wild Horses / Midnight Rambler / Rip This Joint / Street Fighting Man / Jumpin' Jack Flash / E: Sympathy for the Devil

NOTES: The fourth of five Los Angeles shows.

JULY 13, 1975

TOUR: 1975 Tour of the Americas

VENUE: L.A. Forum, Inglewood, CA, USA

SPECIAL GUESTS: Steel Band Association of America, Jesse Ed Davis (tpt), Steve Madaio (tpt), Trevor Lawrence (sax), Bobby Keys (sax)

OPENING/OTHER ACT(S): Steel Band Association of America

SONGS: Honky Tonk Women / All Down the Line / If You Can't Rock Me → Get Off of My Cloud, LMV / Ain't Too Proud to Beg (Whitfield, Holland) / Star Star / Gimme Shelter / You Gotta Move (McDowell, Davis) / You Can't Always Get What You Want / Happy / Tumbling Dice / Fingerprint File / Brown Sugar / It's Only Rock 'n' Roll / Doo Doo Doo Doo Doo (Heartbreaker) / That's Life (Preston) / Outta Space (Preston, Green) / Angie / Wild Horses / Midnight Rambler / Rip This Joint / Street Fighting Man / Jumpin' Jack Flash / E: Sympathy for the Devil

NOTES: The fifth and final Los Angeles show of the 1975 tour.

JULY 15, 1975

TOUR: 1975 Tour of the Americas

VENUE: Cow Palace, San Francisco, CA, USA

OPENING/OTHER ACT(S): The Wailers

SONGS: Honky Tonk Women / All Down the Line / If You Can't Rock Me → Get Off of My Cloud, LMV / Ain't Too Proud to Beg (Whitfield, Holland) / Star Star / Gimme Shelter / You Gotta Move (McDowell, Davis) / You Can't Always Get What You Want / Happy /

Tumbling Dice / Fingerprint File / Brown Sugar / It's Only Rock 'n' Roll / Doo Doo Doo Doo Doo (Heartbreaker) / That's Life (Preston) / Outta Space (Preston, Green) / Angie / Wild Horses / Midnight Rambler / Rip This Joint / Street Fighting Man / Jumpin' Jack Flash

NOTES: The first of two San Francisco dates on the '75 tour. The Wailers opened for the Stones on both Cow Palace dates. "Sympathy for the Devil" was again removed from the show; the list above is a typical set for the balance of the tour.

JULY 16, 1975

TOUR: 1975 Tour of the Americas

VENUE: Cow Palace, San Francisco, CA, USA

OPENING/OTHER ACT(S): The Wailers

JULY 18, 1975

TOUR: 1975 Tour of the Americas

VENUE: Seattle Center Coliseum, Seattle, WA, USA

OPENING/OTHER ACT(S): The Wailers

NOTES: Again, the opening act was the Wailers.

JULY 19, 1975

TOUR: 1975 Tour of the Americas

VENUE: Hughes Stadium, Fort Collins, CO, USA

SPECIAL GUESTS: Elton John

SONGS: Honky Tonk Women / All Down the Line / If You Can't Rock Me → Get Off of My Cloud, LMV / Ain't Too Proud to Beg (Whitfield, Holland) / Star Star / Gimme Shelter / You Gotta Move (McDowell, Davis) / You Can't Always Get What You Want / Happy / Tumbling Dice / Fingerprint File / Brown Sugar / It's Only Rock 'n' Roll / Doo Doo Doo Doo Doo (Heartbreaker) / That's Life (Preston) / Outta Space (Preston, Green) / Angie / Wild Horses / Midnight Rambler / Rip This Joint / Street Fighting Man / Jumpin' Jack Flash

NOTES: Elton John guests with the Stones on "Honky Tonk Women." Fort Collins is close to Denver.

JULY 23, 1975

TOUR: 1975 Tour of the Americas

VENUE: Chicago Stadium, Chicago, IL, USA

OPENING/OTHER ACT(S): The Crusaders

NOTES: The Crusaders opened for the Stones at this and the next night's Chicago performance.

JULY 24, 1975

TOUR: 1975 Tour of the Americas

VENUE: Chicago Stadium, Chicago, IL, USA

OPENING/OTHER ACT(S): The Crusaders

JULY 26, 1975

TOUR: 1975 Tour of the Americas
VENUE: Indiana State University, University Assembly Center, Bloomington, IN, USA
OPENING/OTHER ACT(S):   The Crusaders
NOTES: The Crusaders opened for the Stones here as they had in Chicago.

JULY 27, 1975

TOUR: 1975 Tour of the Americas
VENUE: Cobo Hall, Detroit, MI, USA
OPENING/OTHER ACT(S):   The Meters
NOTES: The Meters opened for the Stones at this and the next evening's performance in Detroit.

JULY 28, 1975

TOUR: 1975 Tour of the Americas
VENUE: Cobo Hall, Detroit, MI, USA

OPENING/OTHER ACT(S):   The Meters

JULY 30, 1975

TOUR: 1975 Tour of the Americas
VENUE: The Omni, Atlanta, GA, USA
OPENING/OTHER ACT(S):   The Meters
NOTES: The Meters were the opening act again.

JULY 31, 1975

TOUR: 1975 Tour of the Americas
VENUE: Greensboro Auditorium & Coliseum, Greensboro, NC, USA
OPENING/OTHER ACT(S):   The Meters
NOTES: The concert took place in the 50,000-seat outdoor coliseum part of this complex.

AUGUST 2, 1975

TOUR: 1975 Tour of the Americas

Ron Wood, Billy Preston, Mick and Keith at Madison Square Garden, 1975 (USED BY PERMISSION OF BOB GRUEN, ALL RIGHTS RESERVED)

VENUE: The Gator Bowl, Atlantic Beach, Jacksonville, FL, USA

OPENING/OTHER ACT(S): The J. Geils Band, Tower of Power

NOTES: Opening acts were the J. Geils Band and Tower of Power.

AUGUST 4, 1975

TOUR: 1975 Tour of the Americas

VENUE: Freedom Hall Coliseum, Louisville, KY, USA

AUGUST 6, 1975

TOUR: 1975 Tour of the Americas

VENUE: Hampton Roads Coliseum, Hampton, VA, USA

AUGUST 8, 1975

TOUR: 1975 Tour of the Americas

VENUE: Rich Stadium, Buffalo, NY, USA

NOTES: The last gig of the 1975 Tour of the Americas. Nearly a month's worth of Latin American shows, to have begun in Mexico City on August 7, were cancelled due to currency problems in countries south of the U.S. border. The schedule was to have been: August 7–10, National Auditorium, Mexico City, Mexico; August 14–17, Maracanzinho, Rio de Janeiro, Brazil; August 19–21, Convention Hall, São Paulo, Brazil; August 24, Anhembi Hall, São Paulo, Brazil; and August 28–31, El Poliedro, Caracas, Venezuela. Had the shows happened, the name of the tour might have made more sense.

1976

APRIL 28, 1976 – JUNE 23, 1976

TOUR: 1976 European tour

VENUE: West Germany, Belgium, UK, Holland, France, Spain, Switzerland, Yugoslavia and Austria

PERSONNEL: Mick Jagger, Keith Richards, Ron Wood, Charlie Watts, Bill Wyman, Ian Stewart, Billy Preston, Ollie Brown

SPECIAL GUESTS: Eric Clapton

OPENING/OTHER ACT(S): The Meters (indoor shows), the Robin Trower Band and the Meters (outdoor shows), the Kokomo Band, Robin Trower, the Meters (outdoor shows in Belgium and Holland)

SONGS: Honky Tonk Women / If You Can't Rock Me → Get Off of My Cloud, LMV / Hand of Fate / Hey Negrita / Ain't Too Proud to Beg (Whitfield, Holland) / Fool to Cry / Hot Stuff / Star Star / Cherry Oh Baby (Donaldson) / Angie / You Gotta Move (McDowell,

Davis) / Key to the Highway (Broonzy) / You Can't Always Get What You Want / Happy / Tumbling Dice / Nothing for Nothing (Preston) / Outta Space (Preston, Green) / Midnight Rambler / It's Only Rock 'n' Roll / Brown Sugar / Jumpin' Jack Flash / **E1:** Street Fighting Man / **E2:** Sympathy for the Devil

NOTES: Eric Clapton made a guest appearance on May 15 at Grandby Hall, in Leicester, England, sitting in on lead guitar and vocal on "Key to the Highway" (which was added to the list at that one concert only), then returning to the stage at show's end for "Jumpin' Jack Flash" and the encore, "Steet Fighting Man." Billy Preston and Ollie Brown backed the Stones on keyboards and percussion, respectively, with Preston soloing midset—backed by the Stones—on "Nothing for Nothing" and "Outta Space." Mick Jagger literally took flight over European audiences on the second Preston song, grabbing a rope that dangled from the ceiling and swooping out Tarzan-like from the stage, over heads, and back. Outdoors, of course, the stunt couldn't be performed. But, though it was hardly done to compensate stadium audiences for missing the Stone on a rope, two additional acts were added to the opening bill at outdoor shows—the Robin Trower band and the Kokomo band (in Holland). The Meters opened all venues and were the only warmup act at the indoor gigs. "All Down the Line" was only performed in Frankfurt. "Cherry Oh Baby" was only performed in Paris; "Angie" was added there, played in the French and Spanish shows, then removed from the setlist. "Sympathy for the Devil" (designated **E2:** above) was the encore at four of the six Earl's Court shows.

APRIL 28, 1976

TOUR: 1976 European tour

VENUE: Festhalle, Frankfurt, West Germany

OPENING/OTHER ACT(S): The Meters

SONGS: Honky Tonk Women / If You Can't Rock Me → Get Off of My Cloud, LMV / Hand of Fate / Hey Negrita / Ain't Too Proud to Beg (Whitfield, Holland) / Fool to Cry / Hot Stuff / Star Star / You Gotta Move (McDowell, Davis) / You Can't Always Get What You Want / Happy / Tumbling Dice / Nothing for Nothing (Preston) / Outta Space (Preston, Green) / Midnight Rambler / It's Only Rock 'n' Roll / Brown Sugar / Jumpin' Jack Flash / Street Fighting Man

NOTES: First show of the 1976 European tour. This setlist is typical for most shows except those in Paris, Earl's Court Arena in London, and Grandby Hall.

APRIL 29, 1976

TOUR: 1976 European tour

VENUE: Festhalle, Frankfurt, West Germany

OPENING/OTHER ACT(S): The Meters

*Ticket to Stones show in Frankfurt, Germany during the
1976 European tour* (JAMES KARNBACH COLLECTION)

APRIL 30, 1976

TOUR: 1976 European tour
VENUE: Münsterland Halle, Münster, West Germany
OPENING/OTHER ACT(S): The Meters

MAY 2, 1976

TOUR: 1976 European tour
VENUE: Ostseehalle, Kiel, West Germany
OPENING/OTHER ACT(S): The Meters

MAY 3, 1976

TOUR: 1976 European tour
VENUE: Deutschlandhalle, West Berlin, West Germany
OPENING/OTHER ACT(S): The Meters

MAY 4, 1976

TOUR: 1976 European tour
VENUE: Stadthalle, Bremen, West Germany
OPENING/OTHER ACT(S): The Meters

MAY 6, 1976

TOUR: 1976 European tour
VENUE: Forêt Nationale, Brussels, Belgium
OPENING/OTHER ACT(S): The Meters, The Robin
Trower Band

MAY 7, 1976

TOUR: 1976 European tour
VENUE: Forêt Nationale, Brussels, Belgium

OPENING/OTHER ACT(S): The Meters, The Robin
Trower Band

MAY 10, 1976

TOUR: 1976 European tour
VENUE: Apollo Theatre, Glasgow, Scotland
OPENING/OTHER ACT(S): The Meters

MAY 11, 1976

TOUR: 1976 European tour
VENUE: Apollo Theatre, Glasgow, Scotland
OPENING/OTHER ACT(S): The Meters

MAY 12, 1976

TOUR: 1976 European tour
VENUE: Apollo Theatre, Glasgow, Scotland
OPENING/OTHER ACT(S): The Meters

MAY 14, 1976

TOUR: 1976 European tour
VENUE: Grandby Hall, Leicester, Leicestershire, England
OPENING/OTHER ACT(S): The Meters

MAY 15, 1976

TOUR: 1976 European tour
VENUE: Grandby Hall, Leicester, Leicestershire, England
SPECIAL GUESTS: Eric Clapton (gtr, vo)
OPENING/OTHER ACT(S): The Meters
SONGS: Honky Tonk Women / If You Can't Rock Me → Get Off of My Cloud, LMV / Hand of Fate / Hey Negrita / Ain't Too Proud to Beg (Whitfield, Holland) / Fool to Cry / Hot Stuff / Star Star / Key to the Highway (Broonzy) / You Can't Always Get What You Want / Happy / Tumbling Dice / Nothing for Nothing (Preston) / Outta Space (Preston, Green) / Midnight Rambler / It's Only Rock 'n' Roll / Brown Sugar / Jumpin' Jack Flash / E: Street Fighting Man
NOTES: Guitarist Eric Clapton made a guest appearance with the band on "Key to the Highway," "Jumpin' Jack Flash" and "Street Fighting Man." It was thought that Clapton's guest spot began with his joining in on "Brown Sugar," leaving the stage, then returning for a special encore performance of "Key to the Highway." This rumor has no factual basis. "Key to the Highway" is not an encore song in any event; it was inserted mid-set at this show especially for Clapton's cameo (on lead guitar and vocals). He did return to the stage for the last two songs, which included the actual encore, "Street Fighting Man."

MAY 17, 1976

TOUR: 1976 European tour
VENUE: New Bingley Hall, Stafford, Staffordshire, England
OPENING/OTHER ACT(S):   The Meters

MAY 18, 1976

TOUR: 1976 European tour
VENUE: New Bingley Hall, Stafford, Staffordshire, England
OPENING/OTHER ACT(S):   The Meters

MAY 21, 1976

TOUR: 1976 European tour
VENUE: Earls Court Arena, Earls Court, London, England
OPENING/OTHER ACT(S):   The Meters
SONGS: Honky Tonk Women / If You Can't Rock Me → Get Off of My Cloud, LMV1 / Hand of Fate / Hey Negrita / Ain't Too Proud to Beg (Whitfield, Holland) / Fool to Cry / Hot Stuff / Star Star / You Gotta Move (McDowell, Davis) / You Can't Always Get What You Want / Happy / Tumbling Dice / Nothing for Nothing (Preston) / Outta Space (Preston, Green) / Midnight Rambler / It's Only Rock 'n' Roll / Brown Sugar / Jumpin' Jack Flash / Street Fighting Man / E: Sympathy for the Devil, LV2
NOTES: The Stones played six consecutive gigs, with one day off in the middle (on the 24th), at Earl's Court. The concerts were recorded and yielded two tracks for *Love You Live.*

MAY 22, 1976

TOUR: 1976 European tour
VENUE: Earls Court Arena, Earls Court, London, England
OPENING/OTHER ACT(S):   The Meters
NOTES: The second of the Earls Court dates.

MAY 23, 1976

TOUR: 1976 European tour
VENUE: Earls Court Arena, Earls Court, London, England
OPENING/OTHER ACT(S):   The Meters
NOTES: The third of the Earls Court dates.

MAY 25, 1976

TOUR: 1976 European tour
VENUE: Earls Court Arena, Earls Court, London, England
OPENING/OTHER ACT(S):   The Meters

NOTES: After a night off, the Stones played their fourth gig at Earls Court Arena.

MAY 26, 1976

TOUR: 1976 European tour
VENUE: Earls Court Arena, Earls Court, London, England
OPENING/OTHER ACT(S):   The Meters

MAY 27, 1976

TOUR: 1976 European tour
VENUE: Earls Court Arena, Earls Court, London, England
OPENING/OTHER ACT(S):   The Meters
NOTES: The final night of the Stones' six-performance engagement at Earl's Court Arena.

MAY 29, 1976

TOUR: 1976 European tour
VENUE: Zuiderpark, The Hague, Holland
OPENING/OTHER ACT(S):   The Meters, The Robin Trower Band, The Kokomo Band

MAY 30, 1976

TOUR: 1976 European tour
VENUE: Zuiderpark, The Hague, Holland
OPENING/OTHER ACT(S):   The Meters, The Robin Trower Band, The Kokomo Band

JUNE 1, 1976

TOUR: 1976 European tour
VENUE: Westfallenhalle, Dortmund, West Germany
OPENING/OTHER ACT(S):   The Meters

JUNE 2, 1976

TOUR: 1976 European tour
VENUE: Sporthalle, Cologne, West Germany
OPENING/OTHER ACT(S):   The Meters
NOTES: Two shows

JUNE 4, 1976

TOUR: 1976 European tour
VENUE: Les Abattoirs, Paris, France
OPENING/OTHER ACT(S):   The Meters
SONGS: Honky Tonk Women / If You Can't Rock Me → Get Off of My Cloud, LMV / Hand of Fate / Hey Negrita / Ain't Too Proud to Beg (Whitfield, Holland) / Fool to Cry / Hot Stuff / Star Star / Angie /You Gotta Move (McDowell, Davis) / You Can't Always Get What You Want / Happy / Tumbling Dice / Nothing for

Nothing (Preston) / Outta Space (Preston, Green) / Midnight Rambler / It's Only Rock 'n' Roll / Brown Sugar / Jumpin' Jack Flash / **E:** Street Fighting Man

NOTES: The Stones played four dates here, this being the first. Note the addition of "Angie."

JUNE 5, 1976

TOUR: 1976 European tour

VENUE: Les Abattoirs, Paris, France

OPENING/OTHER ACT(S): The Meters

SONGS: Honky Tonk Women, LV2 / If You Can't Rock Me → Get Off of My Cloud, LMV / Hand of Fate / Hey Negrita / Ain't Too Proud to Beg (Whitfield, Holland) / Fool to Cry / Hot Stuff / Star Star / Angie / You Gotta Move (McDowell, Davis), LV1 / You Can't Always Get What You Want / Happy, LV1 / Tumbling Dice / Nothing for Nothing (Preston) / Outta Space (Preston, Green) / Midnight Rambler / It's Only Rock 'n' Roll / Brown Sugar / Jumpin' Jack Flash / **E:** Street Fighting Man

NOTES: Recorded for *Love You Live*. Three tracks came from this show.

JUNE 6, 1976

TOUR: 1976 European tour

VENUE: Les Abattoirs, Paris, France

OPENING/OTHER ACT(S): The Meters

SONGS: Honky Tonk Women / If You Can't Rock Me → Get Off of My Cloud, LMV / Hand of Fate / Hey Negrita / Ain't Too Proud to Beg (Whitfield, Holland) / Fool to Cry / Hot Stuff, LV1 / Star Star, LV1 / Angie / You Gotta Move (McDowell, Davis) / You Can't Always Get What You Want / Happy / Tumbling Dice / Nothing for Nothing (Preston) / Outta Space (Preston, Green) / Midnight Rambler / It's Only Rock 'n' Roll / Brown Sugar, LV1 / Jumpin' Jack Flash, LV2 / **E:** Street Fighting Man

NOTES: *Love You Live* recording took place; four tracks came from this show. See CHRONOLOGY for more information about June 6, 1976.

JUNE 7, 1976

TOUR: 1976 European tour

VENUE: Les Abattoirs, Paris, France

OPENING/OTHER ACT(S): The Meters

SONGS: Honky Tonk Women / If You Can't Rock Me → Get Off of My Cloud, LMV / Hand of Fate / Hey Negrita / Ain't Too Proud to Beg (Whitfield, Holland) / Fool to Cry / Hot Stuff / Star Star / Cherry Oh Baby (Donaldson) / Angie / You Gotta Move (McDowell, Davis) / You Can't Always Get What You Want, LV1 / Happy / Tumbling Dice, LV1 / Nothing for Nothing (Preston) / Outta Space (Preston, Green) / Midnight

Rambler / It's Only Rock 'n' Roll / Brown Sugar / Jumpin' Jack Flash / **E:** Street Fighting Man

NOTES: Final gig of four in as many days in Paris. "Cherry Oh Baby" was added to the set, but did not appear on *Love You Live*. Two tracks on that album originated at this show.

JUNE 9, 1976

TOUR: 1976 European tour

VENUE: Palais des Sports, Lyon, France

OPENING/OTHER ACT(S): The Meters

SONGS: Honky Tonk Women / If You Can't Rock Me Get Off of My Cloud, LMV / Hand of Fate / Hey Negrita / Ain't Too Proud to Beg (Whitfield, Holland) / Fool to Cry / Hot Stuff / Star Star / Angie / You Gotta Move (McDowell, Davis) / You Can't Always Get What You Want / Happy / Tumbling Dice / Nothing for Nothing (Preston) / Outta Space (Preston, Green) / Midnight Rambler / It's Only Rock 'n' Roll / Brown Sugar / Jumpin' Jack Flash / **E:** Street Fighting Man

NOTES: The band removed "Cherry Oh Baby," added during the Paris shows.

JUNE 11, 1976

TOUR: 1976 European tour

VENUE: Plaza des Toros Monumental, Barcelona, Spain

OPENING/OTHER ACT(S): The Meters, Billy Preston, The Robin Trower Band

JUNE 13, 1976

TOUR: 1976 European tour

VENUE: Parc des Sports de l'Ouest, Nice, France

OPENING/OTHER ACT(S): The Meters, The Robin Trower Band

NOTES: "Angie" is played at this show for the last time on this tour.

JUNE 15, 1976

TOUR: 1976 European tour

VENUE: Hallenstadion, Zurich, Switzerland

OPENING/OTHER ACT(S): The Meters, The Robin Trower Band

JUNE 16, 1976

TOUR: 1976 European tour

VENUE: Olympiahalle, Munich, West Germany

OPENING/OTHER ACT(S): The Meters

JUNE 17, 1976

TOUR: 1976 European tour

VENUE: Olympiahalle, Munich, West Germany

OPENING/OTHER ACT(S): The Meters

JUNE 19, 1976

TOUR: 1976 European tour
VENUE: Neckarstadion, Stuttgart, West Germany
OPENING/OTHER ACT(S): The Meters, The Robin Trower Band

JUNE 21, 1976

TOUR: 1976 European tour
VENUE: Domsportova Hall, Zagreb, Yugoslavia
OPENING/OTHER ACT(S): The Meters

JUNE 22, 1976

TOUR: 1976 European tour
VENUE: Domsportova Hall, Zagreb, Yugoslavia
OPENING/OTHER ACT(S): The Meters

JUNE 23, 1976

TOUR: 1976 European tour
VENUE: Stadthalle, Vienna, Austria
OPENING/OTHER ACT(S): The Meters
NOTES: This is the last official gig of the 1976 European tour. The Stones did play another gig in 1976, at Knebworth Park in England in August.

AUGUST 21, 1976

TOUR: Knebworth Fair
VENUE: Knebworth Park, Knebworth, Hertfordshire, England
PERSONNEL: Mick Jagger, Keith Richards, Ron Wood, Charlie Watts, Bill Wyman, Ian Stewart, Billy Preston, Ollie Brown
OPENING/OTHER ACT(S): Don Harrison Band, Utopia, Hot Tuna, 10cc, Lynyrd Skynyrd
SONGS: (I Can't Get No) Satisfaction / Ain't Too Proud to Beg (Whitfield, Holland) / If You Can't Rock Me → Get Off of My Cloud, LMV / Hand of Fate / Around & Around (Berry) / Little Red Rooster (Dixon) / Stray Cat Blues / Hey Negrita / Hot Stuff / Fool to Cry / Star Star / Let's Spend the Night Together / You Gotta Move (McDowell, Davis) / You Can't Always Get What You Want / Dead Flowers / Route 66 (Troup) / Wild Horses / Honky Tonk Women / Tumbling Dice / Happy / Nothing for Nothing (Preston) / Outta Space (Preston, Green) / Midnight Rambler / It's Only Rock 'n' Roll / Brown Sugar / Rip This Joint / Jumpin' Jack Flash / E: Street Fighting Man
NOTES: Todd Rundgren, Lynyrd Skynyrd, Hot Tuna, 10cc and the Don Harrison Band were also on the bill at this outdoor show. This concert seems to have dropped

out of the sky into the Rolling Stones' 1976 tour schedule —about two months after their European tour ended, with no shows to follow it. At the time, the Stones' appearance at the Knebworth festival was explained as the band's response to their European fans, many of whom were left unsatisfied after the Stones' recent continental jaunt. One complaint was that there hadn't been enough seats for all who wanted them at the smallish venues in Europe, however this does not completely explain why they did a big outdoor show in England to compensate the Europeans.

There were 28 songs in the Stones' set at Knebworth, the longest in their performing career. The physical set— the stage itself—was the largest on which they had performed so far. One might say it was also the longest stage, —it was shaped like the Rolling Stones' logo with the tongue portion extending approximately 150 feet out into the audience. That crowd numbered around 200,000 (as of June, 1996), still the largest paid attendance ever at a single Stones show. Both Altamont and Hyde Park had more people, but those were free (in the sense that no tickets were sold) concerts. The Knebworth show was videotaped for a possible TV special and the audio was recorded for a potential live Stones LP. Nothing ever surfaced in either medium, which is curious for this period in the band's career when they were clearly doing a fair amount of advance planning. One would think, with all the hoopla, that something from a 28-song set might have ended up on *Love You Live*, or on a non-album B-side at the very least. Sources close to the band at the time maintain that the audio tracks were technically damaged, which rendered the entire project useless. Win some, lose some. And some you just don't like, maybe.

1977

MARCH 4, 1977

TOUR: El Mocambo shows
VENUE: El Mocambo Club, Toronto, Ontario, Canada
PERSONNEL: Mick Jagger, Keith Richards, Ron Wood, Charlie Watts, Bill Wyman, Ian Stewart, Billy Preston, Ollie Brown
OPENING/OTHER ACT(S): April Wine
SONGS: Route 66 (Troup) / All Down the Line / Around & Around (Berry), LV1 / Brown Sugar / Crazy Mama / Dance Little Sister / Fool to Cry / Hand of Fate / Honky Tonk Women / Hot Stuff / It's Only Rock 'n' Roll / Jumpin' Jack Flash / Let's Spend the Night Together / Little Red Rooster (Dixon), LV1 / Mannish Boy (London, McDaniel, Morganfield) / Cracking Up (McDaniel) / Melody / Star Star / Street Fighting Man / Tumbling Dice / Worried About You

NOTES: The versions of "Mannish Boy," "Cracking Up," "Little Red Rooster" and "Around & Around" on *Love You Live* were recorded at these shows. Eddie Kramer was the live recording engineer at the El Mocambo.

MARCH 5, 1977

TOUR: El Mocambo shows
VENUE: El Mocambo Club, Toronto, Ontario, Canada
OPENING/OTHER ACT(S): April Wine
SONGS: Honky Tonk Women / All Down the Line / Around & Around (Berry), LV1 / Brown Sugar / Crazy Mama / Dance Little Sister / Fool to Cry / Hand of Fate / Route 66 (Troup) / Hot Stuff / It's Only Rock 'n' Roll / Jumpin' Jack Flash / Let's Spend the Night Together / Little Red Rooster (Dixon), LV1 / Mannish Boy (London, McDaniel, Morganfield) / Cracking Up (McDaniel) / Melody / Star Star / Street Fighting Man / Tumbling Dice / Worried About You
NOTES: On this second night at El Mocambo, the band led off the set with "Honky Tonk Women," and the previous night's opener, "Route 66," took its place later on in the show.

1978

JUNE 10 – JULY 26, 1978

TOUR: Ninth (1978) North American tour
VENUE: US
PERSONNEL: Mick Jagger, Keith Richards, Ron Wood, Charlie Watts, Bill Wyman, Ian Stewart, Ian McLagan
SPECIAL GUESTS: Doug Kershaw, Linda Ronstadt, Eddie Money, Sugar Blue, Nicky Hopkins, Bobby Keys
OPENING/OTHER ACT(S): Henry Paul Band, Peter Tosh, Patti Smith, Etta James, Doug Kershaw, Prince, Foreigner, Southside Johnny & the Asbury Jukes, Eddie Money, Santana
SONGS: Let it Rock (Anderson) / All Down the Line / Honky Tonk Women / Star Star / Lies / Miss You / When the Whip Comes Down / Beast of Burden / Just My Imagination (Running Away with Me) (Whitfield, Strong) / Respectable / Far Away Eyes / Love in Vain (Robt. Johnson) / Shattered / Hound Dog (Leiber, Stoller) / Tumbling Dice / Happy / Sweet Little Sixteen (Berry) / Brown Sugar / Jumpin' Jack Flash / Street Fighting Man / (I Can't Get No) Satisfaction
NOTES: The 1978 American tour was the most diverse of any Stones tour up to that point and possibly ever after. For concertgoers, there were many surprises along the road, including numerous variations on what had become standard operating procedure for a Stones tour. Some of the changes came as the band's response to fans calling for smaller shows, others might be ascribed to serendipity, economics, or just because that's what the Stones wanted to do that year. And, for the Rolling Stones, '78 was a fairly strange year. It was no secret nor far from any interested mind that Keith's legal problems loomed heavily over the band's future, perhaps reason enough to do things differently.

Concert sites in 1978 varied in size from 1,800- to 5,000-seat houses to 18,000-seat arenas and 50,000-seat stadiums. Instead of one or two or even three "special" small venues along the way, there were seven: Washington, DC; Detroit, MI; Passaic, NJ; New York, NY; Atlanta, GA; Myrtle Beach, SC; and Fort Worth, TX at the 4,800-seat Will Rogers Auditorium where the band's 1972 performance had been filmed for *Ladies & Gentlemen, the Rolling Stones* (the '78 Fort Worth show was also filmed, though nothing was ever released).

The Stones acquired a couple of weird new identities that year. Some newspapers advertised upcoming Stones shows under their newly assumed names—the Cockroaches at the Fox Theater in Atlanta; the Great Southeast Stoned Out Wrestling Champions in Lakeland, Florida—and that alias was also printed on the Lakeland tickets.

More "special guests" made appearances with the band on this tour than on any other; they included Linda Ronstadt in Tucson, Eddie Money in Lexington, Doug Kershaw in Dallas, and Sugar Blue in Chicago. But this was also the first time guesting worked in reverse, with Mick Jagger coming out *before* Stones' performances in some cities to sing "Keep on Walking—Don't Look Back" with opening (Rolling Stones Records) artist Peter Tosh.

Mick's onstage wardrobe was a major departure from the $1,500 per night designer jumpsuits of '75. This time out, he favored punkish ripped T-shirts and torn vinyl sweatpants patched with masking tape. Stages were nearly bare for the smaller '78 shows, with just the band and their instruments in the spotlight. But "downsizing" hardly affected the tour negatively. On the contrary, it just added more notes to that mix of more, and less, and different. The 1978 North American tour was most definitely memorable, and is still thought of as "special" by fans and the Rolling Stones themselves.

Ian Stewart on piano and Ian McLagan on keyboards backed the Stones throughout the tour. Hopkins and Keys showed up in Oakland to sit in. The songs listed above include all numbers on the 1978 tour setlists. Some titles were performed only once or twice; for example, "Hound Dog," only turned up in Memphis, TN (natch!) and Lexington, KY.

JUNE 10, 1978

TOUR: Ninth (1978) North American tour
VENUE: Civic Center, Lakeland, FL, USA

OPENING/OTHER ACT(S): The Henry Paul Band

SONGS: Let it Rock (Anderson) / All Down the Line / Honky Tonk Women / Star Star / When the Whip Comes Down / Miss You / Beast of Burden / Respectable / Far Away Eyes / Love in Vain (Robt. Johnson) / Shattered / Tumbling Dice / Happy / Brown Sugar / Jumpin' Jack Flash / **E:** Street Fighting Man

NOTES: The Stones were billed as "The Great Southeast Stoned Out Wrestling Champions" at the first gig of the '78 tour.

JUNE 12, 1978

TOUR: Ninth (1978) North American tour

VENUE: Fox Theater, Atlanta, GA, USA

OPENING/OTHER ACT(S): Patti Smith

SONGS: Let it Rock (Anderson) / All Down the Line / Honky Tonk Women / Star Star / Lies / Miss You / When the Whip Comes Down / Beast of Burden / Just My Imagination (Running Away with Me) (Whitfield, Strong) / Respectable / Far Away Eyes / Love in Vain

(Robt. Johnson) / Shattered / Tumbling Dice / Happy / Brown Sugar / **E:** Jumpin' Jack Flash

NOTES: "The Cockroaches," as they were called in local advertisements for this show, was the Stones' second new identity. Patti Smith opened for them. Later, during the Stones' encore, she rushed the stage and was immediately led off by security.

JUNE 14, 1978

TOUR: Ninth (1978) North American tour

VENUE: Capitol Theatre, Passaic, NJ, USA

OPENING/OTHER ACT(S): Etta James

SONGS: Let it Rock (Anderson) / All Down the Line / Honky Tonk Women / Star Star / Lies / Miss You / When the Whip Comes Down / Beast of Burden / Just My Imagination (Running Away with Me) (Whitfield, Strong) / Respectable / Far Away Eyes / Love in Vain (Robt. Johnson) / Shattered / Tumbling Dice / Happy / Sweet Little Sixteen (Berry) / Brown Sugar / Jumpin' Jack Flash / **E:** Street Fighting Man

Onstage at the Palladium, New York City—one of the 1978 tour's small shows (1978, PHYLLIS LATTNER)

NOTES: A miniscule number of tickets went on sale at a very few locations, and for the general public seats for this concert were almost impossible to obtain. Where the bulk of the tickets went was a subject of much debate at the time. Even scalpers were in short supply. There were many reports of scalpers charging up to $900 for a single ticket—more than three times the going rate for a top act. many fans later said they would have been willing to pay such premium prices for a chance to see the Stones in a small venue like this one but couldn't find anyone to take their money.

JUNE 15, 1978

TOUR: Ninth (1978) North American tour
VENUE: Warner Theater, Washington, DC, USA
OPENING/OTHER ACT(S): Peter Tosh, Foreigner
SONGS: Let it Rock (Anderson) / All Down the Line / Honky Tonk Women / Star Star / Miss You / When the Whip Comes Down / Just My Imagination (Running Away with Me) (Whitfield, Strong) / Respectable / Far Away Eyes / Love in Vain (Robt. Johnson) / Shattered / Tumbling Dice / Happy / Sweet Little Sixteen (Berry) / Brown Sugar
NOTES: There was no encore at this show. Jagger became ill.

JUNE 17, 1978

TOUR: Ninth (1978) North American tour
VENUE: JFK Stadium, Philadelphia, PA, USA
OPENING/OTHER ACT(S): Peter Tosh, Foreigner

JUNE 19, 1978

TOUR: Ninth (1978) North American tour
VENUE: The Palladium, New York, NY, USA
OPENING/OTHER ACT(S): Peter Tosh
NOTES: After the June 14 Passaic, NJ experience, an effective, tightly controlled ticket lottery was held for seats at the Palladium show. Lucky winners paid just $10.50 per ticket. This concert was a prize for the Palladium itself, its specialness revealed in one way by the lighting of the landmark theater's unused-for-decades crystal chandelier. "Keep on Walking—Don't Look Back" was performed.

JUNE 21, 1978

TOUR: Ninth (1978) North American tour
VENUE: Hampton Roads Coliseum, Hampton, VA, USA
OPENING/OTHER ACT(S): Peter Tosh
NOTES: Mick joined Peter Tosh during the latter's opening set for a duet on "Keep on Walking—Don't Look Back."

JUNE 22, 1978

TOUR: Ninth (1978) North American tour
VENUE: Myrtle Beach Convention Center, Myrtle Beach, SC, USA
OPENING/OTHER ACT(S): Peter Tosh
NOTES: Again, Mick came onstage during the opening set to sing "Keep on Walking—Don't Look Back" with Peter Tosh.

JUNE 26, 1978

TOUR: Ninth (1978) North American tour
VENUE: War Memorial Coliseum, Greensboro, NC, USA
OPENING/OTHER ACT(S): Peter Tosh

JUNE 28, 1978

TOUR: Ninth (1978) North American tour
VENUE: Mid-South Coliseum, Memphis, TN, USA
OPENING/OTHER ACT(S): Peter Tosh
SONGS: Let it Rock (Anderson) / All Down the Line / Honky Tonk Women / Star Star / Lies / Miss You / When the Whip Comes Down, LV / Beast of Burden / Just My Imagination (Running Away with Me) (Whitfield, Strong) / Respectable / Far Away Eyes / Love in Vain (Robt. Johnson) / Shattered / Hound Dog (Leiber, Stoller) / Tumbling Dice / Happy / Sweet Little Sixteen (Berry) / Brown Sugar / E: Jumpin' Jack Flash
NOTES: This show's setlist—and one other—were rarities. The Stones played Big Mama Thornton and the Johnny Otis Band's 1953 number one billboard R&B chart-topper, "Hound Dog" (Elvis covered it later). "When the Whip Comes Down" on *Sucking in the '70s* was recorded here.

JUNE 29, 1978

TOUR: Ninth (1978) North American tour
VENUE: Rupp Arena, Lexington, KY, USA
SPECIAL GUESTS: Eddie Money
OPENING/OTHER ACT(S): Peter Tosh
NOTES: Eddie Money joins the band on stage for "Miss You." The Stones do "Hound Dog" here also. The setlist is the same as in Memphis.

JULY 1, 1978

TOUR: Ninth (1978) North American tour
VENUE: Cleveland Municipal Stadium, Cleveland, OH, USA
OPENING/OTHER ACT(S): Peter Tosh

JULY 4, 1978

TOUR: Ninth (1978) North American tour

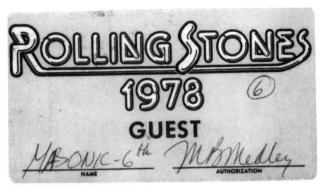

1978 tour pass (JAMES KARNBACH COLLECTION)

VENUE: Rich Stadium, Buffalo, NY, USA
OPENING/OTHER ACT(S): Peter Tosh

JULY 6, 1978

TOUR: Ninth (1978) North American tour
VENUE: Masonic Hall, Detroit, MI, USA
OPENING/OTHER ACT(S): Peter Tosh

JULY 8, 1978

TOUR: Ninth (1978) North American tour
VENUE: Soldiers Field, Chicago, IL, USA
SPECIAL GUESTS: Sugar Blue
OPENING/OTHER ACT(S): Southside Johnny & the Asbury Jukes, Peter Tosh, Journey
NOTES: Sugar Blue guested on "Miss You."

JULY 10, 1978

TOUR: Ninth (1978) North American tour
VENUE: St. Paul Civic Center, St. Paul, MN, USA
OPENING/OTHER ACT(S): Peter Tosh

JULY 11, 1978

TOUR: Ninth (1978) North American tour
VENUE: Checkerdome, St. Louis, MO, USA
OPENING/OTHER ACT(S): Peter Tosh

JULY 13, 1978

TOUR: Ninth (1978) North American tour
VENUE: Superdome, New Orleans, LA, USA
OPENING/OTHER ACT(S): Peter Tosh

JULY 16, 1978

TOUR: Ninth (1978) North American tour
VENUE: Folsom Field, Boulder, CO, USA
OPENING/OTHER ACT(S): Peter Tosh

JULY 18, 1978

TOUR: Ninth (1978) North American tour
VENUE: Will Rogers Auditorium, Fort Worth, TX, USA
SPECIAL GUESTS: Doug Kershaw
OPENING/OTHER ACT(S): Etta James, Peter Tosh
NOTES: Violinist Doug Kershaw joins the Stones onstage on "Far Away Eyes." The show was filmed to be released as a closed-circuit broadcast in movie theaters, but nothing ever came of it.

JULY 19, 1978

TOUR: Ninth (1978) North American tour
VENUE: Hofheinz Pavilion, Houston, TX, USA
OPENING/OTHER ACT(S): Peter Tosh

JULY 21, 1978

TOUR: Ninth (1978) North American tour
VENUE: Tucson Community Center, Tucson, AZ, USA
SPECIAL GUESTS: Linda Ronstadt
OPENING/OTHER ACT(S): Etta James
NOTES: Linda Ronstadt made a special appearance at this show, singing with the band on "Tumbling Dice."

JULY 23, 1978

TOUR: Ninth (1978) North American tour
VENUE: Anaheim Stadium, Anaheim, CA, USA
OPENING/OTHER ACT(S): Peter Tosh, Prince
NOTES: First of two nights at Anaheim Stadium. Anaheim is located in Orange County, about an hour southeast of downtown Los Angeles, and is also the home of the original Disneyland. If that doesn't sound too bizarre, then consider the reports concerning Prince's reception by Stones fans, who booed him offstage three-quarters of the way through his set.

JULY 24, 1978

TOUR: Ninth (1978) North American tour
VENUE: Anaheim Stadium, Anaheim, CA, USA
OPENING/OTHER ACT(S): Peter Tosh

JULY 26, 1978

TOUR: Ninth (1978) North American tour
VENUE: Oakland Coliseum, Oakland, CA, USA
SPECIAL GUESTS: Nicky Hopkins, Bobby Keys
OPENING/OTHER ACT(S): Peter Tosh, Eddie Money, Santana
NOTES: Nicky Hopkins and Bobby Keys joined the Stones at the final gig of the 1978 tour—on Mick's birthday. The last time Santana supported the Stones at a Northern California concert had been nine years earlier —at Altamont.

1979

APRIL 22, 1979

TOUR: C.N.I.B. Benefit Show

VENUE: Oshawa Civic Auditorium, Oshawa, Ontario, Canada

PERSONNEL: Mick Jagger, Keith Richards, Ron Wood, Charlie Watts, Bill Wyman, Ian Stewart

SPECIAL GUESTS: Dan Ackroyd, John Belushi, The New Barbarians

OPENING/OTHER ACT(S): The New Barbarians—Keith Richards, Ron Wood, Bobby Keys, Ian McLagan, Stanley Clarke, Bobby Keys, Joseph Zigaboo Modeliste (a.k.a. Ziggy)

SONGS: Prodigal Son (Rev. Wilkins) / Let it Rock (Anderson) / Respectable / Star Star / Beast of Burden / Just My Imagination (Running Away with Me) (Whitfield, Strong) / When the Whip Comes Down / Shattered / Miss You / Jumpin' Jack Flash

NOTES: Oshawa (20 miles from Toronto), Keith Richards was ordered by Judge Lloyd Graburn to give a special concert for the Canadian National Institute for the Blind (CNIB) as part of his sentence. Billed as "The Keith

Keith onstage at Oshawa (1979, PHYLLIS LATTNER)

Richards Benefit Concert," the show was to be the premiere for the newly formed "New Barbarians," consisting of Keith Richards, Ron Wood, Ian McLagan (keyboards), Stanley Clarke (bass), Bobby Keys (sax), and Joseph Zigaboo Modeliste—a.k.a. "Ziggy" (drums). Although never officially announced, it was widely rumored that the Roll-

Mick and Keith perform an acoustic "Prodigal Son" at Oshawa, April 22, 1979 during Keith's benefit concert for the blind/penance for his Canadian drug conviction of 1977. (1979, PHYLLIS LATTNER)

ing Stones would appear. Canadian Dan Ackroyd and fellow Stones fan John Belushi introduced the New Barbarians. When the Barbarians' set finished, Keith remained onstage taking bows. Then, from a rear corner of the stage, Mick Jagger walked on to greet Keith. After the audience pandemonium subsided, Mick and Keith settled down on two stools to perform an acoustic "Prodigal Son," with Jagger singing and Richards on guitar. At the end of the song, the remaining Stones—Woody, Bill and Charlie—walked onstage and the band jumped into "Let it Rock." They played an abbreviated—50-minute—set at the first, afternoon show. The rest of the New Barbarians came onstage to join the Stones for the last two numbers at both performances, "Miss You" and "Jumpin' Jack Flash." The evening show was identical in other respects, from the Barbarians' opening to Jagger's "surprise" entrance and acoustic duet with Richards, as well as the length and content of the Stones' set and the crowd's response. Seats in the first 15 audience rows were given free to CNIB members. This might not have been such a wonderful idea, in hindsight (no pun intended). When the Stones started to play, a mad dash to the stage from rows 16 to 25 sent canes, glasses and dogs flying through the air.

1981

SEPTEMBER 15, 1981

TOUR: 1981 US tour—Pretour warmup / Thank-you gig

VENUE: Sir Morgan's Cove, Worcester, MA, USA

PERSONNEL: Mick Jagger, Keith Richards, Ron Wood, Charlie Watts, Bill Wyman, Ian Stewart, Ian McLagan, Ernie Watts

OPENING/OTHER ACT(S): Ezmaralda

NOTES: The "unannounced" small club show in which the Stones, billed as "The Cockroaches and Blue Sunday," sharpened their chops for the upcoming three-month tour. Although Toronto's El Mocambo shows in '77 had been the band's North American club debut and they had played small theaters on the '78 tour, this would be their first ever small club show in the United States. Finding the right place for a "warmup" gig—small but equipped to handle them and able to keep the event quiet and its location a secret until showtime—was a challenge. The band checked out a few potential venues in the area but logistical details such as stage size and the proper number of exit doors proved problematic.

Finally, they came upon Sir Morgan's Cove in Worcester. The club could accommodate only 275 to 300 people but appeared to fit the band's requirements. The Stones asked Sir Morgan's management if they wouldn't mind

The ticket for the Stones' (a.k.a. "The Cockroaches") surprise show at Sir Morgan's Cove in Worcester, MA prior to the 1981 tour (JAMES KARNBACH COLLECTION)

their playing there and could the club handle ticket distribution. The response was yes, play but no, they would not want the responsibility of giving out tickets.

A creative solution to the ticket problem came when a local radio station, WAAF, agreed to hold an on-air contest of sorts and, together with members of the Stones' management team, distribute the tickets. The station told listeners that if they were displaying the station's logo—the call letters WAAF—when the station's cars encountered them, they'd get free tickets to a surprise Rolling Stones show. The band's only proviso was firmly stated—they'd cancel the gig if the location was revealed.

All was going just fine—cars with teams of WAAF and Stones staffers drove around looking for logos and handing out tickets. Then, the major rock station in Boston stepped in heavily. Apparently feeling jilted by the Stones for passing them over for a tiny local station, the big-wattage Boston boys (and, probably, girls) gave it all away in a fit of broadcast pique. They began airing "advisories," telling listeners *not* to go to a certain

Rare stub from the 1981 Boston gig that never happened. The show was canceled because of the hoopla at their surprise show at Sir Morgan's Cove in Worcester, Massachusetts. (JAMES KARNBACH COLLECTION)

address—that of Sir Morgan's Cove—because a riot could break out at any time, making the area unsafe for everyone. Naturally, this gave fans all the information they needed about the location of the Stones' secret gig, which drew a huge crowd to the club. It also brought out the police, who reportedly made 11 arrests. Had the Stones arrived at that point, there would surely have been a mass riot.

The band was scheduled to go on at about 10:00 P.M., but when Ezmaralda, the opening act, finished at 9:30, no Stones or members of their management were to be found. They hadn't turned up by 10:30 when it began to rain, which dispersed some of the mob. The 4,000 people gathered outside the club dwindled to 1,500. By 11:30 there were still no Stones, but the 1,500 had shrunk to a more manageable, though still large, crowd of 800. At approximately 11:50 P.M., a van rolled up to the rear entrance and out popped the Rolling Stones. The band, appreciating the tenacity of the fans outside in the weather, opened the doors to the club so they could hear the show along with the luckier, and drier, ticketed ones inside. Beginning with "Everybody Needs Someone to Love (Russell, Burke, Wexler)," the Stones played a 22-song show, closing it with "Jumpin' Jack Flash." As for the other 20 titles, we can only say that Sir Morgan's Cove had more in common with Stones shows of the early '60s than the size of the venue and the riot outside. All who attended remember how great the music was, but not exactly what it was.

Unfortunately for those in the greater Boston area, there was fallout from the chaos in Worcester. At the same time, the band had scheduled a September 21 performance at Boston's Metropolitan Center. The show had not been officially announced but tickets were already printed and the fan rumor mill was actively reporting that it would happen. However, after Sir Morgan's Cove, Boston city officials got a major case of riot paranoia and nixed the Metro Center concert. And this all happened because of a jealous radio station? We can't really "blame it on the Stones," can we?

SEPTEMBER 25, 1981– DECEMBER 19, 1981

TOUR: 1981 US tour

VENUE: US

PERSONNEL: Mick Jagger, Keith Richards, Ron Wood, Charlie Watts, Bill Wyman, Ian Stewart, Ian McLagan, Ernie Watts, Bobby Keys

SPECIAL GUESTS: Tina Turner, Sugar Blue, Chuck Leavell, Mick Taylor

OPENING/OTHER ACT(S): George Thorogood, Journey, Heart, The Go-Go's, Prince, The J. Geils Band, The Greg Kihn Band, Henry Paul Band, Van Halen, The Stray Cats, The Fabulous Thunderbirds, ZZ Top, The Neville Brothers, Tina Turner, Garland Jeffreys, Screamin' Jay Hawkins, Joe Ely, Etta James, George Duke & Stanley Clark, Molly Hatchet, Iggy Pop, Santana, Bobby Womack, The Meters

SONGS: Under My Thumb / When the Whip Comes Down / Let's Spend the Night Together / Just My Imagination (Running Away with Me) (Whitfield, Strong) / Shattered / Neighbours / Black Limousine (Jagger, Richards, Wood) / Down the Road Apiece (Raye) / Mona (I Need You Baby) (McDaniel) / Twenty Flight Rock (Fairchild, Cochran) / Going to À Go Go (Robinson, Johnson, Moore, Rogers) / Let Me Go / She's So Cold / Time Is on My Side (Meade) / Beast of Burden / Waiting on a Friend / Let It Bleed / Tops / You Can't Always Get What You Want / Tumbling Dice / Little T & A / Hang Fire / Star Star / Start Me Up / Miss You / Honky Tonk Women / All Down the Line / Brown Sugar / Jumpin' Jack Flash / (I Can't Get No) Satisfaction

NOTES: Regularly backing the Stones were Ian Stewart on piano, Ian McLagan on keyboards and Ernie Watts on saxophone. Ernie played in the Doc Severenson Orchestra on "The Johnny Carson Show." Bobby Keys joined the backup musicians on saxophone on October 9 in Los Angeles and remained for the rest of the tour. Guest appearances were made at single shows by Chuck Leavell, Tina Turner, Sugar Blue, and Mick Taylor. Opening acts varied from city to city and are listed with the appropriate shows. This list of songs contains all numbers played on this tour; not all were performed each night. The set developed with the progress of the tour, and songs were added, subtracted or moved in the lineup; sets of particular note will be included with the applicable performance. Various tracks on *Some Girls* were recorded during the tour. The Washington (Largo, MD), Kansas City, and Pontiac concerts were all taped for "The King Biscuit Flower Hour" radio program; the best cuts were used in a 60-minute special Stones broadcast.

SEPTEMBER 25, 1981

TOUR: 1981 US tour
VENUE: JFK Stadium, Philadelphia, PA, USA
OPENING/OTHER ACT(S): George Thorogood, Journey
SONGS: Under My Thumb / When the Whip Comes Down / Neighbors / Just My Imagination (Running Away with Me) (Whitfield, Strong) / Shattered / Let's Spend the Night Together / Black Limousine (Jagger, Richards, Wood) / She's So Cold / Time Is on My Side (Meade) / Beast of Burden / Waiting on a Friend / Let It Bleed / You Can't Always Get What You Want / Tops / Tumbling Dice / Hang Fire / Let Me Go / Little T & A / Start Me Up / Miss You / Honky Tonk Women / All Down the Line / Brown Sugar / Jumpin' Jack Flash / Street Fighting Man / **E:** (I Cant't Get No) Satisfaction

SEPTEMBER 26, 1981

TOUR: 1981 US tour
VENUE: JFK Stadium, Philadelphia, PA, USA
OPENING/OTHER ACT(S): George Thorogood, Journey
SONGS: Under My Thumb / When the Whip Comes Down / Let's Spend the Night Together / Just My Imagination (Running Away with Me) (Whitfield, Strong) / Shattered / Neighbours / Black Limousine (Jagger, Richards, Wood) / Down the Road Apiece (Raye) / Mona (I Need You Baby) (McDaniel) / Twenty Flight Rock (Fairchild, Cochran) / She's So Cold / Time Is on My Side (Meade) / Beast of Burden / Waiting on a Friend / Let It Bleed / You Can't Always Get What You Want / Tumbling Dice / Little T & A / Hang Fire / Start Me Up / Miss You / Honky Tonk Women / All Down the Line / Brown Sugar / Jumpin' Jack Flash / **E:** Street Fighting Man

SEPTEMBER 27, 1981

TOUR: 1981 US tour
VENUE: Rich Stadium, Buffalo, NY, USA
OPENING/OTHER ACT(S): George Thorogood, Journey

OCTOBER 1, 1981

TOUR: 1981 US tour
VENUE: Metro Center, Rockfold, IL, USA
SPECIAL GUESTS: Lee Allen
OPENING/OTHER ACT(S): The Go-Go's
SONGS: Under My Thumb / When the Whip Comes Down / Let's Spend the Night Together / Shattered / Neighbours / Black Limousine (Jagger, Richards, Wood) / Just My Imagination (Running Away with Me) (Whitfield, Strong) / Twenty Flight Rock (Fairchild, Cochran) / Let Me Go / Time Is on My Side (Meade) / Beast of Burden / Waiting on a Friend / Let It Bleed / You Can't Always Get What You Want / Tumbling Dice / Little T

& A / She's So Cold / Hang Fire / Miss You / Start Me Up / Honky Tonk Women / Brown Sugar / **E:** Jumpin' Jack Flash
NOTES: Saxophonist Lee Allen was a special guest at this gig and went on to Colorado with the band. His performance at this gig was something to see!

OCTOBER 3, 1981

TOUR: 1981 US tour
VENUE: Folsom Field, Boulder, CO, USA
SPECIAL GUESTS: Lee Allen
OPENING/OTHER ACT(S): George Thorogood, Heart
SONGS: Under My Thumb / When the Whip Comes Down / Let's Spend the Night Together / Shattered / Neighbours / Black Limousine (Jagger, Richards, Wood) / Just My Imagination (Running Away with Me) (Whitfield, Strong) / Twenty Flight Rock (Fairchild, Cochran) / Let Me Go / Time Is on My Side (Meade) / Beast of Burden / Waiting on a Friend / Let It Bleed / Tops / You Can't Always Get What You Want / Tumbling Dice / Little T & A / She's So Cold / All Down the Line / Hang Fire / Star Star / Miss You / Start Me Up / Honky Tonk Women / Brown Sugar / Jumpin' Jack Flash / **E:** (I Can't Get No) Satisfaction
NOTES: Order of the set changed and "Tops" was added. Lee Allen travelled with the band from Rockford, Illinois and was again a special guest on tenor saxophone at both Colorado performances. Allen had recorded with Little Richard, Etta James and Fats Domino in the late '50s–early '60s.

OCTOBER 4, 1981

TOUR: 1981 US tour
VENUE: Folsom Field, Boulder, CO, USA
SPECIAL GUESTS: Lee Allen
OPENING/OTHER ACT(S): George Thorogood, Heart
NOTES: Lee Allen was special guest on sax, as on previous day.

OCTOBER 7, 1981

TOUR: 1981 US tour
VENUE: Jack Murphy Stadium, San Diego, CA, USA
OPENING/OTHER ACT(S): George Thorogood, The J. Geils Band
SONGS: Under My Thumb / When the Whip Comes Down / Let's Spend the Night Together / Shattered / Black Limousine (Jagger, Richards, Wood) / Neighbours / Just My Imagination (Running Away with Me) (Whitfield, Strong) / Twenty Flight Rock (Fairchild, Cochran) / Let Me Go / Time Is on My Side (Meade) / Beast of Burden / Waiting on a Friend / Let It Bleed / You Can't Always Get What You Want / Little T & A / Tumbling

167

Dice / She's So Cold / All Down the Line / Hang Fire / Star Star / Miss You / Start Me Up / Honky Tonk Women / Brown Sugar / Jumpin' Jack Flash / **E:** Street Fighting Man

OCTOBER 9, 1981

TOUR: 1981 US tour

VENUE: Los Angeles Memorial Coliseum, Los Angeles, CA, USA

PERSONNEL: Mick Jagger, Keith Richards, Ron Wood, Charlie Watts, Bill Wyman, Ian Stewart, Ian McLagan, Ernie Watts, Bobby Keys

OPENING/OTHER ACT(S): Prince, The J. Geils Band, George Thorogood

SONGS: Under My Thumb / When the Whip Comes Down / Let's Spend the Night Together / Shattered / Neighbours / Black Limousine (Jagger, Richards, Wood) / Just My Imagination (Running Away with Me) (Whitfield, Strong) / Twenty Flight Rock (Fairchild, Cochran) / Let Me Go / Time Is on My Side (Meade) / Beast of Burden / Waiting on a Friend / Let It Bleed / You Can't Always Get What You Want / Little T & A / Tumbling Dice / All Down the Line / Hang Fire / Star Star / Miss You / Start Me Up / Honky Tonk Women / Brown Sugar / Jumpin' Jack Flash / Street Fighting Man / **E:** (I Can't Get No) Satisfaction

NOTES: Bobby Keys joined the tour at this performance; the backup musicians now include two sax players. Keys does a solo on "Brown Sugar." But prior to the Stones' show, the fans gave one opening artist the boot: after garbage was thrown at him by a displeased audience, Prince left the stage after four songs.

OCTOBER 11, 1981

TOUR: 1981 US tour

VENUE: Los Angeles Memorial Coliseum, Los Angeles, CA, USA

OPENING/OTHER ACT(S): The J. Geils Band, George Thorogood

OCTOBER 14, 1981

TOUR: 1981 US tour

VENUE: The Kingdome, Seattle, WA, USA

OPENING/OTHER ACT(S): The Greg Kihn Band, The J. Geils Band

OCTOBER 15, 1981

TOUR: 1981 US tour

VENUE: The Kingdome, Seattle, WA, USA

OPENING/OTHER ACT(S): The Greg Kihn Band, The J. Geils Band

OCTOBER 17, 1981

TOUR: 1981 US tour

VENUE: Candlestick Park, San Francisco, CA, USA

OPENING/OTHER ACT(S): George Thorogood, The J. Geils Band

SONGS: Under My Thumb / When the Whip Comes Down / Let's Spend the Night Together / Shattered / Neighbours / Black Limousine (Jagger, Richards, Wood) / Just My Imagination (Running Away with Me) (Whitfield, Strong) / Twenty Flight Rock (Fairchild, Cochran) / Let Me Go / Time Is on My Side (Meade) / Beast of Burden / Waiting on a Friend / Let It Bleed / You Can't Always Get What You Want / Little T & A / Tumbling Dice / She's So Cold / All Down the Line / Hang Fire / Star Star / Miss You / Start Me Up / Honky Tonk Women / Brown Sugar / Jumpin' Jack Flash / **E:** (I Can't Get No) Satisfaction

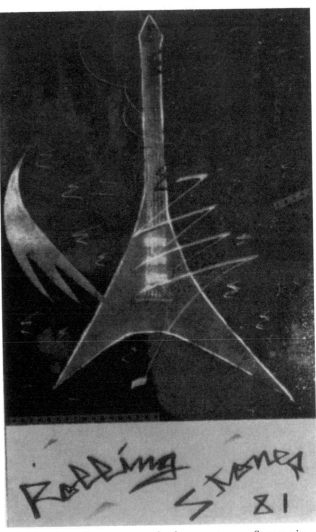

This laminated pass got you backstage at every Stones gig in '81. (JAMES KARNBACH COLLECTION)

OCTOBER 18, 1981

TOUR: 1981 US tour
VENUE: Candlestick Park, San Francisco, CA, USA
OPENING/OTHER ACT(S): George Thorogood, The J. Geils Band

OCTOBER 24, 1981

TOUR: 1981 US tour
VENUE: Tangerine Bowl, Orlando, FL, USA
OPENING/OTHER ACT(S): Henry Paul Band, Van Halen

OCTOBER 25, 1981

TOUR: 1981 US tour
VENUE: Tangerine Bowl, Orlando, FL, USA
OPENING/OTHER ACT(S): Henry Paul Band, Van Halen

OCTOBER 26, 1981

TOUR: 1981 US tour
VENUE: Fox Theater, Atlanta, GA, USA
SPECIAL GUESTS: Chuck Leavell
OPENING/OTHER ACT(S): The Stray Cats
NOTES: The Stray Cats open. Making his debut performance with the Stones, Chuck Leavelll sat in for the entire Atlanta show. Thus, the band had two keyboard players as well as two saxophonists at their performance before the fewest people on the 1981 tour. The Fox Theater was the smallest venue (3,900 seats) the Stones played on this tour, excluding their surprise "warmup" performance in Worcester, MA on September 15, 10 days before the tour officially began.

OCTOBER 28, 1981

TOUR: 1981 US tour
VENUE: Astrodome, Houston, TX, USA
OPENING/OTHER ACT(S): The Fabulous Thunderbirds, ZZ Top

OCTOBER 29, 1981

TOUR: 1981 US tour
VENUE: Astrodome, Houston, TX, USA
OPENING/OTHER ACT(S): The Fabulous Thunderbirds, ZZ Top

OCTOBER 31, 1981

TOUR: 1981 US tour
VENUE: Cotton Bowl, Dallas, TX, USA
OPENING/OTHER ACT(S): The Fabulous Thunderbirds, ZZ Top

NOVEMBER 1, 1981

TOUR: 1981 US tour
VENUE: Cotton Bowl, Dallas, TX, USA
OPENING/OTHER ACT(S): The Fabulous Thunderbirds, ZZ Top

NOVEMBER 3, 1981

TOUR: 1981 US tour
VENUE: Freedom Hall, Louisville, KY, USA
OPENING/OTHER ACT(S): The Neville Brothers
SONGS: Under My Thumb / When the Whip Comes Down / Let's Spend the Night Together / Shattered / Neighbours / Black Limousine (Jagger, Richards, Wood) / Just My Imagination (Running Away with Me) (Whitfield, Strong) / Down the Road Apiece (Raye) / Going to a Go Go (Robinson, Johnson, Moore, Rogers) / Let Me Go / Beast of Burden / Waiting on a Friend / Let It Bleed / You Can't Always Get What You Want / Little T & A / Tumbling Dice / She's So Cold / All Down the Line / Hang Fire / Miss You / Start Me Up / Honky Tonk Women / Brown Sugar / Jumpin' Jack Flash / E: (I Can't Get No) Satisfaction
NOTES: "Going to À Go Go" was added to the set at this performance.

NOVEMBER 5, 1981

TOUR: 1981 US tour
VENUE: Brendan Byrne Arena, The Meadowlands, East Rutherford, NJ, USA
SPECIAL GUESTS: Tina Turner
OPENING/OTHER ACT(S): Tina Turner
SONGS: Under My Thumb, LV2 / When the Whip Comes Down / Let's Spend the Night Together / Shattered / Neighbours / Black Limousine (Jagger, Richards, Wood) / Just My Imagination (Running Away with Me) (Whitfield, Strong) / Twenty Flight Rock (Fairchild, Cochran) / Going to À Go Go (Robinson, Johnson, Moore, Rogers) / Let Me Go / Time Is on My Side (Meade) / Beast of Burden / Waiting on a Friend / Let It Bleed / You Can't Always Get What You Want / Little T & A / Tumbling Dice / She's So Cold → All Down the Line → Hang Fire → Miss You → Start Me Up → Honky Tonk Women → Brown Sugar → E: Jumpin' Jack Flash
NOTES: Tina Turner opened for the Stones, and made a guest appearance during their set on "Honky Tonk Women." The New Jersey appearances were filmed for *Let's Spend the Night Together*, but Tina's guest spots didn't make the final edit of the film. The concerts at Brendan Byrne arena, a 20,000-seat venue, were all recorded; "Under My Thumb" from this show did make it onto *Still Life*.

NOVEMBER 6, 1981

TOUR: 1981 US tour
VENUE: Brendan Byrne Arena, The Meadowlands, East Rutherford, NJ, USA
SPECIAL GUESTS: Tina Turner
OPENING/OTHER ACT(S):   Tina Turner
NOTES: Tina Turner again joined the Stones on "Honky Tonk Women" and the show was filmed for *Let's Spend the Night Together.*

NOVEMBER 7, 1981

TOUR: 1981 US tour
VENUE: Brendan Byrne Arena, The Meadowlands, East Rutherford, NJ, USA
SPECIAL GUESTS: Tina Turner
OPENING/OTHER ACT(S):   Tina Turner
NOTES: Tina Turner opened for the Stones and again joined them onstage for "Honky Tonk Women." The show, like the other New Jersey concerts, was filmed for *Let's Spend the Night Together.*

NOVEMBER 9, 1981

TOUR: 1981 US tour

Mick agape in Hartford, CT, November 9, 1981 (1981, PHYLLIS LATTNER)

VENUE: Civic Center, Hartford, CT, USA
OPENING/OTHER ACT(S):   Garland Jeffreys
NOTES: Garland Jeffreys opened for the Stones on both Hartford dates.

NOVEMBER 10, 1981

TOUR: 1981 US tour
VENUE: Civic Center, Hartford, CT, USA
OPENING/OTHER ACT(S):   Garland Jeffreys

NOVEMBER 12, 1981

TOUR: 1981 US tour
VENUE: Madison Square Garden, New York, NY, USA
OPENING/OTHER ACT(S):   Screamin' Jay Hawkins
NOTES: Although Screamin' Jay Hawkins opened both Madison Square Garden shows, he was a last-minute substitution. James Brown was originally booked to appear, but missed his plane in Georgia. He phoned promoter Bill Graham with that news and requested a chartered plane to fly him and his band to New York. That alternative had a very expensive price tag and Graham gave Brown a quick two-word expletive—"F***Y**"—as a reply. The promoter then phoned Hawkins's manager in New York and inquired as to Screamin' Jay's plans for the evening. "Why?" asked the manager, unaware. Graham answered him with another question: if his client was available, would he like to open for the Stones that night?

NOVEMBER 13, 1981

TOUR: 1981 US tour
VENUE: Madison Square Garden, New York, NY, USA
OPENING/OTHER ACT(S):   Screamin' Jay Hawkins
NOTES: See Notes for November 12.

NOVEMBER 16, 1981

TOUR: 1981 US tour
VENUE: Richfield Coliseum, Cleveland, OH, USA
OPENING/OTHER ACT(S):   Etta James

NOVEMBER 17, 1981

TOUR: 1981 US tour
VENUE: Richfield Coliseum, Cleveland, OH, USA
OPENING/OTHER ACT(S):   Etta James

NOVEMBER 19, 1981

TOUR: 1981 US tour
VENUE: Checkerdome, St. Louis, MO, USA
OPENING/OTHER ACT(S):   George Duke & Stanley Clark

NOVEMBER 20, 1981

TOUR: 1981 US tour

VENUE: Unidome, Cedar Falls, IA, USA

OPENING/OTHER ACT(S): The Stray Cats

NOVEMBER 21, 1981

TOUR: 1981 US tour

VENUE: St. Paul Civic Center, St. Paul, MN, USA

OPENING/OTHER ACT(S): The Stray Cats

NOVEMBER 23, 1981

TOUR: 1981 US tour

VENUE: Rosemont Horizon, Chicago, IL, USA

OPENING/OTHER ACT(S): The Neville Brothers

NOVEMBER 24, 1981

TOUR: 1981 US tour

VENUE: Rosemont Horizon, Chicago, IL, USA

SPECIAL GUESTS: Sugar Blue

OPENING/OTHER ACT(S): The Neville Brothers

NOTES: Sugar Blue made a guest appearance on "Miss You," playing harmonica as he had on the studio version that appears on *Some Girls.*

NOVEMBER 25, 1981

TOUR: 1981 US tour

VENUE: Rosemont Horizon, Chicago, IL, USA

OPENING/OTHER ACT(S): The Neville Brothers

SONGS: Under My Thumb / When the Whip Comes Down / Let's Spend the Night Together / Shattered / Neighbours / Black Limousine (Jagger, Richards, Wood) / Just My Imagination (Running Away with Me) (Whitfield, Strong) / Twenty Flight Rock (Fairchild, Cochran) / Going to À Go Go (Robinson, Johnson, Moore, Rogers) / Let Me Go / Time Is on My Side (Meade) / Beast of Burden, LV / Waiting on a Friend / Let It Bleed / You Can't Always Get What You Want / Little T & A / Tumbling Dice / She's So Cold / Hang Fire / Miss You / Honky Tonk Women / Brown Sugar / Start Me Up, LV / Jumpin' Jack Flash / E: (I Can't Get No) Satisfaction

NOTES: *Still Life* tracks "Beast of Burden" and "Start Me Up" came from this show.

NOVEMBER 27, 1981

TOUR: 1981 US tour

VENUE: Carrier Dome, Syracuse, NY, USA

OPENING/OTHER ACT(S): Molly Hatchet

NOTES: Molly Hatchet opened for the Stones at both Syracuse performances in the 42,000-seat Carrier Dome.

NOVEMBER 28, 1981

TOUR: 1981 US tour

VENUE: Carrier Dome, Syracuse, NY, USA

OPENING/OTHER ACT(S): Molly Hatchet

NOVEMBER 30, 1981

TOUR: 1981 US tour

VENUE: Silverdome, Pontiac, MI, USA

OPENING/OTHER ACT(S): Iggy Pop, Santana

NOTES: This show was taped for potential use in a one-hour "King Biscuit Flower Hour" broadcast. The 76,214-seat Silverdome, located some 30 miles outside Detroit, was the third-largest venue (after the Superdome and the Cotton Bowl) of the '81 tour.

DECEMBER 1, 1981

TOUR: 1981 US tour

VENUE: Silverdome, Pontiac, MI, USA

OPENING/OTHER ACT(S): Iggy Pop, Santana

NOTES: This show was taped for potential use in a one-hour "King Biscuit Flower Hour" broadcast.

DECEMBER 5, 1981

TOUR: 1981 US tour

VENUE: Superdome, New Orleans, LA, USA

OPENING/OTHER ACT(S): George Thorogood

DECEMBER 7, 1981

TOUR: 1981 US tour

VENUE: Capitol Center, Largo, MD, USA

OPENING/OTHER ACT(S): Bobby Womack

SONGS: Under My Thumb / When the Whip Comes Down / Let's Spend the Night Together / Shattered / Neighbours / Black Limousine (Jagger, Richards, Wood) / Just My Imagination (Running Away with Me) (Whitfield, Strong) / Twenty Flight Rock (Fairchild, Cochran) / Going to À Go Go (Robinson, Johnson, Moore, Rogers) / Let Me Go, LV / Time Is on My Side (Meade) / Beast of Burden / Waiting on a Friend / Let It Bleed / You Can't Always Get What You Want / Little T & A / Tumbling Dice / She's So Cold / Hang Fire / Miss You / Honky Tonk Women / Brown Sugar / Start Me Up / Jumpin' Jack Flash

NOTES: This show was taped for potential use in a one-hour "King Biscuit Flower Hour" broadcast. The band was recording the concert as well. *Still Life*'s "Let Me Go" live cut came from this performance.

DECEMBER 8, 1981

TOUR: 1981 US tour

VENUE: Capitol Center, Largo, MD, USA

OPENING/OTHER ACT(S): Bobby Womack

SONGS: Under My Thumb / When the Whip Comes Down / Let's Spend the Night Together / Shattered / Neighbours / Black Limousine (Jagger, Richards, Wood) / Just My Imagination (Running Away with Me) (Whitfield, Strong) / Twenty Flight Rock (Fairchild, Cochran), LV / Going to À Go Go (Robinson, Johnson, Moore, Rogers), LV / Let Me Go / Time Is on My Side (Meade) / Beast of Burden / Waiting on a Friend / Let It Bleed / You Can't Always Get What You Want / Little T & A / Tumbling Dice / She's So Cold / Hang Fire / Miss You / Honky Tonk Women / Brown Sugar / Start Me Up / Jumpin' Jack Flash/ E: (I Can't Get No) Satisfaction

NOTES: This show was taped for the "King Biscuit Flower Hour" as well as by the band. The live versions of "Twenty Flight Rock" and "Going to À Go Go" on *Still Life* were recorded here.

DECEMBER 9, 1981

TOUR: 1981 US tour

VENUE: Capitol Center, Largo, MD, USA

OPENING/OTHER ACT(S): Bobby Womack

NOTES: The song, "Little T & A," was not performed at this show. This show was taped for potential use in a one-hour "King Biscuit Flower Hour" broadcast.

DECEMBER 11, 1981

TOUR: 1981 US tour

VENUE: Rupp Arena, Lexington, KY, USA

OPENING/OTHER ACT(S): The Meters

SONGS: Under My Thumb / When the Whip Comes Down / Let's Spend the Night Together / Shattered / Neighbours / Black Limousine (Jagger, Richards, Wood) / Just My Imagination (Running Away with Me) (Whitfield, Strong) / Twenty Flight Rock (Fairchild, Cochran) / Going to À Go Go (Robinson, Johnson, Moore, Rogers) / Let Me Go / Time Is on My Side (Meade) / Beast of Burden / Waiting on a Friend / Let It Bleed / You Can't Always Get What You Want / Little T & A / Tumbling Dice / She's So Cold / Hang Fire / Miss You / Honky Tonk Women / Brown Sugar / Start Me Up / Jumpin' Jack Flash

DECEMBER 13, 1981

TOUR: 1981 US tour

VENUE: Sun Devil Stadium, Tempe, AZ, USA

OPENING/OTHER ACT(S): George Thorogood, Joe Ely

SONGS: Under My Thumb / When the Whip Comes Down / Let's Spend the Night Together / Shattered / Neighbours / Black Limousine (Jagger, Richards, Wood) / Just My Imagination (Running Away with Me) (Whit-field, Strong) / Twenty Flight Rock (Fairchild, Cochran) / Going to À Go Go / Let Me Go / Time Is on My Side (Meade) / Beast of Burden / Waiting on a Friend / Let It Bleed / You Can't Always Get What You Want / Little T & A / Tumbling Dice / She's So Cold / Hang Fire / Miss You / Honky Tonk Women / Brown Sugar / Start Me Up / Jumpin' Jack Flash / (I Can't Get No) Satisfaction, LV2

NOTES: There were two opening acts—Joe Ely, then George Thorogood—at this performance, not a particularly unique occurrence on the tour. But the unannounced appearance onstage of significant Stones females was. Patti Hansen, Jo Wood, Jerry Hall, Shirley Watts and Jane Rose joined the boys on (what else?) "Honky Tonk Women" at this gig only. The live version of "Satisfaction" on *Still Life* was recorded here.

DECEMBER 14, 1981

TOUR: 1981 US tour

VENUE: Kemper Arena, Kansas City, MO, USA

SPECIAL GUESTS: Mick Taylor

OPENING/OTHER ACT(S): George Thorogood

NOTES: George Thorogood opened for the Stones. Mick Taylor made a surprise guest appearance with his former bandmates at this gig. Taylor was in town for a gig of his own and had been hanging out with the band at the hotel. He accompanied them to the arena, just to see the show, but Keith and Ronnie asked him to sit in. He borrowed a guitar and was introduced close to the beginning of the show, and stayed on until the end, which he remembers as "too long." He also remembers others agreeing with that assessment. This show was taped for potential use in a one-hour "King Biscuit Flower Hour" broadcast.

DECEMBER 15, 1981

TOUR: 1981 US tour

VENUE: Kemper Arena, Kansas City, MO, USA

OPENING/OTHER ACT(S): George Thorogood

NOTES: This show was taped for potential use in one-hour "King Biscuit Flower Hour" broadcast.

DECEMBER 18, 1981

TOUR: 1981 US tour

VENUE: Hampton Roads Coliseum, Hampton, VA, USA

OPENING/OTHER ACT(S): George Thorogood

SONGS: Under My Thumb / When the Whip Comes Down / Let's Spend the Night Together, LV / Shattered, LV / Neighbours / Black Limousine (Jagger, Richards, Wood) / Just My Imagination (Running Away with Me) (Whitfield, Strong) / Twenty Flight Rock (Fairchild,

Cochran) / Going to À Go Go (Robinson, Johnson, Moore, Rogers) /Let Me Go / Time Is on My Side (Meade), LV2 / Beast of Burden / Waiting on a Friend / Let It Bleed / You Can't Always Get What You Want / Little T & A / Tumbling Dice / She's So Cold / Hang Fire / Miss You / Honky Tonk Women / Brown Sugar / Start Me Up / Jumpin' Jack Flash / **E:** (I Can't Get No) Satisfaction

NOTES: Three *Still Life* tracks were recorded at this date—"Let's Spend the Night Together," "Shattered," and "Time Is on My Side."

DECEMBER 19, 1981

TOUR: 1981 US tour
VENUE: Hampton Roads Coliseum, Hampton, VA, USA
OPENING/OTHER ACT(S): George Thorogood
SONGS: Under My Thumb / When the Whip Comes Down / Let's Spend the Night Together / Shattered / Neighbours / Black Limousine (Jagger, Richards, Wood) / Just My Imagination (Running Away with Me) (Whitfield, Strong), LV / Twenty Flight Rock (Fairchild, Co-

A surly Ronnie in Largo, MD, December 7, 1981
(1981, PHYLLIS LATTNER)

chran) / Let Me Go / Time Is on My Side (Meade) / Beast of Burden / Waiting on a Friend / Let It Bleed / You Can't Always Get What You Want / Little T & A / Tumbling Dice / She's So Cold / Hang Fire / Miss You / Honky Tonk Women / Brown Sugar / Start Me Up / Jumpin' Jack Flash

NOTES: This was the concert broadcast as the Rolling Stones' first pay-per-view television special. "Just My Imagination" on *Still Life* was recorded at this last performance of the '81 tour.

1982

MAY 26, 1982 – JULY 25, 1982

TOUR: 1982 European tour
VENUE: Scotland, England, Holland, Germany, France, Sweden, Austria, Spain, Switzerland and Ireland
PERSONNEL: Mick Jagger, Keith Richards, Ron Wood, Charlie Watts, Bill Wyman, Ian Stewart, Chuck Leavell, Bobby Keys, Gene Barge
OPENING/OTHER ACT(S): The J. Geils Band, George Thorogood, UB40, Black Uhuru, Joe Jackson, Telefon
SONGS: Under My Thumb / When the Whip Comes Down / Let's Spend the Night Together / Shattered / Neighbours / Black Limousine (Jagger, Richards, Wood) / Just My Imagination (Running Away with Me) (Whitfield, Strong) / Twenty Flight Rock (Fairchild, Cochran) / Going to À Go Go (Robinson, Johnson, Moore, Rogers) / Chantilly Lace (Richardson) / Let Me Go / Time Is on My Side (Meade) / Beast of Burden / Let It Bleed / You Can't Always Get What You Want / Little T & A / Angie / Tumbling Dice / She's So Cold / Hang Fire / Miss You / Honky Tonk Women / Brown Sugar / Start Me Up / Jumpin' Jack Flash / **E:** (I Can't Get No) Satisfaction
NOTES: Backing players for the Stones were Ian Stewart, piano; Chuck Leavell, keyboards; Bobby Keys and Gene Barge, saxophone. The J. Geils Band opened at all large venues, joined occasionally by George Thorogood who also preceded the Stones in some of the smaller houses as the sole warmup act. The other artists joined the bill in various locations. "Chantilly Lace" appeared in a tour setlist for the first time in 1982.

MAY 26, 1982

TOUR: 1982 European tour
VENUE: Capitol Theatre, Aberdeen, Scotland
OPENING/OTHER ACT(S): George Thorogood
SONGS: Under My Thumb / When the Whip Comes Down / Let's Spend the Night Together / Shattered / Neighbours / Black Limousine (Jagger, Richards, Wood)

/ Just My Imagination (Running Away with Me) (Whitfield, Strong) / Twenty Flight Rock (Fairchild, Cochran) / Going to À Go Go (Robinson, Johnson, Moore, Rogers) / Chantilly Lace (Richardson) / Let Me Go / Time Is on My Side (Meade) / Beast of Burden / Let It Bleed / You Can't Always Get What You Want / Tumbling Dice / Little T & A / Hang Fire / Miss You / Honky Tonk Women / Brown Sugar / Start Me Up / Jumpin' Jack Flash / **E:** (I Can't Get No) Satisfaction

MAY 27, 1982

TOUR: 1982 European tour
VENUE: Apollo Theatre, Glasgow, Scotland
OPENING/OTHER ACT(S): George Thorogood

MAY 28, 1982

TOUR: 1982 European tour
VENUE: Edinburgh Playhouse, Edinburgh, Scotland
OPENING/OTHER ACT(S): George Thorogood
SONGS: Under My Thumb / When the Whip Comes Down / Let's Spend the Night Together / Shattered / Neighbours / Black Limousine (Jagger, Richards, Wood) / Just My Imagination (Running Away with Me) (Whitfield, Strong) / Twenty Flight Rock (Fairchild, Cochran) / Going to À Go Go (Robinson, Johnson, Moore, Rogers) / Chantilly Lace (Richardson) / Let Me Go / Time Is on My Side (Meade) / Beast of Burden / You Can't Always Get What You Want / Little T & A / Tumbling Dice / She's So Cold / Hang Fire / Miss You / Honky Tonk Women / Brown Sugar / Start Me Up / Jumpin' Jack Flash / **E:** (I Can't Get No) Satisfaction

MAY 31, 1982

TOUR: 1982 European tour
VENUE: The 100 Club, London, England
OPENING/OTHER ACT(S): None
NOTES: There was *no* opening act at this gig.

JUNE 2, 1982

TOUR: 1982 European tour
VENUE: Feyenoord Stadium, Rotterdam, Holland
OPENING/OTHER ACT(S): The J. Geils Band, UB40, George Thorogood
SONGS: Under My Thumb / When the Whip Comes Down / Let's Spend the Night Together / Shattered / Neighbours / Black Limousine (Jagger, Richards, Wood) / Just My Imagination (Running Away with Me) (Whitfield, Strong) / Twenty Flight Rock (Fairchild, Cochran) / Going to À Go Go (Robinson, Johnson, Moore, Rogers) / Chantilly Lace (Richardson) / Let Me Go / Time Is on My Side (Meade) / Beast of Burden / Let It Bleed / You Can't Always Get What You Want / Little T & A

/ Tumbling Dice / She's So Cold / Hang Fire / Miss You / Honky Tonk Women / Brown Sugar / Start Me Up / Jumpin' Jack Flash / **E:** (I Can't Get No) Satisfaction
NOTES: The first of three dates in Rotterdam, this was the first official concert of the '82 tour.

JUNE 4, 1982

TOUR: 1982 European tour
VENUE: Feyenoord Stadium, Rotterdam, Holland
OPENING/OTHER ACT(S): The J. Geils Band, UB40, George Thorogood
NOTES: The setlist was identical to that of June 2.

JUNE 5, 1982

TOUR: 1982 European tour
VENUE: Feyenoord Stadium, Rotterdam, Holland
OPENING/OTHER ACT(S): The J. Geils Band, UB40, George Thorogood
SONGS: Under My Thumb / When the Whip Comes Down / Let's Spend the Night Together / Shattered / Neighbours / Black Limousine (Jagger, Richards, Wood) / Just My Imagination (Running Away with Me) (Whitfield, Strong) / Twenty Flight Rock (Fairchild, Cochran) / Going to À Go Go (Robinson, Johnson, Moore, Rogers) / Chantilly Lace (Richardson) / Let Me Go / Time Is on My Side (Meade) / Beast of Burden / Let It Bleed / You Can't Always Get What You Want / Little T & A / She's So Cold / Hang Fire / Miss You / Honky Tonk Women / Brown Sugar / Start Me Up / Jumpin' Jack Flash / **E:** (I Can't Get No) Satisfaction
NOTES: Slight change in the set—no "Tumbling Dice."

JUNE 6, 1982

TOUR: 1982 European tour
VENUE: Niedersachsen-Stadion, Hanover, West Germany
OPENING/OTHER ACT(S): The J. Geils Band
SONGS: Under My Thumb / When the Whip Comes Down / Let's Spend the Night Together / Shattered / Neighbours / Black Limousine (Jagger, Richards, Wood) / Just My Imagination (Running Away with Me) (Whitfield, Strong) / Twenty Flight Rock (Fairchild, Cochran) / Going to À Go Go (Robinson, Johnson, Moore, Rogers) / Chantilly Lace (Richardson) / Let Me Go / Time Is on My Side (Meade) / Beast of Burden / Let It Bleed / You Can't Always Get What You Want / Little T & A / Tumbling Dice / She's So Cold / Hang Fire / Miss You / Honky Tonk Women / Brown Sugar / Start Me Up / Jumpin' Jack Flash / (I Can't Get No) Satisfaction
NOTES: "Tumbling Dice" reappears and the set remains as above through June 10.

JUNE 7, 1982

TOUR: 1982 European tour
VENUE: Niedersachsen-Stadion, Hanover, West Germany
OPENING/OTHER ACT(S): The J. Geils Band

JUNE 8, 1982

TOUR: 1982 European tour
VENUE: Waldbühne Halle, West Berlin, Germany
OPENING/OTHER ACT(S): The J. Geils Band

JUNE 10, 1982

TOUR: 1982 European tour
VENUE: Olympiastadion, Munich, West Germany
OPENING/OTHER ACT(S): The J. Geils Band

JUNE 11, 1982

TOUR: 1982 European tour
VENUE: Olympiastadion, Munich, West Germany
OPENING/OTHER ACT(S): The J. Geils Band
SONGS: Under My Thumb / When the Whip Comes Down / Let's Spend the Night Together / Shattered / Neighbours / Black Limousine (Jagger, Richards, Wood) / Twenty Flight Rock (Fairchild, Cochran) / Going to À Go Go (Robinson, Johnson, Moore, Rogers) / Chantilly Lace (Richardson) / Let Me Go / Time Is on My Side (Meade) / Beast of Burden / You Can't Always Get What You Want / Little T & A / Tumbling Dice / She's So Cold / Hang Fire / Miss You / Honky Tonk Women / Brown Sugar / Start Me Up / Jumpin' Jack Flash / E: (I Can't Get No) Satisfaction
NOTES: The set lost "Let It Bleed" and "Just My Imagination" at the second Munich date.

JUNE 13, 1982

TOUR: 1982 European tour
VENUE: Hippodrome d'Auteuil, Paris, France
OPENING/OTHER ACT(S): The J. Geils Band, Telefon, George Thorogood
SONGS: Under My Thumb / When the Whip Comes Down / Let's Spend the Night Together / Shattered / Neighbours / Black Limousine (Jagger, Richards, Wood) / Just My Imagination (Running Away with Me) (Whitfield, Strong) / Twenty Flight Rock (Fairchild, Cochran) / Going to À Go Go (Robinson, Johnson, Moore, Rogers) / Chantilly Lace (Richardson) / Let Me Go / Time Is on My Side (Meade) / Beast of Burden / Let It Bleed / You Can't Always Get What You Want / Little T & A / Tumbling Dice / She's So Cold / Hang Fire / Miss You / Honky Tonk Women / Brown Sugar / Start Me Up / Jumpin' Jack Flash / E: (I Can't Get No) Satisfaction

NOTES: The show again included "Let It Bleed" and "Just My Imagination" after a brief loss of both in Munich. No more setlist changes occurred until Newcastle on June 23.

JUNE 14, 1982

TOUR: 1982 European tour
VENUE: Hippodrome d'Auteuil, Paris, France
OPENING/OTHER ACT(S): The J. Geils Band, Telefon, George Thorogood

JUNE 16, 1982

TOUR: 1982 European tour
VENUE: Stade Gerland, Lyons, France
OPENING/OTHER ACT(S): The J. Geils Band, Telefon, George Thorogood

JUNE 19, 1982

TOUR: 1982 European tour
VENUE: Ullevi Stadium, Gothenburg, Sweden
OPENING/OTHER ACT(S): The J. Geils Band

JUNE 20, 1982

TOUR: 1982 European tour
VENUE: Ullevi Stadium, Gothenburg, Sweden
OPENING/OTHER ACT(S): The J. Geils Band

JUNE 23, 1982

TOUR: 1982 European tour
VENUE: Newcastle United Football Ground, Newcastle-upon-Tyne, Northumberland, England
OPENING/OTHER ACT(S): The J. Geils Band
SONGS: Under My Thumb / When the Whip Comes Down / Let's Spend the Night Together / Shattered / Neighbours / Black Limousine (Jagger, Richards, Wood) / Just My Imagination (Running Away with Me) (Whitfield, Strong) / Twenty Flight Rock (Fairchild, Cochran) / Going to À Go Go (Robinson, Johnson, Moore, Rogers) / Chantilly Lace (Richardson) / Let Me Go / Time Is on My Side (Meade) / Beast of Burden / You Can't Always Get What You Want / Little T & A / Tumbling Dice / She's So Cold / Hang Fire / Miss You / Honky Tonk Women / Brown Sugar / Start Me Up / Jumpin' Jack Flash / E: (I Can't Get No) Satisfaction
NOTES: No "Let It Bleed." A sane choice, considering the venue.

JUNE 25, 1982

TOUR: 1982 European tour
VENUE: Wembley Stadium, Wembley, Middlesex, England

OPENING/OTHER ACT(S): The J. Geils Band, Black Uhuru

SONGS: Under My Thumb / When the Whip Comes Down / Let's Spend the Night Together / Shattered / Neighbours / Black Limousine (Jagger, Richards, Wood) / Just My Imagination (Running Away with Me) (Whitfield, Strong) / Twenty Flight Rock (Fairchild, Cochran) / Going to À Go Go (Robinson, Johnson, Moore, Rogers) / Chantilly Lace (Richardson) / Let Me Go / Time Is on My Side (Meade) / Beast of Burden / Let It Bleed / You Can't Always Get What You Want / Little T & A / Tumbling Dice / She's So Cold / Hang Fire / Miss You / Honky Tonk Women / Brown Sugar / Start Me Up / Jumpin' Jack Flash / E: (I Can't Get No) Satisfaction

NOTES: The set returned to "normal" at the Wembley dates.

JUNE 26, 1982

TOUR: 1982 European tour

VENUE: Wembley Stadium, Wembley, Middlesex, England

OPENING/OTHER ACT(S): The J. Geils Band, Black Uhuru

JUNE 27, 1982

TOUR: 1982 European tour

VENUE: Ashton Gate Park, Bristol, Gloucestershire, England

OPENING/OTHER ACT(S): The J. Geils Band

SONGS: Under My Thumb / When the Whip Comes Down / Let's Spend the Night Together / Shattered / Neighbours / Black Limousine (Jagger, Richards, Wood) / Just My Imagination (Running Away with Me) (Whitfield, Strong) / Twenty Flight Rock (Fairchild, Cochran) / Going to À Go Go (Robinson, Johnson, Moore, Rogers) / Chantilly Lace (Richardson) / Let Me Go / Time Is on My Side (Meade) / Beast of Burden / Let It Bleed / You Can't Always Get What You Want / Little T & A / Tumbling Dice / She's So Cold / Hang Fire / Jumpin' Jack Flash / E: (I Can't Get No) Satisfaction

NOTES: The Bristol show was shorter by four songs— "Miss You," "Honky Tonk Women," "Brown Sugar" and "Start Me Up" weren't performed.

JUNE 29, 1982

TOUR: 1982 European tour

VENUE: Festhalle, Frankfurt, West Germany

OPENING/OTHER ACT(S): The J. Geils Band

SONGS: Under My Thumb / When the Whip Comes Down / Let's Spend the Night Together / Shattered / Neighbours / Black Limousine (Jagger, Richards, Wood)

Ticket to show at Frankfurt's Festhalle during the 1982 European tour (JAMES KARNBACH COLLECTION)

/ Just My Imagination (Running Away with Me) (Whitfield, Strong) / Twenty Flight Rock (Fairchild, Cochran) / Going to À Go Go (Robinson, Johnson, Moore, Rogers) / Chantilly Lace (Richardson) / Let Me Go / Time Is on My Side (Meade) / Beast of Burden / Let It Bleed / You Can't Always Get What You Want / Little T & A / Tumbling Dice / She's So Cold / Hang Fire / Miss You / Honky Tonk Women / Brown Sugar / Start Me Up / Jumpin' Jack Flash / E: (I Can't Get No) Satisfaction

NOTES: The four songs removed in Bristol returned to the show in Frankfurt and the set stayed the same until the third performance in that city.

JUNE 30, 1982

TOUR: 1982 European tour

VENUE: Festhalle, Frankfurt, West Germany

OPENING/OTHER ACT(S): The J. Geils Band

JULY 1, 1982

TOUR: 1982 European tour

VENUE: Festhalle, Frankfurt, West Germany

OPENING/OTHER ACT(S): The J. Geils Band

SONGS: Under My Thumb / When the Whip Comes Down / Let's Spend the Night Together / Shattered / Neighbours / Black Limousine (Jagger, Richards, Wood) / Just My Imagination (Running Away with Me) (Whitfield, Strong) / Twenty Flight Rock (Fairchild, Cochran) / Going to À Go Go (Robinson, Johnson, Moore, Rogers) / Let Me Go / Time Is on My Side (Meade) / Beast of Burden / You Can't Always Get What You Want /

Little T & A / Tumbling Dice / She's So Cold / Hang Fire / Miss You / Honky Tonk Women / Brown Sugar / Start Me Up / Jumpin' Jack Flash / **E:** (I Can't Get No) Satisfaction

NOTES: "Let It Bleed" and "Chantilly Lace" were not performed here, nor in any shows on the balance of the tour. This was the setlist for the Austrian and German performances that immediately followed Frankfurt; small, interesting changes cropped up in Spain and thereafter.

JULY 3, 1982

TOUR: 1982 European tour

VENUE: Prater Stadion, Vienna, Austria

OPENING/OTHER ACT(S): The J. Geils Band

JULY 4, 1982

TOUR: 1982 European tour

VENUE: Mungersdorfer-Stadion, Cologne, West Germany

OPENING/OTHER ACT(S): The J. Geils Band

JULY 5, 1982

TOUR: 1982 European tour

VENUE: Mungersdorfer-Stadion, Cologne, West Germany

OPENING/OTHER ACT(S): The J. Geils Band

JULY 7, 1982

TOUR: 1982 European tour

VENUE: Estadio Vincent Calderon, Madrid, Spain

OPENING/OTHER ACT(S): The J. Geils Band

SONGS: Under My Thumb / When the Whip Comes Down / Let's Spend the Night Together / Shattered / Neighbours / Black Limousine (Jagger, Richards, Wood) / Just My Imagination (Running Away with Me) (Whitfield, Strong) / Twenty Flight Rock (Fairchild, Cochran) / Going to À Go Go (Robinson, Johnson, Moore, Rogers) / Let Me Go / Time Is on My Side (Meade) / Beast of Burden / You Can't Always Get What You Want / Little T & A / Angie / Tumbling Dice / She's So Cold / Hang Fire / Miss You / Honky Tonk Women / Brown Sugar / Start Me Up / Jumpin' Jack Flash / **E:** (I Can't Get No) Satisfaction

NOTES: "Angie" is added to the show and remains until the end of the tour.

JULY 9, 1982

TOUR: 1982 European tour

VENUE: Estadio Vincent Calderon, Madrid, Spain

OPENING/OTHER ACT(S): The J. Geils Band

SONGS: Under My Thumb / When the Whip Comes Down / Let's Spend the Night Together / Shattered / Neighbours / Black Limousine (Jagger, Richards, Wood) / Just My Imagination (Running Away with Me) (Whitfield, Strong) / Twenty Flight Rock (Fairchild, Cochran) / Going to À Go Go (Robinson, Johnson, Moore, Rogers) / Let Me Go / Time Is on My Side (Meade) / Beast of Burden / You Can't Always Get What You Want / Little T & A / Angie / Tumbling Dice / She's So Cold / Hang Fire / Miss You / Honky Tonk Women / Brown Sugar / Start Me Up / Jumpin' Jack Flash / **E:** (I Can't Get No) Satisfaction

JULY 11, 1982

TOUR: 1982 European tour

VENUE: Stadio Comunale, Turin, Italy

OPENING/OTHER ACT(S): The J. Geils Band

SONGS: Under My Thumb / When the Whip Comes Down / Let's Spend the Night Together / Shattered / Neighbours / Black Limousine (Jagger, Richards, Wood) / Just My Imagination (Running Away with Me) (Whitfield, Strong) / Twenty Flight Rock (Fairchild, Cochran) / Going to À Go Go (Robinson, Johnson, Moore, Rogers) / Let Me Go / Time Is on My Side (Meade) / Beast of Burden / You Can't Always Get What You Want / Angie / Tumbling Dice / She's So Cold / Hang Fire / Miss You / Honky Tonk Women / Brown Sugar / Start Me Up / Jumpin' Jack Flash / (I Can't Get No) Satisfaction

NOTES: No "T & A" in Turin, initially.

JULY 12, 1982

TOUR: 1982 European tour

VENUE: Stadio Comunale, Turin, Italy

OPENING/OTHER ACT(S): The J. Geils Band

SONGS: Under My Thumb / When the Whip Comes Down / Let's Spend the Night Together / Shattered / Neighbours / Black Limousine (Jagger, Richards, Wood) / Just My Imagination (Running Away with Me) (Whitfield, Strong) / Twenty Flight Rock (Fairchild, Cochran) / Going to À Go Go (Robinson, Johnson, Moore, Rogers) / Let Me Go / Time Is on My Side (Meade) / Beast of Burden / You Can't Always Get What You Want / Little T & A / Angie / Tumbling Dice / She's So Cold / Hang Fire / Miss You / Honky Tonk Women / Brown Sugar / Start Me Up / Jumpin' Jack Flash

NOTES: Turin's July 12 audience got "Little T & A" but no "Satisfaction." Closing this show with "Jumpin' Jack Flash" was unique for this tour.

JULY 15, 1982

TOUR: 1982 European tour

VENUE: St. Jakob Stadion, Basel, Switzerland
OPENING/OTHER ACT(S): The J. Geils Band
SONGS: Under My Thumb / When the Whip Comes Down / Let's Spend the Night Together / Shattered / Neighbours / Black Limousine (Jagger, Richards, Wood) / Just My Imagination (Running Away with Me) (Whitfield, Strong) / Twenty Flight Rock (Fairchild, Cochran) / Going to À Go Go (Robinson, Johnson, Moore, Rogers) / Let Me Go / Time Is on My Side (Meade) / Beast of Burden / You Can't Always Get What You Want / Little T & A / Angie / Tumbling Dice / She's So Cold / Hang Fire / Miss You / Honky Tonk Women / Brown Sugar / Jumpin' Jack Flash / (I Can't Get No) Satisfaction

JULY 17, 1982

TOUR: 1982 European tour
VENUE: Stadio San Paolo, Naples, Italy
OPENING/OTHER ACT(S): The J. Geils Band
SONGS: Under My Thumb / When the Whip Comes Down / Let's Spend the Night Together / Shattered / Neighbours / Black Limousine (Jagger, Richards, Wood) / Just My Imagination (Running Away with Me) (Whitfield, Strong) / Twenty Flight Rock (Fairchild, Cochran) / Going to À Go Go (Robinson, Johnson, Moore, Rogers) / Let Me Go / Time Is on My Side (Meade) / Beast of Burden / You Can't Always Get What You Want / Little T & A / Angie / Tumbling Dice / She's So Cold / Hang Fire / Miss You / Honky Tonk Women / Brown Sugar / Start Me Up / Jumpin' Jack Flash / **E:** (I Can't Get No) Satisfaction
NOTES: The setlist returned to the one used before the alterations in Turin and Basel and remained stable until the tour ended.

JULY 20, 1982

TOUR: 1982 European tour
VENUE: Parc des Sports de l'Ouest, Nice, France
OPENING/OTHER ACT(S): The J. Geils Band

JULY 24, 1982

TOUR: 1982 European tour
VENUE: Slane Castle, Slane, Ireland
OPENING/OTHER ACT(S): The J. Geils Band

JULY 25, 1982

TOUR: 1982 European tour
VENUE: Roundhay Park, Leeds, Yorkshire, England
OPENING/OTHER ACT(S): The J. Geils Band, Joe Jackson, George Thorogood

SONGS: Under My Thumb / When the Whip Comes Down / Let's Spend the Night Together / Shattered / Neighbours / Black Limousine (Jagger, Richards, Wood) / Just My Imagination (Running Away with Me) (Whitfield, Strong) / Twenty Flight Rock (Fairchild, Cochran) / Going to À Go Go (Robinson, Johnson, Moore, Rogers) / Let Me Go / Time Is on My Side (Meade) / Beast of Burden / You Can't Always Get What You Want / Little T & A / Angie / Tumbling Dice / She's So Cold / Hang Fire / Miss You / Honky Tonk Women / Brown Sugar / Start Me Up / Jumpin' Jack Flash / **E:** (I Can't Get No) Satisfaction
NOTES: The last gig of the 1982 tour.

1986

FEBRUARY 23, 1986

TOUR: Ian Stewart memorial
VENUE: The 100 Club, London, England
PERSONNEL: Mick Jagger, Keith Richards, Ron Wood, Charlie Watts, Bill Wyman
SPECIAL GUESTS: Eric Clapton, Pete Townshend, Jeff Beck, Jack Bruce, Simon Kirk
OPENING/OTHER ACT(S): Rocket 88
SONGS: Route 66 (Troup) / Down the Road Apiece (Raye) / Key to the Highway (Segar, Broonzy) / Confessin' the Blues (McShann, Brown) / Mannish Boy (London, McDaniel, Morganfield) / Bye Bye Johnny (Berry) / Harlem Shuffle (Relf, Nelson) / Little Red Rooster (Dixon) / Down in the Bottom (Dixon) / I Believe I'll Dust My Broom (Robt. Johnson) / Little Queenie (Berry)
NOTES: A select audience of 100 family and very close friends attended to honor Ian Stewart, who had died suddenly of a massive heart attack on December 12, 1985. Rocket 88, Stu's band, performed first. Note that the

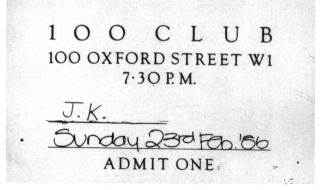

*The invitation/ticket to the Stones' only show in 1986—
Ian Stewart's wake* (JAMES KARNBACH COLLECTION)

Stones' set contained no Jagger/Richards tunes. It was composed entirely of Stu's favorite old blues numbers. Many musicians were there, including Stu's old friend and Stones bassist from the early days, Collin Golding. A few sat in, including Simon Kirk, who played drums on "Route 66," "Down the Road Apiece," "Key to the Highway," "Confessin' the Blues" and "Mannish Boy." Eric Clapton joined the band for "Key to the Highway," "Bye Bye Johnny" (as did Jeff Beck), and "I Believe I'll Dust My Broom" (a.k.a. "Dust My Blues," a.k.a. "Dust My Broom" —commonly thought to have been written by Elmore James who popularized it, actually a Robert Johnson original). Beck also appeared with Pete Townshend as guest on "Harlem Shuffle," "Little Red Rooster," and "Down in the Bottom."

1989

AUGUST 12, 1989 – DECEMBER 19, 1989

TOUR: Steel Wheels—North America

VENUE: US & Canada

PERSONNEL: Mick Jagger, Keith Richards, Ron Wood, Charlie Watts, Bill Wyman, Matt Clifford, Chuck Leavell, Bobby Keys, the Uptown Horns (Arno Hecht/Paul Litteral/Bob Funk/Crispen Cioe), Bernard Fowler, Lisa Fischer, Cindy Mizelle

SPECIAL GUESTS: Living Colour, Eric Clapton, John Lee Hooker, Axl Rose, Izzy Stradlin

OPENING/OTHER ACT(S): Living Colour, Guns 'n' Roses, Sons of Bob

SONGS: Continental Drift, V2 / Start Me Up / Bitch / Sad Sad Sad / Shattered / Undercover of the Night / Harlem Shuffle (Relf, Nelson) / Tumbling Dice / Miss You / Terrifying / Almost Hear You Sigh / Ruby Tuesday / Play with Fire (Nanker Phelge) / Angie / Rock and a Hard Place / Salt of the Earth / Dead Flowers / One Hit (to the Body) / Mixed Emotions / Honky Tonk Women / Midnight Rambler / You Can't Always Get What You Want / Little Red Rooster (Dixon) / Boogie Chillin' (Hooker) / Before They Make Me Run / Happy / Can't Be Seen / Paint It, Black / 2000 Light Years from Home / Sympathy for the Devil / Street Fighting Man /

Steel Wheels takes off

Gimme Shelter / It's Only Rock 'n' Roll / Brown Sugar / (I Can't Get No) Satisfaction / **E:** Jumpin' Jack Flash

NOTES: On July 11, the band rolled into a sweltering Grand Central Station aboard a private train car and announced plans for a world tour, their first in seven years, and previewed their new album to some 500 sweaty press and more screaming fans. The first official gig of Steel Wheels was in Philadelphia on August 31, but on August 12 the band played an "impromptu" show for 500 at Toad's Place in New Haven, CT. This is a listing of all songs played on the US/Canada portion of Steel Wheels. Backing the Stones throughout were: Matt Clifford, keyboards and French horn: Chuck Leavell, keyboards; Bobby Keys, saxophone; the Uptown Horns, brass; Bernard Fowler, Lisa Fischer and Cindy Mizelle, backing vocals. Axl Rose, Izzy Stradlin, Eric Clapton and John Lee Hooker appeared in Atlantic City on December 19 only. Living Colour opened throughout the tour up to and including Montreal on December 14, and joined the Stones onstage for one number at that last show. Guns 'n' Roses were added to the bill in Los Angeles only.

AUGUST 12, 1989

TOUR: Steel Wheels—North America

VENUE: Toad's Place, New Haven, CT, USA

PERSONNEL: Mick Jagger, Keith Richards, Ron Wood, Charlie Watts, Bill Wyman, Matt Clifford, Chuck Leavell, Bobby Keys

OPENING/OTHER ACT(S): Sons of Bob

SONGS: Start Me Up / Bitch / Tumbling Dice / Sad Sad Sad / Miss You / Little Red Rooster (Dixon) /Honky Tonk Women / Mixed Emotions / It's Only Rock 'n' Roll / Brown Sugar / Jumpin' Jack Flash

NOTES: It had become a tradition for the Stones to begin each tour with a "thank you" show for the community that put up with them and the associated mania of pretour rehearsals. The band had been rehearsing in a girls' school in nearby Washington, Connecticut since mid-July, much to the dismay of many local citizens. Toad's Place, in nearby New Haven (home of Yale University), is an established northeast tour stop for many well-known artists. And Toad's provided the venue for the Stones to try out their Steel Wheels set on 500 lucky folks. The Rolling Stones' appearance was unannounced to the public and unbilled. The Stones (minus the Uptown Horns and backing vocalists Fowler, Fischer and Mizelle) would play following that night's regularly scheduled act, a local band called Sons of Bob.

AUGUST 31, 1989

TOUR: Steel Wheels—North America

VENUE: Veterans Stadium, Philadelphia, PA, USA

PERSONNEL: Mick Jagger, Keith Richards, Ron Wood, Charlie Watts, Bill Wyman, Matt Clifford, Chuck Leavell, Bobby Keys, the Uptown Horns (Arno Hecht/Paul Litteral/Bob Funk/Crispen Cioe), Bernard Fowler, Lisa Fischer, Cindy Mizelle

OPENING/OTHER ACT(S): Living Colour

SONGS: Continental Drift, V2 / Start Me Up / Bitch / Shattered / Sad Sad Sad / Undercover of the Night / Harlem Shuffle (Relf, Nelson) / Tumbling Dice / Miss You / Ruby Tuesday / Play with Fire (Nanker Phelge) / Dead Flowers / One Hit (to the Body) / Mixed Emotions / Honky Tonk Women / Midnight Rambler / You Can't Always Get What You Want / Little Red Rooster (Dixon) / Before They Make Me Run / Happy / Paint It, Black / 2000 Light Years from Home / Sympathy for the Devil / Gimme Shelter / It's Only Rock 'n' Roll / Brown Sugar / (I Can't Get No) Satisfaction / **E:** Jumpin' Jack Flash

NOTES: Official opening concert of the Steel Wheels tour. Rampant pretour press skepticism as to whether a "middle-aged" Mick Jagger could cut it was fairly well silenced after this first gig. Reviews were overwhelmingly favorable, despite a noticeable opening-night glitch. During the beginning of "Shattered," the third song in the set, the power to the band's instruments onstage went out, forcing them to stop playing. The juice was restored 10 minutes later and the Stones picked up where they left off. But "Shattered" was never played again on Steel Wheels.

SEPTEMBER 1, 1989

TOUR: Steel Wheels—North America

VENUE: Veterans Stadium, Philadelphia, PA, USA

OPENING/OTHER ACT(S): Living Colour

SONGS: Continental Drift, V2 / Start Me Up / Bitch / Sad Sad Sad / Undercover of the Night / Harlem Shuffle (Relf, Nelson) / Tumbling Dice / Miss You / Ruby Tuesday / Play with Fire (Nanker Phelge) / Dead Flowers / One Hit (to the Body) / Mixed Emotions / Honky Tonk Women / Midnight Rambler / You Can't Always Get What You Want / Little Red Rooster (Dixon) / Before They Make Me Run / Happy / Paint It, Black / 2000 Light Years from Home / Sympathy for the Devil / Gimme Shelter / It's Only Rock 'n' Roll / Brown Sugar / (I Can't Get No) Satisfaction / **E:** Jumpin' Jack Flash

NOTES: "Shattered" was no more from this point on, and the Steel Wheels setlist stayed the same until the shows at Alpine Valley Stadium in East Troy, WI, began on September 8.

SEPTEMBER 3, 1989

TOUR: Steel Wheels—North America

VENUE: Exhibition Stadium, Toronto, Ontario, Canada

OPENING/OTHER ACT(S): Living Colour

SEPTEMBER 4, 1989

TOUR: Steel Wheels—North America
VENUE: Exhibition Stadium, Toronto, Ontario, Canada
OPENING/OTHER ACT(S): Living Colour

SEPTEMBER 6, 1989

TOUR: Steel Wheels—North America
VENUE: Three Rivers Stadium, Pittsburgh, PA, USA
OPENING/OTHER ACT(S): Living Colour
NOTES: The MTV video awards, broadcast that night from New York, featured the Stones playing "Mixed Emotions" "live." Actually, their performance had been taped three days earlier.

SEPTEMBER 8, 1989

TOUR: Steel Wheels—North America
VENUE: Alpine Valley Music Theater, East Troy, WI, USA
OPENING/OTHER ACT(S): Living Colour
SONGS: Continental Drift, V2 / Start Me Up / Bitch / Sad Sad Sad / Undercover of the Night / Harlem Shuffle (Relf, Nelson) / Tumbling Dice / Miss You / Ruby Tuesday / Play with Fire (Nanker Phelge) / Dead Flowers / Rock and a Hard Place / One Hit (to the Body) / Mixed Emotions / Honky Tonk Women / Midnight Rambler / You Can't Always Get What You Want / Little Red Rooster (Dixon) / Before They Make Me Run / Happy / Paint It, Black / 2000 Light Years from Home / Sympathy for the Devil / Gimme Shelter / It's Only Rock 'n' Roll / Brown Sugar / (I Can't Get No) Satisfaction / E: Jumpin' Jack Flash
NOTES: The addition of "Rock and a Hard Place" solidified the set, which will not change until the very end of the tour in Atlantic City.

SEPTEMBER 9, 1989

TOUR: Steel Wheels—North America
VENUE: Alpine Valley Music Theater, East Troy, WI, USA
OPENING/OTHER ACT(S): Living Colour

SEPTEMBER 11, 1989

TOUR: Steel Wheels—North America
VENUE: Alpine Valley Music Theater, East Troy, WI, USA
SPECIAL GUESTS: Sugar Blue
OPENING/OTHER ACT(S): Living Colour
SONGS: Continental Drift, V2 / Start Me Up / Bitch / Sad Sad Sad / Undercover of the Night / Harlem Shuffle (Relf, Nelson) / Tumbling Dice / Miss You / Ruby Tuesday / Play with Fire (Nanker Phelge) / Dead Flowers / Rock and a Hard Place / One Hit (to the Body) / Mixed Emotions / Honky Tonk Women / Midnight Rambler / You Can't Always Get What You Want / Little

Ron Wood, Steel Wheels tour 1989 (USED BY PERMISSION OF BOB GRUEN, ALL RIGHTS RESERVED)

Red Rooster (Dixon) / Before They Make Me Run / Happy / Paint It, Black / 2000 Light Years from Home / Sympathy for the Devil / Gimme Shelter / It's Only Rock 'n' Roll / Brown Sugar / (I Can't Get No) Satisfaction / E: Jumpin' Jack Flash
NOTES: Sugar Blue, on harp, makes a special guest appearance with the Stones on "Miss You."

SEPTEMBER 14, 1989

TOUR: Steel Wheels—North America
VENUE: Riverfront Stadium, Cincinnati, OH, USA
OPENING/OTHER ACT(S): Living Colour

SEPTEMBER 16, 1989

TOUR: Steel Wheels—North America
VENUE: Carter-Finley Stadium, Raleigh, NC, USA
OPENING/OTHER ACT(S): Living Colour

SEPTEMBER 17, 1989

TOUR: Steel Wheels—North America
VENUE: Busch Stadium, St. Louis, MO, USA
SPECIAL GUESTS: Johnny Johnson

Mick and Bobby Keys, Steel Wheels tour 1989

OPENING/OTHER ACT(S): Living Colour
NOTES: Famed blues pianist Johnny Johnson made a special guest appearance here in St. Louis, joining the band onstage for "Little Red Rooster."

SEPTEMBER 19, 1989

TOUR: Steel Wheels—North America
VENUE: Cardinal Stadium, Louisville, KY, USA
OPENING/OTHER ACT(S): Living Colour

SEPTEMBER 21, 1989

TOUR: Steel Wheels—North America
VENUE: Carrier Dome, Syracuse, NY, USA
OPENING/OTHER ACT(S): Living Colour

SEPTEMBER 22, 1989

TOUR: Steel Wheels—North America

VENUE: Carrier Dome, Syracuse, NY, USA
OPENING/OTHER ACT(S): Living Colour

SEPTEMBER 24, 1989

TOUR: Steel Wheels—North America
VENUE: Robert F. Kennedy Memorial Stadium, Washington, DC, USA
OPENING/OTHER ACT(S): Living Colour

SEPTEMBER 25, 1989

TOUR: Steel Wheels—North America
VENUE: Robert F. Kennedy Memorial Stadium, Washington, DC, USA
OPENING/OTHER ACT(S): Living Colour

SEPTEMBER 27, 1989

TOUR: Steel Wheels—North America

VENUE: Cleveland Municipal Stadium, Cleveland, OH, USA

OPENING/OTHER ACT(S): Living Colour

SEPTEMBER 29, 1989

TOUR: Steel Wheels—North America

VENUE: Sullivan Stadium, Foxboro, MA, USA

OPENING/OTHER ACT(S): Living Colour

OCTOBER 1, 1989

TOUR: Steel Wheels—North America

VENUE: Sullivan Stadium, Foxboro, MA, USA

OPENING/OTHER ACT(S): Living Colour

OCTOBER 3, 1989

TOUR: Steel Wheels—North America

VENUE: Sullivan Stadium, Foxboro, MA, USA

OPENING/OTHER ACT(S): Living Colour

OCTOBER 5, 1989

TOUR: Steel Wheels—North America

VENUE: Legion Field, Birmingham, AL, USA

OPENING/OTHER ACT(S): Living Colour

OCTOBER 7, 1989

TOUR: Steel Wheels—North America

VENUE: Cyclone Field, Ames, IA, USA

OPENING/OTHER ACT(S): Living Colour

OCTOBER 8, 1989

TOUR: Steel Wheels—North America

VENUE: Arrowhead Stadium, Kansas City, MO, USA

OPENING/OTHER ACT(S): Living Colour

OCTOBER 10, 1989

TOUR: Steel Wheels—North America

VENUE: Shea Stadium, Queens, NY, USA

OPENING/OTHER ACT(S): Living Colour

SONGS: Continental Drift, V2 / Start Me Up / Bitch / Sad Sad Sad / Undercover of the Night / Harlem Shuffle (Relf, Nelson) / Tumbling Dice / Miss You / Ruby Tuesday / Rock and a Hard Place / Angie / Mixed Emotions / Honky Tonk Women / Midnight Rambler / You Can't Always Get What You Want / Little Red Rooster (Dixon) / Before They Make Me Run / Happy / Paint It, Black / 2000 Light Years from Home / Sympathy for the Devil / Gimme Shelter / It's Only Rock 'n' Roll / Brown Sugar / (I Can't Get No) Satisfaction / **E:** Jumpin' Jack Flash

OCTOBER 11, 1989

TOUR: Steel Wheels—North America

VENUE: Shea Stadium, Queens, NY, USA

OPENING/OTHER ACT(S): Living Colour

OCTOBER 18, 1989

TOUR: Steel Wheels—North America

VENUE: Los Angeles Memorial Coliseum, Los Angeles, CA, USA

OPENING/OTHER ACT(S): Living Colour, Guns 'n' Roses

SONGS: Continental Drift, V2 / Start Me Up / Bitch / Sad Sad Sad / Undercover of the Night / Harlem Shuffle (Relf, Nelson) / Tumbling Dice / Miss You / Ruby Tuesday / Play with Fire (Nanker Phelge) / Rock and a Hard Place / Mixed Emotions / Honky Tonk Women / Midnight Rambler / You Can't Always Get What You Want / Little Red Rooster (Dixon) / Happy / Paint It, Black / 2000 Light Years from Home / Sympathy for the Devil / Gimme Shelter / It's Only Rock 'n' Roll / Brown Sugar / (I Can't Get No) Satisfaction / **E:** Jumpin' Jack Flash

OCTOBER 19, 1989

TOUR: Steel Wheels—North America

VENUE: Los Angeles Memorial Coliseum, Los Angeles, CA, USA

OPENING/OTHER ACT(S): Living Colour, Guns 'n' Roses

OCTOBER 21, 1989

TOUR: Steel Wheels—North America

VENUE: Los Angeles Memorial Coliseum, Los Angeles, CA, USA

OPENING/OTHER ACT(S): Living Colour, Guns 'n' Roses

OCTOBER 22, 1989

TOUR: Steel Wheels—North America

VENUE: Los Angeles Memorial Coliseum, Los Angeles, CA, USA

OPENING/OTHER ACT(S): Living Colour, Guns 'n' Roses

OCTOBER 25, 1989

TOUR: Steel Wheels—North America

VENUE: Shea Stadium, Queens, NY, USA

OPENING/OTHER ACT(S): Living Colour / Dou Doun' Diaye Rose

OCTOBER 26, 1989

TOUR: Steel Wheels—North America

VENUE: Shea Stadium, Queens, NY, USA

OPENING/OTHER ACT(S): Living Colour / Dou Doun' Diaye Rose

OCTOBER 28, 1989

TOUR: Steel Wheels—North America
VENUE: Shea Stadium, Queens, NY, USA
OPENING/OTHER ACT(S): Living Colour / Dou Doun' Diaye Rose
SONGS: Continental Drift, V2 / Start Me Up / Bitch / Sad Sad Sad / Undercover of the Night / One Hit (to the Body) / Tumbling Dice / Miss You / Ruby Tuesday / Angie / Rock and a Hard Place / Mixed Emotions / Honky Tonk Women / Midnight Rambler / You Can't Always Get What You Want / Can't Be Seen / Happy / Paint It, Black / 2000 Light Years from Home / Sympathy for the Devil / Gimme Shelter / It's Only Rock 'n' Roll / Brown Sugar / (I Can't Get No) Satisfaction / **E:** Jumpin' Jack Flash

OCTOBER 29, 1989

TOUR: Steel Wheels—North America
VENUE: Shea Stadium, Queens, NY, USA
OPENING/OTHER ACT(S): Living Colour / Dou Doun' Diaye Rose

NOVEMBER 1, 1989

TOUR: Steel Wheels—North America
VENUE: B.C. Place, Vancouver, British Columbia, Canada
OPENING/OTHER ACT(S): Living Colour

NOVEMBER 2, 1989

TOUR: Steel Wheels—North America
VENUE: B.C. Place, Vancouver, British Columbia, Canada
OPENING/OTHER ACT(S): Living Colour

NOVEMBER 4, 1989

TOUR: Steel Wheels—North America
VENUE: Alameda Stadium, Oakland, CA, USA
OPENING/OTHER ACT(S): Living Colour

NOVEMBER 5, 1989

TOUR: Steel Wheels—North America
VENUE: Alameda Stadium, Oakland, CA, USA
OPENING/OTHER ACT(S): Living Colour

NOVEMBER 8, 1989

TOUR: Steel Wheels—North America
VENUE: Astrodome, Houston, TX, USA

OPENING/OTHER ACT(S): Living Colour

NOVEMBER 10, 1989

TOUR: Steel Wheels—North America
VENUE: Texas Stadium, Dallas, TX, USA
OPENING/OTHER ACT(S): Living Colour

NOVEMBER 11, 1989

TOUR: Steel Wheels—North America
VENUE: Texas Stadium, Dallas, TX, USA
OPENING/OTHER ACT(S): Living Colour

NOVEMBER 13, 1989

TOUR: Steel Wheels—North America
VENUE: Superdome, New Orleans, LA, USA
OPENING/OTHER ACT(S): Living Colour

NOVEMBER 15, 1989

TOUR: Steel Wheels—North America
VENUE: Orange Bowl, Miami, FL, USA
OPENING/OTHER ACT(S): Living Colour

NOVEMBER 16, 1989

TOUR: Steel Wheels—North America
VENUE: Orange Bowl, Miami, FL, USA
OPENING/OTHER ACT(S): Living Colour

NOVEMBER 18, 1989

TOUR: Steel Wheels—North America
VENUE: Tampa Stadium, Tampa, FL, USA
OPENING/OTHER ACT(S): Living Colour

NOVEMBER 21, 1989

TOUR: Steel Wheels—North America
VENUE: Grant Field, Atlanta, GA, USA
OPENING/OTHER ACT(S): Living Colour

NOVEMBER 25, 1989

TOUR: Steel Wheels—North America
VENUE: The Gator Bowl, Atlantic Beach, Jacksonville, FL, USA
OPENING/OTHER ACT(S): Living Colour
SONGS: Continental Drift, V2 / Start Me Up / Bitch / Sad Sad Sad / Undercover of the Night / One Hit (to the Body) / Tumbling Dice / Miss You, LV / Ruby Tuesday / Angie / Rock and a Hard Place, LV / Mixed Emotions / Honky Tonk Women / Midnight Rambler / You Can't Always Get What You Want, LV2 / Can't Be Seen / Happy / Paint It, Black / 2000 Light Years from Home / Sympathy for the Devil / Gimme Shelter

/ It's Only Rock 'n' Roll / Brown Sugar / (I Can't Get No) Satisfaction / **E:** Jumpin' Jack Flash
NOTES: The live tracks on the *Flashpoint* era releases included "Miss You," "Rock and a Hard Place," and "You Can't Always Get What You Want" from this show.

NOVEMBER 26, 1989

TOUR: Steel Wheels—North America
VENUE: Death Valley Stadium, Clemson, SC, USA
OPENING/OTHER ACT(S): Living Colour
SONGS: Continental Drift, V2 / Start Me Up, LV / Bitch / Sad Sad Sad / Undercover of the Night / One Hit (to the Body) / Tumbling Dice / Miss You / Ruby Tuesday / Play with Fire (Nanker Phelge), LV / Rock and a Hard Place / Mixed Emotions / Honky Tonk Women / Midnight Rambler / You Can't Always Get What You Want / Can't Be Seen / Happy / Paint It, Black / 2000

Light Years from Home / Sympathy for the Devil / Gimme Shelter / It's Only Rock 'n' Roll / Brown Sugar / (I Can't Get No) Satisfaction, LV3 / **E:** Jumpin' Jack Flash
NOTES: This show was added late to the tour. A portion of the proceeds of this concert went to benefit victims of Hurricane Hugo. As it happened, three songs recorded here were later released during the *Flashpoint* period: "Start Me Up," "Satisfaction" and "Play with Fire."

NOVEMBER 29, 1989

TOUR: Steel Wheels—North America
VENUE: The Metrodome, Minneapolis, MN, USA
OPENING/OTHER ACT(S): Living Colour

NOVEMBER 30, 1989

TOUR: Steel Wheels—North America
VENUE: The Metrodome, Minneapolis, MN, USA
OPENING/OTHER ACT(S): Living Colour

Ronnie, Chuck Leavell (c) and Keith, working Steel Wheels

DECEMBER 3, 1989

TOUR: Steel Wheels—North America
VENUE: Skydome, Toronto, Ontario, Canada
OPENING/OTHER ACT(S): Living Colour

DECEMBER 4, 1989

TOUR: Steel Wheels—North America
VENUE: Skydome, Toronto, Ontario, Canada
OPENING/OTHER ACT(S): Living Colour

DECEMBER 6, 1989

TOUR: Steel Wheels—North America
VENUE: The Hoosier Dome, Indianapolis, IN, USA
OPENING/OTHER ACT(S): Living Colour

DECEMBER 7, 1989

TOUR: Steel Wheels—North America
VENUE: The Hoosier Dome, Indianapolis, IN, USA
OPENING/OTHER ACT(S): Living Colour

DECEMBER 9, 1989

TOUR: Steel Wheels—North America
VENUE: Silverdome, Pontiac, MI, USA
OPENING/OTHER ACT(S): Living Colour

DECEMBER 10, 1989

TOUR: Steel Wheels—North America
VENUE: Silverdome, Pontiac, MI, USA
OPENING/OTHER ACT(S): Living Colour

DECEMBER 14, 1989

TOUR: Steel Wheels—North America
VENUE: Olympic Stadium, Montreal, Quebec, Canada
SPECIAL GUESTS: Living Colour
OPENING/OTHER ACT(S): Living Colour
NOTES: This was Living Colour's last gig on Steel Wheels as the opening act for the Stones. Mick brought them onstage for an impromptu jam on "It's Only Rock 'n' Roll"—not as an encore number, but in its regular place in the setlist.

DECEMBER 16, 1989

TOUR: Steel Wheels—North America
VENUE: Atlantic City Convention Center, Atlantic City, NJ, USA
OPENING/OTHER ACT(S): None

DECEMBER 17, 1989

TOUR: Steel Wheels—North America

VENUE: Atlantic City Convention Center, Atlantic City, NJ, USA
OPENING/OTHER ACT(S): None

DECEMBER 19, 1989

TOUR: Steel Wheels—North America
VENUE: Atlantic City Convention Center, Atlantic City, NJ, USA
SPECIAL GUESTS: Axl Rose, Izzy Stradlin, John Lee Hooker, Eric Clapton
OPENING/OTHER ACT(S): None
SONGS: Continental Drift, V2 / Start Me Up / Bitch / Sad Sad Sad, LV / Undercover of the Night, LV / Harlem Shuffle (Relf, Nelson), LV / Tumbling Dice / Miss You / Terrifying / Ruby Tuesday / Salt of the Earth / Rock and a Hard Place / Mixed Emotions / Honky Tonk Women / Midnight Rambler / You Can't Always Get What You Want / Little Red Rooster (Dixon), LV2 / Boogie Chillin' (Hooker) / Can't Be Seen / Happy / Paint It, Black / 2000 Light Years from Home / Sympathy for the Devil / Gimme Shelter / It's Only Rock 'n' Roll / Brown Sugar / (I Can't Get No) Satisfaction / **E:** Jumpin' Jack Flash
NOTES: The final concert of the North American portion of the Steel Wheels tour, broadcast live via pay-per-view television, and featuring special guests Axl Rose, Izzy Stradlin, Eric Clapton and John Lee Hooker. The Stones invited Axl and Izzy to appear with them and gave them their choice of songs—"Salt of the Earth" was it. Clapton joined the band for "Little Red Rooster" (recorded that night and later released on *Flashpoint*), and Hooker came onstage for his "Boogie Chillin'." In addition to "Little Red Rooster," three other live tracks from this concert—"Harlem Shuffle," "Sad Sad Sad" and "Undercover"—found their way onto *Flashpoint*-period releases.

1990

FEBRUARY 14, 1990 – FEBRUARY 27, 1990

TOUR: Steel Wheels—Japan
VENUE: Korakuen Dome, Tokyo, Japan
PERSONNEL: Mick Jagger, Keith Richards, Ron Wood, Charlie Watts, Bill Wyman, Matt Clifford, Chuck Leavell, Bobby Keys, the Uptown Horns (Arno Hecht/Paul Litteral/Bob Funk/Crispen Cioe), Bernard Fowler, Lisa Fischer, Cindy Mizelle
SONGS: Continental Drift, V2 / Start Me Up / Bitch / Sad Sad Sad / Harlem Shuffle (Relf, Nelson) / Tumbling Dice / Miss You / Almost Hear You Sigh / Ruby

Tuesday / Play with Fire (Nanker Phelge) / Angie / Rock and a Hard Place / Mixed Emotions / Honky Tonk Women / Midnight Rambler / You Can't Always Get What You Want / Little Red Rooster (Dixon) / Can't Be Seen / Happy / Paint It, Black / 2000 Light Years from Home / Sympathy for the Devil / Gimme Shelter / It's Only Rock 'n' Roll / Brown Sugar / (I Can't Get No) Satisfaction / Jumpin' Jack Flash

NOTES: This setlist includes all numbers played at the 10 Tokyo concerts. Certain songs were alternated at various performances—"Miss You" with "Almost Hear You Sigh," and "Play With Fire" with "Angie." "Little Red Rooster" was played only once, at the February 20 concert.

FEBRUARY 14, 1990

TOUR: Steel Wheels—Japan
VENUE: Korakuen Dome, Tokyo, Japan

FEBRUARY 16, 1990

TOUR: Steel Wheels—Japan
VENUE: Korakuen Dome, Tokyo, Japan

FEBRUARY 17, 1990

TOUR: Steel Wheels—Japan
VENUE: Korakuen Dome, Tokyo, Japan

FEBRUARY 19, 1990

TOUR: Steel Wheels—Japan
VENUE: Korakuen Dome, Tokyo, Japan

FEBRUARY 20, 1990

TOUR: Steel Wheels—Japan
VENUE: Korakuen Dome, Tokyo, Japan

FEBRUARY 21, 1990

TOUR: Steel Wheels—Japan
VENUE: Korakuen Dome, Tokyo, Japan

FEBRUARY 23, 1990

TOUR: Steel Wheels—Japan
VENUE: Korakuen Dome, Tokyo, Japan

FEBRUARY 24, 1990

TOUR: Steel Wheels—Japan
VENUE: Korakuen Dome, Tokyo, Japan

FEBRUARY 26, 1990

TOUR: Steel Wheels—Japan

VENUE: Korakuen Dome, Tokyo, Japan
SONGS: Continental Drift, V2 / Start Me Up / Bitch / Sad Sad Sad / Harlem Shuffle (Relf, Nelson) / Tumbling Dice / Miss You / Ruby Tuesday / Play with Fire (Nanker Phelge) / Rock and a Hard Place / Mixed Emotions / Honky Tonk Women / Midnight Rambler / You Can't Always Get What You Want / Little Red Rooster (Dixon) / Can't Be Seen / Happy / Paint It, Black / 2000 Light Years from Home / Sympathy for the Devil, LV3 / Gimme Shelter / It's Only Rock 'n' Roll / Brown Sugar / (I Can't Get No) Satisfaction / Jumpin' Jack Flash
NOTES: The live, released "Sympathy for the Devil" was recorded at this show.

FEBRUARY 27, 1990

TOUR: Steel Wheels—Japan
VENUE: Korakuen Dome, Tokyo, Japan
SONGS: Continental Drift, V2 / Start Me Up / Bitch / Sad Sad Sad / Harlem Shuffle (Relf, Nelson) / Tumbling Dice / Almost Hear You Sigh / Ruby Tuesday, LV / Angie / Rock and a Hard Place / Mixed Emotions / Honky Tonk Women / Midnight Rambler / You Can't Always Get What You Want / Little Red Rooster (Dixon) / Can't Be Seen / Happy / Paint It, Black / 2000 Light Years from Home / Sympathy for the Devil / Gimme Shelter / It's Only Rock 'n' Roll / Brown Sugar / (I Can't Get No) Satisfaction / Jumpin' Jack Flash, LV3
NOTES: The final performance of Steel Wheels/Japan. "Ruby Tuesday" and "Jumpin' Jack Flash" from this show would become *Flashpoint*-era releases.

MAY 18, 1990 – AUGUST 25, 1990

TOUR: Urban Jungle European tour
VENUE: Holland, Germany, Portugal, Spain, France, Switzerland, Italy, Austria, Sweden, Norway, Denmark, Czechoslovakia, UK
PERSONNEL: Mick Jagger, Keith Richards, Ron Wood, Charlie Watts, Bill Wyman, Matt Clifford, Chuck Leavell, Bobby Keys, The Uptown Horns (Arno Hecht/Paul Litteral/Bob Funk/Crispen Cioe), Bernard Fowler, Lorelei McBroom, Sophia Jones
SONGS: Continental Drift, V2 / Start Me Up / Bitch / Sad Sad Sad / Harlem Shuffle (Relf, Nelson) / Tumbling Dice / Miss You / Terrifying / Almost Hear You Sigh / Ruby Tuesday / Factory Girl / Angie / Dead Flowers / Rock and a Hard Place / Mixed Emotions / Honky Tonk Women / Midnight Rambler / You Can't Always Get What You Want / I Just Want to Make Love to You (Dixon) / Little Red Rooster (Dixon) / Can't Be Seen / Before They Make Me Run / Happy / Paint It, Black / 2000 Light Years from Home / Sympathy for the

Mick with vocalist Lisa Fischer on the Steel Wheels tour

Devil / Street Fighting Man / Gimme Shelter / It's Only Rock 'n' Roll / Brown Sugar / **E1:** Jumpin' Jack Flash / **E2:** (I Can't Get No) Satisfaction

NOTES: This is a listing of all songs played on the Urban Jungle tour. A few numbers such as "Factory Girl," "Angie," "Terrifying," "I Just Want to Make Love to You," "Before They Make Me Run," and "Can't Be Seen" were rotated in and out of the set as the tour progressed. "Dead Flowers" and "Little Red Rooster" only showed up in the German performances early in the tour. Urban Jungle sets contained 23–25 songs, plus the "Continental Drift" intro. Notice the personnel change: Lorelei McBroom and Sophia Jones replaced backup singers Lisa Fischer and Cindy Mizelle on the Urban Jungle leg of the tour.

MAY 18, 1990

TOUR: Urban Jungle European tour
VENUE: Feyenoord Stadium, Rotterdam, Holland

MAY 19, 1990

TOUR: Urban Jungle European tour
VENUE: Feyenoord Stadium, Rotterdam, Holland

MAY 21, 1990

TOUR: Urban Jungle European tour
VENUE: Feyenoord Stadium, Rotterdam, Holland

MAY 23, 1990

TOUR: Urban Jungle European tour
VENUE: Niedersachsen-Stadion, Hanover, West Germany
SONGS: Continental Drift, V2 / Start Me Up / Bitch / Sad Sad Sad / Tumbling Dice / Miss You / Almost Hear You Sigh / Ruby Tuesday / Rock and a Hard Place / Mixed Emotions / Honky Tonk Women / Midnight Rambler / You Can't Always Get What You Want / Can't Be Seen / Happy / Paint It, Black / 2000 Light Years

from Home / Sympathy for the Devil / Street Fighting Man / Gimme Shelter / It's Only Rock 'n' Roll / Brown Sugar / (I Can't Get No) Satisfaction / **E:** Jumpin' Jack Flash

MAY 24, 1990

TOUR: Urban Jungle European tour
VENUE: Niedersachsen-Stadion, Hanover, West Germany
SONGS: Continental Drift, V2 / Start Me Up / Bitch / Sad Sad Sad / Tumbling Dice / Miss You / Almost Hear You Sigh / Ruby Tuesday / Factory Girl / Rock and a Hard Place / Mixed Emotions / Honky Tonk Women / You Can't Always Get What You Want / I Just Want to Make Love to You (Dixon) / Before They Make Me Run / Happy / Paint It, Black / 2000 Light Years from Home / Sympathy for the Devil / Street Fighting Man / Gimme Shelter / It's Only Rock 'n' Roll / Brown Sugar / (I Can't Get No) Satisfaction / **E:** Jumpin' Jack Flash

MAY 26, 1990

TOUR: Urban Jungle European tour
VENUE: Wald Stadium, Frankfurt, West Germany
SONGS: Continental Drift, V2 / Start Me Up / Bitch / Sad Sad Sad / Tumbling Dice / Miss You / Almost Hear You Sigh / Ruby Tuesday / Factory Girl / Rock and a Hard Place / Mixed Emotions / Honky Tonk Women / Midnight Rambler / You Can't Always Get What You Want / Can't Be Seen / Happy / Paint It, Black / 2000 Light Years from Home / Sympathy for the Devil / Street Fighting Man / Gimme Shelter / It's Only Rock 'n' Roll / Brown Sugar / (I Can't Get No) Satisfaction / **E:** Jumpin' Jack Flash

MAY 27, 1990

TOUR: Urban Jungle European tour
VENUE: Wald Stadium, Frankfurt, West Germany
SONGS: Continental Drift, V2 / Start Me Up / Bitch / Sad Sad Sad / Harlem Shuffle (Relf, Nelson) / Tumbling Dice / Miss You / Almost Hear You Sigh / Ruby Tuesday / Dead Flowers / Rock and a Hard Place / Mixed Emotions / Honky Tonk Women / You Can't Always Get What You Want / Little Red Rooster (Dixon) / Before They Make Me Run / Happy / Paint It, Black / 2000 Light Years from Home / Sympathy for the Devil / Street Fighting Man / Gimme Shelter / It's Only Rock 'n' Roll / Brown Sugar / (I Can't Get No) Satisfaction / **E:** Jumpin' Jack Flash
NOTES: Both "Dead Flowers" and "Little Red Rooster" were performed at the second Frankfurt show of Urban Jungle.

MAY 30, 1990

TOUR: Urban Jungle European tour
VENUE: Mungersdorfer-Stadion, Cologne, West Germany
SONGS: Continental Drift, V2 / Start Me Up / Bitch / Sad Sad Sad / Harlem Shuffle (Relf, Nelson) / Tumbling Dice / Miss You / Almost Hear You Sigh / Ruby Tuesday / Factory Girl / Rock and a Hard Place / Mixed Emotions / Honky Tonk Women / Midnight Rambler / You Can't Always Get What You Want / Can't Be Seen / Happy / Paint It, Black / 2000 Light Years from Home / Sympathy for the Devil / Street Fighting Man / Gimme Shelter / It's Only Rock 'n' Roll / Brown Sugar / (I Can't Get No) Satisfaction / **E:** Jumpin' Jack Flash

MAY 31, 1990

TOUR: Urban Jungle European tour
VENUE: Mungersdorfer-Stadion, Cologne, West Germany

JUNE 2, 1990

TOUR: Urban Jungle European tour
VENUE: Olympiastadion, Munich, West Germany
SONGS: Continental Drift, V2 / Start Me Up / Sad Sad Sad / Harlem Shuffle (Relf, Nelson) / Tumbling Dice / Miss You / Almost Hear You Sigh / Ruby Tuesday / Factory Girl / Rock and a Hard Place / Mixed Emotions / Honky Tonk Women / Midnight Rambler / You Can't Always Get What You Want / Little Red Rooster (Dixon) / Can't Be Seen / Happy / Paint It, Black / 2000 Light Years from Home / Sympathy for the Devil / Street Fighting Man / Gimme Shelter / It's Only Rock 'n' Roll / Brown Sugar / (I Can't Get No) Satisfaction / **E:** Jumpin' Jack Flash
NOTES: "Bitch" was dropped from the set. "Little Red Rooster" appears once more.

JUNE 3, 1990

TOUR: Urban Jungle European tour
VENUE: Olympiastadion, Munich, West Germany
SONGS: Continental Drift, V2 / Start Me Up / Sad Sad Sad / Harlem Shuffle (Relf, Nelson) / Tumbling Dice / Miss You / Almost Hear You Sigh / Ruby Tuesday / Angie / Rock and a Hard Place / Mixed Emotions / Honky Tonk Women / Midnight Rambler / You Can't Always Get What You Want / Before They Make Me Run / Happy / Paint It, Black / 2000 Light Years from Home / Sympathy for the Devil / Street Fighting Man / Gimme Shelter / It's Only Rock 'n' Roll / Brown Sugar / (I Can't Get No) Satisfaction / **E:** Jumpin' Jack Flash
NOTES: "Angie" replaced "Factory Girl" at the second Munich show.

JUNE 6, 1990

TOUR: Urban Jungle European tour

VENUE: Olympic Stadium, West Berlin, Germany

SONGS: Continental Drift, V2 / Start Me Up / Sad Sad Sad / Harlem Shuffle (Relf, Nelson) / Tumbling Dice / Miss You / Almost Hear You Sigh / Ruby Tuesday / Angie / Rock and a Hard Place / Mixed Emotions / Honky Tonk Women / Midnight Rambler / You Can't Always Get What You Want / Can't Be Seen / Happy / Paint It, Black / 2000 Light Years from Home / Sympathy for the Devil / Street Fighting Man / Gimme Shelter / It's Only Rock 'n' Roll / Brown Sugar / Jumpin' Jack Flash / **E:** (I Can't Get No) Satisfaction

NOTES: "Satisfaction" was played as the encore, following "Jumpin' Jack Flash."

JUNE 10, 1990

TOUR: Urban Jungle European tour

VENUE: Alvalade, Lisbon, Portugal

JUNE 13, 1990

TOUR: Urban Jungle European tour

VENUE: Olympic Stadium, Barcelona, Spain

JUNE 14, 1990

TOUR: Urban Jungle European tour

VENUE: Olympic Stadium, Barcelona, Spain

SONGS: Continental Drift, V2 / Start Me Up / Sad Sad Sad / Harlem Shuffle (Relf, Nelson) / Tumbling Dice / Miss You / Almost Hear You Sigh / Ruby Tuesday / Angie / Rock and a Hard Place / Mixed Emotions / Honky Tonk Women / Midnight Rambler / You Can't Always Get What You Want / Can't Be Seen / Happy / Paint It, Black, LV / 2000 Light Years from Home, LV / Sympathy for the Devil / Street Fighting Man / Gimme Shelter / It's Only Rock 'n' Roll / Brown Sugar / Jumpin' Jack Flash / **E:** (I Can't Get No) Satisfaction

NOTES: *Flashpoint* era, post-tour releases included "Paint It Black" and "2000 Light Years" from this performance.

JUNE 16, 1990

TOUR: Urban Jungle European tour

VENUE: Estadio Vincent Calderon, Madrid, Spain

JUNE 17, 1990

TOUR: Urban Jungle European tour

VENUE: Estadio Vincent Calderon, Madrid, Spain

JUNE 20, 1990

TOUR: Urban Jungle European tour

VENUE: Velodrom, Marseille, France

JUNE 22, 1990

TOUR: Urban Jungle European tour

VENUE: Parc des Princes, Paris, France

SONGS: Continental Drift, V2 / Start Me Up / Sad Sad Sad / Harlem Shuffle (Relf, Nelson) / Tumbling Dice / Miss You / Terrifying / Ruby Tuesday / Angie / Rock and a Hard Place / Mixed Emotions / Honky Tonk Women / Midnight Rambler / You Can't Always Get What You Want / I Just Want to Make Love to You (Dixon) / Can't Be Seen / Happy / Paint It, Black / 2000 Light Years from Home / Sympathy for the Devil / Street Fighting Man / Gimme Shelter / It's Only Rock 'n' Roll / Brown Sugar / Jumpin' Jack Flash / **E:** (I Can't Get No) Satisfaction

NOTES: "Terrifying" appeared in the set.

JUNE 23, 1990

TOUR: Urban Jungle European tour

VENUE: Parc des Princes, Paris, France

SONGS: Continental Drift, V2 / Start Me Up / Sad Sad Sad / Harlem Shuffle (Relf, Nelson) / Tumbling Dice / Miss You / Terrifying / Ruby Tuesday / Angie / Rock and a Hard Place / Mixed Emotions / Honky Tonk Women / Midnight Rambler / You Can't Always Get What You Want / Can't Be Seen / Happy / Paint It, Black / 2000 Light Years from Home / Sympathy for the Devil / Street Fighting Man / Gimme Shelter / It's Only Rock 'n' Roll / Brown Sugar / Jumpin' Jack Flash / (I Can't Get No) Satisfaction

JUNE 25, 1990

TOUR: Urban Jungle European tour

VENUE: Parc des Princes, Paris, France

SONGS: Continental Drift, V2 / Start Me Up / Sad Sad Sad / Harlem Shuffle (Relf, Nelson) / Tumbling Dice / Miss You / Terrifying / Ruby Tuesday / Angie / Factory Girl / Rock and a Hard Place / Mixed Emotions / Honky Tonk Women / Midnight Rambler / You Can't Always Get What You Want / Can't Be Seen / Happy / Paint It, Black / 2000 Light Years from Home / Sympathy for the Devil / Street Fighting Man / Gimme Shelter / It's Only Rock 'n' Roll / Jumpin' Jack Flash / Brown Sugar / (I Can't Get No) Satisfaction

JUNE 27, 1990

TOUR: Urban Jungle European tour

VENUE: St. Jakob Stadion, Basel, Switzerland

JULY 4, 1990

TOUR: Urban Jungle European tour
VENUE: Wembley Stadium, Wembley, Middlesex, England
SONGS: Continental Drift, V2 / Start Me Up / Sad Sad Sad / Harlem Shuffle (Relf, Nelson) / Tumbling Dice / Miss You / Almost Hear You Sigh / Ruby Tuesday / Rock and a Hard Place / Mixed Emotions / Honky Tonk Women / Midnight Rambler / You Can't Always Get What You Want / Little Red Rooster (Dixon) / Can't Be Seen / Happy / Paint It, Black / 2000 Light Years from Home / Sympathy for the Devil / Street Fighting Man / Gimme Shelter / It's Only Rock 'n' Roll / Brown Sugar / Jumpin' Jack Flash / (I Can't Get No) Satisfaction

JULY 6, 1990

TOUR: Urban Jungle European tour
VENUE: Wembley Stadium, Wembley, Middlesex, England
SONGS: Continental Drift, V2 / Start Me Up / Sad Sad Sad / Harlem Shuffle (Relf, Nelson) / Tumbling Dice / Miss You / Almost Hear You Sigh / Ruby Tuesday / Factory Girl, LV / Rock and a Hard Place / Mixed Emotions / Honky Tonk Women / Midnight Rambler / You Can't Always Get What You Want / I Just Want to Make Love to You (Dixon), LV / Can't Be Seen / Happy / Paint It, Black / 2000 Light Years from Home / Sympathy for the Devil / Street Fighting Man / Gimme Shelter / It's Only Rock 'n' Roll / Brown Sugar / Jumpin' Jack Flash / **E:** (I Can't Get No) Satisfaction
NOTES: The live versions of "Factory Girl" and "I Just Want to Make Love to You" were recorded at this Wembley concert.

JULY 7, 1990

TOUR: Urban Jungle European tour
VENUE: Wembley Stadium, Wembley, Middlesex, England
SONGS: Continental Drift, V2 / Start Me Up / Sad Sad Sad / Harlem Shuffle (Relf, Nelson) / Tumbling Dice / Miss You / Almost Hear You Sigh / Ruby Tuesday / Angie / Rock and a Hard Place / Mixed Emotions / Honky Tonk Women / Midnight Rambler / You Can't Always Get What You Want / Before They Make Me Run / Happy / Paint It, Black / 2000 Light Years from Home / Sympathy for the Devil / Street Fighting Man / Gimme Shelter / It's Only Rock 'n' Roll / Brown Sugar / Jumpin' Jack Flash / **E:** (I Can't Get No) Satisfaction

JULY 9, 1990

TOUR: Urban Jungle European tour
VENUE: Hampden Park, Glasgow, Scotland

SONGS: Continental Drift, V2 / Start Me Up / Sad Sad Sad / Harlem Shuffle (Relf, Nelson) / Tumbling Dice / Miss You / Almost Hear You Sigh / Ruby Tuesday / Rock and a Hard Place / Mixed Emotions / Honky Tonk Women / Midnight Rambler / You Can't Always Get What You Want / Can't Be Seen / Happy / Paint It, Black / 2000 Light Years from Home / Sympathy for the Devil / Street Fighting Man / Gimme Shelter / It's Only Rock 'n' Roll / Brown Sugar / Jumpin' Jack Flash / **E:** (I Can't Get No) Satisfaction

JULY 16, 1990

TOUR: Urban Jungle European tour
VENUE: Arms Park, Cardiff, Wales
SONGS: Continental Drift, V2 / Start Me Up / Sad Sad Sad / Harlem Shuffle (Relf, Nelson) / Tumbling Dice / Miss You / Almost Hear You Sigh / Ruby Tuesday / Rock and a Hard Place / Mixed Emotions / Honky Tonk Women / Midnight Rambler / You Can't Always Get What You Want / Can't Be Seen / Happy / Paint It, Black / 2000 Light Years from Home / Sympathy for the Devil / Street Fighting Man / Gimme Shelter / It's Only Rock 'n' Roll / Brown Sugar / Jumpin' Jack Flash / (I Can't Get No) Satisfaction

JULY 18, 1990

TOUR: Urban Jungle European tour
VENUE: St. James Park, Newcastle-upon-Tyne, Northumberland, England
SONGS: Continental Drift, V2 / Start Me Up / Sad Sad Sad / Harlem Shuffle (Relf, Nelson) / Tumbling Dice / Miss You / Almost Hear You Sigh / Ruby Tuesday / Rock and a Hard Place / Mixed Emotions / Honky Tonk Women / Midnight Rambler / You Can't Always Get What You Want / Can't Be Seen / Happy / Paint It, Black / 2000 Light Years from Home / Sympathy for the Devil / Street Fighting Man / Gimme Shelter / It's Only Rock 'n' Roll / Brown Sugar / Jumpin' Jack Flash / (I Can't Get No) Satisfaction

JULY 20, 1990

TOUR: Urban Jungle European tour
VENUE: Manchester City Football Ground, Maine Road, Moss Side, Manchester, Lancashire, England
SONGS: Continental Drift, V2 / Start Me Up / Sad Sad Sad / Harlem Shuffle (Relf, Nelson) / Tumbling Dice / Miss You / Almost Hear You Sigh / Ruby Tuesday / Factory Girl / Rock and a Hard Place / Mixed Emotions / Honky Tonk Women / Midnight Rambler / You Can't Always Get What You Want / Can't Be Seen / Happy / Paint It, Black / 2000 Light Years from Home / Sympathy for the Devil / Street Fighting Man / Gimme Shelter

/ It's Only Rock 'n' Roll / Brown Sugar / Jumpin' Jack Flash / (I Can't Get No) Satisfaction

JULY 21, 1990

TOUR: Urban Jungle European tour
VENUE: Manchester City Football Ground, Maine Road, Moss Side, Manchester, Lancashire, England
SONGS: Continental Drift, V2 / Start Me Up / Sad Sad Sad / Harlem Shuffle (Relf, Nelson) / Tumbling Dice / Miss You / Almost Hear You Sigh / Ruby Tuesday / Factory Girl / Rock and a Hard Place / Mixed Emotions / Honky Tonk Women / Midnight Rambler / You Can't Always Get What You Want / Before They Make Me Run / Happy / Paint It, Black / 2000 Light Years from Home / Sympathy for the Devil / Street Fighting Man / Gimme Shelter / It's Only Rock 'n' Roll / Brown Sugar / Jumpin' Jack Flash / E: (I Can't Get No) Satisfaction

JULY 25, 1990

TOUR: Urban Jungle European tour
VENUE: Stadio Flaminio, Rome, Italy
SONGS: Continental Drift, V2 / Start Me Up / Sad Sad Sad / Harlem Shuffle (Relf, Nelson) / Tumbling Dice / Miss You / Ruby Tuesday / Angie / Rock and a Hard Place / Mixed Emotions / Honky Tonk Women / Midnight Rambler / You Can't Always Get What You Want / Happy / Paint It, Black / 2000 Light Years from Home / Sympathy for the Devil / Street Fighting Man / Gimme Shelter / It's Only Rock 'n' Roll / Brown Sugar / Jumpin' Jack Flash / E: (I Can't Get No) Satisfaction
NOTES: The Stones performed 22 songs at both Rome performances, the shortest setlists of the tour.

JULY 26, 1990

TOUR: Urban Jungle European tour
VENUE: Stadio Flaminio, Rome, Italy
SONGS: Continental Drift, V2 / Start Me Up / Sad Sad Sad / Harlem Shuffle (Relf, Nelson) / Tumbling Dice / Miss You / Ruby Tuesday / Angie / Rock and a Hard Place / Mixed Emotions / Honky Tonk Women / Midnight Rambler / You Can't Always Get What You Want / Happy / Paint It, Black / 2000 Light Years from Home / Sympathy for the Devil / Street Fighting Man / Gimme Shelter / It's Only Rock 'n' Roll / Brown Sugar / Jumpin' Jack Flash / E: (I Can't Get No) Satisfaction

JULY 28, 1990

TOUR: Urban Jungle European tour
VENUE: Stadio Delle Alpi, Turin, Italy
SONGS: Continental Drift, V2 / Start Me Up / Sad Sad Sad / Harlem Shuffle (Relf, Nelson) / Tumbling Dice / Miss You / Ruby Tuesday / Angie / Rock and a Hard

Place / Mixed Emotions / Honky Tonk Women / Midnight Rambler / You Can't Always Get What You Want / Before They Make Me Run / Paint It, Black / 2000 Light Years from Home / Sympathy for the Devil / Street Fighting Man / Gimme Shelter / It's Only Rock 'n' Roll / Brown Sugar, LV2 / Jumpin' Jack Flash / E: (I Can't Get No) Satisfaction

JULY 31, 1990

TOUR: Urban Jungle European tour
VENUE: Prater Stadion, Vienna, Austria

AUGUST 3, 1990

TOUR: Urban Jungle European tour
VENUE: Eriksberg, Gothenburg, Sweden

AUGUST 4, 1990

TOUR: Urban Jungle European tour
VENUE: Eriksburg, Gothenburg, Sweden

AUGUST 6, 1990

TOUR: Urban Jungle European tour
VENUE: Valle Hovin, Oslo, Norway

AUGUST 7, 1990

TOUR: Urban Jungle European tour
VENUE: Valle Hovin, Oslo, Norway

AUGUST 9, 1990

TOUR: Urban Jungle European tour
VENUE: Idretspark, Copenhagen, Denmark

AUGUST 13, 1990

TOUR: Urban Jungle European tour
VENUE: Weisensee, East Berlin, Germany
SONGS: Continental Drift, V2 / Start Me Up / Sad Sad Sad / Harlem Shuffle (Relf, Nelson) / Tumbling Dice / Miss You / Almost Hear You Sigh / Ruby Tuesday / Rock and a Hard Place / Mixed Emotions / Honky Tonk Women / Midnight Rambler / You Can't Always Get What You Want / Can't Be Seen / Happy / Paint It, Black / 2000 Light Years from Home / Sympathy for the Devil / Street Fighting Man / Gimme Shelter / It's Only Rock 'n' Roll / Brown Sugar / Jumpin' Jack Flash / E: (I Can't Get No) Satisfaction

AUGUST 14, 1990

TOUR: Urban Jungle European tour
VENUE: Weisensee, East Berlin, Germany

AUGUST 16, 1990

TOUR: Urban Jungle European tour
VENUE: Gelsenkirchen Parkstadion, Gelsenkirchen, West Germany

AUGUST 18, 1990

TOUR: Urban Jungle European tour
VENUE: Straiiov Stadium, Prague, Czechoslovakia

AUGUST 24, 1990

TOUR: Urban Jungle European tour
VENUE: Wembley Stadium, Wembley, Middlesex, England
SONGS: Continental Drift, V2 / Start Me Up / Sad Sad Sad / Harlem Shuffle (Relf, Nelson) / Tumbling Dice / Miss You / Ruby Tuesday / Angie / Rock and a Hard Place / Mixed Emotions / Honky Tonk Women / Midnight Rambler / You Can't Always Get What You Want / Can't Be Seen / Happy / Paint It, Black / 2000 Light Years from Home / Sympathy for the Devil / Street Fighting Man / Gimme Shelter / It's Only Rock 'n' Roll / Brown Sugar / Jumpin' Jack Flash / **E:** (I Can't Get No) Satisfaction

AUGUST 25, 1990

TOUR: Urban Jungle European tour
VENUE: Wembley Stadium, Wembley, Middlesex, England
SONGS: Continental Drift, V2 / Start Me Up / Sad Sad Sad / Harlem Shuffle (Relf, Nelson) / Tumbling Dice / Miss You / Ruby Tuesday / Angie / Rock and a Hard Place / Mixed Emotions / Honky Tonk Women / Midnight Rambler / You Can't Always Get What You Want / Before They Make Me Run / Happy / Paint It, Black / 2000 Light Years from Home / Sympathy for the Devil / Street Fighting Man / Gimme Shelter / It's Only Rock 'n' Roll / Brown Sugar / Jumpin' Jack Flash / **E:** (I Can't Get No) Satisfaction
NOTES: The last gig of the Urban Jungle tour. In all, the so-called "middle-aged" Rolling Stones gave 117 high-energy performances in high-capacity stadiums on their year-long Steel Wheels/Urban Jungle world tour. There were 45 concerts in Europe, 10 in Japan, and 62 in North America.

1994

JULY 19, 1994

TOUR: Voodoo Lounge tour—North America
VENUE: RPM Club, Toronto, Ontario, Canada

PERSONNEL: Mick Jagger, Keith Richards, Ron Wood, Charlie Watts, Darryl Jones, Chuck Leavell, Bobby Keys, Lisa Fischer, Bernard Fowler
SPECIAL GUESTS: Jeff Healy
OPENING/OTHER ACT(S): Jeff Healy
SONGS: Live with Me / You Got Me Rocking / Tumbling Dice / Shattered / Rocks Off / Sparks Willll Fly / Monkey Man / No Expectations / Love Is Strong / Brand New Car / Honky Tonk Women / I Go Wild / Start Me Up / Street Fighting Man / Brown Sugar / I Can't Get Next to You (Holland, Dozier, Holland)
NOTES: This traditional thank-you-for-putting-up-with-us-while-we-rehearsed/warmup-for-the-tour small show was Darryl Jones's first public performance as the Stones' new bassist. Chuck Leavell played keyboards, Bobby Keys was on sax, and Bernard Fowler and Lisa Fischer sang backup as they all would do on the 1994 Voodoo Lounge tour that followed. Rehearsals had taken place in Toronto for two months; this "surprise" performance was announced to the public on the morning of the show. Admission was $5.00 (Canadian) to the small (1,000-capacity) venue and all proceeds went to Covenant House to benefit runaway teens. Five songs—"Brand New Car," "Love Is Strong" (featuring Jagger on harmonica), "You Got Me Rocking," "Sparks Will Fly," and "I Go Wild,"—came from the *Voodoo Lounge* album. Except for a slow, bluesy—à la Al Green—rendition of the old Temptations song "I Can't Get Next to You," the rest of the set came from the *Let It Bleed*, *Beggars Banquet*, *Exile on Main Street*, *Sticky Fingers* and *Some Girls* LP's. Other musical tidbits from the show: Jagger played guitar on "No Expectations," "Brand New Car" and "I Go Wild" and Woody played pedal steel guitar on "No Expectations." Other items: two women threw their bras onstage during "Honky Tonk Women"—Mick stuffed one under his belt and threw it back at the end of the number, but Keith kept the other. Blind slide guitarist Jeff Healy, a Toronto native, opened for the Stones, and played with them on "I Can't Get Next to You," their RPM Club encore. The show lasted 85 minutes.

AUGUST 1, 1994 – DECEMBER 18, 1994

TOUR: Voodoo Lounge—North America
VENUE: US and Canada
PERSONNEL: Mick Jagger, Keith Richards, Ron Wood, Charlie Watts, Darryl Jones, Chuck Leavell, Bobby Keys, Bernard Fowler, Lisa Fischer, The New West Horns (Andy Snitzer, Michael Davis, Kent Smith)
SPECIAL GUESTS: Sheryl Crow, Robert Cray, Bo Diddley, Lenny Kravitz, Whoopi Goldberg

OPENING/OTHER ACT(S): Counting Crows, Stone Temple Pilots, Lenny Kravitz, Bryan Adams, Ian Moore, Seal, Spin Doctors, Blind Melon, Colin James

SONGS: Not Fade Away (Petty, Hardin) / Undercover of the Night / Tumbling Dice / Live with Me / You Got Me Rocking / Rocks Off / Sparks Will Fly / Shattered / (I Can't Get No) Satisfaction / Beast of Burden / Memory Motel / Out of Tears / No Expectations / All Down the Line / Miss You / Sad Sad Sad / Wild Horses / Far Away Eyes / Doo Doo Doo Doo Doo (Heartbreaker) / Angie / Dead Flowers / Sweet Virginia / Hot Stuff / I Can't Get Next to You (Holland, Dozier, Holland) / It's All Over Now (Womack, Womack) / Who Do You Love (McDaniel) / Stop Breaking Down (Robt. Johnson; arr: Jagger, Richards, Taylor, Wyman, Watts) / Brand New Car / Honky Tonk Women / Before They Make Me Run / The Worst / Happy / Sympathy for the Devil / Love Is Strong / Monkey Man / I Go Wild / Start Me Up / It's Only Rock'n"Roll / Street Fighting Man / Brown Sugar / **E:** Jumpin' Jack Flash

NOTES: This listing's opening act and special guest entries reflect data for all shows on this portion of the tour. Similarly, Songs includes all numbers played on the North American leg of Voodoo Lounge. Setlists of official concerts varied from 22 to 27 songs in length, including the encore, "Jumpin' Jack Flash." The "secret" RPM Club pretour gig on July 19 had a 16-song set.

AUGUST 1, 1994

TOUR: Voodoo Lounge—North America

VENUE: Robert F. Kennedy Memorial Stadium, Washington, DC, USA

ADDITIONAL PERSONNEL: Stilt Walkers

OPENING/OTHER ACT(S): Counting Crows

SONGS: Not Fade Away (Petty, Hardin) / Undercover of the Night / Tumbling Dice / Live with Me / You Got Me Rocking / Rocks Off / Sparks Will Fly / Shattered / (I Can't Get No) Satisfaction / Beast of Burden / Memory Motel / Out of Tears / All Down the Line / Hot Stuff / I Can't Get Next to You (Holland, Dozier, Holland) / Brand New Car / Honky Tonk Women / Before They Make Me Run / The Worst / Love Is Strong / Monkey Man / I Go Wild / Start Me Up / It's Only Rock 'n' Roll / Street Fighting Man / Brown Sugar / **E:** Jumpin' Jack Flash

NOTES: During rehearsals at RFK before this first arena show of the Voodoo Lounge tour, both "Slave" and "Sister Morphine" were scratched, per Jagger. Planned "spontaneous" event during the performance: Mick would select someone from the audience at random to come onstage and request his or her favorite tune (via a prop "jukebox"), the indication being that each show of the tour would feature a different extra number. It never

happened. This information came via the Internet from a stagehand at the arena, who also reported that a "2 million dollar jumbo TV . . . fell 60 feet," but missed hitting anyone. The jumbotron did, in fact, fall. No one was injured, though it was chillingly close. The Stones missed being killed by mere minutes—they had just left the stage when the accident happened. The ruined jumbotron was the top-of-the-line model—the only one then in existence. An inferior backup unit had to be substituted for nearly half the US tour until a replacement could be delivered. The stagehand, who identified him- or herself as "Ayatollah3" in electronic messages, indicated that tempers were a bit ragged ("oneee testy Mick") and some rehearsals had been fairly "sloppy." But, the Internet reports concluded, the "tour list is finally set"; lights and video had been programmed for the above titles for the August 1 show. Though that jukebox idea never materialized, the RFK concerts did feature the unexpected appearance onstage (no warning from the erstwhile Cyber-Deep-Throat!) of two hayseed-costumed stiltwalkers during "Monkey Man." That curious production bit was scrapped after DC.

AUGUST 3, 1994

TOUR: Voodoo Lounge—North America

VENUE: Robert F. Kennedy Memorial Stadium, Washington, DC, USA

OPENING/OTHER ACT(S): Counting Crows

SONGS: Not Fade Away (Petty, Hardin) / Undercover of the Night / Tumbling Dice / Live with Me / You Got Me Rocking / Rocks Off / Sparks Will Fly / Shattered / (I Can't Get No) Satisfaction / Beast of Burden / Out of Tears / Memory Motel / All Down the Line / Miss You / I Can't Get Next to You (Holland, Dozier, Holland) / Brand New Car / Honky Tonk Women / Happy / The Worst / Love Is Strong / Monkey Man / I Go Wild / Start Me Up / It's Only Rock 'n' Roll / Street Fighting Man / Brown Sugar / **E:** Jumpin' Jack Flash

AUGUST 6, 1994

TOUR: Voodoo Lounge—North America

VENUE: Legion Field Stadium, Birmingham, AL, USA

OPENING/OTHER ACT(S): Counting Crows

SONGS: Not Fade Away (Petty, Hardin) / Tumbling Dice / Live with Me / You Got Me Rocking / Rocks Off / Sparks Will Fly / Shattered / (I Can't Get No) Satisfaction / Beast of Burden / Out of Tears / Memory Motel / All Down the Line / Miss You / I Can't Get Next to You (Holland, Dozier, Holland) / I Go Wild / Honky Tonk Women / Before They Make Me Run / The Worst / Love Is Strong / Monkey Man / Start Me Up / It's Only Rock 'n' Roll / Street Fighting Man / Brown Sugar / **E:** Jumpin' Jack Flash

AUGUST 10, 1994

TOUR: Voodoo Lounge—North America

VENUE: The Hoosier Dome, Indianapolis, IN, USA

OPENING/OTHER ACT(S): Counting Crows

SONGS: Not Fade Away (Petty, Hardin) / Tumbling Dice / You Got Me Rocking / Shattered / Rocks Off / Sparks Will Fly / (I Can't Get No) Satisfaction / Beast of Burden / Out of Tears / Wild Horses / All Down the Line / Miss You / I Can't Get Next to You (Holland, Dozier, Holland) / I Go Wild / Honky Tonk Women / Happy / The Worst / Love Is Strong / Monkey Man / Start Me Up / It's Only Rock 'n' Roll / Street Fighting Man / Brown Sugar / E: Jumpin' Jack Flash

AUGUST 12, 1994

TOUR: Voodoo Lounge—North America

VENUE: Giants Stadium, The Meadowlands, East Rutherford, NJ, USA

OPENING/OTHER ACT(S): Counting Crows

SONGS: Not Fade Away (Petty, Hardin) / Tumbling Dice / You Got Me Rocking / Shattered / Rocks Off / Sparks Will Fly / (I Can't Get No) Satisfaction / Beast of Burden / Out of Tears / Wild Horses / All Down the Line / Miss You / I Can't Get Next to You (Holland, Dozier, Holland) / I Go Wild / Honky Tonk Women / Before They Make Me Run / The Worst / Love Is Strong / Monkey Man / Start Me Up / It's Only Rock 'n' Roll / Street Fighting Man / Brown Sugar / E: Jumpin' Jack Flash

AUGUST 14, 1994

TOUR: Voodoo Lounge—North America

VENUE: Giants Stadium, The Meadowlands, East Rutherford, NJ, USA

OPENING/OTHER ACT(S): Counting Crows

SONGS: Not Fade Away (Petty, Hardin) / Tumbling Dice / You Got Me Rocking / Shattered / Rocks Off / Sparks Will Fly / (I Can't Get No) Satisfaction / Beast of Burden / Out of Tears / Wild Horses / All Down the Line / Miss You / I Can't Get Next to You (Holland, Dozier, Holland) / I Go Wild / Honky Tonk Women / Happy / The Worst / Love Is Strong / Monkey Man / Start Me Up / It's Only Rock 'n' Roll / Street Fighting Man / Brown Sugar / E: Jumpin' Jack Flash

AUGUST 15, 1994

TOUR: Voodoo Lounge—North America

VENUE: Giants Stadium, The Meadowlands, East Rutherford, NJ, USA

OPENING/OTHER ACT(S): Counting Crows

SONGS: Not Fade Away (Petty, Hardin) / Tumbling Dice / You Got Me Rocking / Shattered / Rocks Off /

Sparks Will Fly / (I Can't Get No) Satisfaction / Beast of Burden / Out of Tears / Memory Motel / All Down the Line / Miss You / Brand New Car / I Go Wild / Honky Tonk Women / Before They Make Me Run / The Worst / Love Is Strong / Monkey Man / Start Me Up / It's Only Rock 'n' Roll / Street Fighting Man / Brown Sugar / E: Jumpin' Jack Flash

AUGUST 17, 1994

TOUR: Voodoo Lounge—North America

VENUE: Giants Stadium, The Meadowlands, East Rutherford, NJ, USA

OPENING/OTHER ACT(S): Counting Crows

SONGS: Not Fade Away (Petty, Hardin) / Tumbling Dice / You Got Me Rocking / Shattered / Rocks Off / Sparks Will Fly / (I Can't Get No) Satisfaction / Beast of Burden / Out of Tears / Memory Motel / All Down the Line / Miss You / I Go Wild / Honky Tonk Women / Happy / The Worst / Love Is Strong / Monkey Man / Start Me Up / Street Fighting Man / It's Only Rock 'n' Roll / Brown Sugar / E: Jumpin' Jack Flash

AUGUST 19, 1994

TOUR: Voodoo Lounge—North America

VENUE: Canadian National Exhibition Stadium, Toronto, Ontario, Canada

OPENING/OTHER ACT(S): Stone Temple Pilots

SONGS: Not Fade Away (Petty, Hardin) / Tumbling Dice / You Got Me Rocking / Shattered / Rocks Off / Sparks Will Fly / (I Can't Get No) Satisfaction / Beast of Burden / Out of Tears / Wild Horses / All Down the Line / Miss You / Sad Sad Sad / I Go Wild / Honky Tonk Women / Before They Make Me Run / The Worst / Love Is Strong / Monkey Man / Start Me Up / Street Fighting Man / It's Only Rock 'n' Roll / Brown Sugar / E: Jumpin' Jack Flash

AUGUST 20, 1994

TOUR: Voodoo Lounge—North America

VENUE: Canadian National Exhibition Stadium, Toronto, Ontario, Canada

OPENING/OTHER ACT(S): Stone Temple Pilots

SONGS: Not Fade Away (Petty, Hardin) / Tumbling Dice / You Got Me Rocking / Shattered / Rocks Off / Sparks Will Fly / (I Can't Get No) Satisfaction / Beast of Burden / Out of Tears / Memory Motel / All Down the Line / Miss You / I Can't Get Next to You (Holland, Dozier, Holland) / I Go Wild / Honky Tonk Women / Happy / The Worst / Love Is Strong / Monkey Man / Start Me Up / Street Fighting Man / It's Only Rock 'n' Roll / Brown Sugar / E: Jumpin' Jack Flash

AUGUST 23, 1994

TOUR: Voodoo Lounge—North America

VENUE: Winnipeg Stadium, Winnipeg, Manitoba, Canada

OPENING/OTHER ACT(S): Stone Temple Pilots

SONGS: Not Fade Away (Petty, Hardin) / Tumbling Dice / You Got Me Rocking / Shattered / Rocks Off / Sparks Will Fly / (I Can't Get No) Satisfaction / Beast of Burden / Out of Tears / Wild Horses / All Down the Line / Miss You / It's All Over Now (Womack, Womack) / I Go Wild / Honky Tonk Women / Happy / The Worst / Love Is Strong / Monkey Man / Street Fighting Man / Start Me Up / It's Only Rock 'n' Roll / Brown Sugar / **E:** Jumpin' Jack Flash

AUGUST 26, 1994

TOUR: Voodoo Lounge—North America

VENUE: University of Wisconsin, Madison, WI, USA

OPENING/OTHER ACT(S): Lenny Kravitz

SONGS: Not Fade Away (Petty, Hardin) / Tumbling Dice / You Got Me Rocking / Shattered / Rocks Off / Sparks Will Fly / (I Can't Get No) Satisfaction / Beast of Burden / Out of Tears / Memory Motel / All Down the Line / Miss You / It's All Over Now (Womack, Womack) / I Go Wild / Honky Tonk Women / Before They Make Me Run / The Worst / Love Is Strong / Monkey Man / Street Fighting Man / Start Me Up / It's Only Rock 'n' Roll / Brown Sugar / **E:** Jumpin' Jack Flash

AUGUST 28, 1994

TOUR: Voodoo Lounge—North America

VENUE: Cleveland Municipal Stadium, Cleveland, OH, USA

SPECIAL GUESTS: Lenny Kravitz

OPENING/OTHER ACT(S): Lenny Kravitz

SONGS: Not Fade Away (Petty, Hardin) / Tumbling Dice / You Got Me Rocking / Shattered / Rocks Off / Sparks Will Fly / (I Can't Get No) Satisfaction / Beast of Burden / No Expectations / Memory Motel / All Down the Line / Miss You / I Can't Get Next to You (Holland, Dozier, Holland) / I Go Wild / Honky Tonk Women / Happy / The Worst / Love Is Strong / Monkey Man / Street Fighting Man / Start Me Up / It's Only Rock 'n' Roll / Brown Sugar / **E:** Jumpin' Jack Flash

NOTES: Lenny Kravitz opened for the Stones and joined them later onstage for one number, "No Expectations."

AUGUST 30, 1994

TOUR: Voodoo Lounge—North America

VENUE: Riverfront Stadium, Cincinnati, OH, USA

OPENING/OTHER ACT(S): Lenny Kravitz

SONGS: Not Fade Away (Petty, Hardin) / Tumbling Dice / You Got Me Rocking / Shattered / Rocks Off / Sparks Will Fly / (I Can't Get No) Satisfaction / Beast of Burden / Out of Tears / Memory Motel / All Down the Line / Miss You / I Go Wild / Honky Tonk Women / Before They Make Me Run / The Worst / Love Is Strong / Monkey Man / Street Fighting Man / Start Me Up / It's Only Rock 'n' Roll / Brown Sugar / **E:** Jumpin' Jack Flash

SEPTEMBER 4, 1994

TOUR: Voodoo Lounge—North America

VENUE: Foxboro Stadium, Foxboro, MA, USA

OPENING/OTHER ACT(S): Lenny Kravitz

SONGS: Not Fade Away (Petty, Hardin) / Tumbling Dice / You Got Me Rocking / Shattered / Rocks Off / Sparks Will Fly / (I Can't Get No) Satisfaction / Beast of Burden / Out of Tears / Wild Horses / All Down the Line / Miss You / Brand New Car / I Go Wild / Honky Tonk Women / Before They Make Me Run / The Worst / Love Is Strong / Monkey Man / Street Fighting Man / Start Me Up / It's Only Rock 'n' Roll / Brown Sugar / **E:** Jumpin' Jack Flash

SEPTEMBER 5, 1994

TOUR: Voodoo Lounge—North America

VENUE: Foxboro Stadium, Foxboro, MA, USA

OPENING/OTHER ACT(S): Lenny Kravitz

SONGS: Not Fade Away (Petty, Hardin) / Tumbling Dice / You Got Me Rocking / Shattered / Rocks Off / Sparks Will Fly / (I Can't Get No) Satisfaction / Beast of Burden / Memory Motel / All Down the Line / I Go Wild / Miss You / Honky Tonk Women / Happy / The Worst / Love Is Strong / Monkey Man / Street Fighting Man / It's Only Rock 'n' Roll / Start Me Up / Brown Sugar / **E:** Jumpin' Jack Flash

SEPTEMBER 7, 1994

TOUR: Voodoo Lounge—North America

VENUE: Carter-Finley Stadium, Raleigh, NC, USA

OPENING/OTHER ACT(S): Counting Crows

SONGS: Not Fade Away (Petty, Hardin) / Tumbling Dice / You Got Me Rocking / Shattered / Rocks Off / Sparks Will Fly / (I Can't Get No) Satisfaction / Beast of Burden / Memory Motel / All Down the Line / I Go Wild / Miss You / Honky Tonk Women / Before They Make Me Run / The Worst / Love Is Strong / Monkey Man / Street Fighting Man / Start Me Up / It's Only Rock 'n' Roll / Brown Sugar / **E:** Jumpin' Jack Flash

NOTES: Carter-Finley Stadium is on the campus of North Carolina State University.

SEPTEMBER 9, 1994

TOUR: Voodoo Lounge—North America

VENUE: Spartan Stadium, Michigan State University, East Lansing, MI, USA

OPENING/OTHER ACT(S): Lenny Kravitz

SONGS: Not Fade Away (Petty, Hardin) / Tumbling Dice / You Got Me Rocking / Shattered / Rocks Off / Sparks Will Fly / (I Can't Get No) Satisfaction / Beast of Burden / Out of Tears / All Down the Line / I Go Wild / Miss You / Honky Tonk Women / Happy / The Worst / Love Is Strong / Monkey Man / Street Fighting Man / Start Me Up / It's Only Rock 'n' Roll / Brown Sugar / **E:** Jumpin' Jack Flash

SEPTEMBER 11, 1994

TOUR: Voodoo Lounge—North America

VENUE: Soldiers Field, Chicago, IL, USA

OPENING/OTHER ACT(S): Lenny Kravitz

SONGS: Not Fade Away (Petty, Hardin) / Tumbling Dice / You Got Me Rocking / Shattered / Rocks Off / Sparks Will Fly / (I Can't Get No) Satisfaction / Beast of Burden / Memory Motel / All Down the Line / I Go Wild / Miss You / Honky Tonk Women / Before They Make Me Run / The Worst / Love Is Strong / Monkey Man / Street Fighting Man / Start Me Up / It's Only Rock 'n' Roll / Brown Sugar / **E:** Jumpin' Jack Flash

SEPTEMBER 12, 1994

TOUR: Voodoo Lounge—North America

VENUE: Soldiers Field, Chicago, IL, USA

OPENING/OTHER ACT(S): Lenny Kravitz

SONGS: Not Fade Away (Petty, Hardin) / Tumbling Dice / You Got Me Rocking / Shattered / Rocks Off / Sparks Will Fly / (I Can't Get No) Satisfaction / Beast of Burden / Wild Horses / All Down the Line / I Go Wild / Miss You / Honky Tonk Women / Happy / The Worst / Love Is Strong / Monkey Man / Street Fighting Man / Start Me Up / It's Only Rock 'n' Roll / Brown Sugar / **E:** Jumpin' Jack Flash

SEPTEMBER 15, 1994

TOUR: Voodoo Lounge—North America

VENUE: Mile High Stadium, Denver, CO, USA

OPENING/OTHER ACT(S): Lenny Kravitz

SONGS: Not Fade Away (Petty, Hardin) / Tumbling Dice / You Got Me Rocking / Shattered / Rocks Off / Sparks Will Fly / (I Can't Get No) Satisfaction / Beast of Burden / Wild Horses / Live with Me / I Go Wild / It's All Over Now (Womack, Womack) / Miss You / Honky Tonk Women / Before They Make Me Run / The Worst / Love Is Strong / Monkey Man / Street Fighting Man

/ Start Me Up / It's Only Rock 'n' Roll / Brown Sugar / **E:** Jumpin' Jack Flash

SEPTEMBER 18, 1994

TOUR: Voodoo Lounge—North America

VENUE: Faurot Field, University of Missouri, Columbia, MO, USA

OPENING/OTHER ACT(S): Blind Melon

SONGS: Not Fade Away (Petty, Hardin) / Tumbling Dice / You Got Me Rocking / Shattered / Rocks Off / Sparks Will Fly / (I Can't Get No) Satisfaction / Beast of Burden / Memory Motel / Live with Me / I Go Wild / It's All Over Now (Womack, Womack) / Miss You / Honky Tonk Women / Before They Make Me Run / The Worst / Love Is Strong / Monkey Man / Street Fighting Man / Start Me Up / It's Only Rock 'n' Roll / Brown Sugar / **E:** Jumpin' Jack Flash

SEPTEMBER 22, 1994

TOUR: Voodoo Lounge—North America

VENUE: Veterans Stadium, Philadelphia,. PA, USA

OPENING/OTHER ACT(S): Blind Melon

SONGS: Not Fade Away (Petty, Hardin) / Tumbling Dice / You Got Me Rocking / Shattered / Rocks Off / Sparks Will Fly / (I Can't Get No) Satisfaction / Beast of Burden / Memory Motel / All Down the Line / I Go Wild / It's All Over Now (Womack, Womack) / Miss You / Honky Tonk Women / Before They Make Me Run / The Worst / Love Is Strong / Monkey Man / Street Fighting Man / Start Me Up / It's Only Rock 'n' Roll / Brown Sugar / **E:** Jumpin' Jack Flash

SEPTEMBER 23, 1994

TOUR: Voodoo Lounge—North America

VENUE: Veterans Stadium, Philadelphia, PA, USA

OPENING/OTHER ACT(S): Blind Melon

SONGS: Not Fade Away (Petty, Hardin) / Tumbling Dice / You Got Me Rocking / Shattered / Rocks Off / Sparks Will Fly / (I Can't Get No) Satisfaction / Beast of Burden / Wild Horses / All Down the Line / I Go Wild / Doo Doo Doo Doo Doo (Heartbreaker) / Miss You / Honky Tonk Women / Happy / The Worst / Love Is Strong / Monkey Man / Street Fighting Man / Start Me Up / It's Only Rock 'n' Roll / Brown Sugar / **E:** Jumpin' Jack Flash

NOTES: "Doo Doo Doo Doo Doo (Heartbreaker)" makes its first appearance in a Voodoo Lounge setlist.

SEPTEMBER 25, 1994

TOUR: Voodoo Lounge—North America

VENUE: Williams Brice Stadium, University of South Carolina, Columbia, SC, USA

OPENING/OTHER ACT(S): Blind Melon

SEPTEMBER 27, 1994

TOUR: Voodoo Lounge—North America
VENUE: Liberty Bowl, Memphis, TN, USA
OPENING/OTHER ACT(S): Blind Melon

SEPTEMBER 29, 1994

TOUR: Voodoo Lounge—North America
VENUE: Three Rivers Stadium, Pittsburgh, PA, USA
OPENING/OTHER ACT(S): Blind Melon
SONGS: Not Fade Away (Petty, Hardin) / Tumbling Dice / You Got Me Rocking / Shattered / Rocks Off / Sparks Will Fly / (I Can't Get No) Satisfaction / Beast of Burden / Out of Tears / Doo Doo Doo Doo Doo (Heartbreaker) / I Go Wild / It's All Over Now (Womack, Womack) / Miss You / Honky Tonk Women / Happy / The Worst / Love Is Strong / Monkey Man / Street Fighting Man / Start Me Up / It's Only Rock 'n' Roll / Brown Sugar / **E:** Jumpin' Jack Flash

OCTOBER 1, 1994

TOUR: Voodoo Lounge—North America
VENUE: Cyclone Field, Ames, IA, USA
OPENING/OTHER ACT(S): Blind Melon
SONGS: Not Fade Away (Petty, Hardin) / Tumbling Dice / You Got Me Rocking / Shattered / Rocks Off / Sparks Will Fly / (I Can't Get No) Satisfaction / Beast of Burden / Out of Tears / Doo Doo Doo Doo Doo (Heartbreaker) / I Go Wild / It's All Over Now (Womack, Womack) / Miss You / Honky Tonk Women / Before They Make Me Run / The Worst / Love Is Strong / Monkey Man / Street Fighting Man / Start Me Up / It's Only Rock 'n' Roll / Brown Sugar / **E:** Jumpin' Jack Flash

OCTOBER 4, 1994

TOUR: Voodoo Lounge—North America
VENUE: Commonwealth Stadium, Edmonton, Alberta, Canada
OPENING/OTHER ACT(S): Colin James
SONGS: Not Fade Away (Petty, Hardin) / Tumbling Dice / You Got Me Rocking / Shattered / Rocks Off / Sparks Will Fly / (I Can't Get No) Satisfaction / Beast of Burden / Out of Tears / Doo Doo Doo Doo Doo (Heartbreaker) / I Go Wild / It's All Over Now (Womack, Womack) / Miss You / Honky Tonk Women / Happy / The Worst / Love Is Strong / Monkey Man / Street Fighting Man / Start Me Up / It's Only Rock 'n' Roll / Brown Sugar / **E:** Jumpin' Jack Flash

OCTOBER 5, 1994

TOUR: Voodoo Lounge—North America
VENUE: Commonwealth Stadium, Edmonton, Alberta, Canada
OPENING/OTHER ACT(S): Colin James
SONGS: Not Fade Away (Petty, Hardin) / Tumbling Dice / You Got Me Rocking / Shattered / Rocks Off / Sparks Will Fly / (I Can't Get No) Satisfaction / Beast of Burden / Out of Tears / Doo Doo Doo Doo Doo (Heartbreaker) / I Go Wild / It's All Over Now (Womack, Womack) / Miss You / Honky Tonk Women / Before They Make Me Run / The Worst / Love Is Strong / Monkey Man / Street Fighting Man / Start Me Up / It's Only Rock 'n' Roll / Brown Sugar / **E:** Jumpin' Jack Flash

OCTOBER 10, 1994

TOUR: Voodoo Lounge—North America
VENUE: Superdome, New Orleans, LA, USA
OPENING/OTHER ACT(S): Bryan Adams
SONGS: Not Fade Away (Petty, Hardin) / Tumbling Dice / You Got Me Rocking / Shattered / Rocks Off / Sparks Will Fly / (I Can't Get No) Satisfaction / Beast of Burden / Out of Tears / Doo Doo Doo Doo Doo (Heartbreaker) / I Go Wild / It's All Over Now (Womack, Womack) / Miss You / Honky Tonk Women / Before They Make Me Run / The Worst / Love Is Strong / Monkey Man / Street Fighting Man / Start Me Up / It's Only Rock 'n' Roll / Brown Sugar / **E:** Jumpin' Jack Flash
NOTES: The New Orleans concert was broadcast "live" (delayed in some markets) nationwide on FM radio.

OCTOBER 14, 1994

TOUR: Voodoo Lounge—North America
VENUE: MGM Grand Hotel & Casino, Las Vegas, NV, USA
OPENING/OTHER ACT(S): Seal
SONGS: Not Fade Away (Petty, Hardin) / Tumbling Dice / You Got Me Rocking / Shattered / Rocks Off / Sparks Will Fly / (I Can't Get No) Satisfaction / Beast of Burden / Out of Tears / I Can't Get Next to You (Holland, Dozier, Holland) / I Go Wild / It's All Over Now (Womack, Womack) / Miss You / Honky Tonk Women / Before They Make Me Run / The Worst / Love Is Strong / Monkey Man / Street Fighting Man / Start Me Up / It's Only Rock 'n' Roll / Brown Sugar / **E:** Jumpin' Jack Flash

OCTOBER 15, 1994

TOUR: Voodoo Lounge—North America

VENUE: MGM Grand Hotel & Casino, Las Vegas, NV, USA

OPENING/OTHER ACT(S): Seal

SONGS: Not Fade Away (Petty, Hardin) / Tumbling Dice / You Got Me Rocking / Shattered / Rocks Off / Sparks Will Fly / (I Can't Get No) Satisfaction / Beast of Burden / Memory Motel / Love Is Strong / It's All Over Now (Womack, Womack) / I Go Wild / Miss You / Honky Tonk Women / Happy / The Worst / Sympathy for the Devil / Monkey Man / Street Fighting Man / Start Me Up / It's Only Rock 'n' Roll / Brown Sugar / E: Jumpin' Jack Flash

NOTES: Note the change in the order of songs and the first appearance of "Sympathy for the Devil" in the setlist. The song remained in Voodoo Lounge shows from this point on.

OCTOBER 17, 1994

TOUR: Voodoo Lounge—North America

VENUE: Jack Murphy Stadium, San Diego, CA, USA

OPENING/OTHER ACT(S): Seal

SONGS: Not Fade Away (Petty, Hardin) / Tumbling Dice / You Got Me Rocking / Shattered / Rocks Off / Sparks Will Fly / (I Can't Get No) Satisfaction / Beast of Burden / Out of Tears / Doo Doo Doo Doo Doo (Heartbreaker) / Love Is Strong / It's All Over Now (Womack, Womack) / I Go Wild / Miss You / Honky Tonk Women / Before They Make Me Run / The Worst / Sympathy for the Devil / Monkey Man / Street Fighting Man / Start Me Up / It's Only Rock 'n' Roll / Brown Sugar / E: Jumpin' Jack Flash

NOTES: The rearranged, amplified (by the addition of "Sympathy for the Devil") 24-song set of the middle portion of the North American tour took shape here and at the second Las Vegas show.

OCTOBER 19, 1994

TOUR: Voodoo Lounge—North America

VENUE: The Rose Bowl, Pasadena, CA, USA

OPENING/OTHER ACT(S): Buddy Guy, The Red Hot Chili Peppers

SONGS: Not Fade Away (Petty, Hardin) / Tumbling Dice / You Got Me Rocking / Shattered / Rocks Off / Sparks Will Fly / (I Can't Get No) Satisfaction / Beast of Burden / Out of Tears / Doo Doo Doo Doo Doo (Heartbreaker) / Love Is Strong / It's All Over Now (Womack, Womack) / I Go Wild / Miss You / Honky Tonk Women / Before They Make Me Run / The Worst / Sympathy for the Devil / Monkey Man / Street Fighting Man / Start Me Up / It's Only Rock 'n' Roll / Brown Sugar / E: Jumpin' Jack Flash

OCTOBER 21, 1994

TOUR: Voodoo Lounge—North America

VENUE: The Rose Bowl, Pasadena, CA, USA

OPENING/OTHER ACT(S): Buddy Guy, The Red Hot Chili Peppers

SONGS: Not Fade Away (Petty, Hardin) / Tumbling Dice / You Got Me Rocking / Shattered / Rocks Off / Sparks Will Fly / (I Can't Get No) Satisfaction / Beast of Burden / Memory Motel / All Down the Line / Love Is Strong / It's All Over Now (Womack, Womack) / I Go Wild / Miss You / Honky Tonk Women / Happy / The Worst / Sympathy for the Devil / Monkey Man / Street Fighting Man / Start Me Up / It's Only Rock 'n' Roll / Brown Sugar / E: Jumpin' Jack Flash

OCTOBER 23, 1994

TOUR: Voodoo Lounge—North America

VENUE: Rice Stadium, Salt Lake City, UT, USA

NOTES: The set was identical to that of the second L.A. (Pasadena) show.

OCTOBER 26, 1994

TOUR: Voodoo Lounge—North America

VENUE: Alameda County Stadium, Oakland, CA, USA

OPENING/OTHER ACT(S): Seal

SONGS: Not Fade Away (Petty, Hardin) / Tumbling Dice / You Got Me Rocking / Shattered / Rocks Off / Sparks Will Fly / (I Can't Get No) Satisfaction / Beast of Burden / Out of Tears / Doo Doo Doo Doo Doo (Heartbreaker) / Love Is Strong / It's All Over Now (Womack, Womack) / I Go Wild / Miss You / Honky Tonk Women / Before They Make Me Run / The Worst / Sympathy for the Devil / Monkey Man / Street Fighting Man / Start Me Up / It's Only Rock 'n' Roll / Brown Sugar / E: Jumpin' Jack Flash

OCTOBER 28, 1994

TOUR: Voodoo Lounge—North America

VENUE: Alameda County Stadium, Oakland, CA, USA

OPENING/OTHER ACT(S): Seal

SONGS: Not Fade Away (Petty, Hardin) / Tumbling Dice / You Got Me Rocking / Shattered / Rocks Off / Sparks Will Fly / (I Can't Get No) Satisfaction / Beast of Burden / Wild Horses / Doo Doo Doo Doo Doo (Heartbreaker) / Love Is Strong / It's All Over Now (Womack, Womack) / I Go Wild / Miss You / Honky Tonk Women / Happy / The Worst / Sympathy for the Devil / Monkey Man / Street Fighting Man / Start Me Up / It's Only Rock 'n' Roll / Brown Sugar / E: Jumpin' Jack Flash

NOTES: "Wild Horses" was played only at this second Oakland show, in the ninth slot on the list lately occupied by either "Out of Tears" or "Memory Motel."

OCTOBER 29, 1994

TOUR: Voodoo Lounge—North America
VENUE: Alameda County Stadium, Oakland, CA, USA
OPENING/OTHER ACT(S): Seal
SONGS: Not Fade Away (Petty, Hardin) / Tumbling Dice / You Got Me Rocking / Shattered / Rocks Off / Sparks Will Fly / (I Can't Get No) Satisfaction / Beast of Burden / Memory Motel / All Down the Line / Love Is Strong / It's All Over Now (Womack, Womack) / I Go Wild / Miss You / Honky Tonk Women / Before They Make Me Run / The Worst / Sympathy for the Devil / Monkey Man / Street Fighting Man / Start Me Up / It's Only Rock 'n' Roll / Brown Sugar / **E:** Jumpin' Jack Flash

OCTOBER 31, 1994

TOUR: Voodoo Lounge—North America
VENUE: Alameda County Stadium, Oakland, CA, USA
OPENING/OTHER ACT(S): Seal
SONGS: Not Fade Away (Petty, Hardin) / Tumbling Dice / You Got Me Rocking / Shattered / Rocks Off / Sparks Will Fly / (I Can't Get No) Satisfaction / Beast of Burden / Out of Tears / Doo Doo Doo Doo Doo (Heartbreaker) / Love Is Strong / It's All Over Now (Womack, Womack) / I Go Wild / Miss You / Honky Tonk Women / Before They Make Me Run / The Worst / Sympathy for the Devil / Monkey Man / Street Fighting Man / Start Me Up / It's Only Rock 'n' Roll / Brown Sugar / **E:** Jumpin' Jack Flash
NOTES: In Oakland, the last show had the same set as the first.

NOVEMBER 3, 1994

TOUR: Voodoo Lounge—North America
VENUE: The Sun Bowl, El Paso, TX, USA
OPENING/OTHER ACT(S): Bryan Adams
SONGS: Not Fade Away (Petty, Hardin) / Tumbling Dice / You Got Me Rocking / Shattered / Rocks Off / Sparks Will Fly / (I Can't Get No) Satisfaction / Beast of Burden / Out of Tears / Doo Doo Doo Doo Doo (Heartbreaker) / Love Is Strong / It's All Over Now (Womack, Womack) / I Go Wild / Miss You / Honky Tonk Women / Before They Make Me Run / The Worst / Sympathy for the Devil / Monkey Man / Street Fighting Man / Start Me Up / It's Only Rock 'n' Roll / Brown Sugar / **E:** Jumpin' Jack Flash

NOVEMBER 5, 1994

TOUR: Voodoo Lounge—North America
VENUE: The Alamo Dome, San Antonio, TX, USA
OPENING/OTHER ACT(S): Bryan Adams
SONGS: Not Fade Away (Petty, Hardin) / Tumbling Dice / You Got Me Rocking / Shattered / Rocks Off / Sparks Will Fly / (I Can't Get No) Satisfaction / Beast of Burden / Far Away Eyes / Doo Doo Doo Doo Doo (Heartbreaker) / Love Is Strong / It's All Over Now (Womack, Womack) / I Go Wild / Miss You / Honky Tonk Women / Happy / The Worst / Sympathy for the Devil / Monkey Man / Street Fighting Man / Start Me Up / It's Only Rock 'n' Roll / Brown Sugar / **E:** Jumpin' Jack Flash
NOTES: "Far Away Eyes" was played for the first time on Voodoo Lounge.

NOVEMBER 11, 1994

TOUR: Voodoo Lounge—North America
VENUE: War Memorial Stadium, Little Rock, AR, USA
OPENING/OTHER ACT(S): Bryan Adams
SONGS: Not Fade Away (Petty, Hardin) / Tumbling Dice / You Got Me Rocking / Shattered / Rocks Off / Sparks Will Fly / (I Can't Get No) Satisfaction / Beast of Burden / Far Away Eyes / Doo Doo Doo Doo Doo (Heartbreaker) / Love Is Strong / It's All Over Now (Womack, Womack) / I Go Wild / Miss You / Honky Tonk Women / Before They Make Me Run / The Worst / Sympathy for the Devil / Monkey Man / Street Fighting Man / Start Me Up / It's Only Rock 'n' Roll / Brown Sugar / **E:** Jumpin' Jack Flash

NOVEMBER 13, 1994

TOUR: Voodoo Lounge—North America
VENUE: Astrodome, Houston, TX, USA
OPENING/OTHER ACT(S): Bryan Adams
SONGS: Not Fade Away (Petty, Hardin) / Tumbling Dice / You Got Me Rocking / Shattered / Rocks Off / Sparks Will Fly / (I Can't Get No) Satisfaction / Beast of Burden / Out of Tears / Doo Doo Doo Doo Doo (Heartbreaker) / Love Is Strong / It's All Over Now (Womack, Womack) / I Go Wild / Miss You / Honky Tonk Women / Before They Make Me Run / The Worst / Sympathy for the Devil / Monkey Man / Street Fighting Man / Start Me Up / It's Only Rock 'n' Roll / Brown Sugar / **E:** Jumpin' Jack Flash

NOVEMBER 15, 1994

TOUR: Voodoo Lounge—North America
VENUE: The Georgia Dome, Atlanta, GA, USA
OPENING/OTHER ACT(S): Bryan Adams

SONGS: Not Fade Away (Petty, Hardin) / Tumbling Dice / You Got Me Rocking / Shattered / Rocks Off / Sparks Will Fly / (I Can't Get No) Satisfaction / Beast of Burden / Out of Tears / Doo Doo Doo Doo Doo (Heartbreaker) / Love Is Strong / It's All Over Now (Womack, Womack) / I Go Wild / Miss You / Honky Tonk Women / Before They Make Me Run / The Worst / Sympathy for the Devil / Monkey Man / Street Fighting Man / Start Me Up / It's Only Rock 'n' Roll / Brown Sugar / E: Jumpin' Jack Flash

NOVEMBER 16, 1994

TOUR: Voodoo Lounge—North America
VENUE: The Georgia Dome, Atlanta, GA, USA
OPENING/OTHER ACT(S): Bryan Adams
SONGS: Not Fade Away (Petty, Hardin) / Tumbling Dice / You Got Me Rocking / Shattered / Rocks Off / Sparks Will Fly / (I Can't Get No) Satisfaction / Beast of Burden / Far Away Eyes / All Down the Line / Love Is Strong / It's All Over Now (Womack, Womack) / I Go Wild / Miss You / Honky Tonk Women / Happy / The Worst / Sympathy for the Devil / Monkey Man / Street Fighting Man / Start Me Up / It's Only Rock 'n' Roll / Brown Sugar / E: Jumpin' Jack Flash

NOVEMBER 18, 1994

TOUR: Voodoo Lounge—North America
VENUE: Cotton Bowl, Dallas, TX, USA
OPENING/OTHER ACT(S): Bryan Adams, Ian Moore
SONGS: Not Fade Away (Petty, Hardin) / Tumbling Dice / Live with Me / You Got Me Rocking / Shattered / Rocks Off / Sparks Will Fly / (I Can't Get No) Satisfaction / Beast of Burden / Far Away Eyes / Doo Doo Doo Doo Doo (Heartbreaker) / Love Is Strong / It's All Over Now (Womack, Womack) / I Go Wild / Miss You / Honky Tonk Women / Before They Make Me Run / The Worst / Sympathy for the Devil / Monkey Man / Start Me Up / It's Only Rock 'n' Roll / Street Fighting Man / Brown Sugar / E: Jumpin' Jack Flash
NOTES: A 25-song set, with "Live with Me" plus a bit of a shuffle in the order of things.

NOVEMBER 22, 1994

TOUR: Voodoo Lounge—North America
VENUE: Tampa Stadium, Tampa, FL, USA
OPENING/OTHER ACT(S): The Spin Doctors
SONGS: Not Fade Away (Petty, Hardin) / Tumbling Dice / You Got Me Rocking / Shattered / Rocks Off / Sparks Will Fly / (I Can't Get No) Satisfaction / Beast of Burden / Far Away Eyes / All Down the Line / Out of Tears / Love Is Strong / It's All Over Now (Womack, Womack) / I Go Wild / Miss You / Honky Tonk Women

/ Happy / The Worst / Sympathy for the Devil / Monkey Man / Street Fighting Man / Start Me Up / It's Only Rock 'n' Roll / Brown Sugar / E: Jumpin' Jack Flash

NOVEMBER 25, 1994

TOUR: Voodoo Lounge—North America
VENUE: Joe Robbie Stadium, Miami, FL, USA
SPECIAL GUESTS: Whoopi Goldberg, Sheryl Crow, Robert Cray, Bo Diddley
OPENING/OTHER ACT(S): The Spin Doctors
SONGS: Not Fade Away (Petty, Hardin) / Tumbling Dice / You Got Me Rocking / Shattered / Rocks Off / Sparks Will Fly / Live with Me / (I Can't Get No) Satisfaction / Beast of Burden / Angie / Dead Flowers / Sweet Virginia / Doo Doo Doo Doo Doo (Heartbreaker) / It's All Over Now (Womack, Womack) / Stop Breaking Down (Robt. Johnson; arr: Jagger, Richards, Taylor, Wyman, Watts) / Who Do You Love (McDaniel) / I Go Wild / Miss You / Honky Tonk Women / Before They Make Me Run / The Worst / Sympathy for the Devil / Monkey Man / Street Fighting Man / Start Me Up / It's Only Rock 'n' Roll / Brown Sugar / E: Jumpin' Jack Flash
NOTES: The Voodoo Lounge concert which was broadcast live on pay-per-view television and later became a commercial video. Whoopi Goldberg introduced the band "that brought music to us that our parents told us we probably shouldn't be listening to, but a lot of our parents are here tonight. A lot of people have tried to mimic this band, but couldn't do it, because there is only one." Whoopi returned at encore time to chime in on "Jumpin' Jack Flash." The show was notable in other respects. Three special guest artists joined the Stones onstage for one number each: Sheryl Crow duetted with Mick on "Live with Me," Robert Cray came in on "Stop Breaking Down" and Bo Diddley appeared for his "Who Do You Love." Most remarkably, the Miami performance featured a mini "acoustic set" in the middle of the show—and almost in the middle of the audience. After "Beast of Burden," the band jumped onto a truck-bed platform that propelled them amidst the floor-level crowd while they performed "Angie," "Dead Flowers" and "Sweet Virginia." It was a long show, with 27 numbers. The Spin Doctors opened; their set was not part of the television broadcast.

NOVEMBER 27, 1994

TOUR: Voodoo Lounge—North America
VENUE: University of Florida, Gainesville, FL, USA
OPENING/OTHER ACT(S): The Spin Doctors
SONGS: Not Fade Away (Petty, Hardin) / Tumbling Dice / You Got Me Rocking / Shattered / Rocks Off / Sparks Will Fly / (I Can't Get No) Satisfaction / Beast of

Burden / Far Away Eyes / Doo Doo Doo Doo Doo (Heartbreaker) / Love Is Strong / It's All Over Now (Womack, Womack) / I Go Wild / Miss You / Honky Tonk Women / Happy / The Worst / Sympathy for the Devil / Monkey Man / Street Fighting Man / Start Me Up / It's Only Rock 'n' Roll / Brown Sugar / **E:** Jumpin' Jack Flash

DECEMBER 1, 1994

TOUR: Voodoo Lounge—North America
VENUE: Silverdome, Pontiac, MI, USA
OPENING/OTHER ACT(S): The Spin Doctors
SONGS: Not Fade Away (Petty, Hardin) / Tumbling Dice / You Got Me Rocking / Rocks Off / Live With Me / Sparks Will Fly / (I Can't Get No) Satisfaction / Beast of Burden / Memory Motel / I Go Wild / Love Is Strong / I Can't Get Next to You (Holland, Dozier, Holland) / It's All Over Now (Womack, Womack) / Miss You / Honky Tonk Women / Before They Make Me Run / The Worst / Sympathy for the Devil / Monkey Man / Street Fighting Man / Start Me Up / It's Only Rock 'n' Roll / Brown Sugar / **E:** Jumpin' Jack Flash

DECEMBER 3, 1994

TOUR: Voodoo Lounge—North America
VENUE: Skydome, Toronto, Ontario, Canada
OPENING/OTHER ACT(S): The Spin Doctors
SONGS: Not Fade Away (Petty, Hardin) / Tumbling Dice / You Got Me Rocking / Rocks Off / Live with Me / Sparks Will Fly / (I Can't Get No) Satisfaction / Beast of Burden / Far Away Eyes / Doo Doo Doo Doo Doo (Heartbreaker) / Love Is Strong / It's All Over Now (Womack, Womack) / I Go Wild / Miss You / Honky Tonk Women / Happy / The Worst / Sympathy for the Devil / Monkey Man / Street Fighting Man / Start Me Up / It's Only Rock 'n' Roll / Brown Sugar / **E:** Jumpin' Jack Flash

DECEMBER 5, 1994

TOUR: Voodoo Lounge—North America
VENUE: Olympic Stadium, Montreal, Quebec, Canada
OPENING/OTHER ACT(S): The Spin Doctors
SONGS: Not Fade Away (Petty, Hardin) / Tumbling Dice / You Got Me Rocking / Shattered / Rocks Off / Sparks Will Fly / (I Can't Get No) Satisfaction / Beast of Burden / Out of Tears / Doo Doo Doo Doo Doo (Heartbreaker) / Love Is Strong / It's All Over Now (Womack, Womack) / I Go Wild / Miss You / Honky Tonk Women / Before They Make Me Run / The Worst / Sympathy for the Devil / Monkey Man / Street Fighting Man / Start Me Up / It's Only Rock 'n' Roll / Brown Sugar / **E:** Jumpin' Jack Flash

DECEMBER 6, 1994

TOUR: Voodoo Lounge—North America
VENUE: Olympic Stadium, Montreal, Quebec, Canada
OPENING/OTHER ACT(S): The Spin Doctors

DECEMBER 8, 1994

TOUR: Voodoo Lounge—North America
VENUE: Carrier Dome, Syracuse, NY, USA
PERSONNEL: Mick Jagger, Keith Richards, Ron Wood, Charlie Watts, Darryl Jones, Chuck Leavell, Lisa Fischer, Bernard Fowler, The New West Horns (Andy Snitzer, Michael Davis, Kent Smith)
OPENING/OTHER ACT(S): The Spin Doctors
SONGS: Not Fade Away (Petty, Hardin) / Tumbling Dice / You Got Me Rocking / Shattered / Rocks Off / Sparks Will Fly / (I Can't Get No) Satisfaction / Beast of Burden / Memory Motel / Doo Doo Doo Doo Doo (Heartbreaker) / Love Is Strong / It's All Over Now (Womack, Womack) / I Go Wild / Miss You / Honky Tonk Women / Before They Make Me Run / The Worst / Sympathy for the Devil / Monkey Man / Street Fighting Man / Start Me Up / It's Only Rock 'n' Roll / Brown Sugar / **E:** Jumpin' Jack Flash
NOTES: Bobby Keys did not appear at this performance.

DECEMBER 11, 1994

TOUR: Voodoo Lounge—North America
VENUE: The Metrodome, Minneapolis, MN, USA
PERSONNEL: Mick Jagger, Keith Richards, Ron Wood, Charlie Watts, Darryl Jones, Chuck Leavell, Bobby Keys, Lisa Fischer, Bernard Fowler, The New West Horns (Andy Snitzer, Michael Davis, Kent Smith)
OPENING/OTHER ACT(S): The Spin Doctors
SONGS: Not Fade Away (Petty, Hardin) / Tumbling Dice / You Got Me Rocking / Shattered / Rocks Off / Sparks Will Fly / (I Can't Get No) Satisfaction / Beast of Burden / Far Away Eyes / Doo Doo Doo Doo Doo (Heartbreaker) / Love Is Strong / It's All Over Now (Womack, Womack) / I Go Wild / Miss You / Honky Tonk Women / Before They Make Me Run / The Worst / Sympathy for the Devil / Monkey Man / Street Fighting Man / Start Me Up / It's Only Rock 'n' Roll / Brown Sugar / **E:** Jumpin' Jack Flash

DECEMBER 15, 1994

TOUR: Voodoo Lounge—North America
VENUE: The Kingdome, Seattle, WA, USA
OPENING/OTHER ACT(S): The Spin Doctors
SONGS: Not Fade Away (Petty, Hardin) / Tumbling Dice / You Got Me Rocking / Shattered / Rocks Off / Sparks Will Fly / (I Can't Get No) Satisfaction / Beast of

Burden / Far Away Eyes / Doo Doo Doo Doo Doo (Heartbreaker) / Love Is Strong / It's All Over Now (Womack, Womack) / I Go Wild / Miss You / Honky Tonk Women / Before They Make Me Run / The Worst / Sympathy for the Devil / Monkey Man / Street Fighting Man / Start Me Up / It's Only Rock 'n' Roll / Brown Sugar / **E:** Jumpin' Jack Flash

DECEMBER 17, 1994

TOUR: Voodoo Lounge—North America
VENUE: B.C. Place, Vancouver, British Columbia, Canada

OPENING/OTHER ACT(S): The Spin Doctors
SONGS: Not Fade Away (Petty, Hardin) / Tumbling Dice / You Got Me Rocking / Shattered / Rocks Off / Sparks Will Fly / (I Can't Get No) Satisfaction / Beast of Burden / Far Away Eyes / Doo Doo Doo Doo Doo (Heartbreaker) / Love Is Strong / It's All Over Now (Womack, Womack) / I Go Wild / Miss You / Honky Tonk Women / Before They Make Me Run / The Worst / Sympathy for the Devil / Monkey Man / Street Fighting Man / Start Me Up / It's Only Rock 'n' Roll / Brown Sugar / **E:** Jumpin' Jack Flash

DECEMBER 18, 1994

TOUR: Voodoo Lounge—North America
VENUE: B.C. Place, Vancouver, British Columbia, Canada

OPENING/OTHER ACT(S): The Spin Doctors
SONGS: Not Fade Away (Petty, Hardin) / Tumbling Dice / You Got Me Rocking / Shattered / Rocks Off / Sparks Will Fly / (I Can't Get No) Satisfaction / Beast of Burden / Out of Tears / Doo Doo Doo Doo Doo (Heartbreaker) / Love Is Strong / It's All Over Now (Womack, Womack) / I Go Wild / Miss You / Honky Tonk Women / Happy / The Worst / Sympathy for the Devil / Monkey Man / Street Fighting Man / Start Me Up / It's Only Rock 'n' Roll / Brown Sugar / **E:** Jumpin' Jack Flash
NOTES: The last North American gig of the Voodoo Lounge tour.

1995

JANUARY 14 – APRIL 17, 1995

JANUARY 14, 1995

TOUR: Voodoo Lounge tour (Part 2)—Latin America
VENUE: Autodromo Hermanos Rodriguez, Mexico City, Mexico

OPENING/OTHER ACT(S): Caifanes
SONGS: Not Fade Away (Petty, Hardin) / Tumbling Dice / You Got Me Rocking / Rock and a Hard Place / Rocks Off / (I Can't Get No) Satisfaction / Angie / You Can't Always Get What You Want / Doo Doo Doo Doo Doo (Heartbreaker) / Love Is Strong / It's All Over Now (Womack, Womack) / I Go Wild / Miss You / Honky Tonk Women / Before They Make Me Run / The Worst / Sympathy for the Devil / Monkey Man / Street Fighting Man / Start Me Up / It's Only Rock 'n' Roll / Brown Sugar / Jumpin' Jack Flash

JANUARY 16, 1995

TOUR: Voodoo Lounge (Part 2)—Latin America
VENUE: Autodromo Hermanos Rodriguez, Mexico City, Mexico

OPENING/OTHER ACT(S): Caifanes
SONGS: Not Fade Away (Petty, Hardin) / Tumbling Dice / You Got Me Rocking / Rock and a Hard Place, LV / Rocks Off / (I Can't Get No) Satisfaction / Beast of Burden / Angie / You Can't Always Get What You Want / Just My Imagination (Running Away with Me) (Whitfield, Strong) / Love Is Strong / I Go Wild / Miss You / Honky Tonk Women / Happy / The Worst / Sympathy for the Devil / Gimme Shelter / Street Fighting Man / Start Me Up / It's Only Rock 'n' Roll / Brown Sugar / Jumpin' Jack Flash

JANUARY 18, 1995

TOUR: Voodoo Lounge (Part 2)—Latin America
VENUE: Autodromo Hermanos Rodriguez, Mexico City, Mexico

OPENING/OTHER ACT(S): Caifanes
SONGS: Not Fade Away (Petty, Hardin) / Tumbling Dice / You Got Me Rocking / Rock and a Hard Place / Rocks Off / (I Can't Get No) Satisfaction / Beast of Burden / Angie / Midnight Rambler / Just My Imagination (Running Away with Me) (Whitfield, Strong) / Love Is Strong / I Go Wild / Miss You / Honky Tonk Women / Before They Make Me Run / The Worst / Sympathy for the Devil / Monkey Man / Street Fighting Man / Start Me Up / It's Only Rock 'n' Roll / Brown Sugar / Jumpin' Jack Flash

JANUARY 20, 1995

TOUR: Voodoo Lounge (Part 2)—Latin America
VENUE: Autodromo Hermanos Rodriguez, Mexico City, Mexico

OPENING/OTHER ACT(S): Caifanes
SONGS: Not Fade Away (Petty, Hardin) / Tumbling Dice / You Got Me Rocking / Rock and a Hard Place / Rocks Off / (I Can't Get No) Satisfaction / Beast of

Burden / Angie / You Can't Always Get What You Want / Love Is Strong / I Go Wild / Miss You / Honky Tonk Women / Happy / The Worst / Sympathy for the Devil / Gimme Shelter / Street Fighting Man / Start Me Up / It's Only Rock 'n' Roll / Brown Sugar / **E:** Jumpin' Jack Flash

JANUARY 27, 1995

TOUR: Voodoo Lounge (Part 2)—Latin America
VENUE: Morumbi Stadium, São Paulo, Brazil
OPENING/OTHER ACT(S): Red Baron, Rita Lee, Spin Doctors

JANUARY 28, 1995

TOUR: Voodoo Lounge (Part 2)—Latin America
VENUE: Morumbi Stadium, São Paulo, Brazil
OPENING/OTHER ACT(S): Red Baron, Rita Lee, Spin Doctors
SONGS: Not Fade Away (Petty, Hardin) / Tumbling Dice / You Got Me Rocking / Rock and a Hard Place / (I Can't Get No) Satisfaction / Beast of Burden / Angie / Midnight Rambler / Let It Bleed / Just My Imagination (Running Away with Me) (Whitfield, Strong) / Love Is Strong / I Go Wild / Miss You / Honky Tonk Women / Before They Make Me Run / The Worst / Sympathy for the Devil / Street Fighting Man / Start Me Up / It's Only Rock 'n' Roll / Brown Sugar / **E:** Jumpin' Jack Flash

FEBRUARY 2, 1995

TOUR: Voodoo Lounge (Part 2)—Latin America
VENUE: Maracana Stadium, Rio de Janeiro, Brazil

FEBRUARY 4, 1995

TOUR: Voodoo Lounge (Part 2)—Latin America
VENUE: Maracana Stadium, Rio de Janeiro, Brazil
SONGS: Not Fade Away (Petty, Hardin) / Tumbling Dice / You Got Me Rocking / It's All Over Now (Womack, Womack) / Live with Me / Sparks Will Fly / (I Can't Get No) Satisfaction / Angie / Midnight Rambler / Rock and a Hard Place / I Go Wild / Miss You / Honky Tonk Women / Happy / The Worst / Sympathy for the Devil / Monkey Man / Street Fighting Man / Start Me Up / It's Only Rock 'n' Roll / Brown Sugar / Jumpin' Jack Flash

FEBRUARY 9, 1995

TOUR: Voodoo Lounge (Part 2)—Latin America
VENUE: River Plate Stadium, Buenos Aires, Argentina
OPENING/OTHER ACT(S): Los Ratones Paranoicos

SONGS: Not Fade Away (Petty, Hardin) / Tumbling Dice / You Got Me Rocking / It's All Over Now (Womack, Womack) / Undercover of the Night / Sparks Will Fly / (I Can't Get No) Satisfaction / Out of Tears / Angie / Rock and a Hard Place / Love Is Strong / I Go Wild / Miss You / Honky Tonk Women / Before They Make Me Run / The Worst / Sympathy for the Devil / Gimme Shelter / Street Fighting Man / Start Me Up / It's Only Rock 'n' Roll / Brown Sugar / Jumpin' Jack Flash
NOTES: Los Ratones Paranoicos (The Paranoid Rats) opened for the band in Argentina and Chile. They are managed by none other than Andrew Loog Oldham.

FEBRUARY 11, 1995

TOUR: Voodoo Lounge (Part 2)—Latin America
VENUE: River Plate Stadium, Buenos Aires, Argentina
OPENING/OTHER ACT(S): Los Ratones Paranoicos

FEBRUARY 12, 1995

TOUR: Voodoo Lounge (Part 2)—Latin America
VENUE: River Plate Stadium, Buenos Aires, Argentina
OPENING/OTHER ACT(S): Los Ratones Paranoicos

FEBRUARY 14, 1995

TOUR: Voodoo Lounge (Part 2)—Latin America
VENUE: River Plate Stadium, Buenos Aires, Argentina
OPENING/OTHER ACT(S): Los Ratones Paranoicos

FEBRUARY 16, 1995

TOUR: Voodoo Lounge (Part 2)—Latin America
VENUE: River Plate Stadium, Buenos Aires, Argentina
OPENING/OTHER ACT(S): Los Ratones Paranoicos

FEBRUARY 19, 1995

TOUR: Voodoo Lounge (Part 2)—Latin America
VENUE: Estadio Nacionale, Santiago, Chile
OPENING/OTHER ACT(S): Los Ratones Paranoicos
SONGS: Not Fade Away (Petty, Hardin) / Tumbling Dice / You Got Me Rocking / Rocks Off / Rock and a Hard Place / Sparks Will Fly / (I Can't Get No) Satisfaction / Angie / Out of Tears / Love Is Strong / It's All Over Now (Womack, Womack) / I Go Wild / Miss You / Honky Tonk Women / Before They Make Me Run / Slipping Away / Sympathy for the Devil / Monkey Man / Street Fighting Man / Start Me Up / It's Only Rock 'n' Roll / Brown Sugar / Jumpin' Jack Flash
NOTES: Keith sings "Slipping Away" for the first time.

FEBRUARY 24, 1995

TOUR: Voodoo Lounge (Part 2)—South Africa

VENUE: Ellis Park Stadium, Johannesburg, South Africa
SONGS: Not Fade Away (Petty, Hardin) / Tumbling Dice / You Got Me Rocking / It's All Over Now (Womack, Womack) / Live with Me / Sparks Will Fly / (I Can't Get No) Satisfaction / Out of Tears / Angie / Rock and a Hard Place / Midnight Rambler / I Go Wild / Miss You / Honky Tonk Women / Happy / Slipping Away / Sympathy for the Devil / Monkey Man / Street Fighting Man / Start Me Up / It's Only Rock 'n' Roll / Brown Sugar / Jumpin' Jack Flash
NOTES: The cost to transport the most dominant feature of the Voodoo Lounge set was so prohibitive (it took two jumbo jets to ferry the snake) that the South African stage had everything but the cobra. This was the origin of bootleg CD titles from the two South African shows ("Everything but the Cobra").

FEBRUARY 25, 1995

TOUR: Voodoo Lounge (Part 2)—South Africa
VENUE: Ellis Park Stadium, Johannesburg, South Africa
SONGS: Not Fade Away (Petty, Hardin) / Tumbling Dice / You Got Me Rocking / It's All Over Now (Womack, Womack) / Live with Me / Sparks Will Fly / (I Can't Get No) Satisfaction / Out of Tears / Angie / Rock and a Hard Place / Midnight Rambler / I Go Wild / Miss You / Honky Tonk Women / Happy / Slipping Away / Sympathy for the Devil / Monkey Man / Street Fighting Man / Start Me Up / It's Only Rock 'n' Roll / Brown Sugar / Jumpin' Jack Flash
NOTES: "One Hit (to the Body)" and no "Miss You."

MARCH 6, 1995

TOUR: Voodoo Lounge tour (Part 2)—Japan
VENUE: Tokyo Dome, Tokyo, Japan
SONGS: Not Fade Away (Petty, Hardin) / Tumbling Dice / You Got Me Rocking / It's All Over Now (Womack, Womack) / Live with Me / Sparks Will Fly / (I Can't Get No) Satisfaction / Angie / Sweet Virginia / Doo Doo Doo Doo Doo (Heartbreaker) / Love Is Strong / I Go Wild / Miss You / Honky Tonk Women / Before They Make Me Run / Slipping Away / Sympathy for the Devil / Monkey Man / Street Fighting Man / Start Me Up / It's Only Rock 'n' Roll / Brown Sugar / Jumpin' Jack Flash

MARCH 8, 1995

TOUR: Voodoo Lounge (Part 2)—Japan
VENUE: Tokyo Dome, Tokyo, Japan
SONGS: Not Fade Away (Petty, Hardin) / Tumbling Dice / You Got Me Rocking / Shattered / Rocks Off / Sparks Will Fly / (I Can't Get No) Satisfaction / Love in Vain (Robt. Johnson), AV / Dead Flowers / It's All Over

Now (Womack, Womack) / Love Is Strong / I Go Wild / Miss You / Honky Tonk Women / Happy / Slipping Away / Sympathy for the Devil / Monkey Man / Street Fighting Man / Start Me Up / It's Only Rock 'n' Roll / Brown Sugar / Jumpin' Jack Flash

MARCH 9, 1995

TOUR: Voodoo Lounge tour (Part 2)—Japan
VENUE: Tokyo Dome, Tokyo, Japan
SONGS: Not Fade Away (Petty, Hardin) / Tumbling Dice / You Got Me Rocking / All Down the Line / Rocks Off / Sparks Will Fly / (I Can't Get No) Satisfaction / No Expectations / Let It Bleed / Rock and a Hard Place / Love Is Strong / I Go Wild / Miss You / Honky Tonk Women / Before They Make Me Run / The Worst / Sympathy for the Devil / Monkey Man / Street Fighting Man / Start Me Up / It's Only Rock 'n' Roll / Brown Sugar / Jumpin' Jack Flash

MARCH 12, 1995

TOUR: Voodoo Lounge (Part 2)—Japan
VENUE: Tokyo Dome, Tokyo, Japan
SONGS: Not Fade Away (Petty, Hardin) / Tumbling Dice / You Got Me Rocking / All Down the Line / Rocks Off / Sparks Will Fly / (I Can't Get No) Satisfaction / Angie / Sweet Virginia / Rock and a Hard Place / Love Is Strong / I Go Wild / Miss You / Honky Tonk Women / Before They Make Me Run / Slipping Away / Sympathy for the Devil / Monkey Man / Street Fighting Man / Start Me Up / It's Only Rock 'n' Roll / Brown Sugar / Jumpin' Jack Flash

MARCH 14, 1995

TOUR: Voodoo Lounge (Part 2)—Japan
VENUE: Tokyo Dome, Tokyo, Japan
SONGS: Not Fade Away (Petty, Hardin) / Tumbling Dice / You Got Me Rocking / Shattered / Rocks Off / Sparks Will Fly / (I Can't Get No) Satisfaction / Beast of Burden / Out of Tears / Doo Doo Doo Doo Doo (Heartbreaker) / Love Is Strong / I Go Wild / Miss You / Honky Tonk Women / Happy / The Worst / Sympathy for the Devil / Monkey Man / Street Fighting Man / Start Me Up / It's Only Rock 'n' Roll / Brown Sugar / Jumpin' Jack Flash

MARCH 16, 1995

TOUR: Voodoo Lounge (Part 2)—Japan
VENUE: Tokyo Dome, Tokyo, Japan
SONGS: Not Fade Away (Petty, Hardin) / Tumbling Dice / You Got Me Rocking / Live with Me / Rocks Off / Sparks Will Fly / (I Can't Get No) Satisfaction / Beast of Burden / Angie / It's All Over Now (Womack,

Womack) / Love Is Strong / I Go Wild / Miss You / Honky Tonk Women / Before They Make Me Run / Slipping Away / Sympathy for the Devil / Monkey Man / Street Fighting Man / Start Me Up / It's Only Rock 'n' Roll / Brown Sugar / Jumpin' Jack Flash

MARCH 17, 1995

TOUR: Voodoo Lounge (Part 2)—Japan
VENUE: Tokyo Dome, Tokyo, Japan
SONGS: Not Fade Away (Petty, Hardin) / Tumbling Dice / You Got Me Rocking / It's All Over Now (Womack, Womack) / Rocks Off / Sparks Will Fly / (I Can't Get No) Satisfaction / Beast of Burden / Memory Motel / Rock and a Hard Place / Love Is Strong / I Go Wild / Miss You / Honky Tonk Women / Happy / Slipping Away / Sympathy for the Devil / Monkey Man / Street Fighting Man / Start Me Up / It's Only Rock 'n' Roll / Brown Sugar / Jumpin' Jack Flash

MARCH 22, 1995

TOUR: Voodoo Lounge (Part 2)—Japan
VENUE: Fukuoka Dome, Fukuoka, Japan
SONGS: Not Fade Away (Petty, Hardin) / Tumbling Dice / You Got Me Rocking / It's All Over Now (Womack, Womack) / Rocks Off / Sparks Will Fly / (I Can't Get No) Satisfaction / Beast of Burden / Angie / Rock and a Hard Place / Love Is Strong / I Go Wild / Miss You / Honky Tonk Women / Before They Make Me Run / Slipping Away / Sympathy for the Devil / Monkey Man / Street Fighting Man / Start Me Up / It's Only Rock 'n' Roll / Brown Sugar / Jumpin' Jack Flash

MARCH 23, 1995

TOUR: Voodoo Lounge (Part 2)—Japan
VENUE: Fukuoka Dome, Fukuoka, Japan
SONGS: Not Fade Away (Petty, Hardin) / Tumbling Dice / You Got Me Rocking / It's All Over Now (Womack, Womack) / Shattered / Sparks Will Fly / (I Can't Get No) Satisfaction / Love In Vain (Robt. Johnson), AV / Sweet Virginia / Doo Doo Doo Doo Doo (Heartbreaker) / Love Is Strong / I Go Wild / Miss You / Honky Tonk Women / Happy / The Worst / Sympathy for the Devil / Monkey Man / Street Fighting Man / Start Me Up / It's Only Rock 'n' Roll / Brown Sugar / Jumpin' Jack Flash
NOTES: Last performance of Voodoo Lounge in Japan.

MARCH 27, 1995

TOUR: Voodoo Lounge (Part 2)—Australia/New Zealand
VENUE: Melbourne Cricket Ground, Melbourne, Australia

OPENING/OTHER ACT(S): The Cruel Sea
SONGS: Not Fade Away (Petty, Hardin) / Tumbling Dice / You Got Me Rocking / It's All Over Now (Womack, Womack) / Live with Me / Sparks Will Fly / (I Can't Get No) Satisfaction / Angie / Sweet Virginia / Rock and a Hard Place, LV / Love Is Strong / I Go Wild / Miss You / Honky Tonk Women / Before They Make Me Run / Slipping Away / Sympathy for the Devil / Monkey Man / Street Fighting Man / Start Me Up / It's Only Rock 'n' Roll / Brown Sugar / Jumpin' Jack Flash

MARCH 28, 1995

TOUR: Voodoo Lounge (Part 2)—Australia/New Zealand
VENUE: Melbourne Cricket Ground, Melbourne, Australia
OPENING/OTHER ACT(S): The Cruel Sea
SONGS: Not Fade Away (Petty, Hardin) / Tumbling Dice / You Got Me Rocking / It's All Over Now (Womack, Womack) / Shattered / Sparks Will Fly / (I Can't Get No) Satisfaction / Beast of Burden / Love In Vain (Robt. Johnson), AV / Midnight Rambler / Love Is Strong / I Go Wild / Miss You / Honky Tonk Women / Happy / The Worst / Sympathy for the Devil / Gimme Shelter / Street Fighting Man / Start Me Up / It's Only Rock 'n' Roll / Brown Sugar / Jumpin' Jack Flash

APRIL 1, 1995

TOUR: Voodoo Lounge (Part 2)—Australia/New Zealand
VENUE: Sydney Cricket Ground, Sydney, Australia
OPENING/OTHER ACT(S): The Cruel Sea
SONGS: Not Fade Away (Petty, Hardin) / Tumbling Dice / You Got Me Rocking / It's All Over Now (Womack, Womack) / Shattered / Sparks Will Fly / (I Can't Get No) Satisfaction / Love In Vain (Robt. Johnson), AV / Sweet Virginia / Midnight Rambler / I Go Wild / Miss You / Honky Tonk Women / Before They Make Me Run / Slipping Away / Sympathy for the Devil / Monkey Man / Street Fighting Man / Start Me Up / It's Only Rock 'n' Roll / Brown Sugar / Jumpin' Jack Flash

APRIL 2, 1995

TOUR: Voodoo Lounge (Part 2)—Australia/New Zealand
VENUE: Sydney Cricket Ground, Sydney, Australia
OPENING/OTHER ACT(S): The Cruel Sea

APRIL 5, 1995

TOUR: Voodoo Lounge (Part 2)—Australia/New Zealand

VENUE: Adelaide Football Park, Adelaide, Australia
OPENING/OTHER ACT(S):   The Cruel Sea

APRIL 8, 1995

TOUR: Voodoo Lounge (Part 2)—Australia/New Zealand
VENUE: Perry Lakes Stadium, Perth, Western Australia
OPENING/OTHER ACT(S):   The Cruel Sea
SONGS: Not Fade Away (Petty, Hardin) / Tumbling Dice / You Got Me Rocking / Shattered / Rocks Off / Sparks Will Fly / (I Can't Get No) Satisfaction / Beast of Burden / Angie / Rock and a Hard Place / I Go Wild / Miss You / Honky Tonk Women / Before They Make Me Run / Slipping Away / Sympathy for the Devil / Gimme Shelter / Street Fighting Man / Start Me Up / It's Only Rock 'n' Roll / Brown Sugar / Jumpin' Jack Flash

APRIL 12, 1995

TOUR: Voodoo Lounge (Part 2)—Australia/New Zealand
VENUE: ANZ Stadium, Brisbane, Australia
OPENING/OTHER ACT(S):   The Cruel Sea
SONGS: Not Fade Away (Petty, Hardin) / Tumbling Dice / You Got Me Rocking / Live with Me / Just My Imagination (Running Away with Me) (Whitfield, Strong) / Sparks Will Fly / (I Can't Get No) Satisfaction / Beast of Burden / Angie / Rock and a Hard Place / I Go Wild / Miss You / Honky Tonk Women / Before They Make Me Run / The Worst / Sympathy for the Devil / Gimme Shelter / Street Fighting Man / Start Me Up / It's Only Rock 'n' Roll / Brown Sugar / Jumpin' Jack Flash

APRIL 16, 1995

TOUR: Voodoo Lounge (Part 2)—Australia/New Zealand
VENUE: Western Springs Stadium, Auckland, New Zealand
OPENING/OTHER ACT(S):   The Exponents
SONGS: Not Fade Away (Petty, Hardin) / Tumbling Dice / It's All Over Now (Womack, Womack) / Shattered / All Down the Line / Sparks Will Fly / (I Can't Get No) Satisfaction / Angie / Sweet Virginia / Doo Doo Doo Doo Doo (Heartbreaker) / I Go Wild / Miss You / Honky Tonk Women / Before They Make Me Run / Slipping Away / Sympathy for the Devil / Gimme Shelter / Street Fighting Man / Start Me Up / It's Only Rock 'n' Roll / Brown Sugar / Jumpin' Jack Flash

APRIL 17, 1995

TOUR: Voodoo Lounge (Part 2)—Australia/New Zealand
VENUE: Western Springs Stadium, Auckland, New Zealand
OPENING/OTHER ACT(S):   The Exponents
SONGS: Not Fade Away (Petty, Hardin) / Tumbling Dice / You Got Me Rocking / Live with Me / All Down the Line / Sparks Will Fly / (I Can't Get No) Satisfaction / Beast of Burden / Wild Horses / Rock and a Hard Place / I Go Wild / Miss You / Honky Tonk Women / Happy / The Worst / Sympathy for the Devil / Monkey Man / Street Fighting Man / Start Me Up / It's Only Rock 'n' Roll / Brown Sugar / Jumpin' Jack Flash
NOTES: The last gig on the Australia/New Zealand leg of Voodoo Lounge.

MAY 26, 1995 – MAY 27, 1995

TOUR: The Foot Tappers and Wheel Shunters Club Gig
VENUE: Paradiso Club, Amsterdam, The Netherlands
PERSONNEL: Mick Jagger, Keith Richards, Ron Wood, Charlie Watts, Darryl Jones, Chuck Leavell, Bobby Keys, Lisa Fischer, Bernard Fowler, The New West Horns (Andy Snitzer, Michael Davis, Kent Smith)
SPECIAL GUESTS: Don Was (kb), Andy Snitzer (org)
OPENING/OTHER ACT(S):   None
SONGS: Not Fade Away (Petty, Hardin) / It's All Over Now (Womack, Womack) / Live with Me / Let It Bleed / The Spider and the Fly (Nanker Phelge) / Beast of Burden / Angie / Wild Horses / Sweet Virginia / Dead Flowers / Shine a Light / Still a Fool (Dixon) / Down in the Bottom (Dixon) / Like a Rolling Stone (Dylan) / Jump on Top of Me / Connection / Before They Make Me Run / Slipping Away / The Worst / Monkey Man / Gimme Shelter / I Can't Get Next to You (Holland, Dozier, Holland) / All Down the Line / Respectable / Rip This Joint / Street Fighting Man
NOTES: Prior to setting out on the European segment of Voodoo Lounge, the Stones played a two-night surprise engagement for audiences of just 800 per show at the Paradiso, a smallish club in Amsterdam. Both concerts were recorded for an upcoming CD long rumored to be an "unplugged" album, and taped for later broadcast and video release. Some, but not all, of the numbers were acoustic, and some were semi-acoustic. Still, the shows were striking departures from "regular" Stones concerts in other ways. There were new versions of old songs in both sets, and a few Stones favorites the band had never played live. Not to mention the big setlist shocker "Like a Rolling Stone," which they had never publicly performed—or played—before, and which Jagger introduced as "a song Bob Dylan wrote for us." Bobby Keys had more sax solos than in the usual

The banner across the entranceway of Amsterdam's Paradiso Club on May 26, 1995 announces the evening's "surprise" attraction. (1995, JAMES KARNBACH)

Voodoo Lounge set, producer Don Was sat in on keyboards for "Shine a Light," and Andy Snitzer left his sax to sit in on organ on "Slipping Away." This is a list of all songs performed at both Paradiso gigs; actual setlists are given with the appropriate dates.

MAY 26, 1995

TOUR: The Foot Tappers and Wheel Shunters Club Gig

VENUE: Paradiso Club, Amsterdam, The Netherlands

SPECIAL GUESTS: Don Was

SONGS: Not Fade Away (Petty, Hardin) / It's All Over Now (Womack, Womack) / Live with Me / Let It Bleed / The Spider and the Fly (Nanker Phelge) / Beast of Burden / Angie / Wild Horses / Sweet Virginia / Dead Flowers / Shine a Light / Like a Rolling Stone (Dylan) / Connection / Slipping Away / The Worst / Gimme Shelter / All Down the Line / Respectable / Rip This Joint / E: Street Fighting Man

NOTES: The show opened with the usual "Not Fade Away," but, unusually, Darryl Jones played standup bass and Ron Wood acoustic guitar. "The Spider and the Fly" was another surprise, with Jagger on harmonica. Then, a few acoustic songs later, came the Stones' first public performance of "Shine a Light" (with producer Don Was

making an unexpected guest appearance on organ) followed by Dylan's "Like a Rolling Stone." Mick and Keith did the vocals on "Connection" as a duet. That song would become a Keith solo during the European tour. "Street Fighting Man" was the encore on this first night at the Paradiso.

MAY 27, 1995

TOUR: The Foot Tappers and Wheel Shunters Club Gig

VENUE: Paradiso Club, Amsterdam, The Netherlands

SPECIAL GUESTS: Don Was

OPENING/OTHER ACT(S): None

SONGS: Not Fade Away (Petty, Hardin) / It's All Over Now (Womack, Womack) / Live with Me / Let It Bleed / Beast of Burden / Angie / Wild Horses / Sweet Virginia / Dead Flowers / Still A Fool (Dixon) / Down in the Bottom (Dixon) / Shine a Light / Like a Rolling Stone (Dylan) / Jump on Top of Me / Connection / Before They Make Me Run / Slipping Away / Monkey Man / I Can't Get Next to You (Holland, Dozier, Holland) / All Down the Line / Street Fighting Man / **E1:** Rip This Joint / **E2:** Respectable

NOTES: "Jump on Top of Me," the B-side of the various "You Got Me Rocking" single releases and featured on the soundtrack of the Robert Altman film *Ready to Wear (Pret a Porter)* was performed for the first time at the second Paradiso show. Willie Dixon's "Still a Fool"—a *Beggars Banquet* outtake—was another live premiere and his "Down in the Bottom" (a.k.a. "Meet Me in the Bottom") was wildly received by those who remembered (or had heard of) the Stones last playing it—in 1964. It was an outtake from the Chess sessions that year. The evening ended with a two-song encore—"Rip This Joint" and "Respectable."

JUNE 31 – AUGUST 30, 1995

JUNE 3, 1995

TOUR: Voodoo Lounge (Part 2)—Europe
VENUE: Olympic Stadium, Stockholm, Sweden
OPENING/OTHER ACT(S): Robert Cray
SONGS: Not Fade Away (Petty, Hardin) / Tumbling Dice / You Got Me Rocking / Respectable / Rocks Off / Live with Me / Sparks Will Fly / (I Can't Get No) Satisfaction / Wild Horses / Like a Rolling Stone (Dylan) / Rock and a Hard Place / I Go Wild / Miss You / Honky Tonk Women / Before They Make Me Run / Slipping Away / Sympathy for the Devil / Monkey Man / Street Fighting Man / Start Me Up / It's Only Rock 'n' Roll / Brown Sugar / E: Jumpin' Jack Flash
NOTES: This was the first gig of the Voodoo Lounge (Part 2)—Europe tour, as the European portion was designated by the Stones organization. The setlist had some striking differences from Voodoo Lounge shows prior to the Paradiso Club, beginning with the addition of "Like a Rolling Stone." Robert Cray opened.

JUNE 6, 1995

TOUR: Voodoo Lounge (Part 2)—Europe
VENUE: Olympic Stadium, Helsinki, Finland
OPENING/OTHER ACT(S): Robert Cray
SONGS: Not Fade Away (Petty, Hardin) / Tumbling Dice / You Got Me Rocking / Rocks Off / Live with Me / Sparks Will Fly / (I Can't Get No) Satisfaction / Beast of Burden / Wild Horses / Like a Rolling Stone (Dylan) / Rock and a Hard Place / I Go Wild / Miss You / Honky Tonk Women / Before They Make Me Run / Slipping Away / Sympathy for the Devil / Gimme Shelter / Street Fighting Man / Start Me Up / It's Only Rock 'n' Roll / Brown Sugar / E: Jumpin' Jack Flash

JUNE 9, 1995

TOUR: Voodoo Lounge (Part 2)—Europe
VENUE: Valle Hovin, Oslo, Norway
OPENING/OTHER ACT(S): Robert Cray

SONGS: Not Fade Away (Petty, Hardin) / Tumbling Dice / You Got Me Rocking / All Down the Line / Live with Me / Sparks Will Fly / (I Can't Get No) Satisfaction / Let It Bleed / Wild Horses / Like a Rolling Stone (Dylan) / Doo Doo Doo Doo Doo (Heartbreaker) / I Go Wild / Miss You / Honky Tonk Women / Happy / The Worst / Sympathy for the Devil / Monkey Man / Street Fighting Man / Start Me Up / It's Only Rock 'n' Roll / Brown Sugar / E: Jumpin' Jack Flash

JUNE 11, 1995

TOUR: Voodoo Lounge (Part 2)—Europe
VENUE: Parken, Copenhagen, Denmark
OPENING/OTHER ACT(S): Robert Cray
SONGS: Not Fade Away (Petty, Hardin) / Tumbling Dice / You Got Me Rocking / Rocks Off / Live with Me / Sparks Will Fly / (I Can't Get No) Satisfaction / Sweet Virginia / Fool to Cry / Like a Rolling Stone (Dylan) / Doo Doo Doo Doo Doo (Heartbreaker) / I Go Wild / Miss You / Honky Tonk Women / Before They Make Me Run / Slipping Away / Sympathy for the Devil / Gimme Shelter / Street Fighting Man / Start Me Up / It's Only Rock 'n' Roll / Brown Sugar / E: Jumpin' Jack Flash
NOTES: An acoustic "Sweet Virginia" and the inclusion of "Fool to Cry" were setlist highlights at the Copenhagen show.

JUNE 13, 1995

TOUR: Voodoo Lounge (Part 2)—Europe
VENUE: Parc de Goffert, Nijmegen, The Netherlands
OPENING/OTHER ACT(S): Robert Cray
SONGS: Not Fade Away (Petty, Hardin) / Tumbling Dice / You Got Me Rocking / It's All Over Now (Womack, Womack) / Live with Me / Sparks Will Fly / (I Can't Get No) Satisfaction / Beast of Burden / Wild Horses / Like a Rolling Stone (Dylan) / Gimme Shelter / Rock and a Hard Place / I Go Wild / Miss You / Honky Tonk Women / Before They Make Me Run / The Worst / Sympathy for the Devil / Street Fighting Man / Start Me Up / It's Only Rock 'n' Roll / Brown Sugar / E: Jumpin' Jack Flash

JUNE 14, 1995

TOUR: Voodoo Lounge (Part 2)—Europe
VENUE: Parc de Goffert, Nijmegen, The Netherlands
OPENING/OTHER ACT(S): Robert Cray
SONGS: Not Fade Away (Petty, Hardin) / Tumbling Dice / You Got Me Rocking / All Down the Line / Live with Me / Sparks Will Fly / (I Can't Get No) Satisfaction / Beast of Burden / Fool to Cry / Like a Rolling Stone (Dylan) / Doo Doo Doo Doo Doo (Heartbreaker) /

Monkey Man / I Go Wild / Miss You / Honky Tonk Women / Happy / Slipping Away / Sympathy for the Devil / Street Fighting Man / Start Me Up / It's Only Rock 'n' Roll / Brown Sugar / **E:** Jumpin' Jack Flash
NOTES: Six songs in the set differed from those played the night before in Nijmegen.

JUNE 18, 1995

TOUR: Voodoo Lounge (Part 2)—Europe
VENUE: Pink Pop Site, Landgraaf, The Netherlands
OPENING/OTHER ACT(S): Robert Cray
SONGS: Not Fade Away (Petty, Hardin) / Tumbling Dice / You Got Me Rocking / Rocks Off / Live with Me / Sparks Will Fly / (I Can't Get No) Satisfaction / Love Is Strong / Love in Vain (Robt. Johnson), AV / Like a Rolling Stone (Dylan) / Rock and a Hard Place / Gimme Shelter / I Go Wild / Miss You / Honky Tonk Women / Before They Make Me Run / Slipping Away / Sympathy for the Devil / Street Fighting Man / Start Me Up / It's Only Rock 'n' Roll / Brown Sugar / **E:** Jumpin' Jack Flash
NOTES: The evening was marked, though not marred from most reports, by intermittent heavy rain.

JUNE 20, 1995

TOUR: Voodoo Lounge (Part 2)—Europe
VENUE: Mungersdorfer-Stadion, Cologne, Germany
OPENING/OTHER ACT(S): The Tragically Hip
SONGS: Not Fade Away (Petty, Hardin) / Tumbling Dice / You Got Me Rocking / It's All Over Now (Womack, Womack) / Live with Me / Sparks Will Fly / (I Can't Get No) Satisfaction / Beast of Burden / Wild Horses / Like a Rolling Stone (Dylan) / Rock and a Hard Place / Monkey Man / I Go Wild / Miss You / Honky Tonk Women / Happy / Slipping Away / Sympathy for the Devil / Street Fighting Man / Start Me Up / It's Only Rock 'n' Roll / Brown Sugar / **E:** Jumpin' Jack Flash

JUNE 22, 1995

TOUR: Voodoo Lounge (Part 2)—Europe
VENUE: Niedersachsen-Stadion, Hannover, Germany
OPENING/OTHER ACT(S): The Tragically Hip
SONGS: Not Fade Away (Petty, Hardin) / Tumbling Dice / You Got Me Rocking / It's All Over Now (Womack, Womack) / Live with Me / Sparks Will Fly / (I Can't Get No) Satisfaction / Beast of Burden / Angie / Like a Rolling Stone (Dylan) / Rock and a Hard Place / Monkey Man / I Go Wild / Miss You / Honky Tonk Women / Before They Make Me Run / The Worst / Sympathy for the Devil / Street Fighting Man / Start Me Up / It's Only Rock 'n' Roll / Brown Sugar / Jumpin' Jack Flash

JUNE 24, 1995

TOUR: Voodoo Lounge (Part 2)—Europe
VENUE: Werchter Festival Ground, Werchter, Belgium
OPENING/OTHER ACT(S): The Tragically Hip
SONGS: Not Fade Away (Petty, Hardin) / Tumbling Dice / You Got Me Rocking / It's All Over Now (Womack, Womack) / Rocks Off / Sparks Will Fly / (I Can't Get No) Satisfaction / Let It Bleed / Angie / Like a Rolling Stone (Dylan) / Doo Doo Doo Doo Doo (Heartbreaker) / Gimme Shelter / I Go Wild / Miss You / Honky Tonk Women / Before They Make Me Run / Slipping Away / Sympathy for the Devil / Street Fighting Man / Start Me Up / It's Only Rock 'n' Roll / Brown Sugar / Jumpin' Jack Flash

JUNE 25, 1995

TOUR: Voodoo Lounge (Part 2)—Europe
VENUE: Werchter Festival Ground, Werchter, Belgium
OPENING/OTHER ACT(S): The Tragically Hip
SONGS: Not Fade Away (Petty, Hardin) / Tumbling Dice / You Got Me Rocking / It's All Over Now (Womack, Womack) / Live with Me / Sparks Will Fly / (I Can't Get No) Satisfaction / Beast of Burden / Angie / Like a Rolling Stone (Dylan) / Doo Doo Doo Doo Doo (Heartbreaker) / Monkey Man / I Go Wild / Miss You / Honky Tonk Women / Happy / The Worst / Sympathy for the Devil / Street Fighting Man / Start Me Up / It's Only Rock 'n' Roll / Brown Sugar / Jumpin' Jack Flash
NOTES: This second show in Werchter was a late addition to the tour itinerary, after proposed concerts in Italy were cancelled and tickets for the previous night's show sold out quickly. This outdoor venue was filled to its 70,000 capacity both evenings.

JUNE 30, 1995

TOUR: Voodoo Lounge (Part 2)—Europe
VENUE: Hippodrome de Longchamps, Paris, France
OPENING/OTHER ACT(S): Bon Jovi, Eric LaPointe
SONGS: Not Fade Away (Petty, Hardin) / Tumbling Dice / You Got Me Rocking / It's All Over Now (Womack, Womack) / Live with Me / Sparks Will Fly / (I Can't Get No) Satisfaction / Beast of Burden / Angie / Like a Rolling Stone (Dylan) / Rock and a Hard Place / Gimme Shelter / I Go Wild / Miss You / Honky Tonk Women / Connection / Slipping Away / Sympathy for the Devil / Street Fighting Man / Start Me Up / Brown Sugar / Jumpin' Jack Flash
NOTES: Eric LaPointe was the first to perform, then Bon Jovi opened for the Stones.

JULY 1, 1995

TOUR: Voodoo Lounge (Part 2)—Europe

VENUE: Hippodrome de Longchamps, Paris, France

OPENING/OTHER ACT(S): Bon Jovi, Eric LaPointe

SONGS: Not Fade Away (Petty, Hardin) / Tumbling Dice / You Got Me Rocking / It's All Over Now (Womack, Womack) / Rocks Off / Sparks Will Fly / (I Can't Get No) Satisfaction / Beast of Burden / Angie / Like a Rolling Stone (Dylan) / Doo Doo Doo Doo Doo (Heartbreaker) / Monkey Man / I Go Wild / Miss You / Honky Tonk Women / Before They Make Me Run / The Worst / Sympathy for the Devil / Street Fighting Man / Start Me Up / It's Only Rock 'n' Roll / Brown Sugar / Jumpin' Jack Flash

NOTES: French artist Eric LaPointe and band preceded Bon Jovi on the opening bill. The Stones' show took place almost entirely in the rain, which began falling torrentially with "Tumbling Dice," and continued in varying amounts before finally tapering off with "Sympathy for the Devil."

JULY 3, 1995

TOUR: Voodoo Lounge (Part 2)—Europe

VENUE: Olympia Theatre, Paris, France

OPENING/OTHER ACT(S): Eric LaPointe, La Place

SONGS: Honky Tonk Women / Tumbling Dice / You Got Me Rocking / All Down the Line / Shattered / Beast of Burden / Let It Bleed / Angie / Wild Horses / Down in the Bottom (Dixon) / Shine a Light / Like a Rolling Stone (Dylan) / I Go Wild / Miss You / Connection / Slipping Away / Midnight Rambler / Rip This Joint / Start Me Up / It's Only Rock 'n' Roll / Brown Sugar / Jumpin' Jack Flash

NOTES: Announced only a week before the date, the Stones returned after 28 years to perform again at l'Olympia. The lucky and the plucky who braved an all-night wait to buy tickets/wristbands at the Champs Elysees Virgin Megastore on July 2, attended a unique show in the 4,000-seat theater. In a departure from other live performances, Ron Wood opened "Let It Bleed" with the slide guitar riff heard on studio recordings of the song. Keith sang "Connection" as a solo vocalist—not in the usual duet with Mick. "Midnight Rambler" was a special, long version. And, as with the other small shows on the tour, the Stones did *not* play "Satisfaction."

JULY 9, 1995

TOUR: Voodoo Lounge (Part 2)—Europe

VENUE: Don Valley Stadium, Sheffield, South Yorkshire, England

OPENING/OTHER ACT(S): Del Amitri

SONGS: Not Fade Away (Petty, Hardin) / Tumbling Dice / You Got Me Rocking / It's All Over Now (Womack, Womack) / Rocks Off / Sparks Will Fly / (I Can't Get No) Satisfaction / Beast of Burden / Angie / Like a Rolling Stone (Dylan) / Rock and a Hard Place / Gimme Shelter / I Go Wild / Miss You / Honky Tonk Women / Connection / Slipping Away / Sympathy for the Devil / Street Fighting Man / Start Me Up / It's Only Rock 'n' Roll / Brown Sugar / Jumpin' Jack Flash

NOTES: The first UK concert of Voodoo Lounge. A Scottish band, Del Amitri, opened this concert in the newly constructed stadium in the north of England.

JULY 11, 1995

TOUR: Voodoo Lounge (Part 2)—Europe

VENUE: Wembley Stadium, Wembley, Middlesex, England

OPENING/OTHER ACT(S): The Black Crowes

SONGS: Not Fade Away (Petty, Hardin) / Tumbling Dice / You Got Me Rocking / It's All Over Now (Womack, Womack) / Live with Me / Sparks Will Fly / (I Can't Get No) Satisfaction / Sweet Virginia / Wild Horses / Like a Rolling Stone (Dylan) / Rock and a Hard Place / Gimme Shelter / I Go Wild / Miss You / Honky Tonk Women / Connection / The Worst / Sympathy for the Devil / Street Fighting Man / Start Me Up / It's Only Rock 'n' Roll / Brown Sugar / Jumpin' Jack Flash

NOTES: The first of three Wembley dates.

JULY 15, 1995

TOUR: Voodoo Lounge (Part 2)—Europe

VENUE: Wembley Stadium, Wembley, Middlesex, England

OPENING/OTHER ACT(S): The Black Crowes

SONGS: Not Fade Away (Petty, Hardin) / Tumbling Dice / You Got Me Rocking / It's All Over Now (Womack, Womack) / Love Is Strong / Sparks Will Fly / Beast of Burden / Angie / Like a Rolling Stone (Dylan) / Doo Doo Doo Doo Doo (Heartbreaker) / Gimme Shelter / I Go Wild / Miss You / Honky Tonk Women / Before They Make Me Run / Slipping Away / Sympathy for the Devil / Street Fighting Man / Start Me Up / It's Only Rock 'n' Roll / Brown Sugar / Jumpin' Jack Flash

JULY 16, 1995

TOUR: Voodoo Lounge (Part 2)—Europe

VENUE: Wembley Stadium, Wembley, Middlesex, England

OPENING/OTHER ACT(S): The Black Crowes

SONGS: Not Fade Away (Petty, Hardin) / Tumbling Dice / You Got Me Rocking / It's All Over Now (Womack, Womack) / All Down the Line / Sparks Will Fly / (I Can't Get No) Satisfaction / Beast of Burden /

Wild Horses / Like a Rolling Stone (Dylan) / Rock and a Hard Place / Monkey Man / I Go Wild / Miss You / Honky Tonk Women / Happy / Slipping Away / Sympathy for the Devil / Street Fighting Man / Start Me Up / It's Only Rock 'n' Roll / Brown Sugar / Jumpin' Jack Flash

NOTES: This was the first time since 1962 that Bill Wyman had seen the Rolling Stones perform. The band's former bassist and his wife Suzanne sat in the royal box at this third and final Wembley concert. Onstage (other than enough special effects smoke to obscure the stage for the first half of "Not Fade Away"), there were few real surprises, merely a rock 'n' roll show honed to a fine edge by nearly a year on the road performed by a band having what appeared to be a real good time. "Satisfaction" featured an intense Keith Richards guitar solo. Jagger took his own high-energy performance of the song down into the field-level audience, cranking up the already hyper hometown crowd. "See you in Brixton," were Mick's closing words after "Jumpin' Jack Flash," referring to the Stones' final Voodoo Lounge gig in the UK three days later, which only 3,000 fans could see. Afterward, tales were told of Stones fans leaving Wembley Sunday night to queue up for the coveted Brixton tickets, which went on sale Tuesday morning. Of course, there also were stories of happy Brixton ticketholders who had arrived 40 minutes before the windows opened that day. . . .

JULY 19, 1995

TOUR: Voodoo Lounge (Part 2)—Europe

VENUE: Brixton Academy, Brixton, London, England

OPENING/OTHER ACT(S): Reef

SONGS: Honky Tonk Women / Tumbling Dice / You Got Me Rocking / Live with Me / Black Limousine (Jagger, Richards, Wood) / Dead Flowers / Sweet Virginia / Far Away Eyes / Love in Vain (Robt. Johnson) / Down in the Bottom (Dixon) / Shine a Light / Like a Rolling Stone (Dylan) / Monkey Man / I Go Wild / Miss You / Connection / Slipping Away / Midnight Rambler / Rip This Joint / Start Me Up / Brown Sugar / Jumpin' Jack Flash

NOTES: This "surprise" small show at the domed, down-at-the-heels South London Brixton Academy theater was the hot ticket during the UK portion of Voodoo Lounge. General admission (standing) floor level tickets and mandatory wristbands (one set per customer) were sold the day before to some 3,500 fans, many of whom had camped out all night at the single sales point, the Virgin Records Megastore at Oxford Street and Tottenham Court Road. In saying "See you in Brixton," at the end of the July 16 Wembley concert, Mick Jagger had semi-offhandedly confirmed the fan-grapevine rumor of a Brixton show. There was no official announcement, nor

was there any indication of where to purchase tickets until the morning of the 18th. An additional 800 balcony seats were filled by corporate, music-industry, and band-related types. The house was packed and sweltering on an unusually hot day for London; the temperature was nearly 90°F. It was an atypical '90s event, anyway, more akin to Stones shows of the '60s; that is, low-key on glitz and high on excitement. Celebrities like Jack Nicholson were present, but not obviously. Jerry Hall with son James and daughter Elizabeth Jagger, accompanied by Bob Geldof and other friends, trouped through the queue of ticketholders encircling the building and entered via the stage door. Both Marianne Faithfull and Anita Pallenberg (plus offspring Marlon and Angela Richards) were in the audience as well as Mick's brother, Chris Jagger, and both of Keith Richards's parents. Reef, a young UK rock 'n' roll band, opened for the Stones, who came onstage only 20 minutes after their advertised start time. The funky stage was nearly bare, set and lighting design was minimal, consisting only of a Voodoo Lounge-style animal print swag curtain and a couple of drops. Minimal, but highly focused and effective. The entire show was filmed and recorded, a continuation of the band's production of their as yet unnamed "unplugged"/live CD scheduled for an October 1995 release. And the crowd was alive. Fainting fans were carried out regularly from the beginning of "Honky Tonk Women," whether from excitement or the heat, or both.

JULY 22, 1995

TOUR: Voodoo Lounge (Part 2)—Europe

VENUE: El Molinon, Gijon, Spain

SONGS: Not Fade Away (Petty, Hardin) / Tumbling Dice / You Got Me Rocking / It's All Over Now (Womack, Womack) / Rocks Off / Sparks Will Fly / (I Can't Get No) Satisfaction / Beast of Burden / Angie / Like a Rolling Stone (Dylan) / Rock and a Hard Place / Gimme Shelter / I Go Wild / Miss You / Honky Tonk Women / Before They Make Me Run / Slipping Away / Sympathy for the Devil / Street Fighting Man / Start Me Up / It's Only Rock 'n' Roll / Brown Sugar / Jumpin' Jack Flash

JULY 24, 1995

TOUR: Voodoo Lounge (Part 2)—Europe

VENUE: Estadio Jose Alvalade, Lisbon, Portugal

SONGS: Not Fade Away (Petty, Hardin) / Tumbling Dice / You Got Me Rocking / It's All Over Now (Womack, Womack) / Live with Me / Sparks Will Fly / (I Can't Get No) Satisfaction / Beast of Burden / Angie / Like a Rolling Stone (Dylan) / Doo Doo Doo Doo Doo (Heartbreaker) / Gimme Shelter / I Go Wild / Miss You / Honky Tonk Women / Happy / Slipping Away / Sympathy for the Devil / Street Fighting Man / Start Me

Up / It's Only Rock 'n' Roll / Brown Sugar / Jumpin' Jack Flash

JULY 27, 1995

TOUR: Voodoo Lounge (Part 2)—Europe
VENUE: Amphitheatre du Chateau Grammont, Montpellier, France
SPECIAL GUESTS: Bob Dylan
OPENING/OTHER ACT(S): Bob Dylan, The Black Crowes
SONGS: Not Fade Away (Petty, Hardin) / Tumbling Dice / You Got Me Rocking / It's All Over Now (Womack, Womack) / All Down the Line / Sparks Will Fly / (I Can't Get No) Satisfaction / Let It Bleed / Angie / Like a Rolling Stone (Dylan) / Rock and a Hard Place / Gimme Shelter / I Go Wild / Miss You / Honky Tonk Women / Connection / The Worst / Sympathy for the Devil / Start Me Up / It's Only Rock 'n' Roll / Brown Sugar / Jumpin' Jack Flash
NOTES: Bob Dylan's appearance as the Stones' opening act (following the Black Crowes) was a first, and anticipation of his guesting with the boys on "Like a Rolling Stone" was rewarded. Though he appeared reluctant to do so, Dylan sang the song's second verse with Jagger.

JULY 29, 1995

TOUR: Voodoo Lounge (Part 2)—Europe
VENUE: Fussballstadion St. Jakob, Basel, Switzerland
OPENING/OTHER ACT(S): The Black Crowes
SONGS: Not Fade Away (Petty, Hardin) / Tumbling Dice / You Got Me Rocking / It's All Over Now (Womack, Womack) / Sparks Will Fly / (I Can't Get No) Satisfaction / Beast of Burden / Let It Bleed / Angie / Like a Rolling Stone (Dylan) / Rock and a Hard Place / Monkey Man / I Go Wild / Miss You / Honky Tonk Women / Before They Make Me Run / Slipping Away / Sympathy for the Devil / Street Fighting Man / Start Me Up / It's Only Rock 'n' Roll / Brown Sugar / Jumpin' Jack Flash
NOTES: The Black Crowes' keyboard player joined Chuck Leavell on keyboards during "Start Me Up."

JULY 30, 1995

TOUR: Voodoo Lounge (Part 2)—Europe
VENUE: Fussballstadion St. Jakob Stadion, Basel, Switzerland
OPENING/OTHER ACT(S): The Black Crowes
SONGS: Not Fade Away (Petty, Hardin) / Tumbling Dice / You Got Me Rocking / It's All Over Now (Womack, Womack) / Sparks Will Fly / (I Can't Get No) Satisfaction / Sweet Virginia / Angie / Shine a Light / Like a Rolling Stone (Dylan) / Doo Doo Doo Doo Doo (Heartbreaker) / Gimme Shelter / I Go Wild / Miss You

/ Honky Tonk Women / Connection / The Worst / Sympathy for the Devil / Street Fighting Man / Start Me Up / It's Only Rock 'n' Roll / Brown Sugar / Jumpin' Jack Flash
NOTES: Keyboardist Chuck Leavell sat in with the Black Crowes and their keyboard player returned the favor on the Stones' "Start Me Up." Andy Snitzer left his saxophone to play keyboards on "Angie" and "Shine a Light."

AUGUST 1, 1995

TOUR: Voodoo Lounge (Part 2)—Europe
VENUE: Osterreich Ring, Zeltweg, Austria
OPENING/OTHER ACT(S): Andrew Strong
SONGS: Not Fade Away (Petty, Hardin) / Tumbling Dice / You Got Me Rocking / It's All Over Now (Womack, Womack) / Sparks Will Fly / (I Can't Get No) Satisfaction / Beast of Burden / Let It Bleed / Angie / Like a Rolling Stone (Dylan) / Rock and a Hard Place / Gimme Shelter / I Go Wild / Miss You / Honky Tonk Women / Connection / Slipping Away / Sympathy for the Devil / Street Fighting Man / Start Me Up / It's Only Rock 'n' Roll / Brown Sugar / Jumpin' Jack Flash

AUGUST 3, 1995

TOUR: Voodoo Lounge (Part 2)—Europe
VENUE: Olympiastadion, Munich, Germany
OPENING/OTHER ACT(S): Andrew Strong
SONGS: Not Fade Away (Petty, Hardin) / Tumbling Dice / You Got Me Rocking / It's All Over Now (Womack, Womack) / Sparks Will Fly / (I Can't Get No) Satisfaction / Beast of Burden / Angie / Shine a Light / Like a Rolling Stone (Dylan) / Rock and a Hard Place / Monkey Man / I Go Wild / Miss You / Honky Tonk Women / Connection / Slipping Away / Sympathy for the Devil / Street Fighting Man / Start Me Up / It's Only Rock 'n' Roll / Brown Sugar / Jumpin' Jack Flash

AUGUST 5, 1995

TOUR: Voodoo Lounge (Part 2)—Europe
VENUE: Stadion Praha-Strahov, Prague, Czech Republic
OPENING/OTHER ACT(S): Andrew Strong
SONGS: Not Fade Away (Petty, Hardin) / Tumbling Dice / You Got Me Rocking / It's All Over Now (Womack, Womack) / Sparks Will Fly / (I Can't Get No) Satisfaction / Beast of Burden / Sweet Virginia / Angie / Like a Rolling Stone (Dylan) / Rock and a Hard Place / Gimme Shelter / I Go Wild / Miss You / Honky Tonk Women / Connection / Slipping Away / Sympathy for the Devil / Street Fighting Man / Start Me Up / It's Only Rock 'n' Roll / Brown Sugar / Jumpin' Jack Flash
NOTES: Czech President and Stones fan Vaclav Havel attended this show.

AUGUST 8, 1995

TOUR: Voodoo Lounge (Part 2)—Europe
VENUE: Nepstadion, Budapest, Hungary
OPENING/OTHER ACT(S): Andrew Strong, Takacs Tamas Dirty Blues Band
SONGS: Not Fade Away (Petty, Hardin) / Tumbling Dice / You Got Me Rocking / It's All Over Now (Womack, Womack) / Sparks Will Fly / (I Can't Get No) Satisfaction / Beast of Burden / Angie / Like a Rolling Stone (Dylan) / Doo Doo Doo Doo Doo (Heartbreaker) / Gimme Shelter / I Go Wild / Miss You / Honky Tonk Women / Before They Make Me Run / Slipping Away / Sympathy for the Devil / Street Fighting Man / Start Me Up / It's Only Rock 'n' Roll / Brown Sugar / Jumpin' Jack Flash
NOTES: The lead singer of first opening act, the Takacs Tamas Dirty Blues Band, was a guy named Hobo, dubbed the "Hungarian Jagger."

AUGUST 12, 1995

TOUR: Voodoo Lounge (Part 2)—Europe
VENUE: Festival Site, Schuettorf, Germany
OPENING/OTHER ACT(S): Aktion Direkt, Rudiger Hoffmann, Big Country, Jimmy Barnes
SONGS: Not Fade Away (Petty, Hardin) / Tumbling Dice / You Got Me Rocking / It's All Over Now (Womack, Womack) / Sparks Will Fly / (I Can't Get No) Satisfaction / Beast of Burden / Angie / Shine a Light / Like a Rolling Stone (Dylan) / Rock and a Hard Place / Monkey Man / I Go Wild / Miss You / Honky Tonk Women / Connection / Slipping Away / Sympathy for the Devil / Street Fighting Man / Start Me Up / It's Only Rock 'n' Roll / Brown Sugar / Jumpin' Jack Flash
NOTES: Four opening acts.

AUGUST 15, 1995

TOUR: Voodoo Lounge (Part 2)—Europe
VENUE: Festwiese am Zentralstadion, Leipzig, Germany
OPENING/OTHER ACT(S): Big Country
SONGS: Not Fade Away (Petty, Hardin) / Tumbling Dice / You Got Me Rocking / It's All Over Now (Womack, Womack) / Sparks Will Fly / (I Can't Get No) Satisfaction / Beast of Burden / Let It Bleed / Angie / Like a Rolling Stone (Dylan) / Doo Doo Doo Doo Doo (Heartbreaker) / Gimme Shelter / I Go Wild / Miss You / Honky Tonk Women / Connection / Slipping Away / Sympathy for the Devil / Street Fighting Man / Start Me Up / It's Only Rock 'n' Roll / Brown Sugar / Jumpin' Jack Flash

AUGUST 17, 1995

TOUR: Voodoo Lounge (Part 2)—Europe

VENUE: Olympiastadion, Berlin, Germany
OPENING/OTHER ACT(S): Big Country
SONGS: Not Fade Away (Petty, Hardin) / Tumbling Dice / You Got Me Rocking / It's All Over Now (Womack, Womack) / Sparks Will Fly / (I Can't Get No) Satisfaction / Beast of Burden / Shine a Light / Angie / Like a Rolling Stone (Dylan) / Rock and a Hard Place / Monkey Man / I Go Wild / Miss You / Honky Tonk Women / Connection / Slipping Away / Sympathy for the Devil / Street Fighting Man / Start Me Up / It's Only Rock 'n' Roll / Brown Sugar / Jumpin' Jack Flash

AUGUST 19, 1995

TOUR: Voodoo Lounge (Part 2)—Europe
VENUE: Hockenheimring, Hockenheim, Germany
OPENING/OTHER ACT(S): Big Country
SONGS: Not Fade Away (Petty, Hardin) / Tumbling Dice / You Got Me Rocking / It's All Over Now (Womack, Womack) / Sparks Will Fly / (I Can't Get No) Satisfaction / Beast of Burden / Sweet Virginia / Angie / Like a Rolling Stone (Dylan) / Rock and a Hard Place / Gimme Shelter / I Go Wild / Miss You / Honky Tonk Women / Before They Make Me Run / Slipping Away / Sympathy for the Devil / Street Fighting Man / Start Me Up / It's Only Rock 'n' Roll / Brown Sugar / Jumpin' Jack Flash

AUGUST 22, 1995

TOUR: Voodoo Lounge (Part 2)—Europe
VENUE: Maimarkt, Mannheim, Germany
OPENING/OTHER ACT(S): Big Country
SONGS: Not Fade Away (Petty, Hardin) / Tumbling Dice / You Got Me Rocking / Rocks Off / Sparks Will Fly / (I Can't Get No) Satisfaction / Beast of Burden / Wild Horses / Dead Flowers / Like a Rolling Stone (Dylan) / Doo Doo Doo Doo Doo (Heartbreaker) / Gimme Shelter / I Go Wild / Miss You / Honky Tonk Women / Connection / The Worst / Sympathy for the Devil / Street Fighting Man / Start Me Up / It's Only Rock 'n' Roll / Brown Sugar / Jumpin' Jack Flash

AUGUST 25, 1995

TOUR: Voodoo Lounge (Part 2)—Europe
VENUE: Volkswagen Festival Site, Wolfsburg, Germany
OPENING/OTHER ACT(S): Big Country, Andrew Strong
SONGS: Not Fade Away (Petty, Hardin) / Tumbling Dice / You Got Me Rocking / It's All Over Now (Womack, Womack) / Sparks Will Fly / (I Can't Get No) Satisfaction / Beast of Burden / Shine A Light / Angie / Like a Rolling Stone (Dylan) / Rock and a Hard Place / Monkey Man / I Go Wild / Miss You / Honky Tonk Women / Connection / Slipping Away / Sympathy for

the Devil / Street Fighting Man / Start Me Up / It's Only Rock 'n' Roll / Brown Sugar / Jumpin' Jack Flash

NOTES: Some 90,000 fans attended this concert in what was actually one of the Volkswagen factory's parking lots. Wolfsburg is a company town near what used to be the East/West German border.

AUGUST 27, 1995

TOUR: Voodoo Lounge (Part 2)—Europe

VENUE: Kirchberg Stadium, Luxembourg City, Luxembourg

OPENING/OTHER ACT(S): Big Country

SONGS: Not Fade Away (Petty, Hardin) / Tumbling Dice / You Got Me Rocking / It's All Over Now (Womack, Womack) / Sparks Will Fly / (I Can't Get No) Satisfaction / Beast of Burden / Angie / Like a Rolling Stone (Dylan) / Rock and a Hard Place / Gimme Shelter / I Go Wild / Miss You / Honky Tonk Women / Happy / Slipping Away / Sympathy for the Devil / Street Fighting Man / Start Me Up / It's Only Rock 'n' Roll / Brown Sugar / Jumpin' Jack Flash

NOTES: The setlist was only 22 songs.

AUGUST 29, 1995

TOUR: Voodoo Lounge (Part 2)—Europe

VENUE: Feyenoord Stadium, Rotterdam, The Netherlands

OPENING/OTHER ACT(S): Big Country

SONGS: Not Fade Away (Petty, Hardin) / Tumbling Dice / You Got Me Rocking / Shattered / Sparks Will Fly / (I Can't Get No) Satisfaction / Let It Bleed / Angie / Shine a Light / Like a Rolling Stone (Dylan) / Rock and a Hard Place / Monkey Man / I Go Wild / Miss You / Honky Tonk Women / Connection / Slipping Away / Sympathy for the Devil / Street Fighting Man / Start Me Up / It's Only Rock 'n' Roll / Brown Sugar / Jumpin' Jack Flash

NOTES: This concert was broadcast on Belgian radio. It was the penultimate show of Voodoo Lounge, despite persistent rumors (based on wishful thinking and a few seemingly well-founded factoids) that the tour would continue into indoor arena-sized venues in North America in early 1996. The June and July issues of the US fanzine, *Beggars Banquet*, reported that the Stones were considering this option, but broke the bad news on August 11. The Stones, said the *Banquet*, held a band meeting in London on July 20, the day after their Brixton show. They decided that while they might do some '96 dates in Asia and South America, they wouldn't be appearing at Madison Square Garden in January or February (or elsewhere in the US), as had been the summertime buzz along the international fan network.

AUGUST 30, 1995

TOUR: Voodoo Lounge (Part 2)—Europe

VENUE: Feyenoord Stadium, Rotterdam, The Netherlands

OPENING/OTHER ACT(S): Big Country

SONGS: Not Fade Away (Petty, Hardin) / Tumbling Dice / You Got Me Rocking / It's All Over Now (Womack, Womack) / Sparks Will Fly / (I Can't Get No) Satisfaction / Dead Flowers / Far Away Eyes / Like a Rolling Stone (Dylan) / Gimme Shelter / Midnight Rambler / I Go Wild / Miss You / Honky Tonk Women / Happy / Slipping Away / Sympathy for the Devil / Street Fighting Man / Start Me Up / It's Only Rock 'n' Roll / Brown Sugar / **E**: Jumpin' Jack Flash

NOTES: There were only 22 songs in the last setlist of Voodoo Lounge, possibly because this particular "Midnight Rambler" rumbled on for some 11 minutes. Neither that song nor "Far Away Eyes" had been played in stadium Voodoo Lounge shows in Europe—both were major surprises. But the most surprised that night might have been the band, during "Honky Tonk Women." A group of women they knew well came out to dance in the pit in front of the stage—Stones staff members and Ronnie's daughter (Jerry Hall and Jo Wood were spotted in the wings)—wearing costumes ranging from not too much to the garb of a Dutch farm woman.

1997–1998

1997–1998

TOUR: Bridges to Babylon—World tour

NOTES: At press time, the Rolling Stones held a press conference to announce their plans for a year-long world tour and the concurrent release of their new album, both entitled "Bridges to Babylon." On August 18, 1997, the band crossed the Brooklyn Bridge in a 1955 red Cadillac convertible (with Jagger at the wheel) and, with Manhattan as a backdrop, spoke to the media from a stage set up beneath the century-old landmark span. Sprint, the telecommunications giant, sponsored the tour, and the company's CEO was present at the press conference.

Kicking off with a concert on September 23, 1997 at Soldier Field in Chicago, the North American portion of the Bridges to Babylon tour was scheduled to continue through February 1998, with dates in Canada, the United States (including Hawaii) and Mexico City. The band stated that it hoped to then proceed further into Latin America, the Far East and Australia, and later to Europe, although no precise dates for these performances were finalized. Despite earlier rumors of many small shows, the official itinerary of some 30 concerts listed primarily stadium-size venues, with the smallest being the MGM

Grand Garden Arena (c. 5,000 seats) in Las Vegas. It should be noted, however, that as usual, the official itinerary announced at the press conference was expected to change as additional dates became finalized. Opening acts announced for the US leg of the tour included Blues Traveler, the Dave Matthews Band, Foo Fighters, Sheryl Crow and Smashing Pumpkins.

Sessionography

Recording sessions are listed chronologically. Relevant details are included for each entry, broken down into the following categories:

DATE   (or date range)
LOCATION   following the date, indicating the studio or live performance where the listed songs were recorded
SONG(S)   of officially released and unreleased titles (*unreleased song are in italics*) along with version numbers where applicable.

Multiple versions, both studio (V1, V2, etc.) and live (LV1, LV2), exist of many Stones songs, particularly the well-known titles. The differences, beyond the obvious distinctions of "studio" and "live," vary greatly in amount and characteristics, and many are not apparent except to the serious collector. In the early years, US and UK records occasionally contained different versions of the same song: one studio version might include a guitar (for example, "2120 South Michigan Avenue" [Nanker Phelge]) or other instrumental solo while another might not; a song's introduction on one album might differ from the same title on another album or single (for example, "Time Is on My Side"); or the UK version might be two minutes longer than the US version, which may have been edited to conform to American recording technology, perceived tastes, or a record label's marketing strategy.

Throughout the Stones' history, selected additional mixes or truly different tracks of a particular song or collection of songs in general release have been specially released to radio stations, jukeboxes, limited editions or promotion. This adds to an already complicated situation, of course. A few songs have been recorded more than once, in different studios and on different dates, and the resulting tracks released during the same time period. Or, as has happened often in the later years, as many as six takes of one title have come from the same session but have been released in a plethora of formats and combinations with other songs over a longer period. Some versions are more alike than others, and there are easily as many reasons for, and even false claims of, the existence of multiples as there are (official Rolling Stones) versions. It is a confusing subject at best, and we have endeavored to sort it out once and for all.

Where songs (and multiple versions) are listed, they correspond exactly to our listings of titles released on official records (as found in the DISCOGRAPHY) or to known unreleased tracks and outtakes from particular sessions, but not to spurious recordings that have merely found their way onto illegal (bootleg) releases. Similarly, rumored and/or unverifiable tracks or sessions are not listed. To find the source session of a specific version number, simply match the numbers using the INDEX. If it is a live song (LV), the session location will have (Live) in its name. "TV" after a song title indicates a version recorded for television, "PV" indicates a song recorded for a promotional video, and "WT" indicates a working title.

PERSONNEL In general, this category will not be listed, except when there were changes in the group's membership, as when Mick Taylor replaced Brian Jones, or during periods of transition. During the year after Taylor's resignation, however, Ron Wood worked with the Stones in the studio and on tour but not as an official Rolling Stone (he was still a member of The Faces). Hence, during 1975 Wood is listed under Additional Personnel. In this manner, we have attempted to further clarify the band's history.

ADDITIONAL PERSONNEL Non-Stones musicians present and contributing to a particular session or live performance.

PRODUCER(S) If this category and that of Engineer are not present in a listing, either there were none or the names are unknown.

ENGINEER(S) This refers to recording engineers, though if a mixing engineer's name is relevant, it will also be found here.

NOTES: We have provided specific information that will be of interest, either for further clarification of prior categories or to bring to light little-known details of that particular recording session. In addition, some of the facts in Notes may help to resolve many of the raging arguments that have captivated Stones afficionados over the past 30 years and set the historical record straight.

1962

SEPTEMBER 29, 1962[*]
CURLY CLAYTON SOUND STUDIOS,
LONDON, ENGLAND

SONGS: *You Can't Judge a Book (by Looking at the Cover* (Dixon) / *Soon Forgotten* (Oden) / *Close Together* (Reed)
PERSONNEL: Mick Jagger, Keith Richards, Brian Jones, Dick Taylor, Tony Chapman, Ian Stewart
PRODUCER: Curly Clayton/Rolling Stones
ENGINEER: Curly Clayton
NOTES: Live studio recording—no mixing, overdubbing, or other frills. The nucleus of the group that would become the Rolling Stones in their first recording session. Tony Chapman was on drums, Dick Taylor was on bass —he had not yet left the group to prepare for entrance to the Royal School of Art (a decision he made at the end of September as well as returning to his studies at Sidcup College).

1963

MARCH 11, 1963
IBC STUDIOS, PORTLAND PLACE,
LONDON, ENGLAND

SONGS: *Road Runner* (McDaniel) / *Diddley Daddy* (McDaniel, Faqua) / *I Want to Be Loved* (Dixon), V1 / *Honey What's Wrong?* (Dixon) / *Bright Lights, Big City* (Reed)
PERSONNEL: Mick Jagger, Keith Richards, Brian Jones, Charlie Watts, Bill Wyman, Ian Stewart
PRODUCER: Glyn Johns
ENGINEER: Glyn Johns
NOTES: This was the band's first professional recording session and came as a direct result of their meeting Glyn Johns. It was Glyn who booked the Stones into the Red Lion Pub in Surrey in November 1962. Earlier that year, Johns had persuaded the pub's owner that live music on Friday evenings would be good for business and that he should hire the Presidents—the group that Glyn managed —to appear each week. After a while, the Presidents got so busy that they couldn't keep up the weekly schedule, began missing gigs and the landlord threatened to cancel the live music altogether. Ian Stewart, who just happened to be Glyn's flatmate, suggested that Glyn hire his band—the Stones—to play a "Rhythm & Blues Night" every other Friday at the Red Lion. Though Glyn made a record or two of his own during the "British Invasion" period, he'd occasionally sing with the Presidents, his ambition was decidedly focused toward producing and recording others and he had a day job as a recording engineer at IBC Studios in London. After a couple of months of Red Lion gigs, Glyn offered the Stones his studio expertise for this session at IBC. This was the start of a long-standing association with the band; it was not exactly a smooth takeoff, however. At the beginning of May 1963, Glyn chanced to run into the band outside IBC. Unbeknownst to him, the Stones had just bought back the tape from this session on the advice of their new managers, Easton and Oldham. When Johns learned he'd been out of the loop, he was miffed, to say the least. It was some seven months before he'd associate with the Stones again. Nevertheless, Glyn would eventually assume a much larger role in the Stones' recordings and the friendship exists to this day. (See also TOURS AND CONCERTS, DISCOGRAPHY, CHRONOLOGY)

---

[*]The date is approximate. Earlier histories have placed this session on October 27, and the acetates made from this session's tapes may have carried that date. However, Taylor has confirmed his presence at Curly Clayton's as well as his status with the Stones at the time of the session. It always seemed curious that no one had ever included a bass player in the lineup at the band's first recording date. True, the bass is hardly audible on the final tracks, but Taylor was there. Acetates were sent to several recording companies and were rejected by all of them for varoius reasons: that the singer sounded "too colored" was one of the more memorable nuggets of 1962 music business "wisdom."

APRIL 16, 1963
R. G. JONES STUDIO, LONDON, ENGLAND

SONGS: *Pretty Thing* (McDaniel) / *It's All Right Babe* (McDaniel)
PRODUCER: Giorgio Gomelsky
ENGINEER: R. G. Jones, Jr.
NOTES: Recorded to be used in the sound track of a promotional film documentary on the band by Giorgio Gomelsky that was never released. "Pretty Thing" was one of the more popular songs the Stones played at Giorgio's club in Richmond. (See CHRONOLOGY and TOURS AND CONCERTS)

APRIL 23, 1963
BBC STUDIOS, LONDON, ENGLAND

SONGS: *I'm Moving On* (Snow) / *I'm a Hog for You, Baby* (Leiber, Stoller)
PERSONNEL: Mick Jagger, Keith Richards, Brian Jones, Ricky Brown, Carlo Little
PRODUCER: BBC (union) staff
ENGINEER: BBC (union) staff
NOTES: This recording session was booked to produce an audition tape for the BBC's radio shows. Wyman, Watts and Stewart couldn't participate because it was a weekday—a Tuesday—and all three had day jobs. Bassist Ricky Brown (a.k.a. Ricky Fenson) and drummer Carlo Little were thus recruited; both had played with the band in 1962 and knew the material. In the end, the BBC didn't like the sound—they considered it "unsuitable for their programming" (another case where Jagger sounded "too black" for the British music establishment)—and the tape was rejected. The above two songs were among the tracks recorded for the audition.

MAY 10, 1963
OLYMPIC STUDIOS, LONDON, ENGLAND

SONGS: Come On (Berry) / I Want to Be Loved (Dixon) / *Love Potion #9* (Leiber, Stoller)
PRODUCER: Andrew Loog Oldham
ENGINEER: Roger Savage
NOTES: Even though two tracks recorded here would become the Stones' first single—"Come On" b/w "I Want to Be Loved"—there was a second session for "Come On" six days later. When this recording was played to Decca Records honchos on May 14, 1963 (their regular Tuesday pre-release listening session), it was rejected. At Decca's request, the Stones were sent to rerecord "Come On" at Decca Studios on May 16. Interestingly, Decca's May 14 rejection meant that the Stones were no longer legally bound to their contract with Andrew Loog Oldham and Eric Easton. Had Decca wanted to do so, it could have signed the Stones to an exclusive deal, excluding Oldham and Easton—and most likely Allen Klein in the

future—hence changing (Stones) history as we know it. But, again, Decca missed their chance to have another future super group all to themselves, and Andrew Oldham succeeded in keeping the Stones under his direction and management control.

MAY 16, 1963
DECCA STUDIOS, WEST HAMPSTEAD, LONDON, ENGLAND

SONGS: *Come On* (Berry), V2
PRODUCER: Michael Barclay
ENGINEER: Gus Dudgeon
NOTES: Based on their opinion of the tape recorded at the band's session at Olympic on May 10, Decca booked a second session for what was to become the Stones' first single. But, the record came from the Olympic date anyway. The Decca Studios effort has never surfaced, so this version of "Come On" remains unreleased.

AUGUST 1 OR AUGUST 8, 1963
DECCA STUDIOS, WEST HAMPSTEAD, LONDON, ENGLAND

SONGS: Fortune Teller (Neville) / Poison Ivy (Leiber, Stoller), V1 / *What Kind of Girl*
PRODUCER: Michael Barclay
ENGINEER: Gus Dudgeon
NOTES: "I'm a Hog for You, Baby" (Leiber, Stoller) may or may not have been recorded. But, sources close to the Rolling Stones say that had it been done, it would have been recorded as a track to be featured on a future radio broadcast rather than for a record release. This take of "Poison Ivy" was first released along with "Fortune Teller" on the *Saturday Club* LP.

OCTOBER 1963
IBC STUDIOS, PORTLAND PLACE, LONDON, ENGLAND

SONGS: *Wake Up in the Morning* (B. Jones, J.W. Thompson)
PRODUCER: Jonathan Rollands
ENGINEER: Glyn Johns
NOTES: This was a jingle for Rice Krispies cereal, music by Brian Jones and lyrics by members of the J. Walter Thompson ad agency creative team. The tune was performed by the Stones and recorded here for a 30-second European television commercial. The group's fee was approximately four to five times what they were then receiving for a single gig, which wasn't much in October '63 (nowhere near the tens of thousands of pounds or dollars that's been mentioned in the past). In addition, the parties agreed contractually that the identity of the group

performing the music in the commercial was not to be made public. The spot did run in Europe. However, since the song was never officially released on record, we are calling it an unreleased track.

OCTOBER 7, 1963
DE LANE LEA RECORDING STUDIOS, KINGSWAY, LONDON, ENGLAND

SONGS: I Wanna Be Your Man (Lennon, McCartney) / Stoned (Nanker Phelge)

PRODUCER: Eric Easton

NOTES: The session at which the band recorded its second single, the A-side a gift from the Beatles. Andrew Oldham was out of town, so Eric Easton produced. A point of clarification: this studio is located on a street named "Kingsway" in central London, across from the Holborn underground station. A British English-speaker might state that fact as: "De Lane Lea is in Kingsway." The De Lane Lea company's facility is often referred to, by musicians, discographers and journalists, as "the Kingsway studios" and sometimes by its proper name. De Lane Lea Studios might also be identified as being "in Holborn." This has resulted in marked confusion and the mistaken idea that there were two separate studios—De Lane Lea and Kingsway. Nope. They are the same place. Nanker Phelge denoted a group effort at co-writing a song. Interestingly, as it applied to the first couple of songs, Nanker Phelge referred to the five Stones and Ian Stewart. But later Nanker Phelge compositions were registered only in the names of the five Rolling Stones.

NOVEMBER 14, 1963
DE LANE LEA RECORDING STUDIOS, KINGSWAY, LONDON, ENGLAND

SONGS: Money (Gordy, Jr., Bradford) / Poison Ivy (Leiber, Stoller), V2 / Bye Bye Johnny (Berry) / You Better Move On (Alexander) / Go Home, Girl (Alexander)

PRODUCER: Eric Easton

NOTES: Not many bands were doing Arthur Alexander material in 1963—the Beatles had "Anna," but that was about it. Of the two Arthur Alexander songs recorded at this session, the Stones released "You Better Move On." Their outtake, "Go Home, Girl," hasn't been heard since.

NOVEMBER 20–21, 1963
REGENT SOUND STUDIOS, LONDON, ENGLAND

SONGS: Will You Be My Lover Tonight / It Should Be You / Shang a Doo Lang / That Girl Belongs to Yesterday

(a.k.a. My Only Girl) / Leave Me Alone / Sure I Do (B. Jones) / So Much in Love

PRODUCER: Andrew Loog Oldham, Eric Easton

ENGINEER: Bill Farley

NOTES: All but one of the songs in the "unreleased" category were written by Mick and Keith. All of them, though, are demos of original compositions intended for possible sale to other artists that were never released by the Rolling Stones themselves. George Bean recorded "It Should Be You" and "Will You Be My Lover Tonight," and Gene Pitney did "That Girl Belongs to Yesterday" (the latter produced by Andrew Oldham shortly after this demo date). Both artists released the Jagger/Richards tracks on singles at the end of 1963. Teen singer Adrienne Posta cut "Shang a Doo Lang" as her second single. "Sure I Do" features Brian Jones on vocals and is one of the two demos made of songs written by Jones and recorded by the Rolling Stones. At the behest of Andrew Oldham, Gene Pitney assisted Brian in completing the tunes. Neither was released. The Mighty Avengers picked up and put out "So Much in Love." The unreleased "Leave Me Alone" is an up-tempo track with lots of piano and is similar in beat to Ray Charles's "What'd I Say."

DECEMBER 7 OR 9, 1963
REGENT SOUND STUDIOS, LONDON, ENGLAND

SONGS: Give Me Your Hand (and I'll Hold It Tight) / You Must Be the One / When a Girl Loves a Boy / I Want You to Know (B. Jones) & (Jagger, Richards)

PERSONNEL: Mick Jagger, Keith Richards, Brian Jones, Charlie Watts, Bill Wyman, Ian Stewart

ADDITIONAL PERSONNEL: Eric Ford (bass), Andy White (drums), Reg Guest (piano)

PRODUCER: Andrew Loog Oldham

ENGINEER: Bill Farley

NOTES: "Give Me Your Hand (and I'll Hold It Tight)" was written for the Beatles to record, in appreciation for "I Wanna Be Your Man." The Beatles offered a second song to the Stones, "One After 909" (which Mick called "Outside 909" in a 1965 interview), but the Stones wouldn't record it unless the Beatles cut "Give Me Your Hand." The end result was that neither song was released by the group that received it as a gift (but the Beatles released their own "One After 909").

Like the other unreleased songs above, "I Want You to Know" was made into an acetate demo to be shopped around to other bands. The composers' credits on this particular label look like someone couldn't make up his mind. Handwritten, it says: Jagger/Richard (crossed out) Brian Jones (crossed out), then Jagger/Richard. The label on the acetate of "When a Girl Loves a Boy" bore that exact title. In the past, that tune has been erroneously called "When a Boy Meets a Girl," one likely reason being that only the first verse of the song has been bootlegged. Almost certainly, the bootleggers neither had the acetate nor had heard the entire song. The lyrics have more to do with the girl's point of view, as opposed to the boy's, when one listens to all of them!

"You Must Be the One" was later recorded by the Greenbeats and released in November 1964 on the Pye Label. Not all of the Stones were necessarily present at this session, although it is likely they were. The authors believe, however, that the band went to Regent on the 9th (and not the 7th), since that date reflects a break in their very busy tour schedule and they usually recorded on their days off. They did two shows on the 7th. Andrew Oldham was also recording material for his orchestra LP at Regent at this time, using the non-Stones personnel listed above. Thus, while not absolutely confirmed, the musicians' names listed in italics in both personnel categories were most likely involved in this session.

1964

JANUARY 2, 1964
REGENT SOUND STUDIOS,
LONDON, ENGLAND

SONGS: To Know Him Is to Love Him (Spector) (InstBkTk) / There Are but Five Rolling Stones (Leander, Oldham)
PRODUCER: Andrew Loog Oldham
MUSICAL DIRECTOR: Mike Leander
ENGINEER: Bill Farley
NOTES: The Stones did the instrumental backing track for Cleo Sylvestre's vocal of "To Know Him Is to Love Him." They also recorded the instrumental cut, "There Are but Five Rolling Stones," to be used as the B-side of her single. Cleo Sylvestre does not appear at all on the flipside—a fairly novel idea in any event—but it is "The Andrew Oldham Orchestra," *not* the Rolling Stones, which is credited on this song. This was the beginning of Andrew Oldham's short and idiosyncratic, but nonetheless innovative and prolific career as an artist's manager/record producer modeled after the legendary Phil Spector.

JANUARY 3, 1964
REGENT SOUND STUDIOS,
LONDON, ENGLAND

SONGS: Carol (Berry) / Route 66 (Troup) / Mona (I Need You Baby) (McDaniel) / Walking the Dog (Thomas) / You Can Make It If You Try (Jarrett)

PRODUCER: Andrew Loog Oldham
ENGINEER: Bill Farley

JANUARY 10, 1964
REGENT SOUND STUDIOS,
LONDON, ENGLAND

SONGS: I Just Want to Make Love to You (Dixon) / I'm a King Bee (Moore) / Honest I Do (Reed) / *Not Fade Away* (Petty, Hardin), ET
ADDITIONAL PERSONNEL: Phil Spector
PRODUCER: Andrew Loog Oldham
ENGINEER: Bill Farley
NOTES: "Not Fade Away" was recorded here but redone later. This January 10, 1964 early take (ET) was not the released version.

JANUARY 13, 1964
REGENT SOUND STUDIOS,
LONDON, ENGLAND

SONGS: 365 Rolling Stones (One for Each Day of the Year) (Oldham, Leander) / Oh, I Do Like to See Me on the B-Side (Oldham, Watts, Wyman) / Funky and Fleopatra (Oldham)
PERSONNEL: Mick Jagger, Keith Richards, Brian Jones, Charlie Watts, Bill Wyman, *Eric Ford, Andy White*
PRODUCER: Andrew Loog Oldham
ENGINEER: Bill Farley
NOTES: The Stones had come in to help cut demos for Andrew Loog Oldham's Orchestra and new artists Jeannie & the Redheads. It is not certain that the entire group played on every song, but the members did act as session men here and were paid accordingly.

JANUARY 28, FEBRUARY 3, 4, 1964
REGENT SOUND STUDIOS,
LONDON, ENGLAND

SONGS: Little by Little (Phelge, Spector) / Can I Get a Witness (Holland, Holland, Dozier) / Now I've Got a Witness (Nanker Phelge) / Tell Me / Not Fade Away (Petty, Hardin), V1 / *Andrew's Blues* (Nanker Phelge, Spector) / *Spector & Pitney Came Too* (Inst.) (Nanker Phelge, Spector)
ADDITIONAL PERSONNEL: Phil Spector, Graham Nash, Gene Pitney, Allan Clark
PRODUCER: Andrew Loog Oldham
ENGINEER: Bill Farley
NOTES: "Tell Me" was the first original Jagger/Richards song to be released by the Stones. Although it is said that "Not Fade Away" was recorded on January 10, 1964, that particular track—which we have categorized as an unreleased early take (ET)—was most likely not the final, released version. Gene Pitney was present at

the "Fade Away" session but he did not arrive in the UK until February 4, 1964! This is confirmed. In published interviews, the singer told of the session, mentioning that it was his birthday and since Pitney family tradition required much toasting with Cognac on such occasions, he'd brought his own and they all got drunk. (The authors, however, believe this little embellishment was more of a ploy to loosen up the band.) Gene Pitney was born on February 17—close enough to celebrate, and to further contradict the January 10 theory.

FEBRUARY 25, 1964
REGENT SOUND STUDIOS,
LONDON, ENGLAND

SONGS: Susie Q (Broadwater, Lewis, Hawkins) / Good Times, Bad Times / *Over You* (Toussaint, Orange)
PRODUCER: Andrew Loog Oldham
ENGINEER: Bill Farley
NOTES: "Over You" is a cover of an Aaron Neville tune (a collaboration between Neville and Allen Toussaint) recorded in 1960 and released on the tiny Minit label. Neville's single made it to Number 21 on the US R&B charts that October. But the Stones recording didn't surface until an acetate on the Regent Sound label appeared at an auction of rock 'n' roll memorabilia in late 1995. We believe it was recorded here. "Good Times, Bad Times" may have been recorded twice—once here and again at Chess in Chicago during the June 10–11, 1964 sessions.

MARCH 11 OR 12, 1964
DE LANE LEA RECORDING STUDIOS,
KINGSWAY, LONDON, ENGLAND

SONGS: *As Time Goes By / No One Knows*
PERSONNEL: Mick Jagger, Keith Richards
ADDITIONAL PERSONNEL: Jim Sullivan (guitar), Erik Ford (bass)
PRODUCER: Andrew Loog Oldham
ENGINEER: Jim Mine
NOTES: Don't look for Bogie. The first unreleased track is an early take of "As Tears Go By," not the tune from *Casablanca*. This was another demo session. It is commonly believed that "As Tears Go By" was written especially for Marianne Faithfull. That is only partly true. Mick and Keith cut this demo two weeks before ever meeting her—the song had been written as far back as November/December 1963 (see CHRONOLOGY). Following her first encounter with the Stones at Adrienne Posta's 16th birthday party, Marianne went to Olympic Studios to follow up on Andrew Oldham's "I can make you a star"

party patter. Oldham convinced her to try a session and gave Marianne this March 1964 demo to work with. Then, to avoid any association or comparison with the well-known identically titled *Casablanca* tune, Jagger and Richards changed their song's title and rewrote some of its lyrics before Faithfull recorded it. So, they did write some of "As Tears Go By" for Marianne.

JUNE 10–11, 1964
CHESS STUDIOS, CHICAGO, IL, USA

SONGS: It's All Over Now (Womack, Womack)* / Down the Road Apiece (Raye)* / I Can't Be Satisfied (Morganfield)* / Confessin' the Blues (McShann, Brown)** / Around & Around (Berry)** / Good Times, Bad Times** / Tell Me Baby (Broonzy)** / If You Need Me (Pickett, Bateman, Sanders)** / Empty Heart (Nanker Phelge)** / Don't Lie to Me (Berry)** / Now Look What You've Done (Morganfield)** / 2120 South Michigan Avenue (Nanker Phelge), V1** / 2120 South Michigan Avenue (Nanker Phelge), V2** *Stewed and Keefed* (Inst.) (Nanker Phelge)* / *High Heel Sneakers* (Higginbotham)** / *Down in the Bottom* (Dixon)** / *Reelin' & Rockin'* (Berry)**
PRODUCER: Andrew Loog Oldham
ENGINEER: Ron Malo
NOTES: "Tell Me Baby" (Broonzy) (the full title is "Tell Me Baby How Many Times") was only released—by accident—on the 1983 West German *The Rest of the Best (The Rolling Stones Story—Part 2)–Teldec (Telefunken/German Decca) 6.30125FX instead of the Jagger/Richards song "Tell Me." Teldec personnel* apparently knew it wasn't the same "Tell Me" track that the Stones had released nearly 20 years earlier, since the German LP's label lists the song as "Tell Me, v2." The Stones, in fact, released three studio versions of Mick and Keith's "Tell Me" (on their first LPs in both the US and UK and as a single in the US), but this is not one of them. The Broonzy song is unavailable on any other official recording. "2120 South Michigan Avenue" (Nanker Phelge), V2 is a shorter, edited version of this song and lacks the guitar solo of V1. "2120 South Michigan Avenue, V1" appears only on the German LP, Around & Around. The song's title is an homage to hallowed ground—it is the street address of Chess Studios, where many of band's R&B idols had recorded. After a disappointing (at best) first half of their inaugural American tour, the Stones were brought to Chicago for these sessions. The first day, June 10, the Stones were thrilled by the appearance of several visitors in the studio—Buddy Guy, Chuck Berry and Willie Dixon. When the band arrived the next day, none other

---

* = songs recorded on June 10
** = songs recorded on June 11

than Muddy Waters helped them lug guitars and amps into the studio, and stayed around to chat with the boys, who were astonished by the whole experience.

JUNE 24–26, 1964
REGENT SOUND STUDIOS,
LONDON, ENGLAND

SONGS: Congratulations / Time Is on My Side (Meade), V1 / Off the Hook (Nanker Phelge) / You Can't Catch Me (Berry) / *You've Just Made My Day*

PRODUCER: Andrew Loog Oldham

ENGINEER: Bill Farley

NOTES: Previously, this session was thought to have taken place right before the first US Tour. However, a look at the Stones' schedule for that time period would make that a difficult task, at best. "Time Is on My Side, v1" is often called the "organ version" because it features a solo organ in the song's intro instead of the solo electric guitar on v2. It has also been dubbed the "single version," since v1 was the track released on the *first* "Time Is on My Side" single. There were later single releases of "Time Is on My Side," however, some of which were not exact duplicates of the first. For example, London Records rereleased the "Time Is on My Side" single in the early 1970s and some pressings mistakenly used the guitar version (v2), not the organ/single version (v1). ABKCO's 1989 *Rolling Stones Singles Collection—The London Years* includes the "Time Is on My Side" single, the guitar version. "Off the Hook" has the distinct honor of being the only song the Stones recorded for which they were sued for copyright infringement—by Chess Records. The Stones lost the case and 50% of the royalties for the song, which in actuality belonged to Chess Records.

JUNE 29–JULY 7, 1964
REGENT SOUND STUDIOS AND DECCA
RECORDING STUDIOS, LONDON, ENGLAND

SONGS: Heart of Stone, DV / Try a Little Harder, DV / Some Things Just Stick in Your Mind, DV

PERSONNEL: Mick Jagger, Keith Richards, *Brian Jones, Charlie Watts, Bill Wyman,* Jim Sullivan (12-string guitar)

ADDITIONAL PERSONNEL: Jimmy Page (gtr, bs), John McLaughlin (gtr), Andy White (ds), Reg Guest (pi), Joe Morretti (gtr)

PRODUCERS: Andrew Loog Oldham, Michael Barclay

ENGINEERS: Bill Farley (Regent), Gus Dudgeon (Decca)

NOTES: More demos. The tracks were released on *Metamorphosis*, 11 years later. "Some Things Just Stick in Your Mind" appeared only on the UK album. It features Big Jim Sullivan on 12-string guitar. This version of "Heart of Stone," however, was first used in the soundtrack of *Charlie Is My Darling* and features Jimmy

Page on guitar (see FILMS and PROMOTIONAL FILMS AND VIDEOS).

JULY 1964
REGENT SOUND STUDIOS,
LONDON, ENGLAND

SONGS: Heart of Stone, DV

PERSONNEL: Mick Jagger, Jimmy Page, John McLaughlin, Clem Cattini

PRODUCER: Andrew Loog Oldham

ENGINEER: Bill Farley

NOTES: This is the version of "Heart of Stone" released on *Metamorphosis.*

AUGUST 31–SEPTEMBER 1, 3, 4, 1964
PYE STUDIOS AND DECCA
RECORDING STUDIOS,
LONDON, ENGLAND

SONGS: We're Wasting Time, DV / (Walking Thru the) Sleepy City, DV / Each and Every Day of the Year, DV / Da Doo Ron Ron (Spector), DV / *Hear It,* DV / *Blue Turns to Grey,* DV

PERSONNEL: Mick Jagger, Keith Richards, John McLaughlin, Jimmy Page, Joe Morretti, John Paul Jones, Andy White, Mike Leander (arranger)

PRODUCERS: Andrew Loog Oldham and Michael Barclay

ENGINEERS: Bill Farley (Regent) and Gus Dudgeon (Decca)

NOTES: "Da Doo Ron Ron" was released, not on a Rolling Stones album, but on the 1964 Andrew Oldham Orchestra LP entitled *16 Hip Hits*, recorded at Regent Sound. Whenever there was studio time left over during the making of this LP, Oldham would phone and ask Mick and Keith to come in and record any newly written songs with the session musicians. Thus these sessions, like others in 1963, 1964 and 1965, produced demos of the various Jagger/Richards tracks that ended up on *Metamorphosis* in 1975 ("We're Wasting Time" only appears on the European release of this LP). *"Hear It"* is an instrumental track featuring Big Jim Sullivan on 12-string guitar and Keith Richards on guitar.

SEPTEMBER 2, 1964
REGENT SOUND STUDIOS,
LONDON, ENGLAND

SONGS: Little Red Rooster (Dixon) / Off the Hook (Nanker Phelge) / You Can't Catch Me (Berry)

PRODUCER: Andrew Loog Oldham

ENGINEER: Bill Farley

SEPTEMBER 28–29, 1964
REGENT SOUND STUDIOS,
LONDON, ENGLAND

SONGS: Surprise Surprise / Grown Up Wrong / Under the Boardwalk (Broadwater, Lewis, Hawkins) / *I'm Relying on You / We Were Falling in Love*
PRODUCER: Andrew Loog Oldham
ENGINEER: Bill Farley
NOTES: The outtake "I'm Relying on You" is the same song as one that has erroneously been titled "I'm Just a Funny Guy" (or variations on that title) by many people. "We Were Falling in Love" has also been mistitled "Waving Hair" by many people in the bootleg circuit.

OCTOBER 27–NOVEMBER 2, 1964
RCA STUDIOS, HOLLYWOOD, CA, USA

SONGS: Hitch Hike (Gaye, Stevenson, Paul) / Pain in My Heart (Neville) / Down Home Girl (Leiber, Butler) / Heart of Stone / Oh Baby (We Got a Good Thing Goin') (Ozen) / Everybody Needs Somebody to Love (Russell, Burke, Wexler), V1 / Everybody Needs Somebody to Love (Russell, Burke, Wexler), V2
ADDITIONAL PERSONNEL: Jack Nitzsche
PRODUCER: Andrew Loog Oldham
ENGINEER: David Hassinger
NOTES: Ian Stewart played piano on "Everybody Needs Somebody to Love" and Jack Nitzsche played piano on "Down Home Girl" and Nitzsche-phone (a keyboard instrument of his own invention) on "Pain in My Heart."

NOVEMBER 8, 1964
CHESS STUDIOS, CHICAGO, IL, USA

SONGS: What a Shame / Time Is on My Side (Meade), V2 / Little Red Rooster (Dixon)* / *Mercy Mercy* (Covay, Miller), V1 / *Key to the Highway* (Segar, Broonzy) / *Good Bye Girl* (Wyman) / *Fanny Mae* (Brown, Robinson)
PRODUCER: Andrew Loog Oldham
ENGINEER: Ron Malo
NOTES: This version of "Mercy Mercy" is more uptempo, jazzier, and has different vocals from the released track, "Mercy Mercy," V2, which the Stones recorded six months after this session, on May 10, 1965. The well-known guitar version of "Time Is on My Side" was done here as was the little-known outtake "Good Bye Girl," the first Bill Wyman composition the Stones recorded in the studio. Wyman wrote "Good Bye Girl" but it features Jagger on vocals as usual, lest there be any confusion. "Good Bye Girl" has gone under the incorrect

title of "Get Back to the One You Love," a verse repeated many times in the song but not the title of it.

1965

JANUARY 11–12, 1965
DE LANE LEA RECORDING STUDIOS,
KINGSWAY, LONDON, ENGLAND

SONGS: *The Last Time*, ET / *A Mess of Fire*, WT a.k.a. *Play with Fire* (Nanker Phelge), ET
PRODUCER: Andrew Loog Oldham
NOTES: These were early takes of "The Last Time" and "Play with Fire." The released tracks were primarily cut a week later in the US. Mick and Keith wrote "The Last Time" at their flat in Hampstead in December 1964. This take didn't work at all; they used the instrumental track from RCA, and the vocals had to be rerecorded at yet another RCA session one month after that.

JANUARY 17–18, 1965
RCA STUDIOS, HOLLYWOOD, CA, USA

SONGS: The Last Time / Play with Fire (Nanker Phelge)
ADDITIONAL PERSONNEL: Phil Spector, Jack Nitzsche
PRODUCER: Andrew Loog Oldham
ENGINEER: David Hassinger
NOTES: Vocals on "The Last Time" were rerecorded on February 17, 1965 at RCA Studios in Hollywood, CA. The whole band worked on that track. But there was a unique lineup of personnel on "Play with Fire": Mick Jagger, vocals; Keith Richards, acoustic guitar; Jack Nitzsche, keyboards; Phil Spector, guitar (tuned down for a bass effect). Charlie Watts, Brian Jones, Bill Wyman and Ian Stewart did not play on this version of "Play with Fire," although Jones played harpsichord on a version used on the "Shindig" show taped on May 20, 1965 and aired on May 26. The backing track for the "Shindig" version of "Play with Fire" (among other titles) was recorded during sessions beginning on May 18 at RCA (see below).

FEBRUARY 17, 1965
RCA STUDIOS, HOLLYWOOD, CA, USA

SONGS: The Last Time
PERSONNEL: Mick Jagger, Keith Richards
PRODUCER: Andrew Loog Oldham
ENGINEER: David Hassinger
NOTES: Vocals on "The Last Time" were rerecorded at this session and the song was remixed.

---

* Whether or not this track was actually done here is a matter of much debate.

LATE FEBRUARY, 1965
DECCA STUDIOS, LONDON, ENGLAND

SONGS: I'd Much Rather Be with the Boys (Oldham, Richards), DV

PERSONNEL: Mick Jagger, Keith Richards, Andy White (drums), John McLaughlin (guitar), Joe Morretti (guitar), Mike Leander, Art Greenslade

PRODUCER: Andrew Loog Oldham

ENGINEER: Gus Dudgeon

NOTES: Keith and Andrew wrote "I'd Much Rather Be with the Boys" on the beach in Australia, as a congratulatory gift for Bob Crewe commemorating his hit.

MARCH 5, 1965
REGAL THEATRE, EDMONTON, LONDON, ENGLAND (LIVE)

MARCH 6, 1965
EMPIRE THEATER, LIVERPOOL, LANCASHIRE, ENGLAND (LIVE)

MARCH 7, 1965
PALACE THEATER, MANCHESTER, LANCASHIRE, ENGLAND (LIVE)

MARCH 16, 1965
GRANADA THEATRE, GREENFORD, MIDDLESEX, ENGLAND

SONGS: Everybody Needs Somebody to Love (Russell, Burke, Wexler) → Pain in My Heart (Neville), LMV / Route 66 (Troup), LV1 / I'm Moving On (Snow), LV1 / I'm Alright (McDaniel), LV1 / We Want the Stones (Nanker Phelge) / *Down the Road Apiece* (Raye) / *Little Red Rooster* (Dixon

PERSONNEL: Mick Jagger, Keith Richards, Brian Jones, Charlie Watts, Bill Wyman, Ian Stewart

PRODUCER: Andrew Loog Oldham

ENGINEER: Glyn Johns

NOTES: The four shows recorded for the Stones' EP, *Got Live If You Want It*. However, only three performances produced the material that ended up being released; the tracks from the Edmonton concert were not used.

MAY 10, 1965
CHESS STUDIOS, CHICAGO, IL, USA

SONGS: That's How Strong My Love Is (Jamison) / The Under-Assistant West Coast Promotion Man (Nanker Phelge) / Mercy Mercy (Covay, Miller), V2 / *Try Me* (Brown) / (I Can't Get No) Satisfaction, ET

PRODUCER: Andrew Loog Oldham

ENGINEER: Ron Malo

NOTES: This version of "(I Can't Get No) Satisfaction" is an early, unreleased take of the song. It is all acoustic, and has a harmonica solo, which the released, famous version does not. The cut that would become one of the best-known songs in rock 'n' roll was recorded in sessions which began the following day in Hollywood, CA.

MAY 11–12, 1965
RCA STUDIOS, HOLLYWOOD, CA, USA

SONGS: (I Can't Get No) Satisfaction / My Girl (Robinson, White) / Good Times (Cooke) / Cry to Me (Russell) / I've Been Loving You Too Long (Redding, Butler) / The Spider and the Fly (Nanker Phelge) / One More Try

PRODUCER: Andrew Loog Oldham

ENGINEER: David Hassinger

NOTES: "(I Can't Get No) Satisfaction" is actually the second recorded version of this famous track; an early, unreleased, take went onto tape at Chess Studios in Chicago the day before these LA sessions.

MAY 18–19, 1965
RCA STUDIOS, HOLLYWOOD, CA, USA

SONGS: *Little Red Rooster* (Dixon), TV / *(I Can't Get No) Satisfaction*, TV / *Play with Fire*, TV / *The Last Time*, TV

PRODUCER: Andrew Loog Oldham

ENGINEER: David Hassinger

NOTES: These were backing tracks to be used on "Shindig," hence the designation "TV" for television version and the classification of the songs as "unreleased" (as in unreleased on any official record). The "Shindig" program was taped on May 20 and aired on May 26, 1965. Brian Jones played harpsichord on this version of "Play with Fire" but not on the record release version, and harmonica on "Satisfaction."

SEPTEMBER 6–7, 1965
RCA STUDIOS, HOLLYWOOD, CA, USA

SONGS: I'm Free / Get Off of My Cloud / The Singer Not the Song / She Said Yeah (Christy, Jackson) / Gotta Get Away / Blue Turns to Grey

ADDITIONAL PERSONNEL: J. W. Alexander, (tambourine), Jack Nitzche

PRODUCER: Andrew Loog Oldham

ENGINEER: David Hassinger

NOTES: This was the Stones' version of "Blue Turns to Grey," as opposed to the demo version of August 31–September 1, 3, 4, 1964. Guest tambourine player J. W. Alexander had managed the late Sam Cooke (died December 11, 1964) and ran Kags Music.

Keith Richards at the piano during 1966 session (TOM BEACH COLLECTION)

OCTOBER 26, 1965
IBC STUDIOS, PORTLAND PLACE, LONDON, ENGLAND

SONGS: As Tears Go By (Jagger, Richards, Oldham)
PERSONNEL: Mick Jagger, Keith Richards
ADDITIONAL PERSONNEL: Mike Leander, Mike Leander Orchestra (strings)
PRODUCER: Andrew Loog Oldham
ENGINEER: Glyn Johns
NOTES: Strings arranged by Mike Leander and Keith Richards. Mick and Keith were the only Stones present. The basic instrumental track is essentially the same for both "As Tears Go By" and "Con le mie lacrime," the Italian version of the song that was recorded the following year—with one other difference (see March 15, 1966).

DECEMBER 3–8, 1965
RCA STUDIOS, HOLLYWOOD, CA, USA

SONGS: Mother's Little Helper / Sittin' on a Fence / Goin' Home / Doncha Bother Me / Think / Sad Day / Take It or Leave It / 19th Nervous Breakdown / Ride On Baby / *Looking Tired* / *Aftermath*
ADDITIONAL PERSONNEL: Jack Nitzsche
PRODUCER: Andrew Loog Oldham
ENGINEER: David Hassinger
NOTES: Jack Nitzsche played piano on "Sad Day." Brian Jones played harpsichord on "Take It or Leave It," "Sittin' on a Fence," and "Ride On Baby." Ian Stewart played on "Looking Tired." "Aftermath" is a blues-y instrumental outtake track. "Doncha Bother Me" was originally called "Don't You Follow Me" when planned for release on the ill-fated *Could You Walk on the Water* LP in February 1966. After the myriad hassles with the album title, the song was renamed "Doncha Bother Me" for *Aftermath*, released in March. (See CHRONOLOGY)

1966

MARCH 6–9, 1966
RCA STUDIOS, HOLLYWOOD, CA, USA

SONGS: Lady Jane / Paint It, Black / Flight 505 / High & Dry / It's Not Easy / I Am Waiting / Long Long While / Out of Time, V1 / Out of Time, V2 / Stupid Girl / Under My Thumb / What to Do / *Tracks of My Tears* (Robinson)
ADDITIONAL PERSONNEL: Jack Nitzsche
PRODUCER: Andrew Loog Oldham
ENGINEER: David Hassinger
NOTES: Brian Jones played dulcimer on "Lady Jane," marimbas on "Under My Thumb" and sitar on "Paint It, Black" in addition to acoustic and electric guitars and keyboards throughout these session dates. Jack Nitzsche played harpsichord on "Stupid Girl," piano on "Paint It, Black" and "Out of Time" and various percussion instruments on other tracks. Ian Stewart played organ on "Stupid Girl" and "Out of Time."

MARCH 15, 1966
IBC STUDIOS, PORTLAND PLACE, LONDON, ENGLAND

SONGS: Con le mie lacrime (Jagger, Richards, Danpa)
PERSONNEL: Mick Jagger, Keith Richards
ADDITIONAL PERSONNEL: Mike Leander, Mike Leander Orchestra (harpsichord)
ARRANGERS: Keith Richards, Mike Leander
PRODUCER: Andrew Loog Oldham
ENGINEER: Glyn Johns
NOTES: "Con le mie lacrime" is an Italian version of "As Tears Go By," with the same basic backing track. Mick recorded the Italian-language vocal at this session and overdubbed harpsichord to complete this version.

MAY 6, 1966
PYE STUDIOS, LONDON, ENGLAND

SONGS: Out of Time, DV

PERSONNEL: Mick Jagger, Eric Ford (bs), Reg Guest (pi), Joe Morretti (gtr), Andy White (ds), Syd Sax (string leader), Chris Farlowe

ARRANGER: Art Greenslade

PRODUCER: Mick Jagger

ENGINEER: Alan Florence

NOTES: This version of "Out of Time," with Mick Jagger on vocals, was released on *Metamorphosis*. Note that the rest of the Stones were not present. The instrumental backing track—without Jagger's vocals—is the identical backing used in singer Chris Farlowe's version of "Out of Time," which was released as a single at the end of May 1966. Chris Farlowe's record was produced by Mick Jagger.

AUGUST 3–11, 1966
RCA STUDIOS, HOLLYWOOD, CA, USA

SONGS: Have You Seen Your Mother, Baby, Standing in the Shadow? / Who's Driving Your Plane / Who's Been Sleeping Here? / Miss Amanda Jones / Connection / Back Street Girl / All Sold Out / Please Go Home / Let's Spend the Night Together / Something Happened to Me Yesterday / Cool, Calm, Collected / Complicated

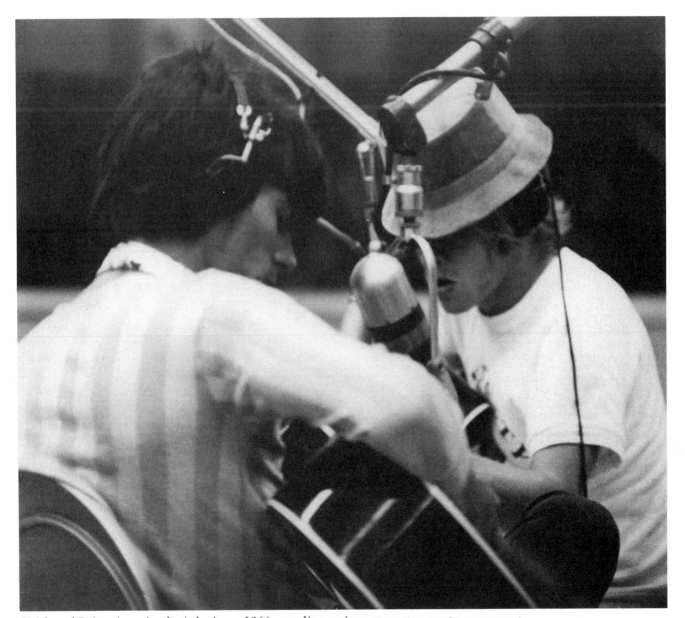

Keith and Brian (wearing hat) during a 1966 recording session (TOM BEACH COLLECTION)

/ Yesterday's Papers / She Smiled Sweetly / My Obsession / *Panama Powder Room* / *Godzi* / *Get Yourself Together* / *Something BB*

ADDITIONAL PERSONNEL: Jack Nitzsche

PRODUCER: Andrew Loog Oldham

ENGINEER: David Hassinger

NOTES: Jack Nitzsche played piano on "Who's Driving Your Plane." That song was actually first released in the US as "Who's Driving My Plane" on the B-side of the "Have You Seen Your Mother, Baby?" single but was titled correctly on the UK single. Another confusing, if slightly ironic, bit of Stones lore: The track was recorded in the US and is registered with BMI and the US Copyright Office as "Who's Driving Your Plane." Most of these are the basic tracks for Between the Buttons that were initially recorded here and not at Olympic, as had been thought previously. Some were reworked later and had vocals or other instrumental finishing touches added—in September 1966 at IBC and in November 1966 at Pye and Olympic Studios—but for the most part, the *Buttons* LP cuts were done here at RCA.

SEPTEMBER 2, 1966
IBC STUDIOS, PORTLAND PLACE, LONDON, ENGLAND

SONGS: Who's Driving Your Plane / Have You Seen Your Mother, Baby, Standing in the Shadow? / My Girl (Robinson, White)

ADDITIONAL PERSONNEL: Mike Leander (horn and string arrangements), Mike Leander Orchestra

PRODUCER: Andrew Loog Oldham

ENGINEER: Glyn Johns

NOTES: Orchestral backing was put on the August '66 RCA tracks—horns on "Have You Seen Your Mother, Baby" and "Who's Driving Your Plane," and strings on "My Girl."

SEPTEMBER 23, 1966
ROYAL ALBERT HALL, LONDON, ENGLAND (LIVE)

NOTES: Contrary to the hype on the cover of the *Got Live If You Want It!* album, this show was *not* recorded for the LP. See October 1, 1966, below.

OCTOBER 1, 1966
CITY HALL, NEWCASTLE, ENGLAND (LIVE)

SONGS: Get Off of My Cloud, LV / 19th Nervous Breakdown, LV / Under My Thumb, LV / The Last Time, LV

PRODUCER: Andrew Loog Oldham

ENGINEER: Glyn Johns

NOTES: For *Got Live If You Want It!*, London PS 493, album. Although this LP's cover boasts: "Recorded Live at The Albert Hall," the Stones did not, in fact, get the hall's permission to record their show. Peter Whitehead did film that performance (see PROMOTIONAL FILMS AND VIDEOS), but without audio. Considering the ambience at Albert Hall that night, it would have been a waste of time and tape, anyway. The album tracks came from two shows here in Newcastle and two shows in Bristol on October 7, where management didn't quibble about a few more mikes and cables. Still, Andrew Oldham believed that "Live at Bristol" (*or* Newcastle) wasn't as hip or stylish a hook for the band's first live album—so "Albert Hall" went on the cover (see also: TOURS AND CONCERTS ; DISCOGRAPHY).

OCTOBER 7, 1966
COLSTON HALL, BRISTOL, ENGLAND (LIVE)

SONGS: Not Fade Away (Petty, Hardin), LV / I'm Alright (McDaniel), LV2 / Have You Seen Your Mother, Baby, Standing in the Shadow?, LV / Lady Jane, LV / Time Is on My Side (Meade), LV1 / (I Can't Get No) Satisfaction, LV1

PRODUCER: Andrew Loog Oldham

ENGINEER: Glyn Johns

NOTES: For *Got Live If You Want It!*, London PS 493, album

OCTOBER 11–20, 1966 (APPROX.)
IBC STUDIOS, PORTLAND PLACE, LONDON, ENGLAND

SONGS: Get Off of My Cloud, LV / Have You Seen Mother, Baby, Standing in the Shadow?, LV / I'm Alright (McDaniel), LV2 / Not Fade Away (Petty, Hardin), LV / The Last Time, LV / Time Is on My Side (Meade), LV1 / 19th Nervous Breakdown, LV / (I Can't Get No) Satisfaction, LV1

PRODUCER: Andrew Loog Oldham

ENGINEER: Glyn Johns

NOTES: Studio recording for *Got Live If You Want It!*, London PS 493, album

NOVEMBER 9–26, 1966
OLYMPIC STUDIOS AND PYE STUDIOS, LONDON, ENGLAND

SONGS: Ruby Tuesday / If You Let Me / Let's Spend the Night Together / She Smiled Sweetly / My Obsession / Yesterday's Papers / Complicated / Something Happened to Me Yesterday / Cool, Calm, Collected / All Sold Out / Miss Amanda Jones / Please Go Home / Who's

Jack Nitzsche (l) with Keith during a session at RCA studios in 1966 (Tom Beach Collection)

Been Sleeping Here? / Connection / Back Street Girl / Dandelion / *Trouble in Mind* (R. Jones) / *Ruby Tuesday, ET* (a.k.a. *Title 8*) / *Sometimes Happy Sometimes Blue* (a.k.a. *Dandelion*) / *Get Yourself Together* / *Godzi* / *English Summer* / *All Part of the Act*

ADDITIONAL PERSONNEL: Jack Nitzsche, Nicky Hopkins

PRODUCER: Andrew Loog Oldham

ENGINEER: Glyn Johns

NOTES: Tracks from the August '66 RCA sessions were brought back to London and finished at Olympic and Pye Studios in November; some new songs were recorded as well. Jack Nitzsche played piano on "She Smiled Sweetly" and "Let's Spend the Night Together" and Ian Stewart played piano on "Connection." Brian Jones played trombone on "Something Happened to Me Yesterday" and recorder on "Ruby Tuesday." "English Summer" was to have been released as a single in June or July of 1967, but was put on the back burner due to the band's arrests and the rush release of "We

Love You"/"Dandelion"—and was never heard of again. The outtake "All Part of the Act" later became "All Sold Out." Pye Studios was used for overdubs and arrangements only, such as for "Something Happened to Me Yesterday."

DECEMBER 13, 1966
OLYMPIC STUDIOS, LONDON, ENGLAND

SONGS: Who's Been Sleeping Here? / Miss Amanda Jones / My Obsession / Back Street Girl / Something Happened to Me Yesterday / All Sold Out / *It's Been Quiet Here at Home*

ADDITIONAL PERSONNEL: Jack Nitzsche, Nicky Hopkins

PRODUCER: Andrew Loog Oldham

ENGINEER: Glyn Johns

NOTES: Brian Jones played trombone on "Something Happened to Me Yesterday." More overdubbing and mixing.

Keith Richards during a recording session (with bow), 1966–1967 (TOM BEACH COLLECTION)

1967

JANUARY 3–6, 1967
OLYMPIC STUDIOS, LONDON, ENGLAND

ENGINEER: Glyn Johns
ASSISTANT ENGINEER: Eddie Kramer
NOTES: The Stones were present, but this session was primarily devoted to final mixing and last-minute overdubs on *Between the Buttons* tracks.

JANUARY 18–19, 1967
OLYMPIC STUDIOS, LONDON, ENGLAND

SONGS: *Let's Spend the Night Together*, TV / *Ruby Tuesday*, TV / *It's All Over Now* (Womack, Womack), TV / *Connection* TV
PRODUCER: Rolling Stones
ENGINEER: Glyn Johns
NOTES: These are the instrumental backing tracks the Stones recorded to use in their January 22, 1967 appearance on the "Sunday Night at the London Palladium" television show. This particular version of "It's All Over Now" is totally different from the released track, but the other three songs are essentially just instrumental versions of the familiar recordings. (See TELEVISION APPEARANCES)

FEBRUARY 11, 1967
OLYMPIC STUDIOS, LONDON, ENGLAND

SONGS: *Blues 1* (WT)
PRODUCER: Rolling Stones
ENGINEER: Glyn Johns
NOTES: The letters "WT" following this and other unreleased song titles denote a working title for a composition-in-progress.

FEBRUARY 14, 1967
OLYMPIC STUDIOS, LONDON, ENGLAND

SONGS: *Title 9* (a.k.a. *Rock 'n' Roll Track*), WT / *Title 10*, WT / *Bill's Tune* (Wyman), WT
PRODUCER: Rolling Stones
ENGINEER: Glyn Johns
NOTES: The letters "WT" following this and other unreleased song titles denote a working title for a composition-in-progress. "Bill's Tune" was a working title for Wyman's "Acid in the Grass," which became "In Another Land" during final sessions in July '67. In spite of many stories of the song having been written *and* recorded in July, both working titles are listed on dated master tapes from the February 1967 Olympic sessions. See February 22 and July 12–13, 1967.

FEBRUARY 16, 1967
OLYMPIC STUDIOS, LONDON, ENGLAND

SONGS: *Blues III*, WT
PRODUCER: Rolling Stones
ENGINEER: Glyn Johns

FEBRUARY 17, 1967
OLYMPIC STUDIOS, LONDON, ENGLAND

SONGS: *Title 5*, WT
PRODUCER: Rolling Stones
ENGINEER: Glyn Johns

FEBRUARY 22, 1967
OLYMPIC STUDIOS, LONDON, ENGLAND

SONGS: *Acid in the Grass* (Wyman), WT / *(I Believe I'll) Dust My Broom* (Robt. Johnson) / *Trouble in Mind* (R. Jones) / *You Can't Always Get What You Want* (Inst.) ET / *Blues Jam*
PRODUCER: Rolling Stones
ENGINEER: Glyn Johns
NOTES: "Acid in the Grass" was the next title given to the earlier "Bill's Tune," the song that became "In Another Land." See February 14 and July 12–13, 1967. The "You Can't Always Get What You Want" track recorded here was a very early instrumental take of this now quintessentially Stones song.

MARCH 10, 1967
OLYMPIC STUDIOS, LONDON, ENGLAND

SONGS: *Blow Me Mama*
PRODUCER: Rolling Stones
ENGINEER: Glyn Johns
NOTES: An unreleased Jagger/Richards song.

MAY 18, 1967
OLYMPIC STUDIOS, LONDON, ENGLAND

SONGS: She's a Rainbow
ADDITIONAL PERSONNEL: Nicky Hopkins, John Paul Jones
PRODUCER: Rolling Stones
ENGINEER: Glyn Johns
NOTES: Nicky Hopkins, piano; strings arranged by John Paul Jones.

JUNE 9, 1967
OLYMPIC STUDIOS, LONDON, ENGLAND

SONGS: Citadel
PRODUCER: Rolling Stones
ENGINEER: Glyn Johns

Keith on bass and wearing sunglasses with Mick in the studio during the Satanic *sessions, 1967* (TOM BEACH COLLECTION)

JUNE 12–13, 1967
OLYMPIC STUDIOS, LONDON, ENGLAND

SONGS: We Love You / Dandelion / *Lady Fair,* WT / *Fairground,* WT

ADDITIONAL PERSONNEL: Nicky Hopkins

PRODUCER: Andrew Loog Oldham

ENGINEER: Glyn Johns

ASSISTANT ENGINEER: Eddie Kramer

NOTES: "We Love You" was written as a thank-you to Stones fans for their concern and support during the period of Mick's, Keith's, and Brian's multiple drug busts and resultant trials. Piano by Nicky Hopkins. John Lennon and Paul McCartney contributed additional backing vocals as their gesture of support for the Stones; these were recorded one month later at Olympic Studios after the Redlands trial (over drug charges resulting from the arrests of Mick, Keith, and Robert Fraser at Keith's West

Sussex home). Also overdubbed and added to the song's final mix after the trial was the sound of a prison door slamming. "Fairground" is the working title of "Dandelion."

JULY 7–22, 1967
OLYMPIC STUDIOS, LONDON, ENGLAND

SONGS: In Another Land (Wyman) / Sing This All Together / Sing This All Together (See What Happens) / The Lantern / On with the Show / We Love You

ADDITIONAL PERSONNEL: Nicky Hopkins, Steve Marriott, Ronnie Lane, John Lennon, Paul McCartney

PRODUCER: Rolling Stones

ENGINEER: Glyn Johns

ASSISTANT ENGINEER: Eddie Kramer

NOTES: "In Another Land" (Wyman), also known as "Acid in the Grass" (Wyman), features Bill Wyman on lead vocals and bass, Charlie Watts on drums, Steve Marriott and Ronnie Lane on vocals, guitars, and Nicky Hopkins on harpsichord. "Sing This All Together" (and "Sing This All Together [See What Happens]") has Nicky Hopkins on piano and John Lennon and Paul McCartney providing backing vocals. The two Beatles also recorded their vocal contribution to "We Love You" at these sessions. (See June 12–13, 1967 entry, above.) "The Lantern" and "On with the Show" also feature Nicky Hopkins on piano.

AUGUST 10–30, SEPTEMBER 1–7,1967
OLYMPIC STUDIOS, LONDON, ENGLAND

SONGS: Gomper / 2000 Light Years from Home / 2000 Man

ADDITIONAL PERSONNEL: Nicky Hopkins (piano), Eddie Dramer (claves)

PRODUCER: Rolling Stones

ENGINEER: Glyn Johns

ASSISTANT ENGINEER: Eddie Kramer

NOTES: "2000 Light Years from Home" featured Brian Jones on Mellotron and assistant engineer Eddie Kramer on claves. Remixed at Bell Sound Studios, NYC in mid-September 1967. This song almost didn't appear on *Satanic*; it was not until the addition of Brian's Mellotron that it was even considered to be a contender. After it was mixed at Olympic, it still needed work: the band still wasn't satisfied. A protracted mixing session at Bell Sound produced the track the Stones had envisioned and —at the 11th hour—"2000 Light Years from Home" made it onto the album. As for "Gomper," it has no such convoluted history, as far as we know. All we can report is that in a 1976 interview with author James Karnbach, the late Ian Stewart said that he detested the song. Unfortunately, there is no way to know for certain whether Stu was speaking frankly—or pulling James's leg.

OCTOBER 2–5, 1967
OLYMPIC STUDIOS AND DE LANE LEA
RECORDING STUDIOS, LONDON, ENGLAND

SONGS: The Lantern / Citadel / *Manhole Cover*, WT / *Surprise Me* / *She's Doing Her Thing*

ADDITIONAL PERSONNEL: Nicky Hopkins (piano)

PRODUCER: Rolling Stones

ENGINEER: Glyn Johns

ASSISTANT ENGINEER: Eddie Kramer

NOTES: In addition to the recording of finished versions of "The Lantern" and "Citadel," these sessions were devoted to the final mixing of tracks for *Their Satanic Majesties Request*. Almost concurrently with work done at Olympic, *Satanic* tracks were also fine-tuned and mixed in sessions at De Lane Lea during this same week.

OCTOBER 3, 1967
OLYMPIC STUDIOS, LONDON, ENGLAND

SONGS: *Manhole Cover*, WT / *Surprise Me* / *She's Doing Her Thing*

ADDITIONAL PERSONNEL: Nicky Hopkins (piano)

PRODUCER: Rolling Stones

ENGINEER: Glyn Johns

OCTOBER 11, 1967
OLYMPIC STUDIOS, LONDON, ENGLAND

SONGS: Snoring (Wyman) / *Bathroom/Toilet*, WT

ADDITIONAL PERSONNEL: Nicky Hopkins (piano)

PRODUCER: Rolling Stones

ENGINEER: Glyn Johns, Andy Johns

NOTES: "Snoring" is not exactly a "song." It is merely the sound of Bill Wyman sleeping in the studio, caught on tape. It was released on *Satanic*—as "In Another Land" fades out, Wyman's snoring is heard, then "2000 Man" begins.

OCTOBER 16, 21, 23, 1967
OLYMPIC STUDIOS, LONDON, ENGLAND

SONGS: 2000 Man / Cosmic Christmas / *Gold Painted Nails* / *Fly High as a Kite*, WT / *Child of the Moon* (inst. take)

ADDITIONAL PERSONNEL: Nicky Hopkins

PRODUCER: Rolling Stones

ENGINEER: Glyn Johns, Andy Johns

NOTES: "Cosmic Christmas" is a title present but not listed on *Their Satanic Majesties Request*.

1968

FEBRUARY–MARCH 1968
REDLANDS, SUSSEX, ENGLAND
(KEITH RICHARDS'S HOME)

SONGS: *Primo Grande* / *Rock Me Baby* / *Hold On, I'm Coming*

PERSONNEL: Mick Jagger, Keith Richards, Brian Jones, Bill Wyman, Charlie Watts

PRODUCER: Jimmy Miller

ENGINEER: Eddie Kramer

NOTES: "Primo Grande" is the embryonic instrumental backing track for the unreleased "Did Everybody Pay Their Dues," which eventually became "Street Fighting Man." It was recorded on a cassette machine at Keith's house and used on the final release. Keith liked the funky sound quality of those early takes on cassette—with Charlie on a toy drum—and so did the rest of the band. But the raw feeling of the tune wasn't there after they rere-

Keith relaxes between takes during a session at Olympic Studios in 1968. (COURTESY OF ABKCO)

corded the track on studio equipment. Instead of spending many more hours trying to make a multi-track professional machine duplicate the sound of a portable cassette recorder, Jimmy Miller, their new producer, opted for a simple solution. He recorded Keith and Charlie on Keith's cassette machine, then dubbed that track onto four-track and recording proceeded from there, finally ending up on an eight-track master at Olympic.

When Jimmy Miller was brought in to produce, he insisted on bringing along his own engineer, Eddie Kramer. This meant booting out Glyn Johns, who had told the band about Miller when they decided to look for an American producer. Kramer left after finishing his work on *Beggars Banquet*, and Glyn was back in the engineer's chair beginning from April 7. Both engineers worked on the LP.

MARCH 17–APRIL 1, 1968
OLYMPIC STUDIOS, LONDON, ENGLAND

SONGS: Jigsaw Puzzle / Child of the Moon / Parachute Woman / Jumpin' Jack Flash / *Pay Your Dues (Street Fighting Man*, ET) / [a.k.a.] *Primo Grande / Child of the Moon* (acoustic version), ET / *Title 5*

ADDITIONAL PERSONNEL: Dave Mason, Rick Grech, Roger Chapman, Jim King, Rocky Dijon (a.k.a. Kwazi Dzidzornu), Nicky Hopkins, Jimmy Miller

PRODUCER: Jimmy Miller

ENGINEER: Eddie Kramer

NOTES: Brian Jones, saxophone on "Child of the Moon" and sitar on "Pay Your Dues." Also on "Child of the Moon" were Rocky Dijon (whose real name was

Kwazi Dzidzornu) on percussion and Jimmy Miller on vocal. Miller's falsetto can be heard at the beginning of "Child of the Moon." The song was first recorded as an acoustic number; that version was never used; the released track was done on March 29. "Parachute Woman" was completed on March 25; "Title 5" was also recorded on March 25, but was renamed when the finished track was laid down on March 29. "Title 5" was the working title for "Jumpin' Jack Flash." The song "Jigsaw Puzzle" —which loosely originated out of Mick and Marianne's penchant for doing real jigsaws at home—got put together in the studio and onto tape on March 23.

The development of "Pay Your Dues" into the well-known "Street Fighting Man" was an unusually complex process and quite unique among Jagger/Richards songs. Written during November–December 1967, "Pay Your Dues" is also a good deal more than an early take of "Street Fighting Man." The working title "Primo Grande" listed above is the precursor to "Pay Your Dues," probably the best full take of the basic instrumental track, transferred from cassette to four-track (see February–March 1968 entry). "Pay Your Dues" is the basis for "Street Fighting Man," with nearly the same music but different lyrics. New words were written after "Pay Your Dues" was in the can. The Stones worked on the song ("Pay Your Dues") throughout these March Olympic sessions, finally finishing it (or so they thought at the time) in an all-night marathon, March 31–April 1. In addition to Brian on sitar, "Pay Your Dues" featured Dave Mason on shehani—an Indian reed instrument similar to a clarinet—plus Rick Grech on electric violin, and Roger Chapman and Jim King on backup vocals. Chapman and King were members of the group Family, who just happened to be booked into Olympic that last night, as was Mason.

"Pay Your Dues" was actually scheduled for release on May 26, 1968 as the band's next single (with that title) backed with "Child of the Moon." It had even been announced in the trade press on May 4. One week later, though, the band had a change of heart and, they thought, a potentially better tune for a single. On May 11 the original single was withdrawn and reconfigured —"Jumpin' Jack Flash" was released in the UK on May 24 (May 31 in the US) in place of "Pay Your Dues"; "Child of the Moon" remained the B-side. Meanwhile, "Pay Your Dues" continued to develop conceptually (one line is: "Did everybody pay their dues?") amidst the student uprisings and anti–Vietnam War upheaval of the spring and early summer of 1968. Jagger wrote new lyrics, discarded the original vocal track and recorded a new one —the result was "Street Fighting Man," destined to become a Stones classic and one of the world's best-known songs from the '60's. Rick Grech's electric violin on "Pay Your Dues" seems to have gotten lost in the transformation to "Street Fighting Man." For obvious reasons, the vocals by Family members Roger Chapman (*another Chapman on a Stones track!*) and Jim King went the way of Jagger's own "Pay Their Dues" effort. Although Eddie Kramer left Britain for the US on April 17, 1968, he received the engineering credit on "Street Fighting Man." Glyn Johns actually recorded Jagger's new vocal, but Kramer had shepherded the track from its cassette-deck beginning until "Pay Your Dues" was completed.

APRIL 3, 1968
OLYMPIC STUDIOS, LONDON, ENGLAND

SONGS: Stray Cat Blues / *Pay Your Dues*
PRODUCER: Jimmy Miller
ENGINEER: Eddie Kramer

APRIL 20, 1968
OLYMPIC STUDIOS, LONDON, ENGLAND

SONGS: Jumpin' Jack Flash
PRODUCER: Jimmy Miller
ENGINEER: Glyn Johns

APRIL 27, 1968
OLYMPIC STUDIOS, LONDON, ENGLAND

SONGS: Jumpin' Jack Flash, PV
PRODUCER: Jimmy Miller
ENGINEER: Glyn Johns
NOTES: This version was made for use in a "Jumpin' Jack Flash" promo video (hence, the designation "PV")

Mick Jagger and Charlie Watts at Olympic Studios in June '68 (COURTESY OF ABKCO)

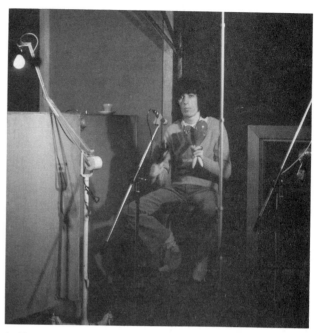

Bill Wyman on maracas at Olympic Studios, June '68
(COURTESY OF ABKCO)

and was never released on record. Instrumentally, it is a more up-tempo track from the record version. Mick sings the song differently as well. However, one of the "Jumpin' Jack Flash" promo films actually suffered as a result of this new take. (See PROMOTIONAL FILMS AND VIDEOS)

MAY 9–10, 1968
OLYMPIC STUDIOS, LONDON, ENGLAND

SONGS: *Silver Blanket*, WT
ADDITIONAL PERSONNEL: Nicky Hopkins (piano)
PRODUCER: Jimmy Miller
ENGINEER: Glyn Johns
NOTE: At this stage, the eight-track master labelled "Silver Blanket" had no vocals. "Silver Blanket" was the working title for "Salt of the Earth."

MAY 13–21, 1968
OLYMPIC STUDIOS, LONDON, ENGLAND

SONGS: Factory Girl / Prodigal Son (Rev. Wilkins) / Salt of the Earth / Family / No Expectations / Stray Cat Blues / Downtown Suzie (Wyman) / Dear Doctor / Sister Morphine (Jagger, Richards, Faithfull) / Street Fighting Man / *Blood Red Wine / Hamburger to Go / Lady / Silver Blanket*, WT / *Still a Fool* (Morganfield)
ADDITIONAL PERSONNEL: Nicky Hopkins, Jack Nitzsche
PRODUCER: Jimmy Miller
ENGINEER: Glyn Johns

NOTES: Nicky Hopkins played piano on "Family" and "Salt of the Earth." "Sister Morphine" is a Jagger/Richards/Faithfull composition, though some recordings credit only Jagger/Richards. The song was written during these sessions. Marianne Faithfull recorded her solo version on January 30, 1969 and released it before the Stones did theirs. "Silver Blanket" (working title of "Salt of the Earth") developed from early takes into its final form at these sessions. And "Did Everybody Pay Their Dues" became "Street Fighting Man."

MAY 23, 1968
OLYMPIC STUDIOS, LONDON, ENGLAND

SONGS: Love in Vain (Robt. Johnson)
ADDITIONAL PERSONNEL: Ry Cooder, Nicky Hopkins (keyboards)
PRODUCER: Jimmy Miller
ENGINEER: Glyn Johns
NOTES: Ry Cooder played mandolin. "Love in Vain" is usually credited "Traditional" but was actually written by Robert Johnson, but not copyrighted. Some pressings of *Let It Bleed* lead one to believe it's a Jagger/Richards

composition. They created the arrangement, maybe, but they didn't write it. Note that Brian Jones was not present.

JUNE 4, 5, 6–10, 1968
OLYMPIC STUDIOS, LONDON, ENGLAND

SONGS: Sympathy for the Devil / No Expectations
ADDITIONAL PERSONNEL: Nicky Hopkins, Rocky Dijon, Anita Pallenberg, Marianne Faithfull
PRODUCER: Jimmy Miller
ENGINEER: Glyn Johns
NOTES: Jean-Luc Godard films the Stones recording "Sympathy for the Devil," following its development from start to finished track, for *Sympathy for the Devil* a.k.a. *One Plus One*. As the song evolved from a folk-y tune with Jagger on acoustic guitar through a blues-y number to a samba, the players took various parts on various instruments. And the final released version features some out-of-the-ordinary combinations, as follows: Keith Richards, bass; Bill Wyman, maracas; backup vocals Charlie Watts, Keith Richards, Bill Wyman, Brian Jones, Nicky Hopkins, Anita Pallenberg and Marianne Faithfull. Rocky Dijon is on congas. Besides singing backup, Nicky Hopkins is on

Mick Jagger (center) on acoustic guitar with Bill Wyman on bass (left, rear) and Brian Jones (back to camera). Charlie Watts is on the right (rear). (COURTESY OF ABKCO)

keyboards, his more customary slot. Similarly, Brian Jones also plays guitar and Charlie Watts, drums.

JUNE 24, 1968
OLYMPIC STUDIOS, LONDON, ENGLAND

SONGS: Prodigal Son (Rev. Wilkins)
PRODUCER: Jimmy Miller
ENGINEER: Glyn Johns

JUNE 28, 1968
OLYMPIC STUDIOS, LONDON, ENGLAND

SONGS: Family / *Power Cut / Too Far to Walk / Thief for the Blues*
ADDITIONAL PERSONNEL: Nicky Hopkins
PRODUCER: Jimmy Miller
ENGINEER: Glyn Johns
NOTES: Nicky Hopkins played piano on "Family"

JUNE 30–JULY 1968
SUNSET SOUND STUDIOS, LOS ANGELES, CA, USA

SONGS: Street Fighting Man / Jigsaw Puzzle / Parachute Woman / Salt of the Earth
PERSONNEL: Mick Jagger, Keith Richards, Brian Jones, *Charlie Watts, Bill Wyman,* Ian Stewart.
PRODUCER: Jimmy Miller
ENGINEER: Glyn Johns (and most likely "Gene" of the unknown surname)
NOTES: Vocals recorded and mixing done, for the most part. Charlie and Bill might have been there, though not necessarily. Hence, the italics.

NOVEMBER 16, 1968
MORGAN STUDIOS, LONDON, ENGLAND

SONGS: You Can't Always Get What You Want
PERSONNEL: Mick Jagger, Keith Richards, Brian Jones, Charlie Watts, Bill Wyman, Ian Stewart
PRODUCER: Jimmy Miller
ENGINEER: Andy Johns
NOTES: This was the first attempt at recording this song. It didn't work out particularly well here; the next day they went to Olympic Studios.

NOVEMBER 17, 1968
OLYMPIC STUDIOS, LONDON, ENGLAND

SONGS: You Can't Always Get What You Want / Memo from Turner
PERSONNEL: Mick Jagger, Keith Richards, Brian Jones, Charlie Watts, Bill Wyman, Ian Stewart

ADDITIONAL PERSONNEL: Al Kooper, Jimmy Miller, Madelaine Bell, Doris Troy, Nanette Newman, Rocky Dijon, Jack Nitzsche
PRODUCER: Jimmy Miller
ENGINEER: Glyn Johns, George Chkiantz
NOTES: The players on "You Can't Always Get What You Want" were as follows: Al Kooper—piano, French horn, organ; Jimmy Miller—drums (no Charlie Watts); Madelaine Bell, Doris Troy and Nanette Newman—additional vocals; Rocky Dijon—percussion. "Brian [Jones's] contribution to that session was to lie on his stomach most of the night, reading an article on botany," wrote Bill Wyman in *Stone Alone.* Al Kooper played keyboards on "Memo from Turner." This is the version of "Memo" that appears on the album *Metamorphosis.* The title "Memo from Turner," JV refers to Jagger's solo version that was used in the soundtrack of the film *Performance.* Mick recorded that track at another, earlier session of his own.

DECEMBER 10–11, 1968
INTERTEL STUDIOS,
LONDON, ENGLAND WITH OLYMPIC
MOBILE RECORDING TRUCK (LIVE)

SONGS: Jumpin' Jack Flash, LV4 / Parachute Woman, LV1 / You Can't Always Get What You Want, LV3 / No Expectations, LV1 / Sympathy for the Devil, LV4 / Salt of the Earth, LV1 / Yer Blues (Lennon, McCartney), LV1 / Whole Lotta Yoko (Ono), LV1 / *Route 66* (Troup), LV2 / *Confessin' the Blues* (McShann, Brown) / *Yonder Wall* (Clark), LV1 / *Walkin' Blues* (Robert Johnson), LV1
ADDITIONAL PERSONNEL: Rocky Dijon, Nicky Hopkins, John Lennon, Eric Clapton, Mitch Mitchell, Yoko Ono, Ivry Gitlis
PRODUCER: Jimmy Miller
ENGINEER: Glyn Johns
NOTES: The live recording of the *The Rolling Stones Rock and Roll Circus* soundtrack at the time of performance and filming. Only released and outtake Stones and Dirty Mac tracks are listed. "Yer Blues" and "Whole Lotta Yoko" were performed by the "instant supergroup" comprising John Lennon (guitar, vocals), Eric Clapton (lead guitar), Keith Richards (bass) and Mitch Mitchell (drums). The Dirty Mac also backed Yoko and "perpetual violinist" Ivry Gitlis on "Whole Lotta Yoko."

Additional personnel involved in post-production for the final October 15, 1996 releases of *The Rolling Stones Rock and Roll Circus* soundtrack cassette/CD and the video and laserdisc of the film are listed in the DISCOGRAPHY and PROMOTIONAL FILMS AND VIDEOS, respectively, along with additional information about the Circus itself.

1969

FEBRUARY 9–10, 1969
OLYMPIC STUDIOS, LONDON, ENGLAND

SONGS: You Got the Silver / Midnight Rambler / *You Got the Silver* (inst.)
ADDITIONAL PERSONNEL: Nicky Hopkins
PRODUCER: Jimmy Miller
ENGINEER: Glyn Johns
NOTES: For *Let It Bleed*. Piano and organ were played by Nicky Hopkins, autoharp by Brian Jones on "You Got the Silver." Keith did the guitars and vocals. The released version of "You Got the Silver" was the first song that Mick Jagger was *not* on. "Midnight Rambler" featured Mick Jagger on harp and vocals, Brian on percussion, and Keith, Charlie and Bill in their regular spots.

FEBRUARY 17, 1969
OLYMPIC STUDIOS, LONDON, ENGLAND

SONGS: *You Got the Silver*, JV
PRODUCER: Jimmy Miller
ENGINEER: Glyn Johns
NOTES: This take of "You Got the Silver" features Mick Jagger on vocals (hence: JV).

FEBRUARY 18, 1969
OLYMPIC STUDIOS, LONDON, ENGLAND

SONGS: You Got the Silver
PRODUCER: Jimmy Miller
ENGINEER: Glyn Johns
NOTES: This session included a Stones "first," with Keith Richards making his debut as a vocalist on "You Got the Silver."

FEBRUARY 23–25, 1969
OLYMPIC STUDIOS, LONDON, ENGLAND

SONGS: Gimme Shelter
PERSONNEL: Mick Jagger, Keith Richards, Charlie Watts, Bill Wyman, Ian Stewart
PRODUCER: Jimmy Miller (percussion)
ENGINEER: Glyn Johns
NOTES: "Gimme Shelter," or so the longstanding story goes, was written by Keith Richards while in his car outside the location where Anita Pallenberg and Mick Jagger were filming *Performance*. Supposedly, Keith was not particularly pleased with the onscreen pairing and refused to go inside, instead stewing in the car and writing "Gimme Shelter" until shooting had finished each day.

MARCH 9, 1969
OLYMPIC STUDIOS, LONDON, ENGLAND

SONGS: Let It Bleed / *If You Need Someone*, WT
PERSONNEL: Mick Jagger, Keith Richards, Charlie Watts, Bill Wyman, Ian Stewart
PRODUCER: Jimmy Miller
ENGINEER: Glyn Johns
NOTES: For *Let It Bleed*. "If You Need Someone" was the working title for the song "Let It Bleed."

MARCH 10–11, 1969
OLYMPIC STUDIOS, LONDON, ENGLAND

SONGS: Midnight Rambler / *Honky Tonk Women*, ET
PRODUCER: Jimmy Miller
ENGINEER: Glyn Johns
NOTES: For *Let It Bleed*. Jones played on both tracks, although the released "Honky Tonk Women" did not contain his guitar track.

MARCH 15, 1969
OLYMPIC STUDIOS, LONDON, ENGLAND

SONGS: Gimme Shelter / You Can't Always Get What You Want
PERSONNEL: Mick Jagger, Keith Richards, Charlie Watts, Bill Wyman, Ian Stewart
ADDITIONAL PERSONNEL: The London Bach Choir, Jack Nitzsche, Al Cooper, Rocky Dijon, Madeline Bell, Doris Troy, Nannette Newman
PRODUCER: Jimmy Miller
ENGINEER: Glyn Johns
NOTES: Jack Nitzsche did the choral arrangements. Note that Brian wasn't present. There was a visitor in the studio during this session—John Mayall. He and Mick Jagger had a long conversation about guitarists.

MARCH 16, 1969
OLYMPIC STUDIOS, LONDON, ENGLAND

SONGS: *The Jimmy Miller Show* / *Pennies from Heaven*, WT / *Honky Tonk Women*, ET
PERSONNEL: Mick Jagger, Keith Richards, *Brian Jones*, Charlie Watts, Bill Wyman, Ian Stewart
PRODUCER: Jimmy Miller
ENGINEER: Glyn Johns
NOTES: *Let It Bleed*—period session. "The Jimmy Miller Show" is an actual song title, but "Pennies from Heaven" was probably a working title.

MARCH 22–23, 1969
OLYMPIC STUDIOS, LONDON, ENGLAND

SONGS: Sister Morphine (Jagger, Richards, Faithfull) / *I Was Just a Country Boy*

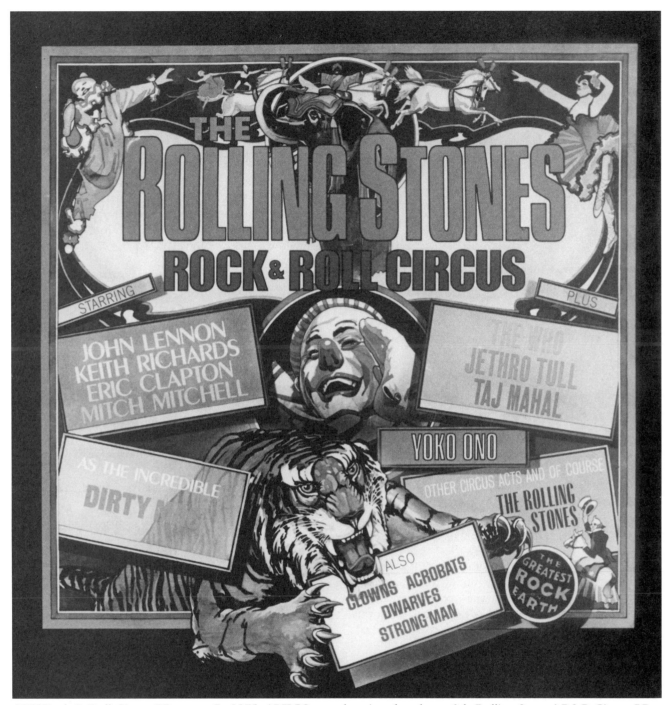

1975 Rock & Roll Circus *LP cover—In 1975, ABKCO was planning the release of the* Rolling Stones' R&R Circus *LP. It had gone as far as making the LP cover, but the project was put on hold—until 1996—and the cover was redesigned.* (TOM BEACH COLLECTION)

PRODUCER: Jimmy Miller

ENGINEER: Glyn Johns

NOTES: *Let It Bleed* sessions continue. "Sister Morphine" is an early take for the Stones' version, recorded on 22 March. The unreleased "I Was Just a Country Boy" was laid down on 23 March.

MARCH 24, 26, 27, 1969
OLYMPIC STUDIOS, LONDON, ENGLAND

SONGS: Love in Vain (Robt. Johnson)

PERSONNEL: Mick Jagger, Keith Richards, Charlie Watts, Bill Wyman, Ian Stewart

ADDITIONAL PERSONNEL: Ry Cooder (mandolin)

PRODUCER: Jimmy Miller
ENGINEER: Glyn Johns
NOTES: For *Let It Bleed*. No Brian.

MARCH 28, 1969
OLYMPIC STUDIOS, LONDON, ENGLAND

SONGS: Sister Morphine (Jagger, Richards, Faithfull)
PERSONNEL: Mick Jagger, Keith Richards, Charlie Watts, Bill Wyman, Ian Stewart
ADDITIONAL PERSONNEL: Ry Cooder
PRODUCER: Jimmy Miller
ENGINEER: Glyn Johns

MARCH 30, 1969
OLYMPIC STUDIOS, LONDON, ENGLAND

SONGS: Sister Morphine (Jagger, Richards, Faithfull) / *Busk Up* (Jam)
PERSONNEL: Mick Jagger, Keith Richards, Charlie Watts, Bill Wyman, Ian Stewart
ADDITIONAL PERSONNEL: Ry Cooder
PRODUCER: Jimmy Miller
ENGINEER: Glyn Johns

MARCH 31, 1969
OLYMPIC STUDIOS, LONDON, ENGLAND

SONGS: Shine a Light / Sister Morphine (Jagger, Richards, Faithfull) / *French Gig* / *Aladdin Story*
PERSONNEL: Mick Jagger, Keith Richards, Charlie Watts, Bill Wyman, Ian Stewart
ADDITIONAL PERSONNEL: Ry Cooder, Nicky Hopkins
PRODUCER: Jimmy Miller
ENGINEER: Glyn Johns
NOTES: This exemplifies the danger of assigning specific album titles to particular recording sessions; there are always exceptions like these songs. Spring to early summer of 1969 was the period in which the Stones produced *Let It Bleed*. But neither of these two released tracks came out on that LP. "Shine a Light" is on *Exile on Main Street*, and "Sister Morphine" on *Sticky Fingers*.

APRIL 17, 19, 20, 22, 1969
OLYMPIC STUDIOS, LONDON, ENGLAND

SONGS: Monkey Man / *Positano Primo*, WT / *When Old Glory Comes Along*
PERSONNEL: Mick Jagger, Keith Richards, Charlie Watts, Bill Wyman, Ian Stewart
ADDITIONAL PERSONNEL: Nicky Hopkins (kb), Jimmy Miller (tambourine)
PRODUCER: Jimmy Miller
ENGINEER: Glyn Johns (chief engineer), Vic Smith
NOTES: "Positano Primo" was "Monkey Man"'s working title. Mick and Keith had been to Positano, Italy earlier in the year and there they wrote the track that would become "Monkey Man." Producer Jimmy Miller used his percussionist's skills at this session by playing tambourine on "Monkey Man"; Nicky Hopkins was on keyboards. Vic Smith was the engineer on the basic track of "Monkey Man."

APRIL 23, 1969
OLYMPIC STUDIOS, LONDON, ENGLAND

SONGS: Blow with Ry (Hopkins, Cooder, Watts) / Boudoir Stomp (Hopkins, Cooder, Watts) / Edward's Thrump Up (Hopkins, Cooder, Watts) / Interlude a la El Hopo (Hopkins, Cooder, Watts) / Highland Fling (Hopkins, Cooder, Watts) / It Hurts Me Too (James) / Downtown Suzie (Wyman) / *Curtis Meets Smokey* / *So Fine*
PERSONNEL: Mick Jagger, Charlie Watts, Bill Wyman
ADDITIONAL PERSONNEL: Ry Cooder, Nicky Hopkins
PRODUCER: Jimmy Miller
ENGINEER: Glyn Johns
NOTES: This session's output, except for Bill Wyman's "Downtown Suzie" and the two unreleased tracks, ended up on the *Jammin' with Edward* LP. As the story goes, neither Keith nor Brian had turned up at the studio that night, so, rather than waiting around, those who were there just started playing. "Edward" was a nickname for Nicky Hopkins, hence the title.

APRIL 29, 1969
OLYMPIC STUDIOS, LONDON, ENGLAND

SONGS: *Mucking About*
PERSONNEL: Mick Jagger, Keith Richards, Charlie Watts, Bill Wyman, Ian Stewart
PRODUCER: Jimmy Miller
ENGINEER: Glyn Johns

MAY 12, 1969
OLYMPIC STUDIOS, LONDON, ENGLAND

SONGS: Country Honk
PERSONNEL: Mick Jagger, Keith Richards, Charlie Watts, Bill Wyman, Ian Stewart
PRODUCER: Jimmy Miller
ENGINEER: Glyn Johns

MAY 12–JUNE 7, 1969
OLYMPIC STUDIOS, LONDON, ENGLAND

SONGS: Live with Me / Honky Tonk Women / Country Honk
PERSONNEL: Mick Jagger, Keith Richards, Mick Taylor, Charlie Watts, Bill Wyman, Ian Stewart
PRODUCER: Jimmy Miller
ENGINEER: Glyn Johns

NOTES: May 12–June 7, 1969. *Let It Bleed* sessions. Brian Jones was not present. May 24 was Mick Taylor's first real session with the Stones, though he was not officially named as Brian's replacement until June 9 and did not appear in public with the band until a press conference on June 13. See individual date listings below.

MAY 14, 1969
OLYMPIC STUDIOS, LONDON, ENGLAND

SONGS: Honky Tonk Women / *Blues Jam*
PERSONNEL: Mick Jagger, Keith Richards, Charlie Watts, Bill Wyman, Ian Stewart
ADDITIONAL PERSONNEL: Mick Taylor
PRODUCER: Jimmy Miller
ENGINEER: Glyn Johns
NOTES: This was most likely the true date of Mick Taylor's first session with the Stones. When he arrived at Olympic for what he believed was just a "one-off" session gig, the band was working on "Honky Tonk Women." He recalls joining in on that song, but because there was no serious recording done that first night, he just jammed with the band (see June 5, 1969, below). The session was *so* loose that Taylor was seriously bored after a couple of hours, and recalls telling the others, "Well, if you're not going to play, I'm going home." At that point, he found out that the session had been his audition, and that he'd gotten the *real* gig; that is, Brian Jones's place in the Rolling Stones. *Then* he went home.

MAY 24, 1969
OLYMPIC STUDIOS, LONDON, ENGLAND

SONGS: Live with Me
PERSONNEL: Mick Jagger, Keith Richards, Mick Taylor, Charlie Watts, Bill Wyman, Ian Stewart
PRODUCER: Jimmy Miller
ENGINEER: Glyn Johns
NOTES: Mick Taylor's first "real" recording session with the Stones. He'd auditioned, unknowingly, for the band 10 days earlier (see May 14 above) at Olympic Studios. Tape was rolling that night, but the Stones' covert agenda was to check out the 20-year-old guitarist that John Mayall had recommended, not to record tracks for *Let It Bleed*. When Taylor returned to Olympic on May 24, it was as a Rolling Stone. "Live with Me" was the first song he recorded as a bona fide, salaried member of the band.

JUNE 5, 1969
OLYMPIC STUDIOS, LONDON, ENGLAND

SONGS: Honky Tonk Women
PERSONNEL: Mick Taylor
PRODUCER: Jimmy Miller
ENGINEER: Glyn Johns

NOTES: Overdub session. Mick Taylor added guitar to the previously recorded track.

JUNE 10–JULY 2, 1969
OLYMPIC STUDIOS, LONDON, ENGLAND

SONGS: Let It Bleed / Monkey Man / Jiving Sister Fanny / I'm Going Down / I Don't Know Why (Wonder, Riser, Hunter, Hardaway) / Country Honk / Sweet Virginia / All Down the Line / Stop Breaking Down (Trad; Arr: Jagger, Richards, Taylor, Wyman, Watts) / Shine a Light / Loving Cup / *I Don't Know the Reason Why / Toss the Coin / The Vulture / All Down the Line,* AV
PERSONNEL: Mick Jagger, Keith Richards, Mick Taylor, Charlie Watts, Bill Wyman, Ian Stewart
ADDITIONAL PERSONNEL: Nicky Hopkins, Jimmy Miller
PRODUCER: Jimmy Miller
ENGINEER: Glyn Johns; on "Jiving Sister Fanny," Andy Johns, Glyn Johns, George Chkiantz
NOTES: *Let It Bleed* LP sessions. Ian Stewart—piano, Bill Wyman—bass and autoharp on "Let It Bleed," Nicky Hopkins—piano, Jimmy Miller—tambourine, Bill Wyman—vibes on "Monkey Man" (Mick Taylor did not play on either cut). The overdubs on "Loving Cup" (Jimmy Miller—percussion, Nicky Hopkins—piano, Clydie King and Vanetta Fields—backup vocals) were not done here, but in 1971 at Sunset Sound in Los Angeles. "All Down the Line" started out as an acoustic track, not the rock 'n' roll electric version eventually released on *Exile on Main Street*. The acoustic version (AV) remains unreleased. Engineer George Chkiantz got a weird credit on *Let It Bleed*. It read: "George—alias 'Irish O'Duffy' Chkiantz." Irish O'Duffy and George Chkiantz are not the same person, nor was this a nickname, but an O'Duffy actually existed (Alan O'Duffy), and he and Chkiantz weren't seeing eye-to-eye at the time. The credit was a bit of an inside joke—a good natured ribbing by the Stones. Now, about that "Gene" . . .

JULY 5, 1969
HYDE PARK CONCERT, HYDE PARK, LONDON, ENGLAND (LIVE)
PYE MOBILE RECORDING STUDIO

ADDITIONAL PERSONNEL: Rocky Dijon (a.k.a. Kwasi Dzidzornu), Nicky Hopkins, Ginger Johnson & His African Drummers
PRODUCER: Granada Television
ENGINEER: Ray Prickett
NOTES: The entire Hyde Park free concert was recorded for Granada Television's documentary, using the 8-track facilities of the Pye Mobile Recording Stu-

dio. (See TOURS AND CONCERTS, FILMS, TELEVISION APPEARANCES)

OCTOBER 18, 1969
SUNSET SOUND STUDIOS,
LOS ANGELES, CA, USA

SONGS: Gimme Shelter
PRODUCER: Jimmy Miller

OCTOBER 17–26, 1969
SUNSET SOUND STUDIOS,
LOS ANGELES, CA, USA

PRODUCER: Jimmy Miller
ENGINEER: Glyn Johns
NOTES: Mixing and overdubs on tracks for the *Let It Bleed* LP.

OCTOBER 28–NOVEMBER 2, 1969
ELEKTRA STUDIOS,
LOS ANGELES, CA, USA

SONGS: Gimme Shelter
PRODUCER: Jimmy Miller
ENGINEER: Glyn Johns and Bruce Botnick

NOVEMBER 2–3, 1969
SUNSET SOUND STUDIOS,
LOS ANGELES, CA, USA

SONGS: Gimme Shelter / Live with Me / Country Honk
PERSONNEL: Mick Jagger
ADDITIONAL PERSONNEL: Nicky Hopkins, Jimmy Miller, Merry Clayton, Leon Russell, Byron Berline, Nanette Newman, Sam Cutler
PRODUCER: Jimmy Miller
ENGINEER: Glyn Johns
NOTES: The Stones as a group did not play at this session, which consisted primarily of Jagger supervising the overdubbing process. Merry Clayton's vocal track and Leon Russell's piano were recorded here, for example. In the final versions "Gimme Shelter" features Mick Jagger on harp, Nicky Hopkins on piano, Jimmy Miller on percussion; additional vocals by Merry Clayton. "Live with Me" has Leon Russell and Nicky Hopkins on piano; horns were arranged by Leon Russell. "Live with Me" and "Country Honk" were begun at the end of May 1969 at Olympic Studios in London. Those songs featured Nanette Newman on additional vocals, Mick Taylor on slide guitar, Byron Berline on fiddle, and Sam Cutler on automobile horn on "Country Honk." Yes, it was tour manager Sam Cutler on that car horn. That was part of the session. And, in order to capture the sound quality the Stones wanted, noted fiddler Byron Berline took his axe

out of the studio. Honest. Engineers set up Berline's microphone outside the building and the musician, a true pro, did his part amid the ambient sounds of Hollywood's streetlife and traffic. Bonnie Bramlett was to sing backup vocals on "Gimme Shelter" but was unable to do so. At the suggestion of Bruce Botnick, the Stones hired Merry Clayton, wife of Curtis Amy—the sax player on the Doors' track "Touch Me."

NOVEMBER 26, 1969
BALTIMORE CIVIC CENTER (LIVE),
BALTIMORE, MD, USA

SONGS: Love in Vain (Robt. Johnson), LV / *Jumpin' Jack Flash / Carol* (Berry) / *Sympathy for the Devil / Stray Cat Blues / You Gotta Move* (McDowell, Davis) / *Under My Thumb / I'm Free / Midnight Rambler / Live with Me / Little Queenie* (Berry) / *(I Can't Get No) Satisfaction / Honky Tonk Women / Street Fighting Man*
PRODUCER: The Rolling Stones and Glyn Johns
ENGINEER: Glyn Johns
NOTES: Although the album's notes may say otherwise, it is probable that "Love in Vain" on *Get Yer Ya-Ya's Out* was recorded here. The entire show was recorded.

NOVEMBER 27 AND 28, 1969
MADISON SQUARE GARDEN (LIVE),
NEW YORK CITY, NY, USA

SONGS: Jumpin' Jack Flash, LV / Carol (Berry), LV / Stray Cat Blues, LV / Love in Vain (Robt. Johnson), LV / Midnight Rambler, LV / Sympathy for the Devil, LV / Live with Me, LV / Little Queenie, LV / Honky Tonk Women, LV / Street Fighting Man, LV
PRODUCER: The Rolling Stones and Glyn Johns
ENGINEER: Glyn Johns
NOTES: November 27 and 28, 1969 live recordings (using Wally Heider's mobile studio) of the 1969 US tour concerts at New York's Madison Square Garden. The above songs appear on *Get Yer Ya-Ya's Out*, but as with the live taping in Baltimore on November 26 and in Boston on November 29, the entire show was recorded at each of the three performances in New York City. There were two shows on November 28, and one the day before. For setlist information for these NYC dates, see TOURS AND CONCERTS.

NOVEMBER 29, 1969
THE BOSTON GARDEN (LIVE),
BOSTON, MA, USA

SONGS: Jumpin' Jack Flash, LV / Carol (Berry), LV / Stray Cat Blues, LV / Love in Vain (Robt. Johnson), LV / Midnight Rambler, LV / Sympathy for the Devil, LV

/ Live with Me, LV / Little Queenie, LV / Honky Tonk Women, LV / Street Fighting Man, LV

PRODUCER: The Rolling Stones and Glyn Johns

ENGINEER: Glyn Johns

NOTES: The live recording of this concert completed the taping for *Get Yer Ya-Ya's Out*. (See TOURS AND CONCERTS and DISCOGRAPHY)

DECEMBER 2–3, 1969
MUSCLE SHOALS SOUND STUDIOS, SHEFFIELD, AL, USA

SONGS: Brown Sugar / You Gotta Move (McDowell, Davis) / Wild Horses

ADDITIONAL PERSONNEL: Jim Dickenson

PRODUCER: Jimmy Miller

ENGINEER: Jimmy Johnson

NOTES: Saxophone by Bobby Keys on "Brown Sugar." Electric piano by Bill Wyman on "You Gotta Move" (McDowell, Davis). Jim Dickenson played piano on "Wild Horses."

DECEMBER 9–10, 1969
OLYMPIC STUDIOS, LONDON, ENGLAND

SONGS: You Gotta Move (McDowell, Davis) / Brown Sugar / Wild Horses / Love in Vain (Robt. Johnson), LV/ Honky Tonk Women, LV1 / Live with Me, LV / Gimme Shelter, LV

ADDITIONAL PERSONNEL: Bobby Keys

PRODUCER: Jimmy Miller

ENGINEER: Glyn Johns

NOTES: Overdub and mixing sessions for both the Muscle Shoals material and the live tapes from the 1969 tour concerts.

1970

JANUARY–FEBRUARY 1970
TRIDENT STUDIOS AND OLYMPIC STUDIOS, LONDON, ENGLAND

SONGS: Jumpin' Jack Flash, LV1 / Carol (Berry), LV / Stray Cat Blues, LV / Love in Vain (Robt. Johnson), LV / Midnight Rambler, LV / Sympathy for the Devil, LV1 / Live with Me, LV1 / Little Queenie (Berry), LV / Honky Tonk Women, LV1 / Street Fighting Man, LV1

PRODUCER: Jimmy Miller

ENGINEER: Glyn Johns, Andy Johns

NOTES: Mixing and overdubbing of the 1969 US tour LP, *Get Yer Ya-Ya's Out*.

FEBRUARY 17, 1970
OLYMPIC STUDIOS, LONDON, ENGLAND

SONGS: Wild Horses

PRODUCER: Jimmy Miller

ENGINEER: Glyn Johns, Andy Johns

NOTES: Final studio session and mixing of the first version of this song.

MARCH–MAY 1970
ROLLING STONES MOBILE (RSM), STARGROVES, NEWBURY, ENGLAND AND OLYMPIC STUDIOS, LONDON, ENGLAND

SONGS: Sway / Can't You Hear Me Knocking / Bitch / I Got the Blues / Moonlight Mile / Dead Flowers / Sweet Black Angel / Waiting for a Friend (a.k.a. Waiting on a Friend) / *Who Am I / Good Time Women / As Now / Rock It / Travelling Tiger / Dancing in the Light / Bent Green Needles*, WT

ADDITIONAL PERSONNEL: Bobby Keys, Jim Price, Paul Buckmaster, Nicky Hopkins, Jimmy Miller, Rocky Dijon, Billy Preston

PRODUCER: Jimmy Miller

ENGINEER: Glyn Johns, Andy Johns, Chris Kimsey

NOTES: *Sticky Fingers* sessions. For the most part, the work proceeded as follows: backing tracks were recorded at Stargroves (Mick Jagger's home) during March 1970 using the Rolling Stones mobile (RSM) studio. Most of the songs were finished in sessions at Olympic Studios in April and May 1970. Naturally, there were deviations from this path, exceptions suggesting that there weren't really any rules. Some examples: "Sweet Black Angel" was recorded here under the working title "Bent Green Needles" but wasn't completed until 1972; "Wild Horses" was finished in February—Andy Johns remembers mixing that tune and "Dead Flowers" while at Stargroves; "Good Time Women" is actually an unreleased early take of "Tumbling Dice," and was recorded in late May at Olympic Studios. Some personnel credits: Paul Buckmaster arranged the strings on "Sway"; "Can't You Hear Me Knocking" features Rocky Dijon on congas and Billy Preston on organ. Preston also plays organ on "I Got the Blues" along with Bobby Keys on sax and Jim Price on trumpet. The piano on "Dead Flowers" was done by Ian Stewart. Jimmy Miller contributed percussion to "Sweet Black Angel." "Waiting for a Friend" was begun here; the track developed in later sessions over the years until completion and a minor title change to "Waiting on a Friend."

APRIL 24, 1970
OLYMPIC STUDIOS, LONDON, ENGLAND

SONGS: Brown Sugar, V2 / Wild Horses, V2 / Dead Flowers

PRODUCER: Jimmy Miller
ENGINEER: Glyn Johns, Andy Johns, Chris Kimsey
NOTES: Most likely a final mixing session. A master tape containing these titles is archived with this studio date, along with another "Wild Horses" tape, both dated February 17, 1970 and marked "final" (see February 17, 1970, and March through May 1970, above). Those are facts. The authors theorize that this particular tape was the source of the alternate version of "Brown Sugar" used in the film, *Gimme Shelter* and that both songs were inadvertently used in alternate versions on the first pressing of the *Hot Rocks* LP ("Brown Sugar," V2 is the same in both places).

JUNE 16, 1970
OLYMPIC STUDIOS, LONDON, ENGLAND

SONGS: Stop Breaking Down (Trad; Arr: Jagger, Richards, Taylor, Wyman, Watts)
PRODUCER: Jimmy Miller
ENGINEER: Glyn Johns, Andy Johns
NOTES: Stu played piano on this track. Jagger played harmonica on "Stop Breaking Down."

JUNE 22, 1970
OLYMPIC STUDIOS, LONDON, ENGLAND

SONGS: *Leather Jacket* (Taylor)
PRODUCER: Jimmy Miller
ENGINEER: Glyn Johns, Chris Kimsey
NOTES: The Stones never released this song. After leaving the group, Mick Taylor finished it and included it on his first solo album (*Mick Taylor*, CBS, 1979).

JUNE 30, 1970
OLYMPIC STUDIOS, LONDON, ENGLAND

SONGS: Sweet Virginia / *Candlewick Bedspread*
PRODUCER: Jimmy Miller
ENGINEER: Glyn Johns, Andy Johns
NOTES: Ian Stewart was again on piano; Jagger on harmonica.

JULY 14–15, 1970
OLYMPIC STUDIOS, LONDON, ENGLAND

SONGS: I'm Going Down / All Down the Line / *Who Am I*
ADDITIONAL PERSONNEL: Stephen Stills, Bill Plummer
PRODUCER: Jimmy Miller
ENGINEER: Glyn Johns, Andy Johns
NOTES: Stephen Stills played guitar on "I'm Going Down," which was released on *Metamorphosis*. Bill Plummer played upright bass.

JULY 20, 1970
OLYMPIC STUDIOS, LONDON, ENGLAND

SONGS: Sweet Virginia / *Aladdin Stomp*
PRODUCER: Jimmy Miller
ENGINEER: Glyn Johns, Andy Johns
NOTES: Jagger played harmonica on "Sweet Virginia."

JULY 23, 1970
OLYMPIC STUDIOS, LONDON, ENGLAND

SONGS: All Down the Line / Shine a Light
ADDITIONAL PERSONNEL: Billy Preston (organ)
PRODUCER: Jimmy Miller
ENGINEER: Glyn Johns, Andy Johns

JULY 27, 1970
OLYMPIC STUDIOS, LONDON, ENGLAND

SONGS: Hip Shake a.k.a. Shake Your Hips (Moore)
PRODUCER: Jimmy Miller
ENGINEER: Glyn Johns, Andy Johns

OCTOBER 17–31, 1970
OLYMPIC STUDIOS, LONDON, ENGLAND

SONGS: Hide Your Love / Shake Your Hips / Sweet Virginia / Stop Breaking Down (Trad; Arr: Jagger, Richards, Taylor, Wyman, Watts) / *Travellin' Man* (Jagger, Richards, Taylor) / *Aladdin Story* / *Potted Shrimp* / *All Down the Line*, AV / *Good Time Women*
ADDITIONAL PERSONNEL: Bobby Keys, Jim Price, Paul Buckmaster, Nicky Hopkins, Jimmy Miller
PRODUCER: Jimmy Miller
ENGINEER: Glyn Johns
NOTES: These sessions occurred after the band's European tour ended. Finishing touches were added to the *Sticky Fingers* cuts recorded during the spring and new tracks like "Hide Your Love" (which was released in 1973 on *Goat's Head Soup* and featured Mick Jagger on piano) were laid down. The unreleased "Travellin' Man" and "Potted Shrimp" were recorded at Olympic Studios in 1970, not during the *Exile on Main Street* sessions in the south of France, or elsewhere, as other researchers have maintained. In fact, "Aladdin Story" (also unreleased), was begun at the March 31, 1969 Olympic session. Those tracks were added to material from this 1970 session and the latter song was mixed here. These outtakes are often associated with the *Exile* sessions, in large part because they show up on bootleg releases along with other illegally obtained tracks that appear to be alternate takes of official LP cuts. As bootleggers combine and recombine tracks and release "new" titles, the amount of incorrect or misleading information grows exponentially.

1971

MARCH 13, 1971
LEEDS UNIVERSITY,
LEEDS, ENGLAND (LIVE)

SONGS: Let It Rock (Anderson), LV

ADDITIONAL PERSONNEL: Nicky Hopkins, Bobby Keys, Jim Price

PRODUCER: Jimmy Miller

ENGINEER: Glyn Johns

NOTES: This is the only version of "Let It Rock" ever officially released. The record was the UK maxi single, RSR RS 19100 (also the first picture sleeve in the UK); it also contains studio versions of "Brown Sugar" and "Bitch." The whole show was, in fact, recorded; the other songs were: "Jumpin' Jack Flash," "Live with Me," "Dead Flowers," "Stray Cat Blues," "Love in Vain" (Robt. Johnson), "Midnight Rambler," "Little Queenie," "Bitch," "Brown Sugar," "Honky Tonk Women," "(I Can't Get No) Satisfaction" and "Street Fighting Man." These other live versions from Leeds have not been released on any official Stones record.

JULY–SEPTEMBER 30, 1971
OCTOBER 15–NOVEMBER 23, 1971
ROLLING STONES MOBILE (RSM),
NELLCÔTE, VILLEFRANCHE-SUR-MER,
FRANCE

NOTES: The only other non-Stones musicians at the Nellcôte sessions were Jim Price, Bobby Keys and Nicky Hopkins—and Gram Parsons (although he did not record for the LP).

NOVEMBER–DECEMBER 1971
JANUARY, FEBRUARY, MARCH 1972
SUNSET SOUND STUDIOS AND WALLY
HEIDER STUDIOS, LOS ANGELES,
CA, USA

ADDITIONAL PERSONNEL: Clydie King, Jerry Kirkland, Shirley Goodman, Mac Rebennack (a.k.a. Dr. John), Vanetta Fields, Tammi Lynn, Al Perkins, Richard Washington, Kathy McDonald, Bill Plummer, Joe Green

PRODUCER: Jimmy Miller

ENGINEER: Andy Johns, Joe Zagarino

NOTES: Mixing and overdubs for *Exile*, from all reports, were arduous. After taking a Christmas break, Andy Johns was not asked back. Joe Zagarino, from the Jimmy Miller camp, had come in while Andy was in England for the holidays. Sometime in February, though, Andy was asked to come back to finish the LP.

DECEMBER 1971–MARCH 1972
(RECORDING/OVERDUBBING AND FINAL
MIXING) SUNSET SOUND STUDIOS,
HOLLYWOOD, CA, USA

SONGS: Rocks Off / Rip This Joint / Shake Your Hips (Moore) / Casino Boogie / Tumbling Dice / Torn and Frayed / Sweet Black Angel / Happy / Turd on the Run / Ventilator Blues (Jagger, Richards, Taylor) / Just Wanna See His Face / Let It Loose / Soul Survivor / Loving Cup / Shine a Light / *Sophia Loren / I'm Not Signifying / Fragile / Fast Talking Slow Walking / Rip This Joint*, KV

ADDITIONAL PERSONNEL: Nicky Hopkins, Bobby Keys, Jim Price, Bill Plummer, Clydie King, Vanetta Fields, Jerry Kirkland, Tammi Lynn, Shirley Goodman, Dr. John, Shine Robinson, Joe Green, Kathi McDonald, Al Perkins. Billy Preston, Jimmy Miller, "Amy and Nitrate" (see below)

PRODUCER: Jimmy Miller

ENGINEER: Glyn Johns, AndyJohns

NOTES: Recorded using the Rolling Stones mobile studio at Keith Richards's house in the south of France. Some recording, overdubbing and the final mixing took place at Sunset Sound in LA. Additional players and their instruments are as follows: Nicky Hopkins, piano; Bobby Keys, saxophone and percussion; Jim Price, trumpet, trombone and organ; Bill Plummer, upright bass and electric bass; Al Perkins, steel guitar; Billy Preston, organ and piano; Jimmy Miller, drums and percussion. Clydie King, Vanetta Fields, Jerry Kirkland, Tammi Lynn, Shirley Goodman, Dr. John (a.k.a. Mac Rebennack, also on keyboards), Joe Green, and Kathi McDonald provided backup vocals.

The true identity of those two speedy marimba players, "Amy & Nitrate," is no longer a secret. In his autobiography, *Under a Hoodoo Moon* (St. Martin's Press, 1994), Dr. John cracked the case wide open. Hardly difficult for him, since he'd been the one who brought all the backup singers and other musicians (including guitarist Shine Robinson, a member of Dr. John's band) down to Sunset Sound when Keith phoned for help. The marimba twins on "Sweet Black Angel" are actually *one* person, and *he* was not at all amused when *Exile* came out. Richard Washington, also known as "Didimus," was irate. He almost popped a voodoo curse on the band for not crediting him for his marimba work, according to Dr. John. Crudely disguising him as a drug (amyl nitrate) wasn't so much the issue. Receiving proper credit for his musical contributions had always been a "thing" with Washington/Didimus.

Mick Jagger played additional guitar on "Tumbling Dice," and harp on "Shake Your Hips," "Sweet Black Angel" and "Turd on the Run." Keith did lead vocals, guitar and bass on "Happy," bass on "Casino Boogie" and piano on

"Just Wanna See His Face." Mick Taylor played bass on "Tumbling Dice," "Torn and Frayed" and "Just Wanna See His Face." Ian Stewart played piano on "Shake Your Hips." "Loving Cup" was overdubbed and mixed at Sunset Sound; the backup vocals of Clydie King and Vanetta Fields, Hopkins's piano and Jimmy Miller's percussion were added to the track begun Olympic Studios in 1969.

The unreleased "Rip This Joint," KV is a version with Keith on lead vocal (KV = Keith Vocal).

1972

MARCH 24–25, 1972
WALLY HEIDER STUDIOS,
LOS ANGELES, CA, USA

PERSONNEL: Mick Jagger, Keith Richards
PRODUCER: Jimmy Miller
ENGINEER: Andy Johns
NOTES: The *final* final mixes for the entire *Exile on Main St.* LP are done in a marathon 36-hour session at Wally Heider's.

MARCH 28, 1972
SUNSET SOUND STUDIOS,
LOS ANGELES, CA, USA

SONGS: Exile on Main St. Blues / *I Don't Care*
PERSONNEL: Mick Jagger (piano and vocals)
ENGINEER: Andy Johns
NOTES: Mick Jagger records a promo spot for the Stones' new LP, *Exile on Main St.* "Exile on Main St. Blues" will appear on a flexi-disc insert in the April 29, 1972 issue of *New Musical Express* to promote the album's release, scheduled for May 12, 1972. During the early planning for this promo, the band had discussed hiring Stevie Wonder, Billy Preston or Carole King to play the piano on this track, but nothing ever came of the idea. Jagger does both the vocals and the piano. The song "I Don't Care" is an unreleased track that also features Jagger's piano playing.

NOVEMBER 25–30, 1972 AND
DECEMBER 6–21, 1972
DYNAMIC SOUND STUDIOS,
KINGSTON, JAMAICA

SONGS: Dancing With Mr. D / 100 Years Ago / Coming Down Again / Doo Doo Doo Doo Doo (Heartbreaker) / Angie / Winter / Can You Hear the Music /

Star Star / Short and Curlies / Waiting on a Friend[*] / Tops / *Criss Cross / Separately* (Jagger, Richards, Taylor) / *You Should Have Seen Her Ass / Four and In / Give Us a Break / First Thing / Miami / Man-Eating Woman / Brown Leaves / After Muddy & Charlie / Jamaica I / Zabadoo*

ADDITIONAL PERSONNEL: Nicky Hopkins
PRODUCER: Jimmy Miller
ENGINEER: Andy Johns
ASSISTANT ENGINEER: Carlton Lee
NOTES: *Goat's Head Soup* LP sessions. Only Nicky Hopkins was present at Dynamic Studios in Jamaica. However, additional tracks were overdubbed at Island and Olympic Studios in May 1973. In addition to Nicky Hopkins on piano, musicians included: Billy Preston, clavinet and piano; Bobby Keys, saxophone; Chuck Finley, trumpet; Jim Horn, horns and flute. Strings on "Angie" and "Winter" were arranged by Nicky Harrison. Ian Stewart played piano on "Short and Curlies" and percussion on "Star Star." Jagger was on piano on "Hide Your Love," which started out at Olympic in October 1970 and was pulled out of the can and worked on here, but not finished (the version of "Hide Your Love" that appears on *Goat's Head* was recorded in *May 1973* at Olympic, as the final mixing and overdub sessions began [see below]). Mick Taylor played bass on "Dancing With Mr. D." Sonny Rollins was on sax on "Waiting on a Friend."

1973

Live 16–24-track recordings were made at the following performances during 1973. The material was archived for possible use in a future live album release.

September 3, 1973—Sporthalle, Cologne, Germany
September 7, 8, 9, 1973—Empire Pool, Wembley, Middlesex, England
September 11–12, 1973—King's Hall, Belle Vue, Manchester, Lancashire, England
October 9, 10, 11, 1973—Gruga Halle, Essen, Germany
October 15, 1973—Palais des Sports, Antwerp, Belgium
Octover 17, 1973—Foret Nationale, Brussels, Belgium

JANUARY 13–15, 1973
VILLAGE RECORDERS,
LOS ANGELES, CA, USA

SONGS: *Windmill / Tops,* AT / *Star Star,* AT / *Doo Doo Doo Doo Doo (Heartbreaker),* AT / *Dancing with Mr. D,* AT

---

[*]A title which was not released until 1981, well after Mick Taylor had left the Stones. The unreleased "Criss Cross" is the correct title of the song called (erroneously) "Save Me" included on many unofficial (i.e., bootleg) releases and in print sessionographies based on unverified data.

PRODUCER: Jimmy Miller

ENGINEER: Rob Fraboni, Baker Bigsley

NOTES: The above three *Goat's Head Soup* titles—"Star Star" [a.k.a. "Starfucker"], "Dancing With Mr. D" and "Heartbreaker"—were worked on here, but these are not the actual tracks that appeared on the album. Similarly, "Tops" is a released *song*, but this alternate take wasn't. We have listed these four as "unreleased," and as A(lternate)T(ake)s, since that best describes these tapes. On the other hand, "Windmill" is a true outtake, an unreleased song.

MAY 23, 26, 1973
OLYMPIC STUDIOS, LONDON, ENGLAND

SONGS: Hide Your Love

ADDITIONAL PERSONNEL: Billy Preston, Nicky Hopkins

PRODUCER: Jimmy Miller

ENGINEER: Andy Johns, Doug Bennett

NOTES: The version of "Hide Your Love" on *Goat's Head Soup* comes from this session at Olympic and was recorded as final mixing and overdubbing sessions for the album began. It features Mick Jagger on piano.

MAY 28–JUNE 20, 1973
ISLAND RECORDING STUDIOS, LONDON, ENGLAND

SONGS: Dancing With Mr. D / 100 Years Ago / Coming Down Again / Doo Doo Doo Doo Doo (Heartbreaker) / Angie / Hide Your Love / Winter / Can You Hear the Music / Star Star / Silver Train

ADDITIONAL PERSONNEL: Nicky Harrison, Chuck Finley, Billy Preston, Pascal, Rebop, Jimmy Miller, Jim Price, Bobby Keys, Jim Horn, Nicky Hopkins, Ray Cooper

PRODUCER: Jimmy Miller

ENGINEER: Andy Johns

ASSISTANT ENGINEER: Howard Kilgour

NOTES: These are the final mixing and overdub sessions for *Goat's Head Soup*—and the recording of "Silver Train" as it appears on the album. That one track, which features Mick Jagger on harp and Ian Stewart on piano, was laid down at the beginning of this block of time and mixed here along with the others.

NOVEMBER 13–24, 1973
MUSICLAND STUDIOS, MUNICH, GERMANY

SONGS: If You Can't Rock Me* / Ain't Too Proud to Beg (Whitfield, Holland) / Till the Next Goodbye / Time Waits for No One / Luxury / Dance Little Sister * / If You Really Want to Be My Friend / Fingerprint File / Black Limousine (Jagger, Richards, Wood) / Through the Lonely Nights / *Drift Away (Williams)* / *Living in the Heart of Love*

PERSONNEL: Mick Jagger, Keith Richards, Mick Taylor, Charlie Watts, Bill Wyman, Ian Stewart

ADDITIONAL PERSONNEL: Billy Preston, Nicky Hopkins

PRODUCER: The Glimmer Twins

ENGINEER: Andy Johns,* Keith Harwood

NOTES: The beginning of recording for what was to become *It's Only Rock 'n' Roll* (the song of that name hadn't been written as of yet, however); these sessions continued in January. Only the band was present (plus Nicky and Billy Preston); Mick Taylor was ill and was not present for the entire period at Musicland.

DECEMBER 2–10, 1973
THE WICK (RON WOOD'S HOME), LONDON, ENGLAND

SONGS: It's Only Rock 'n' Roll / Instrumental Jam

PERSONNEL: Mick Jagger, Keith Richards

ADDITIONAL PERSONNEL: Ron Wood, David Bowie, Willie Weeks, Kenny Jones

ENGINEER: George Chkiantz

NOTES: The embryonic stage of what many believe to be the seminal Rolling Stones song. Clearly a British rocker's tune, "It's Only Rock 'n' Roll" developed as friends jammed at Ronnie Wood's house—well before there was a vacant spot in the Stones lineup. When Mick Jagger realized they had something happening that ought to be preserved properly on tape, he phoned Olympic Studios recording engineer George Chkiantz at home and asked him if he could come down to Woody's and record the session. At the time, Chkiantz had just become a father and, when interviewed 23 years later, in 1997, clearly remembered the call—and the session—quite well: "He was very serious about my coming down," Chkiantz said with a chuckle, "he even offered to pay for a babysitter." After the Wick session, Chkiantz, who worked on this song all the way through its evolution, took the tape from there to Olympic, where further work was done on it; that was merely a technical stopover for the track. The personnel on the basic track recorded at Ronnie's were: Mick Jagger and David Bowie, vocals; Keith Richards and Ron Wood, guitars; Willie Weeks, bass; Kenny Jones, drums.

1974

JANUARY 14–28, 1974
MUSICLAND STUDIOS
MUNICH, WEST GERMANY

SONGS: If You Can't Rock Me* / Ain't Too Proud to Beg (Whitfield, Holland) / It's Only Rock 'n' Roll / Till the Next Goodbye / Time Waits for No One / Luxury /

Dance Little Sister* / If You Really Want to Be My Friend / Fingerprint File / Black Limousine (Jagger, Richards, Wood) / Through the Lonely Nights / *Drift Away (Williams)* / *Living in the Heart of Love*

PERSONNEL: Mick Jagger Keith Richards, Mick Taylor, Charlie Watts, Bill Wyman, Ian Stewart

ADDITIONAL PERSONNEL: Billy Preston, Nicky Hopkins

PRODUCER: The Glimmer Twins

ENGINEER: Andy Johns*, Keith Harwood

NOTES: The continuation of sessions at Musicland, begun in November 1973. Again, only the band was present (plus Nicky Hopkins and Billy Preston). Keith Richards was on bass and Mick Jagger on rhythm guitar on "If You Can't Rock Me." Nicky Hopkins did piano on "Till the Next Goodbye" and Mick Taylor played bass on "Fingerprint File." FYI: the last song Mick Taylor recorded with the Rolling Stones was (drum roll, please) "Till the Next Goodbye." We're not making this up.

MARCH 1–2, 1974 (APPROX.)
OLYMPIC STUDIOS, LONDON, ENGLAND

SONGS: It's Only Rock 'n' Roll

ENGINEER: George Chkiantz

ASSISTANT ENGINEER: Rod Thear

NOTES: The basic track recorded in Woody's home studio is transferred to multitrack, to permit the Stones to add onto it.

APRIL 10–15, 1974
ROLLING STONES MOBILE (RSM),
STARGROVES, NEWBURY, UK

SONGS: It's Only Rock 'n' Roll / Fingerprint File / Luxury

ADDITIONAL PERSONNEL: Nicky Hopkins, Billy Preston

PRODUCER: The Glimmer Twins

ENGINEERS: George Chkiantz, Keith Harwood

ASSISTANT ENGINEER: Tapani Tapanainen

NOTES: Overdubbing and mixing on "It's Only Rock 'n' Roll" and other cuts on the album of the same name. It was at these sessions that the rest of the Stones got a crack at working on the title song for their next album (the "It's Only Rock 'n' Roll" track initially recorded at Ron Wood's house in February), although not all members played on either. Guitar, vocal and piano overdubs were added: Jagger contributed more sing-along-with-Bowie; Ian Stewart laid down his distinctive piano and Mick Taylor augmented the guitar parts. But, Willie Weeks's bass and Kenny Jones's drums stayed

—Charlie Watts said he couldn't do any better, for one thing. George Chkiantz continued in his role as engineer on "It's Only Rock 'n' Roll," but did not work on the other cuts. As to other songs, this is not a complete listing. Billy Preston played piano and clavinet and Mick Taylor played bass on "Fingerprint File"; Nicky Hopkins played piano on "Luxury." However, it is likely that most additional recording done here on tracks such as "Fingerprint File" and "Luxury" was of the fine-tuning variety. This was the last session in which any recording on these tracks was done before the final mixing of this LP at Island Studios, May 20–25 (see below).

MAY 20–25, 1974
ISLAND STUDIOS, LONDON, ENGLAND

SONGS: If You Can't Rock Me / Ain't Too Proud to Beg (Whitfield, Holland) / It's Only Rock 'n' Roll / Till the Next Goodbye / Time Waits for No One / Luxury / Dance Little Sister / If You Really Want to Be My Friend / Short & Curlies / Fingerprint File

PERSONNEL: Mick Jagger, Keith Richards

ADDITIONAL PERSONNEL: Ray Cooper (percussion), Ed Leach (cowbell), Charlie Jolly (tabla), Blue Magic (bkg. vocals)

PRODUCER: The Glimmer Twins

ENGINEER: Keith Harwood, Glyn Johns**

ASSISTANT ENGINEERS: George Chkiantz (overdub engineer), Howard Kilgour

NOTES: Final mixing for the entire *It's Only Rock 'n' Roll* album.

DECEMBER 7–15, 1974
MUSICLAND STUDIOS,
MUNICH, WEST GERMANY

SONGS: Fool to Cry / Cherry Oh Baby (Donaldson) / Slave / Hand of Fate / Hey Negrita / Worried About You

PERSONNEL: Mick Jagger, Keith Richards, Charlie Watts, Bill Wyman, Ian Stewart

ADDITIONAL PERSONNEL: Ron Wood, Nicky Hopkins

PRODUCER: The Glimmer Twins

ENGINEERS: Keith Harwood, Mac

NOTES: For *Black & Blue* LP. Ron Wood, electric guitar; Nicky Hopkins, organ; Jagger and Richards, vocals on "Cherry Oh Baby" (Donaldson). Nicky Hopkins, piano and string synthesizer; Jagger, electric piano and lead vocal on "Fool to Cry." Mick Taylor was not present; his resignation was announced to the press on December 12.

**"Fingerprint File" was mixed by Glyn Johns, the balnce by Keith Harwood.

1975

Live 16–24-track recordings were done at the folowing concerts this year, for use in a potential live album:

June 14, 1975—Municipal Stadium, Cleveland, OH
June 15, 1975—Buffalo Municipal Auditorium, Buffalo, NY
June 17–18, 1975—Maple Leaf Gardens, Toronto, Ontario, Canada
July 10–July 13, 1975—The Los Angeles Forum, Inglewood, CA
July 15–16, 1975—The Cow Palace, San Francisco, CA
July 27–28, 1975—Cobo Hall, Detroit, MI

JANUARY 23–FEBRUARY 9, 1975
ROLLING STONES MOBILE (RSM),
ROTTERDAM, THE NETHERLANDS

SONGS: Melody* / Worried About You / Slave / *Let's Do It Right / Freeway Jam / English Rose / Shame Shame Shame (Reed)*
PERSONNEL: Mick Jagger, Keith Richards, Charlie Watts, Bill Wyman, Ian Stewart
ADDITIONAL PERSONNEL: Ron Wood, Billy Preston, Arif Mardin
PRODUCER: The Glimmer Twins
ENGINEER: Glyn Johns*, Keith Harwood
NOTES: Rolling Stones mobile studio in Rotterdam, Holland. For *Black & Blue* LP. On "Melody" Billy Preston was on piano and organ and provided additional vocals, and Arif Mardin did the horn arrangement. Mick Jagger did the foot stomp on that tune. Ron Wood was not an official Stone, though he regularly recorded and toured with the band throughout 1975. He was still officially with the Faces. He is listed under the "Additional Personnel" category until after February 1976, when he became an authentic Rolling Stone.

MARCH 25–APRIL 4, 1975
MUSICLAND STUDIOS, MUNICH,
WEST GERMANY

SONGS: Hot Stuff / Hand of Fate / Memory Motel / Hey Negrita / Crazy Mama / *Start Me Up*, reggae version / *I Love Ladies / Munich Hilton*
ADDITIONAL PERSONNEL: Ron Wood, Billy Preston, Ollie Brown, Harvey Mandel, Wayne Perkins
PRODUCER: The Glimmer Twins
ENGINEER: Keith Harwood
NOTES: *Black & Blue* LP sessions. A few interesting facts about the tunes recorded here: on "Hot Stuff" Harvey Mandel played lead guitar, and Ollie Brown, Bill Wyman, Mick Jagger, Ian Stewart and Charlie Watts did the percussion. Wayne Perkins played solo guitar and Billy Pre-

ston, piano, on "Hand of Fate." On "Memory Motel" Mick Jagger played concert piano and provided lead vocals; Keith Richards was on electric piano and vocals (lead harmony and backup); Mandel and Perkins were on guitar; and Preston, string synthesizer and backup vocals. Ron Wood played lead guitar on "Hey Negrita."

JUNE 17, 1975
MAPLE LEAF GARDENS (LIVE),
TORONTO, ONTARIO, CANADA

SONGS: Fingerprint File, LV1 / It's Only Rock 'n' Roll, LV1
ADDITIONAL PERSONNEL: Ron Wood
PRODUCER: The Glimmer Twins
ENGINEER: Eddie Kramer, Ron Nevison
NOTES: These tracks appear on the *Love You Live* album.

OCTOBER 19–NOVEMBER 30, 1975
MOUNTAIN RECORDING STUDIOS,
MONTREUX, SWITZERLAND

SONGS: Hand of Fate / Fool to Cry / Cherry Oh Baby (Donaldson) / Crazy Mama / Hot Stuff / Memory Motel
NOTES: Final overdubbing and mixing for the *Black & Blue* LP.
ENGINEER: Keith Harwood
ASSISTANT ENGINEER: Lew Hahn

1976

Live 16–24-track recordings were done at the folowing concerts this year, for use in a potential live album:

May 22–23, 1976—Earls Court Arena, Earls Court, London, England
May 29–30, 1976–Zuiderpark, The Hague, Holland
June 1, 1976—Westfallenhalle, Dortmund, Germany
June 2, 1976 (two shows)—Sporthalle, Cologne, West Germany
June 4–5, 1976 (four shows)—Les Abattoirs, Paris, France
June 9, 1976—Palais des Sports, Lyon, France
June 16–17, 1976—Olmpiahalle, Munich, Germany
June 19, 1976—Neckarstadion, Stuttgart, Germany
August 21, 1976—Knebworth House, Knebworth, Hertfordshire, England

JANUARY 18–FEBRUARY 1976
ATLANTIC RECORDING STUDIOS,
STERLING SOUND, NEW YORK, NY, USA

PERSONNEL: Mick Jagger, Keith Richards
PRODUCER: The Glimmer Twins

NOTES: Mixing and final overdubs for *Black & Blue*.
ENGINEER: Chris Kimsey
MASTERING ENGINEERS: Lee Hulko, Gene Paul

MAY 21–MAY 26, 1976
EARL'S COURT ARENA (LIVE),
LONDON, ENGLAND

SONGS: If You Can't Rock Me → Get Off of My Cloud, LMV1 / Sympathy for the Devil, LV2
PERSONNEL: Mick Jagger, Keith Richards, Ron Wood, Charlie Watts, Bill Wyman, Ian Stewart
ADDITIONAL PERSONNEL: Billy Preston, Ollie Brown
PRODUCER: The Glimmer Twins
ENGINEER: Keith Harwood
ASSISTANT ENGINEERS: Mick McKenna, Tapani Tapanainen
NOTES: These tracks appear on *Love You Live*. Ron Wood was finally performing as an official member of the Rolling Stones, per the formal announcement on February 28, 1976.

JUNE 5–7, 1976
LES ABATTOIRS (LIVE),
PARIS, FRANCE

SONGS: Honky Tonk Women, LV2 / You Gotta Move (McDowell, Davis), LV1 / Happy, LV1 / Hot Stuff, LV1 / Star Star, LV1 / Tumbling Dice, LV1 / You Can't Always Get What You Want, LV1 / Brown Sugar, LV1 / Jumpin' Jack Flash, LV2
ADDITIONAL PERSONNEL: Billy Preston, Ollie Brown
PRODUCER: The Glimmer Twins
ENGINER: Keith Harwood
ASSISTANT ENGINEERS: Mick McKenna, Tapani Tapanainen
NOTES: These tracks appear on *Love You Live*.

1977

MARCH 4 AND 5, 1977
EL MOCAMBO CLUB (LIVE),
TORONTO, ONTARIO, CANADA

SONGS: Mannish Boy (London, McDaniel, Morganfield) / Cracking Up (McDaniel) / Little Red Rooster (Dixon), LV / Around & Around (Berry), LV
ADDITIONAL PERSONNEL: Billy Preston, Ollie Brown
PRODUCER: The Glimmer Twins
ENGINEER: Eddie Kramer
NOTES: The tracks recorded at these shows appear on *Love You Live*. Billy Preston was on keyboards and Ollie Brown on percussion. The whole set was recorded on both occasions. The other songs included "Route 66"

(which opened the show on March 4), "Starfucker" a.k.a. "Star Star," "Worried about You," "Dance Little Sister," "Honky Tonk Women" (the opener on March 5), "Let's Spend the Night Together," "All Down the Line," "Hand of Fate," "Jumpin' Jack Flash" and "Crazy Mama."

JUNE 20–JULY 30, 1977
ATLANTIC RECORDING STUDIOS,
NEW YORK, NY, USA

SONGS: Honky Tonk Women, LV2 / If You Can't Rock Me → Get Off of My Cloud, LMV1 / Happy, LV1 / Hot Stuff, LV1 / Star Star, LV1 / Tumbling Dice, LV1 / Fingerprint File, LV1 / You Gotta Move (McDowell, Davis), LV1 / You Can't Always Get What You Want, LV1 / Mannish Boy (London, McDaniel, Morganfield) / Cracking Up (McDaniel) / Little Red Rooster (Dixon), LV1 / Around & Around (Berry), LV / It's Only Rock 'n' Roll, LV1 / Brown Sugar, LV1 / Jumpin' Jack Flash, LV2 / Sympathy for the Devil, LV2
PERSONNEL: Mick Jagger, Keith Richards (plus the rest of the band at various times)
PRODUCER: The Glimmer Twins
REMIX ENGINEERS: Eddie Kramer, Jimmy Douglass
NOTES: Final mixing of the LP *Love You Live*.

OCTOBER 10–DECEMBER 21, 1977
PATHÉ MARCONI, EMI STUDIOS,
PARIS, FRANCE

SONGS: Miss You / When the Whip Comes Down / Just My Imagination (Running Away with Me) (Whitfield, Strong) / Some Girls / Lies / Far Away Eyes / Respectable / Beast of Burden, V1 / Beast of Burden, V2 / Shattered / Everything Is Turning to Gold (Jagger, Richards, Wood) / *Claudine* / *Everlasting Is My Love* / *Jah Wonderful* / *Los Trios Guitarras* (inst.) / *Jah Is Not Dead* / *Covered in Bruises* (Jagger, Richards, Wood)
ADDITIONAL PERSONNEL: Ian McLagan, Mel Collins, Sugar Blue, Boz Scaggs
PRODUCER: The Glimmer Twins
ENGINEER: Chris Kimsey
ASSISTANT ENGINEERS: Benny King, Barry Sage
NOTES: These *Some Girls* sessions took place during two blocks of time within this period. The first was from October 10 through November 25, 1977. Recording then resumed on December 5 and continued through December 21, 1977. Ian McLagan: piano, Hammond organ ("Miss You," "Just My Imagination"). Mel Collins, saxophone and Sugar Blue, harmonica on "Miss You." Sugar Blue also played harmonica on "Some Girls," and on the same song Keith Richards was on bass and acoustic guitar, Ron Wood on acoustic guitar, Mick Jagger on additional guitar and Bill Wyman on synthesizer. Jagger

also contributed additional guitar on "Miss You," "When the Whip Comes Down," "Lies," "Just My Imagination" and "Respectable." Jagger and Richards were both on piano on "Far Away Eyes," and Ron Wood was on pedal steel guitar. Wood played bass, pedal steel and lead guitars on "Shattered." The "Beast of Burden" on vinyl and cassette—the one most of us know—is V1. An entirely different version—V2—went on products for the short-lived eight-track tape player.

1978

JANUARY 5–MARCH 2, 1978
PATHÉ MARCONI, EMI STUDIOS,
PARIS, FRANCE

SONGS: Before They Make Me Run* / *So Young / Fiji Gin / I Can't Help It / Do You Think I Care / The Way She Held Me Tight / I Need You / Let's Go Steady* (Cooke) / *Petrol / Everlasting Is My Love / No Spare Parts / You Win Again / Claudine / It's a Lie / It's All Wrong / Never Let Her Go / Never Make You Cry / Not the Way to Go / Biscuit Blues / Disco Music / When You're Gone / Angeline*
ADDITIONAL PERSONNEL: Keith Moon
PRODUCER: The Glimmer Twins
ENGINEER: Chris Kimsey, Dave Jordon*
NOTES: *Some Girls* sessions, continued. Keith Richards did the vocals and played bass, and electric and acoustic guitars on "Before They Make Me Run." Note that "So Young," which was released in 1994 as the B-side of "Love Is Strong" and was the first single off the *Voodoo Lounge* album, was first recorded here.

MARCH 15–31, 1978
ATLANTIC RECORDING STUDIOS,
NEW YORK, NY

SONGS: Miss You / When The Whip Comes Down / Just My Imagination (Whitfield, Strong) / Some Girls / Lies / Far Away Eyes / Respectable / Before They Make Me Run / Beast of Burden, V1 / Shattered
PRODUCER: The Glimmer Twins
MASTER ENGINEER: Ted Jensen
NOTES: Mixing of the LP *Some Girls*.

JUNE 28, 1978
MID-SOUTH COLISEUM (LIVE),
MEMPHIS, TN, USA

SONGS: When the Whip Comes Down, LV
ADDITIONAL PERSONNEL: Ian McLagan
PRODUCER: The Glimmer Twins
ENGINEER: Bob Clearmountain

NOTES: This is the version of "When the Whip Comes Down" that appears on the album, *Sucking in the 70s.*

AUGUST–SEPTEMBER 1978
WALLY HEIDER STUDIOS (A.K.A. RCA
STUDIOS), HOLLYWOOD, CA, USA

SONGS: *What Am I Living For* (Willis) / *I Ain't Superstitious* (Dixon) / *What Gives You the Right / One Night* (Bartholomew, King) / *Blues with a Feeling* (Jacobs) / *Tallahassee Lassie* (Slay, Crewe, Piccariello) / *My First Plea* (Reed) / *Serious Love* (Dunbar) / *The Harder They Come* (Cliff) / *Your Angel Steps Out of Heaven* (Ripley)
PERSONNEL: Mick Jagger, Keith Richards, Ron Wood, Charlie Watts, Bill Wyman, Ian Stewart
ADDITIONAL PERSONNEL: Ian McLagan (piano)
PRODUCER: The Glimmer Twins
ENGINEER: Michael Carnavale
NOTES: All songs unreleased. In August the band just listened to playbacks of taped performances from the 1978 tour. Then, in September, they started recording in the studio.

1979

JANUARY 18–FEBRUARY 12, 1979
COMPASS POINT STUDIOS,
NASSAU, BAHAMAS

SONGS: Little T & A / All About You / Think I'm Going Mad / She's So Cold / *Let's Go Steady* (Cooke) / *Gangster's Moll / I'll Let You Know / Linda Lu* (R. Sharpe) / *Lonely at the Top / It Won't Be Long / Still in Love / Sweet Home Chicago* (Robt. Johnson) / *What's the Matter / You're So Beautiful (but You Gotta Die Someday) / Break Away / Sands of Time*
ADDITIONAL PERSONNEL: Bobby Keys, Chrissy Kinsey
PRODUCER: The Glimmer Twins
ENGINEER: Chris Kimsey
NOTES: Keith Richards did the vocals on "Little T & A" and "All About You" and on the unreleased "Let's Go Steady" (this is the same song titled "She Left Me" on various bootlegs). Chrissy Kimsey sang back-up vocals on "Let's Go Steady" with Richards. Chrissy is married to engineer Chris Kimsey. Jagger sung lead on "Think I'm Going Mad."

JUNE 10–AUGUST 25, 1979
SEPTEMBER 12–OCTOBER 19, 1979
PATHÉ MARCONI EMI STUDIOS,
PARIS, FRANCE

SONGS: Summer Romance / Let Me Go / Hang Fire / Indian Girl / Where the Boys Go / Worried About You

/If I Was a Dancer (Dance, Pt. 2) (Jagger, Richards, Wood) / Black Limousine (Jagger, Richards, Wood) / No Use in Crying (Jagger, Richards, Wood) / Emotional Rescue / Send It to Me / Down in the Hole / Dance (instr.) (Jagger, Richards, Wood) / Dance (Jagger, Richards, Wood) / Let's Go Steady (Cooke) / *Gangster's Moll* / *I'll Let You Know* / *Linda Lu* (R. Sharpe) / *Lonely at the Top* / *It Won't Be Long* / *Still in Love* / *Sweet Home Chicago* (Robt. Johnson) / What's the Matter

ADDITIONAL PERSONNEL: Jack Nitzsche, Arif Mardin, Bobby Keys, Sugar Blue, Max Romeo, Michael Shrieve

PRODUCER: The Glimmer Twins

ENGINEER: Chris Kimsey

NOTES: *Tatoo You* and *Emotional Rescue* tracks came from the 1979 sessions that began in Nassau in January, then started up again in Paris on June 18, continued through July 5, then resumed on September 12 and ended on October 18. Jack Nitzsche did the horn arrangement and Arif Mardin conducted the horn section on "Indian Girl" and "Let's Go Steady." On "Dance" Bobby Keys played saxophone, among others, and Max Romeo provided backup vocals. Michael Shrieve did percussion on "Down in the Hole" and "She's So Cold." Ron Wood played bass on "Emotional Rescue." Sugar Blue played harmonica on "Down in the Hole."

NOVEMBER–DECEMBER 1979
ELECTRIC LADY STUDIOS,
NEW YORK, NY, USA

SONGS: Little T & A / Start Me Up / Hang Fire / Black Limousine (Jagger, Richards, Wood) / Tops / No Use In Crying (Jagger, Richards, Wood) / Worried About You / Let Me Go / Indian Girl / Summer Romance

PERSONNEL: Mick Jagger, Keith Richards

PRODUCER: The Glimmer Twins

ENGINEER: Chris Kimsey

ASSISTANT ENGINEER: Sean Fullen

NOTES: Overdub and mixing sessions.

1980

APRIL 1980
ELECTRIC LADY STUDIOS,
NEW YORK, NY, USA

SONGS: Dance* (Jagger, Richards, Wood) / Summer Romance / Send It to Me / Let Me Go / Indian Girl / Where the Boys Go / Down in the Hole / Emotional Rescue / She's So Cold / All About You

PERSONNEL: Mick Jagger, Keith Richards

PRODUCER: The Glimmer Twins

ENGINEER: Chris Kimsey, Brad Samuelsohn ("Dance" Remix)

NOTES: Final mixing of *Emotional Rescue*.

OCTOBER 11–NOVEMBER 12, 1980
PATHÉ MARCONI, EMI STUDIOS,
PARIS, FRANCE

SONGS: Slave / Neighbours / Heaven

PRODUCER: The Glimmer Twins

ENGINEER: Chris Kimsey

NOTES: *Tattoo You* sessions, continued. Bill Wyman played synthesizer and guitar on "Heaven."

NOVEMBER 25–DECEMBER 1980
PATHÉ MARCONI, EMI STUDIOS,
PARIS, FRANCE

PERSONNEL: Mick Jagger, Keith Richards

PRODUCER: The Glimmer Twins

ENGINEER: Chris Kimsey

NOTES: Mixing sessions.

1981

APRIL–JUNE 1981
ATLANTIC RECORDING STUDIOS,
NEW YORK, NY

SONGS: Slave / Neighbours / Heaven / Waiting on a Friend

PERSONNEL: Mick Jagger, Keith Richards

PRODUCER: The Glimmer Twins

ENGINEER: Chris Kimsey

NOTES: Final mixing for *Tattoo You*.

NOVEMBER 5, 1981
BRENDAN BYRNE ARENA (LIVE),
THE MEADOWLANDS,
RUTHERFORD, NJ, USA

SONGS: Under My Thumb, LV2

ADDITIONAL PERSONNEL: Ian McLagan, Ernie Watts, Bobby Keys

PRODUCER: The Glimmer Twins

ENGINEER: Chris Kimsey

NOTES: The live version of "Under My Thumb" that appears on *Still Life* was recorded during this performance, which was part of the Stones' 1981 American tour.

NOVEMBER 25, 1981
ROSEMONT HORIZON (LIVE),
CHICAGO, IL, USA

SONGS: Start Me Up, LV / Beast of Burden, LV

ADDITIONAL PERSONNEL: Ian McLagan, Ernie Watts, Bobby Keys
PRODUCER: The Glimmer Twins
ENGINEER: Chris Kimsey
NOTES: This live version of "Start Me Up" appears on *Still Life*. But the "Beast of Burden" recorded live here was used on single and 12" single releases only, and not on *Still Life*.

DECEMBER 7, 1981
CAPITOL CENTER (LIVE),
LARGO, MD, USA

SONGS: Let Me Go, LV
ADDITIONAL PERSONNEL: Ian McLagan, Ernie Watts. Bobby Keys
PRODUCER: The Glimmer Twins
ENGINEER: Chris Kimsey
NOTES: The live version of "Let Me Go" released on *Still Life*.

DECEMBER 8, 1981
CAPITOL CENTER (LIVE),
LARGO, MD

SONGS: Twenty Flight Rock (Fairchild, Cochran), LV / Going to À Go Go (Robinson, Johnson, Moore, Rogers), LV
ADDITIONAL PERSONNEL: Ian McLagan, Ernie Watts, Bobby Keys
PRODUCER: The Glimmer Twins
ENGINEER: Chris Kimsey
NOTES: These two *Still Life* tracks were recorded at this second December performance at the Capitol Center arena during the Stones' 1981 tour.

DECEMBER 13, 1981
SUN DEVIL STADIUM (LIVE),
TEMPE, AZ, USA

SONGS: (I Can't Get No) Satisfaction, LV2
ADDITIONAL PERSONNEL: Ian McLagan, Ernie Watts, Bobby Keys
PRODUCER: The Glimmer Twins
ENGINEER: Chris Kimsey
NOTES: Another *Still Life* album track, recorded during the 1981 North American tour.

DECEMBER 18, 1981
HAMPTON ROADS COLISEUM (LIVE),
HAMPTON, VA, USA

SONGS: Let's Spend the Night Together, LV / Shattered, LV / Time Is on My Side (Meade), LV2
ADDITIONAL PERSONNEL: Ian McLagan, Ernie Watts, Bobby Keys
PRODUCER: The Glimmer Twins

ENGINEER: Chris Kimsey
NOTES: For *Still Life*.

DECEMBER 19, 1981
HAMPTON ROADS COLISEUM (LIVE),
HAMPTON, VA, USA

SONGS: Just My Imagination (Running Away with Me) (Whitfield, Strong), LV
ADDITIONAL PERSONNEL: Ian McLagan, Ernie Watts, Bobby Keys
PRODUCER: The Glimmer Twins
ENGINEER: Chris Kimsey
NOTES: This track appears on *Still Life*.

1982

MARCH–APRIL 1982
THE POWER STATION,
NEW YORK, NY, USA

SONGS: Take the A Train (Strayhorn) / Under My Thumb, LV2 / Let's Spend the Night Together, LV / Shattered, LV / Twenty Flight Rock (Fairchild, Cochran), LV / Going to À Go Go (Robinson, Johnson, Moore, Rogers), LV / Let Me Go, LV / Time Is on My Side (Meade), LV2 / Just My Imagination (Whitfield, Strong), LV / Start Me Up, LV / (I Can't Get No) Satisfaction, LV2 / Star Spangled Banner (Key, Arr: Hendrix)
PERSONNEL: Mick Jagger, Keith Richards, Ron Wood, Charlie Watts
PRODUCER: The Glimmer Twins
ENGINEER: Bob Clearmountain
NOTES: Playback of 1981 tour tapes plus editing and mixing of tracks for *Still Life*.

OCTOBER–NOVEMBER 1982
NOVEMBER 11–DECEMBER 16, 1982
PATHÉ MARCONI, EMI STUDIOS,
PARIS, FRANCE

SONGS: She Was Hot / Wanna Hold You / Too Much Blood, V1 / Too Much Blood, V2 / Too Much Blood, V3 / All the Way Down / Too Tough / It Must Be Hell / Tie You Up (Pain of Love / XXX (Jagger, Richards, Wood) / *Still in Love* / *Crazy Arms*
ADDITIONAL PERSONNEL: Chuck Leavell, Jim Barber, CHOPS
PRODUCER: The Glimmer Twins
ENGINEER: Chris Kimsey
ASSISTANT ENGINEERS: Rod Thear, Steve Lipson
NOTES: Keyboards by Chuck Leavell, piano by Ian Stewart on "She Was Hot." On "Wanna Hold You" vocals

were done by Keith Richards and Ron Wood was on bass. "Too Much Blood" features horns by CHOPS and additional guitar by Jim Barber. These sessions produced tracks that appeared on the *Undercover* album. The outtake "XXX" is a real song—not to be confused with the working title of "Too Tough." Its lyrics were quite explicit. After they were rewritten, the song then became "Pretty Beat Up."

1983

MAY–JUNE 1983
COMPASS POINT STUDIOS,
NASSAU, BAHAMAS

SONGS: Undercover of the Night, V1 / Undercover of the Night, V2 / Tie You Up (Pain of Love) / Feel On Baby / Pretty Beat Up (Jagger, Richards, Wood) / Wanna Hold You / She Was Hot / *All Mixed Up* (Trad.)

PERSONNEL: Mick Jagger, Keith Richards, Ron Wood, Charlie Watts, Bill Wyman, Ian Stewart

ADDITIONAL PERSONNEL: Sly Dunbar, Robbie Shakespeare, Chuck Leavell

PRODUCER: The Glimmer Twins

ENGINEER: Chris Kimsey

NOTES: Chuck Leavell, keyboards; Sly Dunbar, percussion; Robbie Shakespeare, bass (except for "Tie You Up (Pain of Love)" on which Ron Wood played bass, and "Pretty Beat Up" which had Keith Richards on bass). Ian Stewart and Bill Wyman were on piano on "Pretty Beat Up."

1983
HIT FACTORY STUDIOS,
NEW YORK, NY, USA

SONGS: Undercover of the Night, V1 / Undercover of the Night, V2 / Undercover of the Night, V3 / Tie You Up (Pain of Love) / Feel On Baby, V1 / Feel On Baby, V2 / Pretty Beat Up (Jagger, Richards, Wood) / Wanna Hold Up / She Was Hot / All the Way Down / It Must Be Hell / Too Much Blood, V1 / Too Much Blood, V2 / Too Much Blood, V3 / Think I'm Going Mad / Too Tough

ADDITIONAL PERSONNEL: Sly Dunbar, Robbie Shakespeare, Chuck Leavell, David Sanborn, Martin Ditchman, Mustapha Cissie, Brahms Coundoul

PRODUCER: The Glimmer Twins

ENGINEER: Chris Kimsey

MIXING ENGINEER: Brian McGee

NOTES: Final overdubs and mixing of all tracks for the *Undercover* album took place here at the Hit Factory in New York City.

1985

JANUARY 23–MARCH 2, 1985
APRIL–JUNE 1985
PATHÉ MARCONI, EMI STUDIOS,
PARIS, FRANCE

JULY 16–AUGUST 17, 1985
SEPTEMBER 10–OCTOBER 15, 1985
RPM STUDIOS, NEW YORK, NY, USA

NOVEMBER 15–DECEMBER 5, 1985
RIGHT TRACK STUDIOS,
NEW YORK, NY, USA

SONGS: One Hit (to the Body) (Jagger, Richards, Wood), V1 / One Hit (to the Body) (Jagger, Richards, Wood), V2 / One Hit (to the Body) (Jagger, Richards, Wood), V3 / Fight, V1 / Harlem Shuffle (Relf, Nelson), V1 / Harlem Shuffle (Relf, Nelson), V2 / Harlem Shuffle (Relf, Nelson), V3 / Hold Back / Too Rude (Roberts, Dunbar, Shakespeare) / Winning Ugly / Back to Zero (Jagger, Richards, Leavell) / Dirty Work (Jagger, Richards, Wood) / Had It with You / Sleep Tonight / *What Am I Supposed to Do* (?) / *Baby You're Too Much / Deep Love / Sending Out an Invitation* (?) / *Some of Us Are on Our Knees / For Your Precious Love* (Brooks, Brooks, Butler) / *Strictly Memphis* (?) / *What Are You Goin' to Do With My Love*

ADDITIONAL PERSONNEL: Bobby Womack, Don Covay, Chuck Leavell, Jimmy Page, Patti Scialfa, Jimmy Cliff, Tom Waits, Kirsty MacColl, Ivan Neville, Anton Fig, Steve Jordan, Charley Drayton, Philippe Saisse, The Uptown Horns (Arno Hecht, Paul Litteral, Bob Funk, and Crispen Cioe)

PRODUCER: The Glimmer Twins and Steve Lillywhite

ENGINEER: Dave Jordan

NOTES: *Dirty Work* LP sessions. Additional players and their instruments were as follows: Bobby Womack, Don Covay, Patti Scialfa, Jimmy Cliff, Tom Waits, Kirsty MacColl—backing vocals. Chuck Leavell, Ivan Neville—piano and keyboards. Anton Fig, Steve Jordan—drums. Jimmy Page, Philippe Saisse—guitars. Charley Drayton, bass. The Uptown Horns were present at these sessions but the cuts on which they played were not released, which is why their names do not appear in the album credits. Recording took place at Pathé Marconi in Paris from January through June. The album was mixed at two studios in New York: RPM Studios (July 16–August 17 and September 10–October 15) and Right Track Studios (November 15–December 5).

1989

**JANUARY 20, 1989–FEBRUARY 13, 1989
BLUE WAVE STUDIOS,
BARBADOS, WEST INDIES**

**MARCH 29, 1989–MAY 5, 1989
AIR STUDIOS, MONTSERRAT IS., W.I.**

SONGS: Mixed Emotions, V1 / Mixed Emotions, V4 / Almost Hear You Sigh / Terrifying, V1 / Terrifying, V2 / Terrifying, V3 / Wish I Never Met You / Cook Cook Blues / Fancyman Blues / Slipping Away / Sad Sad Sad / Hold On to Your Hat / Hearts for Sale / Blinded by Love / Can't Be Seen / Continental Drift, V1 / Break the Spell / Rock and a Hard Place, V1 / Rock and a Hard Place, V2 / Rock and a Hard Place, V3 / Rock and a Hard Place, V4 / *Hell Hound on My Trail* (Robt. Johnson) / *Three Oceans / Ready Yourself / Giving It Up / Your Precious Love* (Butler) / *Hang On Tonight / Hold On to Yourself / You've Got Some Nerve / Sweet Thing / When I Get to Thinking / Call Girl Blues*, WT (a.k.a. *Cook Cook Blues*) / *Gangster's Moll / Hot Line / Steel Wheels,* (a.k.a. *Rock and a Hard Place*)

ADDITIONAL PERSONNEL: Chuck Leavell, The Kick Horns (Simon Clarke, Roddy Corimer, Tim Sanders, Paul Spong), Bernard Fowler, Luis Jardim, Sara Dash, Lisa Fischer, Matt Clifford, Phil Baer, Chris Jagger, Sonia Morgan, Tessa Niles

PRODUCER: Chris Kimsey and the Glimmer Twins

ENGINEER: Christopher Marc Potter

NOTES: These are the sessions that produced the tracks for the Stones first new album in five years—*Steel Wheels*. Mick and Keith began in Barbados to see if they could still do it "without killing each other," as both explained on many occasions after the album was released. The experiment was a success, and recording was finished at Air Studios on Montserrat Island.

Some of the tracks listed above as released (that is, not italicized), were not on *Steel Wheels*: "Cook Cook Blues," originally titled "Call Girl Blues," came out only on singles until 1991, when it made its way onto the *Collectibles* disc of the *Flashpoint + Collectibles* limited edition double CD set. "Fancyman Blues" was the B-side of the "Mixed Emotions" singles but didn't make it onto the *Steel Wheels* album either, but is also on *Collectibles*. Originally, "Fancyman Blues" was to be donated to a musicians' fundraising effort for hurricane relief on Montserrat.

The opening to "Continental Drift" is Moroccan music performed by the Master Musicians of Joujouka with Bachir Attar (who had been "discovered" by Brian Jones 22 years earlier, in 1967) and was recorded by Mick, Keith and Ron Wood in Tangier after the sessions on Montserrat

Island and added during mixing. Who played what is well documented on the inner sleeve of *Steel Wheels*, and there are a few interesting facts about some of those tracks.

Mick Jagger, in addition to his usual vocals and occasional harmonica and keyboards, played guitar on seven tracks on *Steel Wheels*. But he did not appear *at all* on "Can't Be Seen," though it is a Jagger/Richards composition. Keith did the lead vocal (and background vocals and guitar) on that track and on "Slipping Away" (which had Jagger doing background vocals only). Bill Wyman was not present on "Sad, Sad, Sad," "Hold On to Your Hat," "Continental Drift, or "Break the Spell." Ron Wood played bass guitar on those cuts (acoustic bass guitar on "Continental Drift") and dobro on "Break the Spell." Chris Jagger is credited as "literary editor" on "Blinded by Love" and "Almost Hear You Sigh." The latter track began, in fact, as an outtake from *Talk Is Cheap*, Keith's 1988 solo album. "Almost Hear You Sigh" was redone in these sessions for the band's album. On the other hand, the *Steel Wheels* outtake, "Sweet Thing," didn't make it onto that LP, but Mick Jagger redid it and released it on his own solo effort, *Wandering Spirit*, in 1993. A couple of the Stones' earlier studio outtakes— "Gangster's Moll" from the *Emotional Rescue* and "Your Precious Love" from the *Dirty Work* sessions—were pulled out of memory and/or their respective cans and worked on when the band got together this time. Neither made it, yet again. And there was indeed a song entitled "Steel Wheels," though it was only a working title for "Rock and a Hard Place."

Additional personnel and their instruments in these sessions: Chuck Leavell—piano, organ, keyboards, Wurlitzer. The Kick Horns—brass and horn arrangements. Matt Clifford—keyboards, piano, harmonium, clavinet; strings and electric piano on "Slipping Away," and percussion programming and orchestration on "Continental Drift." Luis Jardim—percussion. Phil Baer—fiddle and mandolin. Bernard Fowler, Sara Dash, and Lisa Fischer—background vocals. Sonia Morgan and Tessa Niles did background vocals on "Continental Drift." Farafina played African instruments and Keith Richards is credited with the instrumental parts of acoustic guitar and bicycle (!) on "Continental Drift."

**MAY 15–JUNE 29, 1989
OLYMPIC SOUND STUDIOS,
LONDON, ENGLAND**

SONGS: Mixed Emotions, V1, V2, V3 / Almost Hear You Sigh / Terrifying, V1 / Terrifying, V2 / Terrifying, V3 / Wish I Never Met You / Cook Cook Blues / Fancyman Blues / Slipping Away / Sad Sad Sad / Hold On to Your Hat / Hearts for Sale / Blinded by Love / Can't Be Seen / Continental Drift, V1 / Break the Spell

/ Rock and a Hard Place, V1 / Rock and a Hard Place, V2 / Rock and a Hard Place, V3 / Rock and a Hard Place, V4

PERSONNEL: Mick Jagger, Keith Richards, Ron Wood, Charlie Watts, Bill Wyman

PRODUCER: The Glimmer Twins and Chris Kimsey

ENGINEER: Christopher Marc Potter

NOTES: Final mixing of the *Steel Wheels* LP. Note that the two days of recording in Morocco fall within these dates. The Master Musicians of Joujouka material was recorded and brought back to London to be mixed with the rest of the album.

JUNE 16–17, 1989*
TANGIER, MOROCCO

SONGS: Continental Drift, V1 / Continental Drift, V2

PERSONNEL: Master Musicians of Joujouka with Bachir Attar

PRODUCER: The Glimmer Twins

ENGINEER: Mick Jagger, Keith Richards, Ron Wood

NOTES: The Moroccan instrumental (pipes, drums, percussion) portion at the beginning of "Continental Drift" was recorded in Tangier by Mick, Keith and Ron and added in the mixing to the tracks already laid down in the studio during the *Steel Wheels* sessions that concluded in April. "Continental Drift, V2" was actually a snippet of this recording played to open each performance on the Steel Wheels/Urban Jungle tour; we have placed the initial session here merely to give the version an originating point.

1989–1991

AUGUST 31, 1989–AUGUST 25, 1990
STEEL WHEELS/URBAN JUNGLE WORLD TOUR, USA, JAPAN AND EUROPE (LIVE RECORDINGS)

SONGS: Start Me Up, LV / Sad, Sad, Sad, LV / Miss You, LV / Rock and a Hard Place, LV / Ruby Tuesday, LV / You Can't Always Get What You Want, LV2 / Factory Girl, LV / Can't Be Seen, LV / Little Red Rooster (Dixon), LV2 / Paint It, Black, LV / Sympathy for the Devil, LV3 / Brown Sugar, LV2 / Jumpin' Jack Flash, LV3 / (I Can't Get No) Satisfaction, LV3 / 2000 Light Years from Home, LV / Play with Fire, LV / I Just Want to Make Love to You (Dixon), LV / Harlem Shuffle (Relf, Nelson), LV / Continental Drift, V2 / Undercover of the Night, LV

PERSONNEL: Mick Jagger, Keith Richards, Ron Wood, Charlie Watts, Bill Wyman

ADDITIONAL PERSONNEL: Matt Clifford, Chuck Leavell, Bobby Keys, The Uptown Horns (Arno Hecht, Paul Litteral, Bob Funk, and Crispen Cioe), Bernard Fowler, Lisa Fischer, Cindy Mizelle, Lorelei McBroom, Sophia Jones, Eric Clapton

PRODUCER: Chris Kimsey and the Glimmer Twins

LIVE RECORDING ENGINEERS: Bob Clearmountain/ David Hewett and Remote Recording Services, Cedric Beatty, Harry Braun and Dierk's Recording Mobile

NOTES: Eric Clapton played guitar on "Little Red Rooster," Matt Clifford—keyboards and French horn; Chuck Leavell—keyboards; Bobby Keys—saxophone; Bernard Fowler, Lisa Fischer and Cindy Mizelle (Steel Wheels) or Lorelei McBroom and Sophia Jones (Urban Jungle)—background vocals.

The above songs were recorded live at various performances during the 1989–1990 Steel Wheels / Urban Jungle world tour and appeared on *Flashpoint* and subsequent releases. The US part of Steel Wheels began on August 31, 1989 in Philadelphia, PA and ended on December 19, 1989 in Atlantic City, NJ. That final US Steel Wheels concert was broadcast as a pay-per-view cable television special. Steel Wheels—Japan was a month of shows in February 1990. The European portion of the Urban Jungle tour began on May 18, 1990 in Rotterdam and concluded in London on August 25. In 1991, the Stones released the album *Flashpoint* and many singles, CD singles, and special limited edition packages in various formats. *Flashpoint* was comprised of live songs recorded during the year of touring, plus two studio tracks recorded after the tour. Live tracks not on the album release, many previously unreleased tracks, and some old favorites were found on the other releases. Individual shows where specific tracks were recorded are detailed below.

NOVEMBER 18, 1990–JANUARY 1991
METROPOLIS STUDIOS, LONDON, ENGLAND

SONGS: Continental Drift, V2 / Start Me Up, LV / Sad Sad Sad, LV / Miss You, LV / Rock and a Hard Place, LV / Ruby Tuesday, LV / You Can't Always Get What You Want, LV2 / Factory Girl, LV / Can't Be Seen, LV / Little Red Rooster (Dixon), LV2 / Pain It, Black, LV / Sympathy for the Devil, LV3 / Brown Sugar, LV2 / Jumpin' Jack Flash, LV3 / (I Can't Get No) Satisfaction, LV3

PERSONNEL: Mick Jagger, Keith Richards

PRODUCER: Chris Kimsey and the Glimmer Twins

ENGINEERS: Chris Kimsey, Christopher Marc Potter

NOTES: Mixing of tracks for the LP Flashpoint. "Highwire" and "Sex Drive," which also appear on the album, were mixed where they were recorded—at the Hit Factory in London—also during the month of January 1991. See below.

NOVEMBER 25, 1989
STEEL WHEELS—NORTH AMERICA (LIVE)
THE GATOR BOWL, ATLANTIC BEACH,
JACKSONVILLE, FL, USA

SONGS: Miss You, LV / Rock and a Hard Place, LV / You Can't Always Get What You Want, LV2

ADDITIONAL PERSONNEL: Matt Clifford, Chuck Leavell, Bobby Keys, The Uptown Horns (Arno Hecht, Paul Litteral, Bob Funk and Crispen Cioe), Bernard Fowler, Lisa Fischer, Cindy Mizelle

PRODUCER: Chris Kimsey and the Glimmer Twins

LIVE RECORDING ENGINEERS: Bob Clearmountain/ David Hewett and Remote Recording Services, Cedric Beatty, Harry Braun and Dierk's Recording Mobile

NOTES: Matt Clifford—keyboards and French horn; Chuck Leavell—keyboards; Bobby Keys—saxophone; and Bernard Fowler, Lisa Fischer and Cindy Mizelle— background vocals.

NOVEMBER 26, 1989
STEEL WHEELS—NORTH AMERICA (LIVE)
DEATH VALLEY STADIUM,
CLEMSON, SC, USA

SONGS: Start Me Up, LV / (I Can't Get No) Satisfaction, LV3 / Play with Fire, LV

ADDITIONAL PERSONNEL: Matt Clifford, Chuck Leavell, Bobby Keys, The Uptown Horns (Arno Hecht, Paul Litteral, Bob Funk, and Crispen Cioe), Bernard Fowler, Lisa Fischer, Cindy Mizelle

PRODUCER: Chris Kimsey and the Glimmer Twins

LIVE RECORDING ENGINEERS: Bob Clearmountain/ David Hewett and Remote Recording Services, Cedric Beatty, Harry Braun and Dierk's Recording Mobile

NOTES: Matt Clifford—keyboards and French horn; Chuck Leavell—keyboards; Bobby Keys—saxophone; and Bernard Fowler, Lisa Fischer and Cindy Mizelle— background vocals.

DECEMBER 19, 1989
STEEL WHEELS—NORTH AMERICA (LIVE)
ATLANTIC CITY CONVENTION CENTER,
ATLANTIC CITY, NJ, USA

SONGS: Sad Sad Sad, LV / Little Red Rooster (Dixon), LV2 / Harlem Shuffle (Relf, Nelson), LV / Undercover of the Night, LV

ADDITIONAL PERSONNEL: Matt Clifford, Chuck Leavell, Bobby Keys, The Uptown Horns (Arno Hecht, Paul Litteral, Bob Funk, and Crispen Cioe), Bernard Fowler, Lisa Fischer, Cindy Mizelle, Eric Clapton

PRODUCER: Chris Kimsey and the Glimmer Twins

LIVE RECORDING ENGINEERS: Bob Clearmountain/ David Hewett and Remote Recording Services, Cedric Beatty, Harry Braun and Dierk's Recording Mobile

NOTES: Matt Clifford—keyboards and French horn; Chuck Leavell—keyboards; Bobby Keys—saxophone; and Bernard Fowler, Lisa Fischer and Cindy Mizelle— background vocals. Eric Clapton—guitar on "Little Red Rooster."

FEBRUARY 26, 1990
STEEL WHEELS—JAPAN (LIVE)
KORAKUEN DOME, TOKYO, JAPAN

SONGS: Sympathy for the Devil, LV3

ADDITIONAL PERSONNEL: Matt Clifford, Chuck Leavell, Bobby Keys, The Uptown Horns (Arno Hecht, Paul Litteral, Bob Funk, and Crispen Cioe), Bernard Fowler, Lisa Fischer, Cindy Mizelle

PRODUCER: Chris Kimsey and the Glimmer Twins

LIVE RECORDING ENGINEERS: Bob Clearmountain/ David Hewett and Remote Recording Services, Cedric Beatty, Harry Braun and Dierk's Recording Mobile

NOTES: Matt Clifford—keyboards and French horn; Chuck Leavell—keyboards; Bobby Keys—saxophone; and Bernard Fowler, Lisa Fischer and Cindy Mizelle— background vocals.

FEBRUARY 27, 1990
STEEL WHEELS—JAPAN (LIVE)
KORAKUEN DOME, TOKYO, JAPAN

SONGS: Ruby Tuesday, LV / Jumpin' Jack Flash, LV3

ADDITIONAL PERSONNEL: Matt Clifford, Chuck Leavell, Bobby Keys, The Uptown Horns (Arno Hecht, Paul Litteral, Bob Funk, and Crispen Cioe), Bernard Fowler, Lisa Fischer, Cindy Mizelle

PRODUCER: Chris Kimsey and the Glimmer Twins

LIVE RECORDING ENGINEERS: Bob Clearmountain/ David Hewett and Remote Recording Services, Cedric Beatty, Harry Braun and Dierk's Recording Mobile

NOTES: Matt Clifford—keyboards and French horn; Chuck Leavell—keyboards; Bobby Keys—saxophone; and Bernard Fowler, Lisa Fischer and Cindy Mizelle— background vocals.

JUNE 14, 1990
URBAN JUNGLE—EUROPE (LIVE)
OLYMPIC STADIUM, BARCELONA, SPAIN

SONGS: Paint It, Black, LV / 2000 Light Years from Home, LV

ADDITIONAL PERSONNEL: Matt Clifford, Chuck Leavell, Bobby Keys, The Uptown Horns (Arno Hecht, Paul Litteral, Bob Funk, and Crispen Cioe), Bernard Fowler, Lorelei McBroom, Sophia Jones

PRODUCER: Chris Kimsey and the Glimmer Twins

LIVE RECORDING ENGINEERS: Bob Clearmountain/ David Hewett and Remote Recording Services, Cedric Beatty, Harry Braun and Dierk's Recording Mobile

NOTES: Matt Clifford—keyboards and French horn; Chuck Leavell—keyboards; Bobby Keys—saxophone; and Bernard Fowler, Lorelei McBroom and Sophia Jones —background vocals.

JULY 6, 1990
URBAN JUNGLE TOUR—EUROPE (LIVE)
WEMBLEY STADIUM, LONDON, ENGLAND

SONGS: Factory Girl, LV / I Just Want to Make Love to You (Dixon), LV

ADDITIONAL PERSONNEL: Matt Clifford, Chuck Leavell, Bobby Keys, The Uptown Horns (Arno Hecht, Paul Litteral, Bob Funk, and Crispen Cioe), Bernard Fowler, Lorelei McBroom, Sophia Jones

PRODUCER: Chris Kimsey and the Glimmer Twins

LIVE RECORDING ENGINEERS: Bob Clearmountain/ David Hewett and Remote Recording Services, Cedric Beatty, Harry Braun and Dierk's Recording Mobile

NOTES: Matt Clifford—keyboards and French horn; Chuck Leavell—keyboards; Bobby Keys—saxophone; and Bernard Fowler, Lorelei McBroom and Sophia Jones —background vocals.

JULY 28, 1990
URBAN JUNGLE—EUROPE (LIVE)
STADIO DELLE ALPI, TURIN, ITALY

SONGS: Brown Sugar, LV2

ADDITIONAL PERSONNEL: Matt Clifford, Chuck Leavell, Bobby Keys, The Uptown Horns (Arno Hecht, Paul Litteral, Bob Funk and Crispen Cioe), Bernard Fowler, Lorelei McBroom, Sophia Jones

PRODUCER: Chris Kimsey and the Glimmer Twins

LIVE RECORDING ENGINEERS: Bob Clearmountain/ David Hewett and Remote Recording Services, Cedric Beatty, Harry Braun and Dierk's Recording Mobile

NOTES: Matt Clifford—keyboards and French horn; Chuck Leavell—keyboards; Bobby Keys—saxophone; and Bernard Fowler, Lorelei McBroom, Sophia Jones— background vocals.

JANUARY 7–18, 1991
HIT FACTORY STUDIO, LONDON, ENGLAND

SONGS: Highwire / Sex Drive, V1 / Sex Drive, V2 / Sex Drive, V3

ADDITIONAL PERSONNEL: Bernard Fowler, Tessa Niles, Katie Kissoon

PRODUCER: Chris Kimsey and the Glimmer Twins

ENGINEER: Mark Stent; mixed by Chris Kimsey and Mark Stent

NOTES: Bernard Fowler—background vocals on "Highwire"; Tessa Niles and Katie Kissoon—background vocals on "Sex Drive." These songs were released on *Flashpoint* along with live tracks recorded on the 1989–1990 Steel Wheels/Urban Jungle world tour. The additional "Sex Drive" versions were released in various combinations in various formats during 1991.

1993

JULY 9–AUGUST 6, 1993 AND
SEPTEMBER 4–30, 1993[*]
RON WOOD'S HOME, DUBLIN, IRELAND

SONGS: Love Is Strong / You Got Me Rocking / Sparks Will Fly / The Worst/ New Faces / Moon Is Up / Out of Tears / I Go Wild / Brand New Car / Sweethearts Together / Suck on the Jugular / Blinded by Rainbows / Baby Break It Down / Thru and Thru / Mean Disposition / The Storm / So Young / *Troubled Man* (Gaye) / *The Nearness of You* (Carmichael) / *It Takes a Lot to Laugh, It Takes a Train to Cry* (Dylan)

PERSONNEL: Mick Jagger, Keith Richards, Ron Wood, Charlie Watts

PRODUCER: Don Was and the Glimmer Twins

NOTES: These were the initial sessions for *Voodoo Lounge*, recorded at Ron's house in Ireland. Note that there was as yet no bass player. Bill Wyman had announced that he didn't "want to do it anymore" on the BBC on January 6, 1993. (See TELEVISION APPEARANCES and CHRONOLOGY)

NOVEMBER 3–DECEMBER 10, 1993
WINDMILL LANE STUDIOS,
DUBLIN, IRELAND

SONGS: Love Is Strong, V1 / Love Is Strong, V2 / Love Is Strong, V3 / Love Is Strong, V4 / Love Is Strong, V5 / Love Is Strong, V6 / Love Is Strong, V7 / Love Is Strong, V8 / Love Is Strong, V9 / Love Is Strong, V10 / Love Is Strong, V11 / You Got Me Rocking / Sparks Will Fly / The Worst / New Faces / Moon Is Up / Out of Tears / I Go Wild / Brand New Car / Sweethearts Together / Suck on the Jugular / Blinded by Rainbows / Baby Break It Down / Thru and Thru / Mean Disposition / The Storm / So Young / Jump on Top of Me / *Hold on You / Got It Made / Make It Now / It's Funny / Ivy League / Honest Man / Yellow Jacket / Bump & Ride / Anything for You / Monsoon Rangoon / Tease Me / Possesses Me / Middle C / Zulu / Samba / Alright Charlie / Another CR*, WT / *Zip Mouth Angel*

ADDITIONAL PERSONNEL: Darryl Jones, Chuck Leavell, Bobby Keys, Bernard Fowler, Lisa Fischer, Ivan

Neville, Bobby Womack, Benmont Tench, Flaco Jiminez, Luis Jardim

PRODUCER: Don Was and the Glimmer Twins

ENGINEER: Bob Clearmountain

NOTES: The Stones' new bassist, Darryl Jones, joined the rest of the band for this final stage of recording for the *Voodoo Lounge* album. Mixing took place from January through April 1994 in Los Angeles. Note that "Mean Disposition" only appeared on CD releases of the album, and "So Young," "The Storm" and "Jump on Top of Me" are non-album B-sides. "Jump on Top of Me" was used in the soundtrack of Robert Altman's film, *Ready to Wear* (*Pret à Porter*).

1995

MARCH 3–4, 1995
TOSHIBA-EMI STUDIOS, TOKYO, JAPAN

SONGS: Love in Vain (Robt. Johnson), V2 / Slipping Away, V2 / The Spider and the Fly (Nanker Phelge), V2 / Wild Horses, V3 / Wild Horses, V4 / Little Baby (Dixon) / *Parachute Woman*, SV (single version) / *No Expectations*, SV / *Let It Bleed*, SV / *Beast of Burden*, SV / *Memory Motel*, SV / *The Worst*, SV / *Honest I Do* (Reed), SV / *Let's Spend the Night Together*, SV / *The Last Time*, SV / *Angie*, SV / *Make No Mistake* (Richards), SV / *Heartbeat* (Petty), SV / *You're Right, I'm Left, She's Gone* (Gayten, Mendelsohn), SV

ADDITIONAL PERSONNEL: Darryl Jones, Chuck Leavell, Lisa Fischer, Bernard Fowler, Bobby Keys, The New West Horns (Andy Snitzer, Michael Davis, Kent Smith)

PRODUCER: Don Was and the Glimmer Twins

ENGINEER: Ed Cherney

NOTES: Five tracks from this rehearsal/recording session ended up on *Stripped* and are listed as released, above. Recorded outtakes from this session are listed as unreleased.

MAY 26, 1995
THE PARADISO, AMSTERDAM,
THE NETHERLANDS (LIVE)

SONGS: Street Fighting Man, LV2 / Gimme Shelter, LV2

ADDITIONAL PERSONNEL: Darryl Jones, Chuck Leavell, Lisa Fischer, Bernard Fowler, Bobby Keys, The New West Horns (Andy Snitzer, Michael Davis, Kent Smith)

PRODUCER: Don Was and the Glimmer Twins

ENGINEER: Ed Cherney

MAY 27, 1995
THE PARADISO, AMSTERDAM,
THE NETHERLANDS (LIVE)

SONGS: All Down the Line, LV2 / Dead Flowers, LV2TV / Shine a Light, LV2TV

ADDITIONAL PERSONNEL: Darryl Jones, Chuck Leavell, Lisa Fischer, Bernard Fowler, Bobby Keys, The New West Horns (Andy Snitzer, Michael Davis, Kent Smith)

PRODUCER: Don Was and the Glimmer Twins

ENGINEER: Ed Cherney

JULY 3, 1995
OLYMPIA THEATRE, PARIS, FRANCE (LIVE)

SONGS: Shine a Light, LV1 / Let It Bleed, LV1 / Angie, LV1

ADDITIONAL PERSONNEL: Darryl Jones, Chuck Leavell, Lisa Fischer, Bernard Fowler, Bobby Keys, The New West Horns (Andy Snitzer, Michael Davis, Kent Smith)

PRODUCER: Don Was and the Glimmer Twins

ENGINEER: Ed Cherney

JULY 19, 1995
BRIXTON ACADEMY, BRIXTON,
LONDON, ENGLAND (LIVE)

SONGS: Like a Rolling Stone (Dylan), LV1 / Like a Rolling Stone (Dylan), LV2 / Dead Flowers, LV1 / Black Limousine (Jagger, Richards, Wood), LV1 / Live with Me, LV2 / Sweet Virginia, LV1TV

ADDITIONAL PERSONNEL: Darryl Jones, Chuck Leavell, Bernard Fowler, Lisa Fischer, Bobby Keys, Andy Snitzer, Michael Davis, Kent Smith

PRODUCER: Don Was and the Glimmer Twins

ENGINEER: Chris Kimsey

NOTES: Bob Dylan's "Like a Rolling Stone" was released on the album *Stripped* in its full 5:39 length—this is V1. The song was only performed *once* at the show, however. An edited version (4:18), V2, appeared on singles and is listed above merely to indicate the source of the released track. "Black Limousine" was included as a bonus track only on the Japanese release of *Stripped*, although it did appear on maxi-single releases with "Like a Rolling Stone" elsewhere in the world. On "Dead Flowers" Chuck Leavell joined in on the backing vocals in addition to his regular keyboard playing and singer Bernard Fowler doubled on percussion. Fowler did both on "Like a Rolling Stone" as well.

JULY 25–26, 1995
ESTUDIOS VALENTIM DE CARVALHO,
LISBON, PORTUGAL

SONGS: Not Fade Away (Petty, Hardin), V2 / I'm Free, V2 / Sweet Virginia, V2

ADDITIONAL PERSONNEL: Darryl Jones, Chuck Leavell, Bernard Fowler, Lisa Fischer, Bobby Keys, Andy Snitzer, Michael Davis, Kent Smith
PRODUCER: Don Was and the Glimmer Twins
ENGINEER: Ed Cherney
NOTES: Jagger played maracas on "Not Fade Away" and Leavell provided backup vocals on "Sweet Virginia."

1996–1997

DECEMBER 1996
WESTSIDE STUDIO, LONDON, ENGLAND

JANUARY 1997
EAST VILLAGE, NEW YORK, NY, USA

APRIL, MAY, JUNE, JULY 1997
OCEAN WAY RECORDING STUDIOS, HOLLYWOOD, CA, USA

SONGS: Low Down / Thief in the Night / Out of Control* / (They'll Never Make a) Saint of Me / Already over Me / Gun Face / How Can I Stop?** / Flip the Switch* / Too Tight / Where'd You Hide My Blues / High or Low / Always Suffering / Might As Well Get Juiced / Nobody's Seen My Baby / *You Don't Have to Mean It / Anyway You Look at It / Precious Lips / Feeling Now** / I'm Cured / Smooth Stuff / Ever-changing World / Baby, You're Too Much*
PERSONNEL: Mick Jagger, Keith Richards, Ron Wood, Charlie Watts
ADDITIONAL PERSONNEL: Darryl Jones (bs), Waddy Wachtel (gtr), Me'shell N'degeocello, Jim Keltner (ds), Blondie Chaplin (vo), Bernie Worrell (kb, vo), Wayne Shorter (sax), Kenny Arnoff
PRODUCERS: Don Was, The Dust Brothers, Babyface, Rob Fraboni
ENGINEER: [Incomplete at press time]

MIXING ENGINEER: Wally Gagel*, Danny Saber
NOTES: These were the sessions for the band's newest album, which was to be released on September 30, 1997, and was being sequenced and pressed as *we* went to press. The record was tentatively titled—at various times, depending on the source of the information: 1) Blessed Poison; 2) Flip the Switch; or 3) Bridges to Babylon. Number 3, Bridges to Babylon, made the final cut. The first single was to be released two weeks earlier, with "Has Anybody Seen My Baby" as the A side. The B side (said to be a non-album cut) was still unconfirmed.

From insider accounts, these sessions were in many ways unlike any the Stones had ever done. All those producers' names on a Rolling Stones album are an obvious new twist. Multi–Grammy Award winners Kenneth "Babyface" Edmonds and the Dust Brothers were, it is said, Jagger's idea for a way to keep current and on the edge. Though he worked on several tracks, Babyface—whose presence in the studio garnered worldwide press attention—ended up with no album tracks to his credit. The L.A.–based Dust Brothers, most recently known for their work on Beck's (that's the single-named '90s superstar, not Jeff) *Odelay* album, . . . not just another bit of Mick's edge-of-pop strategy.

For his part, Keith invited old friend and neighbor producer Rob Fabroni to work on a couple of the songs near and dear to Keith's heart (and vocal cords). Richards had sung lead on two cuts marked with ** above)—only "How Can I Stop" made the short list. As he had done for all of *Voodoo Lounge* and *Stripped*, Don Was handled production on the balance of the album. Was brought in a few of his favorite colleagues, including bassist and master mixing engineer Wally Gagel, who helped out in the latter capacity.

Every member of the band was involved at all stages of the process; each had pet tracks and brought in favorite other musicians; some of whom are listed above and others who you'll have to identify from the liner notes of the CD when it is released.

Discography (US & UK)

INTRODUCTION

On June 7, 1963, the Rolling Stones entered the pop music world with their first single, "Come On," backed by "I Want to Be Loved." By July 12, 1994, with the album *Voodoo Lounge*, they had been releasing records for 31 years, one month . . . and five days. And they didn't stop there.

This chapter deals with legitimate (official) recordings—singles (45 rpm vinyl, cassette and CD), maxi-singles (three songs on a 45), EPs (four to five songs on a 45), cassette and CD versions of maxi-singles and EPs, and albums (33⅓ rpm vinyl LPs, cassette and CD). Included are various promos and the many compilations released in various formats over this 31-plus-year period.

From the beginning, the Stones have had a quirky release history. For instance, the first time they appeared on an album it wasn't theirs. The Stones' first LP, *The Rolling Stones*, Decca LK 4605, was released in the UK on April 17, 1964. But recordings by the band had been released on several British pop music compilation albums as early as the fall of 1963. The first, *Thank Your Lucky Stars Vol. 2*, Decca LK 4554, released on Sept 28, 1963, included "Come On." And on Jan 24, 1964, two more collections containing Stones cuts were issued: *Ready, Steady, Go!*, Decca LK 4577, had "Come On" and "I Wanna Be Your Man" and *Saturday Club*, Decca 4583, included "Fortune Teller" in a different version from the one on the Stones first EP, "Poison Ivy." The Stones had performed on the British pop music television programs

"Ready, Steady, Go!" and "Thank Your Lucky Stars" and on BBC Radio's "Saturday Club" several times before their own album hit the stores.

This chapter will also show how track listings differed on US and UK records. For example, *Aftermath* had 14 tracks in the UK but only 11 in the US (only 10 songs appeared on both). What happened to such "missing tracks" can be traced through the entries in this section. In the case of *Aftermath*, some of those outstanding cuts later appeared on the US LP *Flowers*, which, contrary to most American fans' understanding at the time, was not a new Stones album. The band hadn't gone into the studio to record *Flowers*, it was a semi-compilation of tracks from two previous UK LPs plus a few outtakes.

Song versions also differed in products released in the two markets in the early years, though not as greatly as the actual makeup of the records. Certain titles were released on singles in one country but not the other, or not until much later. A lot of this had to do with marketing strategy. Tastes and taboos were in a state of upheaval in the 1960s, and the Stones were certainly a motive force. But there was still a difference between what would air in Peoria and what would air in Edinburgh, and the record companies—if not the Stones—knew it.

Also listed and of particular interest to collectors of official Stones records are the many promos and alternate mixes that came out by the carload. Some of these are very rare, like the promotional album released in mid-October 1969. This record, issued by London and Decca ostensi-

The Rolling Stones' first single (JPK/CB)

bly as advance promotion for *Let It Bleed*, contained only one cut from that album ("Love in Vain") but included many samples from previous Stones LPs. Only 200 copies were issued in each country, earmarked for DJs.

Then, there's the frequency factor in the Stones' release timeline. The '60s saw the emergent Stones issuing records at a running clip. The tempo slowed to moderato in the '70s and by the '80s and '90s there were large gaps between new offerings. These gaps hardly meant fewer actual releases, since this was the era of highly targeted marketing and the release of special editions catering to emerging outlets such as disco clubs. Thus the "special limited editions" containing three to six versions of the same song in "Disco," "LP," "DJ," "Groove," etc., versions, mixes or edits.

As we noted in the introduction to the PROMOTIONAL FILMS AND VIDEOS chapter, rather than discussing *The Voodoo Lounge CD-ROM* in the Stones' discography, we've chosen to put it with the films and videos because it has more in common with them than with the band's music-only releases. Of course, we have listed the *Stripped* Enhanced CD with the records, tapes and CDs. That's because the *Stripped* ECD or CD+ contains the entire *Stripped* album and can be played on a regular audio CD player. The "enhanced" part—the interactive material on that disk—is a *bonus* to the music and is accessed by putting the same disk into the CD-ROM drive of a home computer. Since the two products were released at the same time, the *Stripped* ECD has a lot of material from *The Voodoo Lounge CD-ROM* within that interactive bonus section —another way to promote that product—in addition to the music videos from *Stripped* parts of the *Stripped* one-hour video and so on.

We have tried as far as humanly possible to list all official Rolling Stones releases to date. We apologize humbly if we've missed something, particularly in the last decade when Rolling Stones Records seemed to have figured out how to produce the maximum output out of the minimum input and confuse just about everyone, ourselves included.

1963

JUNE 7, 1963

WHERE RELEASED: UK
TITLE & CATALOG #: Single, Decca F 11675
SONGS: [A] Come On (Berry) / [B] I Want to Be Loved (Dixon)
NOTES: First Rolling Stones single.

STONED
(Jagger; Phelge)
PROMOTIONAL COPY

LONDON RECORDS

Southern
Music Publ.
Co., Inc.
ASCAP
Time: 2:10

45-LON9641V

THE ROLLING STONES
DR 31955
Made in U.S.A.

Rare and valuable "Stoned" promo single—the disc was withdrawn from general release. (JAMES KARNBACH COLLECTION)

SEPTEMBER 27, 1963

WHERE RELEASED: UK
TITLE & CATALOG #: *Thank Your Lucky Stars, Vol. 2,* Decca LK 4554 (Compilation)
SONGS: [B8] Come On (Berry)
NOTES: This is a compilation album on which the Rolling Stones are represented by the eighth cut on side B, their recording of Chuck Berry's "Come On."

NOVEMBER 1, 1963

WHERE RELEASED: UK
TITLE & CATALOG #: Single, Decca F 11764
SONGS: [A] I Wanna Be Your Man (Lennon, McCartney) / [B] Stoned (Nanker Phelge)
NOTES: Obviously, this was the Stones' second single. Rare are surviving copies of some early pressings of this disc with the B-side title misprinted as "Stones." They do

exist. With some 30 years distance, one might wonder if record company personnel really merely goofed and thought the Stones were writing about themselves, as was the explanation back then, or whether it was a more purposeful decision by Decca to try to change the title.

NOVEMBER 1, 1963

WHERE RELEASED: US
TITLE & CATALOG #: Single, London 9641
SONGS: [A] I Wanna Be Your Man (Lennon, McCartney) / [B] Stoned (Nanker Phelge)
NOTES: This single (identical to Decca F 11764 in the UK) was released solely for promotional purposes in the US, and only about 500 copies were pressed. No picture sleeve came with this record.

1964

JANUARY 10, 1964

WHERE RELEASED: UK
TITLE & CATALOG #: *The Rolling Stones* (EP), Decca DFE 8560
SONGS: [A] Bye Bye Johnny (Berry) / Money (Gordy Jr., Bradford) / [B] You Better Move On (Alexander) / Poison Ivy (Leiber, Stoller), V2
NOTES: The first Stones EP released in the UK; rereleased as 12" EP in 1982. "Poison Ivy," V2 was recorded November 10, 1963 at De Lane Lea Studios, London; "Poison Ivy," V1 was recorded on August 18, 1963 at Decca Studios in London and was first released on the *Saturday Club* compilation album (Decca LK 4583) on January 24, 1964.

JANUARY 24, 1964

WHERE RELEASED: UK
TITLE & CATALOG #: *Ready, Steady, Go!*, Decca LK 4577 (Compilation)
SONGS: [A5] Come On (Berry) / [B1] I Wanna Be Your Man (Lennon, McCartney)
NOTES: The Stones are represented by two tracks on this popular British television show's compilation album, which Decca rereleased in 1983 with the catalog number TAB 60.

JANUARY 24, 1964

WHERE RELEASED: UK
TITLE & CATALOG #: *Saturday Club*, Decca LK 4583 (Compilation)
SONGS: [A8] Fortune Teller (Neville) / [B5] Poison Ivy (Leiber, Stoller), V1

NOTES: Two tracks by the Stones on this compilation album.

FEBRUARY 21, 1964

WHERE RELEASED: UK
TITLE & CATALOG #: Single, Decca 11845
SONGS: [A] Not Fade Away (Petty, Hardin) / [B] Little by Little (Phelge, Spector)

MARCH 6, 1964

WHERE RELEASED: US
TITLE & CATALOG #: Single, London 9657
SONGS: [A] Not Fade Away (Petty, Hardin) / [B] I Wanna Be Your Man (Lennon, McCartney)
NOTES: The Rolling Stones' first US single. Released in a color picture sleeve, with the same cover design and photo as their first US album. UK singles did not have picture sleeves until "Brown Sugar" was released.

APRIL 17, 1964

WHERE RELEASED: UK
TITLE & CATALOG #: *The Rolling Stones*, Decca LK 4605
SONGS: [A] Route 66 (Troup) / I Just Want to Make Love to You (Dixon) / Honest I Do (Reed) / Mona (I Need You Baby) (McDaniel) / Now I've Got a Witness (Phelge) / Little by Little (Phelge, Spector) / [B] I'm a King Bee (Moore) / Carol (Berry) / Tell Me, V1 / Can I Get a Witness (Holland, Holland, Dozier) / You Can Make It If You Try (Jarrett) / Walking the Dog (Thomas)
NOTES: The Rolling Stones' first UK album. Their first LP, containing the first original Jagger/Richards composition to be released by the Stones, the song "Tell Me." (George Bean was the first to record any of the team's songs: "It Should Be You" was released on a single in January 1964 by Decca, backed with "Will You Be My Lover Tonight." Gene Pitney's single version of "That Girl Belongs to Yesterday" beat Bean's disc into record stores by a month, having been released during December 1963.) There are actually three versions of "Tell Me" on the first Stones releases. Version 1, on this LP (there was no UK single), is 4:08 in length and has a guitar break and an extended ending that does not fade out. Another LP version found on various export albums in Europe and elsewhere, "Tell Me," V3, has the same guitar break, but ends with a fadeout at 3:46. The US album and single version is V2. It is one minute and seven seconds shorter than the UK version, at 2:59, has no guitar break and fades out at the end.

This album closely resembles a typical setlist of live Stones performances of this period. The songs on it were recorded in the studio as if the band were playing them live. Unlike later sessions in which vocal and instrumental tracks might be laid down individually and successively for each song, here the band merely set up and played their instruments as if on stage.

A few historically illuminating notes about song credits: On this LP, "Now I've Got a Witness" is credited to Phelge, but on later releases the credit is Nanker Phelge. "Nanker Phelge" was Brian Jones's idea. It was a way to credit songs composed by the whole group (not just Mick and Keith) for which publishing and other song royalties would be shared equally by all band members. The name itself stems from the notorious period when Mick, Keith and Brian shared an apartment in Edith Grove. "Nanker" was their slang for the weird faces they made at each other (as in "pulling a nanker"). Said Brian Jones in a July 1964 interview in *Rave* magazine, "'Nankies' are little men who think they represent authority. We take them off by pulling down the underneath of our eyes and pushing up the end

of the nose." "Phelge" honored another Edith Grove roommate, printer Jimmy Phelge, who was known for his disgusting personal habits. Nanker Phelge Music., Ltd. was the publishing company created in 1964 by Jones and Andrew Oldham to administer such songs.

MAY 29, 1964

WHERE RELEASED: US
TITLE & CATALOG #: *England's Newest Hit Makers— The Rolling Stones*, London PS 375
SONGS: [A] Not Fade Away (Petty, Hardin) / Route 66 (Troup) / I Just Want to Make Love to You (Dixon) / Honest I Do (Reed) / Now I've Got a Witness (Nanker Phelge) / Little by Little (Phelge, Spector) / [B] I'm a King Bee (Moore) / Carol (Berry) / Tell Me, V2 / Can I Get a Witness (Holland, Holland, Dozier) / You Can Make It If You Try (Jarrett) / Walking the Dog (Thomas)

The mastering information for the Stones UK EP, "5 X 5" (JAMES KARNBACH COLLECTION)

MINIMUM RECORDING TIME
ONE DIRECTION | BOTH DIRECTIONS

THIS TAPE IS RECORD[

AT ☐ 1⅞ ☐ 3¾ ☐ 7½ ☐ 15

BELL SOUND STUDIOS, INC.

XER____/RECORDER____/STUDIO____

35MM   J. O. No.____
4T   3T
2T   M   REEL No.____ OF____
              DATE 10/6/64

"Twelve by Five"
RTIST/PRODUCT ROLLING STONES - LONDON RECORDS
LIENT

MASTER NO.	TITLE	TAKE NO.	TIME	COMMENTS
	SIDE 1 ARL 6493			25¼/9 (L) 10/B/33
33759	ROUND + ROUND ✓		3:00	+7/4
33757	CONFESSIN' THE BLUES		2:45	+6/4
33756	EMPTY HEART		2:36	+6/4
34146	TIME IS ON MY SIDE (see 41761) ✗		2:50	+7/40 +6/4 -8/20
33544	GOOD TIMES, BAD TIMES		2:28	-2/40 +4/4
33543	ITS ALL OVER NOW		3:20	+1/40 +7/4
			17:42	
	SIDE 2 ARL 6494			
33758	2120 SOUTH MICHIGAN AVE		2:08	+7/4
	UNDER THE BOARDWALK		2:45	+3/70 +6/4 -4/20
34147	CONGRATULATIONS	+1DB	2:25	+11/30 +6/4
	GROWN UP WRONG		2:04	+4/4 -2/20
33756	IF YOU NEED ME		2:00	+1/30 +4/4
	SUSIE Q		1:59	+2/30 +3/4 -4/20
			13:38	

DR34642 (en Andy + TH 10/9/7c Rm5
1A-1B- Ghoversville-
1C-1D- Pinckneyville-} 10/7/64
1E-1F- Monarch
2A- Col- 12/13/66 - Rm5
ARL 6494 D.20- 3/7/67 Col kit Rm5
    L +6½P 60 +10P/3 - 10P/10
    R ✗- 5P/60 +6.5P/8

F.S. — FALSE START   I.T. — INCOMPLETE TAKE   T.L. — TAIL LEADER   H.L. — HEAD LEADER

RM NC
T5-5

MONAURAL ORIGINAL

TRANSPORT
#T-

The mastering information for the US album 12 X 5 (JAMES KARNBACH COLLECTION)

NOTES: The Stones' first US album—although its first pressings (about 1000 copies) were actually produced in the UK. "Tell Me," V2 appears on US single and album releases. It is 2:59 in length, fades out at the end, and lacks the guitar break of the UK album's V1. See Notes for the April 17, 1964 release of *The Rolling Stones*, Decca LK 4605, above, for more about "Tell Me."

JUNE 12, 1964

WHERE RELEASED: US
TITLE & CATALOG #: Single, London 9682
SONGS: [A] Tell Me, V2 / [B] I Just Want to Make Love to You (Dixon)
NOTES: "Tell Me" was the first Jagger/Richards composition to be released by the Rolling Stones. This is its first single release.

JUNE 26, 1964

WHERE RELEASED: UK
TITLE & CATALOG #: Single, Decca F 11934
SONGS: [A] It's All Over Now (Womack, Womack) / [B] Good Times, Bad Times
NOTES: The first Rolling Stones single to reach number one on the UK charts.

JULY 24, 1964

WHERE RELEASED: US
TITLE & CATALOG #: Single, London 9687
SONGS: [A] It's All Over Now (Womack, Womack) / [B] Good Times, Bad Times
NOTES: Picture sleeve. Many DJ's deleted the words "half-assed game" in order to play "It's All Over Now" in 1964 America. Still, the song was banned from broadcast by many radio stations before their unlucky employees had a chance to clean it up. The record only made it to number 27 on the US charts. Oddly, the idea to cover the Valentinos' (Bobby Womack's group) tune came from the US. It had been suggested to the Stones by popular WMCA-New York DJ Murray the K, who also emceed their first New York date, at Carnegie Hall on June 20, 1964.

AUGUST 14, 1964

WHERE RELEASED: UK
TITLE & CATALOG #: *Five by Five* (EP), Decca DFE 8590
SONGS: [A] If You Need Me (Pickett, Bateman, Sanders) / Empty Heart (Nanker Phelge) / 2120 South Michigan Avenue (Nanker Phelge), V1 / [B] Confessin' the Blues (McShann, Brown) / Around & Around (Berry)
NOTES: Rereleased in the UK in November 1982 as a 12" EP, Decca DFEX 8590. This version of "2120 South Michigan Avenue" is unique to this record and is longer than V2, which appears on all other US and UK releases.

SEPTEMBER 25, 1964

WHERE RELEASED: US
TITLE & CATALOG #: Single, London 9708
SONGS: [A] Time Is on My Side (Meade), V1 / [B] Congratulations
NOTES: "Time Is on My Side" was credited erroneously to Meade, Norman. The author is Norman Meade. The mistake was corrected on the album *12 X 5*, though it tends to crop up on later compilations.

OCTOBER 23, 1964

WHERE RELEASED: US
TITLE & CATALOG #: *12 X 5*, London PS 402
SONGS: [A] Around & Around (Berry) / Confessin' the Blues (McShann, Brown) / Empty Heart (Nanker Phelge) / Time Is on My Side (Meade), V1 / Good Times, Bad Times / It's All Over Now (Womack, Womack) / [B] 2120 South Michigan Avenue (Nanker Phelge), V2 / Under the Boardwalk (Resnick, Young) / Congratulations / Grown Up Wrong / If You Need Me (Pickett, Bateman, Sanders) / Susie Q (Broadwater, Lewis, Hawkins)
NOTES: "Time Is on My Side," V1, which appears on this, the Stones' second US album, first appeared on the US single released the previous month. Version 1 has an organ intro, while V2 has a guitar intro.

NOVEMBER 13, 1964

WHERE RELEASED: UK
TITLE & CATALOG #: Single, Decca F 12014
SONGS: Little Red Rooster (Dixon) / Off the Hook (Nanker Phelge)

DECEMBER 18, 1964

WHERE RELEASED: US
TITLE & CATALOG #: Single, London 9725
SONGS: Heart of Stone / What a Shame
NOTES: Both tracks are Jagger/Richards compositions.

1965

JANUARY 15, 1965

WHERE RELEASED: UK
TITLE & CATALOG #: *The Rolling Stones No. 2*, Decca LK 4661
SONGS: [A] Everybody Needs Somebody to Love (Russell, Burke, Wexler), V2 / Down Home Girl (Leiber,

US single picture sleeve for "Heart of Stone" (James Karnbach Collection/Courtesy of ABKCO)

Butler) / You Can't Catch Me (Berry) / Time Is on My Side (Meade), V1 / What a Shame / Grown Up Wrong / [B] Down the Road Apiece (Raye) / Under the Boardwalk (Resnick, Young) / I Can't Be Satisfied (Morganfield) / Pain in My Heart (Neville) / Off the Hook (Nanker Phelge) / Susie Q (Broadwater, Lewis, Hawkins) NOTES: "Everybody Needs Somebody to Love," V2, which appears on this and all other European albums containing this title, is distinguished from V1 by its slower tempo and its length—V2 is nearly 30 seconds longer than V1. Version 1 was released on *The Rolling Stones, Now!*, London PS 420. Both V1 and V2 are studio, as opposed to live, versions of this song. "Time Is on My Side, V1" on this UK album is the organ intro version (as opposed to guitar intro on V2) first released on the US single, London 9708. It also appears on *12 X 5*, London PS 402. Again, the song's writing credit erroneously reads: Meade, Norman, as it did on the single release.

FEBRUARY 12, 1965

WHERE RELEASED: US

TITLE & CATALOG #: *The Rolling Stones, Now!*, London PS 420

SONGS: [A] Everybody Needs Somebody to Love (Russell, Burke, Wexler), V1 / Down Home Girl (Leiber, Butler) / You Can't Catch Me (Berry) / Heart of Stone / What a Shame / Mona (I Need You Baby) (McDaniel) / [B] Down the Road Apiece (Raye) / Off the Hook (Nanker Phelge) / Pain in My Heart (Neville) / Oh Baby (We Got a Good Thing Goin') (Ozen) / Little Red Rooster (Dixon) / Surprise Surprise

NOTES: This version (V1) of "Everybody Needs Somebody to Love" is faster in tempo and shorter in length by some 30 seconds than V2, which appears on European releases. "Little Red Rooster" had been a major hit for the Stones in the UK, but wasn't released as a single in the US. This virtually guaranteed the tune

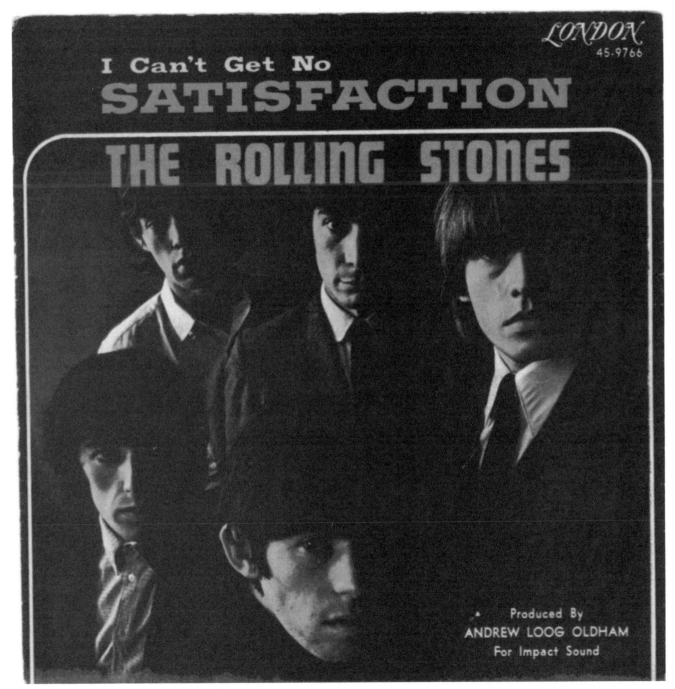

The US picture sleeve for "Satisfaction" (JAMES KARNBACH COLLECTION/COURTESY OF ABKCO)

wouldn't become an American chart-topper, since AM radio almost never played album cuts and FM radio didn't really take off as a force in the industry until some three years later.

FEBRUARY 26, 1965

WHERE RELEASED: UK

TITLE & CATALOG #: Single, Decca F 12104

SONGS: [A] The Last Time / [B] Play with Fire (Nanker Phelge)

MARCH 12, 1965

WHERE RELEASED: US

TITLE & CATALOG #: Single, London 9741

SONGS: [A] The Last Time / [B] Play with Fire (Nanker Phelge)

MAY 21, 1965

WHERE RELEASED: UK

TITLE & CATALOG #: *Fourteen*, Decca LK 4695 (Compilation)

SONGS: [A1] Surprise Surprise

NOTES: Only one track (A1) by the Stones. All profits and artists' royalties were donated to the Lord's Taverners to benefit the National Playing Fields Association. This album, containing single cuts from 14 different British pop acts, was released concurrently in the US under a different title, *England's Greatest Hitmakers*, London PS 430 (see below). The other artists were: The Bachelors, Tom Jones, Billy Fury, Kathy Kirby, Unit 4 +, Dave Berry, the Zombies, Them, Lulu, the Applejacks, Bern Elliott, the Johnny Howard Band, and the Mike Leander Orchestra.

MAY 21, 1965

WHERE RELEASED: US

TITLE & CATALOG #: *England's Greatest Hitmakers*, London PS 430 (Compilation)

SONGS: [A1] Surprise Surprise

NOTES: Only one track (A1) by the Stones. This is the US version of the UK benefit album *Fourteen*, Decca LK 4695 (see above). This US compilation album should not be confused with the similarly titled *England's Newest Hit Makers—The Rolling Stones*, London PS 375—the Stones' own first US album.

JUNE 4, 1965

WHERE RELEASED: US

TITLE & CATALOG #: Single, London 9766

SONGS: [A] (I Can't Get No) Satisfaction / [B] The Under-Assistant West Coast Promotion Man (Nanker Phelge)

NOTES: The first Stones record to reach number one on the US charts. Original pressings of "The Under-Assistant West Coast Promotion Man" on this single and on *Out of Our Heads* (US and UK releases), included the lyric "I have two clerks . . .I break my ass every day." The line had to be deleted from the original tape and subsequent pressings were produced from a new master. Otherwise, the song would never have been broadcast on US AM radio.

JUNE 11, 1965

WHERE RELEASED: UK

TITLE & CATALOG #: *Got Live If You Want It!* (EP), Decca DFE 8620

SONGS: [A] We Want the Stones (Nanker Phelge) / Everybody Needs Somebody to Love (Russell, Burke, Wexler) → Pain in My Heart (Neville), LMV / Route 66 (Troup), LV1 / [B] I'm Moving On (Snow), LV1 / I'm Alright (McDaniel), LV1

NOTES: This EP is comprised of tracks recorded at the Stones' performances on March 6, 1965, at the Empire Theatre, Liverpool, Lancashire; on March 7, 1965, at the Palace Theatre, Manchester, Lancashire; and on March 16, 1965 at the Granada Theatre, Greenford, Middlesex. "Everybody Needs Somebody to Love (Russell, Burke, Wexler) → Pain in My Heart (Neville), LMV" is a *Live Medley Version* of these two songs. Both "I'm Moving On" and "I'm Alright" only exist in live versions.

JULY 30, 1965

WHERE RELEASED: US

TITLE & CATALOG #: *Out of Our Heads*, London PS 429

SONGS: [A] Mercy Mercy (Covay, Miller), V2 / Hitch Hike (Gaye, Stevenson, Paul) / The Last Time / That's How Strong My Love Is (Jamison) / Good Times (Cooke) / I'm Alright (McDaniel), LV1 / [B] (I Can't Get No) Satisfaction / Cry to Me (Russell) / The Under-Assistant West Coast Promotion Man (Nanker Phelge) / Play with Fire (Nanker Phelge) / The Spider and the Fly (Nanker Phelge) / One More Try

NOTES: Early pressings of "The Under-Assistant West Coast Promotion Man" on this album (US and UK releases) included the lyric, "I have two clerks . . . I break my ass every day." The line had to be deleted from the original tape and subsequent pressings were made from a new master. "Satisfaction" was the Stones' first American number one hit. That tune does not appear on the UK *Out of Our Heads*.

AUGUST 20, 1965

WHERE RELEASED: UK

TITLE & CATALOG #: Single, Decca F 12220

SONGS: [A] (I Can't Get No) Satisfaction / [B] The Spider and the Fly (Nanker Phelge)

NOTES: The first pressings of this single were produced with "The Under-Assistant West Coast Promotion Man" as the B-side, like the earlier US release. This was a mistake. Approximately 1,000 copies may have been distributed before the error was caught, thus creating a valuable item for collectors. Their second single ("I Wanna Be Your Man"/"Stoned") was the first such collectible, due to a label misprint.

SEPTEMBER 24, 1965

WHERE RELEASED: UK

"Satisfaction"/"Get Off of My Cloud" single picture sleeve for the Japanese market (JAMES KARNBACH COLLECTION/ COURTESY OF ABKCO)

《ローリング・ストーンズ来日記念発売》

サティスファクション・・・・・・・・・・・・・・・・・・・(I Can't Get No) SATISFACTION (3:48)

一人ぼっちの世界・・・・・・・・・・・・・・・・・・・・・・GET OFF OF MY CLOUD (2:58)

ローリング・ストーンズ/THE ROLLING STONES
Produced by Andrew Loog Oldham

1965年の7月にアメリカで、また同年9月にはイギリスで第1位に達した大ヒット曲「**サティスファクション**」は、いまでもストーンズのコンサートのプログラムに取り上げられる代表作です。ストーンズ最初のミリオン・セラー・ヒットとしても知られ、天才ソウル・シンガー、オーティス・レディングのヒットでもおなじみです。
「**一人ぼっちの世界**」も、1965年11月に英米でNo.1となったストーンズ18番のナンバーです。

(I Can't Get No) SATISFACTION

I can't get no satisfaction
I can't get no satisfaction
I tried, and I tried and I tried, and I tried
I can't get no, I can't get no

When I'm driving in my car, and a man talks on the radio
He's telling me more and more about some useless
    information
That's supposed to fire my imagination

I can't get no, no no no
Hey hey hey
That's what I said

When I'm watching my TV and a man comes on and
    tells me
How white my shirts can be
But he can't be a man, cause he doesn't smoke the same
    cigarettes as me

I can't get no satisfaction
I can't get no reaction
I can't get no
When I'm riding down the world
When I'm doing this and I'm signing that and
I'm trying to make some girl she tell me
I better better better come back maybe next week
'Cause it seems I'm on a losing streak

I can't get no, I can't get no
I can't get no satisfaction
No satisfaction, no satisfaction, no satisfaction
〈3分48秒〉

GET OFF OF MY CLOUD

I live on a cloud,
And all the night,
Night, night,
Fallin' around my block

I sit at home,
And lookin' out the
Window and imagin',
It's the world outside,

And inside,
The guys all dressed,
Up to start,
The union drive,

'Cause I walked,
By and I found out that,
I had the time out,
To give her a good time,

(Repeat)

Hey, Hey, He, He,
Get off of my cloud,
Hey, Hey, He, He,
Get off of my cloud,

Hey, Hey, He, He,
Get off of my cloud,
Gonna ran on,
Through the crowd,

The tompo,
Of the ringin'
I say the high speed,
Was there all of the time,

A boy says he
Hello how are you,
Well I guess,
I'm doin' fine,

'Cause I'm free
Too much noise,
If the people,
Evet want to go yea,

'Cause you,
Feel so good,
You nearly suprised me,
Out of my head,

(Repeat)

Pick a time,
put up with it,
Kind of dangerous,
Slide right down,

So where,
The crowd of people,
There was nobody,
But a soul around.

I raise myself,
Right awake,
So dark that,
I started to dream.

In the mornin',
In the park,
The tickets with,
My drag was,
Stuck on my little tree.

(Repeat)
〈2分58秒〉

MADE IN JAPAN

45r.p.m.   Ⓟ '73·1   発売元 キングレコード株式会社
★レコードから無断でテープその他に録音することは法律で禁じられています。
TOP-1773 Ⓢ

It's difficult enough for a native English speaker to understand the words to Stones' songs—imagine how it must be for the Japanese. Note these lyrics to "Get Off of My Cloud," which bear little resemblance to the actual ones. (JAMES KARNBACH COLLECTION/COURTESY OF ABKCO)

TITLE & CATALOG #: *Out of Our Heads*, Decca LK/SKL 4733

SONGS: [A] She Said Yeah (Christy, Jackson) / Mercy Mercy (Covay, Miller), V2 / Hitch Hike (Gaye, Stevenson, Paul) / That's How Strong My Love Is (Jamison) / Good Times (Cooke) / Gotta Get Away / [B] Talkin' 'Bout You (Berry) / Cry to Me (Russell) / Oh Baby (We Got a Good Thing Goin') (Ozen) / Heart of Stone / The Under-Assistant West Coast Promotion Man (Nanker Phelge) / I'm Free

NOTES: First album released in stereo in the UK. (LK in the catalog number denotes the mono version, SKL indicates stereo) It was actually not *true* stereo, but electronically reprocessed audio that simulated stereo. Early pressings of "The Under-Assistant West Coast Promotion Man" on this album (US and UK releases) included the lyric "I have two clerks . . . I break my ass every day." The line was deleted from the original tape and later pressings were made from a new master.

SEPTEMBER 24, 1965

WHERE RELEASED: US
TITLE & CATALOG #: Single, London 9792
SONGS: [A] Get Off of My Cloud / [B] I'm Free

OCTOBER 22, 1965

WHERE RELEASED: UK
TITLE & CATALOG #: Single, Decca F 12263
SONGS: [A] Get Off of My Cloud / [B] The Singer Not the Song

DECEMBER 3, 1965

WHERE RELEASED: US
TITLE & CATALOG #: *December's Children (and Everybody's)*, London PS 451
SONGS: [A] She Said Yeah (Christy, Jackson) / Talkin' 'Bout You (Berry) / You Better Move On (Alexander) / Look What You've Done (Morganfield) / The Singer Not the Song / Route 66 (Troup), LV1 / [B] Get Off of My Cloud / I'm Free / As Tears Go By (Jagger, Richards, Oldham) / Gotta Get Away / Blue Turns to Grey / I'm Moving On (Snow), LV1
NOTES: This album is made up of unreleased tracks ("Look What You've Done," "Blue Turns to Grey," "As Tears Go By"), tracks released only as singles in both countries, and tracks previously released only in the UK. "Get Off of My Cloud" became the Stones' second US number one hit.

DECEMBER 17, 1965

WHERE RELEASED: US
TITLE & CATALOG #: Single, London 9808
SONGS: [A] As Tears Go By (Jagger, Richards, Oldham) / [B] Gotta Get Away

1966

FEBRUARY 4, 1966

WHERE RELEASED: UK
TITLE & CATALOG #: Single, Decca F 12331
SONGS: [A] 19th Nervous Breakdown / [B] As Tears Go By (Jagger, Richards, Oldham)

NOTES: "As Tears Go By" had been released in the US on a single and on the US album *December's Children* in December 1965.

FEBRUARY 11, 1966

WHERE RELEASED: US
TITLE & CATALOG #: Single, London 9823
SONGS: [A] 19th Nervous Breakdown / [B] Sad Day

APRIL 1, 1966

WHERE RELEASED: US
TITLE & CATALOG #: *Big Hits (High Tide & Green Grass)*, London NPS 1
SONGS: [A] (I Can't Get No) Satisfaction / The Last Time / As Tears Go By (Jagger, Richards, Oldham) / Time Is on My Side (Meade), V2 / It's All Over Now (Womack, Womack) / Tell Me, V2 / [B] 19th Nervous Breakdown / Heart of Stone / Get Off of My Cloud / Not Fade Away (Petty, Hardin) / Good Times, Bad Times / Play with Fire (Nanker Phelge)
NOTES: Compilation of hits, 1964–1966. This was the Stones' first LP in what was to become a long string of "greatest hits" compilations over the next 28 years.

APRIL 15, 1966

WHERE RELEASED: UK
TITLE & CATALOG #: *Aftermath*, Decca SKL 4786
SONGS: [A] Mother's Little Helper / Stupid Girl / Lady Jane / Under My Thumb / Doncha Bother Me / Goin' Home / [B] Flight 505 / High & Dry / Out of Time, V1 / It's Not Easy / I Am Waiting / Take It or Leave It / Think / What to Do
NOTES: The first Rolling Stones album comprised entirely of Jagger/Richards songs. This UK release contains three more tracks (14 versus 11) than the US album of the same name that was released later, on July 2, 1966. A core of 10 songs appears on both records, in different sequences. The UK *Aftermath* does not include "Paint It, Black," while the US version lacks "Mother's Little Helper," "Take It or Leave It," "Out of Time," V1 (the long version, never released in the US), and "What to Do."

MAY 6, 1966

WHERE RELEASED: US
TITLE & CATALOG #: Single, London 901
SONGS: [A] Paint It, Black / [B] Stupid Girl

MAY 13, 1966

WHERE RELEASED: UK

TITLE & CATALOG #: Single, Decca 12395
SONGS: [A] Paint It, Black / [B] Long Long While

JULY 1, 1966

WHERE RELEASED: US
TITLE & CATALOG #: Single, London 902
SONGS: [A] Mother's Little Helper / [B] Lady Jane

JULY 1, 1966

WHERE RELEASED: US
TITLE & CATALOG #: *Aftermath*, London PS 476
SONGS: [A] Paint It, Black / Stupid Girl / Lady Jane / Under My Thumb / Doncha Bother Me / Think / [B] Flight 505 / High & Dry / It's Not Easy /I Am Waiting / Goin' Home
NOTES: First US album comprised wholly of Jagger/ Richards original songs. Not exactly the same as the UK

Rare acetate of "She Said Yeah" (JAMES KARNBACH COLLECTION)

This very rare US LP cover was legally released and then pulled back. The cover artwork was then changed; the background color was altered; and it was not printed on textured stock as it was in this first pressing. (COLLECTION OF JAMES KARNBACH)

Aftermath release of April 15, 1966. See Notes for UK release, above.

SEPTEMBER 23, 1966

WHERE RELEASED: UK
TITLE & CATALOG #: Single, Decca F 12497
SONGS: [A] Have You Seen Your Mother, Baby, Standing in the Shadow? / [B] Who's Driving Your Plane

SEPTEMBER 23, 1966

WHERE RELEASED: US
TITLE & CATALOG #: Single, London 903
SONGS: [A] Have You Seen Your Mother, Baby, Standing in the Shadow? / [B] Who's Driving Your Plane
NOTES: "Who's Driving Your Plane" is actually called "Who's Driving *My* Plane" on the label of this US single,

but not on UK Single, Decca F 12497, or on the *No Stone Unturned* compilation album.

NOVEMBER 4, 1966

WHERE RELEASED: UK
TITLE & CATALOG #: *Big Hits (High Tide & Green Grass,)* Decca TXS 101
SONGS: [A] Have You Seen Your Mother, Baby, Standing in the Shadow? / Paint It, Black / It's All Over Now (Womack, Womack) / The Last Time / Heart of Stone / Not Fade Away (Petty, Hardin) / Come On (Berry) / [B] (I Can't Get No) Satisfaction / Get Off of My Cloud / As Tears Go By (Jagger, Richards, Oldham / 19th Nervous Breakdown / Lady Jane / Time Is on My Side (Meade), V2 / Little Red Rooster (Dixon)
NOTES: This compilation marks the first UK LP release of "Paint It, Black," "Get Off of My Cloud," "Satisfaction," "Little Red Rooster," "The Last Time" and "Not Fade Away." All had previously been released on US albums and singles, but on UK singles only.

DECEMBER 9, 1966

WHERE RELEASED: US
TITLE & CATALOG #: *Got Live If You Want It!*, London PS 493
SONGS: [A] Under My Thumb, LV1 / Get Off of My Cloud, LV / Lady Jane, LV / Not Fade Away (Petty, Hardin), LV / I've Been Loving You Too Long (Redding, Butler) / Fortune Teller (Neville) / [B] The Last Time, LV / 19th Nervous Breakdown, LV / Time Is on My Side (Meade), LV1 / I'm Alright (McDaniel), LV2 / Have You Seen Your Mother, Baby, Standing in the Shadow? LV / (I Can't Get No) Satisfaction, LV1
NOTES: "I've Been Loving You Too Long" (Redding, Butler) and "Fortune Teller" (Neville) are actually studio versions with overdubbed screaming. "Fortune Teller" is the same version as that on the *Saturday Club*, Decca LK 4583 compilation album released January 24, 1964. Both "Under My Thumb" and "Satisfaction" are longer on the "digitally remastered" ABKCO CD (and vinyl and cassette) reissue of 1986.

1967

JANUARY 13, 1967

WHERE RELEASED: UK
TITLE & CATALOG #: Single, Decca F 12546
SONGS: [A] Let's Spend the Night Together / [B] Ruby Tuesday
NOTES: The content of the singles released simultaneously in January 1967 in the UK and US was the same,

except for the A-side/B-side sequence. English DJs and audiences weren't thought to be as Victorian as the Americans.

JANUARY 13, 1967

WHERE RELEASED: US
TITLE & CATALOG #: Single, London 904
SONGS: [A] Ruby Tuesday / [B] Let's Spend the Night Together
NOTES: The record companies' perception of American mores was correct, irony or no irony. See TELEVISION APPEARANCES for Ed Sullivan's solution to the mere suggestion of s-e-x in the Stones' lyrics.

JANUARY 20, 1967

WHERE RELEASED: UK
TITLE & CATALOG #: *Between the Buttons*, Decca SKL 4852
SONGS: [A] Yesterday's Papers / My Obsession / Back Street Girl / Connection / She Smiled Sweetly / Cool, Calm, Collected / [B] All Sold Out / Please Go Home / Who's Been Sleeping Here? / Complicated / Miss Amanda Jones / Something Happened to Me Yesterday
NOTES: "Back Street Girl" and "Please Go Home" do not appear on the US release of *Between the Buttons*, London PS 499. The track sequence also differs. However, this UK album does not contain "Ruby Tuesday" or "Let's Spend the Night Together." The last Stones album to be produced by Andrew Loog Oldham.

FEBRUARY 10, 1967

WHERE RELEASED: US
TITLE & CATALOG #: *Between the Buttons*, London PS 499
SONGS: [A] Let's Spend the Night Together / Yesterday's Papers / Ruby Tuesday / Connection / She Smiled Sweetly / Cool, Calm, Collected / [B] All Sold Out / My Obsession / Who's Been Sleeping Here? / Complicated / Miss Amanda Jones / Something Happened to Me Yesterday
NOTES: This US album does not contain either "Back Street Girl" or "Please Go Home," which appear on the UK release, but the tunes are on the US-only LP, *Flowers*, London PS 509, released on July 14, 1967. *Between the Buttons* was the last Stones album to be produced by Andrew Oldham. The ABKCO 1986 CD reissue included the original Charlie Watts drawings that had accompanied the initial vinyl release.

JULY 14, 1967

WHERE RELEASED: US
TITLE & CATALOG #: *Flowers*, London PS 509

SONGS: [A] Ruby Tuesday / Have You Seen Your Mother, Baby, Standing in the Shadow? / Let's Spend the Night Together / Lady Jane / Out of Time, V2 / My Girl (Robinson, White) / [B] Back Street Girl / Please Go Home / Mother's Little Helper / Take It or Leave It / Ride on Baby / Sittin' on a Fence

NOTES: This album was never released in the UK, but was issued for export (to Europe and elsewhere) on Decca, SKL 4888. "Sittin' on a Fence" is a first release. "My Girl" and "Ride on Baby" were released here for the first and only time. "Mother's Little Helper," "Ruby Tuesday," "Let's Spend the Night Together," and "Have You Seen Your Mother, Baby" had only been released as US singles. The remaining tracks had been released on the UK versions of *Between the Buttons* and *Aftermath*.

Rare acetate of "We Love You." The Bell Sound label refers to the facility in New York City used frequently by the Stones.
(JAMES KARNBACH COLLECTION)

"In Another Land"/"The Lantern" picture sleeve. In a rare move for the Stones, Bill Wyman got top billing. (JAMES KARNBACH COLLECTION/COURTESY OF ABKCO)

AUGUST 18, 1967

WHERE RELEASED: UK
TITLE & CATALOG #: Single, Decca F 12654
SONGS: [A] We Love You / [B] Dandelion

AUGUST 18, 1967

WHERE RELEASED: US

TITLE & CATALOG #: Single, London 905
SONGS: [A] Dandelion / [B] We Love You

DECEMBER 1, 1967

WHERE RELEASED: US
TITLE & CATALOG #: Single, London 907
SONGS: [A] In Another Land (Wyman) / [B] The Lantern

DECEMBER 8, 1967

WHERE RELEASED: UK

TITLE & CATALOG #: *Their Satanic Majesties Request*, Decca TXS 103

SONGS: [A] Sing This All Together / Citadel / In Another Land (Wyman) / 2000 Man / Sing This All Together (See What Happens) / [B] She's a Rainbow / The Lantern / Gomper / 2000 Light Years from Home / On with the Show

NOTES: This album represents a series of "firsts" for the Rolling Stones. *Satanic* featured the debut of another member of the Rolling Stones as a lead vocalist and songwriter—Bill Wyman. His song, "In Another Land," was also released the same week as the A-side of a single (London 907) backed with "The Lantern." This was the first original LP to be packaged in a gatefold cardboard sleeve (the first greatest-hits LP, *Big Hits (High Tide & Green Grass)*, also had one, but that was not an original release. The cover was shot in Mt. Vernon, New York, in September 1967 by photographer Michael Cooper. The image is a 3-D photograph, believed to be the first of its kind on an album cover. At the time, technical support and processing facilities for 3-D photography existed only in Japan, where the camera was made, and in New York. A warehouse studio in Mt. Vernon was decided on as the more feasible location for the band to work. They all—the band and Cooper—gathered props and set up the shot. The final cover art includes (very discreetly) the faces of the Beatles within the flowers. Many speculated that this was a response to the doll sporting a Stones sweater pictured on the 1966 *Sergeant Pepper* cover, but Lennon and McCartney had, in fact, done background vocals on "Sing This Altogether" and "We Love You." The latter was included along with "Dandelion" on the original acetate pressing of this LP, but both were removed at the last minute. This could explain *Satanic*'s 10-track total, instead of the usual 12 on Stones LPs. And, there are two versions of the same song on the album ("Sing This Altogether" and "Sing This Altogether [See What Happens]"), possibly another "first" for any band. It was also the Stones' first LP issued without the producer credit of Andrew Loog Oldham, and the first and last produced by the "Rolling Stones." Oldham was with the Stones at the beginning of the *Satanic* sessions; it is not known why he did not receive some sort of credit. Finally, this is the first Stones album with identical track listings on both US and UK releases.

DECEMBER 8, 1967

WHERE RELEASED: US

TITLE & CATALOG #: *Their Satanic Majesties Request*, London NPS 2

SONGS: [A] Sing This All Together / Citadel / In Another Land (Wyman) / 2000 Man / Sing This All Together (See What Happens) / [B] She's a Rainbow / The Lantern / Gomper / 2000 Light Years from Home / On with the Show

NOTES: For the first time, the tracks were identical on both the US and UK albums. See Notes for the UK release of *Satanic*, above.

DECEMBER 22, 1967

WHERE RELEASED: US

TITLE & CATALOG #: Single, London 906

SONGS: [A] She's a Rainbow / [B] 2000 Light Years from Home

NOTES: "She's a Rainbow" was a US Top 40 hit.

1968

MAY 24, 1968

WHERE RELEASED: UK

TITLE & CATALOG #: Single, Decca 12782

SONGS: [A] Jumpin' Jack Flash / [B] Child of the Moon

MAY 31, 1968

WHERE RELEASED: US

TITLE & CATALOG #: Single, London 908

SONGS: [A] Jumpin' Jack Flash / [B] Child of the Moon

AUGUST 30, 1968

WHERE RELEASED: US

TITLE & CATALOG #: Single, London 909

SONGS: [A] Street Fighting Man / [B] No Expectations

NOTES: Early pressings had a different mix of "Street Fighting Man" from the one found on later editions of this single. The early version was replaced with the track that appears on *Beggars Banquet*, and never showed up again on an official release.

DECEMBER 6, 1968

WHERE RELEASED: UK

TITLE & CATALOG #: *Beggars Banquet*, Decca SKL 4955

SONGS: [A] Sympathy for the Devil / No Expectations / Dear Doctor / Parachute Woman / Jigsaw Puzzle / [B] Street Fighting Man / Prodigal Son (Rev. Wilkins) / Stray Cat Blues / Factory Girl / Salt of the Earth

NOTES: The first Stones LP produced by Jimmy Miller. The original cover photo—a grungy graffiti-covered bathroom wall (with toilet)—was rejected by Decca and the album was released in an off-white sleeve adorned only with black script lettering. The toilet cover finally saw the light of day when ABKCO digitized and reissued the first 17 albums on CD, cassette and vinyl in 1986.

DECEMBER 6, 1968

WHERE RELEASED: US

TITLE & CATALOG #: *Beggars Banquet*, London PS 539

SONGS: [A] Sympathy for the Devil / No Expectations / Dear Doctor / Parachute Woman / Jigsaw Puzzle / [B] Street Fighting Man / Prodigal Son (Rev. Wilkins) / Stray Cat Blues / Factory Girl / Salt of the Earth

NOTES: London Records also refused the original toilet/graffiti cover photo: US record buyers had to wait nearly 20 years for the ABKCO 1986 reissue to see it. The cover photo hassles had delayed the original album's release for more than two months. Contrary to one popular rumor at the time, the use of a simple white cover was

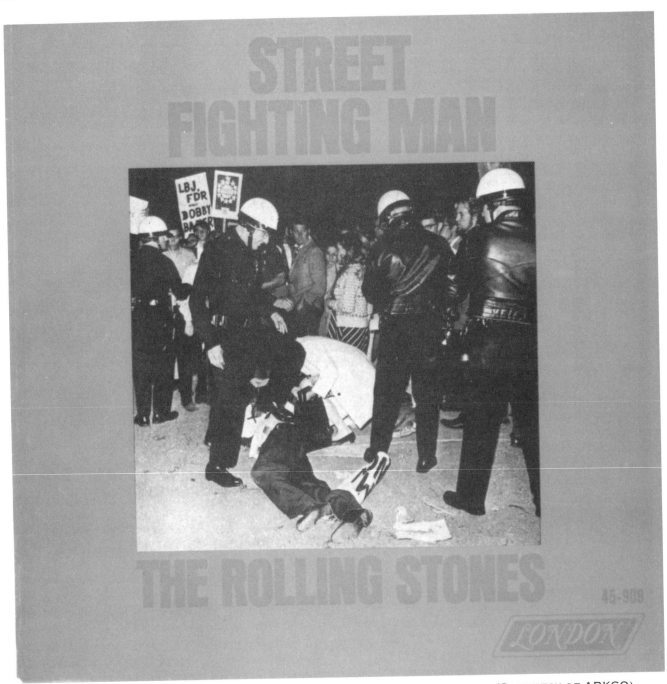

The very rare "Street Fighting Man" US picture sleeve (JAMES KARNBACH COLLECTION/COURTESY OF ABKCO)

merely a measure to prevent further delay and had nothing to do with the Beatles' *White Album*.

1969

JULY 3, 1969

WHERE RELEASED: UK
TITLE & CATALOG #: Single, Decca F 12952
SONGS: [A] Honky Tonk Women / [B] You Can't Always Get What You Want

JULY 3, 1969

WHERE RELEASED: US
TITLE & CATALOG #: Single, London 910
SONGS: [A] Honky Tonk Women / [B] You Can't Always Get What You Want

SEPTEMBER 12, 1969

WHERE RELEASED: UK
TITLE & CATALOG #: *Through the Past, Darkly (Big Hits Vol. 2)*, Decca SKL 5019
SONGS: [A] Jumpin' Jack Flash / Mother's Little Helper / 2000 Light Years from Home / Let's Spend the Night Together / You Better Move On [Alexander] / We Love You / [B] Street Fighting Man / She's a Rainbow / Ruby Tuesday / Dandelion / Sittin' on a Fence / Honky Tonk Women
NOTES: The songs "We Love You" and "You Better Move On" were replaced by "Paint It, Black" and "Have You Seen Your Mother, Baby, Standing in the Shadow?" on the US release of this "greatest hits" album. ("You Better Move On" (Alexander) was recorded in 1963). Also, the track sequencing here on the Decca offering differs from the London Records release. The album was dedicated to Brian Jones, who had died on July 3, 1969.

SEPTEMBER 12, 1969

WHERE RELEASED: US
TITLE & CATALOG #: *Through the Past, Darkly (Big Hits Vol. 2)*, London NPS 3
SONGS: [A] Paint It, Black / Ruby Tuesday / She's a Rainbow / Jumpin' Jack Flash / Mother's Little Helper / Let's Spend the Night Together / [B] Honky Tonk Women / Dandelion / 2000 Light Years from Home / Have You Seen Your Mother, Baby, Standing in the Shadow? / Street Fighting Man
NOTES: See Notes (above) on UK version of this album, released on September 12, 1969. Both were dedicated to the late Brian Jones.

OCTOBER 31, 1969

WHERE RELEASED: US & UK
TITLE & CATALOG #: *The Rolling Stones (The Promotional Album)*, London/Decca RSD 1
SONGS: [A] Route 66 (Troup) / Walking the Dog (Thomas) / Around & Around (Berry) / Everybody Needs Somebody to Love (Russell, Burke, Wexler), V1 / Off the Hook (Nanker Phelge) / Susie Q (Broadwater, Lewis, Hawkins) / I'm Free / She Said Yeah (Christy, Jackson) / [B] Under My Thumb / Stupid Girl / 2000 Man / Sympathy for the Devil / Prodigal Son (Rev. Wilkins) / Love in Vain (Robt. Johnson)
NOTES: A limited edition of 200 records was released by each label as the Rolling Stones' promotional album for DJs in the US and UK. Note that "Love in Vain" was not released to the general public by the Stones until December 1969. This tune, though often credited "(Trad.)" and credited to Woody Payne by the Stones on the *Let It Bleed* albums, was actually written by Robert Johnson. Johnson's songs were never copyrighted.

DECEMBER 5, 1969

WHERE RELEASED: UK
TITLE & CATALOG #: *Let It Bleed*, Decca SKL 5025
SONGS: [A] Gimme Shelter / Love in Vain (Robt. Johnson) / Country Honk / Live with Me / Let It Bleed / [B] Midnight Rambler / You Got the Silver / Monkey Man / You Can't Always Get What You Want
NOTES: This is Mick Taylor's first LP with the Stones. The album, both in its cover and its content, symbolizes the Stones in transition (for the first time). Brian Jones is present on some tracks, other cuts feature only four Stones, and Taylor plays on two cuts—"Country Honk" and "Live with Me"—and the "new" group appears. The album's cover has some fairly heavy (-handed?) symbolism. The front photo is a pristine still-life showing a Stones record (with the title *Let It Bleed* with photos of the non-Jones Stones on its label) seemingly being played by an antique tone arm; atop and skewered by the phonograph's spindle are a movie film can, a clock face, a pizza, a vehicle tire, and finally a decorated cake with five mostly unsmiling plastic musicians. The band was going on tour, being reborn or at least changing, and doing a movie (*Gimme Shelter*) while releasing this album. Those are facts, however one wishes to deconstruct symbols. The back cover, however, is more obviously descriptive of rock 'n' roll chaos. The record is smashed and covered with pizza and broken crockery; the tire is punctured, sliced and wrapped with bandages; blank film spews out of the can; and the only figure left standing on the partially eaten cake is the one resembling Taylor—and he's sunk halfway into the icing.

Let It Bleed was the last Stones record to be available to the general public in either mono or stereo versions. See also Notes for the US *Let It Bleed*, below.

DECEMBER 5, 1969

WHERE RELEASED: US
TITLE & CATALOG #: *Let It Bleed*, London NPS 4
SONGS: [A] Gimme Shelter / Love in Vain (Robt. Johnson) / Country Honk / Live with Me / Let It Bleed / [B] Midnight Rambler / You Got the Silver / Monkey Man / You Can't Always Get What You Want
NOTES: Authorship of the song "Love in Vain" was credited to Woody Payne on the inner sleeve of this album (and on the UK release). However, the tune was actually written by Robert Johnson, whose songs were never copyrighted. This was the first time the Stones did not release a single with an album track as the A-side. "Honky Tonk Women" (backed with "You Can't Always Get What You Want") *was* released as a single in July 1969, but the song is not on *Let It Bleed*. "Country Honk" is the album track. Still a B-side, "You Can't Always Get What You Want" became a hit single when it was rereleased by Decca in 1973 (with "Sad Day" as the A-side). See also Notes for UK release, above.

1970

SEPTEMBER 4, 1970

WHERE RELEASED: UK
TITLE & CATALOG #: *Get Yer Ya-Ya's Out! The Rolling Stones in Concert*, Decca SKL 5065
SONGS: [A] Jumpin' Jack Flash, LV1 / Carol (Berry), LV / Stray Cat Blues, LV / Love in Vain (Robt. Johnson), LV / Midnight Rambler, LV / [B] Sympathy for the Devil, LV1 / Live with Me, LV1 / Little Queenie (Berry), LV / Honky Tonk Women, LV1 / Street Fighting Man, LV1
NOTES: The last non-compilation Stones album released on Decca. All tracks were supposedly recorded at New York City's Madison Square Garden during the 1969 US tour; many were later overdubbed and edited. From the time of its release, there has been an ongoing debate over the actual performances that yielded the *Ya-Ya's* tracks. (See SESSIONOGRAPHY and TOURS AND CONCERTS)

SEPTEMBER 4, 1970

WHERE RELEASED: US
TITLE & CATALOG #: *Get Yer Ya-Ya's Out! The Rolling Stones in Concert*, London NPS 5

SONGS: [A] Jumpin' Jack Flash, LV1 / Carol (Berry), LV / Stray Cat Blues, LV / Love in Vain (Robt. Johnson), LV / Midnight Rambler, LV / [B] Sympathy for the Devil, LV1 / Live with Me, LV1 / Little Queenie (Berry), LV / Honky Tonk Women, LV1 / Street Fighting Man, LV1
NOTES: The live performances were recorded, according to the LP credits, at Madison Square Garden, NYC, during the Stones 1969 tour; many tracks were overdubbed and edited prior to release. See Notes for the UK release, above. This is London Records' last release of an original (non-compilation) Stones album.

1971

From 1971 onward, all new Rolling Stones recordings were released on Rolling Stones Records (RSR), the band's own label with the now-familiar tongue logo. Album covers and picture sleeves are identical for RSR product released in both the UK and US, though catalog numbers differ. London and Decca continued to issue singles and compilations of previously released songs after the Stones had left.

JANUARY 1971

WHERE RELEASED: Export Only/RARE
TITLE & CATALOG #: Single (Export), Decca F 13126
SONGS: [A] Love in Vain (Robt. Johnson), LV / [B] Little Queenie (Berry), LV
NOTES: This rare live single was packaged in a picture sleeve, for export only, by Decca after the Stones left the label.

MARCH 5, 1971

WHERE RELEASED: UK
TITLE & CATALOG #: *Stone Age*, Decca SKL 5084
SONGS: [A] Look What You've Done (Morganfield) / It's All Over Now (Womack, Womack) / Confessin' the Blues (McShann, Brown) / One More Try / As Tears Go By (Jagger, Richards, Oldham) / The Spider and the Fly (Nanker Phelge) / [B] My Girl (Robinson, White) / Paint It, Black / If You Need Me (Pickett, Bateman, Sanders) / The Last Time / Blue Turns to Grey / Around & Around (Berry)
NOTES: This compilation album (and all Stones records on Decca from 1971 on) was released after the band left the label. When this record came out, the Rolling Stones took out ads in music industry trade papers voicing their intense disapproval. They disavowed having had any part in the *Stone Age* release, and said the album was "below

the standard we try to keep up, both in choice of content and cover design."

APRIL 16, 1971

WHERE RELEASED: UK
TITLE & CATALOG #: Maxi-single, RSR RS 19100
SONGS: [A] Brown Sugar / [B] Bitch / Let It Rock (Anderson), LV
NOTES: First picture sleeve in the UK. "Let It Rock" is a live track that was recorded in concert at Leeds University, UK, on March 13, 1971, and was never released on any other US or UK record. Note that this maxi-single has the same catalog number as (regular) US Single, RSR RS 19100, released May 8, which contained only "Brown Sugar" and "Bitch."

APRIL 23, 1971

WHERE RELEASED: US & UK
TITLE & CATALOG #: *Sticky Fingers*, RSR COC 59100
SONGS: [A] Brown Sugar / Sway / Wild Horses / Can't You Hear Me Knocking / You Gotta Move (McDowell, Davis) / [B] Bitch / I Got the Blues / Sister Morphine / Dead Flowers / Moonlight Mile
NOTES: The first album released on Rolling Stones Records. The record and its "zipper and underwear" cover designed by Andy Warhol sparked worldwide controversy. See the May 15, 1971 release of the Spanish version, below. "Sister Morphine" was credited to Jagger/Richards on some pressings, but later editions of *Sticky Fingers* around the time of its original release gave songwriting credit to Jagger/Richards/[Marianne] Faithfull. But rereleases of *Sticky Fingers* on CD and cassette credit the song to Jagger/Richards only. Marianne Faithfull actually recorded and released the song before the Stones (as she had done with "As Tears Go By").

MAY 7, 1971

WHERE RELEASED: US
TITLE & CATALOG #: Single, RSR RS 19100
SONGS: [A] Brown Sugar / [B] Bitch

MAY 14, 1971

WHERE RELEASED: Spain
TITLE & CATALOG #: *Sticky Fingers*, RSR HRSS 591-01
SONGS: [A] Brown Sugar / Sway / Wild Horses / Can't You Hear Me Knocking / You Gotta Move (McDowell, Davis) / [B] Bitch / I Got the Blues / Let It Rock (Anderson), LV / Dead Flowers / Moonlight Mile
NOTES: Spain banned "Sister Morphine" from release in that country. The Stones replaced it with "Let It Rock" on this special Spanish release of *Sticky Fingers*, and inserted 30 seconds of silence at the beginning of the cut to protest the ban. The Franco government also forbade the use of the original zipper and underwear cover. The Warhol design was replaced with a photo of disembodied female fingers emerging from a messily opened can of treacle.

JUNE 11, 1971

WHERE RELEASED: US
TITLE & CATALOG #: Single, RSR RS 19101
SONGS: [A] Wild Horses / [B] Sway
NOTES: US only.

JUNE 25, 1971

WHERE RELEASED: UK
TITLE & CATALOG #: Maxi-single, Decca F 13195
SONGS: [A] Street Fighting Man / Surprise Surprise / [B] Everybody Needs Somebody to Love (Russell, Burke, Wexler), V2
NOTES: This maxi-single, with picture sleeve, marked the first time "Surprise Surprise" was released on a Rolling Stones record in Britain. The track was used as the band's contribution to the benefit compilation album *Fourteen*, Decca LK 4695 but had not been part of an actual Stones LP or single in the UK. It had appeared on their third US album, *The Rolling Stones, Now!*, London PS 420, in 1965.

JULY 20, 1971

WHERE RELEASED: UK
TITLE & CATALOG #: Single, Decca F 13203
SONGS: [A] Street Fighting Man / [B] Surprise Surprise

AUGUST 27, 1971

WHERE RELEASED: UK
TITLE & CATALOG #: *Gimme Shelter*, Decca SKL 5101
SONGS: [A] Jumpin' Jack Flash / Love in Vain (Robt. Johnson) / Honky Tonk Women / Street Fighting Man / Sympathy for the Devil / Gimme Shelter / [B] Under My Thumb, LV1 / Time Is on My Side (Meade), LV1 / I've Been Loving You Too Long (Redding, Butler) / Fortune Teller (Neville) / Lady Jane / (I Can't Get No) Satisfaction, LV1
NOTES: This album's release by Decca (after the Stones had left the label) was timed to coincide with the British release of the movie *Gimme Shelter*, but has nothing to do with the film. The A-side is comprised of studio cuts that coincide (by accident or on purpose) with live songs in the movie. The B-side contains live cuts recorded at performances in the UK, and the studio versions of "I've Been Loving You Too Long" and "Fortune Teller"—all of which had been released on the 1966 LP, *Got Live If You Want It!*, London PS 493.

1972

JANUARY 11, 1972

WHERE RELEASED: US

TITLE & CATALOG #: *Hot Rocks 1964–1971*, London 2PS 606/607

SONGS: [A] Time Is on My Side (Meade), V2 / Heart of Stone / Play with Fire (Nanker Phelge) / (I Can't Get No) Satisfaction / As Tears Go By (Jagger, Richards, Oldham) / Get Off of My Cloud / [B] Mother's Little Helper / 19th Nervous Breakdown / Paint It, Black / Under My Thumb / Ruby Tuesday / Let's Spend the Night Together / [C] Jumpin' Jack Flash / Street Fighting Man / Sympathy for the Devil / Honky Tonk Women / Gimme Shelter / [D] Midnight Rambler, LV / You

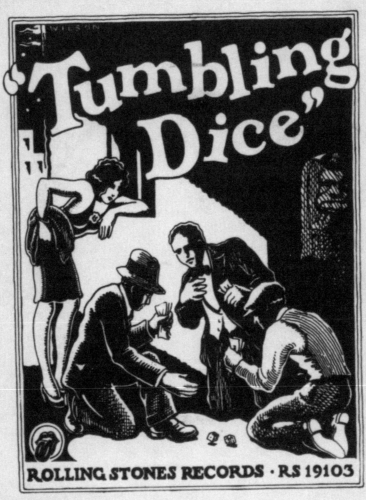

Another variation in the way Stones records appear to international fans. The sleeve of "Tumbling Dice"/"Sweet Black Angel" as it looked in Israel. (JAMES KARNBACH COLLECTION)

Can't Always Get What You Want / Brown Sugar [Brown Sugar, V2 *] / Wild Horses [Wild Horses, V2 *]

NOTES: Double ABKCO-years anthology album. Released after the Stones had left ABKCO and the London/Decca labels. At same time, another album entitled "Hot Rocks" was set to be issued by Atlantic, the Stones new label. ABKCO sought and was awarded an injunction preventing the Atlantic release. *Hot Rocks* was finally released by ABKCO in the UK in 1990, containing (inadvertently) true stereo versions of "Satisfaction," "Heart of Stone," "Paint It, Black," and "Get Off of My Cloud."

FEBRUARY 18, 1972

WHERE RELEASED: UK

TITLE & CATALOG #: *Milestones*, Decca SKL 5098

SONGS: [A] (I Can't Get No) Satisfaction / She's a Rainbow / Under My Thumb / I Just Want to Make Love to You (Dixon) / Yesterday's Papers / I Wanna Be Your Man (Lennon, McCartney) / [Bl Time Is on My Side (Meade), V2 / Get Off of My Cloud / Not Fade Away (Petty, Hardin) / Out of Time, V1 / She Said Yeah (Christy, Jackson) / Stray Cat Blues

NOTES: Compilation

APRIL 14, 1972

WHERE RELEASED: US & UK

TITLE & CATALOG #: Single, RSR RS 19103

SONGS: [A] Tumbling Dice / [B] Sweet Black Angel

APRIL 29, 1972

WHERE RELEASED: UK

TITLE & CATALOG #: *Exile on Main Street* 5" Flexi-Disc (Promo), RSR/SFI 107A

SONGS: [A] Exile on Main St. Blues / All Down the Line / Tumbling Dice / Shine a Light / Happy

NOTES: This record was a freebie insert in the April 29, 1972 issue of the music tabloid, *New Musical Express*. The Stones titles were on the A-side only; two new releases by other artists were promoted on the B-side. "Exile on Main St. Blues" is a little ditty consisting of Mick Jagger on piano, singing a blues-y introduction to the about-to-be-released *Exile on Main Street*; three segments of the song, in 20–45 second bits, are interspersed with the other four cuts, which are excerpts of only about one minute each. The title "Exile on Main St. Blues" is not printed on the label and the song never appears on another official Stones release.

MAY 12, 1972

WHERE RELEASED: UK

TITLE & CATALOG #: *Exile on Main Street*, RSR COC 69 100

SONGS: [A] Rocks Off / Rip this Joint / Shake Your Hips (Moore) / Casino Boogie / Tumbling Dice / [B] Sweet Virginia / Torn and Frayed / Sweet Black Angel / Loving Cup / [C] Happy / Turd on the Run / Ventilator Blues (Jagger, Richards, Taylor) / Just Wanna See His Face / Let It Loose / [D] All Down the Line / Stop Breaking Down (Trad.; Arr: Jagger, Richards, Taylor, Wyman, Watts) / Shine a Light / Soul Survivor

NOTES: Double album, and the *only* double album of new studio tracks (as opposed to live tracks or compilation albums) released by the Stones until *Voodoo Lounge* (yes, it did come out on vinyl) in 1994. In 1993, *New Musical Express* ranked *Exile* number 11 on its list of the "Greatest Albums of All Time."

MAY 12, 1972

WHERE RELEASED: US

TITLE & CATALOG #: *Exile on Main Street*, RSR COC 2-2900

SONGS: [A] Rocks Off / Rip this Joint / Shake Your Hips (Moore) / Casino Boogie / Tumbling Dice / [B] Sweet Virginia / Torn and Frayed / Sweet Black Angel / Loving Cup / [C] Happy / Turd on the Run / Ventilator Blues (Jagger, Richards, Taylor) / Just Wanna See His Face / Let It Loose / [D] All Down the Line / Stop Breaking Down (Trad.; Arr: Jagger, Richards, Taylor, Wyman, Watts) / Shine a Light / Soul Survivor

NOTES: The only double album of new studio work released by the Stones until *Voodoo Lounge*. Digitally remastered and rereleased by Virgin Records in 1994.

JUNE 9, 1972

WHERE RELEASED: US

TITLE & CATALOG #: EP (Promo), Atlantic/RSR COC-7 22900

SONGS: [A] Rocks Off / Sweet Virginia / [B] Rip this Joint / Shake Your Hips (Moore) / Tumbling Dice

NOTES: Atlantic Records promotional EP, released after *Exile on Main Street* in the US only.

JULY 14, 1972

WHERE RELEASED: US

TITLE & CATALOG #: Single, RSR RS 19104

SONGS: [A] Happy / [B] All Down the Line

---

*Two boo-boos cropped up on this original US *Hot Rocks*, but were corrected after the first pressing: a different version of "Brown Sugar" (45 seconds of which is on the *Gimme Shelter* film soundtrack) and an alternate mix of "Wild Horses" made it onto the first edition of the LP.

OCTOBER 13, 1972

WHERE RELEASED: UK

TITLE & CATALOG #: *Rock 'n' Rolling Stones*, Decca SKL 5149

SONGS: [A] Route 66 (Troup) / The Under-Assistant West Coast Promotion Man (Nanker Phelge) / Come On (Berry) / Talkin' 'Bout You (Berry) / Bye Bye Johnny (Berry) / Down the Road Apiece (Raye) / [B] I Just Want to Make Love to You (Dixon) / Everybody Needs Somebody to Love (Russell, Burke, Wexler), V2 / Oh Baby (We Got a Good Thing Goin') (Ozen) / 19th Nervous Breakdown / Little Queenie (Berry), LV / Carol (Berry), LV

NOTES: Another repackaging of previously released Stones songs on Decca Records.

DECEMBER 1, 1972

WHERE RELEASED: US

TITLE & CATALOG #: *More Hot Rocks (Big Hits & Fazed Cookies)*, London 2PS 626/627

SONGS: [A] Tell Me / Not Fade Away (Petty, Hardin) / The Last Time / It's All Over Now (Womack, Womack) / Good Times, Bad Times / I'm Free / [B] Out of Time, V1 / Lady Jane / Sittin' on a Fence / Have You Seen Your Mother, Baby, Standing in the Shadow? / Dandelion / We Love You / [C] She's a Rainbow / 2000 Light Years from Home / Child of the Moon (rmk) / No Expectations / Let It Bleed / [D] What to Do / Money (Gordy Jr., Bradford) / Come On (Berry) / Fortune Teller (Neville) / Poison Ivy (Leiber, Stoller), V2 / Bye Bye Johnny (Berry) / I Can't Be Satisfied (Morganfield) / Long Long While

NOTES: Double album—another repackaging for the US market on London Records. Most of the songs had been previously released, but "Come On," "Bye Bye Johnny," "I Can't Be Satisfied," "Long Long While," "Money," "What to Do" and "Poison Ivy" had never appeared on a US album before. "Child of the Moon" was released here for the first time on *any* album—the "(rmk)" means that this is a remix of the original single track. *More Hot Rocks* was not released in the UK until 1990.

1973

APRIL 27, 1973

WHERE RELEASED: UK

TITLE & CATALOG #: Single, Decca F 13404

SONGS: [A] Sad Day / [B] You Can't Always Get What You Want

NOTES: Released after the Stones had left the label.

AUGUST 21, 1973

WHERE RELEASED: US & UK

TITLE & CATALOG #: Single, RSR RS 19105

SONGS: [A] Angie / [B] Silver Train

AUGUST 31, 1973

WHERE RELEASED: US & UK

TITLE & CATALOG #: *Goat's Head Soup*, RSR COC 59101

SONGS: [A] Dancing with Mr. D / 100 Years Ago / Coming Down Again / Doo Doo Doo Doo Doo (Heartbreaker) / Angie / [B] Silver Train / Hide Your Love / Winter / Can You Hear the Music / Star Star

NOTES: The UK album contains the censored version of "Star Star" (a.k.a. "Starfucker")—one verse was deleted.

SEPTEMBER 14, 1973

WHERE RELEASED: US

TITLE & CATALOG #: EP (Jukebox), Atlantic/RSR COC-7 22900

SONGS: [A] Star Star / Hide Your Love / [B] Can You Hear the Music / 100 Years Ago

SEPTEMBER 14, 1973

WHERE RELEASED: US

TITLE & CATALOG #: EP (Promo), RSR COC 7 59101

SONGS: [A] Star Star / Hide Your Love / [B] Can You Hear the Music / 100 Years Ago

NOTES: Atlantic Records Promo EP.

OCTOBER 5, 1973

WHERE RELEASED: UK

TITLE & CATALOG #: *No Stone Unturned*, Decca SKL 5173

SONGS: [A] Poison Ivy (Leiber, Stoller), V2 / The Singer Not the Song / Surprise Surprise / Child of the Moon (rmk) / Stoned (Nanker Phelge) / Sad Day / [B] Money (Gordy Jr., Bradford) / Congratulations / I'm Moving On (Snow), LV1 / 2120 South Michigan Avenue (Nanker Phelge), V1 / Long Long While / Who's Driving Your Plane

NOTES: A compilation of previously released Stones songs, all recorded between 1963 and 1966, repackaged after the Stones had left label. This was the *first* time "Sad Day" was released on any album.

DECEMBER 14, 1973

WHERE RELEASED: US

TITLE & CATALOG #: Single, RSR RS 19109

Discover Stones—*Japanese LP—note the guy on the left hand side is standing in for Bill Wyman. Bill wasn't there, but they shot the photo anyway and used it.* (JAMES KARNBACH COLLECTION)

SONGS: [A] Doo Doo Doo Doo Doo (Heartbreaker) / [B] Dancing with Mr. D

1974

JANUARY 11, 1974

WHERE RELEASED: UK
TITLE & CATALOG #: Maxi-single, Atlantic K 19107
SONGS: [A] Brown Sugar / [Bl Happy / Rocks Off
NOTES: Promotional record released in conjunction with Radio Luxembourg to commemorate the 25th anniversary of Atlantic Records.

JULY 26, 1974

WHERE RELEASED: UK
TITLE & CATALOG #: Single, RSR RS 19114
SONGS: [A] It's Only Rock 'n' Roll / [B] Through the Lonely Nights
NOTES: B-side "Through the Lonely Nights" had not yet appeared on a Rolling Stones LP.

JULY 26, 1974

WHERE RELEASED: US
TITLE & CATALOG #: Single, RSR RS 19301
SONGS: [A] It's Only Rock 'n' Roll / [B] Through the Lonely Nights

NOTES: B-side "Through the Lonely Nights" had not yet appeared on a Rolling Stones LP.

OCTOBER 18, 1974

WHERE RELEASED: UK
TITLE & CATALOG #: *It's Only Rock 'n' Roll*, RSR COC 59103
SONGS: [A] If You Can't Rock Me / Ain't Too Proud to Beg (Whitfield, Holland) / It's Only Rock 'n' Roll / Till the Next Goodbye / Time Waits for No One / [B] Luxury / Dance Little Sister / If You Really Want to Be My Friend / Short & Curlies / Fingerprint File
NOTES: The first album produced by the Glimmer Twins. As the story goes, the name comes from Mick and Keith's adventures aboard a cruise ship bound for South America in December of 1968. Following the filming of the "Rock and Roll Circus" BBC-TV special, they, together with Anita Pallenberg and Marianne Faithfull (and son Nicholas), decided to vacation in style with a Lisbon to Rio cruise. An older woman passenger who, like Jagger and Richards, spent most of the voyage in the bar, kept asking them who they were. Increasingly frustrated with their not answering, she begged them to "give us a glimmer" of their identities.

OCTOBER 18, 1974

WHERE RELEASED: US
TITLE & CATALOG #: *It's Only Rock 'n' Roll*, RSR COC 79101

SONGS: [A] If You Can't Rock Me / Ain't Too Proud to Beg (Whitfield, Holland) / It's Only Rock 'n' Roll / Till the Next Goodbye / Time Waits for No One / [B] Luxury / Dance Little Sister / If You Really Want to Be My Friend / Short & Curlies / Fingerprint File

NOTES: The first album produced by the Glimmer Twins. See Notes on the UK release of this record, above.

OCTOBER 25, 1974

WHERE RELEASED: US

TITLE & CATALOG #: Single, RSR RS 19302

SONGS: [A] Ain't Too Proud to Beg (Whitfield, Holland) / [B] Dance Little Sister

NOTES: This single was released only in the US.

OCTOBER 29, 1974

WHERE RELEASED: US

TITLE & CATALOG #: Single (Promo), RSR PR 228

SONGS: [A] Time Waits for No One / [B] Time Waits for No One

NOTES: This single, with mono and stereo mixes of "Time Waits for No One," was released for promotional use only.

1975

MAY 23, 1975

WHERE RELEASED: UK

TITLE & CATALOG #: Single, Decca F 13584

SONGS: [A] I Don't Know Why (Wonder, Riser, Hunter, Hardaway) / [B] Try a Little Harder, OOV

NOTES: The Stevie Wonder tune "I Don't Know Why" was credited on this single's first pressing to Jagger/Richards/Taylor. It was subsequently corrected to read Wonder/Riser/Hunter/Hardaway. "Try a Little Harder" was recorded at the July 1964 Andrew Oldham Orchestra sessions in London. See Notes for the June 6, 1975 releases of *Metamorphosis* for information about tracks from those sessions.

MAY 27, 1975

WHERE RELEASED: US

TITLE & CATALOG #: Single, ABKCO ABK 4701

SONGS: [A] I Don't Know Why (Wonder, Riser, Hunter, Hardaway) / [B] Try a Little Harder, OOV

NOTES: Released after the Stones had left ABKCO. See Notes above for the UK release of this single on Decca Records, May 23, 1975.

JUNE 6, 1975

WHERE RELEASED: US

TITLE & CATALOG #: *Metamorphosis*, ABKCO ANA 1

SONGS: [A] Out of Time, V3 / Don't Lie to Me (Berry) / Each and Every Day of the Year, OOV / Heart of Stone, OOV / I'd Much Rather Be with the Boys (Oldham, Richards), OOV / (Walkin' thru the) Sleepy City, OOV / Try a Little Harder, OOV / [B] I Don't Know Why (Wonder, Riser, Hunter, Hardaway) / If You Let Me / Jiving Sister Fanny / Downtown Suzie (Wyman) / Family / Memo from Turner / I'm Going Down

NOTES: *Metamorphosis* was released after the Stones had left ABKCO—the OOV (and V3 for "Out of Time") versions of songs on this record were recorded at the Andrew Oldham Orchestra sessions, with Jagger on vocals backed by the Oldham Orchestra, not the Stones. On the other hand, this "Memo from Turner" is the *only* Rolling Stones version of this particular song ever released. The "Memo from Turner" on the soundtrack of *Performance* is an entirely different version; it was recorded with Mick Jagger on vocals backed by studio musicians (Jimmy Page and others), not the Stones.

JUNE 6, 1975

WHERE RELEASED: UK

TITLE & CATALOG #: *Metamorphosis*, Decca SKL 5212

SONGS: [A] Out of Time, V3 / Don't Lie to Me (Berry) / Some Things Just Stick in Your Mind, OOV / Each and Every Day of the Year, OOV / Heart of Stone, OOV / I'd Much Rather Be with the Boys (Oldham, Richards), OOV / (Walkin' thru the) Sleepy City, OOV / We're Wastin' Time, OOV / Try a Little Harder, OOV / [B] I Don't Know Why (Wonder, Riser, Hunter, Hardaway) / If You Let Me / Jiving Sister Fanny / Downtown Suzie (Wyman) / Family / Memo from Turner / I'm Going Down

NOTES: Released after the Stones had left label. The OOV (and V3 of "Out of Time") versions of songs on this record were recorded at the Andrew Oldham Orchestra sessions with Jagger on vocals backed by the Oldham Orchestra, not the Stones. On the other hand, this "Memo from Turner" is the *only* Rolling Stones version ever released. An entirely different "Memo from Turner" is featured in the film *Performance*, and was released on the movie's soundtrack recordings, but not on *Metamorphosis*. The *Performance* version—or "Memo From Turner, JV" (for Jagger Version)—had Mick Jagger on vocals backed by studio musicians (Jimmy Page and others), not the Stones.

JUNE 6, 1975

WHERE RELEASED: UK

TITLE & CATALOG #:   *Made in the Shade*, RSR COC 59104
SONGS: [A] Brown Sugar / Tumbling Dice / Happy / Dance Little Sister / Wild Horses / [B] Angie / Bitch / It's Only Rock 'n' Roll / Doo Doo Doo Doo Doo (Heartbreaker) / Rip this Joint
NOTES: A "greatest hits" album released by Rolling Stones Records in the UK.

JUNE 6, 1975

WHERE RELEASED: US

TITLE & CATALOG #:   *Made in the Shade*, RSR COC 79102
SONGS: [A] Brown Sugar / Tumbling Dice / Happy / Dance Little Sister / Wild Horses / [B] Angie / Bitch

1975 Decca single release (long after the band had left the label) of "Out of Time" b/w "Jiving Sister Fanny" (JAMES KARNBACH COLLECTION/COURTESY OF ABKCO)

/ It's Only Rock 'n' Roll / Doo Doo Doo Doo Doo (Heartbreaker) / Rip this Joint
NOTES: Rolling Stones Records' US release of this "greatest hits" album.

AUGUST 12, 1975

WHERE RELEASED: US
TITLE & CATALOG #: Single, ABKCO SN 4702
SONGS: [A] Out of Time, V3 / [B] Jiving Sister Fanny
NOTES: This version of "Out of Time" came from the Andrew Oldham Orchestra sessions. See Notes for the June 6, 1975 releases of *Metamorphosis* for information about tracks from those sessions.

SEPTEMBER 5, 1975

WHERE RELEASED: UK
TITLE & CATALOG #: Single, Decca F 13597
SONGS: [A] Out of Time, V3 / [B] Jiving Sister Fanny
NOTES: This version of "Out of Time" came from the Andrew Oldham Orchestra sessions. See Notes for the June 6, 1975 releases of *Metamorphosis* for information about tracks from those sessions.

NOVEMBER 14, 1975

WHERE RELEASED: UK
TITLE & CATALOG #: *Rolled Gold,* Decca ROST 1/2
SONGS: [A] Come On (Berry) / I Wanna Be Your Man (Lennon, McCartney) / Not Fade Away (Petty, Hardin) / Carol (Berry) / It's All Over Now (Womack, Womack) / Little Red Rooster (Dixon) / Time Is on My Side (Meade), V2 / The Last Time / (I Can't Get No) Satisfaction / [B] Get Off of My Cloud / 19th Nervous Breakdown / As Tears Go By (Jagger, Richards, Oldham) / Under My Thumb / Lady Jane / Out of Time, V1 / Paint It, Black / [C] Have You Seen Your Mother, Baby, Standing in the Shadow? / Let's Spend the Night Together / Ruby Tuesday / Yesterday's Papers / We Love You / She's a Rainbow / Jumpin' Jack Flash / [D] Honky Tonk Women / Sympathy for the Devil / Street Fighting Man / Midnight Rambler / Gimme Shelter
NOTES: Double anthology album of songs from the Stones' years with Decca. Not released in the US.

1976

JANUARY 27, 1976

WHERE RELEASED: UK
TITLE & CATALOG#: *By Invitation Only,* Atlantic K60112 (Compilation)
SONGS: [A2] It's Only Rock 'n' Roll / [D2] Angie

NOTES: Compilation album. Among the other artists invited by Atlantic Records were Yes; Emerson, Lake & Palmer; and Led Zeppelin.

FEBRUARY 12, 1976

WHERE RELEASED: UK
TITLE & CATALOG #: *Supertracks,* Phonogram SPORT 1 (Compilation)
SONGS: [A1] Brown Sugar
NOTES: "Brown Sugar" is track A1 on this compilation album.

APRIL 6, 1976

WHERE RELEASED: US
TITLE & CATALOG #: Single, RSR RS 19303 (withdrawn)
SONGS: [A] Fool to Cry / [B] Crazy Mama
NOTES: This single was withdrawn in the US; RSR 19304 was released in its place.

APRIL 13, 1976

WHERE RELEASED: US
TITLE & CATALOG #: Single, RSR RS 19304
SONGS: [A] Fool to Cry / [B] Hot Stuff

APRIL 15, 1976

WHERE RELEASED: UK
TITLE & CATALOG #: Single, Decca F 13635
SONGS: [A] Honky Tonk Women / [B] Sympathy for the Devil

APRIL 16, 1976

WHERE RELEASED: UK
TITLE & CATALOG #: Single, RSR RS 19121
SONGS: [A] Fool to Cry / [B] Crazy Mama

APRIL 16, 1976

WHERE RELEASED: US
TITLE & CATALOG #: 12" Single (Promo), RSR RS 4070
SONGS: [A] Hot Stuff / [B] Crazy Mama
NOTES: The Stones' first US 12" single. Released for promotional purposes in connection with the impending release of the album *Black & Blue,* it was pressed on black and blue vinyl.

APRIL 20, 1976

WHERE RELEASED: UK
TITLE & CATALOG #: *Black & Blue,* RSR COC 59106

SONGS: [A] Hot Stuff / Hand of Fate / Cherry Oh Baby (Donaldson) / Memory Motel / [B] Hey Negrita / Melody / Fool to Cry / Crazy Mama

NOTES: Ron Wood's album debut as an official Stone. The formal announcement had been made on February 28, 1976.

APRIL 20, 1976

WHERE RELEASED: US

TITLE & CATALOG #: *Black & Blue*, RSR COC 79104

SONGS: [A] Hot Stuff / Hand of Fate / Cherry Oh Baby (Donaldson) / Memory Motel / [B] Hey Negrita / Melody / Fool to Cry / Crazy Mama

NOTES: The first album to which Ron Wood contributed as an official member of the band.

1977

SEPTEMBER 23, 1977

WHERE RELEASED: UK

TITLE & CATALOG #: *Love You Live*, RSR COC 89101

SONGS: [A] Honky Tonk Women, LV2 / If You Can't Rock Me → Get Off of My Cloud, LMV1 / Happy, LV1 / Hot Stuff, LV1 / Star Star, LV1 / [B] Tumbling Dice, LV1 / Fingerprint File, LV1 / You Gotta Move (McDowell, Davis), LV1 / You Can't Always Get What You Want, LV1 / [C] Mannish Boy (London, McDaniel, Morganfield) / Cracking Up (McDaniel) / Little Red Rooster (Dixon), LV1 / Around & Around (Berry), LV / [D] It's Only Rock 'n' Roll, LV1 / Brown Sugar, LV1 / Jumpin' Jack Flash, LV2 / Sympathy for the Devil, LV2

NOTES: Cut A1 is preceded by an excerpt from "Fanfare for the Common Man" by Aaron Copland. Vocal overdubbing was done later on several tracks, notably "Happy," "Star Star," "Brown Sugar," "If You Can't Rock Me → Get Off of My Cloud" (LMV1 indicates that this is a *Live Medley Version*), and "You Can't Always Get What You Want." The album is dedicated to Keith Harwood, who, in addition to his studio work on *Black & Blue* and *It's Only Rock 'n' Roll*, engineered the recording of the band's performances in Paris and Earl's Court, London that produced many of these tracks. Harwood was killed in a car accident in September 1976. Other tracks came from 1975–1977 performances in Toronto, Canada.

SEPTEMBER 23, 1977

WHERE RELEASED: US

TITLE & CATALOG #: *Love You Live*, RSR COC 2-9001

SONGS: [A] Honky Tonk Women, LV2 / If You Can't Rock Me → Get Off of My Cloud, LMV1 / Happy, LV1 / Hot Stuff, LV1 / Star Star, LV1 / [B] Tumbling Dice, LV1 / Fingerprint File, LV1 / You Gotta Move (McDowell, Davis), LV1 / You Can't Always Get What You Want, LVl / [C] Mannish Boy (London, McDaniel, Morganfield) / Cracking Up (McDaniel) / Little Red Rooster (Dixon), LVl / Around & Around (Berry), LV / [D] It's Only Rock 'n' Roll, LV1 / Brown Sugar, LV1 / Jumpin' Jack Flash, LV2 / Sympathy for the Devil, LV2

NOTES: See Notes for the UK release, above.

SEPTEMBER 30, 1977

WHERE RELEASED: US

TITLE & CATALOG #: EP (Promo), RSR EP 287

SONGS: [A] If You Can't Rock Me → Get Off of My Cloud, LMV1 / [B] Brown Sugar, LVl / Jumpin' Jack Flash, LV2 / Hot Stuff, LV1

NOTES: US promo only—for the release of *Love You Live*.

OCTOBER 21, 1977

WHERE RELEASED: UK

TITLE & CATALOG #: *Get Stoned—30 Greatest Hits, 30 Original Tracks*, Arcade ADEP 32

SONGS: [A] Not Fade Away (Petty, Hardin) / It's All Over Now (Womack, Womack) / Tell Me / Good Times, Bad Times / Time Is on My Side (Meade), V2 / Little Red Rooster (Dixon) / The Last Time / Play with Fire (Nanker Phelge) / (I Can't Get No) Satisfaction / [B] Get Off of My Cloud / I Wanna Be Your Man (Lennon, McCartney) / As Tears Go By (Jagger, Richards, Oldham) / 19th Nervous Breakdown / Mother's Little Helper / Have You Seen Your Mother, Baby, Standing in the Shadow? / Paint It, Black / [C] Lady Jane / Let's Spend the Night Together / Ruby Tuesday / Dandelion / We Love You / She's a Rainbow / 2000 Light Years from Home / [D] Jumpin' Jack Flash / Gimme Shelter / Street Fighting Man / Honky Tonk Women / Sympathy for the Devil / Wild Horses / Brown Sugar

NOTES: This anthology of Stones favorites was released by ABKCO, marketed via television ads and sold by mail order only. The first "TV LP" for the Stones.

1978

MAY 19, 1978

WHERE RELEASED: UK

TITLE & CATALOG #: Single, RSR EMI 2802

SONGS: [A] Miss You / [B] Far Away Eyes

NOTES: EMI 2802 is a regular single with picture sleeve.

MAY 19, 1978

WHERE RELEASED: UK

TITLE & CATALOG #: 12" Single, RSR 12EMI 2802

SONGS: [A] MissYou / [B] Far Away Eyes

NOTES: This 12" single, pressed in pink vinyl, has a picture sleeve and was released at the same time as the regular single, RSR EMI 2802.

JUNE 2, 1978

WHERE RELEASED: US

TITLE & CATALOG #: Single, RSR RS 19307

SONGS: [A] Miss You / [B] Far Away Eyes

NOTES: RS 19307 is a regular single that was released in the US; DK 4609 is a 12" single that was released concurrently. Disco-crossover "Miss You" was one of the hottest selling singles in the band's history.

JUNE 2, 1978

WHERE RELEASED: US

TITLE & CATALOG #: 12" Single, RSR DK 4609

SONGS: [A] Miss You / [B] Far Away Eyes

NOTES: Released concurrently with single, RSR RS 19307.

JUNE 9, 1978

WHERE RELEASED: UK

TITLE & CATALOG #: *Some Girls*, RSR CUN 39108

SONGS: [A] Miss You / When the Whip Comes Down / Just My Imagination (Whitfield, Strong) / Some Girls / Lies / [B] Far Away Eyes / Respectable / Before They Make Me Run / Beast of Burden, V1 / Shattered

NOTES: The Stones first non-compilation album in two years, *Some Girls* was issued with three different cover variations. The basic design was the same, but accent colors and the sequencing of those colors varied. The design itself caused quite a bit of flack and yet another reworking of an album cover. The front is a takeoff of magazine ads for cheap wigs. The faces of the "models" on the outer sleeve are die-cut out and photos on the inner sleeve show through the holes. The inner sleeve art is a collage of paparazzi photos of famous faces including, but not limited to, the Stones. Lucille Ball, Sophia Loren and Farrah Fawcett, among others pictured there, protested the initial release, which resulted in the Stones' altering and substituting inner sleeve images in subsequent printings. A first edition *Some Girls* cover is thus a rarity.

JUNE 9, 1978

WHERE RELEASED: US

TITLE & CATALOG #: *Some Girls*, RSR COC 39108

SONGS: [A] Miss You / When the Whip Comes Down / Just My Imagination (Whitfield, Strong) / Some Girls / Lies / [B] Far Away Eyes / Respectable / Before They Make Me Run / Beast of Burden, V1 / Shattered

NOTES: Both this LP's cover and the title track's lyrics whipped up a bit of public frenzy. In the US, the words to "Some Girls" were attacked as being both racist and sexist. The cut stayed on the album, but the cover had to be reworked. See Notes for the UK release of *Some Girls*, above.

JUNE 9, 1978

WHERE RELEASED: US

TITLE & CATALOG #: *Some Girls*, RSR TP 39108

SONGS: [A] Miss You / When the Whip Comes Down / Just My Imagination (Whitfield, Strong) / Some Girls / Lies / [B] Far Away Eyes / Respectable / Before They Make Me Run / Beast of Burden, V2 / Shattered

NOTES: The *Some Girls* album in an eight-track tape format. Amazingly, "Beast of Burden" is a totally different version on this eight-track from the same title released in all other formats. A different tempo, and even different words in several verses are apparent in the eight-track "Beast of Burden"—V2—compared to the "Beast of Burden" most of us (authors included) believed was the *only Some Girls*-era studio version released. Clearly, that was an incorrect assumption. As to the reason for V2, most likely it was a mistake—the wrong master take may have been used for the eight-track. But, that's an assumption, too.

AUGUST 29, 1978

WHERE RELEASED: US

TITLE & CATALOG #: Single, RSR RS 19309

SONGS: [A] Beast of Burden, V1 / [B] When the Whip Comes Down

NOTES: This single was originally issued with a picture sleeve, but the black-and-white photo generated a great deal of controversy and the sleeve (only) was withdrawn. The image of a lion sitting on a smiling, reclining young woman was criticized as symbolizing bestiality, though more probably it was the word and image-play with the song title of the A Side that caused offense. This sleeve is very rare.

SEPTEMBER 15, 1978

WHERE RELEASED: UK

TITLE & CATALOG #: Single, RSR EMI 2861

SONGS: [A] Respectable / [B] When the Whip Comes Down

NOTES: Released with a picture sleeve.

NOVEMBER 28, 1978

WHERE RELEASED: US

TITLE & CATALOG #: Single, RSR RS 19310

SONGS: [A] Shattered / [B] Everything Is Turning to Gold (Jagger, Richards, Wood), V1

NOTES: This US-only single was issued with a full-color picture sleeve.

1979

1979

WHERE RELEASED: US

TITLE & CATALOG #: 12" Single, RSR DK 4616

SONGS: [A] Miss You / [B] Hot Stuff

NOTES: Issued as 12" Single only. This was actually a double A-side—both were hits.

1979

WHERE RELEASED: US

TITLE & CATALOG #: *Songs of The Rolling Stones* (Promo), London MPD 1

SONGS: [A] Under My Thumb / I'm Free / Sittin' on a Fence / Ride On Baby / Salt of the Earth / No Expectations / Wild Horses / Paint It, Black / Let's Spend the Night Together / Midnight Rambler / You Can't Always Get What You Want / Stupid Girl / One More Try / The Last Time / Sing This All Together / [B] Jumpin' Jack Flash / You Got the Silver / All Down the Line / (I Can't Get No) Satisfaction / Play with Fire (Nanker Phelge) / Live with Me / Yesterday's Papers / Something Happened to Me Yesterday / Sweet Virginia / Blue Turns to Grey / Out of Time, V2 / Shine a Light / Loving Cup / Ruby Tuesday / Honky Tonk Women

NOTES: Promotional album for radio stations only. Cuts are two-to-three-minute excerpts from these songs, all from the ABKCO/London/Decca years.

JUNE 1, 1979

WHERE RELEASED: UK

TITLE & CATALOG #: *Time Waits for No One—Anthology 1971–1977*, RSR COC 59107

SONGS: [A] Time Waits for No One / Bitch / All Down the Line / Dancing with Mr. D / Angie / [B] Star Star / If You Can't Rock Me / Get Off of My Cloud, LMV1 / Hand of Fate / Crazy Mama / Fool to Cry

1980

1980

WHERE RELEASED: UK

TITLE & CATALOG #: *The Rolling Stones Album Collection*, Decca ROLL 1

NOTES: This is a limited edition boxed set of the Stones' first eight studio LPs on Decca. These are: 1. *The Rolling Stones*, 2. *The Rolling Stones # 2*, 3. *Out of Our Heads*, 4. *Aftermath*, 5. *Between the Buttons*, 6. *Their Satanic Majesties Request*, 7. *Beggars Banquet*, 8. *Let It Bleed*. This release marked a milestone of sorts. It occurred 10 years after the Stones left the label.

JUNE 20, 1980

WHERE RELEASED: UK

TITLE & CATALOG #: Single, RSR RSR 105

SONGS: [A] Emotional Rescue / [B] Down in the Hole

NOTES: Picture sleeve

JUNE 20, 1980

WHERE RELEASED: US & UK

TITLE & CATALOG #: 12" Single (Promo), RSR PR 367

SONGS: [A] Emotional Rescue / [B] Down in the Hole

NOTES: Promotional release only

JUNE 20, 1980

WHERE RELEASED: US

TITLE & CATALOG #: Single, RSR RS 20001

SONGS: [A] Emotional Rescue / [B] Down in the Hole

NOTES: Picture sleeve

JUNE 24, 1980

WHERE RELEASED: UK

TITLE & CATALOG #: *Emotional Rescue*, RSR CUN 39111

SONGS: [A] Dance (Jagger, Richards, Wood) / Summer Romance / Send It to Me / Let Me Go / Indian Girl / [B] Where the Boys Go / Down in the Hole / Emotional Rescue / She's So Cold / All About You

NOTES: Early copies included a large color poster with thermographic images. This rarity was included in the Virgin/EMI special limited edition CD reissue of June 1994. Radio stations in 1980, as had been true since the 1960s, were still receiving edited versions of songs that might offend their listeners. That was the case with the DJ promo edit of "She's So Cold," from which the line "God damn cold" was deleted. The track was otherwise the same on the album. The promo edit of "Emotional Rescue" was merely shortened for airplay. It is customary and often necessary for labels to issue special DJ releases on which tracks from singles or albums have been edited to fit radio time format requirements. Generally speaking, tracks are identical in version and mix to those on the public releases, only shorter.

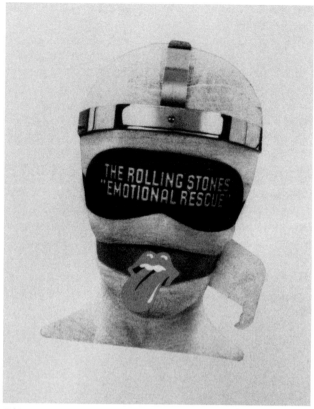

This promotional sticker was made for the release of the Emotional Rescue *LP and was given out at the record release party in New York City.* (JAMES KARNBACH COLLECTION)

JUNE 24, 1980

WHERE RELEASED: US
TITLE & CATALOG #: *Emotional Rescue,* RSR COC 16015
SONGS: [A] Dance (Jagger, Richards, Wood) / Summer Romance / Send It to Me / Let Me Go / Indian Girl / [B] Where the Boys Go / Down in the Hole / Emotional Rescue / She's So Cold / All About You
NOTES: Early copies included a large color poster with thermographic photos. This rare art work was included in the Virgin/EMI special limited edition CD reissue of June 1994. See Notes, above, for the UK release of *Emotional Rescue* for additional information.

SEPTEMBER 5, 1980

WHERE RELEASED: UK
TITLE & CATALOG #: *Singles Collection,* Decca STONE 1–12
SONGS: [A] Come On (Berry) / I Wanna Be Your Man (Lennon, McCartney) / [B] It's All Over Now (Womack, Womack) / I Want to Be Loved (Dixon) / [C] (I Can't Get No) Satisfaction / Little by Little (Phelge, Spector)

/ [D] Not Fade Away (Petty, Hardin) / Little Red Rooster (Dixon) / [E] The Last Time / Paint It, Black / [F] Get Off of My Cloud / Play with Fire (Nanker Phelge) / [G] Jumpin' Jack Flash / As Tears Go By (Jagger, Richards, Oldham) / [H] 19th Nervous Breakdown / Have You Seen Your Mother, Baby, Standing in the Shadow? / [I] Let's Spend the Night Together / You Can't Always Get What You Want / [J] Honky Tonk Women / Ruby Tuesday / [K] Street Fighting Man / Out of Time, V3 / [L] Sympathy for the Devil / Gimme Shelter
NOTES: A boxed set of 12" singles, that came with a poster and a badge.

SEPTEMBER 19, 1980

WHERE RELEASED: UK
TITLE & CATALOG #: Single, RSR 106
SONGS: [A] She's So Cold / [B] Send It to Me
NOTES: Picture sleeve

SEPTEMBER 19, 1980

WHERE RELEASED: US & UK
TITLE & CATALOG #: 12" Single, RSR 12RSR 111
SONGS: [A] She's So Cold / [B] Send It to Me

OCTOBER 10, 1980

WHERE RELEASED: UK
TITLE & CATALOG #: *Solid Rock,* Decca TAB 1
SONGS: [A] Carol (Berry) / Route 66 (Troup) / Fortune Teller (Neville) / I Wanna Be Your Man (Lennon, McCartney) / Poison Ivy (Leiber, Stoller), V2 / Not Fade Away (Petty, Hardin) / (I Can't Get No) Satisfaction / Get Off of My Cloud / [B] Jumpin' Jack Flash / Connection / All Sold Out / Citadel / Parachute Woman / Live with Me / Honky Tonk Women
NOTES: This anthology spans the entire Decca period.

1981

MARCH 12, 1981

WHERE RELEASED: US
TITLE & CATALOG #: *Sucking in the Seventies,* RSR COC 16028
SONGS: [A] Shattered / Everything Is Turning to Gold (Jagger, Richards, Wood), V1 / Hot Stuff, DJV / Time Waits For No One, EV / Fool to Cry, DJV / [B] Mannish Boy (London, McDaniel, Morganfield), EV / When the Whip Comes Down, LV, EV / If I Was a Dancer (Dance, Pt. 2) (Jagger, Richards, Wood) / Crazy Mama, EV / Beast of Burden, DJV

NOTES: This is a compilation, but only "Shattered" is identical (in length, version and mix) to the originally released LP version. DJV stands for DJ Version; EV stands for Edited Version. "Everything Is Turning to Gold" is a first release. "If I Was a Dancer (Dance, Pt. 2)" appears elsewhere only on a 12" promo single.

APRIL 14, 1981

WHERE RELEASED: UK

TITLE & CATALOG #: *Sucking in the Seventies*, RSR CUN 39112

SONGS: [A] Shattered / Everything Is Turning to Gold (Jagger, Richards, Wood), V1 / Hot Stuff, DJV / Time Waits for No One, EV / Fool to Cry, DJV / [B] Mannish Boy (London, McDaniel, Morganfield), EV / When the Whip Comes Down, LV, EV / If I Was a Dancer (Dance, Pt. 2) (Jagger, Richards, Wood) / Crazy Mama, EV / Beast of Burden, DJV

NOTES: As was the US release of March 12, this is a compilation, but only "Shattered" is identical (in length, version and mix) to the originally released LP version. DJV stands for DJ Version; EV stands for Edited Version. "Everything Is Turning to Gold" is a first release. "If I Was a Dancer (Dance, Pt. 2)" appears elsewhere only on a 12" promo single.

AUGUST 14, 1981

WHERE RELEASED: UK

TITLE & CATALOG #: Single, RSR RSR 108

SONGS: [A] Start Me Up / [B] No Use in Crying (Jagger, Richards, Wood)

NOTES: Picture sleeve

AUGUST 14, 1981

WHERE RELEASED: US & UK

TITLE & CATALOG #: 12" Single (Promo), RSR PR 347

SONGS: [A] Start Me Up / [B] No Use in Crying (Jagger, Richards, Wood)

AUGUST 14, 1981

WHERE RELEASED: US

TITLE & CATALOG #: Single, RSR RS 21003

SONGS: [A] Start Me Up / [B] No Use in Crying (Jagger, Richards, Wood)

AUGUST 25, 1981

WHERE RELEASED: UK

TITLE & CATALOG #: *Tattoo You*, RSR CUN 39114

SONGS: [A] Start Me Up / Hang Fire / Slave / Little T & A / Black Limousine (Jagger, Richards, Wood) / Neighbours / [B] Worried About You / Tops / Heaven / No Use in Crying (Jagger, Richards, Wood) / Waiting on a Friend

NOTES: Songs on this album came from various sessions as far back as 1972. Mick Taylor is on "Tops" and "Waiting on a Friend"—both were recorded in Jamaica along with tracks that ended up on *Goat's Head Soup*.

AUGUST 25, 1981

WHERE RELEASED: US

TITLE & CATALOG #: *Tattoo You*, RSR COC 16052

SONGS: [A] Start Me Up / Hang Fire / Slave / Little T & A / Black Limousine (Jagger, Richards, Wood) / Neighbours / [B] Worried About You / Tops / Heaven / No Use in Crying (Jagger, Richards, Wood) / Waiting on a Friend

NOTES: See Notes for UK release, above.

NOVEMBER 6, 1981

WHERE RELEASED: UK

TITLE & CATALOG #: *Slow Rollers*, Decca TAB 30

SONGS: [A] You Can't Always Get What You Want / Take It or Leave It / You Better Move On (Alexander) / Time Is on My Side (Meade), V2 / Pain in My Heart (Neville) / Dear Doctor / Con le mie lacrime (Jagger, Richards, Danpa) / [B] Ruby Tuesday / Play with Fire (Nanker Phelge) / Lady Jane / Sittin' on a Fence / Back Street Girl / Under the Boardwalk (Resnick, Young) / Heart of Stone

NOTES: There were quite a few errors in the crediting and listing of songs on this anthology. The first track, "You Can't Always Get What You Want," was given the title "Con le mie lagrime cosi" and credited to Andrew Oldham. "Con le mie lacrime" is "As Tears Go By" in Italian and this was its only official release in either the UK or the US. "Time Is on My Side" was again miscredited to Meade, Norman. The author is Norman Meade. This mistake began with the Stones' first US release of the song on the single, London 9708 on September 25, 1964; they later corrected the error on the album *12 X 5*, but it resurfaced on their second UK album, *The Rolling Stones No. 2*, Decca LK 4661, and has persisted in various repackagings.

DECEMBER 1, 1981

WHERE RELEASED: UK

TITLE & CATALOG #: Single, RSR RSR 109

SONGS: [A] Waiting on a Friend / [B] Little T & A

NOTES: Picture sleeve

DECEMBER 1, 1981

WHERE RELEASED: US & UK

TITLE & CATALOG #: 12" Single (Promo), RSR DMD 253
SONGS: [A] If I Was a Dancer (Dance, Pt. 2) (Jagger, Richards, Wood) / [B] Dance (Instr.) (Jagger, Richards, Wood)
NOTES: Promo only

DECEMBER 1, 1981

WHERE RELEASED: US
TITLE & CATALOG #: Single, RSR RS 21004
SONGS: [A] Waiting on a Friend / [B] Little T & A

1982

JANUARY 12, 1982

WHERE RELEASED: US
TITLE & CATALOG #: Single, RSR RS 21300
SONGS: [A] Hang Fire / [B] Neighbours
NOTES: This single replaced a scheduled single containing "Hang Fire" b/w "Worried About You" that was not released and had no catalog number assigned to it. RSR RS 21300 was a US-only release.

JUNE 1, 1982

WHERE RELEASED: UK
TITLE & CATALOG #: Single, RSR RSR 110
SONGS: [A] Going to À Go Go (Robinson, Johnson, Moore, Rogers), LV / [B] Beast of Burden, LV
NOTES: Picture sleeve

JUNE 1, 1982

WHERE RELEASED: UK
TITLE & CATALOG #: *Still Life (American Concert 1981)*, RSR CUN 39115
SONGS: [A] Under My Thumb, LV2 / Let's Spend the Night Together, LV / Shattered, LV / Twenty Flight Rock (Fairchild, Cochran), LV / Going to À Go Go (Robinson, Johnson, Moore, Rogers), LV / [B] Let Me Go, LV / Time Is on My Side (Meade), LV2 / Just My Imagination (Whitfield, Strong), LV / Start Me Up, LV / (I Can't Get No) Satisfaction, LV2
NOTES: "Under My Thumb" is preceded by a 27-second intro of "Take the A Train" (Strayhorn), performed by Duke Ellington & His Orchestra; "(I Can't Get No) Satisfaction" is followed by a 44-second "outro" of "The Star Spangled Banner" (Key; Arr: Hendrix), performed by Jimi Hendrix. Also released in the UK as a picture disc—that is, a disc with a photo or other image embedded in the vinyl of the record—RSR CUNP 39115 (see below).

JUNE 1, 1982

WHERE RELEASED: UK
TITLE & CATALOG #: *Still Life (American Concert 1981)*, picture disc, RSR CUNP 39115
SONGS: [A] Under My Thumb, LV2 / Let's Spend the Night Together, LV / Shattered, LV / Twenty Flight Rock (Fairchild, Cochran), LV / Going to À Go Go (Robinson, Johnson, Moore, Rogers), LV / [B] Let Me Go, LV / Time Is on My Side (Meade), LV2 / Just My Imagination (Whitfield, Strong), LV / Start Me Up, LV / (I Can't Get No) Satisfaction, LV2
NOTES: "Under My Thumb" is preceded by a 27-second intro of "Take the A Train" (Strayhorn), performed by Duke Ellington & His Orchestra; "(I Can't Get No) Satisfaction" is followed by a 44-second "outro" of "The Star Spangled Banner" (Key; Arr: Hendrix), performed by Jimi Hendrix. This picture disc has a collage of photographs of the Stones performing live embedded in the vinyl of the record.

JUNE 1, 1982

WHERE RELEASED: Europe
TITLE & CATALOG #: 12" Single, RSR RS 64820 (EMI K052-64820)
SONGS: [A] Going to À Go Go (Robinson, Johnson, Moore, Rogers), LV / [B] Beast of Burden, LV
NOTES: Released as a 12" single in Europe only. The disc has a picture sleeve that makes use of the *Still Life* cover art. This live version of "Beast of Burden" did not appear on an album in either the US or UK until 1991.

JUNE 1, 1982

WHERE RELEASED: US
TITLE & CATALOG #: Single, RSR RS 21301
SONGS: [A] Going to À Go Go (Robinson, Johnson, Moore, Rogers), LV / [B] Beast of Burden, LV
NOTES: Picture sleeve. This live version of "Beast of Burden" did not appear on an album in either the US or UK until 1991.

JUNE 1, 1982

WHERE RELEASED: US
TITLE & CATALOG #: *Still Life (American Concert 1981)*, RSR COC 39113
SONGS: [A] Under My Thumb, LV2 / Let's Spend the Night Together, LV / Shattered, LV / Twenty Flight Rock (Fairchild, Cochran), LV / Going to À Go Go (Robinson, Johnson, Moore, Rogers), LV / [B] Let Me Go, LV / Time Is on My Side (Meade), LV2 / Just My Imagination (Whitfield, Strong), LV / Start Me Up, LV / (I Can't Get No) Satisfaction, LV2

NOTES: "Under My Thumb" is preceded by a 27-second intro of "Take the A Train" (Strayhorn), performed by Duke Ellington & His Orchestra; "(I Can't Get No) Satisfaction" is followed by a 44-second "outro" of "The Star Spangled Banner" (Key; Arr: Hendrix), performed by Jimi Hendrix. Also released in the US was a special limited edition picture disc, RSR COC 39114, below. In 1984, *Still Life* became the Stones' first American CD release—by mistake.

JUNE 1, 1982

WHERE RELEASED: US

TITLE & CATALOG #: *Still Life (American Concert 1981)*, special limited edition picture disc, RSR COC 39114

SONGS: [A] Under My Thumb, LV2 / Let's Spend the Night Together, LV / Shattered, LV / Twenty Flight Rock (Fairchild, Cochran), LV / Going to À Go Go (Robinson, Johnson, Moore, Rogers), LV / [B] Let Me Go, LV / Time Is on My Side (Meade), LV2 / Just My Imagination (Whitfield, Strong), LV / Start Me Up, LV / (I Can't Get No) Satisfaction, LV2

NOTES: See Notes for UK release, above.

JUNE 1, 1982

WHERE RELEASED: US

TITLE & CATALOG #: The Rolling Stones: The First Eleven London Albums, ABKCO

NOTES: Limited edition of individually numbered wooden boxed sets.

SEPTEMBER 14, 1982

WHERE RELEASED: UK

TITLE & CATALOG #: Single, RSR RSR 111

SONGS: [A] Time Is on My Side (Meade), LV2 / [B] Twenty Flight Rock (Fairchild, Cochran), LV

NOTES: Picture sleeve

SEPTEMBER 14, 1982

WHERE RELEASED: UK

TITLE & CATALOG #: 12" Maxi-single, RSR 12RSR 111

SONGS: [A] Time Is on My Side (Meade), LV2 / [B] Twenty Flight Rock (Fairchild, Cochran), LV / Under My Thumb, LV2

NOTES: Note bonus track—"Under My Thumb." Picture sleeve.

SEPTEMBER 14, 1982

WHERE RELEASED: US

TITLE & CATALOG #: Single, RSR RS 21302

SONGS: [A] Time Is on My Side (Meade), LV2 / [B] Twenty Flight Rock (Fairchild, Cochran), LV

NOTES: Picture sleeve

NOVEMBER 23, 1982

WHERE RELEASED: UK

TITLE & CATALOG #: *Story of the Stones*, K-Tel Records NE 1201

SONGS: [A] (I Can't Get No) Satisfaction / It's All Over Now (Womack, Womack) / Time Is on My Side (Meade), V2 / Play with Fire (Nanker Phelge) / Off the Hook (Nanker Phelge) / Little Red Rooster (Dixon) / Let It Bleed / Have You Seen Your Mother, Baby, Standing in the Shadow? / [B] Paint It, Black / The Last Time / We Love You / You Better Move On (Alexander) / Under My Thumb / Come On (Berry) / I Just Want to Make Love to You (Dixon) / Honky Tonk Women / [C] Jumpin' Jack Flash / Route 66 (Troup) / I Wanna Be Your Man (Lennon, McCartney) / Mother's Little Helper / You Can't Always Get What You Want / Carol (Berry) / Let's Spend the Night Together / [D] Get Off of My Cloud / 19th Nervous Breakdown / Not Fade Away (Petty, Hardin) / Walking the Dog (Thomas) / Heart of Stone / Ruby Tuesday / Street Fighting Man

NOTES: "Time Is on My Side" (Meade) was again credited to Meade, Norman. "19th Nervous Breakdown" (Jagger/Richards) was credited to B&S Womack.

NOVEMBER 26, 1982

WHERE RELEASED: UK

TITLE & CATALOG #: 12" EP, Decca DFEX 8560

SONGS: [A] Bye Bye Johnny (Berry) / Money (Gordy Jr., Bradford) / [B] You Better Move On (Alexander) / Poison Ivy (Leiber, Stoller), V2

NOTES: Rerelease of *The Rolling Stones* (EP); Decca DFE 8560

DECEMBER 10, 1982

WHERE RELEASED: UK

TITLE & CATALOG #: *Thank Your Lucky Stars*, Decca Tab 51 (Compilation)

SONGS: [B8] Come On (Berry)

NOTES: This is a rerelease of the 1963 *Thank Your Lucky Stars, Vol. 2*; Decca LK 4554 compilation album on which the Rolling Stones are represented by the eighth cut on side B, their recording of Chuck Berry's "Come On."

1983

FEBRUARY 11, 1983

WHERE RELEASED: UK

TITLE & CATALOG #: Single (Promo), RSR RSR 112A-DJ

SONGS: [A] Let's Spend the Night Together / [B] Start Me Up

NOTES: Picture sleeve. Promotional release only; coincided with release date of movie *Let's Spend the Night Together*.

NOVEMBER 1, 1983

WHERE RELEASED: UK

TITLE & CATALOG #: Single, RSR RSR 113

SONGS: [A] Undercover of the Night, V1 / All the Way Down

NOTES: Picture sleeve

NOVEMBER 1, 1983

WHERE RELEASED: UK

TITLE & CATALOG #: 12" Single, RSR 12RSR 113

SONGS: [A] Undercover of the Night, V2 / [B] Feel On Baby, V2

NOTES: "Undercover of the Night, V2" is called "Dub Version" on this disc; V2 of "Feel On Baby" is labelled "Instrumental Dub Version."

NOVEMBER 1, 1983

WHERE RELEASED: US

TITLE & CATALOG #: 12" Single (Promo), RSR DMD 685

SONGS: [A] Undercover of the Night, V3 / [B] Undercover of the Night, V1

NOTES: V3 is an "extended version." V1 is the LP version of "Undercover of the Night."

NOVEMBER 1, 1983

WHERE RELEASED: US

TITLE & CATALOG #: Single, RSR 7-99813

SONGS: [A] Undercover of the Night, V1 / [B] All the Way Down

NOTES: Picture sleeve

NOVEMBER 8, 1983

WHERE RELEASED: UK

TITLE & CATALOG #: *Undercover*, RSR CUN 1654361

SONGS: [A] Undercover of the Night, V1 / She Was Hot / Tie You Up (Pain of Love) / Wanna Hold You / Feel On Baby, V1 / [B] Too Much Blood, V1 / Pretty Beat Up (Jagger, Richards, Wood) / Too Tough / All the Way Down / It Must Be Hell

NOVEMBER 8, 1983

WHERE RELEASED: US

TITLE & CATALOG #: *Undercover*, RSR 90120

SONGS: [A] Undercover of the Night, V1 / She Was Hot / Tie You Up (Pain of Love) / Wanna Hold You / Feel On Baby, V1 / [B] Too Much Blood, V1 / Pretty Beat Up (Jagger, Richards, Wood) / Too Tough / All the Way Down / It Must Be Hell

DECEMBER 16, 1983

WHERE RELEASED: West Germany

TITLE & CATALOG #: *The Rest of the Best (The Rolling Stones Story—Part 2)*, Teldec 6.30125FX

SONGS: Memphis Tennessee (Berry), OOV / Bright Lights, Big City (Reed) / Tell Me Baby (Broonzy) / Cocksucker Blues

NOTES This is not a complete track listing for this four-LP boxed set issued by Telenfunken Decca (German Decca); its first release on December 16, 1983 included a bonus single of "Cocksucker Blues." That edition was stopped, the single was taken out and the set was rereleased in January 1984.

"Tell Me Baby" was listed as "Tell Me" (V2). This was a major error, since the track is actually "Tell Me Baby How Many Times" (Broonzy). This is the first release of that song, as well as "Bright Lights, Big City" and "Cocksucker Blues," on an official Stones record. Also, "Memphis Tennessee," OOV is not the Stones. This track was recorded by the Andrew Oldham Orchestra in 1964 and released in October 1964 on an album entitled *16 Hip Hits*, (Ace of Clubs 1180).

1984

JANUARY 24, 1984

WHERE RELEASED: UK

TITLE & CATALOG #: Single, RSR RSR 114

SONGS: [A] She Was Hot / [B] Think I'm Going Mad

NOTES: The single RSR 114 has a picture sleeve.

JANUARY 24, 1984

WHERE RELEASED: UK

TITLE & CATALOG #: Single, RSR RSR P114

SONGS: [A] She Was Hot / [B] Think I'm Going Mad

NOTES: RSR P114 is a UK picture disc single; that is, it has a picture embedded in the vinyl of the disc.

JANUARY 24, 1984

WHERE RELEASED: US

TITLE & CATALOG #: Single, RSR 7-99788

SONGS: [A] She Was Hot / [B] Think I'm Going Mad

NOTES: Picture sleeve

JUNE 29, 1984

WHERE RELEASED: UK
TITLE & CATALOG #:   Single, RSR SUGAR 1
SONGS: [A] Brown Sugar / [B] Bitch
NOTES: "RSR SUGAR 1" (single) has a picture sleeve.

JUNE 29, 1984

WHERE RELEASED: UK
TITLE & CATALOG #:   Single, RSR SUGAR P1
SONGS: [A] Brown Sugar / [B] Bitch
NOTES: RSR Sugar P1 is a picture disc single; that is, it has a picture in the vinyl of the disc itself.

JUNE 29, 1984

WHERE RELEASED: UK
TITLE & CATALOG #:   *Rewind (1971–1984)*, RSR CUN 1
SONGS: [A] Miss You / Brown Sugar / Undercover of the Night, V1 / Start Me Up / Tumbling Dice / Hang Fire / [B] Emotional Rescue / Beast of Burden, V1 / Fool to Cry / Waiting on a Friend / Angie / It's Only Rock 'n' Roll / She's So Cold
NOTES: The UK release date differs from that of the US version, which occurred on July 3, 1984. Note also that there are two more tracks ("It's Only Rock 'n' Roll" and "She's So Cold") on the British album.

JULY 3, 1984

WHERE RELEASED: US
TITLE & CATALOG #:   Single, RSR 7-99724
SONGS: [A] Too Tough / [B] Miss You
NOTES: This single was released in the US only.

JULY 3, 1984

WHERE RELEASED: US
TITLE & CATALOG #:   *Rewind (1971–1984)*, RSR RS 7-90176-1
SONGS: [A] Miss You / Brown Sugar / Undercover of the Night, V1 / Start Me Up / Tumbling Dice / Hang Fire / [B] Emotional Rescue / Beast of Burden, V1 / Fool to Cry / Waiting on a Friend / Angie
NOTES: The UK release of this album, with two additional tracks, was June 29, 1984.

DECEMBER 1984

WHERE RELEASED: US
TITLE & CATALOG #:   12" Maxi-single RSR 0-96902
SONGS: [A] Too Much Blood, V2 / [B] Too Much Blood, V3 / Too Much Blood, V1
NOTES: Version 2 is a 12:33 "Dance Version," V3 is a "Dub Version." Both differ from "Too Much Blood," V1, which is the same as that on the *Undercover* LP.

1986

MARCH 4, 1986

WHERE RELEASED: UK
TITLE & CATALOG #:   Single, RSR A 6864
SONGS: [A] Harlem Shuffle (Relf, Nelson), V1 / [B] Had It with You
NOTES: The first release by CBS, the Stones' new label. From 1971 until this point, all Stones recordings (on the Rolling Stones Records "tongue" label) were distributed and promoted by Atlantic Records. CBS's term lasted nearly six years, from this single until the 1991 LP, *Flashpoint*. The band's mega-deal with Virgin Records began with the release of the *Jump Back* compilation in 1993.

MARCH 4, 1986

WHERE RELEASED: UK
TITLE & CATALOG #:   12" Single, RSR TA 6864
SONGS: [A] Harlem Shuffle (Relf, Nelson), V2 / [A] Harlem Shuffle (Relf, Nelson), V3
NOTES: These are different versions from the single and album releases of "Harlem Shuffle." "NY Mix" by Steve Thompson and Michael Barbiero is V2; "London Mix" by Steve Lillywhite is V3. This is a double-A-side single.

MARCH 4, 1986

WHERE RELEASED: UK
TITLE & CATALOG #:   Single, RSR QA 6864
SONGS: [A] Harlem Shuffle (Relf, Nelson), V1 / [B] Had It with You
NOTES: The same as RSR A 6864 but packaged with a wraparound poster.

MARCH 4, 1986

WHERE RELEASED: US
TITLE & CATALOG #:   Single, RSR 38-05802
SONGS: [A] Harlem Shuffle (Relf, Nelson), V1 / [B] Had It with You

MARCH 4, 1986

WHERE RELEASED: US
TITLE & CATALOG #:   12" Single, RSR 44-05365
SONGS: [A] Harlem Shuffle (Relf, Nelson), V2 / [A] Harlem Shuffle (Relf, Nelson), V3
NOTES: As with UK single releases of these titles, the 12" single has different versions (mixes) of the 7" single's A-side. "NY Mix" by Steve Thompson and Michael Barbiero is V2; "London Mix" by Steve Lillywhite is V3. Another double-A-side disc.

MARCH 25, 1986

WHERE RELEASED: UK

TITLE & CATALOG #: *Dirty Work*, RSR 86321

SONGS: [A] One Hit (to the Body) (Jagger, Richards, Wood), V1 / Fight (Jagger, Richards, Wood) / Harlem Shuffle (Relf, Nelson), V1 / Hold Back / Too Rude (Roberts, Dunbar, Shakespeare) / [B] Winning Ugly / Back to Zero (Jagger, Richards, Leavell) / Dirty Work (Jagger, Richards, Wood) / Had It with You / Sleep Tonight

NOTES: The last cut, "Sleep Tonight," is followed by a boogie-woogie piano fadeout as a memorial to Ian Stewart, who died on December 12, 1975. The album is dedicated to him.

MARCH 25, 1986

WHERE RELEASED: US

TITLE & CATALOG #: *Dirty Work*, RSR 40250 (CD: RSR CK 40250)

SONGS: [A] One Hit (to the Body) (Jagger, Richards, Wood), V1 / Fight (Jagger, Richards, Wood) / Harlem Shuffle (Relf, Nelson), V1 / Hold Back / Too Rude (Roberts, Dunbar, Shakespeare) / [B] Winning Ugly / Back to Zero (Jagger, Richards, Leavell) / Dirty Work (Jagger, Richards, Wood) / Had It with You / Sleep Tonight

NOTES: See notes for UK release, above.

MAY 20, 1986

WHERE RELEASED: UK

TITLE & CATALOG #: Single, RSR A 7160

SONGS: [A] One Hit (to the Body) (Jagger, Richards, Wood), V1 / [B] Fight (Jagger, Richards, Wood)

MAY 20, 1986

WHERE RELEASED: UK

TITLE & CATALOG #: 12" Single, RSR TA 7160

SONGS: [A] One Hit (to the Body) (Jagger, Richards, Wood), V1 / [B] Fight (Jagger, Richards, Wood)

MAY 20, 1986

WHERE RELEASED: US

TITLE & CATALOG #: Single, RSR 38-05906

SONGS: [A] One Hit (to the Body) (Jagger, Richards, Wood), V1 / [B] Fight (Jagger, Richards, Wood)

MAY 20, 1986

WHERE RELEASED: US

TITLE & CATALOG #: 12" Maxi-single, RSR 44-05388

SONGS: [A] One Hit (to the Body) (Jagger, Richards, Wood), V2 / [B] One Hit (to the Body) (Jagger, Richards, Wood), V3 / Fight (Jagger, Richards, Wood)

NOTES: In the US, this 12" maxi-single, with picture sleeve, was released containing two additional mixes of "One Hit (to the Body)" plus the single's B-side, "Fight." V2 is a seven-minute "London Mix" and V3 is an "Edit" of 4:04.

NOVEMBER 14, 1986

WHERE RELEASED: US

TITLE & CATALOG #: *The Rolling Stones—The First 17 Albums*, ABKCO

NOTES: ABKCO "digitally remastered" and reissued on CD (and cassette and vinyl) the Stones' first 17 albums. The album covers are the same as the originals, but the banned *Beggars Banquet* toilet-and-graffiti cover was used this time. The catalog numbers are the same except for the addition of the letters "CD" where appropriate and the inclusion of the ABKCO name as the issuing label. For example: *England's Newest Hit Makers—The Rolling Stones* is ABKCO CD 375 (original release was London PS 375). There are a few minor differences between the contents of these reissues and the original vinyl products. For example, on *Got Live If You Want It*, the intro to "Under My Thumb" is 20 seconds longer than the track on the original vinyl. The "outro" of "Satisfaction" is also longer here. These albums were advertised as "digitally remastered," giving the impression that the old mono versions were now stereo. In fact, the original analog masters were digitized and some electronic reprocessing was done to mimic stereo. So, those tracks that were originally released in mono are not true stereo here either.

1987

MAY 28, 1987

WHERE RELEASED: UK

TITLE & CATALOG #: Single, Decca F 102

SONGS: [A] Jumpin' Jack Flash / [B] Child of the Moon (rmk)

MAY 28, 1987

WHERE RELEASED: UK

TITLE & CATALOG #: 12" Maxi-single, Decca FX 102

SONGS: [A] Jumpin' Jack Flash / [B] Child of the Moon (rmk) / Sympathy for the Devil

1989

AUGUST 15, 1989

WHERE RELEASED: US

TITLE & CATALOG #: *The Rolling Stones Singles Collection—The London Years*, ABKCO 1218-2
SONGS: Gotta Get Away / 19th Nervous Breakdown / Sad Day / Paint It, Black / Stupid Girl / Long Long While / Mother's Little Helper / Lady Jane / Have You Seen Your Mother, Baby, Standing in the Shadow? / Who's Driving Your Plane / Let's Spend the Night Together / Ruby Tuesday / We Love You / Dandelion / She's a Rainbow / 2000 Light Years from Home / In Another Land (Wyman) / The Lantern / Jumpin' Jack Flash / Child of the Moon (rmk) / Come On (Berry) / I Want to Be Loved (Dixon) / I Wanna Be Your Man (Lennon, McCartney) / Stoned (Nanker Phelge) / Not Fade Away (Petty, Hardin) / Little by Little (Phelge, Spector) / It's All Over Now (Womack, Womack) / Good Times, Bad Times / Tell Me / I Just Want to Make Love to You (Dixon) / Time Is on My Side (Meade), V1 / Congratulations / Little Red Rooster (Dixon) / Off the Hook (Nanker Phelge) / Heart of Stone / What a Shame / The Last Time / Play with Fire (Nanker Phelge) / (I Can't Get No) Satisfaction / The Under-Assistant West Coast Promotion Man (Nanker Phelge) / The Spider and the Fly (Nanker Phelge) / Get Off of My Cloud / I'm Free / The Singer Not the Song / As Tears Go By (Jagger, Richards, Oldham)

AUGUST 17, 1989

WHERE RELEASED: UK
TITLE & CATALOG #: CD Single (Ltd. Ed.), RSR 655214-2
SONGS: Mixed Emotions, V1 / Fancyman Blues / Shattered / Waiting on a Friend
NOTES: This is the second limited edition CD single released on this date. It is also packaged in a tin and contains "Mixed Emotions" and "Fancyman Blues," but the two bonus tracks differ from the first limited edition CD single.

AUGUST 18, 1989

WHERE RELEASED: UK
TITLE & CATALOG #: Single, RSR 655193-7
SONGS: [A] Mixed Emotions, V1 / [B] Fancyman Blues
NOTES: Version 1 of "Mixed Emotions" is the 4:00 edited single version of the album track (which is 4:38).

AUGUST 18, 1989

WHERE RELEASED: UK
TITLE & CATALOG #: 12" Single, RSR TA 655193-8
SONGS: [A] Mixed Emotions, V3 / [B] Fancyman Blues
NOTES: "Mixed Emotions," V3 is "Chris Kimsey's 12" Mix," a 6:12 version of this song.

AUGUST 18, 1989

WHERE RELEASED: UK
TITLE & CATALOG #: Cassette Single, RSR 655193-4
SONGS: [A] Mixed Emotions, V1 / [B] Fancyman Blues
NOTES: The regular single on cassette.

AUGUST 18, 1989

WHERE RELEASED: UK
TITLE & CATALOG #: CD Single, RSR 655193-2
SONGS: Mixed Emotions, V1 / Mixed Emotions, V3 /Fancyman Blues
NOTES: Again, V3 of "Mixed Emotions" is "Chris Kimsey's 12" Mix," which is 6:12 long.

AUGUST 18, 1989

WHERE RELEASED: UK
TITLE & CATALOG #: CD Single (Ltd. Ed.), RSR 655193-5
SONGS: Mixed Emotions, V1 / Fancyman Blues / Tumbling Dice / Miss You
NOTES: This is a limited edition CD single with regular single release versions of "Mixed Emotions" and "Fancyman Blues," plus two bonus tracks, packaged in a tin with a Stones' tongue-logo sticker.

AUGUST 18, 1989

WHERE RELEASED: US
TITLE & CATALOG #: Single, RSR 38-69008
SONGS: [A] Mixed Emotions, V1 / [B] Fancyman Blues
NOTES: This is the US single release.

AUGUST 21, 1989

WHERE RELEASED: US
TITLE & CATALOG #: 12" Maxi-single (Promo), RSR/Columbia CAS 1765
SONGS: [A] Mixed Emotions, V3 / Mixed Emotions, V1
NOTES: V3 = Chris Kimsey's 12" mix—6:12; V4 = Edited 7" Version—4:00.

AUGUST 29, 1989

WHERE RELEASED: UK
TITLE & CATALOG #: *Steel Wheels*, RSR 465752-1 (CD —465752-2)
SONGS: Sad Sad Sad / Mixed Emotions, V2 / Terrifying, V1 / Hold On to Your Hat / Hearts for Sale / Blinded by Love / Rock and a Hard Place, V1 / Can't Be Seen / Almost Hear You Sigh (Jagger, Richards, Jordan), V1 / Continental Drift, V1 / Break the Spell / Slipping Away

AUGUST 29, 1989

WHERE RELEASED: US

TITLE & CATALOG #: *Steel Wheels*, RSR 45333

SONGS: Sad Sad Sad / Mixed Emotions, V2 / Terrifying, V1 / Hold On to Your Hat / Hearts for Sale / Blinded by Love / Rock and a Hard Place, V1 / Can't Be Seen / Almost Hear You Sigh (Jagger, Richards, Jordan), V1 / Continental Drift, V1 / Break the Spell / Slipping Away

NOTES: US catalog number applies to LP, CD, cassette formats with appropriate prefixes. RSR/Columbia OC 45333 = vinyl LP; CK 45333 = CD.

SEPTEMBER 1989

WHERE RELEASED: US

TITLE & CATALOG #: 5" CD single (promo), CSK 1755

SONGS: Mixed Emotions, V1 / Mixed Emotions, V2 / Mixed Emotions, V3

NOTES: V1 = 4:00 edited single version; V2 = 4:38 album version; V3 = 6:12 "Chris Kimsey's 12" Mix"

SEPTEMBER 1989

WHERE RELEASED: US

TITLE & CATALOG #: *Say Ahhh*, promo CD, RSR/Columbia CSK 1827

SONGS: [1] Mixed Emotions, V1 / [2] It's Only Rock 'n' Roll / [3] Start Me Up / [4] Brown Sugar / [5] Bitch / [6] Harlem Shuffle (Relf, Nelson), V1 / [7] Tumbling Dice / [8] Can't You Hear Me Knocking / [9] One Hit (to the Body) (Jagger, Richards, Wood), V1 / [10] Shattered / [11] Beast of Burden, V1 / [12] Happy / [13] Undercover of the Night, V1 / [14] Miss You / [15] Dead Flowers / [16] Hand of Fate / [17] Fancyman Blues

OCTOBER 24, 1989

WHERE RELEASED: UK

TITLE & CATALOG #: Single, RSR 655422-7

SONGS: [A] Rock and a Hard Place, V1 / [B] Cook Cook Blues

OCTOBER 24, 1989

WHERE RELEASED: UK

TITLE & CATALOG #: 12" single, RSR 655422-8

SONGS: [A] Rock and a Hard Place, V3 / [B] Rock and a Hard Place, V4 / Cook Cook Blues

NOTES: "Rock and a Hard Place" versions are as follows: V3 = 6:54 Dance Mix and V4 = 6:50 Oh Oh Hard Dub Mix.

OCTOBER 24, 1989

WHERE RELEASED: UK

TITLE & CATALOG #: CD single, RSR 655422-2

SONGS: Rock and a Hard Place, V1 / Cook Cook Blues

OCTOBER 24, 1989

WHERE RELEASED: UK

TITLE & CATALOG #: Cassette Single, RSR 655422-4

SONGS: [A] Rock and a Hard Place, V1 / [B] Cook Cook Blues

OCTOBER 24, 1989

WHERE RELEASED: UK

TITLE & CATALOG #: CD Single (Ltd. Ed.), RSR 655448-5

SONGS: Rock and a Hard Place, V1 / Cook Cook Blues / Emotional Rescue / Some Girls

NOTES: Limited edition CD single packaged in tongue-shaped sleeve. Same A/B side tracks as were released on the UK single plus two bonus tracks.

OCTOBER 24, 1989

WHERE RELEASED: UK

TITLE & CATALOG #: CD Single (Ltd. Ed.), RSR 655448-2

SONGS: Rock and a Hard Place, V1 / Cook Cook Blues / It's Only Rock 'n' Roll / Rocks Off

NOTES: This is the second UK limited edition CD single release, with the "Rock and a Hard Place"/ "Cook Cook Blues" single tracks and two different bonus tracks. This edition was packaged in a box and included a poster.

OCTOBER 24, 1989

WHERE RELEASED: US

TITLE & CATALOG #: Single, RSR 38-73057

SONGS: Rock and a Hard Place, V1 / Cook Cook Blues

OCTOBER 24, 1989

WHERE RELEASED: US

TITLE & CATALOG #: 12" EP, RSR 44-73133

SONGS: [A] Rock and a Hard Place, V3 / Rock and a Hard Place, V4 / [B] Rock and a Hard Place, V5 / Rock and a Hard Place, V6

NOTES: Four different mixes of "Rock and a Hard Place"—these are different from album, regular single and CD single versions (V1 and V2). V3 = 6:54 "Dance Mix"; V4 = 6:50 "Oh Oh Hard Dub Mix"; V5 = 6:57 "Michael Brauer Mix"; V6 = 4:15 "Bonus Beat Mix."

NOVEMBER

WHERE RELEASED: US

TITLE & CATALOG #: 5" CD Single, RSR/Columbia CSK 73057

SONGS: Rock and a Hard Place, V1 / Rock and a Hard Place, V2

NOTES: Version 2 is the 5:20 "Rock and a Hard Place" album track.

NOVEMBER 27, 1989

WHERE RELEASED: UK

TITLE & CATALOG #: 12" Maxi-single, RSR 655422-5

SONGS: [A] Rock and a Hard Place, V5 / [B] Rock and a Hard Place, V6 / Rock and a Hard Place, V1

NOTES: Versions are as noted in the US 12" EP, RSR 44-73133 of October 24, above.

1990

JANUARY

WHERE RELEASED: US

TITLE & CATALOG #: Single, RSR 38-37093

SONGS: Almost Hear You Sigh (Jagger, Richards, Jordan), V1 / Break the Spell

JANUARY

WHERE RELEASED: US

TITLE & CATALOG #: 5" CD Single, RSR/Columbia CSK 73093

SONGS: Almost Hear You Sigh (Jagger, Richards, Jordan), V2 / Almost Hear You Sigh (Jagger, Richards, Jordan), V1

NOTES: V2 = 4:00 Radio Edit Mix; V1 = 4:35 single/album track.

JANUARY

WHERE RELEASED: US

TITLE & CATALOG #: *The Rolling Stones Collection 1971–1989* (Ltd. Ed.), CBS

JUNE 11, 1990

WHERE RELEASED: US

TITLE & CATALOG #: Single, London LON 264

SONGS: [A] Paint It, Black / [B] Honky Tonk Women

NOTES: Reissue

JUNE 11, 1990

TITLE & CATALOG #: US

TITLE & CATALOG #: Maxi-single, London LONX 264

SONGS: Paint It, Black / Honky Tonk Women / Sympathy for the Devil

JUNE 11, 1990

WHERE RELEASED: US

TITLE & CATALOG #: 12" Maxi-single, London LONX 12 264

SONGS: Paint It, Black / Honky Tonk Women / Sympathy for the Devil

JUNE 11, 1990

WHERE RELEASED: US

TITLE & CATALOG #: Cassette Single, London LONCS 264

SONGS: Paint It, Black / Honky Tonk Women

JUNE 18, 1990

WHERE RELEASED: UK

TITLE & CATALOG #: Maxi-single, RSR 656065-7

SONGS: [A] Almost Hear You Sigh (Jagger, Richards, Jordan), V1 / [B] Wish I Never Met You / Mixed Emotions, V1

JUNE 18, 1990

WHERE RELEASED: UK

TITLE & CATALOG #: 12" EP, RSR 656065-6

SONGS: [A] Almost Hear You Sigh (Jagger, Richards, Jordan), V1 / Beast of Burden, V1 / [B] Angie / Fool to Cry

NOTES: 12" EP with gatefold sleeve

JUNE 18, 1990

WHERE RELEASED: UK

TITLE & CATALOG #: Cassette Single, RSR 656065-3

SONGS: [A] Almost Hear You Sigh (Jagger, Richards, Jordan), V1 / [B] Wish I Never Met You / Mixed Emotions, V1

JUNE 18, 1990

WHERE RELEASED: UK

TITLE & CATALOG #: CD Single (Ltd. Ed, Gold CD), RSR 656065-2

SONGS: Almost Hear You Sigh (Jagger, Richards, Jordan), V1 / Wish I Never Met You / Mixed Emotions, V1

JUNE 25, 1990

WHERE RELEASED: UK

TITLE & CATALOG #: CD Single (Ltd. Ed.), RSR 656065-5

SONGS: Almost Hear You Sigh (Jagger, Richards, Jordan), V1 / Wish I Never Met You / Mixed Emotions, V1 / Miss You / Waiting on a Friend

NOTES: This limited edition was packaged in a tin with "Urban Jungle" stickers; two bonus tracks.

JULY 30, 1990

WHERE RELEASED: UK
TITLE & CATALOG #: Single, RSR 656122-7
SONGS: [A] Terrifying, V1 / [B] Rock and a Hard Place, V1

JULY 30, 1990

WHERE RELEASED: UK
TITLE & CATALOG #: 12" Single, RSR 656122-6
SONGS: [A] Terrifying, V1 / [B] Rock and a Hard Place, V1

JULY 30, 1990

WHERE RELEASED: UK
TITLE & CATALOG #: CD Single, RSR 656122-2
SONGS: Terrifying, V2 / Terrifying, V3 / Rock and a Hard Place, V1 / Harlem Shuffle (Relf, Nelson), V1

JULY 30, 1990

WHERE RELEASED: UK
TITLE & CATALOG #: Cassette Single, RSR 656122-4
SONGS: [A] Terrifying, V1 / [B] Rock and a Hard Place, V1

JULY 30, 1990

WHERE RELEASED: Europe
TITLE & CATALOG #: 3" CD Single, RSR 6556613 LC0149
SONGS: Terrifying (12"remix) / Wish I'd Never Met You / Terrifying (7" remix edit, V2) / Terrifying (V1)

JULY 30, 1990

WHERE RELEASED: UK
TITLE & CATALOG #: CD Single, RSR 656122-5
SONGS: Terrifying, V1 / Start Me Up / Shattered / If You Can't Rock Me

1991

MARCH 5, 1991

WHERE RELEASED: US
TITLE & CATALOG #: Single, RSR 38-73742

SONGS: [A] Highwire / [B] 2000 Light Years from Home, LV

MARCH 11, 1991

WHERE RELEASED: UK
TITLE & CATALOG #: Single, RSR 656756-7
SONGS: [A] Highwire / [B] 2000 Light Years from Home, LV

MARCH 21, 1991

WHERE RELEASED: UK
TITLE & CATALOG #: 12" Single, RSR 656756-6
SONGS: Highwire / 2000 Light Years from Home, LV
NOTES: Gatefold sleeve

MARCH 21, 1991

WHERE RELEASED: UK
TITLE & CATALOG #: Cassette Single, RSR 656756-4
SONGS: Highwire / 2000 Light Years from Home, LV

MARCH 21, 1991

WHERE RELEASED: UK
TITLE & CATALOG #: CD Single, RSR 656756-5
SONGS: Highwire / 2000 Light Years from Home, LV / Play with Fire (Nanker Phelge), LV / Factory Girl, LV

MARCH 21, 1991

WHERE RELEASED: UK
TITLE & CATALOG #: Single, RSR 656892-7
SONGS: [A] Ruby Tuesday, LV / [B] Play with Fire (Nanker Phelge), LV

MARCH 21, 1991

WHERE RELEASED: UK
TITLE & CATALOG #: 12" Single, RSR 656892-6
SONGS: [A] Ruby Tuesday, LV / [B] Play with Fire (Nanker Phelge), LV

MARCH 21, 1991

WHERE RELEASED: UK
TITLE & CATALOG #: Cassette Single, RSR 656892-4
SONGS: Ruby Tuesday, LV / Play with Fire (Nanker Phelge), LV

MARCH 21, 1991

WHERE RELEASED: UK
TITLE & CATALOG #: CD Single (picture disc), RSR 656892-5

SONGS: Ruby Tuesday, LV / Play with Fire (Nanker Phelge), LV / Harlem Shuffle (Relf, Nelson), LV / Winning Ugly

MARCH 21, 1991

WHERE RELEASED: UK

TITLE & CATALOG #: CD Single, RSR 656892-2

SONGS: Ruby Tuesday, LV / Play with Fire (Nanker Phelge), LV / You Can't Always Get What You Want, LV2 / Undercover of the Night, LV

MARCH 21, 1991

WHERE RELEASED: UK

TITLE & CATALOG #: CD Single, RSR 656756-2

SONGS: Highwire / 2000 Light Years from Home, LV / Sympathy for the Devil, LV3 / I Just Want to Make Love to You (Dixon), LV

APRIL 2, 1991

WHERE RELEASED: US

TITLE & CATALOG #: *Flashpoint*, RSR RS 47456 (LP)

SONGS: [A] Continental Drift, V2 / Start Me Up, LV / Sad, Sad, Sad, LV / Miss You, LV / Ruby Tuesday, LV / You Can't Always Get What You Want, LV2 / Factory Girl, LV / Little Red Rooster (Dixon), LV2 / [B] Paint It, Black, LV / Sympathy for the Devil, LV3 / Brown Sugar, LV2 / Jumpin' Jack Flash, LV3 / (I Can't Get No) Satisfaction, LV3 / Highwire / Sex Drive, V1

NOTES: "Continental Drift," V2 (which is actually 27 seconds of V1) is entitled "(Intro) Continental Drift" on this and other releases of *Flashpoint*. LP (vinyl) lacks "Rock and a Hard Place" and "Can't Be Seen."

APRIL 2, 1991

WHERE RELEASED: US

TITLE & CATALOG #: *Flashpoint*, RSR CK 47456 (CD)

SONGS: Continental Drift, V2 / Start Me Up, LV / Sad, Sad, Sad, LV / Miss You, LV / Rock and a Hard Place, LV / Ruby Tuesday, LV / You Can't Always Get What You Want, LV2 / Factory Girl, LV / Can't Be Seen, LV / Little Red Rooster (Dixon), LV2 / Paint It, Black, LV / Sympathy for the Devil, LV3 / Brown Sugar, LV2 / Jumpin' Jack Flash, LV3 / (I Can't Get No) Satisfaction, LV3 / Highwire / Sex Drive, V1

NOTES: The CD has two more tracks ("Rock and a Hard Place" and "Can't Be Seen") than the vinyl.

APRIL 8, 1991

WHERE RELEASED: UK

TITLE & CATALOG #: *Flashpoint*, RSR 468135-1

SONGS: Continental Drift, V2 / Start Me Up, LV / Sad, Sad, Sad, LV / Miss You, LV / Rock and a Hard Place, LV / Ruby Tuesday, LV / You Can't Always Get What You Want, LV2 / Factory Girl, LV / Can't Be Seen, LV / Little Red Rooster (Dixon), LV2 / Paint It, Black, LV / Sympathy for the Devil, LV3 / Brown Sugar, LV2 / Jumpin' Jack Flash, LV3 / (I Can't Get No) Satisfaction, LV3 / Highwire / Sex Drive, V1

MAY 20, 1991

WHERE RELEASED: US

TITLE & CATALOG #: *Flashpoint + Collectibles*, RSR CT2K 47880

SONGS: [Disc 1] Continental Drift, V2 / Start Me Up, LV / Sad, Sad, Sad, LV / Miss You, LV / Rock and a Hard Place, LV / Ruby Tuesday, LV / You Can't Always Get What You Want, LV2 / Factory Girl, LV / Can't Be Seen, LV / Little Red Rooster (Dixon), LV2 / Paint It, Black, LV / Sympathy for the Devil, LV3 / Brown Sugar, LV2 / Jumpin' Jack Flash, LV3 / (I Can't Get No) Satisfaction, LV3 / Highwire / Sex Drive, V1 / [Disc 2] Rock and a Hard Place, V5 / Miss You, V4 / Cook Cook Blues / Everything Is Turning to Gold (Jagger, Richards, Wood), V2 / Winning Ugly, V6 / Beast of Burden, LV / Fancyman Blues / Harlem Shuffle (Relf, Nelson), V6 / Wish I Never Met You / Mixed Emotions, V4

NOTES: This is a limited edition double CD set, packaged in a leather-bound case, and consisting of the regular "Flashpoint" CD plus an additional CD that includes rare versions of tracks previously released only on 12" singles and as single B sides.

JUNE 1991

WHERE RELEASED: US

TITLE & CATALOG #: Single, RSR 38-73789

SONGS: [A] Sex Drive, V1 / [B] Undercover of the Night, LV

JUNE 1991

WHERE RELEASED: The Netherlands

TITLE & CATALOG #: 5" CD Maxi-single, Sony Music COL RSR 6575972

SONGS: Jumpin' Jack Flash (Flashpoint at the IMAX) / Tumblin' Dice, LV-Maxi / Street Fighting Man, LV-Maxi

1993

NOVEMBER 22, 1993

WHERE RELEASED: UK

TITLE & CATALOG #: *Jump Back—The Best of the Rolling Stones*, Virgin CDV2726

SONGS: Start Me Up / Brown Sugar / Harlem Shuffle (Relf, Nelson), V1 / It's Only Rock 'n' Roll / Mixed Emotions, V2 / Angie / Tumbling Dice / Fool to Cry / Rock and a Hard Place, V2 / Miss You, V1 / Hot Stuff / Emotional Rescue / Respectable / Beast of Burden, V1 / Waiting on a Friend / Wild Horses / Bitch / Undercover of the Night

NOTES: This compilation of 20-bit digitally remastered hits was the Stones' first release on Virgin Records. Interestingly, this was only a UK release and while available as an import in the US and elsewhere, it was allowed to sell out and was not restocked or was actually pulled back from record stores in early June 1994, to allow demand to build for the release of the Stones' new LP, *Voodoo Lounge*.

1994

JULY 5, 1994

WHERE RELEASED: UK

TITLE & CATALOG #: 7" Single (Ltd. Ed.), Virgin VS 1503

SONGS: [A] Love Is Strong, V1 / [B] The Storm

NOTES: Limited and individually numbered edition of 7,000. V1 is the album version of "Love Is Strong" and "The Storm" is a non-album track. Produced by Don Was and the Glimmer Twins.

JULY 5, 1994

WHERE RELEASED: UK

TITLE & CATALOG #: Cassette Single, Virgin VSC 1503

SONGS: [A] Love Is Strong, V1 / [B] The Storm

NOTES: Essentially the same as the 7" vinyl single, but not a limited edition.

JULY 5, 1994

WHERE RELEASED: UK

TITLE & CATALOG #: CD Single, Virgin VSCDT 1503

SONGS: [1] Love Is Strong, V1 / [2] The Storm / [3] So Young / [4] Love Is Strong, V2

NOTES: V2 = Bob Clearmountain Remix. "So Young" dates back to the *Some Girls* sessions, and (per the credits on this CD) was produced and mixed by Chris Kimsey for Chris Kimsey Productions. Some copies of this CD single have a black sticker on the jewel case with the legend "Special Collectors CD, available for a strictly limited period only—includes two songs 'The Storm' and 'So Young' not available on any album—ever!"

JULY 5, 1994

WHERE RELEASED: UK

TITLE & CATALOG #: CD Single, Virgin VSCDX 1503

SONGS: [1] Love Is Strong, V3 / [2] Love Is Strong, V4 / [3] Love Is Strong, V5 / [4] Love Is Strong, V6 / [5] Love Is Strong, V7 / [6] Love Is Strong, V8

NOTES: V3 = Teddy Riley Radio Remix: V4 = Teddy Riley Extended Remix; V5 = Teddy Riley Extended Rock Remix; V6 = Teddy Riley Dub Remix; V7 = Joe The Butcher Club Mix: V8 = Teddy Riley Instrumental. Jewel case with sticker saying "Features the Teddy Riley Dance Remixes." Remix and additional production on those remixes by Teddy Riley and Sprague Williams, engineered by John Hanes George Mayers and Serban Ghenea. Dance remix by Joe "The Butcher" Nicolo, mixed by Joe and Phil Nicolo, engineered by Dirk Grobelny and Taj Walton.

JULY 5, 1994

WHERE RELEASED: US

TITLE & CATALOG #: CD Single, Virgin V25H 38446

SONGS: [1] Love Is Strong, V1 / [2] Love Is Strong, V4 / [3] Love Is Strong, V6 / [4] Love Is Strong, V5 / [5] The Storm

NOTES: V1 = Album Version; V4 = Teddy Riley Extended Remix; V6 = Teddy Riley Dub Remix; V5 = Teddy Riley Extended Rock Remix.

JULY 5, 1994

WHERE RELEASED: US

TITLE & CATALOG #: 7" EP, Virgin NR 38446

SONGS: [A] Love Is Strong, V1 / [B] The Storm / Love Is Strong, V4

NOTES: V4 = Teddy Riley Extended Remix.

JULY 5, 1994

WHERE RELEASED: US

TITLE & CATALOG #: Cassette Single, Virgin 4KM 38446

SONGS: [A] Love Is Strong, V1 / [B] The Storm / Love Is Strong, V4

NOTES: Contains the same tracks as the US 7" vinyl EP.

JULY 5, 1994

WHERE RELEASED: US

TITLE & CATALOG #: 12" Maxi-single, Virgin Y 38446

SONGS: [A] Love Is Strong, V4 / Love Is Strong, V5 / Love Is Strong, V6 / [B] Love Is Strong, V7 / Love Is Strong, V1 / Love Is Strong, V8

NOTES: V4 = Teddy Riley Extended Remix; V5 = Teddy Riley Extended Rock Remix; V6 = Teddy Riley Dub

Remix; V7 = Joe The Butcher Club Remix; V1 = Album Version; V8 = Teddy Riley Instrumental.

JULY 5, 1994

WHERE RELEASED: US

TITLE & CATALOG #: Promo CD Single, Virgin DPRO 14155

SONGS: [1] Love Is Strong, V1 / [2] Love Is Strong / [3] Love Is Strong / [4] Love Is Strong

NOTES: Four-track promo CD. Actual versions unknown.

JULY 5, 1994

WHERE RELEASED: US

TITLE & CATALOG #: Promo CD Single, Virgin DPRO 14180

SONGS: [1] Love Is Strong, V1 / [2] Love Is Strong

NOTES: Two-track promo CD. Actual versions unknown.

JULY 12, 1994

WHERE RELEASED: UK

TITLE & CATALOG #: *Voodoo Lounge,* Virgin CDV 2750 (CD)

SONGS: [1] Love Is Strong / [2] You Got Me Rocking / [3] Sparks Will Fly / [4] The Worst / [5] New Faces / [6] Moon Is Up / [7] Out of Tears / [8] I Go Wild / [9] Brand New Car / [10] Sweethearts Together / [11] Suck on the Jugular / [12] Blinded by Rainbows / [13] Baby Break It Down / [14] Thru and Thru / [15] Mean Disposition

NOTES: The Stones' 36th album, their 22nd studio album, and their first original album for Virgin Records. *Voodoo Lounge* and its singles are the first Stones records without bassist Bill Wyman. His immediate replacement was Darryl Jones, whose resumé included stints on bass with Miles Davis and Sting, among others. Jones was not hired as an official member of the band.

JULY 12, 1994

WHERE RELEASED: UK

TITLE & CATALOG #: *Voodoo Lounge,* Virgin TCV 2750 (Cassette)

SONGS: [A] Love Is Strong / You Got Me Rocking / Sparks Will Fly / The Worst / New Faces / Moon Is Up / Out of Tears / [B] I Go Wild / Brand New Car / Sweethearts Together / Suck on the Jugular / Blinded by Rainbows / Baby Break It Down / Thru and Thru

NOTES: "Mean Disposition" does not appear on non-CD releases of *Voodoo Lounge.*

JULY 12, 1994

WHERE RELEASED: UK

TITLE & CATALOG #: *Voodoo Lounge,* Virgin V2750 (Vinyl LP)

SONGS: [A] Love Is Strong / You Got Me Rocking / Sparks Will Fly / [B] The Worst / New Faces / Moon Is Up / Out of Tears / [C] I Go Wild / Brand New Car / Sweethearts Together / Suck on the Jugular / [D] Blinded by Rainbows / Baby Break It Down / Thru and Thru

NOTES: "Mean Disposition" does not appear on non-CD releases of *Voodoo Lounge.* Of 22 career studio albums, this is only the second (vinyl) double LP (after *Exile on Main Street*) of new Stones studio work. Gatefold sleeve. Not released on vinyl in the US.

JULY 12, 1994

WHERE RELEASED: US

TITLE & CATALOG #: *Voodoo Lounge,* Virgin 39782 (CD)

SONGS: [1] Love Is Strong / [2] You Got Me Rocking / [3] Sparks Will Fly / [4] The Worst / [5] New Faces / [6] Moon Is Up / [7] Out of Tears / [8] I Go Wild / [9] Brand New Car / [10] Sweethearts Together / [11] Suck on the Jugular / [12] Blinded by Rainbows / [13] Baby Break It Down / [14] Thru and Thru / [15] Mean Disposition

NOTES: The 15th track, "Mean Disposition," only appears on the CD release of *Voodoo Lounge,* not on cassette or, in the UK and elsewhere in the world, on vinyl. This album was not released on vinyl in the US.

JULY 12, 1994

WHERE RELEASED: US

TITLE & CATALOG #: *Voodoo Lounge,* Virgin 39782 (Cassette)

SONGS: [A] Love Is Strong / You Got Me Rocking / Sparks Will Fly / The Worst / New Faces / Moon Is Up / Out of Tears / [B] I Go Wild / Brand New Car / Sweethearts Together / Suck on the Jugular / Blinded by Rainbows / Baby Break It Down / Thru and Thru

NOTES: "Mean Disposition" does not appear on non-CD releases of *Voodoo Lounge. Voodoo Lounge* and its singles are the first Stones records without bassist Bill Wyman. Wyman's replacement, Darryl Jones, made his debut with the band on this album, though not as an official Rolling Stone.

JULY 12, 1994

WHERE RELEASED: US

TITLE & CATALOG #: *Voodoo Lounge—A Sampler,* (Picture Disc) Virgin DPRO-14158 (Promo CD)

NOTES: An eight-track US promo CD for *Voodoo Lounge*. A full 15-track US promo CD was also distributed, but it had the same catalog number (39782) as the mass market release and was indistinguishable from it except for promo stickers on the case and label.

SEPTEMBER 1994

WHERE RELEASED: UK
TITLE & CATALOG #: Single, Virgin VS 1518
SONGS: [A] You Got Me Rocking, V1 / [B] Jump on Top of Me, V2
NOTES: Produced by Don Was and the Glimmer Twins. "You Got Me Rocking," V1 is the album version. "Jump on Top of Me," V2 is a non-album track, but was remixed by Bob Clearmountain—V1 being the version appearing in the soundtrack of *Ready to Wear* (*Pret a Porter*), the Robert Altman film—hence the V2 designation. This vinyl single was issued in a limited, numbered edition of 7,000 only in the UK.

SEPTEMBER 1994

WHERE RELEASED: UK
TITLE & CATALOG #: 12" Maxi-single, Virgin VST 1518
SONGS: [A] You Got Me Rocking, V2 / [B] You Got Me Rocking, V3 / You Got Me Rocking, V3
NOTES: "You Got Me Rocking," V2 = Perfecto Mix; V3 = Sexy Disco Dub Mix; V4 = Trance Mix. Produced by Don Was and the Glimmer Twins. Additional production and remix by Paul Oakenfeld and Steve Osborne; programming and engineering by Ben Hillier; additional vocals by Anita Jarrett; additional percussion by Steve Sidelnyk.

SEPTEMBER 1994

WHERE RELEASED: UK
TITLE & CATALOG #: Cassette Single, Virgin VSC 1518
SONGS: [A] You Got Me Rocking, V1 / [B] Jump on Top of Me, V2
NOTES: Produced by Don Was and the Glimmer Twins. The same as the 7" UK vinyl single, only not a limited edition.

NOVEMBER 28, 1994

WHERE RELEASED: UK
TITLE & CATALOG #: Single, Virgin VS 1524
SONGS: [A] Out of Tears, V2 / [B] I'm Gonna Drive
NOTES: 7" vinyl single. V2 of "Out of Tears" edited by producer Don Was.

NOVEMBER 28, 1994

WHERE RELEASED: UK
TITLE & CATALOG #: Cassette Single, Virgin VSC 1524
SONGS: [A] Out of Tears, V2 / [B] I'm Gonna Drive
NOTES: The same as the 7" single, but on cassette.

NOVEMBER 28, 1994

WHERE RELEASED: UK
TITLE & CATALOG #: CD Single, Virgin VSCDE 1524
SONGS: [A] Out of Tears, V2 / [B] I'm Gonna Drive
NOTES: The same as the 7" single, but on CD.

NOVEMBER 28, 1994

WHERE RELEASED: UK
TITLE & CATALOG #: CD Single, Virgin VSCDT 1524
SONGS: [1] Out of Tears, V2 / [2] I'm Gonna Drive / [3] Sparks Will Fly, V2 / [4] Out of Tears, V3
NOTES: "Sparks Will Fly," V2 is the "radio clean" version, with the line "I'm gonna fuck your sweet ass" removed. "Out of Tears," V3 is the "Bob Clearmountain Remix Edit."

NOVEMBER 28, 1994

WHERE RELEASED: UK
TITLE & CATALOG #: CD Single, Virgin VSCDX 1524 (tear-shaped sleeve)
SONGS: [1] Out of Tears, V2 / [2] I'm Gonna Drive / [3] Sparks Will Fly, V2 / [4] Out of Tears, V3
NOTES: This 5" CD single was issued in a special tear-shaped sleeve, but has the same tracks as VSCDT 1524.

NOVEMBER 28, 1994

WHERE RELEASED: UK
TITLE & CATALOG #: CD Single, (Ltd. Ed.), Virgin VSCDG 1524 (Digipak)
SONGS: [1] Out of Tears, V2 / [2] I'm Gonna Drive / [3] So Young / [4] The Storm / [5] Jump on Top of Me
NOTES: Limited, numbered edition of 4,000. A compilation of *Voodoo Lounge* non-album tracks up to this release date.

1995

JULY 1995

WHERE RELEASED: US
TITLE & CATALOG #: CD Single, Virgin V25H 38478
SONGS: [1] I Go Wild, V1 / [2] I Go Wild, V2 / [3] I Go Wild, LV1 / [4] I Go Wild, V3

NOTES: Produced by Don Was and the Glimmer Twins. Recorded by Don Smith, mixed by Bob Clearmountain. "I Go Wild," V1 = Album Version; V2 = Scott Litt Remix (remixed by Scott Litt at Louie's Clubhouse, Los Angeles, CA); LV1 = Live version recorded at Joe Robbie Stadium, Miami, FL on November 25, 1994 (see TOURS AND CONCERTS)—recorded by David Hewitt and mixed by Bob Clearmountain; V3 = Luis Resto Straight Vocal Mix —remix and additional production by Luis Resto; mixed and played by Luis Resto and recorded at Chomsky Ranch, Los Angeles, CA. Studio versions personnel: Mick Jagger, vocal, guitar; Keith Richards, guitar; Charlie Watts, drums; Ron Wood, b-bender electric guitar and solo; Darryl Jones, bass; Chuck Leavell, B-3 organ; Phil Jones, percussion; Bernard Fowler, Ivan Neville, Mick Jagger, Keith Richards, background vocals. Live version personnel/instrumentation: Mick Jagger, vocals, guitar; Keith Richards, guitar; Charlie Watts, drums; Ron Wood, guitar; Darryl Jones, bass guitar; Chuck Leavell, keyboards; Lisa Fischer and Bernard Fowler, vocals.

JULY 1995

WHERE RELEASED: UK
TITLE & CATALOG #: Promo CD Single, Virgin VSCDJ 1539
SONGS: I Go Wild, V1
NOTES: Single track promo

OCTOBER 30, 1995

WHERE RELEASED: UK
TITLE & CATALOG #: CD Single, Virgin VSCDT 1562
SONGS: [1] Like a Rolling Stone (Dylan), LV1 / [2] Black Limousine (Jagger, Richards, Wood), LV1 / [3] All Down the Line, LV1 / [4] Like a Rolling Stone (Dylan), LV2
NOTES: "Black Limousine" was recorded at the Stones' Brixton Academy show on July 19, 1995, and "All Down the Line" came from their first Paradiso gig in Amsterdam on May 26, 1995.

OCTOBER 30, 1995

WHERE RELEASED: UK
TITLE & CATALOG #: Promo CD Single, Virgin VSCDJ 1562
SONGS: [1] Like a Rolling Stone (Dylan), LV2 / [2] Like a Rolling Stone (Dylan), LV1
NOTES: Two-track promo CD, the first single off the Stones' upcoming album, *Stripped*. The second version of the Bob Dylan tune is an edited one (4:20); the album track (V1) is 5:39 long.

OCTOBER 30, 1995

WHERE RELEASED: UK
TITLE & CATALOG #: CD Single, Virgin VSCDE 1562
SONGS: [1] Like a Rolling Stone (Dylan), LV1 / [2] Black Limousine (Jagger, Richards, Wood), LV1

NOVEMBER 10, 1995

WHERE RELEASED: Japan
TITLE & CATALOG #: *Stripped*, Virgin/Toshiba-EMI VJCP-25202 (CD)
SONGS: Street Fighting Man, LV2 / [2] Like a Rolling Stone (Dylan), LV1 / [3] Not Fade Away (Petty, Hardin), V2 / [4] Shine a Light, LV1 / [5] The Spider and the Fly (Nanker Phelge), V2 / [6] I'm Free, V2 / [7] Wild Horses, V3 / [8] Let It Bleed, LV1 / [9] Dead Flowers, LV1 / [10] Slipping Away, V2 / [11] Angie, LV1 / [12] Love in Vain (Robt. Johnson), V2 / [13] Sweet Virginia, V2 / [14] Little Baby (Dixon) / [15] Black Limousine (Jagger, Richards, Wood), LV1
NOTES: The Japanese release of *Stripped* contained the bonus track "Black Limousine," recorded at the Brixton Academy show on July 19.

NOVEMBER 10, 1995

WHERE RELEASED: UK
TITLE & CATALOG #: *Stripped*, Virgin IVDG 2801 Double CD Promo
SONGS: Disc #1: [1] Street Fighting Man, LV2 / [2] Like a Rolling Stone (Dylan), LV1 / [3] Not Fade Away (Petty, Hardin), V2 / [4] Shine a Light, LV1 / [5] The Spider and the Fly (Nanker Phelge), V2 / [6] I'm Free, V2 / [7] Wild Horses, V3 / [8] Let It Bleed, LV1 / [9] Dead Flowers, LV1 / [10] Slipping Away, V2 / [11] Angie, LV1 / [12] Love in Vain (Robt. Johnson), V2 / [13] Sweet Virginia, V2 / [14] Little Baby (Dixon)
NOTES: Disc number two includes an interview with Mick and Keith conducted by Paul Sexton.

NOVEMBER 13, 1995

WHERE RELEASED: UK (used worldwide)
TITLE & CATALOG #: *Stripped*, Virgin V2801 (Double Vinyl LP)
SONGS: [A] Street Fighting Man, LV2 / Like a Rolling Stone (Dylan), LV1 / Not Fade Away (Petty, Hardin), V2 / Shine a Light, LV1 / [B] The Spider and the Fly (Nanker Phelge), V2 / I'm Free, V2 / Wild Horses, V3 /[C] Let It Bleed, LV1 / Dead Flowers, LV1 / Slipping Away, V2 / Angie, LV1 / [D] Love in Vain (Robt. Johnson), V2 / Sweet Virginia, V2 / Little Baby (Dixon)

NOVEMBER 13, 1995

WHERE RELEASED: UK

TITLE & CATALOG #: *Stripped*, Virgin CDV2801 (CD+)

SONGS: [1] Street Fighting Man, LV2 / [2] Like a Rolling Stone (Dylan), LV1 / [3] Not Fade Away (Petty, Hardin), V2 / [4] Shine a Light, LV1 / [5] The Spider and the Fly (Nanker Phelge), V2 / [6] I'm Free, V2 / [7] Wild Horses, V3 / [8] Let It Bleed, LV1 / [9] Dead Flowers, LV1 / [10] Slipping Away, V2 / [11] Angie, LV1 / [12] Love in Vain (Robt. Johnson), V2 / [13] Sweet Virginia, V2 / [14] Little Baby (Dixon) /interactive material

NOTES: CD+ indicates that additional interactive material is accessible when the disk is played on a computer CD-ROM drive (Macintosh or Windows).

1996

FEBRUARY 9, 1996

WHERE RELEASED: UK

TITLE & CATALOG #: Promo CD Single, Virgin VSCDJ 1578

SONGS: Wild Horses, V4

NOTES: This is an edited (4:07) version of the *Stripped* album track (V3), which was recorded at Toshiba EMI Studios in Tokyo in March 1995. The first studio version of "Wild Horses" appeared on *Sticky Fingers*, the second showed up by mistake on the first pressing of *Hot Rocks*.

MARCH 1996

WHERE RELEASED: UK

TITLE & CATALOG #: CD Single, Virgin VSCDE 1578

SONGS: Wild Horses, V4 / Live with Me, LV2

APRIL 1996

WHERE RELEASED: UK

TITLE & CATALOG #: CD Single, Virgin VSCDT 1578

SONGS: Wild Horses, V4 / Live with Me, LV2 / Tumbling Dice, LV2 / Gimme Shelter, LV2

NOTES: This live version of "Tumbling Dice" appears to have originated, in part, at the Joe Robbie Stadium pay-per-view show in Miami on November 25, 1994. The track begins with just Jagger's vocal and Chuck Leavell's piano with other voices chiming in. The balance is from a backstage rehearsal at the Olympia Theatre, as seen in the "Stripped" Video. "Gimme Shelter" is from the first Paradiso show on May 26, 1995.

OCTOBER 15, 1996

WHERE RELEASED: US & UK

TITLE & CATALOG #: *The Rolling Stones Rock and Roll Circus* Soundtrack CD ABKCO 1268-2

SONGS: [1] Mick Jagger's introduction of *Rock and Roll Circus* / [2] Entry of the Gladiators (Fucik) / [3] Mick Jagger's introduction of Jethro Tull / [4] Song for Jeffrey (Anderson)[1] / [5] Keith Richard's introduction to the Who / [6] A Quick One While He's Away (Townshend)[2] / [7] Over the Waves (Rosas) / [8] Ain't That a Lot of Love (Parker, Banks)[3] / [9] Charlie Watts's introduction of Marianne Faithfull / [10] Something Better (Mann, Goffin)[4] / [11] Mick Jagger's and John Lennon's introduction of the Dirty Mac / [12] Yer Blues (Lennon, McCartney)[5] / [13] Whole Lotta Yoko (Ono)[6] / [14] John Lennon's introduction of the Rolling Stones [and] Jumping Jack Flash / [15] Parachute Woman / [16] No Expectations [17] You Can't Always Get What You Want / [18] Sympathy for the Devil / [19] Salt of the Earth

NOTES: The non-Rolling Stones artists and their respective tracks are identified by the numbers following the track titles as follows: 1 = Jethro Tull (Ian Anderson: lead vocal, flute; Glen Cornic: bass, harmonica; Clive Bunker: drums; Mick Abrahams: guitar); 2 = The Who (Pete Townshend: guitar, vocals; Roger Daltrey: vocals; Keith Moon: drums; John Entwhistle: bass, vocals); 3= Taj Mahal (Taj Mahal: lead vocal; Jesse Ed Davis: guitar; Gary Gilmore: bass; Chuck Blackwell: drums); 4 = Marianne Faithfull: vocal; 5 = The Dirty Mac (John Lennon: lead vocal, guitar; Eric Clapton: lead guitar; Keith Richards: bass; Mitch Mitchell: drums); 6 = Yoko Ono, vocal, and Ivry Gitlis, "perpetual" (electric) violin—backed by the Dirty Mac. The Stones tracks should be obvious.

The audio companion to the long-awaited videocassette and laserdisc release of the Stones' 1968 erstwhile made-for-TV special, the *Rock and Roll Circus*. Like the original film's rebirth as a 1996 home video (discussed in PROMOTIONAL FILMS AND VIDEO) the soundtrack has been digitally remastered, cleaned up and otherwise received all the blessings of '90s technological magic; as a result, the audio quality of this CD stands up quite nicely against most contemporary releases. Technically, a very costly proposition. A great deal of thinking must have preceded production of this entire project, potentially a very risky venture after so many years—the mythological status of the *Circus* amongst fans being only one consideration. That the band didn't care for it back then—merely another minor variable. What would satisfy the aesthetic of the somewhat sloppy psychedelic '60s might not approach the expectations of the sophisticated '90s consumer. Clearly, ABKCO put a lot of effort and a great deal of money into the release of the *Rock and Roll Circus* —but, as they say in the movie business, it's all there on

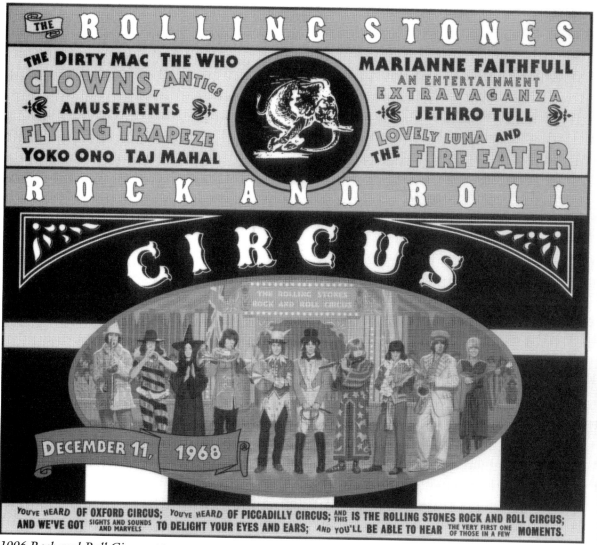

1996 Rock and Roll Circus (COURTESY OF ABKCO)

the screen—or coming out of the speakers, in the case of this CD. The production credits for this audio disc are a clue to just how much was involved in the transformation. Nice touch: the 40-page booklet inside the jewel case —lots of black-and-white photos and two essays about the *Circus* by author David Dalton, one reprinted from the March 19, 1970 issue of *Rolling Stone* magazine (his first-person account of the filming of the *Circus),* the other written for ABKCO in 1995. Produced by Jimmy Miller, Jody Klein and Lenne Allik. Recording engineer: Glyn Johns; mixing engineer: Steve Rosenthal; assistant engineer: Teri Landi; second assistant engineer: Joe Warda; analog to digital transfer engineer: Pascal Byrne; master engineer: Ricky Essig; recording coordinator: Maria Christie. Facilities included Olympic Mobil Recording Truck (1968), The Magic Shop, Decca Studios, Frankford Wayne, Sound One and the Hit Factory. Additional post

production: Jonathan Porath; sound mixing: Magdaline Voliatis; sound editor: John Battiloro; audio consultant: Roger Talkov; sonic solution, art and package design director: Iris Keitel; cover illustration: Marvin Mattelson; package design: Cody Rasmussen. Art-wise, *Circus* is all circus motif—you have to look closely for anything that says rock 'n' roll. The whole project is slickly designed '90s-style, all of a piece, down to the silkscreened CD label (the videocassette and laserdisc received the same treatment, as did ABKCO's promotional items like T-shirts, etc.)—with just enough funkiness in the artwork itself to keep it from being overbearing. The end result: kind of a keepsake from another time, both in form and substance. Which, one supposes, was the idea. The last paragraph on the credits page is one line: "remembering: brian/jesse/ ed/jimmy/john/keith/nicky/stu" (Jones/Davis/Miller /Lennon/Moon/Hopkins/Stewart).

Films

This chapter is a catalog of the cinematic (and videographic) appearances and contributions of the Rolling Stones, including some of the many cameos made by individual band members over the years, in feature-length (25 minutes or more) works. Many of the films listed are now available on home videocassette and many recent titles were made expressly for video. No illegal—bootleg—video titles are included here. This does not mean that bootlegs do not exist, they do. There are simply no unauthorized original works listed in this section.

In addition to Stones films initiated by the band, this directory details anthology films containing Stones footage, period and music documentaries in which the band is represented, and dramatic or documentary features made by others that focus on the group. Also listed are movies in which individual band members had dramatic roles and those to which a Stone made other singular contributions, such as scoring or musical direction. Finally, we have included the films or videos made by individual members. Thus, the listings contain just about every feature-length motion picture with Stones content. If we have omitted something, we apologize; it was not intentional.

In terms of the Rolling Stones' endeavors beyond making records and performing onstage, the feature film has not necessarily been the band's strongest field. There have not been a great number of long-form Stones films made or even planned. This is an understandable situation,

given that the Rolling Stones are musicians first, not actors or filmmakers. Yet, like every other facet of their work, each film project was an attempt to go beyond what musicians had done before, which meant trying whatever new creative tools or techniques were available at the time and employing other creative minds to help achieve something unique. The release, in 1995, of the *Voodoo Lounge* CD-ROM is a prime example of this attitude. We are including it in this category on account of its length, its use of full-motion video and sound, and the fact that its production has more in common with the way a film is made than an audio-only compact disc.

The Stones have hardly been afraid of taking chances, cinematic or musical—or personal, for that matter. The threat of industry gossip did not keep them from holding back a much touted project like *The Rock and Roll Circus* when it did not meet their expectations, nor did the art world's likely disdain prevent them from reining in Robert Frank's film, *Cocksucker Blues*, when it was much more than they ever wanted (both of these are discussed in the listings). But they did take the artistic leap to begin with, as they do every time they mount the concert stage. All art is risk—sometimes it works, sometimes it doesn't.

Often, however, it's more than entertainment and even the Rolling Stones sometimes need to be reminded of that. *Gimme Shelter* has to be one of the top 10 rock 'n' roll documentaries ever made and not only because of its content; it is an amazingly well-crafted piece of cinema. The Stones could easily have prevented its release precisely because of the subject matter; instead they put their own image aside for the reality of their colleagues' view that this was more than just a rock 'n' roll movie; it was history, straightforward and candid. Many of the Stones' other home videos are probably just nice home entertainment —still, always entertaining.

SUNDAY AT RICHMOND

YEAR MADE OR RELEASED: 1961

CREDITS: Director: Giorgio Gomelsky

STONES/FEATURED PERSONNEL: Charlie Watts, Jack Bruce, Alexis Korner's Blues Incorporated

DESCRIPTION: Giorgio Gomelsky's film about the first National Jazz Festival (commonly known as the Richmond Jazz Festival). One of the bands featured on the bill and in the film was Alexis Korner's group, Blues Incorporated. At the time, Charlie Watts played drums and Jack Bruce, bass, with Blues Inc. This film predates both the formation of and Gomelsky's involvement with the Rolling Stones.

THE T.A.M.I. SHOW

YEAR MADE OR RELEASED: 1964

CREDITS: Director: Steve Binder; Producer: Lee Savin; Executive Producer: Bill Sargent; Musical Director: Phil Spector; Arranger: Jack Nitzsche

STONES/FEATURED PERSONNEL: Mick Jagger, Keith Richards, Brian Jones, Bill Wyman, Charlie Watts, Chuck Berry, James Brown & the Famous Flames, the Barbarians, Lesley Gore, The Supremes, The Beach Boys, Smokey Robinson & the Miracles, Marvin Gaye with the Blossoms, Jan & Dean, Gerry & the Pacemakers, Billy J. Kramer & the Dakotas

DESCRIPTION: T.A.M.I. is the acronym for the Teenage American Music International awards show of 1964. The T.A.M.I. show was produced by Bill Sargent, Jr., under the musical direction of Phil Spector, and took place over two days, October 28 and 29, at the Santa Monica Civic Auditorium. Through their acquaintance with Spector, the Stones had secured a place on T.A.M.I.'s incredibly diverse—for 1964—bill that combined Motown stars like the Supremes with American chart-toppers like Jan and Dean and the "Godfather of Soul," James Brown, along with other "British Invasion" artists.

Though these concerts were performed in front of a live audience, a film for commercial release was the planned end product. The Rolling Stones appeared in 1964 and the film entitled *The T.A.M.I. Show* is of *only that program*. However, *The T.A.M.I. Show* was later released under other titles, such as *Gather No Moss* and *That Was Rock*, and the renaming resulted in some degree of confusion. *That Was Rock* is an edited video combination of footage from *The T.A.M.I. Show* and its sequel film,

The Big TNT Show, which documented similar concerts in 1965.

The T.A.M.I. film's technical credits are somewhat curious. It was a black-and-white movie, but the stock was processed by Technicolor Laboratories. Also interesting is the legend, "Filmed In Electronovision," which would lead one to believe that some early videotape equipment was used. *The T.A.M.I. Show* was shot on black-and-white film, not videotape, and was never in color. "Electronovision" was producer Bill Sargent's proprietary system for directing and instantly editing a multiple camera production using film, not videotape. Technicolor Laboratories was involved in Sargent's company. Videotape technology in 1964 was in its infancy, and cameras and other gear were still cumbersome and expensive, particularly what was available for use outside a fully-equipped television studio. Hence, film was usually the medium of choice on location shoots like The *T.A.M.I. Show*. The filmmaker's (usually ungratifiable) goal was to produce an edited feature film of the same quality as could be achieved in a studio control room using video, and this was what Sargent's innovative "Electronovision" was designed to achieve.

This movie could have been a stellar example of pop music cinema, had it not been for the pervasive obnoxious overdubbed audio of audience screaming. In addition to their five songs included in the film, the Stones rehearsed "Not Fade Away," "Tell Me," and "2120 South Michigan Avenue" for their T.A.M.I. show performances, although those three numbers were not included in the film. The finale of *The T.A.M.I. Show* is an orchestra and playback jam entitled "Get Together," featuring all cast members, dancers, *et al.*, and Mick Jagger doing an ad lib live vocal, while the credits roll.

CHARLIE IS MY DARLING

YEAR MADE OR RELEASED: 1965

CREDITS: Director: Peter Whitehead; Producer: Peter Whitehead (ABKCO)

STONES/FEATURED PERSONNEL: Mick Jagger, Keith Richards, Brian Jones, Bill Wyman, Charlie Watts

DESCRIPTION: Shot in Ireland while on tour in September 1965, this *Hard Day's Night*-style documentary shows the Stones at work—onstage, backstage, travelling through the countryside, interacting with each other and fans young and old, and flying home. Three different versions were made, or cut, of this film. None was ever commercially released or aired in its entirety on television. Making *Charlie Is My Darling* was the brainchild of Andrew Loog Oldham; the film's soundtrack includes many musical numbers recorded by the Andrew Oldham Orchestra. Various production difficulties delayed the film's release. Also, the impending start of the Stones' never-begun *Only Lovers Left Alive* film put *Charlie* on the back burner, and rendered it out of date and useless as either a commercial or promotional vehicle when a chance to market it finally arose. A black-and-white cinema-verité slice of the band's life on tour in 1965 was decidedly passé by the late 1960s, when hip films had to be both colorful and psychedelic. It's now time for a full version to be officially released! Just a suggestion, not a prediction.

DEADLY BEES

YEAR MADE OR RELEASED: 1965
CREDITS: Director: Freddie Francis
STONES/FEATURED PERSONNEL: Ron Wood
DESCRIPTION: Woody, with his first band, the Birds, have a small cameo in this British horror flick. Released in 1967.

VIER SCHLUESSEL (FOUR KEYS)

YEAR MADE OR RELEASED: 1966
CREDITS: Director unknown—Germany
STONES/FEATURED PERSONNEL: Mick Jagger, Keith Richards, Brian Jones, Bill Wyman, Charlie Watts, Ian Stewart, Andrew Loog Oldham
DESCRIPTION: The Rolling Stones serendipitously became part of this German-language movie when they arrived at the airport where a crucial scene was being shot. The filmmakers wove footage of the band and Oldham deplaning and being met by a mass gathering of fans into the plot of this black-and-white thriller.

WHAT'S ON THE FLIP SIDE?

YEAR MADE OR RELEASED: 1966
CREDITS: Director: Peter Clifton
STONES/FEATURED PERSONNEL: Mick Jagger, Keith Richards, Brian Jones, Bill Wyman, Charlie Watts
DESCRIPTION: A very rare 16mm black-and-white documentary on the Stones' 1966 Australian tour. One highlight is the Stones onstage, performing "I'm Moving On." Approximately 45 minutes in length.

A DEGREE OF MURDER (MORD UND TOTSCHLAG)

YEAR MADE OR RELEASED: 1967
CREDITS: Director: Volker Schlöndorff
STONES/FEATURED PERSONNEL: Anita Pallenberg, score by Brian Jones
DESCRIPTION: Pallenberg stars in the German-language (subtitled) murder mystery-thriller for which Jones wrote, produced and recorded the soundtrack. (See CHRONOLOGY)

MONTEREY POP

YEAR MADE OR RELEASED: 1967
CREDITS: Director: D. A. Pennebaker
STONES/FEATURED PERSONNEL: Brian Jones
DESCRIPTION: Brian is seen walking around backstage, digging the vibes with pal Jimi Hendrix. However, Pennebaker made another film from his Monterey Pop Festival footage (*Otis & Jimmy at Monterey*) that has a bit more of Brian in it.

OTIS & JIMMY LIVE AT MONTEREY

YEAR MADE OR RELEASED: 1967
CREDITS: Director: D. A. Pennebaker
STONES/FEATURED PERSONNEL: Brian Jones
DESCRIPTION: Otis Redding and Jimi Hendrix at the Monterey Pop Festival. Pennebaker's second film from footage shot at the '67 festival includes Brian Jones's onstage introduction of Hendrix.

TONITE LET'S ALL MAKE LOVE IN LONDON

YEAR MADE OR RELEASED: 1967
CREDITS: Director: Peter Whitehead
STONES/FEATURED PERSONNEL: Mick Jagger, Keith Richards, Brian Jones, Bill Wyman, Charlie Watts, Andrew Loog Oldham
DESCRIPTION: A documentary portrait/pastiche of "Swinging London" of the '60s, set to—and often against—its music. It includes many interviews with current cultural icons on topical issues. Jagger talks about revolution, and Oldham ponders his own future while sitting in a recording studio. Others (Julie Christie, Michael Caine, novelist Edna O'Brien) discuss sex. Many musicians provide audio. The Rolling Stones appear to be performing one song. In fact, the viewer *hears* "Lady Jane" while *seeing*, in slow motion, the band's "Have You Seen Your Mother, Baby?" promo film that Whitehead had shot while fans rioted at the Stones' September 23, 1966 performance at the Royal Albert Hall. (See PROMOTIONAL FILMS &VIDEOS)

NOW TIME

YEAR MADE OR RELEASED: 1968
CREDITS: Director and Producer: Peter Clifton
STONES/FEATURED PERSONNEL: Rolling Stones pre-1968, Procol Harum, Vanilla Fudge, Bee Gees, Ike & Tina Turner, Ten Years After, Russel Morris, Cream, Beach Boys, Move, Traffic, P. P. Arnold, Small Faces, Mary Hopkins, Keith West, The Animals, Gene Washington, Chris Farlowe
DESCRIPTION: This is a TV series—13 half-hour episodes—on music, film and the arts in '60s London.

PERFORMANCE

YEAR MADE OR RELEASED: 1968

CREDITS: Directors: Donald Cammell and Nicholas Roeg

STONES/FEATURED PERSONNEL: Mick Jagger, Anita Pallenberg

DESCRIPTION: Jagger stars, as a burnt-out rock star, opposite James Fox's gangster-on-the run. Pallenberg plays the sex-drugs-rock 'n' roll significant other in Turner's (Jagger's) menage à trois, all facets of which are on the screen. (Michele Breton makes the third *chez* Turner). This production marked Nick Roeg's transition from cinematographer to director. He does both here —wonderfully—codirecting with Cammell, who wrote the screenplay. Jagger also contributed "Memo from Turner" to the soundtrack; the scene is a music video before that genre existed. Little known casting tidbit: Julie Driscoll was the first actress to be offered the part that went to Pallenberg after she turned it down. The film was way ahead of its time and Warner Brothers kept it on ice for two years before allowing it limited theatrical release. Available on home video (edited from an X to an R). Very cool, nevertheless.

THE ROLLING STONES ROCK AND ROLL CIRCUS

YEAR MADE OR RELEASED: 1968

CREDITS: Director: Michael Lindsay-Hogg. Newly edited by Robin M. Klein (1995), for 1996 ABKCO release.

STONES/FEATURED PERSONNEL: Mick Jagger, Keith Richards, Brian Jones, Charlie Watts, Bill Wyman, Ian Stewart, Nicky Hopkins, Rocky Dijon, Eric Clapton, the Who, Marianne Faithfull, Jethro Tull, Taj Mahal, Donyale Luna, Mitch Mitchell, John Lennon, Yoko Ono, Ivry Gitlis, Julius Katchen, clowns, jugglers, animals (Robert Possett's Circus)

DESCRIPTION: Rock 'n' Roll meets the big top—that was the band's idea. The *Rock and Roll Circus* was originally designed to be aired as a television special, but was shelved by the Stones shortly after being shot. Nothing was ever released theatrically or aired on television, though a rumor of its imminent release persisted for over 25 years. However, the substance of that rumor seemed more likely to become reality by late 1995. The film was reedited by Ms. Klein (film editor and daughter of Allen) and director Michael Lindsay-Hogg, and reliable reports began surfacing of an official 1996 release on videocassette and laserdisc. The exact date, however, kept changing. Finally, in late summer, ABKCO *and* the Rolling Stones announced that the "new" *Circus* would be premiered at the New York Film Festival beginning on October 12, 1996. An official date of October 15, was announced for laserdisc, VHS cassette and soundtrack CD releases. Skep-

tics were no doubt mortified when the new *Circus* products appeared in stores on time, as promised. The film was very well received by the critics—reviews in the major US dailies clustered on the positive side, ranging from kind nodding interest to raves.

A few members of the original cast listed were not included in the 1996 cut, most notably pianist Julius Katchen. The Stones were filmed performing some 10 songs, but "Route 66," "Confessin' the Blues," "Yonder Wall" and the traditional "Walkin' Blues" were left out. However, included were two numbers by the Dirty Mac Band, a group formed for the occasion, and composed of John Lennon (gtr,voc), Eric Clapton (gtr), Keith Richards (bs) and Mitch Mitchell (ds). This instant supergroup performed "Yer Blues" (Lennon, McCartney) and backed Yoko Ono (voc) and perpetual violinist Ivry Gitlis on "Whole Lotta Yoko" (Ono). The filming of *Rock and Roll Circus* was the last time Brian Jones would ever be seen performing with the Rolling Stones.

SEA OF SUNSHINE

YEAR MADE OR RELEASED: 1968

CREDITS: Independent

STONES/FEATURED PERSONNEL: Mick Jagger, Keith Richards, Brian Jones, Charlie Watts, Bill Wyman

DESCRIPTION: Psychedelic British low-budget small feature, containing an insert of the Stones' "She's a Rainbow" promo.

SYMPATHY FOR THE DEVIL A.K.A. ONE PLUS ONE

YEAR MADE OR RELEASED: 1968

CREDITS: Director: Jean-Luc Godard

STONES/FEATURED PERSONNEL: Mick Jagger, Keith Richards, Brian Jones, Bill Wyman, Charlie Watts, Marianne Faithfull, Anita Pallenberg

DESCRIPTION: Jean-Luc Godard's arty tedium about the (Olympic) studio evolution of the Stones' song "Sympathy for the Devil" combined with something about revolution in an auto junkyard. Released as *One Plus One* in Europe and the UK, and as *Sympathy for the Devil* in the US. The coverage of the Stones at work is unique and revealing. Outtakes from this film became part of another Godard work, *Voices*.

VOICES

YEAR MADE OR RELEASED: 1968

CREDITS: Director: Jean-Luc Godard

STONES/FEATURED PERSONNEL: Mick Jagger, Keith Richards, Brian Jones, Bill Wyman, Charlie Watts, Marianne Faithfull, Anita Pallenberg

DESCRIPTION: Autobiographical documentary on the director-at-work includes outtakes from Godard's *One Plus One/Sympathy for the Devil* coverage of the Stones at Olympic Studios. The best bit—which didn't make it into *One Plus One*—is of Olympic Studios catching fire in the wee hours and, the musicians, engineers and crew fleeing while the cameras still roll—is used in *Voices.*

FIRE IN THE WATER

YEAR MADE OR RELEASED: 1969

CREDITS: Director: Peter Whitehead; Producer: Mark Sursock; Associate Producer & Director of Sound: Peter Clifton

STONES/FEATURED PERSONNEL: Rolling Stones pre-1969, The Animals, Pink Floyd, Jimi Hendrix, Chuck Berry, The Who, The Beatles, The Doors

DESCRIPTION: Another '60s film, also features Nathalie Delon and Edward Niermans and nonmusical appearances by Jagger, Michael Caine, Eric Burdon, Glenda Jackson, Vanessa Redgrave. Musical performances by those "featured personnel" listed above. Two different versions of this film were released: 60 minutes and 90 minutes.

GIMME SHELTER I

YEAR MADE OR RELEASED: 1969

CREDITS: Directors: David and Albert Maysles and Charlotte Zwerin

STONES/FEATURED PERSONNEL: Mick Jagger, Keith Richards, Mick Taylor, Bill Wyman, Charlie Watts, plus the Hells Angels and all others at Altamont, Melvin Belli, Jerry Garcia, Bobby Keys, Allen Klein *et al.*

DESCRIPTION: An excellent documentary on the Stones' 1969 US tour, and unforgettable not just because of Altamont. Released both theatrically and on home video, the latter is now an ABKCO product.

Directed by the Maysles Brothers and Charlotte Zwerin, this is possibly the most well known of all Stones films. What is not common knowledge is that the Maysles were not the Stones' first choice for the project; they had first commissioned Haskell Wexler to document the US tour. However, Wexler, whose critically acclaimed *Medium Cool* had just been released, wanted to make a *world* tour film and include the Stones' 1970 European concerts in addition to the US dates. This wasn't part of the band's plan. With only a week or so to go before Madison Square Garden, the parties still hadn't arrived at a compromise, though relations between them were quite amicable. Wexler, in the end, provided the solution by recommending that the Maysles Brothers be hired in his stead. David and Albert had decent rock 'n' roll filmmaking experience, having made *What's Happening,* which followed the Beatles from their historic US touchdown of February 1964 through their first American concert in Washington, DC.

The Stones' concept for the filming of their '69 tour was far less grandiose than that envisioned by Haskell Wexler, and Jagger's plans for the resulting footage were even less concrete. He wanted documentary material, but would decide what to do with it later. The Stones were already in New York when they hired the Maysles, and asked them to cover only *one* Madison Square Garden show, on the afternoon of November 27. True professionals, David, Albert and company filmed the one performance as agreed, then asked the Stones if they might spend a bit more time with them. The band, evidently, understood the filmmakers' requests for more access: they would gain a better feel for the music and establish tighter rapport with the musicians. The Maysles stayed on the tour, travelling with the band to Baltimore, although they did not film that particular show. They did shoot the Stones' performance at the West Palm Beach Pop Festival as well as their recording sessions at Muscle Shoals Studios in Alabama. When plans for Altamont became a reality, it was thought that coverage of the free concert would provide the perfect focal point for the movie.

Interestingly, the making of this film was one reason for the last minute venue change from Sears Point Raceway to Altamont Speedway. Once the Sears Point owners learned there was a movie being made, they demanded a percentage of the Stones' film. Not surprisingly, this was unacceptable. Raceway officials countered with their own "request"—a fee of $100,000 or the musicians would not be allowed to play. This last one was equally out of the question, and came on Friday, December 5, the day before the advertised event. The Sears Point stage had been set up, with sound equipment and other gear already installed; it was moved to Livermore, CA and rerigged at Altamont Speedway on Saturday, December 6.

Quiz question: Did you know that footage of the West Palm Beach concert *is* in *Gimme Shelter?* Where? Well, we won't tell you. This is one film you must see if you haven't yet done so. If you have, and you don't know the answer, rack your brain or see it again.

Second question: Did you know that there is *another,* shorter, version of *Gimme Shelter?* If not, see below.

GIMME SHELTER II

YEAR MADE OR RELEASED: 1969

CREDITS: Directors: David and Albert Maysles and Charlotte Zwerin

STONES/FEATURED PERSONNEL: Mick Jagger, Keith Richards, Mick Taylor, Bill Wyman, Charlie Watts, plus the Hells Angels and all others at Altamont

DESCRIPTION: The Maysles Brothers made their own cut of the film, which includes some songs not in the 90-minute commercial release. David and Albert's version includes "Prodigal Son," "You Gotta Move" and "Midnight Rambler." Keith rolls a joint during the last one. Unfortunately, the Maysles' original print and its separate mag track have been lost, stolen, or otherwise removed from their owners' control, and have never been located despite many efforts to do so over the years. Happily, the original negatives all exist and are quite secure and intact (and though it's highly unlikely, it could be redone), but anyone out there with knowledge of the whereabouts of this "director's cut" should feel free to contact the authors.

Another piece of unseen—but not missing-in-action—footage from *Gimme Shelter*: seven minutes of film shot backstage at Madison Square Garden includes Jimi Hendrix jamming with the Stones. Southpaw Jimi plays one of Mick Taylor's guitars—upside-down. This is quite nice material, but not likely to be released. A still photograph of this situation was published in 1969 as part of press coverage of the tour; those with sharp eyes might have noticed the lurking cine camera in that frame.

INVOCATION OF MY DEMON BROTHER

YEAR MADE OR RELEASED: 1969
CREDITS: Director: Kenneth Anger
STONES/FEATURED PERSONNEL: Mick Jagger
DESCRIPTION: Jagger wrote and performed the score —on a Moog synthesizer—for this bizarre short that

Mick Jagger as Ned Kelly (STARFILE)

doesn't really qualify for this category at only 12 minutes in length, but fits no other in this book. We are listing it because of Mick's synth soundtrack; the film itself is "late '60s experimental"—like somebody else's acid flashback, you had to be there. Released on video in *The Films of Kenneth Anger, Vol. 3.*

NED KELLY

YEAR MADE OR RELEASED: 1969
CREDITS: Director: Tony Richardson
STONES/FEATURED PERSONNEL: Mick Jagger
DESCRIPTION: Mick took the title role as Australia's favorite 19th-century outlaw son. Jagger also contributed to the soundtrack by singing one song, "Wild Colonial Boy" (Trad., Arr: Silverstein). (See also CHRONOLOGY)

DER REBELL—MICHAEL KOHLHAAS

YEAR MADE OR RELEASED: 1969
CREDITS: Director: Volker Schlöndorff
STONES/FEATURED PERSONNEL: Keith Richards, Anita Pallenberg
DESCRIPTION: Keith's role is that of "Nagel's Man." Filmed in Czechoslovakia.

THE STONES IN THE PARK

YEAR MADE OR RELEASED: 1969
CREDITS: Granada Television
STONES/FEATURED PERSONNEL: Mick Jagger, Keith Richards, Mick Taylor, Bill Wyman, Charlie Watts
DESCRIPTION: The Stones' July 5, 1969 free concert in London's Hyde Park, as filmed by Granada TV. It wasn't a particularly wonderful show, music-wise, but historically speaking, there was more to this concert: it was Mick Taylor's first appearance with the band and had abruptly become a memorial to Brian Jones, who had died on July 3. Granada's 45-minute documentary includes a few bits of behind-the-scenes Stones action that provide a glimpse of the day from the band's point of view. (See TELEVISION APPEARANCES, TOURS AND CONCERTS, CHRONOLOGY)

POPCORN—AN AUDIO-VISUAL THING

YEAR MADE OR RELEASED: 1970
CREDITS: Director: Peter Clifton; Producer: Peter Ryan
STONES/FEATURED PERSONNEL: Mick Jagger, Keith Richards, Mick Taylor, Bill Wyman, Charlie Watts, Ian Stewart
DESCRIPTION: A montage of various promos, interviews, news footage and strange sociopolitical stuff. Stones clips ("2000 Light Years" and "Jumpin' Jack Flash") are included, as well as music by Otis Redding, Jimi Hendrix, the Small Faces and others.

LADIES & GENTLEMEN, THE ROLLING STONES—LIVE AT THE MARQUEE

YEAR MADE OR RELEASED: 1971

CREDITS: Director: Bruce Gower; Producer: Derek Randal

STONES/FEATURED PERSONNEL: Mick Jagger, Keith Richards, Mick Taylor, Bill Wyman, Charlie Watts, Ian Stewart

DESCRIPTION: The Stones were filmed in performance before an audience of friends and family in two shows at London's Marquee Club just prior to their going into tax exile in the south of France. The resultant film was slated for television broadcast—the Stones wanted to make sure they wouldn't be forgotten once they left Britain (fat chance!). There are two cuts of this program—the UK version is 35 minutes, the European edit is 50 minutes. Neither was ever aired in the US.

SUPERSTARS IN FILM CONCERT

YEAR MADE OR RELEASED: 1971

CREDITS: Director: Peter Clifton; Producer: Peter Clifton

STONES/FEATURED PERSONNEL: Mick Jagger, Keith Richards, Mick Taylor, Bill Wyman, Charlie Watts, Ian Stewart

DESCRIPTION: The same format and mishmosh of footage varieties along with many of the same artists that appear in *Popcorn* and *Rock City*, also by Clifton.

COCKSUCKER BLUES

YEAR MADE OR RELEASED: 1972

CREDITS: Directed by Robert Frank

STONES/FEATURED PERSONNEL: Mick Jagger, Keith Richards, Mick Taylor, Bill Wyman, Charlie Watts, Ian Stewart, Bobby Keys, *et al.*

DESCRIPTION: The Stones' infamous behind-the-scenes 1972 tour film, in all its excesses: directed by noted documentary photographer and filmmaker, Robert Frank. Frank's 1958 book, *The Americans*, was a milestone and tradition-breaker in documentary still photography; his film on madness, *Me and My Brother*, was but one of his cinematic efforts. Mick Jagger hired him for the cover of *Exile on Main Street*, and then to memorialize the '72 tour. However, the filmmaker's portrayal of what happened on the road—lots of drugs and sex, some rock 'n' roll, a bit of television repair—gave the Stones pause and they stopped its release. Much of the raunch action in this film was set up, and more has nothing at all to do with the members of the Rolling Stones. There are a few true documentary moments in the lives of the boys on tour, but the film never manages to get inside the real action. It has been described by someone who was there as "almost like a home movie about a movie." Though the Stones would not allow its commercial distribution, the film is screened occasionally in museums and other art-related venues, but only if Frank is physically present.

LADIES & GENTLEMEN, THE ROLLING STONES [#2]

YEAR MADE OR RELEASED: 1972

CREDITS: Director: Rollin Binzer; Producers: Rollin Binzer, Marshall Chess, Bob Fries and Steve Gebhart; Executive Producer: Marshall Chess

STONES/FEATURED PERSONNEL: Mick Jagger, Keith Richards, Mick Taylor, Bill Wyman, Charlie Watts, Ian Stewart, Bobby Keys, Jim Price, Nicky Hopkins

DESCRIPTION: The in-front-of-the-scenes concert film of the 1972 tour that was made at the same time as the *Cocksucker Blues* cameras were rutting around backstage. This was a fortuitous occurrence and/or a damn good backup plan for the Stones. *Ladies & Gentlemen, the Rolling Stones* is all music, 14 songs from shows in Fort Worth and Houston, and was advertised as the "first movie on earth with quadrophonic sound . . . and pounds of paraphernalia."

A true concert film, it was promoted as if it were a concert, with a tour-like schedule. After its premiere at the Ziegfeld Theater in New York City on April 14, 1974, the film itself went on the road: one week in New York, another in Dallas, another in L.A.—with its own special sound system travelling to each city on the route. Tickets —at Stones concert prices—were sold through Ticketron. This sounds gimmicky and it was, but the film did deliver exactly what it said it would—a show, without interviews, without old film clips, without cinematic gimmicks.

ROCKABYE

YEAR MADE OR RELEASED: 1972

CREDITS: National Film Board of Canada

STONES/FEATURED PERSONNEL: Mick Jagger, Keith Richards, *et al.*

DESCRIPTION: A 30-minute Canadian documentary made for television on the business of rock 'n' roll. The Stones' segment was shot at their Montreal Forum show during the '72 tour.

THE LONDON ROCK 'N' ROLL SHOW

YEAR MADE OR RELEASED: 1973

CREDITS: Director: Peter Clifton; Producer: Peter Clifton

STONES/FEATURED PERSONNEL: Mick Jagger

DESCRIPTION: A British documentary on the 1973 Rock 'n' Roll Revival concert at Wembley Stadium. An interview with Jagger is interspersed with performances by

Chuck Berry, Little Richard, Jerry Lee Lewis and various other '50s and early '60s rockers.

ROCK CITY, A.K.A. BOSS CITY A.K.A. SOUNDS OF THE CITY

YEAR MADE OR RELEASED: 1973

CREDITS: Director: Peter Clifton; Producer: Peter Clifton

STONES/FEATURED PERSONNEL: Mick Jagger, Keith Richards, Mick Taylor, Bill Wyman, Charlie Watts, Ian Stewart

DESCRIPTION: The same format as Clifton's *Popcorn* and *Superstars in Film Concert* with a lot of the same material, and many of the same artists, plus a few more.

THE ROLLING STONES DOWN UNDER

YEAR MADE OR RELEASED: 1973

CREDITS Australian TV

STONES/FEATURED PERSONNEL: Mick Jagger, Keith Richards, Mick Taylor, Bill Wyman, Charlie Watts, Ian Stewart

DESCRIPTION: Australian documentary of the Rolling Stones' 1973 Australian tour.

ROD STEWART & THE FACES WITH KEITH RICHARDS

YEAR MADE OR RELEASED: 1974

CREDITS: Director: Roger Grod; Producer: Roger Grod

STONES/FEATURED PERSONNEL: Keith Richards, Ron Wood

DESCRIPTION: Keith makes an onstage cameo appearance with Rod & the Faces in this film of their 1974 concert at the Kilburn State Cinema in London. Woody was still a member of the Faces at the time.

LADIES & GENTLEMEN, THE ROLLING STONES [#3]

YEAR MADE OR RELEASED: 1978

STONES/FEATURED PERSONNEL: Mick Jagger, Keith Richards, Ron Wood, Bill Wyman, Charlie Watts, Ian Stewart

DESCRIPTION: Yes, ladies and gentlemen, there are *three Ladies & Gentlemen* films. This one—90 minutes of the Stones in concert in Fort Worth, TX in 1978 (the same venue as the '72 *Ladies & Gentlemen*)—was never released, however.

THE LAST WALTZ

YEAR MADE OR RELEASED: 1978

CREDITS: Director: Martin Scorcese; Producer: Robbie Robertson

STONES/FEATURED PERSONNEL: Ron Wood

DESCRIPTION: Scorcese's feature-length documentary on The Band's 1976 last concert at Winterland in San Francisco. The soon-to-be- ex- group was not the only act at the show. Other artists included Paul Butterfield, Eric Clapton, Joni Mitchell, Muddy Waters and Van Morrison, among others. Ron Wood appeared with Bob Dylan, Ringo Starr, Eric Clapton and The Band on Dylan's "I Shall Be Released."

THE KIDS ARE ALRIGHT

YEAR MADE OR RELEASED: 1979

CREDITS: Director: Jeff Stein; Producers: Bill Curbishley, Tony Klinger

STONES/FEATURED PERSONNEL: Keith Richards

DESCRIPTION: The Who's career compilation/documentary. The Who's segment from *The Rolling Stones Rock 'n' Roll Circus* is part of this film, marking the first time anything from the *Circus* was officially released. The *Circus* clip begins with Keith Richards introducing the Who's performance. When *The Kids Are Alright* was first released, the entire 1968 piece was included. But, when the film went onto home video, Keith's intro was edited out.

THE WIZARD OF WAUKESHA

YEAR MADE OR RELEASED: 1979

CREDITS: Director: Catherine Orentreich; Producer: Catherine Orentreich

STONES/FEATURED PERSONNEL: Keith Richards, Mick Jagger, Brian Jones, Bill Wyman, Charlie Watts, Ian Stewart

DESCRIPTION: The Les Paul story. A 1965 television clip of the Stones performing "Heart of Stone" with Keith playing a Gibson Les Paul guitar, along with footage of many other guitarists using the solid-body electric instrument invented by "the Wizard of Waukesha." Les Paul also invented a lot of other music-related techno marvels but you'll have to see the one-hour film yourself.

THE RUTLES—ALL YOU NEED IS CASH

YEAR MADE OR RELEASED: 1980

CREDITS: Director: Gary Weis; Producer: Lorne Michaels; Screenplay: Eric Idle

STONES/FEATURED PERSONNEL: Mick Jagger, Ron Wood

DESCRIPTION: The paradigm of pop parody prior to *This Is Spinal Tap!*, written by Monty Python's Eric Idle, that perfectly lampoons the Beatles. Jagger (as himself), talking about how the Rutles gave the Stones a song, and Wood (as himself and as a woman) make cameo appearances that are icing on this sublime, silly cake of a film made for television. Neil Innes (of the Bonzo Dog Band) wrote the score in which some of the song parallels are obvious—"Let It Rot" for "Let It Be"—but many are much subtler Beatlemaniacs' and musicians' in-jokes, all of which work brilliantly.

GREEN ICE

YEAR MADE OR RELEASED: 1981

CREDITS: Director: Ernest Day

STONES/FEATURED PERSONNEL: Bill Wyman

DESCRIPTION: Wyman wrote the soundtrack for this thriller involving spies, government corruption and control of the emerald industry. The cast includes Ryan O'Neal, Anne Archer, Omar Sharif and John Larroquette.

LET'S SPEND THE NIGHT TOGETHER

YEAR MADE OR RELEASED: 1981

CREDITS: Director: Hal Ashby; Producer: Ronald L. Schwary

STONES/FEATURED PERSONNEL: Mick Jagger, Keith Richards, Ron Wood, Bill Wyman, Charlie Watts, Ian Stewart

DESCRIPTION: The Stones' 1981 North American tour movie by the director of *Shampoo, Bound for Glory* and *Coming Home*, among others. Concert footage—some 17 songs*—was shot by Caleb Deschanel and Gerald Fiel at Stones shows at Sun Devil Stadium in Tempe, AZ, and Brendan Byrne Arena in New Jersey. This is a top-of-the-line production, with cinematography as good as it gets. Archival Stones footage and some news clips were inserted in the editing—some of this works, some doesn't —but the film still delivers.

BURDEN OF DREAMS

YEAR MADE OR RELEASED: 1982

CREDITS: Director: Les Blank

STONES/FEATURED PERSONNEL: Mick Jagger

DESCRIPTION: Documentary about the making of *Fitzcarraldo*, director Werner Herzog's film about an Irishman who wanted to build an opera house in the middle of the Amazon jungle. Mick Jagger had to quit the starring role. So many things went wrong on location (Amazon Indian attacks, for example) that the production shut down for several months. Eventually, the filmmaker managed to sort out the problems, but by then Jagger had impending obligations, including a US tour. Reluctantly, he opted not to return to Peru. But Herzog still had

Mick's scenes in the can; some were used in Les Blank's documentary.

THE COMPLEAT BEATLES

YEAR MADE OR RELEASED: 1982

CREDITS: Director: Patrick Montgomery; Producers: Patrick Montgomery and Stephanie Bennett

STONES/FEATURED PERSONNEL: Mick Jagger, Keith Richards, Marianne Faithfull

DESCRIPTION: This chronicle of the life and times of the Fab Four naturally includes the story of the groundbreaking worldwide live broadcast of the Beatles' "All You Need Is Love" recording session. The clip from the Abbey Road event, equally naturally, includes the two Stones plus one, who were seated on the studio floor that day amongst the other "friends of the band."

ROCK GUITAR: A GUIDE WITH THE GREATS

YEAR MADE OR RELEASED: 1982

STONES/FEATURED PERSONNEL: Ron Wood

BILL WYMAN VIDEO 45

YEAR MADE OR RELEASED: 1983

CREDITS: Producer: Bill Wyman

STONES/FEATURED PERSONNEL: Bill Wyman

DESCRIPTION: Three solo Wyman clips—"Si Si Je Suis un Rock Star," "A New Fashion," "Come Back Suzanne" —put together, in the US version. The European release has six songs; it also includes "What a Blow," "White Lightnin'" and "Wanna Get Me a Gun."

DIGITAL DREAMS

YEAR MADE OR RELEASED: 1983

CREDITS: Director: Robert Dornhelm; Producers: Bill and Astrid Wyman

STONES/FEATURED PERSONNEL: Bill Wyman, Astrid Lundstrom

DESCRIPTION: Wyman's autobiographical—"adapted from the computerized diaries of Bill Wyman"—video. Contains some rare Stones footage. With James Coburn. Wyman and Mike Batt cowrote the score.

FAERIE TALE THEATRE— "THE NIGHTINGALE"

YEAR MADE OR RELEASED: 1983

CREDITS: Showtime Entertainment/FoxVideo

---

*An early European version of this movie, released as *Rocks Off*, contained a performance of "When the Whip Comes Down," which *Let's Spend the Night Together* does not. There was a *second* European version without "Whip Comes Down," entitled *Time Is on My Side*, that came out on video (in Europe only). While it has the same track listing as *Let's Spend the Night Together*, *Time Is on My Side* was cut differently; the European video is more like a preliminary edit for the film that ultimately went into worldwide theatrical release.

STONES/FEATURED PERSONNEL: Mick Jagger

DESCRIPTION: Jagger plays the role of the Chinese Emperor in a dramatization of Hans Christian Andersen's "The Nightingale," one segment of Showtime's made-for-TV children's dramatic series. Home video, laserdisc distributed by FoxVideo.

THE ARMS CONCERT, PARTS ONE AND TWO

YEAR MADE OR RELEASED: 1984

CREDITS: Director: Stanley Dorfman; Producer: Glyn Johns

STONES/FEATURED PERSONNEL: Bill Wyman, Charlie Watts, Ronnie Lane, Eric Clapton, Steve Winwood, Kenney Jones, Ray Cooper, Andy Fairweather-Low, Jeff Beck, Jimmy Page

DESCRIPTION: In 1984, former Faces bassist Ronnie Lane staged a concert at the Royal Albert Hall to benefit his Appeal for Action for Research into Multiple Sclerosis (ARMS), the foundation he started after being stricken with MS. Bill and Charlie were among the many British rock 'n' rollers who pitched in. The first concert was a roaring success and the all-star group went on to tour the US. Two 60-minute videos were produced by Glyn Johns and distributed commercially, with the proceeds also going to ARMS. Watts and Wyman are on both tapes, but each video has a different strong performance from others in the ensemble to recommend it—a matter of musical preference only.

BLUES ALIVE—JOHN MAYALL IN CONCERT 1982

YEAR MADE OR RELEASED: 1984

CREDITS: Director: Lew Dell'Amico; Producers: Johnathan Stathakis, Pat Weatherford

STONES/FEATURED PERSONNEL: Mick Taylor

DESCRIPTION: Former Stone Mick Taylor appears with his former bandleader, Mayall, who also released an LP/CD from this show (*John Mayall & the Bluesbreakers—The 1982 Reunion Concert*).

COOL CATS: 25 YEARS OF ROCK 'N' ROLL STYLE

YEAR MADE OR RELEASED: 1984

CREDITS: Director: Terence Dixon; Producers: Stephanie Bennett

STONES/FEATURED PERSONNEL: Mick Jagger, Keith Richards, Brian Jones, Bill Wyman, Charlie Watts, Ian Stewart

DESCRIPTION: Historical documentary with clips of cool rockers from the '50s on up. The Stones segment is from a 1964 Wembley concert.

FATS DOMINO & FRIENDS

YEAR MADE OR RELEASED: 1984

STONES/FEATURED PERSONNEL: Ron Wood

DESCRIPTION: Woody is one of Fats's friends.

THAT WAS ROCK

YEAR MADE OR RELEASED: 1984

CREDITS: Directors: Steve Binder and Larry Peerce; Producers: Lee Savin and Phil Spector

STONES/FEATURED PERSONNEL: Mick Jagger, Keith Richards, Brian Jones, Bill Wyman, Charlie Watts, Ian Stewart

DESCRIPTION: Home video rerelease of *The T.A.M.I. Show* combined with *The Big TNT Show*. The Stones only appear in the former. See the T.A.M.I. entry, above.

VIDEO REWIND

YEAR MADE OR RELEASED: 1984

CREDITS: Director: Julien Temple

STONES/FEATURED PERSONNEL: Mick Jagger, Keith Richards, Mick Taylor, Ron Wood, Charlie Watts, Bill Wyman

DESCRIPTION: One hour of the "best of" the Stones' promo films and music videos, 1971–1983, presented when nighttime security guard Bill Wyman uncases a frozen specimen (Jagger) in the "Withdrawn Exhibits" room of a museum and they take a trip down memory lane. Live "Brown Sugar"; "It's Only Rock 'n' Roll" in sailor suits and a bubble-filled tent; "Undercover of the Night" and "Neighbours" uncensored are four of the 10 promos in this reel that also includes other preserved Stones nostalgia, drama and some funny bits.

BRITISH ROCK (THE FIRST WAVE)

YEAR MADE OR RELEASED: 1985

CREDITS: Directors: Patrick Montgomery, Pamela Page; Producer: Patrick Montgomery

STONES/FEATURED PERSONNEL: Mick Jagger, Keith Richards, Brian Jones, Charlie Watts, Bill Wyman

DESCRIPTION: Historical rockumentary from skiffle to Stonesmania, and then some. There are three Stones songs from the early years plus other archival footage of the period.

READY, STEADY, GO! VOLS. 1, 2, & 3

YEAR MADE OR RELEASED: 1985

CREDITS: Directors: Robert Gamble, Daphne Shadwell, Michael Lindsay-Hogg; Producer: Francis Hitchings

STONES/FEATURED PERSONNEL: Mick Jagger, Keith Richards, Brian Jones, Bill Wyman, Charlie Watts, Ian Stewart

Hail! Hail! Rock 'n' Roll—*Chuck Berry with Keith Richards* (LISA SEIFERT/STARFILE)

DESCRIPTION: The famed British television show's greatest hits (sort of), released on home video. The program ran in the UK from 1963–1967, though the content of the three volumes is not in chronological order. The Stones have a segment or two on each tape.

WILLIE & THE POOR BOYS

YEAR MADE OR RELEASED: 1985
CREDITS: Directors: Eddie Arno, Mark Innocenti
STONES/FEATURED PERSONNEL: Bill Wyman, Charlie Watts, Ron Wood, Kenney Jones, Ringo Starr
DESCRIPTION: Bill Wyman and friends play some classic covers from the *Willie & the Poor Boys* album, and Ringo sweeps up after the dance, in a cameo role as a janitor.

ECHO PARK

YEAR MADE OR RELEASED: 1986

CREDITS: Director: Robert Dornhelm
STONES/FEATURED PERSONNEL: Bill Wyman
DESCRIPTION: Wyman was musical director on this film by Robert Dornhelm, who also made Bill's autobiographical *Digital Dreams*. This feature is best described as a lightweight semi-comedy with a decent cast—Tom Hulce, Susan Dey, Christopher Walken, Cheech Marin, among others—set in a now-crumbling, but once quintessential Raymond Chandleresque section of Los Angeles.

MICK TAYLOR—ROCK, BLUES & SLIDE GUITAR

YEAR MADE OR RELEASED: 1986
CREDITS: Director: Mark Kaplan; A Hot Licks Production
STONES/FEATURED PERSONNEL: Mick Taylor

DESCRIPTION: Mick gives you a 60-minute guitar lesson on video. Mick's "master class" on tape is part of the large Hot Licks catalog of training videos produced by noted guitarist/educator Arlen Roth. Roth appears with Taylor in the slide guitar section of the video; Mick takes care of the rock and blues segments himself. "It's easy," he says. "Just practice." Right.

THE REAL BUDDY HOLLY STORY

YEAR MADE OR RELEASED: 1986
STONES/FEATURED PERSONNEL: Keith Richards
DESCRIPTION: An interview with Keith is featured.

RUNNING OUT OF LUCK

YEAR MADE OR RELEASED: 1986
CREDITS: Director: Julien Temple; Producer: Mick Jagger
STONES/FEATURED PERSONNEL: Mick Jagger, Jerry Hall, Dennis Hopper, Rae Dawn Chong
DESCRIPTION: Feature-length music video that's more of a comedy adventure flick. Shot in Rio and accompanied mostly by music from *She's the Boss,* Jagger's first solo album, with a couple of Stones tunes. Mick plays himself, come to Rio with Jerry to shoot a music video with an insane egomaniac director (Dennis Hopper, obviously). Mick and Jerry fight, and Jagger ends up drunk and alone in the jungle after being mugged by three transvestites he picked up to spite Jerry (he thought they were women —duh!). Then comes slavery (sexual and otherwise) on a banana plantation, his love scene with Rae Dawn Chong —who rescues him—and even more funny stuff.

CHUCK BERRY: HAIL! HAIL! ROCK 'N' ROLL

YEAR MADE OR RELEASED: 1987
CREDITS: Director: Taylor Hackford; Producers: Stephanie Bennett, Chuck Berry; Musical Director: Keith Richards
STONES/FEATURED PERSONNEL: Keith Richards (and Chuck Berry, Ingrid Berry, Johnny Johnson, Little Richard, Bo Diddley, The Everly Brothers, Jerry Lee Lewis, Bruce Springsteen, Roy Orbison, Robert Cray, Eric Clapton, Linda Ronstadt, Julian Lennon, Etta James
DESCRIPTION: Chuck Berry's 60th birthday concert, his life and his music, told documentary-style. Keith is the concert's musical director; directing the man who has been his lifetime idol and strongest musical influence is clearly an awesome position for him. Not to mention the fact that both Richards and Berry are fairly strong personalities to begin with. So, they end up butting heads onscreen as they have in life (Berry once punched Keith, kicked him off his stage in L.A. another time, and merely snubbed him on another occasion).

All the tension is actually great for the film, and keeps the reality level on high. Great interviews with Little Richard and Chuck himself, among others, as well as archival clips about Berry and his music, and wonderful birthday concert performances by Chuck, Etta James, Clapton, Cray *et al.*

EAT THE RICH

YEAR MADE OR RELEASED: 1987
CREDITS: Director: Peter Richardson
STONES/FEATURED PERSONNEL: Bill Wyman
DESCRIPTION: Wyman (and various others unrelated to the film, like Paul and Linda McCartney) makes a cameo appearance. This feature is a farcical black comedy, the tasteful title being awfully descriptive of the plot. Guy loses restaurant job; guy becomes a revolutionary; guy returns to job; guy slings human flesh instead of hash.

9½ WEEKS

YEAR MADE OR RELEASED: 1987
CREDITS: Director: Adrian Lyne
STONES/FEATURED PERSONNEL: Ron Wood
DESCRIPTION: Ron Wood makes a tiny cameo, partying, at an art gallery opening—one scene in the film's story of sexual dominance and submission in a slick modern relationship. Mickey Rourke and Kim Basinger play the obsessively unhappy couple. Absolutely nothing to do with the Stones.

QUEEN—THE MAGIC YEARS, VOLUME 2

YEAR MADE OR RELEASED: 1987
CREDITS: Directors: Rudi Dolezal and Hannes Rossacher
STONES/FEATURED PERSONNEL: Mick Jagger, Keith Richards
DESCRIPTION: Interviews with both Stones are part of this documentary about the veteran British hard rock band, Queen, and its recently deceased lead singer, Freddy Mercury. Released by MPI Home Video.

HEARTS OF FIRE

YEAR MADE OR RELEASED: 1988
CREDITS: Director: Richard Marquand; Producers: Richard Marquand, Gerald Abrams, Jennifer Alward, Jennifer Miller
STONES/FEATURED PERSONNEL: Ron Wood
DESCRIPTION: Woody cameos as a band member at a gig in a bar. The film's plot is also a stretch for those in the major roles—Bob Dylan plays a cynical and crusty rock icon.

KEITH RICHARDS & THE X-PENSIVE WINOS LIVE AT THE HOLLYWOOD PALLADIUM

YEAR MADE OR RELEASED: 1988

CREDITS: Producer & Director: Anthony Eaton; Executive Producer: Jane Rose

STONES/FEATURED PERSONNEL: Keith Richards

DESCRIPTION: Filmed at Keith & the Winos' Hollywood Palladium performance on December 15, 1988. Released in 1991.

THE BEGGARS BANQUET GUIDE TO COLLECTIBLE ROLLING STONES

YEAR MADE OR RELEASED: 1989

CREDITS: Producer & Director: Bill German

STONES/FEATURED PERSONNEL: Bill German

DESCRIPTION: Bill German, editor and publisher of the Rolling Stones' official fanzine, *Beggars Banquet*, gives tips on collecting Stones memorabilia. Released in September 1989.

THE ROLLING STONES AT THE MAX

YEAR MADE OR RELEASED: 1990

CEDITS: Director: Julien Temple; Executive Producer: Michael Cohl

STONES/FEATURED PERSONNEL: The Rolling Stones, Urban Jungle tour personnel

DESCRIPTION: The IMAX film of the Stones' 1989 Steel Wheels tour, but shot at three concerts in Europe during the Urban Jungle portion of the world go-round, with the Steel Wheels stage. The European location is not obvious, except for the presence of backup vocalists Lorelei McBroom and Sophia Jones, who replaced Steel Wheels singers Lisa Fischer and Cindy Mizelle for the Urban Jungle leg of the tour. The band's Steel Wheels tour film, their first concert movie in nearly 10 years, was shot in the IMAX format. The Stones were the first rock band to use this medium—it was the first full-length IMAX concert film in any musical genre. The IMAX process uses 140mm film transported horizontally through its cameras and projectors to produce an image 10 times the size of the usual 35mm frame. IMAX films can only be viewed in special IMAX-equipped theaters (only about 120 worldwide) where that supersharp, superwide IMAX image is projected onto a screen five stories high and 70 feet wide, dominating the peripheral vision, while six-channel surround-sound completes the experience. As usual, the Stones wanted to be on the cutting edge technologically with this film, and were, in spite of the limited number of places it could be screened. It had an eight-theater simultaneous worldwide premiere in October 1991. *But*, the film was later released on home video. Go figure. (See page 48.)

25 X 5—THE CONTINUING ADVENTURES OF THE ROLLING STONES

YEAR MADE OR RELEASED: 1990

CREDITS: Director: Nigel Finch; Producer: Andrew Solt Productions for the Rolling Stones; Executive Producer: Lorne Michaels

STONES/FEATURED PERSONNEL: Mick Jagger, Keith Richards, Brian Jones, Mick Taylor, Ron Wood, Charlie Watts, Bill Wyman

DESCRIPTION: Author James Karnbach was director of archival research on the monumental project of documenting 25 years of five guys playing rock 'n' roll on film. Includes much ultra-rare historical material on the band —early performance footage, unreleased promos and films, and interviews and news footage—much of which had never been seen before, let alone officially released. There is also more recent performance footage in the two-hour film, which uses exclusive contemporary interviews with the Stones as a wraparound narrative to this career retrospective.

BLUE ICE

YEAR MADE OR RELEASED: 1992

CREDITS: Director: Russell Mulcahy; Producers: Martin Bregman and Michael Caine

STONES/FEATURED PERSONNEL: Charlie Watts

DESCRIPTION: Charlie and his Big Band (what you can see of them) make a cameo appearance—with Bobby Short on piano—onstage at ex-spy Michael Caine's jazz club as this spy/murder thriller gets underway. Costar Sean Young, as an ambassador's wife, is impressed with the club but is more interested in the club owner, and even more in his espionage skills. A decent movie with a tangled plot. The score is almost all jazz, almost all numbers written by Pete King and performed by Charlie Watts & the Big Band, featuring Bobby Short, Pete King and Steve Williamson.

FREEJACK

YEAR MADE OR RELEASED: 1992

CREDITS: Director: Geoff Murphy

STONES/FEATURED PERSONNEL: Mick Jagger

DESCRIPTION: Mick with Emilio Estevez as time travelling bounty hunters from the year 2009. Someone's stealing bodies to feed the rich—Anthony Hopkins also appears. . . but so does David Johansen. Filmed in Atlanta, GA.

325

Ron Wood and Bo Diddley live at the Ritz, New York City (CHUCK PULIN/STARFILE)

RON & BO AT THE RITZ

YEAR MADE OR RELEASED: 1992

CREDITS: Director: Richie Namm; Producers: Holly St. Lifer, Michael Owen; Executive Producers: John Scher, Neil Cohen

STONES/FEATURED PERSONNEL: Ron Wood

DESCRIPTION: Ron Wood and Bo Diddley live in concert at the Ritz, New York City.

THE VERY BEST OF THE ED SULLIVAN SHOW, VOLS. 1 & 2

YEAR MADE OR RELEASED: 1992

STONES/FEATURED PERSONNEL: Mick Jagger, Keith Richards, Brian Jones, Charlie Watts, Bill Wyman

DESCRIPTION: This home-video compilation of the Ed Sullivan show actually consists of highlights of various programs. In the Stones' case, the excerpts do not always include their entire performance of a song on a particular (original) show. Volume 1 includes "Satisfaction" and "Let's Spend Some *Time* Together" (the famous bleeping); Volume 2 includes "Paint It, Black."

ROD STEWART: UNPLUGGED

YEAR MADE OR RELEASED: 1993

CREDITS: MTV

STONES/FEATURED PERSONNEL: Ron Wood

DESCRIPTION: Woody joins his old Faces mate for Rod's "Unplugged" special on MTV.

SWEET HOME CHICAGO

YEAR MADE OR RELEASED: 1993

CREDITS: Directors: Alan Raymond, Susan Raymond; Producer: Nina Rosenstein

STONES/FEATURED PERSONNEL: Mick Jagger, Keith Richards, Ron Wood, Muddy Waters, Buddy Guy, Junior Wells, Willie Dixon, Sonny Boy Williamson, Chuck Berry, Marshall Chess

DESCRIPTION: Film about the history of Chicago Blues that includes interviews with Marshall Chess and perfromance footage of the Stones with Muddy Waters at the Checkerboard Lounge

HOODOO U VOODOO

YEAR MADE OR RELEASED: 1994

CREDITS: Director: David Mallet; Producers: Rocky Oldham, Eric Liekefet; Executive Producer: Michael Cohl

STONES/FEATURED PERSONNEL: Mick Jagger, Keith Richards, Mick Taylor, Bill Wyman, Ron Wood, Charlie Watts, Robert Cray, Sheryl Crow, Bo Diddley, Whoopi Goldberg

DESCRIPTION: The Stones' November 25, 1994 Voodoo Lounge pay-per-view show at Joe Robbie Stadium, Miami (Dade County), Florida. With special guests Cray, Crow and Bo. Whoopi introduces the band. (See TOURS AND CONCERTS)

LIVE VOODOO LOUNGE

YEAR MADE OR RELEASED: 1994

CREDITS: Executive Producer: Michael Cohl

STONES/FEATURED PERSONNEL: Mick Jagger, Keith Richards, Mick Taylor, Bill Wyman, Charlie Watts, Ian Stewart

DESCRIPTION: This 90-minute concert video was marketed during the tour by Brockum, the merchandising arm of Toronto-based CPI, the Voodoo Lounge tour promoter. The tape was shot at the Stones' four performances at New Jersey's Giants Stadium in August of 1994 and consists of highlights from Voodoo Lounge as performed at that time—the usual show less "Love Is Strong," "Beast of Burden," "I Go Wild," "Happy," and "I Can't Get Next to You." (See TOURS AND CONCERTS)

THE ROLLING STONES AT THE MAX (VIDEOCASSETTE, LASERDISC)

YEAR MADE OR RELEASED: 1994

CREDITS: Director: Julien Temple

STONES/FEATURED PERSONNEL: Mick Jagger, Keith Richards, Mick Taylor, Bill Wyman, Charlie Watts, Ian Stewart, Urban Jungle tour personnel

DESCRIPTION: The IMAX film of the Stones' 1989 Steel Wheels tour released on home video and laserdisc. The sound is good—best when the video is played on a HiFi/Stereo VCR—and they somehow managed to convert from 140mm to something able to be viewed on a television screen. However, at 85 minutes in length, it is shorter than the original. (For a description of IMAX, refer back to the 1990 entry for this title, page 318.)

5 + 1 • JOHNNY HALLYDAY • ROLLING STONES

YEAR MADE OR RELEASED: 1995 (Compilation)

CREDITS: (Hallyday) Guy Job and Michel Taittinger, Producers; (Stones) Jo Burden-Smith and Leslie Woodhead, Producers

STONES/FEATURED PERSONNEL: 1969 Rolling Stones with Mick Taylor, Johnny Hallyday

DESCRIPTION: Two "legendary" concert films on one videocassette—the Stones' July 5, 1969 free concert in Hyde Park and French rocker Johnny Hallyday's 10th anniversary (celebrating his 10-year career as a rock star) concert at the Palais des Sports in Paris. Hallyday's 1970 show is billed as "immortalizing the wild and crazy rock 'n' roll of Europe in the '60s." As the Stones were to Britain and the US in the '60s, so was Hallyday to the French—a rather interesting marketing concept. An ironic historical fact (not connected with this film save for the personalities): Hallyday and the Stones shared a Paris bill in 1966, with Hallyday opening for the Rolling Stones. When Hallyday's set was over, the audience went home. (Distributed by PolyGram Video [France]).

HISTORY OF ROCK 'N' ROLL, VOLUME ONE: ROCK 'N' ROLL

YEAR MADE OR RELEASED: 1995

CREDITS: Director: Andrew Solt; Producer: Andrew Solt; Executive Producers: Quincy Jones and Andrew Solt (Time-Life Video & Television)

STONES/FEATURED PERSONNEL: Mick Jagger, Keith Richards, Brian Jones, Bill Wyman, Charlie Watts, Ian Stewart

DESCRIPTION: The first videocassette in Time-Life's rock history, first broadcast on television. This segment features the very early Rolling Stones performing "I Just Wanna Make Love to You."

HISTORY OF ROCK 'N' ROLL, VOLUME THREE: BRITAIN INVADES

YEAR MADE OR RELEASED: 1995

CREDITS: Director: Andrew Solt; Producer: Andrew Solt; Executive Producers: Quincy Jones and Andrew Solt (Time-Life Video & Television)

STONES/FEATURED PERSONNEL: Mick Jagger, Keith Richards, Brian Jones, Bill Wyman, Charlie Watts, Ian Stewart

DESCRIPTION: The third segment of Time-Life's rock history features more early Rolling Stones performance footage, including "Satisfaction" and "Around & Around."

HISTORY OF ROCK 'N' ROLL, VOLUME SIX: MY GENERATION

YEAR MADE OR RELEASED: 1995

CREDITS: Director: Obie Benz; Producer: Obie Benz; Executive Producers: Quincy Jones and Andrew Solt (Time-Life Video & Television)

STONES/FEATURED PERSONNEL: Mick Jagger, Keith Richards, Mick Taylor, Bill Wyman, Charlie Watts, Ian Stewart

DESCRIPTION: Number six in the Time-Life series. The Stones do "Streetfighting Man."

HISTORY OF ROCK 'N' ROLL, VOLUME SEVEN: GUITAR HEROES

YEAR MADE OR RELEASED: 1995

CREDITS: Director: Marc J. Sachnoff; Producer: Marc J. Sachnoff; Executive Producers: Quincy Jones and Andrew Solt (Time-Life & Television)

STONES/FEATURED PERSONNEL: Mick Jagger, Keith Richards, Brian Jones, Bill Wyman, Charlie Watts, Ian Stewart

DESCRIPTION: The seventh volume in the Time-Life collection. The highlight is an interview with Keith. The whole series seemed not to have much Stones content when the project was originally broadcast on television. For those who are interested in only one (albeit important) part of the entire history of rock 'n' roll and felt dissatisfied, this seventh segment should be a redeeming one. Footage of "The Last Time" is also included in *Guitar Heroes*.

HULLABALOO: A 60s MUSICAL FLASHBACK, VOLUME 6

YEAR MADE OR RELEASED: 1995 (HomeVideo)

CREDITS:

STONES/FEATURED PERSONNEL: Mick Jagger, Keith Richards, Brian Jones, Bill Wyman, Charlie Watts, Ian Stewart

327

DESCRIPTION: 1965 vintage Stones appearance on the compilation series "Hullabaloo," here performing "Get Off of My Cloud."

THE ROLLING STONES VOODOO LOUNGE WORLD TOUR

YEAR MADE OR RELEASED: 1995

STONES/FEATURED PERSONNEL: Mick Jagger, Keith Richards, Ron Wood, Bill Wyman, Charlie Watts, Ian Stewart, tour (Voodoo Lounge) personnel

DESCRIPTION: The Japanese laserdisc of the 1995 Japanese segment of the Voodoo Lounge world tour.

STRIPPED

YEAR MADE OR RELEASED: 1995

CREDITS: Director: Jim Gable; Producer: Ned Doyle (Japan); Director: David Mallet; Producer: Rocky Oldham (Paradiso); Director & Producer: Christine Strand; Asst. Director & Coproducer: Monica Caston (Brixton Academy, London and the Olympia, Paris); Director: Patrick Woodruffe (Location filming, London and Paris); Editorial Director: Jim Gable

STONES/FEATURED PERSONNEL: Mick Jagger, Keith Richards, Ron Wood, Bill Wyman, Charlie Watts, Ian Stewart, Darryl Jones, Bobby Keys, Chuck Leavell, the New West Horns, Lisa Fischer, Bernard Fowler, tour personnel, Jack Nicholson

DESCRIPTION: Made to promote Stripped, the semi-acoustic, semi-live album recorded in the various locations represented in the video and released post-Voodoo Lounge. Tracks on Stripped were recorded in rehearsals at Toshiba-EMI Studios in Tokyo and in Lisbon and at performances at the Paradiso, Amsterdam; the Olympia Theatre, Paris; and the Brixton Academy, London. The video is a mixture of recording/rehearsal/behind-the-scenes footage in black-and-white mixed with color material from the Stones' performances, fan interviews, and location reportage shot in and around the venues of the "surprise" small shows that produced the tracks for the album.

THE VOODOO LOUNGE CD-ROM

YEAR MADE OR RELEASED: 1995

TITLE: The Voodoo Lounge CD-ROM

CREDITS: CD-ROM Production: Second Vision New Media; Distribution: GTE Entertainment and Virgin Records

STONES/FEATURED PERSONNEL: The Rolling Stones/ Voodoo Lounge Tour personnel/various Rolling Stones family members, friends and other persons in the Stones organization

DESCRIPTION: The Voodoo Lounge CD-ROM (unlike the Stripped Enhanced CD [listed in DISCOGRAPHY]) is solely an interactive multimedia product, viewable only by means of a computer (Macintosh or PC) equipped with a CD-ROM drive and the appropriate hard- and software (see below for system requirements). As mentioned earlier, the making of this little morsel of entertainment has more in common with the production of a film or video—it wasn't just the band in the studio with a couple of engineers and a producer. All of these media are multimedia; the CD-ROM adds interactivity, i.e., your participation, to the equation. But, unlike film or video (or the audio CD or any other audio product), the Voodoo Lounge CD-ROM is not a passive piece of entertainment—you must interact with it in order to see or hear anything past the startup screen. Furthermore, the more you get involved in it, the more you will discover.

The band was very much involved (on both sides of the camera, so to speak) in the making of the VLCDR—there are video clips from the "Jagger-cam" (mounted on his head as he did "on-the-street" mini-interviews and commentary in San Francisco) and the "Ronnie-cam" (attached to his sunglasses while onstage during Voodoo Lounge), for example. Much special filming was done (of the Stones and others as well as by them) to produce this first foray into new media. Since the project was conceived and begun less than 18 months prior to its release (October 1995), and production took place primarily in the last six months of that period, most of it was made during the tour.

Fully exploiting the contents of the Voodoo Lounge album and tour, The Voodoo Lounge CD-ROM aims to show you what the Stones and their music are all about, by making the "Voodoo Lounge" a place in which the Rolling Stones are having a very cool private party—to which you have been invited. Since that concept is entertaining and has been realized as well as it could have been in mid-1995, it entices you to explore the Lounge level by level from the concert stage to the VIP room to the private and more down-and-dirty areas. Also, there are a fair amount of in-jokes—the more you know about the Stones, the more you will appreciate those bits, and the more you'll look for them.

The adventure begins when a taxi drops you off at the "Voodoo Lounge," which is housed in a rambling southern plantation-style mansion complete with hanging moss, cicadas and mysterious (Voodoo, get it?) under- and overtones—and you belly up to the bar. Your choice of drinks determines where you go next, and the amount of Stones "tour-smarts" you possess—get yourself a laminated VIP Pass!—determines how easily you can get around and how much you can see in the various parts of the Lounge. There are some 23 rooms or areas—each with a different theme and content. Blues music in the snooker or billiards room, complete with Mick and Keith talking about their musical influences, and very nice black-and-white film clips of those same old blues musicians. Woody and Keith have an acoustic jam on the veranda, and in addition to the music videos for the four singles off the *Voodoo Lounge* album, there are many interviews (not just from the "Jagger-cam"), and performance clips shot from many perspectives (in addition to Ronnie's sunglasses) —for a total of 45. You will even find a minute of the footage of three Stones and Muddy Waters shot at the Checkerboard Lounge in 1981 (see CHRONOLOGY). There are all sorts of audio files—from music (single B-sides and remixes, alternate versions of other *Voodoo Lounge* tracks) to comments from Charlie (but, you'll have to figure out how to activate CharlieSpeak, and we're not telling you) and the rest of the band to jokes (such as one from Keith, upon exiting one of the bathrooms). Some videos or sound clips are easily found and accessed with a point-and-click of the computer's mouse; getting at others requires more thought and trial and error. You interact with the Stones—and with the environment as if you were partying with them at the Lounge. It's not quite virtual reality, but the rooms were constructed with 3-D computer graphics software and you navigate 360° of each of the physical spaces. Which is helpful if you want to investigate the trash on the floor (some of this will take you to song lyrics, if you click on it). Song lyrics are also found by clicking on an object with some correlation to the words of that track. The band's sense of humor is apparent, some of it self-deprecating. And a wry nod and a wink is given to the public's take on the Stones persona (see Mick Jagger have sex—or talk about it, anyway). You can dance with the type of female you might expect to see at a Stones party. But you may be surprised to discover who the real person in the costume of a Cockney serving wench is, or totally unsurprised when you tumble on the true identity of the guy who bounces you from the VIP room

for being without a laminate. And, naturally, a lot of attention has been paid to the music, both foreground and background. There is a lot of content on the CD-ROM, not all of it will be experienced in one sitting. Have fun.

The *Stripped* ECD has a lot of the material contained on *The Voodoo Lounge CD-ROM*—in addition to music videos and other bonus interactive stuff from *Stripped*—at the price of a regular audio CD. The *VLCDR* came out at around US$50) but was sold in computer software and bookstores in addition to record stores and was discounted deeply after its first appearance. Both products were released within two weeks of each other—which meant that the Stones, while not being the first band to release a multimedia product, were the first to release two interactive titles at the same time.

System Requirements (these are reasonable specifications based on published consumer feedback after this CD-ROM was released; information given on the product packaging might differ): Mac (68030 and up) or Power-Mac with System 7.5 or better, 16MB of RAM, CD-ROM drive (4X is best); Pentium PC: Windows 3.1 or 95, 16 MB RAM, 4X CD-ROM drive. Either system requires a color monitor (at least 8-bit/256 colors). Because this product was designed to be played on either platform, there were initial compatibility problems associated with various hardware combinations (computer/various CD-ROM brands). GTE Entertainment and Virgin both maintained web pages for technical support in addition to telephone and fax numbers. When the *Stripped* enhanced CD was released, VirginUK's website address was printed on the inside cover of the CD's inlay card (http://www.vmg.co.uk/stripped). There were more difficulties with the *Stripped* interative material, it seemed, because of the newness of the "enhanced," technology—it was even more difficult to make a single version of the disk that would play on both platforms with innumerable potential hardware configurations.

Television Appearances

Although there are bands that have sold more albums and played more concerts—very, very few, but there are some—none has made as many television appearances as the Rolling Stones over the past 33 years. This section deals primarily with US and UK television shows, although a German, French, Belgian, Japanese or Dutch appearance sneaks in once in a while, particularly during those years when the Stones made themselves scarce on US and/or UK screens.

In general, news-format shows are listed only to mark appearances of individual band members. Or, if the whole band appeared on a news program and the reason they did was really *news*, it has been included whenever possible. However, neither a news nor an occasional European show listing means that these were the only such appearances the Stones made. Hardly. That would take another book. We have, however, tried to list all musical numbers performed or shown as promo films (or videos) with each program detailed in this chapter.

In the early years of the Stones' career, television was the primary broadcast medium by which bands premiered new records and promoted themselves—on both sides of the Atlantic. While groups were regularly featured on the BBC's "Saturday Club" and similar British radio shows, such shows were not part of the US scene in the early 1960s, nor did American FM stations even get going with free-form rock music programming until late 1965. So, in large part, the Stones' early success (and that of other bands of that era) was due to many appearances on a medium that could transmit both sound and picture, simultaneously startling the world with their music and their equally intense visual presence. Whether audiences found the Stones appealing or repulsive was irrelevant—they could not fail to notice them.

Many of the Rolling Stones' "appearances" on the shows detailed in these entries were just that—live or taped performances by or interviews with the band on specific programs. Others were not, and these are not always obvious. Most people think that the birth of MTV brought forth the creation of music promo films. Not true. In actual fact, the '60s was a haven for promo films made on very low budgets, any number of which could stand up quite nicely next to some of today's costly music videos.

Promos were made to push new records in cities and countries the Stones and other artists were not touring at the time. Some films were made to look like a live (or mimed) appearance on a particular television show. Viewers at home would see the band and hear the audience screaming, and, naturally but erroneously, think the Stones (or whoever) were there in the studio. So much for truth in broadcasting. In actuality, that studio audience was watching the band on a television monitor in the studio, and their screaming was being broadcast along with the film insert. "Shindig" was big on that sort of thing. Even Ed Sullivan used inserts in two shows featuring the Stones, in 1966 and 1969, although these were exceptions to the rule for that program.

Not all promos were straight performance documentaries, either. There were some noteworthy early films. The Stones' promo for "Have You Seen Your Mother, Baby?" in which the band appeared in drag, was filmed in New York City, but US television shows refused to air it. It was never broadcast in the US, though it was shown in a few American movie theaters. English broadcasters weren't quite as uptight; "Top of the Pops" aired the promo 10 days after it was shot.

The band even made a Scopitone promo of "Around & Around" to be played on Scopitone Juke Boxes, which were a sort of first take on the "video jukeboxes" of today. These entertainment gadgets were not as popular in the US as they were in Europe in the '50s and '60s. In fact, most Americans are not even aware they existed.

Other promos never got to see the cathode light of day. Films of "Cry to Me" and "That's How Strong My Love Is," with Brian Jones on organ, are such unseen classics. There also exists an extended "She's a Rainbow" film, a 15-minute reel with avant-garde footage wildly cut to playback additional *Satanic Majesties Request* tracks after the title song ends. More about gems like these can be found in PROMOTIONAL FILMS AND VIDEOS.

The early to mid-1970s saw the Stones extracting clips from their 1972 tour film, *Ladies & Gentlemen, the Rolling Stones*, for use on US and UK television shows as promotion for the film's release. These clips were also slated to be used to promote the release of the Stones' live double LP of the same name, had it happened.

The MTV era that dawned in 1981, along with the emergence of the multiple-market cable television industry, did without doubt broaden the music industry's reach. It also made it almost impossible, and probably irrelevant, to catalog each appearance the Stones and every other group were to make on the small screen. Music videos are now aired continuously; the music promo has become no big deal, except for its existence and premiere (and in the budgetary sense). The later listings in this chapter reflect this point of view. However, the PROMOTIONAL FILMS AND VIDEOS section that follows this chapter contains a catalog of all Rolling Stones promotional films and videos made as of the end of 1995, as well as some more lesser-known tidbits about this aspect of the band's output.

HOW TO READ THE TELEVISION APPEARANCE LISTINGS

This section is a directory of the Rolling Stones' three decades of regular appearances on the small screen. As mentioned in the previous pages, we have concentrated on programs aired in the UK and US, but have also chosen to include listings for a number of unique and important shows that originated in other countries. Programs are listed individually in chronological order; each entry contains six categories of detail about a particular show, though all six headings may not appear in every listing if the information is redundant or unknown. The headings are:

DATE OF BROADCAST: If the actual broadcast date is unknown or the program never aired, the entry will reflect that fact, and further information will be provided in subsequent categories (that is, Notes). For most programs, we have listed the first airing only and not reruns, except when there is historical significance attached to the existence of many rebroadcasts of a program or a Stones segment on it. The latter situation is noticeable and relevant in the early years of the Stones' career. Shows like "Top of the Pops" repeatedly used inserts of a band's performance of a hit single—as long as the song was still a hit, it could be included in that week's telecast. Be aware that many US pop music programs—"Midnight Special," "Shivaree" and "Hollywood À Go Go" among them—were independently produced, nationally syndicated shows. This means that the initial air date of an episode of any of these programs often varied from city to city. However, in most cases, we have relied on the original producers' logs in obtaining the broadcast dates of syndicated programs listed in this book. If you disagree with the date we've given for your favorite Stones appearance of the '60s, please check the Program Notes to see if it was a syndicated program.

PROGRAM: The program title. If the exact name is unknown, a descriptive title will be given as well as any known information about the broadcaster or originator of the program. In other words, if a show was known to have been made by the BBC about the Stones in a coal mine, the listing might say, "unknown title—Stones in coal mine (BBC)." That one never happened, but you get the idea.

WHERE BROADCAST: The country or locality in which the program was broadcast. Most entries are for national broadcasts, but there are a few significant local shows as well.

PERSONNEL: The names of the members of the Rolling Stones and other significant Stones-related individuals who appeared on the show. This heading does *not* appear in all listings. Unless otherwise indicated, all *current* (on that show's air date) members of the Rolling Stones appeared on the program—all their names will not appear in every entry except in those instances where the information is necessary for clarification or to avoid confusion. For example, when any other pertinent, Stones-related individuals appeared with them, all band members' names are noted.

If an individual Stone appeared solo on a broadcast, his name only will be listed, even if a current band promo is also part of the show. But, whenever historical footage containing former Stones is broadcast, every band member whose face was seen on that show will be listed by name in Personnel.

We have delineated the major changes in Stones personnel at the beginning of the transitional years of 1969, 1975 and 1993. The Personnel category will list all members of the "new" band. Until an official change occurs, if no names are listed, it should be assumed that the lineup remained the same and that the whole band appeared.

A few broadcasts near the beginning of one era featured the Rolling Stones of the previous incarnation—usually in promos, but occasionally in a taped show that hadn't yet aired. All band members appearing on such programs will be named, of course, and, to minimize confusion, the names of current personnel will be indicated (assuming the whole group appeared) in the entry immediately following the anachronistic one, as a reminder. The Songs/Content and Notes paragraphs should resolve any questions or apparent contradictions in a listing, like those shows where Brian Jones and Mick Taylor *and* Ron Wood are included in Personnel.

SONGS/OTHER CONTENT: Just like it says. Song titles, interviews, archival footage etc.—whatever Stones material was part of the show, briefly described. Individual segments and song titles are separated by a "/". This heading does not always appear. The content may be unknown; whatever else is known about such programs is provided in Notes.

NOTES: Any further information or description not contained in the other five categories. This heading only appears when necessary, but it's the place to look for the cool, the bizarre, and the silly historical tidbits, many previously unpublished, about the Rolling Stones on the box.

1957

MAY 7, 1957

PROGRAM: Seeing Sport
WHERE BROADCAST: UK
PERSONNEL: Joe Jagger, Mike Jagger
SONGS/OTHER CONTENT: Sports instruction
NOTES: The first known television appearance of any member of the Rolling Stones. Physical education expert Joe Jagger was a consultant on this instructional program and appeared on several episodes. He demonstrated such sporting activities as rock climbing and canoeing with the assistance (on at least three episodes) of his teenage son, Mike—as he was then known—and some of Mike's friends. In this show, they climb rocks together. As host John Disley provides running commentary on proper rock climbing procedure, Mike/Mick gets a rope wrapped

around his waist and is hoisted up the rockface. Little did anyone know at the time, of course, that Mick in 1975 and 1976 would again have rope wrapped around his waist and be hoisted up—this time over thousands of cheering fans.1963

1963

From 1962 to mid-1969, the Rolling Stones consisted of Mick Jagger (voc, gtr, harm), Keith Richards (gtr, voc), Brian Jones (gtr, bass, harm, dulcimer, sax, flute, sitar, kbds), Charlie Watts (ds), Bill Wyman (bs)

JULY 13, 1963

PROGRAM: Thank Your Lucky Stars
WHERE BROADCAST: UK
PERSONNEL: Mick Jagger, Keith Richards, Brian Jones, Charlie Watts, Bill Wyman
SONGS/OTHER CONTENT: Come On (Berry)
NOTES: The Rolling Stones' first television appearance.

AUGUST 23, 1963

PROGRAM: Ready, Steady, Go!
WHERE BROADCAST: UK
SONGS/OTHER CONTENT: Come On (Berry)
NOTES: First time on "Ready, Steady, Go!" This BBC program was broadcast each Friday at 6:10 P.M., and opened with the show's motto, "The weekend starts here!"

AUGUST 29, 1963

PROGRAM: Scene At 6:30
WHERE BROADCAST: UK
SONGS/OTHER CONTENT: Come On (Berry)
NOTES: Granada TV's Manchester-based program.

SEPTEMBER 14, 1963

PROGRAM: Thank Your Lucky Stars
WHERE BROADCAST: UK
SONGS/OTHER CONTENT: Come On (Berry)

NOVEMBER 22, 1963

PROGRAM: Ready, Steady, Go!
WHERE BROADCAST: UK
SONGS/OTHER CONTENT: I Wanna Be Your Man (Lennon, McCartney)

NOVEMBER 23, 1963

PROGRAM: Thank Your Lucky Stars
WHERE BROADCAST: UK
SONGS/OTHER CONTENT: I Wanna Be Your Man (Lennon, McCartney)

DECEMBER 27, 1963

PROGRAM: Ready, Steady, Go!
WHERE BROADCAST: UK
PERSONNEL: Mick Jagger, Keith Richards, Brian Jones, Charlie Watts, Bill Wyman, Andrew Loog Oldham
SONGS/OTHER CONTENT: I Wanna Be Your Man (Lennon, McCartney)
NOTES: The Stones meet Stevie Wonder for the first time—he was also featured on this show. Andrew Oldham hosts a segment as "guest DJ."

1964

JANUARY 2, 1964

PROGRAM: Top of the Pops
WHERE BROADCAST: UK
SONGS/OTHER CONTENT: I Wanna Be Your Man (Lennon, McCartney)
NOTES: Taped January 1, 1964

JANUARY 30, 1964

PROGRAM: Top of the Pops
WHERE BROADCAST: UK
SONGS/OTHER CONTENT: You Better Move On (Alexander)
NOTES: Taped January 29, 1964

FEBRUARY 4, 1964

PROGRAM: Town & Around
WHERE BROADCAST: UK
SONGS/OTHER CONTENT: You Better Move On (Alexander)
NOTES: Taped on January 30 in London. Aired sometime in February, exact date unknown.

FEBRUARY 8, 1964

PROGRAM: Arthur Haynes Show
WHERE BROADCAST: UK
SONGS/OTHER CONTENT: You Better Move On (Alexander) / I Wanna Be Your Man (Lennon, McCartney)
NOTES: A Saturday program.

FEBRUARY 14, 1964

PROGRAM: Ready, Steady, Go!
WHERE BROADCAST: UK
SONGS/OTHER CONTENT: Not Fade Away (Petty, Hardin) / You Better Move On (Alexander) / I Wanna Be Your Man (Lennon, McCartney)

FEBRUARY 29, 1964

PROGRAM: Thank Your Lucky Stars
WHERE BROADCAST: UK
SONGS/OTHER CONTENT: Not Fade Away (Petty, Hardin)

MARCH 4, 1964

PROGRAM: Scene At 6:30
WHERE BROADCAST: UK
SONGS/OTHER CONTENT: Not Fade Away (Petty, Hardin)
NOTES: Taped the previous day in Manchester.

MARCH 5, 1964

PROGRAM: Top of the Pops
WHERE BROADCAST: UK
SONGS/OTHER CONTENT: Not Fade Away (Petty, Hardin)

MARCH 12, 1964

PROGRAM: Top of the Pops
WHERE BROADCAST: UK
SONGS/OTHER CONTENT: Not Fade Away (Petty, Hardin)

APRIL 3, 1964

PROGRAM: Ready, Steady, Go!
WHERE BROADCAST: UK
SONGS/OTHER CONTENT: Not Fade Away (Petty, Hardin)

APRIL 8, 1964

PROGRAM: Top of the Pops
WHERE BROADCAST: UK
SONGS/OTHER CONTENT: I Wanna Be Your Man (Lennon, McCartney)

APRIL 10, 1964

PROGRAM: Ready, Steady, Go! Rave Mad Mod Ball
WHERE BROADCAST: UK
SONGS/OTHER CONTENT: Walking the Dog (Thomas) / Not Fade Away (Petty, Hardin) / High Heel Sneakers (Higginbotham) / I'm Alright (McDaniel)

NOTES: Filmed on April 8, 1964 at Wembley. The Stones mimed the first two numbers to playback, but performed both "High Heel Sneakers" and "I'm Alright" live.

APRIL 24, 1964

PROGRAM: Ready, Steady, Go!
WHERE BROADCAST: UK
SONGS/OTHER CONTENT: Mona (I Need You Baby) (McDaniel) / Route 66 (Troup) / Not Fade Away (Petty, Hardin)
NOTES: Shot in Montreux, Switzerland on April 20. Other guests on the show were Kenny Lynch, Petula Clark and Les Surfs.

APRIL 27, 1964

PROGRAM: Top Beat "Pop Prom"
BROADCAST: UK
SONGS/OTHER CONTENT: Not Fade Away (Petty, Hardin) / High Heel Sneakers (Higginbotham) / I'm Alright (McDaniel)

APRIL 29, 1964

PROGRAM: Top of the Pops
WHERE BROADCAST: UK
SONGS/OTHER CONTENT: I Just Want to Make Love to You (Dixon)

MAY 3, 1964

PROGRAM: Big Beat
WHERE BROADCAST: UK
SONGS/OTHER CONTENT: Not Fade Away (Petty, Hardin) / I Just Want to Make Love to You (Dixon) / I'm Alright (McDaniel)
NOTES: NME Poll Winners Concert performance of April 26, 1964. This was a Sunday broadcast. Big Beat's NME show was aired in two parts. This is part one, which featured the Stones' performance. Part two, featuring the Beatles, was aired on May 10, 1964.

MAY 4, 1964

PROGRAM: Scene At 6:30
WHERE BROADCAST: UK
SONGS/OTHER CONTENT: Unknown
NOTES: The content and songs are unknown.

MAY 6, 1964

PROGRAM: Two Go Round
WHERE BROADCAST: UK
SONGS/OTHER CONTENT: Not Fade Away (Petty, Hardin)

NOTES: A daily show. The exact air date in May of 1964 was unknown at the time of writing.

MAY 30, 1964

PROGRAM: Thank Your Lucky Stars
WHERE BROADCAST: UK
SONGS/OTHER CONTENT: You Can Make It If You Try (Jarrett)

JUNE 2, 1964

PROGRAM: Les Crane Show
WHERE BROADCAST: NY/NJ/CT Tri-State area (USA)
SONGS/OTHER CONTENT: Not Fade Away (Petty, Hardin) / I Just Want to Make Love to You (Dixon) / interview / call-in
NOTES: The Stones' first US television appearance. A live late-night show, aired in what is known as the "Tri-State area," those parts of New York, New Jersey and Connecticut within a 150-mile radius of Manhattan. This program featured live interviews with the band and call-in segments in which viewers could "talk to the Stones," interspersed with the introduction and the two Stones records. Neither song was performed live on this very funny, apparently totally unrehearsed, show. Host Crane persistently referred to the first number as "Fade Away" and was corrected each time. There was much discussion of how tired everyone was (it was after midnight), whether they drank coffee or tea, and several references by Crane to "that other British group" (that is, the Beatles). Other quirky bits included Crane's introduction of Jagger as "Mike," a too-long, one-sided discussion about hair (in particular, Brian Jones's "Prince Valiant" hairdo—Jones made out as if he had no idea what Crane was talking about), and a bit of hilarious culture shock prompted by Bill Wyman. It seems that Wyman wanted to smoke, so he asked if he could "pinch some fags." Naturally, the Americans cracked up and Wyman appeared (smilingly) perplexed. Crane explained that the crew had no idea Wyman only wanted to snag a cigarette, then proceeded to expound on the vagaries of British and American slang, and, as it seemed necessary, went on to give the boys some friendly advice about how to conduct themselves in "the colonies."

JUNE 10, 1964

PROGRAM: Unknown title—local show
WHERE BROADCAST: Chicago, IL (USA)
SONGS/OTHER CONTENT: Not Fade Away (Petty, Hardin) / interview

JUNE 13, 1964

PROGRAM: Hollywood Palace

The Stones on "Hollywood Palace," 1964 (TOM BEACH COLLECTION)

WHERE BROADCAST: USA

SONGS/OTHER CONTENT: I Just Want to Make Love to You (Dixon)

NOTES: This was the Stones' first *network* television appearance in the US. They were the first rock/pop group ever to appear on "Hollywood Palace." Three songs were taped on June 3—the above plus "Not Fade Away" and, according to Bill Wyman, "Tell Me"—then split into segments for two shows. "I Just Want to Make Love to You" was aired as part of this June 13 broadcast, the last episode of the season, hosted by Dean Martin. The second Stones segment containing "Not Fade Away" was part of the September 26, 1964 show, which Ed Wynn emceed. Martin's opinion of the Stones was readily apparent. He introduced the band's segment with unfunny quips about their hair and hygiene. Even when his words were neutral, Dino expressed his scorn and derision nonverbally as his eyes rolled to the heavens for a little additional nastiness.

The band had no inkling of the bashing they'd received until the show aired, 10 days after the taping.

Behind the scenes, the show's stage manager and producer had demonstrated ignorance, rather than malice; they knew nothing about the band or its members. Upon observing the Stones' performing attire during rehearsals—street clothes—they concluded that the band was too poor to afford the suits or tuxedos customarily worn by "Hollywood Palace" performers and approached Andrew Oldham and the band with an offer of help. The show would provide each of them with a white cable-knit sweater, white shirt, white trousers, white socks and white shoes. And, best of all, they added, the boys could keep the outfits after the show. Needless to say, the Stones told them where to hang the clothes.

The artist lineup on the June 13, 1964 "Hollywood Palace" show was: Bertha & Tina (an elephant act); Joey Forman; Larry Grizwald; The King Sisters & Daughters;

the Rolling Stones; and the Share Girls (the wives of various motion picture honchos).

JUNE 18, 1964

PROGRAM: Unknown title—local show

WHERE BROADCAST: Cleveland, OH, USA

SONGS/OTHER CONTENT: Carol (Berry) / Interview

NOTES: This was the taping date for a local program during the Stones' first US tour. The name of the program and its air date are unknown.

JUNE 19, 1964

PROGRAM: Clark Race Show

WHERE BROADCAST: Pittsburgh, PA (USA)

SONGS/OTHER CONTENT: Route 66 (Troup) / Interview

NOTES: Another local program done during the first American tour. The Stones taped two different programs on June 17, 1964; this was one of them.

JUNE 20, 1964

PROGRAM: Clay Cole Show

WHERE BROADCAST: NY/NJ/CT Tri-State area (USA)

SONGS/OTHER CONTENT: Tell Me / Not Fade Away (Petty, Hardin) / Carol (Berry)

NOTES: After the Hollywood Palace debacle, Clay Cole was a welcome change for the Stones. A well-known rock 'n' roll booster on the local music scene and an ardent early Stones fan, Cole treated them and their music with the respect he and they felt they deserved. His kindness would be remembered. Other guests who appeared on this same show were Frankie Avalon, Ray Rivers, Myrna March and Chuck McCann. This program was taped in New York City and aired the same day, reaching viewers within a 150-mile radius of Manhattan.

JUNE 26, 1964

PROGRAM: Ready, Steady, Go!

WHERE BROADCAST: UK

SONGS/OTHER CONTENT: It's All Over Now (Womack, Womack) / Good Times, Bad Times / Interview

NOTES: This show was taped and aired the same day.

JULY 1, 1964

PROGRAM: Top of the Pops

WHERE BROADCAST: UK

SONGS/OTHER CONTENT: It's All Over Now (Womack, Womack)

NOTES: Taped in London on June 27, 1964.

JULY 3, 1964

PROGRAM: Ready, Steady, Go!

WHERE BROADCAST: UK

PERSONNEL: Brian Jones, Mick Jagger

SONGS/OTHER CONTENT: Interview

NOTES: Interview with Brian. Jagger was also present, though only Jones was interviewed.

JULY 4, 1964

PROGRAM: Juke Box Jury

WHERE BROADCAST: UK

SONGS/OTHER CONTENT: It's All Over Now (Womack, Womack)

NOTES: The Stones first and last appearance on this show. They received a lot of flak after this broadcast, not for their musical performance but for their rudeness and generally surly attitudes during the "hit or miss" song-judging portion of the show. They verbally put down each song they heard, giving all (except, most likely, one) a rating of "miss." "It's All Over Now" was also on the docket. Taped on June 27.

JULY 4, 1964

PROGRAM: Thank Your Lucky Stars

WHERE BROADCAST: UK

SONGS/OTHER CONTENT: It's All Over Now (Womack, Womack)

JULY 8, 1964

PROGRAM: Top of the Pops

WHERE BROADCAST: UK

SONGS/OTHER CONTENT: It's All Over Now (Womack, Womack)

NOTES: Repeat airing of the Stones' segment first aired on July 1, 1964.

JULY 15, 1964

PROGRAM: Top of the Pops

WHERE BROADCAST: UK

SONGS/OTHER CONTENT: It's All Over Now (Womack, Womack)

NOTES: Taped on the same day in Manchester. "Top of the Pops" was broadcast weekly on Wednesdays.

JULY 22, 1964

PROGRAM: Top of the Pops

WHERE BROADCAST: UK

SONGS/OTHER CONTENT: It's All Over Now (Womack, Womack)

NOTES: Repeat airing of July 15 segment.

JULY 29, 1964

PROGRAM: Top of the Pops

WHERE BROADCAST: UK

SONGS/OTHER CONTENT: It's All Over Now (Womack, Womack)

NOTES: Another repeat of the Stones' segment first aired on July 15. The record was still a hit.

JULY 31, 1964

PROGRAM: Six Ten

WHERE BROADCAST: Belfast, Northern Ireland

PERSONNEL: Mick Jagger, Brian Jones, Charlie Watts, Bill Wyman

SONGS/OTHER CONTENT: Interview

NOTES: Taped, without Keith, and aired the same day. The four Stones were interviewed only; no songs were performed nor were any records played.

AUGUST 5, 1964

PROGRAM: Top of the Pops

WHERE BROADCAST: UK

SONGS/OTHER CONTENT: It's All Over Now (Womack, Womack)

AUGUST 7, 1964

PROGRAM: Ready, Steady, Go!

WHERE BROADCAST: UK

SONGS/OTHER CONTENT: It's All Over Now (Womack, Womack)

NOTES: Taped in London and aired the same day.

AUGUST 8, 1964

PROGRAM: Thank Your Lucky Stars

WHERE BROADCAST: UK

SONGS/OTHER CONTENT: It's All Over Now (Womack, Womack) / If You Need Me (Pickett, Bateman, Sanders)

NOTES: Taped July 28, 1964 in Teddington.

AUGUST 25, 1964

PROGRAM: Here Today

WHERE BROADCAST: UK

SONGS/OTHER CONTENT: It's All Over Now (Womack, Womack)

NOTES: A Tuesday broadcast. Taped in Weston-Super-Mare and aired the same day.

SEPTEMBER 2, 1964

PROGRAM: Top of the Pops

WHERE BROADCAST: UK

SONGS/OTHER CONTENT: If You Need Me (Pickett, Bateman, Sanders)

SEPTEMBER 21, 1964

PROGRAM: BBC World in Action (series)—"The Flipside"

WHERE BROADCAST: UK

SONGS/OTHER CONTENT: High Heel Sneakers (Higginbotham) / Not Fade Away (Petty, Hardin)

NOTES: This segment of the BBC series featured the Rolling Stones performing both of these songs live.

SEPTEMBER 22, 1964

PROGRAM: Red Skelton Hour

WHERE BROADCAST: USA

SONGS/OTHER CONTENT: Carol (Berry) / Tell Me / It's All Over Now (Womack, Womack)

NOTES: Taped on August 5. The Stones mimed the three prerecorded songs in front of Red and a bunch of screaming fans in a stairwell at the London Palladium.

SEPTEMBER 26, 1964

PROGRAM: Hollywood Palace

WHERE BROADCAST: USA

PERSONNEL: Mick Jagger, Keith Richards, Brian Jones, Charlie Watts, Bill Wyman

SONGS/OTHER CONTENT: Not Fade Away (Petty, Hardin)

NOTES: Ed Wynn was the somewhat nicer host of "Hollywood Palace" for the Stones' second appearance on this show. He did, however, put in his own 2¢ about rock 'n' roll. Following the band's performance of "Not Fade Away," Wynn came onstage wearing a Beatles wig, playing a ukulele and singing "I Wanna Hold Your Hand," whereupon he was attacked by three elderly women from the audience. The Stones segment was from the original June 3, 1964 taping that had provided fodder for Dean Martin on June 13. The "Hollywood Palace" guests on September 26 were Jack Carter; Eydie Gorme; Zizi Jeanmaire & Her Parisian Review; the Great Leones (acrobats); Bob Morry; the Nicholas Brothers; the Rolling Stones; and Mitchell Aires & His Orchestra.

OCTOBER 19, 1964

PROGRAM: Qui de Neuf

WHERE BROADCAST: France

SONGS/OTHER CONTENT: It's All Over Now (Womack, Womack) / Carol (Berry) / Around & Around (Berry)

NOTES: Taped in Paris. Broadcast date unknown.

OCTOBER 25, 1964

PROGRAM: Ed Sullivan Show

WHERE BROADCAST: USA
SONGS/OTHER CONTENT: Time Is on My Side (Meade), V1 / Around & Around (Berry)
NOTES: Taped at CBS in New York and aired the same day. On the original broadcast, Ed shakes hands with Mick and asks where the Stones will be performing, since the band is about to embark on their second US tour. Mick replies that they'll be in San Bernardino (CA) later on in the week. Mick and Ed's cordial but dated conversation was edited out of reruns of this episode.

OCTOBER 31, 1964

PROGRAM: Clay Cole Show
WHERE BROADCAST: NY/NJ/CT Tri-State area (USA)
SONGS/OTHER CONTENT: If You Need Me (Pickett, Bateman, Sanders) / Confessin' the Blues (McShann, Brown) / Interview / Q & A
NOTES: This show and one aired the following week were taped in New York on October 24. The program included an interview/discussion portion, with the Stones taking questions from the audience, in addition to the musical segments in which the songs were performed (mimed to the records).

NOVEMBER 7, 1964

PROGRAM: Clay Cole Show
WHERE BROADCAST: NY/NJ/CT Tri-State area (USA)
SONGS/OTHER CONTENT: Time Is on My Side (Meade), V1 / It's All Over Now (Womack, Womack) / Around & Around (Berry) / Interview / Q & A
NOTES: Two shows were taped in New York on October 24, which meant this second broadcast was listed in the *TV Guide*. This program also included an interview portion and audience questions in addition to the (lip-synched) songs. Also appearing on this show were Neil Sedaka and another group, the Eggheads.

NOVEMBER 16, 1964

PROGRAM: "Tienerklaken" (Special–Belgian TV)
WHERE BROADCAST: Belgium
SONGS/OTHER CONTENT: Carol (Berry) / It's All Over Now (Womack, Womack) / Tell Me / Time Is on My Side (Meade), V1 / Not Fade Away (Petty, Hardin) / Walking The Dog (Thomas) / I'm Alright (McDaniel)
NOTES: Taped on October 18, 1964 at the American Theater on the Brussels World's Fair grounds.

NOVEMBER 20, 1964

PROGRAM: Ready, Steady, Go!
WHERE BROADCAST: UK
PERSONNEL: Mick Jagger, Keith Richards, Brian Jones, Charlie Watts, Bill Wyman

SONGS/OTHER CONTENT: Off the Hook (Nanker Phelge) / Little Red Rooster (Dixon) / Around & Around (Berry) / Jagger, Jones interview
NOTES: Taped in London and aired the same day. Only Mick and Brian were interviewed. Burt Bacharach also appeared on this show.

NOVEMBER 25, 1964

PROGRAM: Glad Rag Ball
WHERE BROADCAST: UK
SONGS/OTHER CONTENT: Around & Around (Berry) / Little Red Rooster (Dixon)
NOTES: Taped in Wembley on November 20, 1964.

DECEMBER 5, 1964

PROGRAM: Thank Your Lucky Stars
WHERE BROADCAST: UK
SONGS/OTHER CONTENT: Around & Around (Berry) / Little Red Rooster (Dixon) / Off the Hook (Nanker Phelge) / Empty Heart (Nanker Phelge)
NOTES: Taped in Birmingham on November 29, 1964.

DECEMBER 31, 1964

PROGRAM: Ready, Steady, Go!
WHERE BROADCAST: UK
SONGS/OTHER CONTENT: Off the Hook (Nanker Phelge) / Around & Around (Berry) / Little Red Rooster (Dixon)
NOTES: This was a repeat of the November 20, 1964 broadcast.

1965

JANUARY 6, 1965

PROGRAM: Six Ten
WHERE BROADCAST: Belfast, Northern Ireland
SONGS/OTHER CONTENT: Little Red Rooster (Dixon) / Rehearsals before a gig / Interview
NOTES: Taped and aired the same day.

JANUARY 15, 1965

PROGRAM: Ready, Steady, Go!
WHERE BROADCAST: UK
SONGS/OTHER CONTENT: Time Is on My Side (Meade) / Down the Road Apiece (Raye)
NOTES: Taped in London and aired the same day.

JANUARY 20, 1965

PROGRAM: Shindig

WHERE BROADCAST: USA

SONGS/OTHER CONTENT: Heart of Stone / Down the Road Apiece (Raye) / Oh Baby (We Got a Good Thing Goin') (Ozen)

NOTES: Taped at Shepperton Studios, England, on December 15, 1964. The Stones mimed their performance of all three songs to playback of album cuts. This was the Stones' premiere appearance on "Shindig." It has been written elsewhere that they appeared on "Shindig" in December 1964. Not true. The authors have viewed every episode of this program—January 20, 1965 was the Stones' first appearance on the show.

JANUARY 30, 1965

PROGRAM: Thank Your Lucky Stars

WHERE BROADCAST: UK

SONGS/OTHER CONTENT: Down Home Girl (Leiber, Butler) / Under the Boardwalk (Resnick, Young) / Susie Q (Broadwater, Lewis, Hawkins)

NOTES: Taped on January 13, 1965 in Teddington.

FEBRUARY 12, 1965

PROGRAM: Rolling Stones Special

WHERE BROADCAST: Australia

SONGS/OTHER CONTENT: Walking the Dog (Thomas) / Off the Hook (Nanker Phelge) / Around & Around (Berry) / Heart of Stone

NOTES: Taped in Melbourne on January 29, 1965, during the band's Australia/Far East tour.

FEBRUARY 26, 1965

PROGRAM: Ready, Steady, Go!

WHERE BROADCAST: UK

PERSONNEL: Mick Jagger, Keith Richards, Brian Jones, Charlie Watts, Bill Wyman

SONGS/OTHER CONTENT: The Last Time / Play with Fire (Nanker Phelge) / Everybody Needs Somebody to Love (Russell, Burke, Wexler) / Jagger interview

NOTES: Taped in London and aired the same day. Interview segment with Mick Jagger only.

FEBRUARY 28, 1965

PROGRAM: Eamonn Andrews Show

WHERE BROADCAST: UK

PERSONNEL: Mick Jagger, Keith Richards, Brian Jones, Charlie Watts, Bill Wyman

SONGS/OTHER CONTENT: The Last Time / Jagger interview

NOTES: Taped in Teddington and aired the same day. The show included an interview with Mick Jagger.

MARCH 3, 1965

PROGRAM: Shindig

WHERE BROADCAST: USA

SONGS/OTHER CONTENT: Susie Q (Broadwater, Lewis, Hawkins) / Heart of Stone

NOTES: Taped on December 15, 1964 at Shepperton Studios, England. Mimed to record playback.

MARCH 4, 1965

PROGRAM: Top of the Pops

WHERE BROADCAST: UK

PERSONNEL: Mick Jagger, Keith Richards, Brian Jones, Charlie Watts, Bill Wyman

SONGS/OTHER CONTENT: Everybody Needs Somebody to Love (Russell, Burke, Wexler) / Down the Road Apiece (Raye) / The Last Time / Oh Baby (We Got a Good Thing Goin') (Ozen) / I Can't Be Satisfied (Morganfield) / Jones and Jagger interview

NOTES: The interview with Mick and Brian was one segment of this program on which the whole band appeared.

MARCH 11, 1965

PROGRAM: Scene At 6:30

WHERE BROADCAST: UK

SONGS/OTHER CONTENT: The Last Time

NOTES: Taped in Manchester and aired the same day.

MARCH 25, 1965

PROGRAM: Top of the Pops

WHERE BROADCAST: UK

SONGS/OTHER CONTENT: The Last Time

NOTES: Taped on March 23, in London.

MARCH 27, 1965

PROGRAM: Thank Your Lucky Stars

WHERE BROADCAST: UK

SONGS/OTHER CONTENT: The Last Time / Play with Fire (Nanker Phelge) / Everybody Needs Somebody to Love (Russell, Burke, Wexler)

NOTES: Taped in Birmingham on March 21, 1965.

APRIL 8, 1965

PROGRAM: Special—Swedish TV

WHERE BROADCAST: Sweden

SONGS/OTHER CONTENT: Everybody Needs Somebody to Love (Russell, Burke, Wexler) / Tell Me / Little Red Rooster (Dixon) / The Last Time

NOTES: Taped on April 2, 1965 in Stockholm. Charlie Watts introduces "Little Red Rooster."

APRIL 9, 1965

PROGRAM: Ready Steady Goes Live

WHERE BROADCAST: UK

SONGS/OTHER CONTENT: Everybody Needs Somebody to Love (Russell, Burke, Wexler) / Pain in My Heart (Neville) / I'm Alright (McDaniel)

NOTES: Taped in Wembley and aired the same day. "Goes Live" refers to the band's playing live instead of miming to records, as had been the show's previous practice.

APRIL 18, 1965

PROGRAM: Big Beat '65

WHERE BROADCAST: UK

SONGS/OTHER CONTENT: Everybody Needs Somebody to Love (Russell, Burke, Wexler) → Around & Around (Berry), LMV / The Last Time / Everybody Needs Somebody to Love (Russell, Burke, Wexler)

NOTES: Taped at the NME Poll Winners concert in Wembley on April 11, 1965. "Everybody Needs Somebody to Love → Around & Around" medley started the set, which ended with the full version of "Everybody."

MAY 2, 1965

PROGRAM: Ed Sullivan Show

WHERE BROADCAST: USA

SONGS/OTHER CONTENT: The Last Time / Everybody Needs Somebody to Love (Russell, Burke, Wexler) / Little Red Rooster (Dixon) / 2120 South Michigan Avenue (Nanker Phelge)

NOTES: Taped in New York City and aired the same day. This broadcast was quite unique for the Sullivan show, since the program closed with the Stones performing the instrumental "2120 South Michigan Avenue" while the credits rolled. The credit crawl usually appeared against the background of the Sullivan theater curtain, *not* over a performance visual. Most sources don't list "2120 South Michigan Avenue" as having been performed on the show but it was.

MAY 22, 1965

PROGRAM: Clay Cole Show

WHERE BROADCAST: NY/NJ/CT Tri-State area (USA)

PERSONNEL: Mick Jagger, Keith Richards, Brian Jones, Charlie Watts, Bill Wyman

SONGS/OTHER CONTENT: The Last Time / Little Red Rooster (Dixon)

NOTES: Taped on May 3, 1965, in New York City. The Clay Cole Show was a local program with a limited budget that normally would not have booked the now-famous Rolling Stones. The Stones had not forgotten the kindness and respect Cole had shown them during their first visit

to the US in 1964, when other television hosts had been demeaning, even downright nasty, and the band had been regularly booed off American concert stages. A year later, all that had changed and the Stones were commanding five-figure fees for television appearances. When asked to appear on Clay Cole's program in '65, they made their fee affordable as a way of thanking him for those past kindnesses and his unflagging support.

MAY 22, 1965

PROGRAM: Hollywood À Go Go

WHERE BROADCAST: USA

SONGS/OTHER CONTENT: The Last Time / Oh Baby (We Got a Good Thing Goin') (Ozen) / Play with Fire (Nanker Phelge)

NOTES: This show had been taped in Los Angeles on May 15. "Hollywood À Go Go" was an independently produced, nationally syndicated US program; for this reason, air dates for the same episode often differed from city to city.

MAY 26, 1965

PROGRAM: Shindig

WHERE BROADCAST: USA

SONGS/OTHER CONTENT: Down the Road Apiece (Raye) / Little Red Rooster (Dixon) / The Last Time / Play with Fire (Nanker Phelge) / (I Can't Get No) Satisfaction

NOTES: Taped in Los Angeles on May 20, 1965. The Stones performed "Down the Road Apiece" live during the show's intro. For the other songs, Mick did the vocals live and the rest of the band mimed to prerecorded instrumental backing tracks. The Stones recorded the material especially for this show at RCA Studios in Los Angeles just prior to the taping. On this broadcast, Brian Jones was seen playing (miming) harmonica on "Satisfaction." The version of "Satisfaction" on this episode was the same as the rejected demo version of the song—containing a harmonica solo—first cut at Chess Studios in Chicago.

JUNE 4, 1965

PROGRAM: Ready Steady Goes Live

WHERE BROADCAST: UK

SONGS/OTHER CONTENT: The Last Time / Play with Fire (Nanker Phelge)

NOTES: Taped the same day in Wembley. Burt Bacharach also appeared on this show.

JUNE 5, 1965

PROGRAM: Shivaree (Episode 19)

WHERE BROADCAST: USA

SONGS/OTHER CONTENT: The Last Time / Play with Fire (Nanker Phelge)
NOTES: This show was taped on May 16, in Los Angeles. Syndicated.

JUNE 10, 1965

PROGRAM: Top of the Pops
WHERE BROADCAST: UK
SONGS/OTHER CONTENT: The Last Time
NOTES: Taped the same day in London.

JUNE 12, 1965

PROGRAM: Thank Your Lucky Stars
WHERE BROADCAST: UK
SONGS/OTHER CONTENT: I'm Moving On (Snow) / I'm Alright (McDaniel) / Route 66 (Troup)
NOTES: Taped in Birmingham on June 6, 1965.

JULY 24, 1965

PROGRAM: Shivaree (Episode 26)
WHERE BROADCAST: USA
SONGS/OTHER CONTENT: Down the Road Apiece (Raye) / Little Red Rooster (Dixon)
NOTES: Song inserts for this show were taped on May 16, in Los Angeles. Syndicated.

JULY 31, 1965

PROGRAM: Thank Your Lucky Stars
WHERE BROADCAST: UK
SONGS/OTHER CONTENT: (I Can't Get No) Satisfaction
NOTES: Taped on July 26, 1965, in Birmingham.

AUGUST 11, 1965

PROGRAM: Shindig
WHERE BROADCAST: US
SONGS/OTHER CONTENT: Down the Road Apiece (Raye)
NOTES: This is the studio "promo" insert, *not* the "Down the Road Apiece" the Stones recorded on May 20, 1965 for "Shindig's" May 26, 1965 broadcast.

AUGUST 23, 1965

PROGRAM: Scene At 6:30
WHERE BROADCAST: UK
SONGS/OTHER CONTENT: (I Can't Get No) Satisfaction
NOTES: Taped in Manchester and aired the same day.

AUGUST 27, 1965

PROGRAM: Ready, Steady, Go!
WHERE BROADCAST: UK

SONGS/OTHER CONTENT: Cry to Me (Russell) / Oh Baby (We Got a Good Thing Goin') (Ozen) / (I Can't Get No) Satisfaction / Apache (Lordan)
NOTES: Taped in Wembley, the same day. The program's usual closer, Cliff Richard's instrumental hit from several years back, "Apache," was performed by four Stones—Brian, Keith, Bill and Charlie. A bit out of the ordinary for a Rolling Stones television appearance.

SEPTEMBER 2, 1965

PROGRAM: Top of the Pops
WHERE BROADCAST: UK
SONGS/OTHER CONTENT: (I Can't Get No) Satisfaction / Wyman and Jagger interview
NOTES: Taped on August 19, 1965, in London.

SEPTEMBER 4, 1965

PROGRAM: Thank Your Lucky Stars
WHERE BROADCAST: UK
SONGS/OTHER CONTENT: (I Can't Get No) Satisfaction
NOTES: Taped on August 29, in Birmingham.

SEPTEMBER 10, 1965

PROGRAM: Ready, Steady, Go! The Rolling Stones—Special Show
WHERE BROADCAST: UK
PERSONNEL: Mick Jagger, Keith Richards, Brian Jones, Charlie Watts, Bill Wyman, Andrew Loog Oldham
SONGS/OTHER CONTENT: I Got You Babe (mimed; Bono) / Oh Baby (We Got a Good Thing Goin') (Ozen) / That's How Strong My Love Is (Jamison) / (I Can't Get No) Satisfaction
NOTES: Taped on September 2 in Wembley. Brian Jones and Cathy McGowan (RSG's presenter), along with Andrew Oldham and the rest of the Stones, did a comedy send-up of Sonny & Cher's current hit single—they all mimed to a recording of "I Got You Babe."

SEPTEMBER 16, 1965

PROGRAM: Shindig
WHERE BROADCAST: USA
SONGS/OTHER CONTENT: (I Can't Get No) Satisfaction
NOTES: Network censors bleeped out the words "who tells me" from "Satisfaction," thinking that they meant the girl in the song was pregnant, according to rumors circulating at that time. See the entry PROMOTIONAL FILMS AND VIDEOS for more information and an explanation of how American censors missed the forest when they cut what was only an imagined tree—so to speak.

SEPTEMBER 23, 1965

PROGRAM: Top of the Pops
WHERE BROADCAST: UK
SONGS/OTHER CONTENT: The Spider and the Fly (Nanker Phelge) / (I Can't Get No) Satisfaction / Cry to Me (Russell)
NOTES: Taped in London and aired the same day.

OCTOBER 14, 1965

PROGRAM: Top of the Pops
WHERE BROADCAST: UK
SONGS/OTHER CONTENT: *Charlie Is My Darling*
NOTES: A film clip from the Stones' Irish tour film shot September 5–6, 1965 was included in this show.

OCTOBER 22, 1965

PROGRAM: Ready, Steady, Go!
WHERE BROADCAST: UK
SONGS/OTHER CONTENT: Cry to Me (Russell) / She Said Yeah (Christy, Jackson) / Get Off of My Cloud
NOTES: Taped the same day in Wembley.

OCTOBER 31, 1965

PROGRAM: Beat Club
WHERE BROADCAST: Germany
SONGS/OTHER CONTENT: (I Can't Get No) Satisfaction
NOTES: Performance footage from the Stones' concert at Waldbuhne, Berlin.

NOVEMBER 4, 1965

PROGRAM: Top of the Pops
WHERE BROADCAST: UK
SONGS/OTHER CONTENT: Get Off of My Cloud
NOTES: Taped in London on October 19.

NOVEMBER 6, 1965

PROGRAM: Shindig
WHERE BROADCAST: USA
SONGS/OTHER CONTENT: Good Times (Cooke) / Mercy Mercy (Covay, Miller)

NOVEMBER 15, 1965

PROGRAM: Hullabaloo
WHERE BROADCAST: USA
SONGS/OTHER CONTENT: She Said Yeah (Christy, Jackson) / Get Off of My Cloud / Film clip
NOTES: Taped in Brooklyn, New York on November 11, 1965. Even though both of the Stones' musical numbers were prerecorded, the direction of the group's appearance resulted in a unique episode of the program. The show's usual opener consisted of a shot of the "Hullaballoo" dancers in action while the announcer introduced the program. This was changed for the band's appearance—for a few seconds, the audience saw the Stones walking through the "Hullaballoo" set and the announcer teasingly let viewers know they'd see more of the group if they stuck around. Hullaballoo also used a short clip from *Charlie Is My Darling* on the show, and a few bars of an instrumental "Satisfaction" were heard during the introduction to a musical segment.

DECEMBER 30, 1965

PROGRAM: Man Alive (BBC-TV)
WHERE BROADCAST: UK
SONGS/OTHER CONTENT: "Love 'Em and Leave 'Em" story / Get Off of My Cloud
NOTES: The story title says it all—about "Brian Jones' son and [the child's] mother" Pat Andrews; along with a clip of the Rolling Stones performing "Get Off of My Cloud" taken from the "Top of the Pops" show of November 4, 1965.

DECEMBER 31, 1965/JANUARY 1, 1966

PROGRAM: Ready, Steady, Go!
WHERE BROADCAST: UK
SONGS/OTHER CONTENT: (I Can't Get No) Satisfaction / Get Off of My Cloud
NOTES: Taped on December 17, 1965.

1966

JANUARY 20, 1966

PROGRAM: Top of the Pops
WHERE BROADCAST: UK
SONGS/OTHER CONTENT: As Tears Go By (Jagger, Richards, Oldham)
NOTES: Taped the same day in London.

FEBRUARY 6, 1966

PROGRAM: Eamonn Andrews Show
WHERE BROADCAST: UK
SONGS/OTHER CONTENT: 19th Nervous Breakdown

FEBRUARY 10, 1966

PROGRAM: Top of the Pops
WHERE BROADCAST: UK
PERSONNEL: Mick Jagger, Keith Richards, Brian Jones, Charlie Watts, Bill Wyman

SONGS/OTHER CONTENT: 19th Nervous Breakdown / Jagger and Richards interview
NOTES: Taped on February 3, 1966, in London.

FEBRUARY 13, 1966

PROGRAM: Ed Sullivan Show
WHERE BROADCAST: USA
SONGS/OTHER CONTENT: 19th Nervous Breakdown / As Tears Go By (Jagger, Richards, Oldham) / (I Can't Get No) Satisfaction
NOTES: Taped the same day in New York. This show was rebroadcast on July 10, 1966.

FEBRUARY 20, 1966

PROGRAM: Big Beat (Australian TV)
WHERE BROADCAST: Australia
SONGS/OTHER CONTENT: 19th Nervous Breakdown / Get Off of My Cloud / As Tears Go By (Jagger, Richards, Oldham) / Play with Fire (Nanker Phelge) / (I Can't Get No) Satisfaction

MARCH 3, 1966

PROGRAM: Top of the Pops
WHERE BROADCAST: UK
SONGS/OTHER CONTENT: The Last Time
NOTES: Taped in Brisbane, Australia on February 22, 1966, for UK airing. Silent footage paired with playback of "The Last Time."

APRIL 14, 1966

PROGRAM: Top of the Pops
WHERE BROADCAST: UK
SONGS/OTHER CONTENT: Mother's Little Helper
NOTES: Taped the same day in London.

APRIL 28, 1966

PROGRAM: Top of the Pops
WHERE BROADCAST: UK
SONGS/OTHER CONTENT: Mother's Little Helper

MAY 1, 1966

PROGRAM: Big Beat '66
WHERE BROADCAST: UK
NOTES: Date of the NME Poll-Winner's Concert—at which the Stones performed "Paint It Black" and "Satisfaction"—but not a true broadcast date as it applies to the band, since the Stones did not appear on the television program that aired on May 1. Neither the Rolling Stones nor the Beatles would perform at this event unless the television cameras were turned off, since both groups were involved in disputes with the BBC and the union. Other acts on the bill were filmed for the "Big Beat" program. We hope this will clarify any confusion that may exist—other books have erroneously listed the Stones (and the Beatles, for that matter) as having appeared on this television program. Both groups played the concert, but weren't on the telecast.

MAY 12, 1966

PROGRAM: Top of the Pops
WHERE BROADCAST: UK
SONGS/OTHER CONTENT: Paint It, Black

MAY 13, 1966

PROGRAM: Thank Your Lucky Stars
WHERE BROADCAST: UK
SONGS/OTHER CONTENT: Paint It, Black / Lady Jane
NOTES: Taped on May 8 in Birmingham.

MAY 19, 1966

PROGRAM: Top of the Pops
WHERE BROADCAST: UK
SONGS/OTHER CONTENT: Mother's Little Helper
NOTES: Repeat airing of the April 14, 1966 segment, which had been rebroadcast on May 12. Also repeated on May 26.

MAY 26, 1966

PROGRAM: Top of the Pops
WHERE BROADCAST: UK
SONGS/OTHER CONTENT: Mother's Little Helper
NOTES: Another repeat airing of the April 14, 1966 segment.

MAY 27, 1966

PROGRAM: Ready, Steady, Go!
WHERE BROADCAST: UK
SONGS/OTHER CONTENT: Paint It, Black / Under My Thumb / I Am Waiting
NOTES: Taped in Wembley, the same day. Many books list this show as occurring on September 10, 1966. Not so. First off, "Ready, Steady, Go!" was a Friday program. September 10 was a Saturday. And the September 9 broadcast of "Ready, Steady, Go!" didn't include the Stones at all. Further evidence can be found on Brian Jones's head—his hair was fairly short, as if he'd recently had a haircut—on this episode of "Ready, Steady, Go!" When Jones appeared at Albert Hall on September 23, 1966 his hair was very, very long. There is no way he could have appeared 13 days earlier on "Ready, Steady, Go!" No one's hair grows that fast!

JULY 10, 1966

PROGRAM: Ed Sullivan Show
WHERE BROADCAST: USA
SONGS/OTHER CONTENT: 19th Nervous Breakdown / As Tears Go By (Jagger, Richards, Oldham) / (I Can't Get No) Satisfaction
NOTES: Rerun of the February 13, 1966 "Ed Sullivan Show."

SEPTEMBER 11, 1966

PROGRAM: Ed Sullivan Show
WHERE BROADCAST: USA
SONGS/OTHER CONTENT: Paint It, Black / Have You Seen Your Mother, Baby, Standing in the Shadow? / Lady Jane
NOTES: Taped in New York on September 9, 1966. As a rule, musical guests on the Sullivan show performed live. However, Brian Jones had injured his wrist and was unable to play for real in front of the camera this time. Both "Paint It, Black" and "Lady Jane" relied heavily on Jones's playing—sitar on the former and dulcimer on the latter. So the Stones were filmed two days prior to the show, miming the instrumental parts to prerecorded backing tracks while Jagger did live vocals. Jones's bandaged wrist is quite visible to the viewer.

SEPTEMBER 22, 1966

PROGRAM: Top of the Pops
WHERE BROADCAST: UK
SONGS/OTHER CONTENT: Have You Seen Your Mother, Baby, Standing in the Shadow?
NOTES: The first BBC airing of the US promo for "Have You Seen Your Mother, Baby?" Shot in New York on September 12, the film featured the Stones in drag. (See PROMOTIONAL FILMS AND VIDEOS)

SEPTEMBER 29, 1966

PROGRAM: Top of the Pops
WHERE BROADCAST: UK
SONGS/OTHER CONTENT: Have You Seen Your Mother, Baby, Standing in the Shadow? / Who's Driving Your Plane? / gold disc party footage
NOTES: The program also included footage of a gold disc presentation party filmed on September 23, in Kensington.

OCTOBER 6, 1966

PROGRAM: Top of the Pops
WHERE BROADCAST: UK
SONGS/OTHER CONTENT: Have You Seen Your Mother, Baby, Standing in the Shadow?

NOTES: This is the "Have You Seen Your Mother, Baby?" promo film, Albert Hall version. (See PROMOTIONAL FILMS AND VIDEOS)

OCTOBER 7, 1966

PROGRAM: Ready, Steady, Go!
WHERE BROADCAST: UK
SONGS/OTHER CONTENT: Have You Seen Your Mother, Baby, Standing in the Shadow? (live)
NOTES: Taped in Wembley on October 4. This was a live performance, not a promo.

DECEMBER 22, 1966

PROGRAM: Top of the Pops
WHERE BROADCAST: UK
SONGS/OTHER CONTENT: Have You Seen Your Mother, Baby, Standing in the Shadow?
NOTES: Taped in London on December 17.

DECEMBER 23, 1966

PROGRAM: Ready, Steady, Go!
BROADCAST: UK
SONGS: Out Of Time / (I Can't Get No) Satisfaction
PERSONNEL: Mick Jagger, Chris Farlowe
NOTES: This appearance consisted of Chris Farlowe performing these two numbers with Mick Jagger only. The rest of the Stones did not appear on the show, which was taped on December 20, 1966.

1967

JANUARY 15, 1967

PROGRAM: Ed Sullivan Show
WHERE BROADCAST: USA
SONGS/OTHER CONTENT: Ruby Tuesday / Let's Spend *Some Time* Together
NOTES: "Let's Spend *Some Time* Together" is "Let's Spend the Night Together" with the lyrics changed per Sullivan's request so as not to offend the sensibilities of those virtuous American audiences! Jagger's expression while singing the altered lyrics left little question as to what he thought of this slice of Americana. As the camera panned the studio audience, one shot captured a very young Mackenzie Phillips, screaming along with the rest of the crowd. Song performances were live vocals over prerecorded tracks.

JANUARY 22, 1967

PROGRAM: Sunday Night at the London Palladium
WHERE BROADCAST: UK

Songs/Other Content: Let's Spend the Night Together / Ruby Tuesday / Connection / It's All Over Now (Womack, Womack)

Notes: The Stones' musical segment, with the band performing live vocals over instrumental tracks they'd recorded at Olympic Studios on January 18, was taped the same day as the broadcast, in London. "Sunday Night at the London Palladium" was Britain's "Ed Sullivan"; that is, a mainstream institution. Making an appearance on either program meant recognition by the establishment entertainment industry and was considered a "big thing" for any artist, old or new. By the time of this booking, the Stones were so popular they could not be ignored by even the most conservative programmers, lest they lose their younger viewers. Still, Andrew Oldham felt he had scored a coup for the band when this appearance was scheduled. Even so, the Stones caused a major furor by refusing to participate in the show's traditional finale in which guests waved "bye-bye" to the audience while standing on the Palladium's revolving stage, or "roundabout," calling it "silly and stupid." Oldham himself was not pleased with them, but audience reaction was swift and negative: the Stones had been rude, the roundabout was a sacred tradition. Popular debate over this, the boys' latest sneer at the system, filled newspaper columns for many days after the broadcast.

JANUARY 26, 1967

Program: Top of the Pops

Where Broadcast: UK

Songs/Other Content: Let's Spend the Night Together

Notes: Taped the preceding day in London.

FEBRUARY 2, 1967

Program: Top of the Pops

Where Broadcast: UK

Songs/Other Content: Ruby Tuesday

Notes: Somewhat unique—Keith played the piano as Brian sat on top of it, playing the flute.

FEBRUARY 5, 1967

Program: Eamonn Andrews Show

Where Broadcast: UK

Personnel: Mick Jagger

Songs/Other Content: She Smiled Sweetly (promo) / Jagger interview

Notes: Taped in London the same day. Mick seized the opportunity of a prescheduled appearance on this show to express his outrage at the *News of the World* for its story on pop stars and drugs that had run in this day's paper. The tabloid reported that Jagger once took LSD with the

Moody Blues in their Roehampton house and described an interview with him during which he openly smoked hashish. None of this was true, said Mick; he had been defamed by the newspaper and was, therefore, instructing his attorneys to sue the *News of the World* for libel. (See CHRONOLOGY)

FEBRUARY 12, 1967

Program: Coverage of the Stones on "Sunday Night at the London Palladium" by Italian TV

Where Broadcast: Italy

Songs/Other Content: Footage of the January 22, 1967 BBC broadcast of "Sunday Night at the London Palladium" plus coverage of the Stones backstage, before and after the show.

Notes: Italian TV covers the controversial appearance of the Stones on the BBC's January 22, 1967 episode of "Sunday Night at the London Palladium."

MAY 28, 1967

Program: Look of the Week

Where Broadcast: UK

Personnel: Mick Jagger

Songs/Other Content: Interview

Notes: Mick was interviewed by Professor John Cohen.

JUNE 25, 1967

Program: Our World (Beatles' appearance)

Where Broadcast: Worldwide

Personnel: (Beatles and friends) Mick Jagger, Keith Richards, Marianne Faithfull

Songs/Other Content: All You Need Is Love (Lennon, McCartney)

Notes: Jagger, Richards and Faithfull were shown in the audience during the live coverage of the Beatles recording "All You Need Is Love" at EMI's famed Abbey Road Studios. This program was a landmark in television history; it was the first live global satellite uplink ever attempted. Though the concept originated at and was developed by the BBC, the content of the show was provided by the national networks of 14 countries. An additional dozen nations took the satellite feed to broadcast the program over their airwaves, adding local language narration. The scene at Abbey Road consisted of friends like Mick, Keith, Marianne (and Brian, who was there but not seen), Graham Nash, Eric Clapton, Jane Asher, Keith Moon and many others sitting cross-legged on the studio floor while the band recorded. It was a party atmosphere, complete with streamers. In actuality, though, there were several days of rehearsals beforehand and basic rhythm tracks had been prerecorded. The cameras rolled while the Beatles and a 13-piece orchestra laid down "All You Need Is Love" on tape, while 350 million people watched. The Beatles' sequence, which lasted slightly more than six minutes, was one of only two British contributions to the 125-minute black-and-white show.

JULY 31, 1967

PROGRAM: World in Action (Granada TV)
WHERE BROADCAST: UK
PERSONNEL: Mick Jagger, William Rees-Mogg, Lord Stow Hill, Dr. John Robinson, Father Thomas Curbishley
SONGS/OTHER CONTENT: Debate
NOTES: Mick Jagger debated the straights on sex, drugs and rock 'n' roll. The cast included moderator Rees-Mogg, editor of the *Times*; Lord Hill, former Home Secretary; Robinson, the Bishop of Woolwich; and Father Curbishley, a leading Jesuit priest. Jagger, who arrived at the site in a helicopter, held his own, giving up nothing. Rees-Mogg penned the historic London *Times* editorial "Who Breaks a Butterfly on a Wheel" that roused public opinion—and most likely saved the Stones' collective careers—by suggesting a more rational look at the 1967 Redlands arrests and the subsequent harsh jail sentences handed out to Jagger and Richards. This *têtes aux têtes* took place the day the Appeals Court agreed and, essentially, freed them. (See CHRONOLOGY)

AUGUST 24, 1967

PROGRAM: Top of the Pops
WHERE BROADCAST: UK
SONGS/OTHER CONTENT: We Love You
NOTES: This was *not* the "We Love You" promo film —the program's producers had banned it from broadcast on grounds that the film ridiculed the British judicial system. Instead, "Top of the Pops" showed its own studio audience dancing to the recorded track as images of the Stones flashed on a screen in the studio.

AUGUST 26, 1967

PROGRAM: Beat Club
WHERE BROADCAST: Germany
SONGS/OTHER CONTENT: We Love You / Dandelion
NOTES: Not only was this the world broadcast premiere of the "We Love You" promo (banned by the BBC for what it deemed to be its mocking, impertinent portrayal of the British courts), but it was also the only airing of the "Dandelion" promo. (See PROMOTIONAL FILMS AND VIDEOS)

SEPTEMBER 1, 1967

PROGRAM: ZDF experimental color broadcast
WHERE BROADCAST: Munich, Germany
SONGS/OTHER CONTENT: We Love You

NOTES: The entire "We Love You" promo film, in color, was aired as part of this German television station's weekend-long experiment in color programming. British audiences had yet to see the Stones' promo—in color or black-and-white—as it had been banned from broadcast by the BBC. This was the first color broadcast of the promo; it had premiered in (then-standard) black-and-white on German NDR-TVs "Beat Club" on August 26.

DECEMBER 21, 1967

PROGRAM: Top of the Pops
WHERE BROADCAST: UK
SONGS/OTHER CONTENT: 2000 Light Years from Home / She's a Rainbow
NOTES: The show, taped in London, featured these tracks from *Satanic*.

DECEMBER 28, 1967

PROGRAM: Top of the Pops
WHERE BROADCAST: UK
SONGS/OTHER CONTENT: Let's Spend the Night Together
NOTES: This end-of-the-year wrap-up show featured the Stones' segment from the "Top of the Pops" broadcast of January 26, 1967.

1968

MARCH 9, 1968

PROGRAM: Beat Club (German TV)
WHERE BROADCAST: Germany
SONGS/OTHER CONTENT: 2000 Light Years from Home

MAY 18, 1968

PROGRAM: Time for Blackburn
WHERE BROADCAST: UK
PERSONNEL: Mick Jagger, Keith Richards, Brian Jones, Charlie Watts, Bill Wyman
SONGS/OTHER CONTENT: Jumpin' Jack Flash / (I Can't Get No) Satisfaction / Presentation of gold LP for Jumpin' Jack Flash
NOTES: Stones live NME Poll-Winners Concert performance in Wembley taped on May 12, 1968, was featured. It was Brian Jones's last concert.

MAY 18, 1968

PROGRAM: Big Beat '68
WHERE BROADCAST: UK
PERSONNEL: Mick Jagger, Keith Richards, Brian Jones, Charlie Watts, Bill Wyman

SONGS/OTHER CONTENT: Jumpin' Jack Flash / (I Can't Get No) Satisfaction

NOTES: The NME Poll-Winners Concert featured the Stones, live. This was also Brian Jones's last public performance, and was taped on May 12.

MAY 23, 1968

PROGRAM: Top of the Pops
WHERE BROADCAST: UK
SONGS/OTHER CONTENT: Jumpin' Jack Flash
NOTES: Airing of "Jumpin' Jack Flash" promo film.

MAY 26, 1968

PROGRAM: Late Night Line-Up (BBC-TV)
WHERE BROADCAST: UK
PERSONNEL: Charlie Watts
SONGS/OTHER CONTENT: Watts interview
NOTES: Interview with Charlie Watts.

JUNE 6, 1968

PROGRAM: Top of the Pops
WHERE BROADCAST: UK
SONGS/OTHER CONTENT: Jumpin' Jack Flash
NOTES: Repeat airing of "Jumpin' Jack Flash" promo film.

JUNE 22, 1968

PROGRAM: Beat Club
WHERE BROADCAST: Germany
SONGS/OTHER CONTENT: Jumpin' Jack Flash
NOTES: Promo film

JUNE 27, 1968

PROGRAM: Top of the Pops
WHERE BROADCAST: UK
SONGS/OTHER CONTENT: Jumpin' Jack Flash
NOTES: Airing of the "Jumpin' Jack Flash" promo film, as edited by "Top of the Pops." The show added its own inserts of still photos and film footage of dancers to the Stones' promo.

SEPTEMBER 6, 1968

PROGRAM: David Frost
WHERE BROADCAST: UK
PERSONNEL: Mick Jagger
SONGS/OTHER CONTENT: Jagger interview
NOTES: David Frost interviewed Mick Jagger.

OCTOBER 8, 1968

PROGRAM NAME: It's Happening

WHERE BROADCAST: USA
PERSONNEL: Mick Jagger
SONGS/OTHER CONTENT: Jagger interview
NOTES: Mick was interviewed in Los Angeles for this locally syndicated US weekday show (a weekend version was titled "Happening '68." The only known Stones appearance on US television in 1968.

NOVEMBER 30, 1968

PROGRAM: Frost on Saturday
WHERE BROADCAST: UK
PERSONNEL: Mick Jagger, Keith Richards, Brian Jones, Charlie Watts, Bill Wyman, Rocky Dijon (congas)
SONGS/OTHER CONTENT: Sympathy for the Devil
NOTES: The last broadcast appearance of Brian Jones with the Rolling Stones on a non-news television show. He played keyboards, Keith Richards played guitar and a bit of tambourine. Taped the preceding day in London.

DECEMBER 5, 1968

PROGRAM: News-UK
WHERE BROADCAST: UK
PERSONNEL: Mick Jagger, Brian Jones, Charlie Watts, Bill Wyman
SONGS/OTHER CONTENT: News coverage
NOTES: The British press covered the *Beggars Banquet* LP press reception at the Gore Hotel, London, specifically the famous pie-throwing stunt/promotion. Keith Richards, absent for most of the event, did amble into the hotel at the very end. Most, if not all, television cameras missed him, but some still photos confirm his presence.

DECEMBER 10–12, 1968
(NEVER BROADCAST)

PROGRAM: The Rolling Stones' Rock 'n' Roll Circus
PERSONNEL: Mick Jagger, Keith Richards, Brian Jones, Charlie Watts, Bill Wyman, Ian Stewart, Rocky Dijon, Eric Clapton, The Who, Marianne Faithfull, Jethro Tull, Taj Mahal, Donyale Luna, Mitch Mitchell, John Lennon, Yoko Ono, Ivry Gitlis, Julius Katchen, clowns, jugglers, animals
SONGS/OTHER CONTENT: *Route 66* (Troup) / *Confessin' the Blues* (McShann, Brown) / Jumpin' Jack Flash / Parachute Woman / You Can't Always Get What You Want / No Expectations / Sympathy for the Devil / Salt of the Earth / *Yonder Wall* (Clark) / *Walkin' Blues* (Trad.) / Yer Blues (Lennon, McCartney) / Whole Lotta Yoko (Ono, Lennon)
NOTES: These were the dates of the filming, at London's InterTel Studios, of the Stones' proposed television special, its release and the absence thereof long the subject of myth, rumor, speculation, and even ordinary discussion.

For various reasons, the show never got past an initial rough cut and so was never officially released as planned. Then in August 1996, it was officially announced that the film would be premiered at the New York Film Festival in October of 1996. Stones followers were amazed and a ticket rush was expected. Song titles listed in italics above were not included in ABKCO's finished product. But the two songs performed by the Dirty Mac Band (the RNR Circus's instant "supergroup" of Lennon, Ono, Mitchell, Gitlis, Clapton and Richards) were retained. The InterTel taping was the last time any audience saw Brian Jones performing with the Rolling Stones. (See PROMOTIONAL FILMS AND VIDEOS)

1969

From 1969 through 1974, the band consisted of Mick Jagger (voc, gtr, harm), Keith Richards (gtr, bass, voc), Mick Taylor (gtr, bass, voc, pi), Charlie Watts (ds), Bill Wyman (bs).

JULY 7, 1969

PROGRAM: David Frost Show (US)
WHERE BROADCAST: USA
SONGS/OTHER CONTENT: You Can't Always Get What You Want
NOTES: Taped June 16, 1969 in England.

JULY 10, 1969

PROGRAM: Top of the Pops
WHERE BROADCAST: UK
SONGS/OTHER CONTENT: Honky Tonk Women
NOTES: Taped July 3, 1969

JULY 17, 1969

PROGRAM: Top of the Pops
WHERE BROADCAST: UK
SONGS/OTHER CONTENT: Honky Tonk Women
NOTES: Taped July 3, 1969

JULY 31, 1969

PROGRAM: Top of the Pops
WHERE BROADCAST: UK
SONGS/OTHER CONTENT: Honky Tonk Women
NOTES: Taped July 3, 1969

AUGUST 7, 1969

PROGRAM: Top of the Pops
WHERE BROADCAST: UK
PERSONNEL: Mick Jagger

SONGS/OTHER CONTENT: Jagger interview
NOTES: Interview of Mick Jagger only; taped in June 1969.

AUGUST 21, 1969

PROGRAM: David Frost Show
WHERE BROADCAST: USA
SONGS/OTHER CONTENT: Honky Tonk Women
NOTES: Taped June 16, 1969 in England.

SEPTEMBER 2, 1969

PROGRAM: Hyde Park Concert (Granada TV)
WHERE BROADCAST: UK
PERSONNEL: Mick Jagger, Keith Richards, Mick Taylor, Charlie Watts, Bill Wyman, Ian Stewart, Rocky Dijon, Ginger Johnson & His African Drummers
SONGS/OTHER CONTENT: Concert/Behind-the-scenes
NOTES: One hour broadcast of Granada TV's documentary coverage of the Stones' July 5 free concert in Hyde Park. (See PROMOTIONAL FILMS AND VIDEOS and TOURS AND CONCERTS)

NOVEMBER 23, 1969

PROGRAM: Ed Sullivan Show
WHERE BROADCAST: USA
SONGS/OTHER CONTENT: Honky Tonk Women / Gimme Shelter / Love in Vain (Robt. Johnson)
NOTES: Taped November 18, 1969 in Los Angeles.

DECEMBER 8, 1969

PROGRAM: Newswatch - KRON-TV
WHERE BROADCAST: San Francisco, CA, USA
SONGS/OTHER CONTENT: Jumpin' Jack Flash / Carol (Berry) / Sympathy for the Devil / overall Altamont coverage / footage of Santana performance

Keith Richards, rock 'n' roll's first astronaut. (JAMES KARNBACH COLLECTION)

NOTES: This was an hour-long special on Altamont produced by KRON, the San Francisco NBC affiliate station. It included overall coverage of the event and its participants (on- and offstage), performance footage of Santana at Altamont, as well as the Stones' Altamont performance of the songs listed above.

DECEMBER 21, 1969

PROGRAM: Ed Sullivan Show
WHERE BROADCAST: USA
SONGS/OTHER CONTENT: Honky Tonk Women / Gimme Shelter / Love in Vain (Robt. Johnson)
NOTES: *Repeat* broadcast of the November 23, 1969 "Ed Sullivan Show."

DECEMBER 25, 1969

PROGRAM: Top of the Pops (Christmas Special)
WHERE BROADCAST: UK
SONGS/OTHER CONTENT: Gimme Shelter / Honky Tonk Women
NOTES: "Honky Tonk Women" and "Gimme Shelter" were both taped on December 12, 1969 in London.

DECEMBER 27, 1969

PROGRAM: Child Of The 60s (London Weekend Television)
WHERE BROADCAST: UK
PERSONNEL: Mick Jagger, Keith Richards, Brian Jones, Mick Taylor, Charlie Watts, Bill Wyman
SONGS/OTHER CONTENT: Newsreel footage/Interviews
NOTES: Stones content was in the form of newsreel footage and interviews with band members.

DECEMBER 28, 1969

PROGRAM: BBC's Ten Years of What
WHERE BROADCAST: UK
PERSONNEL: Mick Jagger, Keith Richards, Brian Jones, Charlie Watts, Bill Wyman
SONGS/OTHER CONTENT: Let's Spend the Night Together
NOTES: The song was a 1967 clip from "Top of the Pops."

DECEMBER 31, 1969

PROGRAM: POP Goes the 60s
WHERE BROADCAST: UK
PERSONNEL: Mick Jagger, Keith Richards, Mick Taylor, Charlie Watts, Bill Wyman
SONGS/OTHER CONTENT: Gimme Shelter
NOTES: Taped on December 12, 1969.

1970

MARCH 5, 1970

PROGRAM: Top of the Pops
WHERE BROADCAST: UK
SONGS/OTHER CONTENT: Unknown
NOTES: Unknown songs

SEPTEMBER 15, 1970

PROGRAM: Old Grey Whistle Test
WHERE BROADCAST: UK
SONGS/OTHER CONTENT: Interview / News footage
NOTES: Taped interview with the Stones, plus newsreel footage insert.

SEPTEMBER 23, 1970

PROGRAM: Unknown title (French TV)
WHERE BROADCAST: France
PERSONNEL: Mick Jagger
SONGS/OTHER CONTENT: Jagger interview
NOTES: The name of the show was unknown at the time of writing. Mick spoke French.

OCTOBER 9, 1970

PROGRAM: Twenty-four Hours
WHERE BROADCAST: UK
PERSONNEL: Mick Jagger
SONGS/OTHER CONTENT: Memo from Turner, JV / Jagger interview
NOTES: Mick Jagger was interviewed about his role in the movie *Performance*, which included his performance of "Memo from Turner." A clip from that scene in the movie was shown.

1971

JANUARY 15, 1971

PROGRAM: BBC-TV
WHERE BROADCAST: UK
PERSONNEL: Mick Jagger
SONGS/OTHER CONTENT: Jagger interview
NOTES: Jagger interviewed about the film, *Performance*.

APRIL 15, 1971

PROGRAM: Top of the Pops
WHERE BROADCAST: UK
SONGS/OTHER CONTENT: Brown Sugar / Bitch / Wild Horses

NOTES: This was repeated on April 22, 1971 (one week later).

APRIL 22, 1971

PROGRAM: Top of the Pops
WHERE BROADCAST: UK
SONGS/OTHER CONTENT: Brown Sugar / Bitch / Wild Horses
NOTES: The repeat of the Stones segment from previous week's show.

MAY 24, 1971

PROGRAM: Hyde Park Concert (Granada TV)
WHERE BROADCAST: UK
PERSONNEL: Mick Jagger, Keith Richards, Mick Taylor, Charlie Watts, Bill Wyman, Ian Stewart, Rocky Dijon, Ginger Johnson & His African Drummers
SONGS/OTHER CONTENT: Concert/ Behind-the-scenes
NOTES: Repeat broadcast of the one-hour Hyde Park concert show originally aired on September 2, 1969. (See PROMOTIONAL FILMS AND VIDEOS and TOURS AND CONCERTS)

JUNE 5, 1971

PROGRAM: Ladies & Gentlemen, the Rolling Stones—Live at the Marquee (Special)
WHERE BROADCAST: UK
PERSONNEL: Mick Jagger, Keith Richards, Mick Taylor, Charlie Watts, Bill Wyman, Ian Stewart, Nicky Hopkins, Bobby Keys, Jim Price
SONGS/OTHER CONTENT: Live with Me / Dead Flowers / I Got the Blues / Let It Rock (Anderson) / Midnight Rambler / (I Can't Get No) Satisfaction / Bitch / Brown Sugar
NOTES: The Stones' last gig before exiling themselves from Britain was filmed before an audience of family and friends in two shows on March 26, 1971 at London's Marquee Jazz Club, where they'd done their very first gig in 1962. This 28-minute UK program was shorter than the 52-minutes aired in the rest of Europe. Neither cut was broadcast in the US.

SEPTEMBER 21, 1971

PROGRAM: Old Grey Whistle Test
WHERE BROADCAST: UK
SONGS/OTHER CONTENT: Unknown

OCTOBER 27, 1971

PROGRAM: Beaton on Bailey (BBC)
WHERE BROADCAST: UK
PERSONNEL: Mick Jagger

SONGS/OTHER CONTENT: Interview
NOTES: Mick Jagger was interviewed in this documentary special about photographers Cecil Beaton and David Bailey.

DECEMBER 7, 1971

PROGRAM: Old Grey Whistle Test
WHERE BROADCAST: UK
SONGS/OTHER CONTENT: Honky Tonk Women
NOTES: A clip of the Stones performing "Honky Tonk Women" from the movie, *Gimme Shelter*. (See PROMOTIONAL FILMS AND VIDEOS)

DECEMBER 30, 1971

PROGRAM: Top of the Pops
WHERE BROADCAST: UK
SONGS/OTHER CONTENT: Brown Sugar / Bitch / Wild Horses
NOTES: The Stones segment, originally broadcast on April 15, 1971, was included in this "Top of the Pops" year-end wrap-up show.

1972

APRIL 25, 1972

PROGRAM: Old Grey Whistle Test
WHERE BROADCAST: UK
PERSONNEL: Mick Jagger
SONGS/OTHER CONTENT: Jagger interview
NOTES: Jagger was interviewed about the making of *Exile on Main Street*, mostly.

MAY 21, 1972

PROGRAM: Top of the Pops
WHERE BROADCAST: UK
SONGS/OTHER CONTENT: Tumbling Dice
NOTES: This clip was filmed at the Stones' Montreux rehearsals for their 1972 North American tour.

MAY 27, 1972

PROGRAM: Old Grey Whistle Test
WHERE BROADCAST: UK
SONGS/OTHER CONTENT: Tumbling Dice / Shake Your Hips (Moore) / Tumbling Dice #2 / Jam #1 / Jam #2
NOTES: All songs were performed live and filmed at Montreux rehearsals.

JUNE 3, 1972

PROGRAM: Local show—title unknown
WHERE BROADCAST: Vancouver, BC, Canada
SONGS/OTHER CONTENT: Interview
NOTES: Interview segment concerning the Stones' current tour. No other information is known.

JUNE 24, 1972

PROGRAM: Old Grey Whistle Test
WHERE BROADCAST: UK
SONGS/OTHER CONTENT: Loving Cup / Jam
NOTES: Includes footage of the band miming "Loving Cup" to playback with live vocal, and jamming on the tune. From material shot at Montreux rehearsals.

JULY 11, 1972

PROGRAM: Old Grey Whistle Test
WHERE BROADCAST: UK
PERSONNEL: Mick Jagger, Keith Richards, Brian Jones, Mick Taylor, Charlie Watts, Bill Wyman
SONGS/OTHER CONTENT: I Am Waiting / Under My Thumb / Paint It, Black / Have You Seen Your Mother, Baby, Standing in the Shadow? / Jumpin' Jack Flash / Honky Tonk Women
NOTES: 1966 clip from "Ready, Steady, Go!," showing first three songs; "Have You Seen Your Mother, Baby?" promo; scenes/songs from the free Hyde Park concert and *Gimme Shelter* film. Plus, footage of Stones '72 tour rehearsals in Montreux, Switzerland on May 21, 1972.

AUGUST 4, 1972

PROGRAM: Dick Cavett Show
WHERE BROADCAST: US
SONGS/OTHER CONTENT: Brown Sugar / Street Fighting Man / Wyman and Jagger interviews
NOTES: Footage from the Stones' July 25, 1972 afternoon show at Madison Square Garden—the band performed "Brown Sugar" and "Street Fighting Man"—plus Dick Cavett's backstage interviews with Mick Jagger and Bill Wyman.

SEPTEMBER 5, 1972

PROGRAM: RTL (Belgian TV)
WHERE BROADCAST: Belgium
PERSONNEL: Mick Jagger, Keith Richards
SONGS/OTHER CONTENT: Jagger and Richards interviews

NOVEMBER 7, 1972

PROGRAM: Old Grey Whistle Test
WHERE BROADCAST: UK

SONGS/OTHER CONTENT: All Down the Line
NOTES: "All Down the Line" promo shown. The live '72 US tour performance was the basis of that promo.

1973

JANUARY 23, 1973

PROGRAM: Old Grey Whistle Test
WHERE BROADCAST: UK
SONGS/OTHER CONTENT: Happy / All Down the Line
NOTES: The songs in these promos were live performances filmed during the '72 tour.

FEBRUARY 21, 1973

PROGRAM: Beat Club
WHERE BROADCAST: UK
SONGS/OTHER CONTENT: Rip This Joint

FEBRUARY 26, 1973

PROGRAM: Australian TV
WHERE BROADCAST: Australia
SONGS/OTHER CONTENT: Band interviews
NOTES: Interviews with band members

FEBRUARY 26, 1973

PROGRAM: ABC-TV Australian Tour Documentary
WHERE BROADCAST: Australia
SONGS/OTHER CONTENT: Documentary
NOTES: A 30-minute documentary on the Stones' '73 Australian tour.

JULY 17, 1973

PROGRAM: Top of the Pops
WHERE BROADCAST: UK
SONGS/OTHER CONTENT: Silver Train / Dancing with Mr. D / Angie
NOTES: Promo films aired.

SEPTEMBER 4, 1973

PROGRAM: German TV—Koln, Germany
WHERE BROADCAST: Germany
SONGS/OTHER CONTENT: Gimme Shelter

SEPTEMBER 14, 1973

PROGRAM: Midnight Special
WHERE BROADCAST: USA
SONGS/OTHER CONTENT: Happy / Tumbling Dice / Midnight Rambler

NOTES: These songs appeared in film clips from *Ladies & Gentlemen, the Rolling Stones* and were aired on this syndicated US late-night show.

SEPTEMBER 22, 1973

PROGRAM: Music Machine CBC-TV
WHERE BROADCAST: Canada
SONGS/OTHER CONTENT: Angie
NOTES: Promo clip

SEPTEMBER 28, 1973

PROGRAM: Katschup
WHERE BROADCAST: Germany
SONGS/OTHER CONTENT: Brown Sugar / Gimme Shelter / Street Fighting Man / Interview
NOTES: Also included a band interview.

SEPTEMBER 29, 1973

PROGRAM: Don Kirshner's Rock Concert
WHERE BROADCAST: USA
SONGS/OTHER CONTENT: Angie V1 / Silver Train / Dancing with Mr. D / Angie V2
NOTES: Promos for *Goat's Head Soup* LP. Taped in July 1973. Included two versions of "Angie."

OCTOBER 1, 1973

PROGRAM: Top Pop (AVRO)
WHERE BROADCAST: The Netherlands
SONGS/OTHER CONTENT: Angie
NOTES: "Top Pop" was a Dutch television program and should not be confused with the UK "Top of the Pops." This was an airing of an "Angie" promo film.

OCTOBER 2, 1973

PROGRAM: Old Grey Whistle Test
WHERE BROADCAST: UK
PERSONNEL: Mick Jagger
SONGS/OTHER CONTENT: Silver Train / Dancing with Mr. D / Jagger interview
NOTES: Promo films of both songs plus an interview with Mick Jagger.

OCTOBER 3, 1973

PROGRAM: Musikladen
WHERE BROADCAST: Germany
SONGS/OTHER CONTENT: Silver Train / Angie
NOTES: Promos

OCTOBER 4, 1973

PROGRAM: Top of the Pops

WHERE BROADCAST: UK
PERSONNEL: Mick Jagger
SONGS/OTHER CONTENT: Promo spot
NOTES: Mick Jagger did a promo spot *for* "Top of the Pops" *on* "Top of the Pops."

OCTOBER 12, 1973

PROGRAM: Dutch TV—program title unknown
WHERE BROADCAST: The Netherlands
PERSONNEL: Mick Jagger, Keith Richards, Mick Taylor
SONGS/OTHER CONTENT: Interview
NOTES: The three Stones were interviewed by Elly de Waard.

OCTOBER 23, 1973

PROGRAM: Old Grey Whistle Test
WHERE BROADCAST: UK
PERSONNEL: Mick Jagger, Keith Richards, Mick Taylor, Charlie Watts, Bill Wyman, Bobby Keys (sax), Jim Price (tpt), Trevor Lawrence (sax), Steve Madaio (tpt), Billy Preston (kb)
SONGS/OTHER CONTENT: Street Fighting Man / Billy Preston interview
NOTES: The promo film for "Street Fighting Man," shot at the Stones' live performance in Frankfurt on September 30, 1973 was shown, along with an interview with Billy Preston.

1974

FEBRUARY 16, 1974

PROGRAM: News conference
WHERE BROADCAST: USA
PERSONNEL: Vice President Gerald Ford
SONGS/OTHER CONTENT: News
NOTES: In response to a reporter's question, Gerald R. Ford, US Vice President at the time, stated that he had never heard of Mick Jagger and asked, "Isn't he the motorcycle rider or something?"

MAY 1974

PROGRAM: Don Kirshner's Rock Concert
WHERE BROADCAST: USA
PERSONNEL: Bill Wyman
SONGS/OTHER CONTENT: White Lightnin' (Wyman) / I Wanna Get Me a Gun (Wyman) / What a Blow (Wyman) / Monkey Grip Glue (Wyman)
NOTES: Wyman's *Monkey Grip* album promos.

MAY 8, 1974

PROGRAM: Old Grey Whistle Test
WHERE BROADCAST: UK
PERSONNEL: Bill Wyman
SONGS/OTHER CONTENT: White Lightnin' (Wyman) / Wyman interview
NOTES: Interview with Wyman about his *Monkey Grip* album plus airing of "White Lightnin'" promo.

MAY 25, 1974

PROGRAM: Speak Easy
WHERE BROADCAST: USA
PERSONNEL: Mick Jagger, Keith Richards, Mick Taylor, Charlie Watts, Bill Wyman
SONGS/OTHER CONTENT: You Can't Always Get What You Want / Midnight Rambler / Wyman interview
NOTES: The songs are clips from the film *Ladies & Gentlemen, the Rolling Stones.* There is also an interview with Bill Wyman in the Speak Easy studios with host Chip Monck. Dr. John also appeared on this show.

JULY 9, 1974

PROGRAM: Old Grey Whistle Test
WHERE BROADCAST: UK
PERSONNEL: Mick Jagger, Keith Richards, Brian Jones, Mick Taylor, Charlie Watts, Bill Wyman
SONGS/OTHER CONTENT: Around & Around (Berry) / Off the Hook (Nanker Phelge) / Time Is on My Side (Meade) / It's All Over Now (Womack, Womack) / I'm Alright (McDaniel) / It's Only Rock 'n' Roll
NOTES: IORR promo film. The other songs are contained in archival footage of the Stones on the T.A.M.I. show of October 28, 1964.

AUGUST 8, 1974

PROGRAM: Top of the Pops
WHERE BROADCAST: UK
SONGS/OTHER CONTENT: It's Only Rock 'n' Roll
NOTES: Promo film

SEPTEMBER 13, 1974

PROGRAM: Midnight Special
WHERE BROADCAST: USA
SONGS/OTHER CONTENT: Happy / Tumbling Dice / Midnight Rambler
NOTES: Clips from *Ladies & Gentlemen, the Rolling Stones.*

OCTOBER 1, 1974

PROGRAM: Old Grey Whistle Test
WHERE BROADCAST: UK

PERSONNEL: Keith Richards
SONGS/OTHER CONTENT: Ain't Too Proud to Beg (Whitfield, Holland) / Richards interview
NOTES: Promo film, plus an interview with Keith.

OCTOBER 19, 1974

PROGRAM: Don Kirshner's Rock Concert
WHERE BROADCAST: USA
SONGS/OTHER CONTENT: It's Only Rock 'n' Roll / Ain't Too Proud to Beg (Whitfield, Holland) / Till the Next Goodbye / All Down the Line / Bye Bye Johnny (Berry) / Love in Vain (Robt. Johnson)
NOTES: The last three songs came from footage of live 1972 tour performances.

DECEMBER 1974

PROGRAM: Jukebox (French TV)
WHERE BROADCAST: France
SONGS/OTHER CONTENT: Unknown

1975

From May 1, 1975 through 1992, the band consisted (unofficially, then officially) of Mick Jagger, Keith Richards, Ron Wood, Charlie Watts, Bill Wyman. 1975 is one year in which program information is particularly chaotic. After Mick Taylor's resignation in December of 1974, there was a five-month transitional period for the Stones; Taylor made his own appearances, and Stones promos from the past five-years were aired in which Taylor, naturally, appeared. Where possible, we have tried to provide amplified information under Personnel as well as in the Songs/Other Content and Notes categories in the potentially confusing instances.

JANUARY 10, 1975

PROGRAM: Old Grey Whistle Test
WHERE BROADCAST: UK
PERSONNEL: Mick Taylor
SONGS/OTHER CONTENT: Interview
NOTES: Mick Taylor was interviewed about leaving the Stones. Bassist Jack Bruce, with whom Taylor has announced he will be working, was also present for the interview.

JANUARY 11 , 1975

PROGRAM: Jukebox (French TV)
WHERE BROADCAST: France
PERSONNEL: Mick Jagger, Keith Richards, Mick Taylor, Charlie Watts, Bill Wyman

SONGS/OTHER CONTENT: Interview and promos

FEBRUARY 5, 1975

PROGRAM: Musikladen

WHERE BROADCAST: Germany

PERSONNEL: Mick Jagger, Keith Richards, Mick Taylor, Charlie Watts, Bill Wyman

SONGS/OTHER CONTENT: Ain't Too Proud to Beg (Whitfield, Holland)

NOTES: Promo

JUNE 19, 1975

PROGRAM: Good Night America

WHERE BROADCAST: USA

PERSONNEL: Mick Jagger, Keith Richards, Ron Wood, Brian Jones, Charlie Watts, Bill Wyman

SONGS/OTHER CONTENT: All Down the Line / Honky Tonk Women / Have You Seen Your Mother, Baby, Standing in the Shadow? / Jagger interview

NOTES: "All Down the Line" and "Honky Tonk Women" as filmed in the Stones' 1975 tour rehearsals in Baton Rouge, Los Angeles on June 1, and Jagger interview. The "Have You Seen Your Mother, Baby" promo was also aired.

JUNE 6, 1975

PROGRAM: Old Grey Whistle Test

WHERE BROADCAST: UK

PERSONNEL: Jack Bruce Band: Mick Taylor (guitar), Jack Bruce (vocals, bass), Carla Bley (vocals, keyboards), Bruce Gary (drums), Ronnie Leahy (keyboards)

SONGS/OTHER CONTENT: Can You Follow / Morning Story / Keep It Down / Pieces of Mind / One Spirit / Without a Word / Smiles & Grins

NOTES: The Jack Bruce Band with Mick Taylor, his first stop after leaving the Stones the previous December, performs on British television.

NOVEMBER 18, 1975

PROGRAM: Old Grey Whistle Test

WHERE BROADCAST: UK

PERSONNEL: Mick Jagger, Keith Richards, Ron Wood, Charlie Watts, Bill Wyman

SONGS/OTHER CONTENT: Jumpin' Jack Flash

1976

APRIL–JUNE 1976

PROGRAM: *Black & Blue* promos

WHERE BROADCAST: Europe (various programs, countries)

SONGS/OTHER CONTENT: Crazy Mama / Hot Stuff / Hey Negrita / Fool to Cry

NOTES: Four promos from the Stones' *Black & Blue* LP were aired all over Europe during this period.

MAY 4, 1976

PROGRAM: Musikladen

WHERE BROADCAST: Germany

PERSONNEL: Bill Wyman

SONGS/OTHER CONTENT: Apache Woman (Wyman)

NOTES: Bill Wyman, solo.

MAY 14–15, 1976

PROGRAM: Stones on the Road (Thames TV)

WHERE BROADCAST: UK

SONGS/OTHER CONTENT: Street Fighting Man / Honky Tonk Women / Star Star / Midnight Rambler / Brown Sugar / It's Only Rock 'n' Roll / Jumpin' Jack Flash / Interviews

NOTES: Taped at the Rolling Stones' performances on these dates at the Apollo Theatre in Glasgow, and Grandby Hall in Leicester, this Thames TV special was directed by Bruce Gowers and produced by David Elstein. It was most likely aired sometime in June or July 1976.

MAY 20, 1976

PROGRAM: Top of the Pops

WHERE BROADCAST: UK

SONGS/OTHER CONTENT: Fool to Cry

NOTES: Promo film aired.

JUNE 3, 1976

PROGRAM: Top of the Pops

WHERE BROADCAST: UK

SONGS/OTHER CONTENT: Fool to Cry

NOTES: Repeat airing of promo, as on May 20.

JUNE 3, 1976

PROGRAM: (French TV Antenne-2) EMI Campus

WHERE BROADCAST: France

PERSONNEL: Mick Jagger, Keith Richards, Ron Wood

SONGS/OTHER CONTENT: Interview

NOTES: French TV interviews three Rolling Stones— Mick, Keith and Ronnie.

(PROBABLY) LATE JULY/ EARLY AUGUST 1976

PROGRAM: Les Rolling Stones aux Abattoirs (three broadcasts on French TV Antenne-2)

WHERE BROADCAST: France

SONGS/OTHER CONTENT: Hand of Fate / Honky Tonk Women / Fool to Cry / Hot Stuff / Star Star / You Gotta Move (McDowell, Davis) / You Can't Always Get What You Want / Outta Space (Preston, Green) / Jumpin' Jack Flash / Street Fighting Man / Tumbling Dice / Midnight Rambler / Angie / It's Only Rock 'n' Roll / Brown Sugar / If You Can't Rock Me → Get Off of My Cloud, LMV / Hey Negrita

NOTES: French TV's coverage of the Stones' June 4, 6, and 7 Paris concerts was broken up into three segments aired later in the summer of 1976. The first program was about an hour in long and featured the portion of the set running from "Honky Tonk Women" to "Street Fighting Man" in the above order. The second segment contained "Tumbling Dice" to "Brown Sugar." Sometime later, "Honky Tonk Women," the "If You Can't Rock Me → Get Off of My Cloud" medley, "Hand of Fate" and "Hey Negrita" were aired as the third Les Abattoirs show.

1977

1977

PROGRAM: Aspekte (ZDF-German TV)

WHERE BROADCAST: Germany

PERSONNEL: Mick Jagger

SONGS/OTHER CONTENT: Jagger interview

NOTES: Interview with Mick featured on this German program.

JANUARY/FEBRUARY 1977

PROGRAM: Merv Griffin Show

WHERE BROADCAST: USA

PERSONNEL: Billy Preston, Ron Wood

SONGS/OTHER CONTENT: Outta Space (Preston, Green)

NOTES: Billy Preston and his band, with Ron Wood.

FEBRUARY 5, 1977

PROGRAM: Soul Train

WHERE BROADCAST: USA

PERSONNEL: Billy Preston, Ron Wood

SONGS/OTHER CONTENT: Outta Space (Preston, Green)

NOTES: Billy Preston and his band appeared on "Soul Train" with guest guitarist, Ron Wood.

APRIL 1977

PROGRAM: Midnight Special

WHERE BROADCAST: USA

PERSONNEL: Van Morrison, Ollie Brown

NOTES: Van Morrison appeared with Stones sideman Ollie Brown on drums. Brown toured with the Stones during '75 and '76 and had recently played with them at El Mocambo in Toronto.

SEPTEMBER 20, 1977

PROGRAM: Old Grey Whistle Test

WHERE BROADCAST: UK

SONGS/OTHER CONTENT: Les Abattoirs Concert / Interviews

NOTES: One-hour broadcast of 1976 concert at Les Abattoirs in Paris, plus interviews with Mick, Ron and Charlie on that and other subjects.

1978

JUNE 6, 1978

PROGRAM: 20/20

WHERE BROADCAST: USA

SONGS/OTHER CONTENT: Teaser

NOTES: Brief spot on the Stones' 1978 tour on ABC-TV's 20/20, aired as a tease for Geraldo Rivera's more extensive story aired on June 20.

JUNE 8, 1978

PROGRAM: Top of the Pops

WHERE BROADCAST: UK

SONGS/OTHER CONTENT: Miss You

NOTES: Promo film

JUNE 20, 1978

PROGRAM: 20/20

WHERE BROADCAST: USA

PERSONNEL: Mick Jagger, Keith Richards, Ron Wood, Charlie Watts, Bill Wyman

SONGS/OTHER CONTENT: When the Whip Comes Down / Respectable / Far Away Eyes / Miss You

NOTES: ABC-TV's 20/20. Geraldo Rivera interviewed the Rolling Stones in pretour rehearsal at Bearsville, NY on June 4, 1978, playing "Whip Comes Down." Three promos—"Respectable," "Far Away Eyes" and "Miss You"—were also included in this 20/20 telecast. The 1978 tour had been running for 10 days by June 20.

JULY 25, 1978

PROGRAM: America Alive

WHERE BROADCAST: USA

PERSONNEL: Mick Jagger

SONGS/OTHER CONTENT: Jagger interview

NOTES: Mick was interviewed while in Los Angeles for this syndicated program.

JULY 26, 1978

PROGRAM: Good Morning America
WHERE BROADCAST: USA
PERSONNEL: Mick Jagger
SONGS/OTHER CONTENT: Jagger interview
NOTES: Mick was interviewed—more tour promotion—on ABC's network morning show.

OCTOBER 7, 1978

PROGRAM: Saturday Night Live
WHERE BROADCAST: USA
SONGS/OTHER CONTENT: Beast of Burden / Shattered / Respectable / Skits
NOTES: The Stones performed three songs, Mick and Charlie scampered in skits. Originally, all five Stones were in a skit with John Belushi, but censors deemed the druggy content too "off color" for broadcast after the 7:30 P.M. dress rehearsal. What with Keith's Canadian drug trial coming up, it was probably a good thing. Belushi played the guardian of the backstage guest list at a Stones concert, Keith played himself. They talked about whether Keith would be doing a fictional February gig with Lou Rawls at the "Afro Dome" in Salisbury, Rhodesia (now Harare, Zimbabwe). Keith's response became one of those seeds that sprout into rumor and grow into myth. "I can't," he said, "every February I have to go to Switzerland to get my blood changed."

OCTOBER 19, 1978

PROGRAM: Top of the Pops
WHERE BROADCAST: UK
SONGS/OTHER CONTENT: Respectable
NOTES: Promo film aired.

Keith Richards with Bill Murray (left), Paul Shaffer (who looks like Paul Simon), and John Belushi (far right) on "Saturday Night Live." (JAMES KARNBACH COLLECTION)

OCTOBER 24, 1978

PROGRAM: Old Grey Whistle Test
WHERE BROADCAST: UK
PERSONNEL: Mick Jagger
SONGS/OTHER CONTENT: Jagger interview
NOTES: Interview with Jagger on various subjects.

NOVEMBER 7, 1978

PROGRAM: Old Grey Whistle Test
WHERE BROADCAST: UK
PERSONNEL: Peter Tosh, Mick Jagger
SONGS/OTHER CONTENT: (You Gotta Walk) Don't Look Back (Robinson, White) (promo film)
NOTES: Peter Tosh's promo of "Don't Look Back," which includes a cameo appearance by Mick Jagger.

NOVEMBER 19, 1978

PROGRAM: Rockline (BBC-TV)
WHERE BROADCAST: UK
PERSONNEL: Mick Jagger
SONGS/OTHER CONTENT: Jagger interview
NOTES: Mick Jagger was interviewed by Anne Nightingale.

DECEMBER 16, 1978

PROGRAM: Saturday Night Live
WHERE BROADCAST: USA
PERSONNEL: Peter Tosh, Mick Jagger
SONGS/OTHER CONTENT: (You Gotta Walk) Don't Look Back (Robinson, White)
NOTES: Peter Tosh did "Don't Look Back" and Mick joined him onstage.

1979

FEBRUARY 9, 1979

PROGRAM: Heroes of Rock 'n' Roll
WHERE BROADCAST: USA
PERSONNEL: Mick Jagger, Keith Richards, Brian Jones, Charlie Watts, Bill Wyman
SONGS/OTHER CONTENT: Around & Around (Berry) / (I Can't Get No) Satisfaction / Jumpin' Jack Flash / Archival news and performance footage
NOTES: The eight-minute Rolling Stones segment in this two-hour historical program consisted of a montage of press coverage, television appearances and promotional films from 1964 to 1968. The first major prime-time documentary on rock 'n' roll to appear on US television.

MARCH 20, 1979

PROGRAM: Mike Douglas Show
WHERE BROADCAST: USA
SONGS/OTHER CONTENT: Unknown

MAY 8, 1979

PROGRAM: Old Grey Whistle Test
WHERE BROADCAST: UK
PERSONNEL: Ron Wood, Bobby Keys (sax), Ringo Starr (drums), Ian McLagan (kb)
SONGS/OTHER CONTENT: Buried Alive (Wood)
NOTES: Ron Wood's solo promo (he played guitar and did vocals while his friends backed him up) was aired.

JUNE 8, 1979

PROGRAM: Midnight Special
WHERE BROADCAST: USA
PERSONNEL: Ron Wood, Bobby Keys (sax), Ringo Starr (drums), Ian McLagan (kb)
SONGS/OTHER CONTENT: Buried Alive (Wood)
NOTES: Ron Wood's promo film.

JULY 13, 1979

PROGRAM: PM Magazine
WHERE BROADCAST: USA
PERSONNEL: Ron Wood
SONGS/OTHER CONTENT: Interview
NOTES: Wood was interviewed for this syndicated show.

SEPTEMBER 2, 1979

PROGRAM: Jerry Lewis Telethon
WHERE BROADCAST: USA
PERSONNEL: Bill Wyman, Kiki Dee, Ringo Starr, Todd Rundgren, Dave Mason
SONGS/OTHER CONTENT: Money (Gordy Jr., Bradford) / Jumpin' Jack Flash / Twist & Shout (Berns) / Miss You
NOTES: An all-star band featuring Bill Wyman, Kiki Dee, Ringo Starr, Todd Rundgren and Dave Mason performed five songs, three of which are listed above, on "Jerry Lewis's Telethon for Muscular Dystrophy." The Stones' "Miss You" promo was aired.

OCTOBER 2, 1979

PROGRAM: Old Grey Whistle Test
WHERE BROADCAST: UK
PERSONNEL: Mick Taylor
SONGS/OTHER CONTENT: Taylor interview
NOTES: Interview with Mick Taylor on the release of his solo LP, *Mick Taylor*, plus various past, present and future subjects.

OCTOBER 9, 1979

PROGRAM: The Cleo Laine Show (BBC)
WHERE BROADCAST: UK
PERSONNEL: Charlie Watts, Charly Antolini, Tony Williams
SONGS/OTHER CONTENT: Drum solos
NOTES: Charlie and two other drummers demonstrated the art and their own styles. Sort of a "drum-off."

OCTOBER 21, 1979

PROGRAM: The History of Television
WHERE BROADCAST: USA
PERSONNEL: Mick Jagger, Keith Richards, Brian Jones, Charlie Watts, Bill Wyman
SONGS/OTHER CONTENT: (I Can't Get No) Satisfaction
NOTES: A clip of the Stones performing "Satisfaction" on the "Ed Sullivan Show" was used in ABC-TV's historical look at its own medium.

DECEMBER 1979

PROGRAM: (Paris, 1976) Exact title unknown (CBC)
WHERE BROADCAST: Canada
PERSONNEL: Mick Jagger, Keith Richards, Ron Wood, Charlie Watts, Bill Wyman, Ian Stewart, Billy Preston, Ollie Brown
SONGS/OTHER CONTENT: Les Abattoirs concerts, 1976

1980

JUNE 1980

PROGRAM: Program title unknown—French TV
WHERE BROADCAST: France
PERSONNEL: Mick Jagger
SONGS/OTHER CONTENT: Jagger interview by Patrice Devret—about the Emotional Rescue tour

JUNE 25, 1980

PROGRAM: Countdown—Dutch TV
WHERE BROADCAST: The Netherlands
PERSONNEL: Mick Jagger
SONGS/OTHER CONTENT: Jagger interview

SEPTEMBER 19, 1980

PROGRAM: Midnight Special
WHERE BROADCAST: USA
SONGS/OTHER CONTENT: She's So Cold
NOTES: Promo film

SEPTEMBER 26, 1980

PROGRAM: Midnight Special
WHERE BROADCAST: USA
SONGS/OTHER CONTENT: She's So Cold / Emotional Rescue
NOTES: Both promos

OCTOBER 26, 1980

PROGRAM NAME: Earl Chin's Rockers '80
WHERE BROADCAST: New York City
PERSONNEL: Mick Jagger, Keith Richards
SONGS/OTHER CONTENT: Jagger and Richards interview, Part I / Far Away Eyes promo / Emotional Rescue promo
NOTES: This very laid-back interview of Mick and Keith by reggae DJ Earl Chin was taped in December 1979, one year prior to being broadcast, at Electric Ladyland Studios in the wee hours. Notable, besides the 4:00 A.M. shoot time, are grooming and wardrobe oddities. Keith is wearing a C.N.I.B (Canadian National Institute for the Blind) braille T-shirt from his sentence/benefit concert. Mick has a full beard, an image rarely, if ever, captured on movie film or video. The whisker effect may have had something to do with the year-long gap between the taping and broadcast of Chin's program to a regular NYC community access cable show seen only in Manhattan and nearby sections of Brooklyn and Queens. Two promos were aired, along with the first part of the interview on October 26. One week later, Part II was broadcast.

OCTOBER 26, 1980

PROGRAM: Don Kirshner's Rock Concert
WHERE BROADCAST: USA
SONGS/OTHER CONTENT: Emotional Rescue / She's So Cold
NOTES: Two Stones promos

NOVEMBER 2, 1980

PROGRAM NAME: Earl Chin's Rockers '80
WHERE BROADCAST: New York City
PERSONNEL: Mick Jagger, Keith Richards
SONGS/OTHER CONTENT: Jagger and Richards interview, Part II
NOTES: Reggae DJ Earl Chin's community access cable show aired the second and final part of what may be the most relaxed interview of Mick and Keith ever televised. Chin talked with them as they all hung out, sitting on couches at Electric Ladyland Studios at around 4:00 A.M.. Jagger had a full beard and looked and acted like, well, just a guy, not "Mick Jagger." Refreshing. See October 26, 1980, above.

DECEMBER 12, 1980

PROGRAM: Midnight Special
WHERE BROADCAST: USA
SONGS/OTHER CONTENT: She's So Cold
NOTES: "She's So Cold" promo was aired in the show's "Top Ten" segment.

DECEMBER 1980

PROGRAM: Best of Sullivan
WHERE BROADCAST: USA
PERSONNEL: Mick Jagger, Keith Richards, Brian Jones, Charlie Watts, Bill Wyman
SONGS/OTHER CONTENT: Time Is on My Side (Meade), V1 / Around & Around (Berry)
NOTES: Best-of reruns—the Stones' (edited) appearance of October 25, 1964 is one episode. See listing for that date above.

1981

MAY 1981

PROGRAM: Saturday Night at the Mill (BBC)
WHERE BROADCAST: UK
PERSONNEL: Bill Wyman
SONGS/OTHER CONTENT: Wyman interview

JULY 9, 1981

PROGRAM: Top of the Pops
WHERE BROADCAST: UK
PERSONNEL: Bill Wyman
SONGS/OTHER CONTENT: Wyman interview
NOTES: Bill interviewed by Jimmy Saville.

AUGUST 13, 1981

PROGRAM: Top of the Pops
WHERE BROADCAST: UK
PERSONNEL: Bill Wyman
SONGS/OTHER CONTENT: Wyman interview
NOTES: Repeat of July 9 segment.

AUGUST 27, 1981

PROGRAM: Top of the Pops
WHERE BROADCAST: UK
SONGS/OTHER CONTENT: Start Me Up
NOTES: Promo

SEPTEMBER 10, 1981

PROGRAM: Top of the Pops
WHERE BROADCAST: UK

SONGS/OTHER CONTENT: Start Me Up
NOTES: Repeat airing of the August 27 segment.

OCTOBER 14, 1981

PROGRAM: Entertainment Tonight
WHERE BROADCAST: USA
PERSONNEL: Bill Wyman
SONGS/OTHER CONTENT: Wyman interview

OCTOBER 20, 1981

PROGRAM: Save the Cable Cars (PSA)
WHERE BROADCAST: San Francisco, CA
PERSONNEL: Mick Jagger, Dianne Feinstein
SONGS/OTHER CONTENT: Public service spot
NOTES: Mick appeared in a locally televised public service announcement with San Francisco Mayor Dianne Feinstein in an appeal to save that city's historic cable cars.

NOVEMBER 5, 1981

PROGRAM: Inside Out
WHERE BROADCAST: UK
PERSONNEL: Mick Jagger
SONGS/OTHER CONTENT: Jagger interview
NOTES: Mick interviewed by Rona Barrett on this BBC-TV show.

DECEMBER 1981

PROGRAM: All Night (Fuji TV)
WHERE BROADCAST: Japan
PERSONNEL: Mick Jagger
SONGS/OTHER CONTENT: Jagger interview
NOTES: Taped in New York City on November 11, 1981

DECEMBER 18, 1981

PROGRAM: The Rolling Stones Live in Concert from Hampton Roads (Pay-per-view)
WHERE BROADCAST: USA
PERSONNEL: Mick Jagger, Keith Richards, Ron Wood, Charlie Watts, Bill Wyman, Ian Stewart, Ian McLagan, Ernie Watts, Bobby Keys
SONGS/OTHER CONTENT: 1981 Hampton Roads concert
NOTES: The Stones' first pay-per-view show. Keith's and Bobby Keys's birthday.

1982

FEBRUARY 3, 1982

PROGRAM: Michael Parkinson Show (BBC-TV)

WHERE BROADCAST: UK
PERSONNEL: Bill Wyman
SONGS/OTHER CONTENT: Wyman interview
NOTES: Bill Wyman interviewed on this BBC show.

FEBRUARY 25, 1982

PROGRAM: 20 Years (German documentary)
WHERE BROADCAST: Germany
PERSONNEL: Mick Jagger, Keith Richards, Brian Jones, Mick Taylor, Ron Wood, Charlie Watts, Bill Wyman
SONGS/OTHER CONTENT: Documentary
NOTES: German documentary on the Rolling Stones' 20-year history.

FEBRUARY 25, 1982

PROGRAM: Kenny Everett Show (BBC-TV)
WHERE BROADCAST: UK
PERSONNEL: Bill Wyman
SONGS/OTHER CONTENT: Wyman interview

MARCH 26, 1982

PROGRAM: Program title unknown (Japanese TV)
WHERE BROADCAST: Japan
PERSONNEL: Bill Wyman
SONGS/OTHER CONTENT: Wyman interview

APRIL 15, 1982

PROGRAM: Musikladen
WHERE BROADCAST: Germany
PERSONNEL: Bill Wyman
SONGS/OTHER CONTENT: A New Fashion (Wyman)
NOTES: Wyman, solo work.

APRIL 16, 1982

PROGRAM: WWF Club
WHERE BROADCAST: Germany
PERSONNEL: Bill Wyman
SONGS/OTHER CONTENT: A New Fashion (Wyman)
NOTES: More solo Wyman on German television.

APRIL 24, 1982

PROGRAM: Ligne Rock
WHERE BROADCAST: France
PERSONNEL: Bill Wyman
SONGS/OTHER CONTENT: Wyman interview

APRIL 28, 1982

PROGRAM: Newsnight (BBC2)
WHERE BROADCAST: UK
PERSONNEL: Mick Jagger

SONGS/OTHER CONTENT: Jagger interview

MAY 26, 1982

PROGRAM: The North Today (BBC-TV)
WHERE BROADCAST: UK
PERSONNEL: Mick Jagger, Keith Richards, Ron Wood, Charlie Watts, Bill Wyman, Ian Stewart, Chuck Leavell, Bobby Keys, Gene Barge
SONGS/OTHER CONTENT: Neighbours
NOTES: A segment on the Stones performing live at the Capitol Theatre, Aberdeen, Scotland.

MAY 27, 1982

PROGRAM: Old Grey Whistle Test
WHERE BROADCAST: UK
SONGS/OTHER CONTENT: Going to À Go Go (Robinson, Johnson, Moore, Rogers)
NOTES: Promo

MAY 27, 1982

PROGRAM: Roundtable (BBC)
WHERE BROADCAST: UK
PERSONNEL: Mick Jagger
SONGS/OTHER CONTENT: Jagger interview
NOTES: Mick interviewed in Glasgow.

JUNE 5, 1982

PROGRAM: Houba Houba (French TV)
WHERE BROADCAST: France
PERSONNEL: Mick Jagger
SONGS/OTHER CONTENT: Jagger interview
NOTES: *En français, naturellement.*

JUNE 24, 1982

PROGRAM: Newsnight (BBC2)
WHERE BROADCAST: UK
PERSONNEL: Keith Richards
SONGS/OTHER CONTENT: Richards interview
NOTES: Live Richards interview

JUNE 25, 1982

PROGRAM: 6 O'Clock News (BBC)
WHERE BROADCAST: UK
PERSONNEL: Mick Jagger, Bill Wyman
SONGS/OTHER CONTENT: Jagger and Wyman interview

JUNE 26, 1982

PROGRAM: Rolling Stones: The First Twenty Years (ORF-TV & WDR-TV)

WHERE BROADCAST: Austria and Germany
PERSONNEL: Mick Jagger, Keith Richards, Brian Jones, Mick Taylor, Ron Wood, Charlie Watts, Bill Wyman, Bianca Jagger, Marianne Faithfull, Ian Stewart, Bill Graham, Rod Stewart, Frank Zappa, Alexis Korner
SONGS/OTHER CONTENT: Documentary
NOTES: This one hour, 50 minute compilation of the first 20 years of the Stones' history used archival performance and newsreel footage, Stones promos and films, as well as interviews with band members (past and present) and those close to them. Marianne Faithfull, Bianca Jagger, Frank Zappa and Bill Graham appeared in this excellent documentary, which was narrated by Alexis Korner. Directed by Rudolf Dolezal and Hannes Rossader, the film was co-produced by and for Austrian and German television and was aired simultaneously in both nations.

JULY 5, 1982

PROGRAM: Hier und Heute (German TV)
WHERE BROADCAST: Germany
PERSONNEL: Mick Jagger
SONGS/OTHER CONTENT: Jagger interview
NOTES: Jagger interviewed in Cologne, West Germany. Featured on German television (WDR).

JULY 15, 1982

PROGRAM: Twenty Years On (BBC2)
WHERE BROADCAST: UK
PERSONNEL: Mick Jagger, Keith Richards, Brian Jones, Mick Taylor, Ron Wood, Charlie Watts, Bill Wyman
SONGS/OTHER CONTENT: Documentary
NOTES: Historical documentary on the Rolling Stones.

SEPTEMBER 17, 1982

PROGRAM: Old Grey Whistle Test
WHERE BROADCAST: UK
SONGS/OTHER CONTENT: Time Is on My Side (Meade)
NOTES: Promo

SEPTEMBER 24, 1982

PROGRAM: Old Grey Whistle Test
WHERE BROADCAST: UK
SONGS/OTHER CONTENT: Time Is On My Side (Meade)
NOTES: Promo

DECEMBER 9, 1982

PROGRAM: The Tube
WHERE BROADCAST: UK
PERSONNEL: Mick Jagger
SONGS/OTHER CONTENT: Jagger interview
NOTES: Taped on June 26, 1982

1983

JANUARY 6, 1983

PROGRAM: Good Morning America
WHERE BROADCAST: USA
PERSONNEL: Ron Wood
SONGS/OTHER CONTENT: Wood interview

APRIL 1983

PROGRAM: Good Morning Britain (BBC)
WHERE BROADCAST: UK
PERSONNEL: Bill Wyman
SONGS/OTHER CONTENT: Wyman interview
NOTES: Bill was interviewed on this BBC morning show.

MAY 5, 1983

PROGRAM: Top of the Pops 1000th Show Special
WHERE BROADCAST: UK
PERSONNEL: Mick Jagger, Keith Richards, Brian Jones, Mick Taylor, Charlie Watts, Bill Wyman
SONGS/OTHER CONTENT: Brown Sugar / Get Off of My Cloud
NOTES: Stones segments included "Brown Sugar" from 1971 and "Get Off of My Cloud" from 1965, as "Top of the Pops" celebrated its longevity.

MAY 10, 1983

PROGRAM: The Nightingale/Faerie Tale Theater (Showtime)
WHERE BROADCAST: USA
PERSONNEL: Mick Jagger
SONGS/OTHER CONTENT: Drama
NOTES: Mick, as the Chinese Emperor, filmed his scenes in the Hans Christian Andersen story on January 14, 1983 for this US cable television series.

SEPTEMBER 21, 1983

PROGRAM: Good Morning Britain (BBC)
WHERE BROADCAST: UK
PERSONNEL: Bill Wyman, Ronnie Lane, Eric Clapton
SONGS/OTHER CONTENT: Interview
NOTES: Bill, along with Ronnie Lane and Eric Clapton are interviewed on this BBC morning show.

SEPTEMBER 25, 1983

PROGRAM: Jerry Lee Lewis Special Tribute
WHERE BROADCAST: USA
PERSONNEL: Keith Richards, Jerry Lee Lewis

SONGS/OTHER CONTENT: Your Cheatin' Heart (Williams) / Little Queenie (Berry) / Great Balls of Fire (Hammer, Blackwell) / High School Confidential (Lewis, Hargrave) / Whole Lotta Shakin' Goin' On (Williams, David)

NOTES: Taped on July 4, 1983 in Los Angeles. Keith jamming with Jerry Lee Lewis onstage.

OCTOBER 28, 1983

PROGRAM: The Tube
WHERE BROADCAST: UK
PERSONNEL: Mick Jagger
SONGS/OTHER CONTENT: Interview
NOTES: Jagger interview from the premiere broadcast of Channel 4's rock show.

NOVEMBER 7, 1983

PROGRAM: CBS Morning News
WHERE BROADCAST: USA
PERSONNEL: Bill Wyman
SONGS/OTHER CONTENT: Wyman interview

NOVEMBER 11, 1983

PROGRAM: Breakfast Time
WHERE BROADCAST: UK
PERSONNEL: Bill Wyman
SONGS/OTHER CONTENT: Wyman interview

NOVEMBER 11, 1983

PROGRAM: The Tube
WHERE BROADCAST: UK
PERSONNEL: Mick Jagger, Julien Temple
SONGS/OTHER CONTENT: Undercover of the Night (edited video) / Not Fade Away (Petty, Hardin) / Time Is on My Side (Meade)
NOTES: The preceding day, the BBC deemed the original video for "Undercover" "too violent" and banned it from broadcast on BBC's "Top of the Pops." The Independent Broadcasting Authority, which oversees non-BBC broadcasters in the UK, ruled likewise on November

Keith Richards with Jerry Lee Lewis (RICHARD AARON/STARFILE)

11. The Stones had been slated to be featured on this Channel 4 show on November 11, so Mick Jagger and the video's director, Julien Temple, appeared together on "The Tube" to defend the new promo. The controversial video portrayed a gang of terrorists (led by Keith) abducting a guest (Mick) from a hotel suite in "San Salvador" and, in the original, blindfolding him and shooting him in the head. (See PROMOTIONAL FILMS AND VIDEOS for more detail.) The "Undercover" video was aired on "The Tube" this time, minus the execution scene. The program's historical segment on the Rolling Stones focused on two of the band's guitarists: Brian Jones versus Ron Wood. "Not Fade Away" was a "Top of the Pops" clip from the Jones years, and "Time Is on My Side" pictured Wood at Hampton Roads, VA in 1981.

NOVEMBER 11, 1983

PROGRAM: CBS News Nightwatch
WHERE BROADCAST: USA
PERSONNEL: Bill Wyman
SONGS/OTHER CONTENT: Wyman interview

NOVEMBER 17, 1983

PROGRAM: Top of the Pops
WHERE BROADCAST: UK
SONGS/OTHER CONTENT: Undercover of the Night
NOTES: Edited promo

NOVEMBER 18, 1983

PROGRAM: The Tube
WHERE BROADCAST: UK
PERSONNEL: Mick Jagger, Keith Richards, Brian Jones, Charlie Watts, Bill Wyman
SONGS/OTHER CONTENT: Time Is on My Side (Meade) / Off the Hook (Nanker Phelge) / It's All Over Now (Womack, Womack)
NOTES: Old Stones "T.A.M.I. Show" footage replaced the scheduled airing of the banned original "Undercover of the Night" promo video.

NOVEMBER 19 AND 26, 1983

PROGRAM: Program title unknown—French TV
WHERE BROADCAST: France
PERSONNEL: Mick Jagger
SONGS/OTHER CONTENT: Jagger interview
NOTES: *En français*

DECEMBER 17, 1983

PROGRAM: Program title unknown (Italian TV)
WHERE BROADCAST: Italy
PERSONNEL: Mick Jagger

SONGS/OTHER CONTENT: Jagger interview

1983

PROGRAM: Radio 1990 (USA Network—cable TV)
WHERE BROADCAST: USA
PERSONNEL: Mick Jagger, Keith Richards
SONGS/OTHER CONTENT: Interviews
NOTES: Rock journalist Lisa Robinson conducted in-depth interviews with Mick and Keith. This television program *was* made and broadcast on the American cable channel "USA" in *1983*; also syndicated on broadcast TV.

1984

JANUARY 5, 1984

PROGRAM: Top of the Pops—20th Anniversary Show
WHERE BROADCAST: UK
PERSONNEL: Mick Jagger, Keith Richards, Brian Jones, Charlie Watts, Bill Wyman
SONGS/OTHER CONTENT: Let's Spend the Night Together
NOTES: Stones segment from 1967 rebroadcast on "Top of the Pops"'s 20th anniversary program.

FEBRUARY 3, 1984

PROGRAM: Friday Night Videos
WHERE BROADCAST: USA
PERSONNEL: Mick Jagger
SONGS/OTHER CONTENT: Jagger interview
NOTES: Part one

FEBRUARY 10, 1984

PROGRAM: Friday Night Videos
WHERE BROADCAST: USA
PERSONNEL: Mick Jagger
SONGS/OTHER CONTENT: Interview / She Was Hot
NOTES: The Jagger interview, part two. Plus, a cleaned-up version of the "She Was Hot" video.

MARCH 18, 1984

PROGRAM: Sunday Sunday (BBC)
WHERE BROADCAST: UK
PERSONNEL: Bill Wyman
SONGS/OTHER CONTENT: Wyman interview

APRIL 4, 1984

PROGRAM: CBS News Nightwatch
WHERE BROADCAST: USA
PERSONNEL: Bill Wyman

SONGS/OTHER CONTENT: Wyman interview
NOTES: Bill Wyman was interviewed in response to a story in the British tabloid, *Sun*. He denied having made derogatory statements about other members of the band.

JUNE 16, 1984

PROGRAM: Aspel & Company (BBC)
WHERE BROADCAST: UK
PERSONNEL: Bill Wyman
SONGS/OTHER CONTENT: Wyman interview

AUGUST 27, 1984

PROGRAM: 8 Days A Week (BBC)
WHERE BROADCAST: UK
PERSONNEL: Bill Wyman
SONGS/OTHER CONTENT: Wyman interview

SEPTEMBER 9, 1984

PROGRAM: London Calling (BBC)
WHERE BROADCAST: UK
PERSONNEL: Bill Wyman
SONGS/OTHER CONTENT: Wyman interview

1985

FEBRUARY 21, 1985

PROGRAM: Top of the Pops
WHERE BROADCAST: UK
PERSONNEL: Mick Jagger
SONGS/OTHER CONTENT: Just Another Night (Jagger)
NOTES: Jagger, solo.

APRIL 9, 1985

PROGRAM: Old Grey Whistle Test
WHERE BROADCAST: UK
PERSONNEL: Mick Jagger
SONGS/OTHER CONTENT: Just Another Night (Jagger)

JULY 13, 1985

PROGRAM: Live Aid (MTV)
WHERE BROADCAST: Worldwide
PERSONNEL: Mick Jagger, Darryl Hall, John Oates, Tina Turner, Keith Richards, Ron Wood, Bob Dylan
SONGS/OTHER CONTENT: Just Another Night (Jagger) / Lonely at the Top / Miss You / State of Shock / It's Only Rock 'n' Roll / Dancing in the Street (Stevenson, Hunter, Gaye) (video) / Ballad of Hollis Brown (Dylan) / When the Ship Comes In (Dylan) / Blowin' in the Wind (Dylan)

NOTES: When they were asked to appear at Bob Geldof's transatlantic benefit concert for Ethiopian famine relief, the Stones declined. They were involved with the recording of *Dirty Work* in Paris and weren't scheduled to finish in time to rehearse and perform at the event. As it happened, Mick and Keith were publicly at odds with each other when Live Aid actually took place. Mick had been concentrating on his solo work prior to the Paris sessions and had made it known that he preferred not to tour in support of the Stones' new record, much to Keith's displeasure. Then, the band decided to take a few weeks off —they needed a break. And, on his own, Jagger decided to appear at Live Aid. At the end of June, Mick and David Bowie recorded a single (and shot a video) of Martha & the Vandellas' "Dancing in the Street," hoping to do the number as a satellite duet during the concert—with Bowie at Wembley and Jagger onstage in Philadelphia. That technical nightmare wasn't to be. Instead, the "Dancing in the Street" video was premiered during the worldwide broadcast. Jagger, backed by Darryl Hall and John Oates, took the stage in Philadelphia and performed "Miss You," "Lonely at the Top" and "Just Another Night" as a solo act for the first time. He was then joined by Tina Turner for two more crowd-pleasing numbers. Meanwhile, Keith and Woody ended up performing at Live Aid—also from Philadelphia—but as Bob Dylan's "surprise guests," joining him on three songs to close the show—"The Ballad of Hollis Brown," "When the Ship Comes In" and "Blowin' in the Wind."

SEPTEMBER 19, 1985

PROGRAM: Top of the Pops
WHERE BROADCAST: UK
PERSONNEL: Mick Jagger, David Bowie
SONGS/OTHER CONTENT: Dancing in the Street (Stevenson, Hunter, Gaye)
NOTES: Promo film for the Jagger/Bowie duet single.

SEPTEMBER 26, 1985

PROGRAM: Top of the Pops
WHERE BROADCAST: UK
PERSONNEL: Mick Jagger, David Bowie
SONGS/OTHER CONTENT: Dancing in the Street (Stevenson, Hunter, Gaye)
NOTES: Rebroadcast of promo first aired on September 19.

NOVEMBER 3, 1985

PROGRAM: Sunday Sunday (BBC)
WHERE BROADCAST: UK
PERSONNEL: Bill Wyman
SONGS/OTHER CONTENT: Wyman interview

1986

FEBRUARY 15, 1986

PROGRAM: Saturday Night Live
WHERE BROADCAST: USA
PERSONNEL: Mick Jagger, Jerry Hall
SONGS/OTHER CONTENT: Jagger cameo
NOTES: Jerry Hall's appearance as "Saturday Night Lives"'s guest host included a part in one skit with Jon Lovitz, the latter playing the "world's greatest pathological liar." Liar Lovitz tries to pick up Hall in a bar, telling her how well he knows the Rolling Stones, and even that he manages them. In walks Mick Jagger, in a surprisingly unsurprising cameo appearance.

FEBRUARY 25, 1986

PROGRAM: The Grammy Awards
WHERE BROADCAST: USA
PERSONNEL: Mick Jagger, Keith Richards, Ron Wood, Charlie Watts, Bill Wyman, Eric Clapton
SONGS/OTHER CONTENT: Harlem Shuffle (Relf, Nelson)
NOTES: Linked up live-via-satellite with the televised ceremonies in Los Angeles, Eric Clapton presented the

Stones with the Grammy Lifetime Achievement Award at the Roof Garden Club in Kensington, London. The band revealed their new video of "Harlem Shuffle" on the Grammy telecast.

FEBRUARY 26, 1986

PROGRAM: Good Morning America
WHERE BROADCAST: USA
PERSONNEL: Mick Jagger, Keith Richards, Ron Wood
SONGS/OTHER CONTENT: Jagger, Richards, Wood interview

MARCH 20, 1986

PROGRAM: Top of the Pops
WHERE BROADCAST: UK
SONGS/OTHER CONTENT: Harlem Shuffle (Relf, Nelson)
NOTES: Promo

JUNE 7, 1986

PROGRAM: Countdown (Dutch TV)
WHERE BROADCAST: The Netherlands
PERSONNEL: Bill Wyman
SONGS/OTHER CONTENT: Wyman interview

Keith Richards with Paul Shaffer on "Friday Night Videos" (CHUCK PULIN/STARFILE)

JUNE 13, 1986

PROGRAM: Friday Night Videos
WHERE BROADCAST: USA
PERSONNEL: Keith Richards, Paul Shaffer, Marcus Miller
SONGS/OTHER CONTENT: Richards interview, part one / Honky Tonk Women / Sleep Tonight
NOTES: The first part of an interview with Keith made up one segment of this show; and Richards, Shaffer and bassist Miller have a nice relaxed jam on two tunes.

JUNE 20, 1986

PROGRAM: Friday Night Videos
WHERE BROADCAST: USA
PERSONNEL: Keith Richards
SONGS/OTHER CONTENT: Richards interview / jam
NOTES: Interview with Keith, part two.

AUGUST 28, 1986

PROGRAM: Old Grey Whistle Test
WHERE BROADCAST: UK
PERSONNEL: The Stones
SONGS/OTHER CONTENT: The Making of "One Hit (to the Body)" video (special).

1987

SEPTEMBER 24, 1987

PROGRAM: Top of the Pops
WHERE BROADCAST: UK
PERSONNEL: Mick Jagger
SONGS/OTHER CONTENT: Let's Work (Jagger)
NOTES: Mick Jagger, solo. Taped on September 11.

OCTOBER 16, 1987

PROGRAM: Program title unknown (Belgian TV)
WHERE BROADCAST: Belgium
PERSONNEL: Mick Jagger
SONGS/OTHER CONTENT: Jagger interview

OCTOBER 23, 1987

PROGRAM: The Last Resort—The Jonathan Ross Show
WHERE BROADCAST: UK
PERSONNEL: Ron Wood
SONGS/OTHER CONTENT: Wood interview

NOVEMBER 17, 1987

PROGRAM: Much Music—(Canadian Cable TV)
WHERE BROADCAST: Canada

PERSONNEL: Mick Jagger, Keith Richards, Brian Jones, Mick Taylor, Ron Wood, Charlie Watts, Bill Wyman
SONGS/OTHER CONTENT: Stones Special

NOVEMBER 27, 1987

PROGRAM: Late Night with David Letterman
WHERE BROADCAST: USA
PERSONNEL: Ron Wood
SONGS/OTHER CONTENT: Wood interview
NOTES: Woody's segment was taped on November 25.

1988

MAY 15, 1988

PROGRAM: Nightflight (Swedish TV)
WHERE BROADCAST: Sweden
PERSONNEL: Ron Wood
SONGS/OTHER CONTENT: Wood interview

SEPTEMBER 29, 1988

PROGRAM: London Plus (BBC)
WHERE BROADCAST: UK
PERSONNEL: Ron Wood
SONGS/OTHER CONTENT: Wood interview

OCTOBER 8, 1988

PROGRAM: Saturday Night Live
WHERE BROADCAST: USA
PERSONNEL: Keith Richards, X-Pensive Winos
SONGS/OTHER CONTENT: Take It So Hard (Richards, Jordan) / Struggle (Richards, Jordan)

OCTOBER 23, 1988

PROGRAM: Smile Jamaica
WHERE BROADCAST: UK
PERSONNEL: Keith Richards, U2
SONGS/OTHER CONTENT: When Love Comes to Town (Bono, U2) / Love Rescue Me (Bono, Dylan, U2)
NOTES: The Smile Jamaica benefit concert for Jamaican hurricane relief was held on October 15, 1989 in London, and was filmed for this later broadcast, which included Keith's guest appearance with U2 at the show. Richards's own Jamaican home had sustained storm damage, although he was not on the island at the time.

OCTOBER 26, 1988

PROGRAM: Keith Richards Rollin' On (MTV)
WHERE BROADCAST: US
PERSONNEL: Keith Richards

SONGS/OTHER CONTENT: Take It So Hard (Richards, Jordan) / Struggle (Richards, Jordan) / Happy / It's All Over Now (Womack, Womack) / Honky Tonk Women / Brown Sugar / Miss You / Waiting on a Friend / (I Can't Get No) Satisfaction / One Hit (to the Body) (Jagger, Richards, Wood)

NOTES: An MTV special profile on Keith's career, initially broadcast in the US and later aired worldwide. "Take It So Hard" and "Struggle" were clips from Keith & the X-Pensive Winos recent "Saturday Night Live" appearance. "It's All Over Now" was a very early Stones performance—on the 1964 T.A.M.I. show. "Miss You," "Waiting on a Friend" and "One Hit (to the Body)" came from Stones promos. The balance of the numbers were taken from footage of live Stones performances of the '70s and band's first pay-per-view television special in 1981.

1989

APRIL 28 AND/OR 29, 1989

PROGRAM: Lifestyles of the Rich and Famous
WHERE BROADCAST: USA
PERSONNEL: Ron Wood
SONGS/OTHER CONTENT: Wood profile
NOTES: It had to happen: "Lifestyles of the Rich and Famous" gets to a Rolling Stone. Woody was the first to be so honored (?), but not the last. Next? See February 21, 1992. Ronnie's show aired on these two nights in various areas; such being the vagaries of television syndication.

MAY 16, 1989

PROGRAM: International Rock Awards
WHERE BROADCAST: USA
PERSONNEL: Keith Richards, The X-Pensive Winos, Tina Turner, Eric Clapton, Dave Edmunds, Jeff Healy, Clarence Clemmons
SONGS/OTHER CONTENT: Whip It Up (Richards, Jordan) / You Keep A Knocking (James)
NOTES: Eric Clapton presented the Living Legend Award to Keith, the Winos performed. Keith & the Winos played with Tina, Clapton and others in closing jam on Elmore James's "You Keep A Knocking."

JULY 11, 1989

PROGRAM: Rolling Stones Press Conference—Grand Central Station (MTV)
WHERE BROADCAST: USA
PERSONNEL: Mick Jagger, Keith Richards, Ron Wood, Charlie Watts, Bill Wyman
SONGS/OTHER CONTENT: Steel Wheels Tour announcement

NOTES: MTV covered the Stones' sweaty tour announcement and aired the press conference in its entirety in the US.

SEPTEMBER 6, 1989

PROGRAM: Evening Magazine
WHERE BROADCAST: USA
PERSONNEL: Mick Jagger, Keith Richards, Ron Wood, Charlie Watts, Bill Wyman
SONGS/OTHER CONTENT: Rolling Stones Special

SEPTEMBER 6, 1989

PROGRAM: MTV Video Awards
WHERE BROADCAST: USA
PERSONNEL: Mick Jagger, Keith Richards, Ron Wood, Charlie Watts, Bill Wyman, Matt Clifford, Chuck Leavell, Bobby Keys, The Uptown Horns (Arno Hecht, Paul Litteral, Bob Funk, Crispen Cioe), Bernard Fowler, Lisa Fischer, Cindy Mizelle
SONGS/OTHER CONTENT: Mixed Emotions
NOTES: Advertised as coming to MTV's viewers "live via satellite from Three Rivers Stadium in Pittsburgh," the Stones' performance of "Mixed Emotions" was actually taped three days earlier in Toronto—September 3 at Exhibition Hall—and broadcast on this awards show. The Stones did play Pittsburgh on September 6.

SEPTEMBER 14, 1989

PROGRAM: Top of the Pops
WHERE BROADCAST: UK
SONGS/OTHER CONTENT: Mixed Emotions
NOTES: Promo

SEPTEMBER 22, 1989

PROGRAM: 20/20
WHERE BROADCAST: USA
SONGS/OTHER CONTENT: Stone Phillips interviews the Rolling Stones
NOTES: Barbara Walters anchored ABC's 20/20, while Stone interviewed the Stones during the Steel Wheels tour.

DECEMBER 5, 1989

PROGRAM: 25 X 5 (BBC)
WHERE BROADCAST: UK
PERSONNEL: Mick Jagger, Keith Richards, Brian Jones, Mick Taylor, Ron Wood, Charlie Watts, Bill Wyman
SONGS/OTHER CONTENT: 25 X 5 (Short version)
NOTES: An early cut of the band's career retrospective film got a sneak television preview in Britain. This version is about 30 minutes shorter than the final, official cut that runs for 132 minutes.

DECEMBER 19, 1989

PROGRAM: Pay-Per-View TV—Atlantic City

WHERE BROADCAST: USA

PERSONNEL: Mick Jagger, Keith Richards, Ron Wood, Charlie Watts, Bill Wyman, Eric Clapton, John Lee Hooker, Matt Clifford, Chuck Leavell, Bobby Keys, The Uptown Horns (Arno Hecht, Paul Litteral, Bob Funk, Crispen Cioe), Bernard Fowler, Lisa Fischer, Cindy Mizelle

SONGS/OTHER CONTENT: Continental Drift, V2 / Start Me Up / Bitch / Sad, Sad, Sad / Undercover of the Night / Harlem Shuffle (Relf, Nelson) / Tumbling Dice / Miss You / Terrifying / Ruby Tuesday / Salt of the Earth / Rock and a Hard Place / Mixed Emotions / Honky Tonk Women / Midnight Rambler / You Can't Always Get What You Want / Little Red Rooster (Dixon) / Boogie Chillin' (Hooker) / Can't Be Seen / Happy / Paint It, Black / 2000 Light Years from Home / Sympathy for the Devil / Gimme Shelter / It's Only Rock 'n' Roll / Brown Sugar / (I Can't Get No) Satisfaction / Jumpin' Jack Flash

NOTES: The last show of Steel Wheels, broadcast via pay-per-view cable television; a major event with major hooplah, just like the tour. Clapton played on "Little Red Rooster," Hooker on "Boogie Chillin'."

DECEMBER 27, 1989

PROGRAM: The Arena

WHERE BROADCAST: UK

PERSONNEL: Mick Jagger, Keith Richards, Brian Jones, Mick Taylor, Ron Wood, Charlie Watts, Bill Wyman

SONGS/OTHER CONTENT: *25 X 5* (Short version)

NOTES: The early, shorter version of the film *25 X 5* got another holiday season preview in Britain, this time on the BBC's "The Arena." See December 5, 1989, above.

DECEMBER 28, 1989

PROGRAM: Top of the Pops

WHERE BROADCAST: UK

PERSONNEL: Mick Jagger, David Bowie

SONGS/OTHER CONTENT: Dancing in the Street (Stevenson, Hunter, Gaye)

NOTES: Promo video

1990

?, ? 1990

PROGRAM: The Rolling Stones on Tour—Japan 1990

WHERE BROADCAST: Japan

SONGS/OTHER CONTENT: Steel Wheels—Japan documentary

MAY 30, 1990

PROGRAM: Steel Wheels—Atlantic City (Fox-TV)

WHERE BROADCAST: USA

PERSONNEL: Mick Jagger, Keith Richards, Ron Wood, Charlie Watts, Bill Wyman, Eric Clapton, John Lee Hooker, Matt Clifford, Chuck Leavell, Bobby Keys, The Uptown Horns (Arno Hecht, Paul Litteral, Bob Funk, Crispen Cioe), Bernard Fowler, Lisa Fischer, Cindy Mizelle

SONGS/OTHER CONTENT: Atlantic City pay-per-view plus additional sequences

NOTES: Fox-TV broadcast the final concert of Steel Wheels, originally aired as a pay-per-view show, with additional sequences. The added segments include 3-D footage shot in Japan as well as other sequences of the band filmed on February 16 during the Japanese leg of the tour.

JUNE 6, 1990

PROGRAM: International Rock Awards

WHERE BROADCAST: USA

PERSONNEL: Keith Richards, Eric Clapton

SONGS/OTHER CONTENT: Award presentation

NOTES: Keith presented the Living Legend Award to Eric Clapton.

AUGUST 15, 1990

PROGRAM: Urban Jungle (Barcelona Pay-Per-View)

WHERE BROADCAST: Europe

SONGS/OTHER CONTENT: Barcelona concerts

NOTES: Ninety minutes of highlights of the Stones' June 1990 performances in Barcelona, Spain, broadcast via SkyTV pay-per-view. SkyTV is a cable operator in Europe and the UK. (See TOURS AND CONCERTS)

OCTOBER 28, 1990

PROGRAM: Sunday Sunday (BBC)

WHERE BROADCAST: UK

PERSONNEL: Bill Wyman

SONGS/OTHER CONTENT: Wyman interview

1991

FEBRUARY 19, 1991

PROGRAM: Instant Recall

WHERE BROADCAST: USA

PERSONNEL: Mick Jagger, Keith Richards, Mick Taylor, Charlie Watts, Bill Wyman

SONGS/OTHER CONTENT: Altamont

NOTES: The Rolling Stones at Altamont—one of this show's three historical segments. A syndicated program produced by NBC.

MARCH 21, 1991

PROGRAM: Top of the Pops

WHERE BROADCAST: UK

PERSONNEL: Mick Jagger, Keith Richards, Ron Wood, Charlie Watts

SONGS/OTHER CONTENT: Highwire

NOTES: Another controversial video. The lyrics, written during the Persian Gulf War, fired up critics and censors with unwanted (but true) political references; for example, the West's history of arms sales to Saddam Hussein. The BBC edited out the first verse.

APRIL 5, 1991

PROGRAM: The Jonathan Ross Show

WHERE BROADCAST: UK

PERSONNEL: Charlie Watts

SONGS/OTHER CONTENT: Watts interview

NOTES: Charlie promoted his new book—actually a new edition of *Ode to a High Flying Bird*, first published in 1965—and the Charlie Watts Quintet's new record, *From One Charlie.*

JUNE 6, 1991

PROGRAM: Good Morning America

WHERE BROADCAST: USA

PERSONNEL: Charlie Watts

SONGS/OTHER CONTENT: Watts interview

NOTES: Charlie talks about the Charlie Watts Quintet.

JUNE 20, 1991

PROGRAM: BBC-TV AM

WHERE BROADCAST: UK

PERSONNEL: Bill Wyman

SONGS/OTHER CONTENT: Wyman interview

NOTES: Wyman interviewed on the BBC's morning show.

OCTOBER 5, 1991

PROGRAM: Sound of the Sixties (BBC-TV Series)

WHERE BROADCAST: UK

PERSONNEL: The Stones, c. 1965

SONGS/OTHER CONTENT: The Last Time

NOTES: This first segment of BBC-TV's '60s series broadcast a 1965 clip of the Stones performing "The Last Time" on "Top of the Pops."

OCTOBER 12, 1991

PROGRAM: Sound of the Sixties (BBC-TV Series)

WHERE BROADCAST: UK

PERSONNEL: The Stones, c. 1964

SONGS/OTHER CONTENT: Not Fade Away (Petty, Hardin)

NOTES: This second segment of BBC-TV's '60s series broadcast a 1964 "Top of the Pops" clip of the Stones performing "Not Fade Away."

OCTOBER 19, 1991

PROGRAM: Sound of the Sixties (BBC-TV Series)

WHERE BROADCAST: UK

PERSONNEL: The Stones, c. 1965

SONGS/OTHER CONTENT: Get Off of My Cloud

NOTES: The third segment of this series used a 1965 clip of "Get Off of My Cloud" from "Top of the Pops."

OCTOBER 19, 1991

PROGRAM: Guitar Legends (Pay-Per-View)

WHERE BROADCAST: US

PERSONNEL: Keith Richards, The X-Pensive Winos

SONGS/OTHER CONTENT: Shake Rattle & Roll (Turner) / I'm Going Down (King) / Something Else (Cochran) / Connection / **E:** Can't Turn You Loose (Redding)

NOTES: Keith & the Winos, Bob Dylan, and other guitar legends were covered on this pay cable offering. Taped on October 17 in Spain.

NOVEMBER 2, 1991

PROGRAM: Sound of the Sixties (BBC-TV Series)

WHERE BROADCAST: UK

PERSONNEL: The Stones, c. 1967

SONGS/OTHER CONTENT: Let's Spend the Night Together

NOTES: The fifth segment (there was no Stones in segment four) of "Sound of the Sixties" included a 1967 clip of "Let's Spend the Night Together"—again, from "Top of the Pops."

NOVEMBER 9, 1991

PROGRAM: Sound of the Sixties (BBC-TV Series)

WHERE BROADCAST: UK

PERSONNEL: The Stones, c. 1969

SONGS/OTHER CONTENT: Honky Tonk Women

NOTES: The sixth segment of "Sound of the Sixties" used another "Top of the Pops" clip, "Honky Tonk Women" from 1969.

NOVEMBER 15, 1991

PROGRAM: ABC's In Concert
WHERE BROADCAST: USA
SONGS/OTHER CONTENT: The Making of the IMAX Movie
NOTES: How the Stones' breakthrough concert film was made—what the cameras looked like, where it can be screened, and so on. The first broadcast dates of this program varied from state to state.

DECEMBER 7, 1991

PROGRAM: Sound of the Sixties (BBC-TV Series)
WHERE BROADCAST: UK
PERSONNEL: The Stones, c. 1969
SONGS/OTHER CONTENT: Gimme Shelter
NOTES: The tenth "Sound of the Sixties" show used another Stones clip, "Gimme Shelter," but this time the footage was taken from the 1969 "POP Go the Sixties" end-of-the-decade special.

1992

JANUARY 4, 1992

PROGRAM: ABC's In Concert
WHERE BROADCAST: USA
PERSONNEL: Keith Richards, The X-Pensive Winos
SONGS/OTHER CONTENT: Richards interview / concert footage
NOTES: A portion of Keith & the Wino's Hollywood Palladium show was aired, as well as an interview with Richards.

JANUARY 24, 1992

PROGRAM: ABC's In Concert
WHERE BROADCAST: USA
SONGS/OTHER CONTENT: IMAX film clips
NOTES: Various clips from *The Rolling Stones at the MAX* are shown.

FEBRUARY 21, 1992

PROGRAM: Lifestyles of the Rich and Famous
WHERE BROADCAST: USA
PERSONNEL: Bill Wyman
SONGS/OTHER CONTENT: Wyman profile
NOTES: Why not? (And see April 28, 1989.)

JULY 10, 1992

PROGRAM: ABC's In Concert
WHERE BROADCAST: USA
PERSONNEL: Mick Taylor
SONGS/OTHER CONTENT: *Gimme Shelter* video clips / Taylor profile, interview
NOTES: An artist profile of Mick Taylor, including a recent at-home interview with the former Stones guitarist, accompanied clips from the Maysles' Brothers movie, *Gimme Shelter*, for a major portion of this program. Among other things, Taylor talked about Altamont and the 1969 tour—his first with the Stones—and the film, on the occasion of its release on home video. (See PROMOTIONAL FILMS AND VIDEOS)

JULY 16, 1992
(APPEARANCE CANCELLED)

PROGRAM: Late Night with David Letterman
WHERE BROADCAST: USA
PERSONNEL: Charlie Watts Quintet
SONGS/OTHER CONTENT: None
NOTES: Watts walked out—appearance cancelled. Charlie felt the mandatory Late Night practice of including the show's bandleader Paul Shaffer in the performances of musical guests would throw off the symmetry of his jazz quintet, and, upon learning of it at rehearsal, he splits. The show aired, but not with Charlie.

JULY 22, 1992

PROGRAM: Dennis Miller Show
WHERE BROADCAST: USA
PERSONNEL: Charlie Watts Quintet
SONGS/OTHER CONTENT: Lover Man (Oh Where Can You Be) / Watts interview
NOTES: The Quintet performed "Lover Man" and Dennis talked with Charlie.

SEPTEMBER 9, 1992

PROGRAM: MTV Video Awards
WHERE BROADCAST: Worldwide
PERSONNEL: Mick Jagger
SONGS/OTHER CONTENT: Award presentation
NOTES: Mick presented the award for Best Video of the Year to Van Halen at ceremonies held at UCLA's Pauley Pavilion. MTV broadcast the show via satellite to 150 countries.

OCTOBER 16, 1992

PROGRAM: Bob Dylan Tribute (Pay-per-view)
WHERE BROADCAST: USA
PERSONNEL: Ron Wood

Keith Richards at the Academy, New Year's Eve (BOB GRUEN/STARFILE)

SONGS/OTHER CONTENT: Seven Days (Dylan) / Knocking on Heaven's Door (Dylan)

OCTOBER 28, 1992

PROGRAM: Late Night with David Letterman
WHERE BROADCAST: USA
PERSONNEL: Ron Wood
SONGS/OTHER CONTENT: Stay With Me (Wood, Stewart) / Wood interview
NOTES: Ronnie talked, and played a vintage Faces tune, on Letterman.

NOVEMBER 5, 1992

PROGRAM: Top of the Pops
WHERE BROADCAST: UK
SONGS/OTHER CONTENT: Honky Tonk Women

NOVEMBER 5, 1992

PROGRAM: Later with Bob Costas
WHERE BROADCAST: USA
PERSONNEL: Ron Wood
SONGS/OTHER CONTENT: Wood interview
NOTES: Vacationing Bob Costas was replaced by Matt Lauer (then an anchor of WNBC-NY's "Live at 5" local newscast), who conducted this interview with Ronnie for Costas's late-night NBC network show. Taped on November 2.

NOVEMBER 19, 1992

PROGRAM: Arsenio Hall Show
WHERE BROADCAST: USA
PERSONNEL: Ron Wood
SONGS/OTHER CONTENT: Wood interview / Show Me (Wood)

NOTES: Ron interviewed on Arsenio.

DECEMBER 31, 1992

PROGRAM: CBS' Rock 'n' Roll New Year from the Hard Rock Café
WHERE BROADCAST: USA
PERSONNEL: Keith Richards, The X-Pensive Winos
SONGS/OTHER CONTENT: Take It So Hard (Richards, Jordan) / Time Is on My Side (Meade) / Wicked As It Seems (Richards, Jordan, Drayton) / Gimme Shelter / Eileen (Richards, Jordan) / Happy / I'm Going Down (King)
NOTES: A clip of Keith and the Winos' New Year's Eve performance at New York City's Academy is included in this New Year's Eve show.

1993

The Rolling Stones are officially a foursome as of 1993, with Bill Wyman's public announcement of his resignation coming in the first television appearance of this year. Thus, the current members of the Rolling Stones are now: Mick Jagger, Keith Richards, Ron Wood and Charlie Watts.

JANUARY 6, 1993

PROGRAM: London Tonight
WHERE BROADCAST: UK
PERSONNEL: Bill Wyman
SONGS/OTHER CONTENT: Wyman interview
NOTES: The first official confirmation of myriad rumors finally came from the subject himself. During an interview on this British program, Bill Wyman formally announced that he had quit the Stones.

JANUARY 23, 1993

PROGRAM: ITV's Video Chart Show
WHERE BROADCAST: UK
PERSONNEL: Mick Jagger
SONGS/OTHER CONTENT: Sweet Thing (Jagger), PV
NOTES: British TV premieres Jagger's "Sweet Thing" video. The promo was shot December 10 and 11, 1992 at the Pump Room in Leamington Spa, England.

FEBRUARY 4, 1993

PROGRAM: Late Night with David Letterman
WHERE BROADCAST: USA
PERSONNEL: Mick Jagger
SONGS/OTHER CONTENT: Jagger walk-on

NOTES: During the week of rehearsals prior to this appearance, Mick "just happened" to get caught by Letterman's cameras—for all of one minute.

FEBRUARY 6, 1993

PROGRAM: Saturday Night Live
WHERE BROADCAST: USA
PERSONNEL: Mick Jagger
SONGS/OTHER CONTENT: Sweet Thing (Jagger) / Don't Tear Me Up (Jagger)
NOTES: "Sweet Thing" and "Don't Tear Me Up" live. Plus Mick in skits—doing Keith—perfectly. This was Jagger's idea, not SNL's writers'. He also wore tights, as part of a not-so-sweet SNL sendup of Prince Charles's silly sanitarian yearnings: the newest dirt in the British monarchy's ongoing tabloid scandal was a story (leaked from Buckingham Palace) describing a passionate Charles telling alleged mistress Camilla Parker-Bowles that he wanted to be her tampon. Mick also taped a segment during the show's dress rehearsal for use two weeks later in a "Wayne's World" special.

FEBRUARY 9, L993

PROGRAM: MTV
WHERE BROADCAST: USA
PERSONNEL: Mick Jagger
SONGS/OTHER CONTENT: Sweet Thing (Jagger), PV
NOTES: MTV, a bit behind the UK, premiered the Jagger video.

FEBRUARY 9, 1993

PROGRAM: Live at Webster Hall
WHERE BROADCAST: USA
PERSONNEL: Mick Jagger
SONGS/OTHER CONTENT: Wired All Night (Jagger) / Out of Focus (Jagger) / Sweet Thing (Jagger) / Use Me (Withers) / Don't Tear Me Up (Jagger) / Evening Gown (Jagger) / Angel in My Heart (Jagger) / Wandering Spirit (Jagger) / Put Me in the Trash (Jagger) / Think (Brown) / Mother of a Man (Jagger) / **E1:** Rip this Joint / **E2:** Live with Me / **E3:** Have You Seen Your Mother, Baby, Standing in the Shadow?
NOTES: Mick Jagger, live at Webster Hall. Limited pay-per-view market, a cable offering in selected US cities.

FEBRUARY 20, 1993

PROGRAM: Wayne's World TV Special
WHERE BROADCAST: USA
PERSONNEL: Mick Jagger
SONGS/OTHER CONTENT: Jagger interview skit with Wayne and Garth

NOTES: This skit was taped during the dress rehearsal for "Saturday Night Live"'s February 6 broadcast.

MARCH 2, 1993

PROGRAM: Center Stage (VH1)
WHERE BROADCAST: USA
PERSONNEL: Keith Richards, The X-Pensive Winos
SONGS/OTHER CONTENT: Four songs
NOTES: Keith and the Winos performing at Chicago's WTTW-TV studios, taped on December 28, 1992.

MARCH 5, 1993

PROGRAM: ABC's In Concert
WHERE BROADCAST: USA
PERSONNEL: Mick Jagger

MARCH 19, 1993

PROGRAM: ABC's In Concert
WHERE BROADCAST: USA
PERSONNEL: Keith Richards, The X-Pensive Winos

APRIL 14, 1993

PROGRAM: MTV Unplugged
WHERE BROADCAST: USA
PERSONNEL: Ron Wood, Rod Stewart
SONGS/OTHER CONTENT: Rod Stewart, unplugged concert
NOTES: Rod Stewart unplugged, joined by Ronnie.

APRIL 29, 1993

PROGRAM: Late Night with David Letterman
WHERE BROADCAST: USA
PERSONNEL: Ron Wood, Rod Stewart
SONGS/OTHER CONTENT: Maggie May (Stewart, Quittenton) / Have I Told You Lately that I Love You (Morrison)
NOTES: Ron and Rod performed together on Letterman.

MAY 23, 1993

PROGRAM: Aspel & Company
WHERE BROADCAST: UK
PERSONNEL: Ron Wood, Jerry Lee Lewis
SONGS/OTHER CONTENT: Great Balls of Fire (Hammer, Blackwell) / Whole Lotta Shakin' Goin' On (Williams, David)
NOTES: Woody backed Jerry Lee Lewis.

JUNE 6, 1993

PROGRAM: Good Morning America
WHERE BROADCAST: USA
PERSONNEL: Charlie Watts

SONGS/OTHER CONTENT: Watts interview
NOTES: Charlie on ABC-TV's morning show

JUNE 11, 1993

PROGRAM: Aspel & Company
WHERE BROADCAST: UK
PERSONNEL: Ron Wood, Rod Stewart
SONGS/OTHER CONTENT: Have I Told You Lately that I Love You (Morrison) / Hot Legs (Stewart)
NOTES: Woody in more duets with Rod.

JUNE 20, 1993

PROGRAM: TV-AM
WHERE BROADCAST: UK
PERSONNEL: Bill Wyman
SONGS/OTHER CONTENT: Interview
NOTES: Bill Wyman shared the stage with Leslie Nielsen. An interesting wake-up call.

JULY 19, 1993

PROGRAM: Center Stage (PBS)
WHERE BROADCAST: USA
PERSONNEL: Keith Richards and The X-Pensive Winos
SONGS/OTHER CONTENT: How I Wish (Richards, Jordan) / Wicked as It Seems (Richards, Jordan, Drayton) / Interview / 999 (Richards, Jordan, Wachtel) / Hate It When You Leave (Richards, Jordan, Wachtel) / Time Is on My Side (Meade) / Interview / Gimme Shelter / Whip It Up (Richards, Jordan) / Interview / Eileen (Richards, Jordan) / I Could Have Stood You Up (Richards, Jordan)
NOTES: One-hour PBS concert special. Taped in December 1992 in Chicago. Four songs from this taping were broadcast by VH1 on March 2 (see above).

OCTOBER 13, 1993

PROGRAM: Regis & Kathy Lee
WHERE BROADCAST: USA
PERSONNEL: Charlie Watts
SONGS/OTHER CONTENT: Watts interview / My Foolish Heart
NOTES: Charlie and the Charlie Watts Quintet appeared on Regis & Kathy Lee's ABC morning show.

OCTOBER 14, 1993

PROGRAM: Late Night with Conan O'Brien
WHERE BROADCAST: USA
PERSONNEL: Charlie Watts
SONGS/OTHER CONTENT: Watts interview / Time after Time
NOTES: Charlie did another promo appearance in New York City. NBC's 12:30 A.M. show.

1994

MAY 3, 1994

PROGRAM: Voodoo Lounge press conference—MTV and networks

WHERE BROADCAST: Worldwide

PERSONNEL: Mick Jagger, Keith Richards, Ron Wood, Charlie Watts

SONGS/OTHER CONTENT: Tour / Album announcement press conference

NOTES: The four Rolling Stones, minus Bill Wyman for the first time, sailed down the Hudson River aboard the *Honey Fitz* (once the Kennedy family's cabin cruiser), floated into a press conference at Manhattan's Pier 60 and announced plans for their upcoming world tour. Covered by most major US and foreign print and broadcast news outlets, the announcement featured statements by each band member and a question-and-answer session, as well as the premiere of the first *Voodoo Lounge* single, "Love Is Strong." Bassist Darryl Jones, who participated in the album's recording sessions, was officially named as Wyman's replacement on the tour (though not as a "Stone") and the names of the other musicians in the lineup were filled in. In addition to further delineating the dates and venues on the tour itinerary and the release dates of the *Voodoo Lounge* LP and its singles, both the tour's promoter, Michael Cohl, and Virgin Records' Ken Berry fielded press questions. MTV broadcast some of the event and clips were shown on most news broadcasts worldwide.

JULY 19, 1994

PROGRAM: MTV

WHERE BROADCAST: Worldwide

PERSONNEL: Mick Jagger, Keith Richards, Ron Wood, Charlie Watts

SONGS/OTHER CONTENT: Love Is Strong, PV

NOTES: The premiere of the first promo from *Voodoo Lounge*, shot in Toronto in June.

JULY 31–AUGUST 5, 1994

PROGRAM: All-Week Stones Salute (VH1)

WHERE BROADCAST: USA

PERSONNEL: Mick Jagger, Keith Richards, Ron Wood, Charlie Watts, Darryl Jones, Bobby Keys, Chuck Leavell, Lisa Fischer, Bernard Fowler, The New West Horns, various Voodoo Lounge tour personnel, Dan Aykroyd

SONGS/OTHER CONTENT: Tour rehearsals / Set-up, Background footage / Interviews / Concert footage clips etc. / Various Stones movies and feature-length television broadcasts

NOTES: Dan Aykroyd hosted this week-long "Salute" and buildup to the Voodoo Lounge tour, which included interviews with Jagger, Richards and other band members as they rehearsed and tried out the stage for the August 1 kickoff concert at RFK Stadium in Washington, DC. Plus, coverage of who and what it took to build the stage and how the mammoth tour would transport itself around the world. VH1 aired other bits and bobs for seven days. See detailed VH1 listings, below.

JULY 31, 1994

PROGRAM: The Rolling Stones—At the MAX (VH1)

WHERE BROADCAST: US

SONGS/OTHER CONTENT: *At the MAX* (IMAX FILM), edited: Start Me Up / Tumbling Dice / Honky Tonk Women / Sympathy for the Devil / You Can't Always Get What You Want / Street Fighting Man / Brown Sugar / (I Can't Get No) Satisfaction

NOTES: The first time the Stones' IMAX movie (as converted to video) is aired on US television—although not in its entirety (see PROMOTIONAL FILMS AND VIDEOS.) Part of the week-long VH1 Rolling Stones/Voodoo Lounge special that began on July 31 (see above).

AUGUST 1, 1994

PROGRAM: 25 X 5—The Continuing Adventures of the Rolling Stones (VH1)

WHERE BROADCAST: US

SONGS/OTHER CONTENTS: *25 X 5*—Film

NOTES: Another part of VH1's week-long Rolling Stones/Voodoo Lounge special. (See PROMOTIONAL FILMS AND VIDEOS)

AUGUST 1, 1994

PROGRAM: Opening Night at RFK (FOX Network—Syndicated)

WHERE BROADCAST: US

SONGS/OTHER CONTENT: Concert footage / Interviews

NOTES: Between 9:00 P.M. and 11:00 P.M.. EST, FOX covered the first concert of Voodoo Lounge, at RFK Stadium in Washington, DC, with intermittent reports, concert footage and interview segments. The program was syndicated and may not have appeared in the same time period in all markets.

AUGUST 2, 1994

PROGRAM: Terrifying (VH1)

WHERE BROADCAST: US

SONGS/OTHER CONTENT: 1989 Atlantic City concert

NOTES: The Stones' 1989 Atlantic City pay-per-view broadcast—a.k.a. "Terrifying"—was yet another offering in a week full of Stonesiana on VH1.

AUGUST 3, 1994

PROGRAM: *Gimme Shelter* (VH1)

WHERE BROADCAST: US

SONGS/OTHER CONTENT: *Gimme Shelter*—Film

NOTES: The Maysles Brothers' landmark contribution to rock 'n' roll filmmaking was another segment in VH1's week-long Rolling Stones/Voodoo Lounge special. (See PROMOTIONAL FILMS AND VIDEOS)

AUGUST 4, 1994

PROGRAM: The Rolling Stones at the Tokyo Dome (VH1)

WHERE BROADCAST: US

SONGS/OTHER CONTENT: Stones at Tokyo Dome (Japanese TV special)

NOTES: Japanese TV's 1990 one-hour special from Steel Wheels in Tokyo got its first US airing by VH1 during its week-long Voodoo Lounge promotion.

AUGUST 5, 1994

PROGRAM: *25 X 5* and *Gimme Shelter* (VH1)

WHERE BROADCAST: US

SONGS/OTHER CONTENT: *25 X 5 / Gimme Shelter*

NOTES: Both of these films were rebroadcast on the final day of VH1's week-long Rolling Stones extravaganza.

AUGUST 28, 1994

PROGRAM: *Performance* (ZDF-TV)

WHERE BROADCAST: Germany

PERSONNEL: Mick Jagger, Anita Pallenberg

SONGS/OTHER CONTENT: *Performance*—Film

NOTES: German television airs the classic film. (See PROMOTIONAL FILMS AND VIDEOS)

SEPTEMBER 8, 1994

PROGRAM: MTV Awards

WHERE BROADCAST: US

SONGS/OTHER CONTENT: Love Is Strong / Start Me Up

NOTES: The MTV Music Awards originated from Radio City Music Hall and featured performance footage of these two songs.

OCTOBER 27, 1994

PROGRAM: Conversation with the Stones (VH1)

WHERE BROADCAST: USA

SONGS/OTHER CONTENT: Band interviews/Voodoo Lounge Tour rehearsal footage

NOTES: There were but four Rolling Stones. After 30 years a Maysles returns—Albert Maysles (brother David died in 1987) produced, directed and was the primary cinematographer on this 30-minute special documentary commissioned by VH1. The whole film was shot in one day, July 12, in Toronto, where the Stones were rehearsing prior to the August 1 kickoff of the Voodoo Lounge Tour. Composed primarily of interviews with the four remaining Stones (journalist Kurt Loder assisted Maysles in formulating the questions to ask), the film also includes footage of the band in rehearsal. VH1 had broadcast the other Maysles film, *Gimme Shelter,* during their week-long summer Stones extravaganza at the beginning of the tour and gave it several re-airings along with the premiere showings of this new one, beginning on October 27.

NOVEMBER 13, 1994

PROGRAM: 60 Minutes

WHERE BROADCAST: USA

PERSONNEL: Mick Jagger, Keith Richards, Ron Wood, Charlie Watts, (and Darryl Jones, Bobby Keys, *et al.*)

SONGS/OTHER CONTENT: Interviews / Concert footage / Behind-the-scenes footage

NOTES: Ed Bradley covered the Stones in a 20-minute segment on this CBS Sunday prime-time magazine show. Concert footage from the Stones' New Orleans show, plus reasonably probing interviews with band members, behind-the-scenes backstage and other coverage—such as Mick Jagger dancing in the street during the New Orleans Jazz Festival—all provided a wide-ranging portrait of the band.

NOVEMBER 18, 1994

PROGRAM: MBone Internet Broadcast

WHERE BROADCAST: Worldwide

SONGS/OTHER CONTENT: Not Fade Away (Petty, Hardin) / Tumbling Dice / Live with Me / You Got Me Rocking / Shattered / Rocks Off

NOTES: The first five songs from the Dallas Voodoo Lounge concert were broadcast over the Internet. Not really television, but we haven't got an Internet chapter —yet. (See CHRONOLOGY and TOURS AND CONCERTS)

NOVEMBER 19, 1994

PROGRAM: ABC's In Concert

WHERE BROADCAST: USA

SONGS/OTHER CONTENT: You Got Me Rocking, PV / Sparks Will Fly / Love Is Strong / Honky Tonk Women / Interview / Backstage footage / Love Is Strong, PV

NOTES: This Saturday evening, "In Concert" featured the Rolling Stones in a big way—in the two videos, plus performance ("Sparks Will Fly," "Love Is Strong,"

"Honky Tonk Women") and backstage footage from the band's Voodoo Lounge warmup gig at Toronto's RPM Club.

WEEK OF NOVEMBER 23, 1994

PROGRAM: Naked Cafe (VH1)
WHERE BROADCAST: USA
SONGS/OTHER CONTENT: Stones on tour / "Jagger-cam" eye-view footage
NOTES: An eight-minute segment of VH1's "Naked Cafe" featured tape shot via a camera mounted on Mick Jagger's head during this day-in-the-life—more like a couple of hours—coverage of the Rolling Stones on tour. The "Jagger-cam" point of view was inset into the overall piece that portrayed the band in various situations—on a bus going to and from a concert, shaking hands, etc.

NOVEMBER 23, 1994

PROGRAM: Beverly Hills 90210
WHERE BROADCAST: USA
PERSONNEL: Mick Jagger, Keith Richards, Ron Wood, Charlie Watts, Darryl Jones, *et al.*
SONGS/OTHER CONTENT: Not Fade Away (Petty, Hardin) clip
NOTES: A clip, supposedly from the Stones' October 19–20 concert in LA, but actually from the *Live Voodoo Lounge* home video, was used at the end of this episode. The show, in a somewhat convoluted plot, portrayed its status-conscious characters finally attending the concert like normal people, without backstage passes.

NOVEMBER 25, 1994

PROGRAM: Joe Robbie Stadium, Miami, FL (Pay-per-view)
WHERE BROADCAST: USA
PERSONNEL: Mick Jagger, Keith Richards, Ron Wood, Charlie Watts, tour personnel, Sheryl Crow, Robert Cray, Bo Diddley
SONGS/OTHER CONTENT: Concert
NOTES: The Voodoo Lounge US Pay-per-view show. (See TOURS AND CONCERTS)

DECEMBER 7, 1994

PROGRAM: Billboard Music Awards
WHERE BROADCAST: USA
PERSONNEL: Mick Jagger, Keith Richards, Ron Wood, Charlie Watts
SONGS/OTHER CONTENT: Backstage interview / I Go Wild
NOTES: One segment of this live awards show was a live-via-satellite interview of the band backstage in Montreal, including their acceptance of *Billboard* Magazine's

Lifetime Achievement Award. Later on in the program, viewers were treated to a supposedly live Stones performance of "I Go Wild." In actuality, the "live" concert was a clip from the US Thanksgiving Day (November 25—detailed above) pay-per-view show in Miami, Florida.

THROUGHOUT 1994

PROGRAM: Promo Videos
WHERE BROADCAST: USA and worldwide via MTV, VH1 etc.
PERSONNEL: Mick Jagger, Keith Richards, Ron Wood, Charlie Watts
SONGS/OTHER CONTENT: Love Is Strong / Out of Tears / You Got Me Rocking / I Go Wild
NOTES: Videos of these songs were aired over MTV, VH1 during 1994.

1995

JANUARY 10, 1995

PROGRAM: George Jones—"The Bradley Barn Sessions" (TNN)
WHERE BROADCAST: US
PERSONNEL: Keith Richards
NOTES: This program, broadcast via Nashville-based TNN cable network, featured Keith.

FEBRUARY 4, 1995

PROGRAM: Rio de Janeiro Concert (Live pay-per-view)
WHERE BROADCAST: Brazil
PERSONNEL: Mick Jagger, Keith Richards, Ron Wood, Charlie Watts, Darryl Jones, *et al.*
SONGS/OTHER CONTENT: Maracana Stadium show
NOTES: Pay-per-view of the Stones' second Rio concert. (See TOURS AND CONCERTS)

FEBRUARY 16, 1995

PROGRAM: Buenos Aires Concert (Live pay-per-view)
WHERE BROADCAST: Argentina
PERSONNEL: Mick Jagger, Keith Richards, Ron Wood, Charlie Watts, Darryl Jones, *et al.*
SONGS/OTHER CONTENT: River Plate Stadium show
NOTES: Pay-per-view of the Stones' fifth and final concert in Buenos Aires. (See TOURS AND CONCERTS)

FEBRUARY 25, 1995

PROGRAM: Johannesburg Concert
WHERE BROADCAST: South Africa
PERSONNEL: Mick Jagger, Keith Richards, Ron Wood, Charlie Watts, Darryl Jones, *et al.*

SONGS/OTHER CONTENT: Ellis Park Stadium show

NOTES: Second of two dates in Johannesburg. The television special was two hours, 15 minutes long, and included all 23 titles in the set, except that "Rock and a Hard Place" was only partially broadcast. (See TOURS AND CONCERTS)

MARCH 3, 1995

PROGRAM: Rolling Stones Tokyo Press Conference

WHERE BROADCAST: Japan

PERSONNEL: Mick Jagger, Keith Richards, Ron Wood, Charlie Watts

SONGS/OTHER CONTENT: Press conference

NOTES: The Japan portion of the Voodoo Lounge tour kicked off with this press conference.

APRIL 1, 1995

PROGRAM: Tokyo Dome Concert (NHK)

WHERE BROADCAST: Japan

PERSONNEL: Mick Jagger, Keith Richards, Ron Wood, Charlie Watts, Darryl Jones, *et al.*

SONGS/OTHER CONTENT: March 12 Tokyo Dome concert

NOTES: The fourth of seven Voodoo Lounge dates at the Tokyo Dome, edited and broadcast by NHK-TV. (See TOURS AND CONCERTS)

JUNE 1, 1995

PROGRAM: Stockholm, Sweden Press conference

WHERE BROADCAST: Europe

SONGS/OTHER CONTENT: Press conference

NOTES: The Stones held this press conference to officially open the European leg of Voodoo Lounge.

JUNE 3, 1995

PROGRAM: Voodoo Lounge—Europe—Special

WHERE BROADCAST: Europe

PERSONNEL: Mick Jagger, Keith Richards, Ron Wood, Charlie Watts, Darryl Jones, *et al.*

SONGS/OTHER CONTENT: Not Fade Away (Petty, Hardin) / I Go Wild (Stockholm) / Love Is Strong

NOTES: Kickoff television special for the European portion of Voodoo Lounge, broadcast in European countries by various national networks (in Germany via ZDF and Premiere [pay TV]; in France over Canal Plus). A lot of behind-the-scenes action, some archival footage (eliminating shots of Bill Wyman and Mick Taylor), current interviews with the band, and performance footage from Voodoo Lounge and prior tours. Only the first two songs came from Voodoo Lounge in Stockholm.

OCTOBER 20, 1995

PROGRAM: Most Wanted (MTV—Europe)

WHERE BROADCAST: UK/Europe

PERSONNEL: Mick Jagger, Keith Richards, Ron Wood, Charlie Watts, Darryl Jones, Patricia Arquette

SONGS/OTHER CONTENT: Like a Rolling Stone (Dylan)

NOTES: The promo video for the first single off *Stripped*. The Stones' soon-to-be-released newest album has its European premiere on MTV's "Most Wanted" program. It didn't air in the US until October 28.

OCTOBER 28, 1995

PROGRAM: MAD TV (FOX)

WHERE BROADCAST: USA

PERSONNEL: Mick Jagger, Keith Richards, Ron Wood, Charlie Watts, Darryl Jones, Patricia Arquette

SONGS/OTHER CONTENT: Like a Rolling Stone (Dylan)

NOTES: The US premiere of the Stones' "Like a Rolling Stone" music video was broadcast nationwide not by MTV, but by the non-cable FOX-TV network on its fairly zany "MAD" (as in *MAD* magazine) television show. MTV-US began showing it on October 31.

NOVEMBER 16, 1995

PROGRAM: The British Invade America (CBS-TV Special)

WHERE BROADCAST: USA

PERSONNEL: Mick Jagger, Keith Richards, Brian Jones, Charlie Watts, Bill Wyman

SONGS/OTHER CONTENT: Time Is on My Side (Meade) / (I Can't Get No) Satisfaction

NOTES: This CBS special on the British invasion included clips of the above songs from "The Ed Sullivan Show."

1996

FEBRUARY 10, 1996

PROGRAM: VH1 to One: Keith Richards

WHERE BROADCAST: US/Worldwide

PERSONNEL: Keith Richards

SONGS/OTHER CONTENT: Interview with Keith

NOTES: Anthony deCurtis conducted a one-on-one interview with Keith Richards at Point of View, his home in Jamaica. A few clips from *Stripped* (the one-hour video) were intercut, but most of the 30-minute (including nearly 15 minutes of commercials!) piece was a very relaxed conversation about 33 years of the Stones, rock 'n' roll, life, music, etc. Also a mini-tour of the house, plus footage of Keith playing with local Rasta musicians he'd been jamming with for many years and was finally recording for a commercial release. VH1 repeated this segment once more on the same date and several times in subsequent weeks. The interview was part of VH1's three and a half hour block of Stones-related programming heralding the release of the band's new album, *Stripped*. Interestingly, VH1 chose to air *Gimme Shelter*, the Maysles Brothers' 1969 tour/Altamont movie, as another large chunk of its February 10 Stones special. (See also PROMOTIONAL FILMS AND VIDEOS)

FEBRUARY 10, 1996

PROGRAM: *Stripped* Special (on VH1)
WHERE BROADCAST: US/Worldwide
PERSONNEL: Mick Jagger, Keith Richards, Ron Wood, Charlie Watts, Darryl Jones, *et al.*
SONGS/OTHER CONTENT: *Stripped*

NOTES: *Stripped*, the Rolling Stones' one-hour video special, was premiered by VH1 as the centerpiece of a three and a half hour modular programming block hooked on the release of *Stripped*, the Stones new album. This video is a kind of album-length semi-documentary music video about the making of a semi-acoustic, semi-live album. (See PROMOTIONAL FILMS AND VIDEOS)

OCTOBER 17, 1996

PROGRAM: Top of the Pops
WHERE BROADCAST: UK
PERSONNEL: Mick Jagger, Keith Richards, Brian Jones, Charlie Watts, Bill Wyman, Ian Stewart, Rocky Dijon, Nicky Hopkins
SONGS/OTHER CONTENT: Sympathy for the Devil, LV4
NOTES: A clip from *The Rolling Stones Rock and Roll Circus* video, released (as were the soundtrack CD and cassette) on October 15, 1996, nearly 28 years after the fact.

Promotional Films and Videos

This section lists the Stones' promotional films and music videos by the year each appeared or, in the case of the unaired, unseen clips, the year made.

1963

PRETTY THING

YEAR MADE: 1963
DIRECTOR: Giorgio Gomelsky
NOTES: Shot in April, 1963, in 35mm black-and-white by Giorgio Gomelsky, this was the title of the first Rolling Stones promo. The band had found their potential springboard to fame when Gomelsky booked them to fill in for his regular Sunday evening band at the Station Hotel in Richmond, a London suburb. In less than two months, the one-off gig had become a regular Stones residency at what came to be called the "Crawdaddy Club" (see CHRO-NOLOGY and TOURS AND CONCERTS). The Stones' audience had grown from a half dozen to hundreds, and promoter/filmmaker Gomelsky had emerged as the band's biggest supporter. Drawing on his experience on the British music scene, and intent on managing the group's burgeoning career, Giorgio targeted the 20-minute documentary-style film at record companies and the press, aimed at generating interest in the Stones and in the rising popularity of rhythm and blues in the UK. The action begins with Stu's legendary transit van arriving at the Station Hotel and the band's gear being unloaded. Inside, people are gathered; the Rolling Stones are about to perform. The concert sequence follows, showing the band performing (miming to the prerecorded) two songs —"Pretty Thing" and "It's All Right, Babe"—intercut with footage of the kids dancing wildly to the music (see SESSIONOGRAPHY). One audience cutaway includes a closeup of Linda Lawrence, Brian Jones's current girlfriend. To date, this film has never been released.

1964

NOT FADE AWAY (PETTY, HARDIN)

ALBUM: *England's Newest Hitmakers* (US) / *Big Hits (High Tide & Green Grass)* (UK)

DIRECTOR: Union

NOTES: Black-and-white. The visuals show the Stones running around outdoors, rolling rocks down a hill (!), and generally goofing about. The audio consists of the prerecorded musical track, but there is no lip synching or mimed performance to the song. The clip was first aired on the BBC-TV show "Top of the Pops."

TELL ME

ALBUM: *The Rolling Stones* (UK) / *England's Newest Hitmakers* (US)

DIRECTOR: Union

IF YOU NEED ME (PICKETT, BATEMAN, SANDERS)

ALBUM: *12 X 5* (US) / *The Rolling Stones #2* (UK)

DIRECTOR: Union

NOTES: Mick does some very bad lip-synching on this one. Shot in black-and-white, on a small stage with the Stones "performing" in front of a backdrop of large curtains. The band appears to be playing magic (for 1964) electric guitars—there are no wires or cables attached to any of the instruments, nor are any amps visible on the stage.

IT'S ALL OVER NOW (WOMACK, WOMACK)

ALBUM: *12 X 5* (US) / *The Rolling Stones #2* (UK)

DIRECTOR: Union

CONFESSIN' THE BLUES (McSHANN, BROWN)

ALBUM: *12 X 5* (US) / *The Rolling Stones #2* (UK)

DIRECTOR: Union

AROUND & AROUND (BERRY)

ALBUM: *12 X 5* (US) / *5 X 5—EP* (UK)

DIRECTOR: Union

NOTES: Not to be confused with the Pathé "Gather No Moss" film shot at the Hull Cinema (performance and backstage footage). This is also a color clip. It was shot especially for Scopitone for the Scopitone jukeboxes that were so popular in Europe and nearly unknown in the US.

SUSIE Q (BROADWATER, LEWIS, HAWKINS)

ALBUM: *12 X 5* (US) / *The Rolling Stones #2* (UK)

DIRECTOR: Union

HEART OF STONE

ALBUM: *The Rolling Stones, Now!* (US) / *Out of Our Heads* (UK)

DIRECTOR: Union

DOWN THE ROAD APIECE (RAYE)

ALBUM: *The Rolling Stones, Now!* (US) / *The Rolling Stones #2* (UK)

DIRECTOR: Union

OH BABY (WE GOT A GOOD THING GOIN') (OZEN)

ALBUM: *The Rolling Stones, Now!* (US) / *Out of Our Heads* (UK)

DIRECTOR: Union

CAROL (BERRY)

ALBUM: *The Rolling Stones* (UK) / *England's Newest Hitmakers* (US)

DIRECTOR: Union

1965

GET OFF OF MY CLOUD

ALBUM: *December's Children* (US) / *Big Hits (High Tide & Green Grass)* (UK)

DIRECTOR: Union

I'M FREE

ALBUM: *December's Children* (US) / *Out of Our Heads* (UK)

DIRECTOR: Peter Whitehead

NOTES: The visuals depict the group cavorting in various situations—running down some railroad tracks, frolicking in the woods—while miming to playback of the song. Black-and-white.

(I CAN'T GET NO) SATISFACTION

ALBUM: *Out of Our Heads* (US) / *Big Hits (High Tide & Green Grass)* (UK)

DIRECTOR: Union

NOTES: When this promo was aired as an insert on "Shindig," September 16, 1965 (*not* to be confused with the Stones' "live" performance of "Satisfaction" aired on "Shindig," May 26, 1965), the censors had gotten to it. Rumors had begun circulating when the song was released that the garbled lyric "trying to make some girl *who tells me*" was "trying to make some girl *pregnant*"—it wasn't, and isn't. Unable to decipher Jagger's vocals, the censors opted for the better-safe-than-sorry approach and cut the phrase, "trying to make some girl who tells me." Ironically, it is the *next* phrase that should have been the subject of scrutiny: " . . . make some girl, who tells me, 'Baby, baby come back, maybe next week, *'cause you see I'm on a losing streak.'*" This was English prostitutes' slangy way of telling customers it was the (menstrual) time of the month.

MERCY, MERCY (COVAY, MILLER)

ALBUM: *Out of Our Heads* (US & UK)

DIRECTOR: Union

GOOD TIMES (COOKE)

ALBUM: *Out of Our Heads* (US & UK)

DIRECTOR: Union

HITCH HIKE (GAYE, STEVENSON, PAUL)

ALBUM: *Out of Our Heads* (US & UK)

DIRECTOR: Union

THAT'S HOW STRONG MY LOVE IS (JAMISON)

ALBUM: *Out of Our Heads* (US & UK)

DIRECTOR: Union

NOTES: Shot in the UK, this promo was meant for US television but never got that far, although a still photograph taken from this film—showing Brian Jones on organ—was used in a 1965 US press kit. This and a film for "Cry to Me" were made at the same session, both used visual footage performed and cut to prerecorded backing tracks.

CRY TO ME (RUSSELL)

ALBUM: *Out of Our Heads* (US & UK)

DIRECTOR: Union

NOTES: This 1965 black-and-white promo was shot on a soundstage. The scene is essentially a performance of the song; the vocal is filmed live over playback. The unique feature of this clip is the setting for the performance: the Stones perform while sitting on stools on a nearly bare stage, which is very much like the band's shows of 1962 on the stages and stools of London jazz clubs. There are some very nice closeups of Jagger in this one.

1966

HAVE YOU SEEN YOUR MOTHER, BABY, STANDING IN THE SHADOWS? PV VERSION I (IN DRAG IN NYC)

ALBUM: *Flowers* (US) / *Big Hits (High Tide & Green Grass)* (UK)

DIRECTOR: Peter Whitehead

NOTES: Shot on September 9, 1966 in New York City, in the streets of Manhattan's Upper West Side and in Greenwich Village. In a very radical move for a rock 'n' roll band in 1966, the Stones appear in drag as female characters in this film. The actual shooting, which was directed by Peter Whitehead, must have been an interesting, hopefully amusing, experience for the band. During breaks in filming, the Stones, still in drag, repaired to a bar across the street. This particular Upper West Side tavern was, however, a favorite hangout for local Teamsters Union members. Geographically and sartorially speaking, the Greenwich Village location might have been a better place to have had that drink. This landmark promo was shot on color film, but Whitehead chose to make his final print in black and white. Although originally intended for the US, it was only shown in the UK: Americans never saw either promo for this song on television until various rock music histories were made, beginning more than a decade later. The Albert Hall version (II) was featured in "Heroes of Rock 'n' Roll," first broadcast on February 9, 1979.

HAVE YOU SEEN YOUR MOTHER, BABY, STANDING IN THE SHADOWS? PV VERSION II (ALBERT HALL)

ALBUM: *Flowers* (US) / *Big Hits (High Tide & Green Grass)* (UK)

DIRECTOR: Peter Whitehead

NOTES Shot at the Stones' performance at the Royal Albert Hall, September 23, 1966. The band was filmed backstage before going on and while performing this song live before a frenzied, rioting crowd. The footage provides an excellent view of the intense fan hysteria created by the appearance of the Rolling Stones and the obvious charisma of Jagger, Richards and Jones. Peter Whitehead also filmed the band's subsequent Bristol and Newcastle performances for use in this promo, which was intended for airing in both the UK and the US, but, like the drag version, was never broadcast on American television. British viewers saw both films. Though a live version of this song appears on *Got Live If You Want It!*, the studio version was used as the audio track in these promos (which were all made to hype singles), and that studio version first appeared on the albums listed above.

LADY JANE

ALBUM: *Aftermath* (US & UK)

DIRECTOR: Peter Whitehead

NOTES: This clip is an odd one. It consists of visual footage from another promo, the riotous Albert Hall (that is, non-drag) version II of "Have You Seen Your Mother, Baby?," run in slow motion and cut to the audio track of "Lady Jane" from *Aftermath*. All of this was done by the filmmaker himself—Whitehead directed the film and the promos—with the Stones' approval. Whether the "Lady Jane" amalgam should be considered an actual "promo" is debatable since it never aired on its own. But Peter Whitehead considered it as such and it is the only specific film/video piece on this song, other than performance clips from various television appearances. It can be seen as part of Whitehead's film, *Tonite, Let's All Make Love in London*.

19TH NERVOUS BREAKDOWN

ALBUM: *Big Hits (High Tide & Green Grass)* (US & UK)

DIRECTOR: Union

LET'S SPEND THE NIGHT TOGETHER

ALBUM: *Between The Buttons*

DIRECTOR: Peter Whitehead

NOTES: Footage shot at Olympic Studios in November 1966. To playback. Never released commercially. Extracts were used later for the "We Love You" promo.

1967

WE LOVE YOU

ALBUM: *Through the Past, Darkly* (UK) / *More Hot Rocks (Big Hits & Fazed Cookies)* (US)

DIRECTOR: Peter Whitehead

NOTES: The dramatic action segment of this promo, in which Keith, Mick and Marianne reenact the trial of Oscar Wilde, doesn't include all the Rolling Stones. Peter Whitehead had shot footage of the whole band recording at Olympic Studios; to keep it a "Stones promo," he added this session material to the film for a final edit that is a montage of quick cuts and high speed zooms. Released in August 1967, "We Love You" was the Stones' thank-you gesture to their fans and friends for their unswerving support during a period of intense harassment of the band by the establishment that culminated in a series of drug arrests, trials and the jailing of Mick and Keith. The promo's opening sequence, conceived and tacked on at the last moment, shows a ball-and-chained prisoner—first Jagger, then more generically from about the knees down —walking down a prison corridor, the jail door slamming behind him.

DANDELION

ALBUM: *Through the Past, Darkly* (US & UK)

DIRECTOR: Union

2000 LIGHT YEARS FROM HOME

ALBUM: *Their Satanic Majesties Request*

DIRECTOR: Michael Lindsay-Hogg

NOTES: The sharp-eyed viewer should notice something peculiar about this promo—Bill, Brian and Keith appear to be left-handed guitarists. For some reason, most likely an error when distribution prints were made, the original negative film was flopped (wrong side up), resulting in the left-to-right reversal of the image.

SHE'S A RAINBOW

ALBUM: *Their Satanic Majesties Request*

DIRECTOR: Michael Lindsay-Hogg

NOTES: TELEVISION APPEARANCES for more pertinent info.

1968

JUMPIN' JACK FLASH—PV VERSION I (WITH MAKEUP)

ALBUM: *Through the Past, Darkly* (US & UK)

DIRECTOR: Michael Lindsay-Hogg

NOTES: Mimed to the record. Unfortunately, during post-production, somebody goofed and grabbed the wrong audio track. This is baffling, since the original plan was fairly specific, even simple: the band had been filmed in a studio, miming to the recorded single. Somehow, in editing, instead of mating the studio master tape of the single with this footage, said unknown person used the audio track for the second promo of this song. That tape had been recorded during the film shoot, with Mick's live vocal over the prerecorded instrumental backing track. The resulting visuals were badly out-of-synch with the audio track in this promo film, and there is no promo film in existence whose soundtrack is the single version of the record.

JUMPIN' JACK FLASH—PV VERSION II (WITHOUT MAKEUP)

ALBUM: *Through the Past, Darkly* (UK & US)

DIRECTOR: Michael Lindsay-Hogg

NOTES: Live vocal, the instrumental parts were mimed to the specially recorded (at Olympic Studios, April 27, 1968) up-tempo "Jumpin' Jack Flash," PV. The audio track—Mick singing over the prerecorded backing—was recorded at the same time the film was shot. This was the tape used by mistake as the audio for version I of this promo, above. It's easy to differentiate the two promos: in version II, Mick isn't wearing makeup and his vocals are in synch with the film; in version I, he is wearing makeup and his vocals are out of synch.

CHILD OF THE MOON

ALBUM: *More Hot Rocks (Big Hits & Fazed Cookies)* (US) / *No Stone Unturned* (UK)

DIRECTOR: Michael Lindsay-Hogg

SYMPATHY FOR THE DEVIL

ALBUM: *Beggars Banquet*

DIRECTOR: Union

NOTES: Not the same as, nor is this a clip from, Jean-Luc Godard's film *One Plus One* (a.k.a. *Sympathy for the Devil*). This particular film piece was shown on the David Frost show, and features Brian Jones on piano and Rocky Dijon on congas.

1969

YOU CAN'T ALWAYS GET WHAT YOU WANT

ALBUM: *Let It Bleed*

DIRECTOR: Union

HONKY TONK WOMEN—PV VERSION I

ALBUM: *Through the Past, Darkly* (UK & US)

DIRECTOR: Union

NOTES: Taped June 16, 1969

HONKY TONK WOMEN—PV VERSION II

ALBUM: *Through the Past, Darkly* (UK & US)

DIRECTOR: Union

NOTES: Taped July 3, 1969

HONKY TONK WOMEN—PV VERSION III

ALBUM: *Through the Past, Darkly* (UK & US)

DIRECTOR: Union

NOTES: Taped December 12, 1969

GIMME SHELTER I & II, 1969

ALBUM: *Let It Bleed*

DIRECTOR: Union

NOTES: This 1969 color promo was shot with two different edits; one a complete performance, the other with some insert news footage. Jagger wears his '69 US tour outfit along with the fringed top and scarf he wore at Altamont. The band performed over playback, with live vocals. Wisely, this filming of the band's vocals over playback of the *Gimme Shelter* track used a prerecorded vocal track with Merry Clayton's vocal edited out.

1970

LITTLE QUEENIE—PV VERSION I (FROM SAVILLE THEATRE)

ALBUM: *Get Your Ya Ya's Out!*

DIRECTOR: Union

LOVE IN VAIN (ROBT. JOHNSON)

ALBUM: *Let It Bleed*

DIRECTOR: Maysles Brothers

NOTES: From the movie, *Gimme Shelter*.

LITTLE QUEENIE—PV VERSION II (FROM MSG CONCERT)

ALBUM: *Get Your Ya Ya's Out!*

DIRECTOR: Maysles Brothers

NOTES: Used for Australian television only.

1973

ANGIE—PV VERSION I (WITH HAT)

ALBUM: *Goat's Head Soup*

DIRECTOR: Michael Lindsay-Hogg

ANGIE—PV VERSION II (WITHOUT HAT)

ALBUM: *Goat's Head Soup*

DIRECTOR: Michael Lindsay-Hogg

SILVER TRAIN

ALBUM: *Goat's Head Soup*

DIRECTOR: Michael Lindsay-Hogg

DANCING WITH MR. D

ALBUM: *Goat's Head Soup*
DIRECTOR: Michael Lindsay-Hogg

RIP THIS JOINT

ALBUM: *Exile on Main St.*
DIRECTOR: Rollin Binzer
NOTES: From Fort Worth concert, 1972

1974

IT'S ONLY ROCK 'N' ROLL

ALBUM: *It's Only Rock 'n' Roll*
DIRECTOR: Michael Lindsay-Hogg

TILL THE NEXT GOODBYE

ALBUM: *It's Only Rock 'n' Roll*
DIRECTOR: Michael Lindsay-Hogg

AIN'T TOO PROUD TO BEG (WHITFIELD, HOLLAND)

ALBUM: *It's Only Rock 'n' Roll*
DIRECTOR: Michael Lindsay-Hogg

MIDNIGHT RAMBLER

ALBUM: *Let It Bleed*
DIRECTOR: Rollin Binzer
NOTES: Used as promo for *Ladies & Gentlemen, the Rolling Stones.*

HAPPY

ALBUM: *Exile on Main St.*
DIRECTOR: Rollin Binzer
NOTES: Used as promo for *Ladies & Gentlemen, the Rolling Stones.*

ALL DOWN THE LINE

ALBUM: *Exile on Main St.*
DIRECTOR: Rollin Binzer
NOTES: Used as promo for *Ladies & Gentlemen, the Rolling Stones.*

LOVE IN VAIN (ROBT. JOHNSON) [1974 PROMO]

ALBUM: *Let it Bleed*
DIRECTOR: Rollin Binzer

NOTES: Used as promo for *Ladies & Gentlemen, the Rolling Stones.*

1976

FOOL TO CRY

ALBUM: *Black & Blue*
DIRECTOR: Michael Lindsay-Hogg

CRAZY MAMA

ALBUM: *Black & Blue*
DIRECTOR: Michael Lindsay-Hogg

HOT STUFF

ALBUM: *Black & Blue*
DIRECTOR: Michael Lindsay-Hogg

HEY NEGRITA

ALBUM: *Black & Blue*
DIRECTOR: Michael Lindsay-Hogg

1978

RESPECTABLE

ALBUM: *Some Girls*
DIRECTOR: Michael Lindsay-Hogg

MISS YOU

ALBUM: *Some Girls*
DIRECTOR: Michael Lindsay-Hogg

FAR AWAY EYES

ALBUM: *Some Girls*
DIRECTOR: Michael Lindsay-Hogg

1980

EMOTIONAL RESCUE I (THERMO)

ALBUM: *Emotional Rescue*
DIRECTOR: Adam Friedman
NOTES: Thermographic images—heat-sensitive photography

EMOTIONAL RESCUE II (NON-THERMO)

ALBUM: *Emotional Rescue*

DIRECTOR: Adam Friedman
NOTES: Regular photography

WHERE THE BOYS ALL GO (THERMO)

ALBUM: *Emotional Rescue*
DIRECTOR: Adam Friedman
NOTES: Thermographic images—heat-sensitive photography

SHE'S SO COLD

ALBUM: *Emotional Rescue*
DIRECTOR: Adam Friedman

DOWN IN THE HOLE (THERMO)

ALBUM: *Emotional Rescue*
DIRECTOR: Adam Friedman
NOTES: Thermographic images, or heat-sensitive photography. This one was for use in clubs only.

1981

START ME UP

ALBUM: *Tattoo You*
DIRECTOR: Michael Lindsay-Hogg
NOTES: Unreleased

HANG FIRE

ALBUM: *Tattoo You*
DIRECTOR: Michael Lindsay-Hogg

NEIGHBOURS

ALBUM: *Tattoo You*
DIRECTOR: Michael Lindsay-Hogg

WAITING ON A FRIEND

ALBUM: *Tattoo You*
DIRECTOR: Michael Lindsay-Hogg
NOTES: Shot on New York City's Lower East Side —what is now referred to as the East Village—on the street and at the St. Mark's Bar & Grill, a neighborhood establishment located on the corner of First Avenue and East 8th Street (which is also know as St. Mark's Place). One exterior street scene depicts Mick and Keith sitting on a stoop with a couple of friends. These were, in fact, actual friends, not just actors—one of them a leather artisan who makes custom boots, belts, bags, etc. The last part of the video takes place at the bar, whose outside wall is plastered with *Tattoo You* album covers (all of which were carefully and speedily removed immediately following the shoot by

members of the Stones' entourage, as the album hadn't yet been released). Once inside, the Stones pick up their instruments and half-heartedly (it seems) mime to the song, "Waiting on a Friend." In reality, what happened in St. Mark's Bar & Grill that day was that the Stones played quite a few songs while the cameras rolled, one of which was Jimmy Reed's "Baby, You Don't Have to Go." The audience, the staff of the tiny (legal capacity 80–100 persons) St. Mark's Bar & Grill, had a real treat. And the Stones performed in what is possibly the smallest venue of their entire career.

WORRIED ABOUT YOU

ALBUM: *Tattoo You*
DIRECTOR: Michael Lindsay-Hogg
NOTES: Unreleased

1982

GOING TO À GO-GO (ROBINSON, JOHNSON, MOORE, ROGERS) I

ALBUM: *Still Life*
DIRECTOR: Hal Ashby

GOING TO À GO-GO (ROBINSON, JOHNSON, MOORE, ROGERS) II

ALBUM: *Still Life*
DIRECTOR: Hal Ashby

START ME UP, LV (LSTNT PROMO)

ALBUM: *Still Life*
DIRECTOR: Hal Ashby
NOTES: *Let's Spend the Night Together* promo film

TIME IS ON MY SIDE (MEADE), LV2

ALBUM: *Still Life*
DIRECTOR: Hal Ashby
NOTES: Not from *Let's Spend the Night Together*

1983

UNDERCOVER OF THE NIGHT I (UNEXPURGATED)

ALBUM: *Undercover*
DIRECTOR: Julien Temple
NOTES: Like the raunchier Stones, the political Stones inevitably become the censored Stones—but not without

a fight—situation normal. This video, set in San Salvador (though filmed in Coyoacan, Mexico), portrays Mick in dual roles. As what looks like somebody's idea of a foreign correspondent (in a tropical tan suit and hat, drinking in the Holiday Inn bar), he watches a group of masked "terrorists" (led by Keith) sneak up and abduct another hotel guest, also played by Mick, whose female companion watches from the bed (maybe this Mick's the real journalist!). Mick-the-guest is brought to a suspension bridge and executed with a gunshot to the head. All this is observed by Mick-the-supposed-newsman who blows that cover and saves the day with his 9mm. The execution scene proved too much for the BBC and others in the UK, and was excised. It was widely thought that the masked shooter in the scene was Keith. Not really a major stretch of the imagination, but erroneous nonetheless. Allan Dunn, Mick Jagger's assistant, played one of the executioners.

UNDERCOVER OF THE NIGHT II ("NONVIOLENT")

ALBUM: *Undercover*
DIRECTOR: Julien Temple
NOTES: Filmed at the Bains-Douches club, Paris.

TOO MUCH BLOOD

ALBUM: *Undercover*
DIRECTOR: Julien Temple

SHE WAS HOT I (UNEDITED, UNCENSORED VERSION)

ALBUM: *Undercover*
DIRECTOR: Julien Temple
NOTES: See below for comparison of censored versus uncensored.

SHE WAS HOT II (MTV EDIT)

ALBUM: *Undercover*
DIRECTOR: Julien Temple
NOTES: Many of this one's original segments landed on the cutting room floor before it was considered fit for airplay. The reasons for the editing were various. One bit showed a record company exec holding a can of TAB and visible product names are a no-no for MTV and most other broadcasters. The same exec appears in another sequence. This time, he seems to have popped a few buttons on his trousers, although they don't fall down. The button-popping was also a no-show. But the appearance of a telephone number in a scene with Charlie Watts created another sort of havoc when the unexpurgated video was shown. The prefix was not the non-working 555-exchange permitted in films; this number was a real

one in many area codes. Many unwitting US households were disturbed by calls from sharp-eyed video viewers who dialed the number. The final cut involved flame-haired actress/dancer Anita Morris, the red-sequined vamp who slithers around and through almost every scene and male in this production. As if the point had not been made, repeatedly, some genius decided that viewers still needed to know "she was hot," and added a really bad special effect to Morris's last appearance, the closing scene in the video. There she is, atop a television set, fire shooting from her head and, you guessed it, butt. Thankfully, the bum blowtorch idea got the *coup de gras*—at both ends.

1986

HARLEM SHUFFLE (RELF, NELSON)

ALBUM: *Dirty Work*
DIRECTOR: Ralph Bakshi

ONE HIT (TO THE BODY) (JAGGER, RICHARDS, WOOD)

ALBUM: *Dirty Work*
DIRECTOR: Russell Mulcahy

1989

MIXED EMOTIONS

ALBUM: *Steel Wheels*
DIRECTOR: Jim Signorelli

ROCK AND A HARD PLACE I (CHYRON+ OR "GRAFFITI VERSION")

ALBUM: *Steel Wheels*
DIRECTOR: Wayne Isham
NOTES: Both "Rock and a Hard Place" videos were shot during the Steel Wheels tour at the end of September/beginning of October in Foxboro, Massachusetts (near Boston), where the band played three concerts at Sullivan Stadium. Most of the onstage performance footage in the video was shot in the stadium during the day, without an audience, though the necessary overall concert and audience shots were filmed during the actual show in the evening. The main difference between the two versions of this promo is the post-production addition, in version I, of Chyron graphics over and throughout most of the Foxboro concert film of the Stones. Some of the Chyron is typographic and in transparent layers—song lyrics and recognizable words. Others are opaque inserts of graphic visuals—drawings, logos—ed-

Ron Wood, director Julien Temple, Keith Richards (together at left) and Charlie Watts during the making of the "Highwire" video (VINNIE ZUFFANTE/STARFILE)

ited into the live footage. The net effect is that many people describe this promo as the "graffiti version." Version II of the "Rock and a Hard Place" video lacks most of the graphic effects, but has added inserts of other, non-concert, footage of the Stones.

ROCK AND A HARD PLACE II (CHYRON+ OR "NO GRAFFITI")

ALBUM: *Steel Wheels*
DIRECTOR: Wayne Isham
NOTES: See "Rock and a Hard Place" I above for a full explanation of the difference between the two promos. This video has some Chyron effects, but fewer than version I. Additionally, the basic version II is a different edit, containing scenes that do not appear in version I.

TERRIFYING

ALBUM: *Steel Wheels*
DIRECTOR: Julien Temple

SAD SAD SAD

ALBUM: *Steel Wheels*
DIRECTOR: Julien Temple
NOTES: Shot on September 3 and 4 in Toronto. Aired on the International Rock Awards, June 6, 1990.

ALMOST HEAR YOU SIGH (JAGGER, RICHARDS, JORDAN)

ALBUM: *Steel Wheels*
DIRECTOR: Jake Scott

389

NOTES: Shot on September 27 and 28, 1989, in Cleveland, Ohio. Director Jake Scott is the son of director Ridley Scott.

1990

IT'S ONLY ROCK 'N' ROLL

ALBUM: *It's Only Rock 'n' Roll*
DIRECTOR: Julien Temple
NOTES: A live Urban Jungle performance in Munich was filmed on June 3, 1990 for this promo. The clip was used on the June 6, 1990 International Rock Awards show.

1991

HIGHWIRE

ALBUM: *Flashpoint*
DIRECTOR: Julien Temple
NOTES: Filmed at Pier 3, in Brooklyn, NY on March 1, 1991, without Bill Wyman. Aired on "Top of the Pops" on March 21, 1991, minus the first, controversial, verse.

SEX DRIVE I
("ARTISTIC VERSION")

ALBUM: *Flashpoint*
DIRECTOR: Julien Temple
NOTES: This footage really should have been used to promote "Little T & A," for that's what you do or don't see, depending on whether you're watching the "artistic" or "MTV" version. Charlie Watts portrays a superb, wry psychiatrist to Mick as a supine-on-the-couch and clearly confused patient. Unsurprisingly, there's a lot of semi/pseudo-Freudian imagery, some of which got cut to satisfy MTV. In this case, more was added to tone it down for the masses, like lingerie on the many nude female bodies who traipse through our patient's (waking?) dreams. By the way, Jagger's alleged paramour, model Carla Bruni, was reportedly one of the actresses in this video. Art? Life? What's the difference? Better ask the Stones—or whoever started those rumors.

SEX DRIVE II (MTV EDIT)

ALBUM: *Flashpoint*
DIRECTOR: Julien Temple
NOTES: With lingerie and edited for MTV.

RUBY TUESDAY

ALBUM: *At the MAX*
DIRECTOR: Julien Temple
NOTES: This version of "Ruby Tuesday" came from the IMAX film (see FILMS). In fact, the video itself was clipped directly from that film and was part of its promotion. A live version of "Ruby Tuesday" is on *Flashpoint*, and that's fortunate in a marketing sense, but it's not the same "Ruby Tuesday" track heard on this video.

JUMPIN' JACK FLASH
(PROMO FILM—W/INSERTS & REEDIT)

ALBUM: *Through the Past, Darkly*
DIRECTOR: Maysles Brothers
NOTES: "Jumpin' Jack Flash" from the film, *Gimme Shelter*, but not a straight clip. Additional visuals (other scenes from the movie) were inserted, using the song footage as a starting point, to make a promo to accompany ABKCO's home video release of *Gimme Shelter*.

(I CAN'T GET NO) SATISFACTION
(PROMO FILM—GIMME SHELTER)

ALBUM: *Out of Our Heads* (US)
DIRECTOR: Maysles Brothers
NOTES: Promo for the *Gimme Shelter* film—another part of ABKCO's marketing of the *Gimme Shelter* videocassette. Unlike the "Jumpin' Jack Flash" promo detailed above, this is just a clip of "Satisfaction" as seen in the Maysles' film, nothing more. However, it is considered a promo because it was released in 1991 expressly for use by various broadcast and cable TV music shows to regenerate interest in the film, and thus, the new home video of it.

1994

LOVE IS STRONG

ALBUM: *Voodoo Lounge*
DIRECTOR: David Fincher
NOTES: The biggest Stones—and various models—you'll ever see were filmed in Toronto at Harbourside Studios, June 15–19, 1994 and seamlessly combined with footage of New York City through the magic of image editing by computer. The result was a black-and-white video in which, for example, Charlie nonchalantly plays a rooftop water tank as if it's his drum kit. Only when your mind truly engages do you realize it's all physically impossible. Premiered on MTV on July 19, 1994.

YOU GOT ME ROCKING

ALBUM: *Voodoo Lounge*
DIRECTOR: Jim Gable
NOTES: The primary shooting took place in New Jersey.

OUT OF TEARS

ALBUM: *Voodoo Lounge*
DIRECTOR: Kevin Kerslake

1995

I GO WILD I

ALBUM: *Voodoo Lounge*
NOTES: Shooting took place January 9 and 10, 1995 in Mexico City.

I GO WILD II

ALBUM: *Voodoo Lounge*
NOTES: Shooting took place January 9 and 10, 1995 in Mexico City.

LIKE A ROLLING STONE (DYLAN)

ALBUM: *Stripped*
DIRECTOR: Michael Goudry

WILD HORSES

ALBUM: *Stripped*
DIRECTOR: Jim Gable
NOTES: Filmed at Toshiba-EMI Studios, Tokyo, Japan during the *Stripped* rehearsal/recording sessions and concurrent filming for the full-length *Stripped* video (see PROMOTIONAL FILMS AND VIDEOS). Aired in Europe in 1996 to promote the album/video and the "Wild Horses" single.

Bootlegs

Although the authors of this book do not in any way condone or wish to promote or legitimize the practice of bootlegging, its existence is a fact of life hardly unique to the Stones, and it is a subject that has become increasingly difficult to ignore. Many Rolling Stones fans avidly collect bootlegs and there appears to be a growing number of people who would like to do so, as we discovered while researching this book. To be sure, we also encountered quite a few music lovers who, on principle, wouldn't touch a bootleg with a barge pole—or so they say. These and the infinite other potential points of view on this question are best served, we feel, by our offering a little historical information and perspective on bootlegging in general and on some notable Stones bootlegs in particular. As we have tried to do in the rest of this book, we hope to clear up tenacious bootleg (mis-) information with facts about Stones boots, where possible.

After 1969, when the first Stones bootleg appeared, a parallel universe of unofficial Rolling Stones recordings began to evolve alongside the band's official catalog and in a short time eclipsed it in size. The number of illegal titles available for purchase on either side of the Atlantic outnumbered the legal ones well before the first Stones CD of any origin appeared. This explosive growth of an illicit industry whose illegally obtained raw materials are the product of artistic creativity is not an unprecedented cultural development in itself. Stealing the Rolling Stones' intellectual property—as original work is referred to in the 1990s—is in keeping with a long larcenous tradition in the arts.

Unauthorized copying of original works of art doubtless began on a small scale not with rock 'n' roll, but *on* a rock—at the beginning, as a cave painting was made portable. Even large-scale art piracy for profit in a mass market is centuries older than the Rolling Stones—William Shakespeare was probably the first major artist to be bootlegged, according to scholars. And, music infringement flourished well before anyone envisioned a record player, let alone a portable tape recorder, in the form of black market sheet music and librettos in the Victorian 19th century. These last two examples are a good way to understand the distinction between bootlegging (Shakespeare) and piracy (sheet music), and to illustrate some interesting ongoing historical parallels.

Shakespeare never authorized publication of any of his works—he sold plays as theater scripts and not in printed form. Nor did he make any provision for preserving them in print after his death. However, enterprising 16th-century souls perceived a growing armchair market for popular culture and, as they were performed, new plays—in various editions with widely varying resemblance to the originals of the Globe Theatre stage—were printed and sold to the public. Though some of the Bard's actual handwritten manuscripts managed to land in the hands of play pilferers (one academic theory is that a few were leaked as Shakespeare's own response to some really awful bootlegs), the primary source for the worst of the print versions was clearly not the playwright. The "masters," if you will, came from someone planted in the audience who took down whole shows in shorthand! (Probably the earliest digital masters, pun intended!) This is one of the very few instances where bootlegging can be seen, historically, as a positive act that benefited human culture and continues to do so. Had it not happened, it's likely that Shakespeare's work would not have been preserved at all.

Had Shakespeare wanted to publish his work, he would have had to formally register the plays before anything could be printed. He might then have had some recourse against the bootleggers, but unpublished work was unprotected. The system was rudimentary; it was not "copyright" as we know it. The bootleg publishers also had to register, and did. Since the invention of the printing press, registration had more to do with government control of the press than with who created—or even owned—what. Even when Britain enacted the first copyright law in 1709, the primary goal was to control the presses; the rights of publishers came next. The third-in-line creators of content, the artists, could obtain the protection of copyright and own their work *if* it was published. In theory, giving authors these rights would act as an incentive for the production of new work and be in the public interest. On the other hand, protection for unpublished material was considered bad for the common good—there was no way to ensure that the copyright holder would market or exhibit the work for public consumption. Clearly, if artists owned all their work the legitimate publishers couldn't hope to control the market nor the Crown the presses, which was the real agenda. Great sales pitch!

Copyright issues entered the international arena with the Berne Convention in 1886. This was an attempt, spearheaded by Britain, to forge some sort of reciprocity between nations on the issue of copyright protection. The major European countries and the United States sent delegates to Switzerland to work out an agreement that would guarantee one nation's copyright protection to works produced by citizens of another nation, assuming both countries signed the treaty. The unequal rights of publishers and creators of intellectual property were touted by the organizers as the hot topic of the gathering—protecting authors' rights was the convention's *raison d'être*.

One of the major issues of Berne was music. Not bootleg recordings of concerts—that wasn't practical just yet, though Thomas Edison had proved it technologically possible nine years earlier—but pirate sheet music and librettos. This was the Victorian era of social gatherings and songfests around the piano, public recitals and music hall entertainment. The public demand for such entertainment was high, but the slickly produced, pricey official editions of popular sheet music were beyond the means of the masses. Consequently, the black market trade in cheap, mass-produced, pirated (or counterfeit) printed music was booming worldwide, and the British music industry was most concerned.

The substantive outcome of the Berne Convention was a statutory copyright for published work that lasted until 50 years after the author's death, and a reciprocal copyright protection agreement between those industrialized countries that signed the final pact. In effect, the European publishers maintained control of their industry on paper, but missed their real target. Most pirate sheet music sold in Europe originated in the home of free enterprise, the United States. Unsurprisingly, the US was not a signatory to the Berne Convention. (Note that none of this really has anything to do with music or creativity except as a commodity or a buzzword—it's all about money and power and the artists had the least of both. Keep all of this in mind.)

In Britain, music publishers reaped what they'd sown and lobbied for 20 years after Berne for a copyright law with teeth. In 1906, Parliament finally enacted a statute providing stiff escalating penalties for infringers, effectively destroying the pirate sheet music industry. Despite the dearth of goodwill for its music industry, Britain's lawmakers showed themselves as both enlightened and technologically progressive with passage of the British Copyright Act of 1911, which extended the copyright protection given printed musical work to sound recordings and applied the statute throughout the British Empire.

Over in the colonies at the turn of the century, American ingenuity was speeding ahead, refining Edison's technology almost to the point of usefulness for recording music. The music industry in the US was finally coming up to speed and seeing self-interest rather than a threat to profits in the notion of copyright law. The US Constitution clearly gave individuals the exclusive rights to their original creative work (Art. I, Sec. 8), with the Congress responsible for enacting laws to protect those rights. Copyright law existed, but unfortunately, both the US Supreme Court and the US Congress were a bit slow on the uptake the first time each was asked to extend protection to recorded music. In 1908 the Court couldn't make the new medium fit into the established requirements of the Library of Congress for registering new works, so composers had no way of protecting or controlling recordings of their music. Even more ridiculous, when revising the copyright law in 1909, Congress considered a record to be a physical object or application, but *not* a creative work. The upshot of this idiocy was that there was no true copyright protection for sound recordings in the US until 1976.

A shadow industry of commercial record pirates and counterfeiters grew and found its operating niche in the legal loopholes of inadequate copyright statutes. Prior to World War II, pirate products consisted of out-of-print titles and classics of various genres. The record companies managed to legally protect their new releases as business assets using unfair competition statutes, but rarely went after small-time pirates, who posed little financial threat to the business.

After the war, the situation changed dramatically because of two major developments. First, a growing radio industry took to broadcasting much more music. Second, reel-to-reel tape technology became accessible to individuals. In the late 1940s, units arrived that were small enough to be portable and that were powered by batteries: technology finally supplied the tools for a commercial bootleg industry long waiting to happen. Jazz, blues, opera, classical—every kind of music was bootlegged. The recording industry decided to circle the wagons and form a professional association in order to fight a burgeoning threat to their profits. Just as the bootleg record industry sprang out of nothing to produce recordings of musical performances that no one ever dreamed they'd be able to hear over and over in their living rooms, the pirates' catalog had changed dramatically. However, the pirates had also changed. In the early 1950s, organized crime decided to get into the music business by counterfeiting the hit singles needed for their jukebox businesses operating all over the country. Where music is concerned, "Why pay for it when you don't have to" could have been the motto of the Victorian sheet music pirate, as it could be the rock 'n' roll bootlegger's creed in the digital age. It certainly explains what the Mafia did and why. They took what they wanted, paid nothing to artists or publishers or labels, because they could. Gone were the small-time operators hawking a bunch of dusty old titles newly pirated in vinyl—enter the 500-ton gorilla.

Such was the music scene just prior to rock 'n' roll.

Although historically significant in the early part of the band's career, most of the products of the illicit Stones bootleg trade don't warrant consideration in a responsible reference work. And, bootlegs, with a few exceptions in three decades, haven't garnered much attention from the Stones, their record labels, or their lawyers—on any level, commercial or artistic. At the time of writing, this may have been about to change.

Over the years, the "underground" unsanctioned releases proliferated at a rate far surpassing the issuance of the Stones' real, legal records. Still, until the late 1980s, a large proportion of bootlegs could be summarily dismissed as low-quality ripoffs by all but the most ardent Stones fan or obsessive collector; the balance were most likely counterfeit pressings of official records. In 1997, however, it is difficult to ignore the existence of a large number of expensively packaged, illegally produced CDs—from high quality digital masters of extremely dubious origin—using widely available technology. Two particular boxed CD sets released at the close of the

Voodoo Lounge tour have become quite problematic. Reportedly, these bootlegs have made Mick Jagger extremely angry. The contents of these releases are various versions of songs that appear on the Voodoo Lounge album, along with several tracks that don't. The source material—the master tapes—appear to be DATs (digital audio tape) from the Voodoo Lounge recording sessions. How these tapes got out of the band's control is a very good question, indeed, one the band is doubtless asking, too. Jagger's ire is focused also on the content. Apparently, there were several songs demo'd by the band that they wanted to finish for their next studio album that are now useless for that purpose, since those tracks were on the tapes and are now out on bootleg. This is possibly one of the clearest examples of what bootlegging really is—theft, coupled with invasion of privacy. How would you like the most recent draft of your novel taken from your desk? Or your unfinished painting nicked from your studio? Who gave bootleggers the chutzpah to believe what they're doing is okay when they take a musician's unreleased studio work and put it out on CD, vinyl, cassette, whathaveyou? Absolutely mind-boggling illogic must fuel such individuals' existence. Or perhaps it is merely a criminal need to make money.

Before the advent of the modern commercial bootleg, unauthorized recordings of rare, live or unusual musical material circulated primarily among collectors. This was a small circle of individuals with serious interests in the work of various artists—more like a secret society than anything else, and certainly not a mass market as exists today. The participants were motivated, for the most part, by their love of the music and the personal gratification of finding something new by a favorite band. Discoveries would be made by one individual and passed along to other serious collectors, one by one, via trade or barter. Such transactions were often contingent on the recipient's promising to keep the material out of wider circulation and off the open market. Collectors were often criticized as selfish for keeping a tight rein on their material, however it was originally acquired. But, had all those promises been kept, it could have stopped or at least limited the explosion of bootlegging.

What we now have in bootlegging is an industry made up of many individuals whose only goal is profit, who have little regard for any of those "private use only" provisos of the past, and even less regard for either the consumer or the artist. It is hardly necessary to reiterate the obvious objections to bootlegging—that is, unauthorized releases constitute copyright infringement; bootleggers pay no royalties and rip off the composer, the artist and his or her official record label. This is all true. There may be even more serious legal ramifications and negative consequences for the artist arising out of the release of privately held material, particularly when, for example, he or she

Bootleg LP of IBC studio sessions. (JAMES KARNBACH COLLECTION)

has made a prior agreement *not* to release something and it ends up on a commercial bootleg.

Bootleggers also consistently rip off the consumer in a variety of ways by releasing and rereleasing the same LP under different titles, often with different and/or incorrect liner information—dates and locations of live shows, or song titles and studio names for session material. Arguably, such blatant misrepresentation is more than simply confusing, it is deliberate fraud. For instance, *Liver*

Than You'll Ever Be from the Stones' November 9, 1969 Oakland Coliseum show has been rereleased with the title "ALTAMONT '69." Bootleg CDs today are priced from $20 to $60 (and more for multiple disc packages), and are usually sold under a no-refund policy, so this can become very costly, and confusing, for the unwitting consumer.

This state of affairs makes it quite difficult to understand the reasoning of the fanatic bootleg collector who "has to have" all 20 versions of the same bootleg—like

Liver Than You'll Ever Be—on his or her shelf. Today, illegal CDs can be and are made by anyone with access to the material and a minimum of technology. Your next-door neighbor could issue five different bootlegs of the same show under different titles with different covers. Why collect what has no bounds let alone any relation to the reality of an artist's work? All subsequent bootlegs of already bootlegged material are merely repackaged bootlegs—hardly the same as official reissues.

Granted, there are some very well-packaged bootleg CDs containing excellent rare material, but they are few and far between. Despite the authors' obvious position on bootlegging, we will talk about a few notable titles that fall into this category, hopefully to provide some historical insight for collectors of bootlegs—and because our publisher asked us to do so.

The first commercial bootleg made of the Rolling Stones was *not Liver Than You'll Ever Be*, but one entitled *Stones in the [Hyde] Park*, which came out in September 1969. It was available only by special order as an import from the UK, and had a white label imprinted only with "Side 1" and "Side 2" and a white album cover on which the title *Stones in the [Hyde] Park* was rubber-stamped. Commercially available bootlegs had just been born but this LP did not receive the same fanfare that *Liver* did—and once *Liver* got reviewed in *Rolling Stone*, the Hyde Park boot went virtually unknown.

Liver Than You'll Ever Be on the Rubber Dubber label was the original first pressing of this unauthorized recording of the Stones' November 9, 1969 concert at the Oakland (CA) Coliseum. As we have noted, this boot was then bootlegged by others under many, many labels and titles.

Another first and a very rare one is the original *Hot Rocks* boot EP, with five studio cuts—"High Heel Sneakers," "Down in the Bottom," "Stewed and Keefed," "Tell Me Baby" and "Looking Tired"—without the "skip" and crackle. What we are referring to is the fact that more bootlegs were made from a worn copy of the original vinyl boot EP. The bootleg-bootleggers' "master" had a skip in the song, "Looking Tired," along with the very audible crackle of a worn record throughout. That original bootleg EP was made from a clean tape. All other vinyl bootlegs of this EP—other than the rare, original first pressing—have that crackling and the "skip." In the mid-1980s, bootleg CDs of the *Hot Rocks* material (combined with other tracks) came out with the same quality of studio stereo sound as found on the original tape.

For those who are interested in unofficial releases and want not to be ripped off by the many bootleg reissues, the selections that follow should provide a decent starting point for quality and rarity. Be forewarned, however, this is not a definitive list, just a quick look into another window on Rolling Stones history. Try to get copies from a friend who already owns them rather than purchasing the actual bootleg.

Listen to these:

1. THE BLACK BOX SET—THREE CDS. 1964–1970
Excellent quality. All studio material. A nice cross-section of the Stones' Decca/London years.

2. SATISFACTION Excellent quality. BBC radio and television shows, 1963–1965.

3. THE TRIDENT MIXES Excellent quality. 1968–1972 studio outtakes. As the story goes, the bootleggers allegedly acquired this tape at a postal auction. Supposedly, it was one of those "lost in the mail" deals, whatever that means. An interesting story.

4. GARDEN STATE '78 A soundboard tape of the Passaic, NJ 1978 show has been milked for everything possible under numerous titles (for example, *Out on Bail*). The story behind this one is a bit more interesting. Supposedly, the original source tape was popped right out of the cassette deck at the mixing board by a fan who was situated right next to it. The sound man, one "B.J.," had ejected the cassette right before the encore, "Street Fighting Man," to see how much tape was left. Seeing that there was still room to finish recording the show, he put the tape back in and continued. There is a "glitch" in this bootleg—the audible evidence of B.J.'s checking the tape, at the beginning of "Street Fighting Man." After the performance was over, B.J. turned his back on the tape deck to sort out and stow his various cables and connections—and the "fan" pushed the eject button and took the tape. Needless to say, when all cassettes of the show got turned over to Stu, B.J. was without one. This was a situation that did not sit well with Ian Stewart and was also not very good for B.J., who could have lost his job. A person's job and reputation was jeopardized for profit motive; another reason to hate bootleggers.

As of May 1995, there were approximately 3,000 Stones bootlegs on the market. Only select stores sell them and not the well-known, large chain record stores. The small "collectible" record shops may have a section devoted to bootleg CDs. You'll just have to find them. They're around.

Index

Note: Italicized page numbers indicate artwork. Song titles appear in quotation marks.

A

ABC Theatre
  Carlisle, 100
  Chester, 100
  Kingston-upon-Hull, 101
  Lincoln, 101
  Plymouth, 99
  Romford, 13
  Wigan, 80, 100
ABC-TV's International Rock
    Awards (1990), 47
Academy of Music, New York,
    102–3
Adelphi Theatre, 83, 95
Advertisement, first, *56, 57*
Aftermath (album), 16, 226, 261,
    273–75, 293, 384
AIMS (Ambition, Ideas, Motiva-
    tion, Success), 44
"Ain't That a Lot of Love," 310
"Ain't Too Proud to Beg,"
    247–48, 287–88, 386
Albert Hall, 88
albums
    first greatest hits, 16
    first released on Rolling
        Stones Records, 283
    first UK, 10, 264
    first US, 265–67
Alcove Club, 71
Alexandra Palace, 97
Alexis Korner's Blues Incorporated,
    2, 4–5, 10
"All About You," 251–52, 293–24

"All Down the Line," 241, 244,
    259, 285, 293, 386
All Night Rave, 81
"All Sold Out," 227–228, 230,
    276, 294
All Star '64 (tour), 85–88, *86, 89*
"All the Way Down," 253, 298
Alley, Patrick, 43
"All-Week Stones Salute" (TV
    show), 375
"Almost Hear You Sigh," 255,
    301–2, 389–90
"Already over Me," 260
Altamont concert, 24–5, *25,* 133,
    349–50
"Always Suffering," 260
Andrews, Pat, 6
"Angie," 246–47, 259, 286, 289,
    293, 299, 306, 309–10, 385
"Around & Around," 222, 250,
    267, 281–82, 291, 332, 382
Around & Around (album), 222
articles
    on Jagger, Mick, 4, *4*
    on Rolling Stones, 5, 8–9
"As Tears Go By," 226, 273, 276,
    282, 284, 290–91, 294, 301
Assembly Hall, 90
Assembly Rooms, 80
Astoria Theatre, 100
At the MAX (film), 48, 375, 390
Atlanta Ballroom, 73
Atlantic City concert (1989), 47,
    186, 255, 301–2, 369, 375–76,
    389

Atlantic Records, 27
Australia/Far East tour (1965),
    105–7
Australia/New Zealand tours
    1966, 119–20
    1995, 206–7
Austria, 1965 tour in, 112–13
Avory, Mick, 4–5, 57–58
awards
    ABC-TV's International Rock
        Awards (1990), 47
    Billboard (1994), 377
    Carl Alan Award (1965), 15
    Creem (1973), 30
    Ivor Novello Awards, 48
    New Musical Express (1968),
        22
    New Musical Express (1978),
        38
    Rolling Stone's (1978), 37
    Rolling Stone's (1982), 42

B

"Babyface" (Kenny Edmonds), 260
"Baby Break It Down," 258, 307
"Back Street Girl," 227, 230,
    276–77, 295
"Back to Zero," 254, 300
Baldry. *See* Long John Baldry
Barrowlands Ballroom, 83
Baths, The (club), 80, 91
Battersea Pleasure Gardens, 68

BBC, first stereo broadcast, 10
"Beast of Burden," 250–53, 292,
    294–95, 299, 302, 305–6
Beat City Club, 97
Beatles, The, 8, 44, 75, 92
Beaton, Cecil, 17
Beck, Jeff, 32
"Before They Make Me Run,"
    250–51, 292
Beggars Banquet (album), 22,
    279–81, 293, 385
Beggars Banquet (magazine), 51
*Beggars Banquet Guide to Collectible
    Rolling Stones, The* (film), 325
Belling, Lawrence, 31
Between the Buttons (album), *15,*
    228, 231, 276, 293, 384
"Big Beat" (TV show), 92
Big Hits (High Tide & Green Grass)
    (album), 16, 273, 276, 382–84
Bill Wyman Video 45 (film), 321–22
Billboard Magazine's Lifetime
    Achievement Award, 377
"*Billboard* Music Awards" (TV
    show), 377
Birmingham Town Hall, 90, 95
"Bitch," 243, 245, 283, 289, 293,
    302, 306
Black & Blue (album), 248–50,
    290–91, 386
*The Black Box Set—Three CDs,
    1964–1970* (album), 397
"Black Limousine," 247–48, 252,
    259, 295, 309
Blackbourn, Stan, 19

"Blinded by Love," 255, 301–2
"Blinded by Rainbows," 258, 307
"Blow with Ry," 240
Blue Note Jazz Band, 73
"Blue Turns to Grey," 225, 273, 282
Blues By Six, 60
Blues Incorporated. *See* Alexis Korner's Blues Incorporated
bootlegs, 393–97
    and copyright protection, 394–95
    first Rolling Stones, 393, 397
Botwell House, 72
"Boudoir Stomp," 240
Bradford, Geoff, 4, 57
Bradford Arts Ball, 81
"Brand New Car," 258, 307
"Break the Spell," 255, 301–2
Brian Jones Presents the Pipes of Pan (album), 21, 28
Bricklayer's Arms pub, 4
Bridges to Babylon (album), 215–16, 260
Bridges to Babylon (tour), 215–16, 260
"Bright Lights, Big City," 298
British Legion Hall, 71–72, 75
British tours
    first, 9, 75–79
    second, 82–84
    third, 85–88, *86, 89*
    fourth, 90–95
    fifth, 99–102
    sixth, 107–9
    seventh, 113–16
    eighth, *121,* 125–28
    ninth, 135–36
Brown, Ollie, 147, 155, 159
Brown, Ricky. *See* Fenson, Ricky
"Brown Sugar," 243–45, 250, 256, 258, 283, 285, 289, 291, 299, 302, 305–6
Bruce, Jack, 377
Buenos Aires concert, 377
Burdens of Dreams (film), 321
By Invitation Only (album), 290
"Bye Bye Johnny," 220, 264, 286

C

Caird Hall, 94
California Ballroom, 72, 74, 84
Camden Theatre, 10
"Can I Get a Witness," 221, 264–65
"Can You Hear the Music," 246–47, 286
Canadian National Institute for the Blind (C.N.I.B.) Benefit concert, 37–38, 164, *164*
"Can't Be Seen," 255–56, 301–2, 305
"Can't You Hear Me Knocking," 243, 283, 302
Cantrell, Scott, 38
Capitol Theatre
    Aberdeen, 94
    Cardiff, 76–77, 100
Carlton Ballroom, 92

Carnegie Hall, 11–12, *80,* 97
"Carol," 221, 242–43, 264–65, 282, 286, 290, 294, 382
Carroll, Jim, *39*
"Casino Boogie," 245, 285
Cavern Club, 79
Cellar Club, 74
"Center Stage" (TV show), 374
Chantinghall Hotel, 94
Chapman, Tony, 4, 6–7, 57–64
    last performance with band, 64
Charlie Is My Darling (film), 112, 223, 314–15, 343
Charlie Watts Quintet, 47
Checkerboard Lounge, 41
"Cherry Oh Baby," 248–49, 291
Chess, Marshall, 27, 36
Chess Records, 2, 11
    copyright infringement suit, 223
Chez Don Club, 80
"Child of the Moon," 234, 286, 301, 385
Chiswick Polytechnic Dance, 79
Circus Kronebau, 13
"Citadel," 231, 233, 279, 294
Civil Hall, 81
Clapton, Eric, 33–34
Club À Go-Go, 79
Club Noreik, 85, 90
C.N.I.B. *See* Canadian National Institute for the Blind
Cockroaches, The, 160
"Cocksucker Blues," 298
Cocksucker Blues (film), 35, 39, 313, 319
Cohl, Michael, 45
Collins, Art, 39
Colston Hall, 84, 93, 101
"Come On," 219, 263–64, 276, 286, 290, 294, 301
"Coming Down Again," 246–47, 286
"Complicated," 227–28, 276
"Con le lie lacrime," 226, 295
concerts. *See also specific concert*
    first behind Iron Curtain, 17, 129
    first on European continent, 98
    pay-per-view. *See* pay-per-view concerts
"Confessin' the Blues," 222, 267, 282, 382
"Congratulations," 223, 267, 286, 301
"Connection," 227, 230, 276, 294
"Continental Drift," 255–56, 301–2, 305
"Cook Cook Blues," 255, 305
"Cool, Calm, Collected," 227–28, 276
Co-op Ballroom, 79
copyright infringement suit
    by Chess Records, 223
    against Mick Jagger, 43–44
Corn Exchange, 71, 75, 81
"Cosmic Christmas," 233
Cotchford Farm, 22
"Country Honk," 240–42, 281–82
Coventry Theatre, 84, 94–95

"Cracking Up," 250, 291
"Crane Show, Les" (TV show), 11, 335
Crawdaddy Club, 7–8, 66–75
    move of, 70
"Crazy Mama," 249, 291, 293–95, 386
Creem awards (1973), 30
Crewe Town Hall, 79
"Cry to Me," 225, 270, 272, 383
Cubi-Club, 92
Curly Clayton Sound Studios, 6, 218
Cyril Davies' R&B All-Stars, 64–65, 73

D

"Da Doo Ron Ron," 223
Daily Mirror, 9
"Dance," 252, 293–94
"Dance Little Sister," 247–48, 287–89
"Dancing with Mr. D," 246–47, 286–87, 293, 386
"Dandelion," 230, 232, 281, 286, 291, 301, 384
Danilo Theatre, 95
"David Frost" (TV show), 348–49
Davies, Cyril, 10
    band of, 64–65, 73
De Montfort Hall, 84–86, 97–98
"Dead Flowers," 243, 259, 283, 302, 309–10
"Dear Doctor," 235, 279–80, 295
Debutante Ball, 71
Decca Records, 9, 16, 22, 26, 28
December's Children (and Everybody's) (album), 273, 382
Degree of Murder (Mord und Totschlag) (film), 16, 315
Detours, The, 82
Diddley, Bo, 9, 76
Digital Dreams (film), 321
"Dirty Work," 254, 300
Dirty Work (album), 42, 254, 388
    dedication of, 300
DISC (magazine), 2, *3,* 4, *6*
Doncaster, Patrick, 9
"Doncha Bother Me," 226, 273–74
"Don't Lie to Me," 222, 288
"Doo Doo Doo Doo Doo (Heartbreaker)," 246–47, 286–87, 289–90
"Down Home Girl," 224, 267, 269
"Down in the Hole," 252, 293–94, 387
"Down the Road Apiece," 222, 268–69, 286, 382
"Downtown Suzie," 235, 240, 288
Dreamland Ballroom, 73
Drill Hall, 82
drug use, 17, 29
    Faithfull, Marianne and, 24
    Fraser, Robert and, 18–20
    Hall, Jerry and, 43–44
    Jagger, Mick and, 17–20, 22, 26, 141
    Jones, Brian and, 18, 20–21

Pallenberg, Anita and, 30–31, 35–36
    Richards, Keith and, 17–20, 30, 34–37, 39, 141
    Watts, Charlie and, 29
    Wood, Ron and, 39
    Wyman, Bill and, 29
Dunbar, John, 10, 26
Dunn, Olivia, 92
Dylan, Bob, 12, 978

E

"Each and Every Day of the Year," 223, 288
Ealing Jazz Club, 7, 58–59, 61–62, 65–66
"Earl Chin's Rockers '80" (TV show), 359
Easton, Eric, 8–9, 28, 50, 68, 218
"Ed Sullivan Show" (TV show), 12, 338–39, 341, 344–45, 349–50
"Edward's Thrump Up," 240
Eel Pie Island, 68–75
El Mocambo shows, 35, 159–60
EMI, 35
"Emotional Rescue," 252, 293–94, 299, 306, 386–87
Emotional Rescue (album), 39, 252, 293–94, *294,* 386–87
Empire Pool, 91–92, 95
Empire Theatre, 88
Empress Ballroom, 97
"Empty Heart," 222, 267
England's Greatest Hit Makers (album), 270
England's Newest Hit Makers—The Rolling Stones (album), 12, 265–67, 382
"Entry of the Gladiators," 310
Epsom Baths, The, 81, 83
Essoldo Theatre, 95
European tours
    1966, 120–22
    1967, 128–29
    1970, 134–35
    1973, 144–47
    1976, 155–59, *156*
    1982, 173–78
    1990, 47, 187–93
    1995, 209–15
Everly Brothers, 9, 76
"Everybody Needs Somebody to Love," 224–25, 267–70, 281, 286
"Everything Is Turning to Gold," 250, 294–95, 305
Exile on Main Street (album), 28, 240, 244–46, 285, 386
Exile on Main Street 5 (promo disc), 285
"Exile on Main Street Blues," 246, 285
Ex-Servicemen's Club, 90

F

"Factory Girl," 235, 256, 258, 279–80, 305
Faerie Tale Theatre—"The Nightingale" (film), 321, 362
Fairfield Halls, 81, 91
Faithfull, Marianne, 10, 17–19, 22–23, 26, 362
  drug use, 24
"Family," 235–37
"Fancyman Blues," 255, 302, 305
"Far Away Eyes," 250–51, 292, 386
Far East tours
  1965, 105–7
  1973, 143–44
"Feel On Baby," 254, 298
Fenson, Ricky, 57, 59–65
Ferry, Bryan, 34
"Fight," 254, 300
film, first appearance in, 12
"Fingerprint File," 247–50, 287–88, 291
Fischer, Lisa, *188*
Fitzcarraldo (film), 39, 321
5 + 1 Johnny Hallyday Rolling Stones (film), 329
Five Times Five (5 X 5) (EP), 265–266, 267, 382
Flamingo Ballroom, 98
Flamingo Jazz Club, 64–65
  last gig at, 65
Flashpoint (album), 47, 256, 258, 305, 390
Flashpoint + Collectibles (album), 255, 305
"Flight 505," 226, 273–74
"Flip the Switch," 260
Floral Hall, 80
Flowers (album), 261, 276–77, 383
"Fool to Cry," 248–49, 291, 293–95, 299, 306, 386
Foot Tappers and Wheel Shunters Club, 207–9
"Fortune Teller," 219, 264, 276, 283, 286, 294
Fourteen (album), 270
Fourth National Jazz & Blues Festival, 98
France
  1965 tour in, 109
  band members banned from, 31
  tax exile in, 27
Fraser, Robert, 17
  drug use, 18–20
Freejack (film), 47–48, 325
"Funky and Fleopatra," 221

G

Gallagher, Roy, 32
Garden State '78 (album), 397
Gather No Moss (film), 314
Gaumont Theatre
  Bournemouth, 78, 99
  Bradford, 77–78, 88
  Derby, 77
  Doncaster, 77, 101
  Hanley, 78, 87, 101

Ipswich, 91, 102
  Norwich, 92
  Salisbury, 78
  Sheffield, 78
  Southampton, 78, 102
  Taunton, 78, 99
  Watford, 76, 81, 86, 102
  Weymouth, 99
  Wolverhampton, 77, 88, 102
  Worcester, 77, 80
"Get Off of My Cloud," 225, 228, 250, 271–73, 276, 284–85, 290–91, 293–94, 301, 382
Get Stoned (album), 291
Get Yer Ya-Ya's Out! The Rolling Stones in Concert (album), 26, 132, 242–43, 282, 385
gig, first, 6–7, 57–58
"Gimme Shelter," 238, 242–243, 259, 281–284, 290–291, 294, 385
Gimme Shelter (album), 283
Gimme Shelter (film), 25–26, 28, 133, 244, 313, 317–18, 376, 379, 390
Glenlyn Ballroom, 82
Glimmer Twins, The, 247–60
  origin of, 287
Globe Theatre, 101
Goat's Head Soup (album), 36, 244, 246–47, 286, 385–86
Godard, Jean-Luc, 21
"Goin' Home," 226, 273–274
"Going to À Go Go," 253, 296–97, 387
Golding, Colin, 57, 60–61
Gomelsky, Giorgio, 7–8, 61, 66, 68, 314, 381
"Gomper," 233, 279
"Good Bye Britain" tour, 27, 135–36
Good, Jack, 2, *3*
"Good Times," 225, 270, 272, 383
"Good Times, Bad Times," 222, 267, 273, 286, 291, 301
Got Live If You Want It! (album), 127, 228, 276, 283
Got Live If You Want It! (EP), 13, 107, 225, 270
"Gotta Get Away," 225, 272–73, 301
"Grammy Awards, The" (TV show), 366
Granada Theatre
  Aylesbury, 84
  Bedford, 83
  East Ham, 95
  Greenford, 86
  Harrow-on-the-Hill, 82
  Kettering, 83
  Kingston-upon-Thames, 86
  Maidstone, 83
  Mansfield, 83
  Rugby, 86
  Shrewsbury, 84
  Tooting, 83
  Walthamstow, 83
  Woolwich, 84
Grand Hotel Ballroom, 74
Great Pop Prom, 75
Great Southeast Stoned Out Wrestling Champions, 160–61

Green Man, The (club), 62–63
Greenwich Town Hall, 79–80
"Grown Up Wrong," 224, 267–68
Guildhall
  Portsmouth, 86
  Southampton, 90
"Gun Face," 260

H

"Had It with You," 254, 300
Hail! Hail! Rock 'n' Roll (film), 44
Hall, Jerry, 39
  and drugs, 43–44
Hampstead Country Club, 85
"Hand of Fate," 248–49, 291, 293, 302
"Hang Fire," 251–52, 295, 299, 387
Hansen, Patti, 42
"Happy," 245, 250, 285, 289, 291, 302, 386
"Harlem Shuffle," 254, 256–57, 300, 302, 305–6, 388
Harringay Jazz Club, 66–67
Harris, Steve, 57–59, 61–62, 64
Harrison, George, 9, 78
Harwood, Keith, 34
Hastings Pier Ballroom, 84
"Have You Seen Your Mother, Baby, Standing in the Shadows?," 16, 227–28, 276–77, 281, 286, 290–91, 294, 301, 332, 345, 383–84
"Heart of Stone," 223–24, *268*, 269, 272–73, 276, 284–85, 288, 295, 301, 382
"Heartbreaker," 246–47, 286–87, 289–90
"Hearts for Sale," 255, 301–2
"Heaven," 252, 295
Hell's Angels, 25, 133
Hendrix, Jimi, 21
"Heroes of Rock 'n' Roll" (TV show), 358
"Hey Negrita," 248–49, 291, 386
"Hide Your Love," 244, 247, 286
"High & Dry," 226, 273–74
"High or Low," 260
High Tide & Green Grass (album), 16, 273, 276, 382–84
High Wycombe Town Hall, 73, 79, 81
"Highland Fling," 240
"Highwire," 258, 305, 390
Hillside Ballroom, 81
"Hip Shake." *See* "Shake Your Hips"
Hippodrome Theatre
  Birmingham, 87, 101
  Brighton, 87–88, 97, 102
"Hitch Hike," 224, 270, 272, 383
"Hold Back," 254, 300
"Hold On to Your Hat," 255, 301–2
"Hollywood Palace" (TV show), 11–12, 335–38
"Honest I Do," 221, 264–65
"Honky Tonk Women," 240–42, 250, 281–84, 290–91, 294, 385

Hoodoo U Voodoo (film), 326
Hopkins, Nicky, 49, 135–36, 144
Hot Rocks (album), 244, 397
Hot Rocks 1964–1971 (album), 284–85
"Hot Stuff," 249–50, 291, 294–95, 306, 386
Hove Town Hall, 93
"How Can I Stop?," 260
Howard, Jo, 43
Howard, Peter, 19
Howlin' Wolf, 54
Hunt, Marsha, 30, 32
Hyde Park Free Concert, 23, 130, 241–42, 349, 351

I

"I Am Waiting," 226, 273–74
"I Can't Be Satisfied," 222, 268, 286
"I Don't Know Why," 241, 288
"I Go Wild," 258, 307, 391
"I Got the Blues," 243, 283
"I Just Want to Make Love to You," 256, 258, 264–65, 285–86, 301
"I Wanna Be Your Man," 220, 264, 285, 290–91, 294, 301
"I Want to Be Loved," 219, 294, 301
"I Want to Make Love to You," 221
IBC Studios, 8
"I'd Much Rather Be with the Boys," 225, 288
"If I Was a Dancer (Dance, Pt. 2)," 252, 294–95
"If You Can't Rock Me," 247–48, 250, 287–88, 291, 293
"If You Let Me," 228, 288
"If You Need Me," 222, 267, 282, 382
"If You Really Want to Be My Friend," 247–48, 287–88
Il Rondo Ballroom, 73
"I'm a King Bee," 221, 264–65
"I'm Alright," 225, 228, 270
"I'm Free," 225, 259, 272–73, 281, 286, 301, 309–10, 382
"I'm Going Down," 241, 244, 288
"I'm Moving On," 225, 270, 273, 286
Impact Sound, 8, 28
Imperial Ballroom, 93, 97
"In Another Land," 232–33, *278*, 279, 301
"Indian Girl," 251–52, 293–94
"Interlude a la El Hopo," 240
"International Rock Awards" (TV show), 368
Invicta Ballroom, 88–90
Ireland/UK/West Germany/Austria, 1965 tour, 112–13
Iron Curtain, first concerts behind, 17, 129
"It Hurts Me Too," 240
"It Must Be Hell," 253–54, 298

"It's All Over Now," 222, 267, 273, 276, 282, 286, 290–91, 294, 301, 382
"It's Not Easy," 226, 273–74
"It's Only Rock 'n' Roll," 247–50, 287–91, 299, 302, 306, 386, 390
It's Only Rock 'n' Roll (album), 248, 287–88, 386, 390
"I've Been Loving You Too Long," 225, 276, 283

J

Jagger, Bianca, 26–27, 29, 31, 362
Jagger, Mick, 1, *14–15, 40, 45, 137, 140, 147, 154, 164, 170, 182, 188, 232, 235–36, 239, 318*
   in Blues Incorporated, 4, *4,* 57
   children of, 28, 42–43
   divorce of, 37, 39
   drug use, 17–20, 22, 26, 141
   early career of, 4–5
   grandchildren of, 48
   injuries, 13, 15, 24, 29
   lawsuit against, 43–44
   marriage to Bianca, 27
   marriage to Jerry Hall, 48
   television appearance, 333
Jammin' with Edward (album), 240
Japan
   1990 tour in, 186–87, 369
   1995 tour in, 205–6
   ban in, 30, 143
   first appearance in, 47
Jazz News (periodical), 5, *6*
"Jigsaw Puzzle," 234, 237, 279–80
Jimmy Miller Productions, 31
"Jiving Sister Fanny," 241, 288, *289*
Johns, Andy, 61
Johns, Glyn, 8, 16, 60–61, 218–19, 234
Jones, Brian, 1, *227, 236*
   death of, 23, 130
   drug use, 18, 20–21
   early career of, 2–5
   fired from band, 23
   illness of, 17
   injuries of, 13
   last public performance, 22, 130
   last tour with band, 128
   letter to *DISC* magazine, *2, 3*
   pseudonyms, 63, 66
Jones, Darryl, 259–60
   first performance, 193
   joins the band, 49, 259
Jones, Paul, 2, 4
Jones, Peter, 8
"Juke Box Jury" appearance, 12
Jump Back—The Best of the Rolling Stones (album), 305–6
"Jump on Top of Me," 258–59
"Jumpin' Jack Flash," 234–35, 237, 242–43, 250, 256–57, 281–84, 290–91, 294, 301, 305, 384–85, 390
"Just My Imagination (Running Away with Me)," 250–51, 253, 292, 296–97

"Just Wanna See His Face," 245–46, 285

K

Kardomah Cafe, 45
Kayser Bondor Ballroom, 81
Keith Richards & the X-Pensive Winos Live at the Hollywood Palladium (film), 325
"Keith Richards Rollin' On" (MTV show), 367–68
Ken Colyer Jazz Club, 66–70
Kershaw, Doug, 37
Keys, Bobby, 11, 31, 96, 134–36, 143–44, *182*
Kidderminster Town Hall, 90
King Biscuit Flower Hour (radio show), 166, 171–72
Kings Hall, 74, 80
Klein, Allen, 13, 16, 42
   firing of, 26, 28
Klein, Sheila, 12
Knebworth Fair Concert, 159
Knight, Brian, 60, 66
Korner, Alexis, 6, 42, 54, 362
Kurhaus (Netherlands), 98

L

Ladies & Gentlemen, the Rolling Stones [#2] (film), 31, 137, 319, 332
Ladies & Gentlemen, the Rolling Stones [#3] (film), 320
Ladies & Gentlemen, the Rolling Stones—Live at the Marquee (film), 319
   TV broadcast, 351
"Lady Jane," 226, 228, 273–74, 276–77, 283, 286, 290–91, 295, 301, 384
"Lantern, The," 232–33, *278, 279,* 301
"Last Time, The," 224, 228, 270, 273, 276, 282, 286, 290–91, 294, 301
"Late Night with Letterman" (TV show), 367
Latin American tour (1995), 203–4
Lawrence, Trevor, 144
lawsuits
   copyright infringement, 43–44, 223
   management, 28–29
Leas Cliff Hall, 91
Leavell, Chuck, *185*
Leek Town Hall, 81
Leicester University, 94
Lennon, John, 9
   murder of, 39
"Let It Bleed," 238, 241, 259, 281–82, 286, 309–10
Let It Bleed (album), 24, 130, 236, 238–42, 281–82, 293, 385–86
"Let It Loose," 245, 285
"Let It Rock," 245, 283

"Let Me Go," 251–53, 293–94, 296–97
"Let's Go Steady," 252
"Let's Spend the Night Together," 227–30, 253, 276–77, 281, 284, 290–91, 294, 296–97, 301, 384
Let's Spend the Night Together (film), 42, 169–70, 321
Lewis, Elmo, 5. *See also* Jones, Brian
Lido Ballroom, 81
"Lies," 250–51, 292
"Like a Rolling Stone," 259, 309–10, 391
"Little Baby," 259, 309–10
Little Boy Blue & the Blue Boys, 2, 50
"Little by Little," 221, 264–65, 294, 301
Little, Carlo, 57, 64–65
"Little Queenie," 242–43, 282, 286, 385
"Little Red Rooster," 223–24, 250, 256–57, 269, 276, 290–91, 294, 301, 305
Little Richard, 9
"Little T & A," 251–52, 295
Live Aid, 43, 365
Live Voodoo Lounge (film), 326
"Live with Me," 240–43, 259, 281–82, 294
Liver Than You'll Ever Be (album), 26, 396–97
Locarno Ballroom, 81, 91–92
London Palladium, 13
London Records, 10–11, 13, 26
Long John Baldry, 10, 65, 73
Long John Baldry and His Kansas City Blue Boys, *5,* 57
Long John Baldry & the Hoochie-Coochie Men, 99
"Long Long While," 226, 286, 301
Long View Farm, 40
Longleat House, 98
"Look What You've Done," 273, 282
lotus stage, 33
"Love in Vain," 236, 239–40, 242–43, 259, 281–83, 309–10, 385–86
"Love Is Strong," 258, 307, 390
Love You Live (album), 34, 149, 157–58, 249–50
   dedication of, 291
"Loving Cup," 241, 245–46, 285
"Low Down," 260
Lowestoft Pavilion, 84
"Luxury," 247–48, 287–88

M

Madaio, Steve, 144
Made in the Shade (album), 288–90
Magdalen College Commemorative Ball, 97
Majestic Ballroom, 76, 80, 92
Management lawsuits, 28–29
Mandel, Harvey, 32
"Mannish Boy," 250, 291, 294–295

Manor House Pub, 66–67
Marquee Jazz Club, 6, 57, 59, 64–65
Matrix Ballroom, 79
Mayall, John, 23
"MBone Internet Broadcast," 376
MBONE System on the Internet, 50
McCartney, Paul, 9, 18, 232
McGrath, Earl, 36, 39
McIlroys Ballroom, 79, 83, 91
"Mean Disposition," 258–59, 307
"Melody," 249, 291
"Memo from Turner," 237, 288
Memorial Hall, 73, 80
"Memory Motel," 249, 291
"Memphis Tennessee," 298
"Mercy Mercy," 225, 270, 272, 383
Metamorphosis (album), 33, 223, 227, 237, 244, 288
Metamorphosis (film), 36
Mick Taylor—Rock, Blues & Slide Guitar (film), 324
"Midnight Rambler," 238, 242–43, 281–82, 284, 290, 386
"Might As Well Get Juiced," 260
mighty mobile studio, 26
Milestones (album), 285
Miller, Jimmy, 21, 30, 49, 234
"Miss Amanda Jones," 227–28, 230, 276
"Miss You," 250–251, 256–57, 292, 299, 302, 305–6, 386
"Mixed Emotions," 255, 301–2, 305–6, 388
"Mona (I Need You Baby)," 221, 264, 269
"Money," 220, 264, 286
"Monkey Man," 240–41, 281–82
"Moon Is Up," 258, 307
"Moonlight Mile," 243, 283
Mord und Totschlag (film), 16, 315
More Hot Rocks (Big Hits & Fazed Cookies) (album), 286, 384–85
"Mother's Little Helper," 226, 273, 277, 281, 284, 291, 301
"MTV Video Awards" (TV show), 181, 368, 371
Muddy Waters, 41, 54
"My Girl," 225, 228, 277, 282
"My Obsession," 228, 230, 276

N

Nanker Phelge, 9, 220
   origin of pseudonym, 265
Ned Kelly (film), 23–24, 26, 318
"Neighbours," 252, 295, 387
Nellcôte, 27, 29
New Barbarians, 37–38
New Elizabethan Ballroom, 98
"New Faces," 258, 307
New Musical Express, 28
   1968 awards, 22
   1978 awards, 38
   promo disc, 285
   Winners Concert, 92
New Victoria Theatre, 9, 76

New Zealand. *See* Australia/New Zealand tours
Newcastle-upon-Tyne City Hall, 94
News of the World, 17–19, 35, 346
    charity gala, 9, 68
Nicaraguan earthquake benefit concert, 143
1962 rotation, *56*
"19th Nervous Breakdown," 226, 228, 273, 276, 284, 286, 290–91, 294, 301, 384
"No Expectations," 235–37, 279–80, 286, 310
No Stone Unturned (album), 286, 385
"No Use in Crying," 252, 295
"Nobody's Seen My Baby," 260
North American tours
    first, 95–97
    second, 102–4
    third, 110–11
    fourth, 13, 116–19
    fifth, 122–24
    sixth, 130–33
    seventh (1972), 136–42
    eighth (1975), 32–33, 147–55
    ninth (1978), 160–63, *161*
    1981, 166–73
    1989, *179,* 179–87, *181–82, 185*
    1995, 193–203
    1997, 215
"Not Fade Away," 221–22, 228, 259–60, 265, 273, 276, 285–86, 290–91, 294, 301, 309–10, 382
"Now I've Got a Witness," 221, 264–65
"Now Look at What You've Done," 222

O

Oasis Club, 73–74, 80
Ode to a High Flying Bird (Watts), 13, 47, 370
Odeon Theatre
    Birmingham, 78
    Blackburn, 88
    Bradford, 101
    Cheltenham, 77, 86, 100
    Colchester, 100
    Exeter, 99, 101
    Folkestone, 94
    Glasgow, 77
    Guildford, 76, 86, 101
    Hammersmith, 79
    Ipswich, 79
    Leicester, 100
    Lewisham, 78, 102
    Liverpool, 77
    Luton, 92, 100
    Manchester, 77, 100
    Newcastle-upon-Tyne, 77, 100
    Nottingham, 78
    Rochester, 78–79, 86
    Romford, 80–81, 87
    Southend, 76, 87, 102
    St. Albans, 78

    Streatham, 76
    Weston-super-Mare, 99
"Off the Hook," 223, 268–69, 281, 301
"Oh Baby (We Got a Good Thing Goin')," 224, 269, 272, 286, 382
"Oh, I Do Like to See Me on the B-Side," 221
Oldham, Andrew Loog, 8–10, 12–13, 28, 218, 221, 276, 314–15, 345–46
Olympia Ballroom, 81–82, 90
Olympia Theatre (Paris), 102
Olympic Studios, 16, 18, *20*
"On with the Show," 232–33, 279
Onassis, Jacqueline, 41
"One Hit (to the Body)," 254, 300, 302, 388
"One More Try," 225, 270, 282
One Plus One (film). *See Sympathy for the Devil*
"100 Years Ago," 246–47, 286
102 Edith Grove in Chelsea, 6
"Opening Night at the RFK" (TV show), 375
Opera House, Blackpool, 88
"Out of Control," 260
Out of Our Heads (album), 13, 270–72, 293, 382–83, 390
"Out of Tears," 258, 307, 391
"Out of Time," 226–27, 273, 277, 285–86, 288, *289,* 290, 294
"Over the Waves," 310
Oxford Town Hall, 82
Oxford University, 97

P

"Pain in My Heart," 224–25, 268–70, 295
"Pain of Love," 253–54, 298
"Paint It, Black," 226, 256–57, 274, 276, 281–82, 284–85, 290–91, 294, 301, 305
Palace Ballroom, 98
Palace Theatre, 93
Palais, The, 84, 91, 98
Pallenberg, Anita, 16–17, 22, 28, 31, 34
    drug use, 30–31, 35–36
    weapon possession, 38–39
"Parachute Woman," 234, 237, 279–80, 294, 310
Paradiso Club (Amsterdam), *208*
Parr Hall, 80
Parson, Gram, 30
Pavilion Ballroom, 79
pay-per-view concerts
    Atlantic City concert, 47, 186, 255, 301–2, 369, 375–76, 389
    Buenos Aires concert, 377
    first live, 41, 173, 360
    Rio de Janeiro concert, 377
    Voodoo Lounge, 201, 326, 377
Pendleton, Harold, 5
Performance (film), 22, 27, 237–38, 316, 350, 376

Perkins, Wayne, 32
Perks, Bill. *See* Wyman, Bill
Perrin, Les, 19, 37
Piccadilly Jazz Club, 61–62
Pier Ballroom, 91, 98
pissing incident, 13
"Play with Fire," 224, 256–57, 270, 273, 284, 291, 294–95, 301
Plaza Ballroom. *See* Ricky Tick Club
Plaza Theatre
    Handsworth, 72
    Oldham, 75
    Oldhill, 72
"Please Go Home," 227–28, 276–77
Point of View, Jamaica, 29
"Poison Ivy," 219–20, 264, 286, 294
Poitier, Suki, 21
Pond, Paul, 2, 4
Pop Hit Parade, 95
Pop Prom, 92
Preston, Billy, 144, 147, *154,* 155, 159
"Pretty Beat Up," 254, 298
Price, Jim, 134–36, 143–44
"Prodigal Son," 235, 237, 279–81
Promopub, B.V., 30

Q

Queens Hall, 79
"Quick One While He's Away," 310
Quiet Knight, The, 37

R

Rank Theatre(s)
    Colchester, 87
    Stockon-on-Tees, 87
    Sunderland, 87
R&B, in England, 53–54
Reading Town Hall, 81
Ready, Steady, Go! (album), 261, 264
"Ready Steady, Go!" (TV show), 9
"Ready, Steady, Go! Rave Mad Mod Ball," 91
recording session, first, 218–19
Red Lion Pub, 6, 61–62, 64–67
    first appearance at, 60
Redlands, 17
    fire at, 30, 42
Rees-Mogg, William, 19
Regal Theatre, 76, 85, 94, 101
repertoire
    1962, 56
    1963, 63
    1964, 82
    1965, 104
    1966, 119
"Respectable," 250–51, 292, 306, 386
Rest of the Best, The (The Rolling Stones Story— Part 2) (album), 26, 222, 298
Rewind (album), 299

Rialto Theatre, 87
Rice Krispies cereal jingle, 219–20
Richards, Keith, 1, *15, 20, 38–39, 41, 45, 49, 150, 154, 164, 185, 226–227, 229–30, 232, 234, 239, 323, 349, 357, 363, 366, 372, 389*
    assault charge, 27–28
    banned from France, 31
    children of, 24, 28, 34, 43
    death of son, 34
    drug use, 17–20, 30, 34–37, 39, 141
    early career of, 2–5
    first solo album, 45
    as grandfather, 51
    injuries of, 15, 40, 47, 115
    in Little Boy Blue & the Blues Boys, 2, 50
    Living Legend Award, 46, 368
    marriage to Patti Hansen, 42
    name change, 1
    reckless driving, 33
    weapon possession, 30, 33
Richmond Athletic Ground. *See* Crawdaddy Club; Fourth National Jazz & Blues Festival
Ricky Tick Club, 64, 66–70, 72–75, 90
"Ride On Baby," 226, 277
Rio de Janeiro concert, 377
"Rip this Joint," 245, 285, 289–90, 386
Ritz Ballroom, 74
"Rock and a Hard Place," 255–257, 301–302, 305–306, 388–389
Rock and Roll Hall of Fame, *45,* 46
Rock 'n' Rolling Stones (album), 286
"Rocks Off," 245, 285
Rolled Gold (album), 290
Rolling Stone (magazine)
    Critics Award (1978), 37
    Readers Award (1982), 42
Rolling Stones, *165, 336*
    beginnings of, 4–7, 53–54
    origin of name, 5–6, 57–58
    pseudonyms of, 160–61
Rolling Stones (The Promotional Album), 281
Rolling Stones #2 (album), 13, 267–68, 293, 382
Rolling Stones—The First 17 Albums, 300
Rolling Stones Album Collection, 293
Rolling Stones at the MAX, The (film), 325, 327
"Rolling Stones aux Abattoirs, Les" (TV show), 355–56
Rolling Stones Book, The (magazine), 11, 16
Rolling Stones Collection 1971–1989 (album), 303
Rolling Stones Day, Colorado, 15
Rolling Stones Down Under, The (film), 320
"Rolling Stones Live in Concert from Hampton Roads" (pay-per-view), 41, 173, 360
"Rolling Stones on Tour—Japan 1990" (TV show), 369
Rolling Stones Records, 21, 27

Rolling Stones Rock and Roll Circus (CD), 51, 310–11
Rolling Stones Rock and Roll Circus (film), 22, 51, 237, *311,* 313, 316
    filming of, 348–49
    soundtrack, 51, 310–11
Rolling Stones Singles Collection—The London Years (album), 223, 301
Rolling Stones Voodoo Lounge World Tour (laserdisc), 327
Rolling Stones (album), 10, 261, 264, 267, 293, 382
Rolling Stones (EP), 264
Rolling Stones—England's Newest Hitmakers (album), 10
"Rolling Stones: The First Twenty Years" (TV show), 361–62
Rolling Stones, Now! (album), 268–70, 382
Ron & Bo at the Ritz (film), 326
Ronstadt, Linda, 37
"Route 66," 221, 225, 264–65, 270, 273, 281, 286, 294
Rowe, Dick, 9
Royal Albert Hall, 75, 85, 92
Royal Hotel Ballroom, 91
Royal Lido Ballroom, 74
Royalty Theatre, 92
"Ruby Tuesday," 228–30, 256–57, 276–77, 281, 284, 290–91, 294–95, 301, 305, 390
Running Out of Luck (film), 323
Ryde Pavilion, 90

S

Sacramento (CA) Memorial Auditorium, 15
"Sad Day," 226, 286, 301
"Sad Sad Sad," 255–57, 301–2, 305, 389
"(They'll Never Make a) Saint of Me," 260
St. Georges Hall, 94, 98
St. John's Hall, 75
St. Leonard's Hall, 72
St. Mary's Church Youth Club, 62
St. Mary's Hall, 81
Salisbury City Hall, 83–84, 90
"Salt of the Earth," 235–37, 279–80, 310
Sandover Hall, 62, 64–65
    last gig at, 65
Santana, Carlos, 33
"Satisfaction." *See* "(I Can't Get No) Satisfaction"
"(I Can't Get No) Satisfaction," 225, 228, 253, 256–57, *269,* 270–71, 273, 76, 283–85, 290–91, 294, 296–97, 301, 305, 382–83, 390
Satisfaction (album), 397
Saturday Club (album), 261, 264
Saturday Night (album), 219
"Saturday Night Live" (TV show), 48, 357, *357,* 358, 366–67, 373
Savoy Ballroom, 75, 93
Say Ahhh (promo CD), 302

Scandinavian tours (1965), 109, 111–12
Scene Club, 70–71
Schneidermann, David, 17, 19
Scotland/Scandinavia tour (1965), 111–12
Selby's Restaurant, 81
"Send It to Me," 252, 293–94
Sensational Rolling Stones, The (tour), 113–16, *113–14*
"Sex Drive," 258, 305, 390
"Shake Your Hips," 244–46, 285
"Shattered," 250–51, 253, 292, 294–97, 302
"She Said Yeah," 225, 272–74, 281, 285
"She Smiled Sweetly," 228–30, 276
"She Was Hot," 253–54, 298, 388
"She's a Rainbow," 231, 279, 281, 285–86, 290–91, 301, 384
"She's So Cold," 251–52, 293–94, 299, 387
"Shindig" (TV show), 12, 225, 340–42
"Shine a Light," 240–41, 244–45, 259, 285, 309–10
"Short and Curlies," 246, 248, 287–88
Shrimpton, Chrissie, 16
Sidcup Art College, 62
"Silver Train," 247, 286, 385
"Sing This All Together (See What Happens)," 232–33, 279
"Singer, Not the Song, The," 225, 273, 286, 301
singles
    collection of, 223, 294, 301
    first, 219, 262, *262*
    first in US, 10
    first number one, 12
Singles Collection (album), 294
Sir Morgan's Cove, 40
"Sister Morphine," 235–36, 238–40, 283
"Sittin' on a Fence," 226, 277, 281, 286, 295
"60 Minutes" (TV show), 376
"Slave," 248–49, 252, 295
"Sleep Tonight," 254, 300
"Sleepy City," 223, 288
"(Walking Thru the) Sleepy City," 223, 288
"Slipping Away," 255, 259, 301–2, 309–10
Slow Rollers (album), 295
"Smile Jamaica," 367
"Snoring," 233
"So Young," 251, 258–59
Solid Rock (album), 294
"Some Girls," 250–51, 292
Some Girls (album), 37–38, 166, 250–51, 292, 386
"Some Things Just Stick in Your Mind," 223, 288
"Something Better," 310
"Something Happened to Me Yesterday," 227–30, 276
"Song for Jeffrey," 310
Sophia Gardens, 87
"Soul Survivor," 245, 285

South African tour (1995), 204–5
Spa Royal Hotel, 93, 97
Spain, ban in, 30
"Sparks Will Fly," 258, 307
Spector, Phil, 11, 103, 314
"Spider and the Fly, The," 225, 259, 270, 282, 301, 309–10
Springfield Hall, 99
Stamford Hall, 80
Star and Garter Pub. *See* Ricky Tick Club
"Star Spangled Banner," 253
"Star Star," 246–47, 250, 291, 293
"Starfucker." *See* "Star Star"
"Start Me Up," 252–53, 256–57, 295–97, 299, 302, 305–6, 387
State Ballroom, 79
Station Hotel, 8, 66–67, 69
Steel Wheels (album), 45–46, *49,* 255–56, 301–2, 388–89
"Steel Wheels—Atlantic City" (TV show), 369
Steel Wheels—Japan tour (1990), 186–87, 369
Steel Wheels—North America tour (1989), *179,* 179–87, *181–82, 185*
Stewart, Ian, 1, 4, 40
    album dedicated to, 300
    death of, 43
    memorial service for, 43, 178–179, *178*
    as road manager, 8, 63
Sticky Fingers (album), 24, 27, 240, 243–44, 283
Sticky Fingers restaurant, 46
Still Life (album), 169, 252, 296–97, 387
    recording of songs for, 169, 171–173
Stone Age (album), 27, 282–83
Stone Alone (Wyman), 6, 45
"Stoned," 220, 262, 286, 301
Stones in the (Hyde) Park (album), 397
"Stones on the Road" (TV show), 355
"Stop Breaking Down," 241, 244, 285
"Storm, The," 258–59
Story of the Stones (album), 297
STP tour, 137
Strand Palace Theatre, 74
"Stray Cat Blues," 235, 242–43, 279–80, 282, 285
"Street Fighting Man," 234–37, 242–43, 259, 279–80, *280,* 281–84, 290–91, 294, 309–10
Stripped (album), 50, 259, 309–10, 391
Stripped (film), 329, 379
Studio One, 17
Studio 51, 61–62, 70–75, 80–82, 250–51, 292, 386
    Ken Colyer Jazz Club at, 66–70
"Stupid Girl," 226, 273–74, 281, 301
"Suck on the Jugular," 258, 307
Sucking in the Seventies (album), 251, 294–95
"Summer Romance," 251–52, 293–94

Sunday at Richmond (film), 314
"Sunday Night at the London Palladium" (TV show), 345–46
"Surprise Surprise," 224, 269–70, 286
"Susie Q," 222, 267–68, 281, 382
"Sway," 243, 283
"Sweet Black Angel," 243, 245, *284,* 285
"Sweet Virginia," 241, 244, 259–60, 285, 309–10
"Sweethearts Together," 258, 307
Swing Auditorium, 11, 95–96
"Sympathy for the Devil," 236–37, 242–43, 250, 256–57, 279–84, 290–91, 294, 305, 310, 385
Sympathy for the Devil (film), 21–22, 26, 187, 236, 316

T

"Take It or Leave It," 226, 273, 277, 295
"Take the A Train," 253
Talk Is Cheap (album), 45, 255
"Talkin' 'Bout You," 272–73
T.A.M.I. Show, The (film), 12, 103, 314
Tattoo You (album), 42, 252, 295, 387
tax exile, 27
Taylor, Dick, 6, 57–59, 62
    early career of, 4–5
Taylor, Mick, 2, 26, 41, 44, *137, 172*
    birth of daughter, 27
    first album with band, 281–82
    first performance, 130
    first session with band, 22–23, 241
    first tour, 131
    joins band, 23
    last live concert tour, 30
    last performance, 147
    last US concert appearance, 143
    separation from band, 31
Teen Beat Night (venue), 75
Teen Fair, 96
Teenage Awards Music International Show. *See* T.A.M.I. Show, The (film)
television appearances, 9, 11–12
    first UK, 333
    first US, 335
"Tell Me," 221–22, 264–65, 267, 273, 286, 291, 301, 382
"Tell Me Baby," 222, 298
"Terrifying"
    pay-per-view. *See* Atlantic City concert (1989)
    TV show, 375–76
Texas State Fair, 96
Thames Hotel. *See* Ricky Tick Club
"Thank Your Lucky Stars" (TV show), 333
Thank Your Lucky Stars, Vol.2 (album), 261, 263
    first appearance on LP, 9

Thank Your Lucky Stars (album), 297

That Was Rock (film), 314, 322

"That's How Strong My Love Is," 225, 270, 272, 383

Their Satanic Majesties Request (album), *232*, 233, 279, 293, 384

"There Are but Five Rolling Stones," 221

"Thief in the Night," 260

"Think," 226, 273–74

"Think I'm Going Mad," 251, 254

Third Richmond Jazz Festival, 72–73

"365 Rolling Stones (One for Each Day of the Year)," 221

"Through the Lonely Nights," 247–48

Through the Past, Darkly (Big Hits Vol. 2) (album), 281, 384–85, 390

"Thru and Thru," 258, 307

"Tie You Up (Pain of Love)," 253–54, 298

"Till the Next Goodbye," 247–48, 287–88, 386

"Time Is on My Side," 223–24, 228, 253, 267–68, 273, 276, 283–85, 290–91, 295–97, 301, 387

"Time Waits for No One," 247–48, 287–88, 293–95

Time Waits for No One— Anthology 1971-1977, 293

Times (London newspaper), 19

"To Know Him Is to Love Him," 221

Toad's Place, 46, 180

"Too Much Blood," 253–54, 298, 388

"Too Rude," 254, 300

"Too Tight," 260

"Too Tough," 253–54, 298

Top Rank Ballroom, 79

"Tops," 246, 252, 295

"Torn and Frayed," 245–46, 285

Torquay Town Hall, 99

Tosh, Peter, 37

    murder of, 44

Tour of the Americas (1975), 32–33, 147–15

Tower Ballroom, 98

Trentham Gardens, 94

The Trident Mixes (album), 397

Trudeau, Margaret, 35–36

"Try a Little Harder," 223, 288

"Tumbling Dice," 245–46, 250, *284*, 285, 289, 291, 299, 302, 306

"Turd on the Run," 245, 285

12 X 5 (album), *266*, 267–68, 382

"20/20" (TV show), 356, 368

"Twenty Flight Rock," 253, 296–97

"20 Years" (German documentary), 361

"2120 South Michigan Avenue," 222–223, 267, 286

"Twenty-four Hours," 350

25 X 5 (film), 325, 368–69, 375–76

Twickenham Design College, 71

"2000 Light Years from Home," 233, 256–57, 279, 281, 286, 291, 301, 384

"2000 Man," 233, 279, 281

U

Ulster Hall, 98

"Under My Thumb," 226, 228, 252–53, 273–74, 276, 281, 283–85, 290, 296–97

"Under the Boardwalk," 224, 267–68, 295

"Under-Assistance West Coast Promotion Man, The," 225, 270, 272–73, 286, 301

Undercover (album), 42, 254, 298, 387–88

"Undercover of the Night," 254, 256–57, 298–99, 302, 306, 387–88

United Kingdom. *See also* British tours

    first album in, 10, 264

    first television appearance, 333

United States

    arrest in, 29

    club gig in, 40

    entry into market, 10–13

    Rolling Stones day in, 15

    television appearances in, 11–12, 335

    tours in. *See* North American tours

"Urban Jungle" (TV show), 369

Urban Jungle tour (1990), 47, 187–93

Usher Hall, 101

V

Valentine Charity Pop Show, 85

Vee, Bobby, 11

"Ventilator Blues," 245, 285

"VH1 to One: Keith Richards" (TV show), 378–79

Video Rewind (film), 43, 322

Villefranche-sur-Mer, 27

Virgin Records, 44–45, 48

Voices (film), 21

Voodoo Lounge (album), 49, 251, 258–59, 307–8, 390–91

Voodoo Lounge CD-ROM, The, 327–29

Voodoo Lounge concert (video), 201, 326, 377

Voodoo Lounge tour

    Australia/New Zealand, 206–7

    Europe, 209–15

    Japan, 205–6

    Latin America, 203–4

    North America, 193–203

    South Africa, 204–5

W

"Waiting on a Friend," 243, 246, 252, 295, 299, 306, 387

"Walking the Dog," 221, 264–65, 281

Wallington Public Hall, 92

Walthamstow Assembly Hall, 75

Wandering Spirit (album), 49, 255

"Wanna Hold Up," 254

"Wanna Hold You," 253–54, 298

Watts, Charlie, 1, 7, *15, 20, 41, 235–236, 389*

    in Alexis Korner's Blues Incorporated, 2

    in Blues By Six, 7, 65

    book by, 12

    children of, 21

    drug use, 29

    early career of, 2–5

    injuries of, 43

    joins band, 6, 63, 65–66

    marriage of, 12

    "MVP Drummer" award, 47

    sketches by, *123*

"We Love You," 232–33, *277*, 281, 286, 290–91, 301, 347, 384

"We Want the Stones," 225, 270

Weatherby Arms, 7

"We're Wasting Time," 223, 288

West Cliff Hall, 90

West Germany, 1965 tour in, 112–13

Westview Park, 97

Wetherby Arms, 4

"What a Shame," 224, 268–69, 301

"What to Do," 226, 273, 286

What's on the Flip Side? (film), 315

"When the Whips Come Down," 250–51, 292, 294–95

Where the Boys All Go, (promo), 387

"Where the Boys Go," 251–52, 293–94

"Where'd You Hide My Blues," 260

White Bear pub, 4

Whitehall, 90

Whitehead, Peter, 112, 228

Who, The, 82

"Whole Lotta Yoko," 237, 310

"Who's Been Sleeping Here?," 227–30, 276

"Who's Driving Your Plane," 227–28, 286, 301

"Wild Horses," 243–44, 259, 283, 285, 289, 291, 306, 309–10, 391

Wm. Morris Hall, 58, 60–61

Wilton Hall, 90

Wimbleton. *See* Palais, The

Winehall Ballroom, 85

"Winning Ugly," 254, 300, 305

"Winter," 246–47, 286

Winter Gardens

    Banbury, 73

    Blackpool, 98

    Bournemouth, 87, 94

    Morecambe, 88

"Wish I Never Met You," 255, 305

Wonder, Stevie, *140*

Wood, Ron, 1, 31–32, *38, 154, 173, 181, 185, 326, 389*

    book of, 45

    children of, 35, 37, 42

    divorce of, 37

    drug use, 39

    first album as band member, 290–91

    first tour with band, 148

    injuries of, 48

    marriage of, 43

    and the New Barbarians band, 37

    official member of band, 250

    one-man show of paintings, 44

Wooden Bridge Hotel, 67–70, 72

Woody's on the Beach club, 44

Works, The (book), 45

"World in Action" (TV show), 347

World Wide Web, Rolling Stones on, 50

"Worried About You," 248–49, 251–52, 295, 387

"Worst, The," 258, 307

Wyman, Bill, 1, *11, 235–36*

    AIMS Project, 44

    autobiography, 45

    divorce, 24

    and drugs, 29

    early career of, 6

    first album with band, 279

    first gig with band, 7

    injuries, 13, 37

    joins the band, 62

    marriage of, 46

    name change, 1, 12, 62–63, 66

    quits the band, 48, 373

Wyman, Lee. *See* Wyman, Bill

X

"XXX," 253–54

Y

"Yer Blues," 237, 310

"Yesterday's Papers," 228, 276, 285, 290

"You Better Move On," 220, 264, 273, 281, 295

"You Can Make It If You Try," 221, 264–65

"You Can't Always Get What You Want," 237–38, 250, 256–57, 281–82, 284–85, 291, 294–95, 305, 310, 385

"You Can't Catch Me," 223, 268–69

"You Got Me Rocking," 258, 307, 391

"You Got the Silver," 238, 281–82

"You Gotta Move," 243, 250, 283, 291